Time, Will, and Purpose

Time, Will, and Purpose

Living Ideas from the Philosophy of Josiah Royce

RANDALL E. AUXIER

OPEN COURT
Chicago, Illinois

To order books from Open Court, call toll-free 1-800-815-2280, or visit our website at www.opencourtbooks.com.

Open Court Publishing Company is a division of Carus Publishing Company, dba ePals Media.

Copyright © 2013 by Carus Publishing Company, dba ePals Media

First printing 2013

All rights reserved. No part of this publication may be reproduced, stored in a retrieval system, or transmitted, in any form or by any means, electronic, mechanical, photocopying, recording, or otherwise, without the prior written permission of the publisher, Open Court Publishing Company, 70 East Lake Street, Suite 800, Chicago, Illinois 60601.

Printed and bound in the United States of America.

ISBN: 978-0-8126-9678-3

Library of Congress Control Number: 2013950117

To the memory of Charles M. Sherover (1922–2005):
teacher, mentor, and loyal friend.

Philosophy, in the true sense of that word, never destroys an ideal that is worth preserving.

—JOSIAH ROYCE, 1892

Contents

Preface	ix
Introduction	1
1. Biography	29
2. Ontology	53
3. Immediacy and Mysticism	73
4. Pragmatism	103
5. Individuality	125
6. Temporalism	163
7. Personalism	201
8. Community and Purpose	243
9. Conservatism and Progress	285
10. Teaching	309
Notes	351
Bibliography	397
Index	409

Preface

In recent years the notable resurgence of interest in and work based upon the thought of Josiah Royce is a welcome (if somewhat unexpected) development. About fifteen years ago I was warning an undergraduate student, one who wanted to go on to graduate school in philosophy, that his enthusiasm for Royce would be a professional liability for him. Royce was little studied then, and work that departed from a Roycean platform would attract few readers and might even be unpopular. Yet, due to the efforts of a lot of people, things have changed. It is a pleasant thing now to be able to teach graduate seminars on Royce that fill up with eager and curious students, and that such students may now write on Royce, meeting fewer uncomprehending looks from those whom they encounter in the philosophy profession. And the change happened quickly and continues to grow.

I took it as a very positive sign when, in February of 2007 I was meeting with Hilary and Ruth Anna Putnam about Hilary's forthcoming volume in the Library of Living Philosophers, and, gracious as he always is, Hilary asked "what are *you* working on?" I said "a book on Royce," and his face lit up as he said "I *love* Royce." Hilary Putnam, the defender of realism, convert to the philosophies of James and Dewey from the narrow straits of linguistic philosophy, *loves* Royce? That can only be a good sign.

I had to admit that the "rediscovery" of Royce was becoming truly general when, while on sabbatical in 2007, I was staying at the home of Robert and Beth Neville just outside of Boston, doing research for this book (and writing it). My hosts returned from an evening gathering in celebration of the release of a new book by a *Boston Globe* writer with the happy name of Charles P. Pierce (that is Pierce, not Peirce). His book *Moving the Chains* is a celebratory analysis of the leadership qualities of Tom Brady, the quarterback of the New England Patriots pro football team (Pierce has since gone on to greater celebrity with his more recent book *Idiot America*). As Beth read through the book about Tom Brady in the days following the media event, she was heard to cackle loudly as she arrived at a substantial passage in which Pierce uses Royce's *Philosophy of Loyalty* to explain how Tom Brady leads his team. Of course, she knew I was writing a book on Royce in the attic just above her. Where Mr. Pierce might have encountered Royce I have no idea, but I will say that his summary of Royce's principles is both accurate and subtle, and in fact perhaps only Royce, of all philosophers, could have supplied him with the ideas he needed.[1] But this Pierce book is not philosophy, it is football and sports journalism—which, while it is not to be taken lightly, since sport, when undertaken in the spirit of loyalty, builds communities and character—and there are graver matters to consider.

As I put the last touches on this book, Jerry Brown, elected yet again as governor of California, has given an inaugural address in which Royce's philosophy of loyalty holds pride of place. As he says, and I agree, we have never needed Royce's ideas more than we do now.[2] I have confidence that the democracy in the United States will succeed in curbing the totalitarian impulses that have been recently manifest in the astonishing willingness of the American government to torture prisoners, and to *defend* the practice, to detain human beings for years on end without being charged or being afforded any realistic legal recourse, to deny them the most basic rights of due process in coming to decisions about guilt, to engage in "extra-ordinary rendition" of captives to secret prisons for torture, to spy upon both citizens and non-citizens without court oversight, to circumvent the authority of congress with "signing statements" that amount to a blunt refusal to execute the law, and to lie to the world in order to make war against and among other peoples for reasons we cannot even obtain from our own government.

This list of crimes is far from complete, as history will eventually show. More recently still we have working class dupes of multinational corporations waving guns outside of town hall meetings to intimidate free speech, we have a government that labels as a terrorist someone who simply embarrasses our State Department by exposing its incompetence, we have thinly veiled racism in service of greed, and "news" outlets promoting boisterous dissent from the most ignorant and misinformed of the populace. Yes, some people would rather kill or let die than pay their taxes, an example of the kind of person Royce characterized as believing himself to have more rights than he has duties. But all of this behavior is the well-worn American tradition, and with slight variations, the same sorts of things were happening in the tumultuous first decade of the twentieth century, and the end of the nineteenth century. Royce's time looked only a bit different from our own.[3] We have perpetual need of a rediscovery and revitalization of our communities. We need trust, hope, civility, and to interpret one another more charitably.

The traitors to hope and community are many. For Royce, a traitor is the person who rebels against *his own cause*—for example, not the ideals of America as understood by, in this case, the opposition, but as understood by the loyal individual himself. The traitor is the one who loses his confidence in his own ideals, who sinks below what those ideals require, due to his fear of losing a battle or a war. Having been made a strong individual by a good community, having served his cause, the traitor first twists the cause into something of which he alone is master—judge, jury, and executioner—to the point that it is no longer possible for him (and often others) to distinguish the cause itself from the strong individual who has identified himself with it. Without necessarily intending to, the traitor refuses genuine community with those who could offer any check upon his own ideas. He denies the lessons of history, denies the facts of science, and he occludes the future because he cannot tell the part (himself) from the whole (the community, the cause, the ideal). No such person can be a good servant of ideals because no such person can be any part of a *genuine* community, and so long as he persists in pretending to be a servant rather than confessing his betrayal, it requires courage to face the traitor and name his crimes. Yet, without this profession of treason, no redemption can occur, and no period of grieving for his (and our) misdeeds can begin.

Our present world is brimming with political, corporate, and military traitors of this type, ones who are in a state of denial about their treason. They cannot redeem themselves, only their fellows can, by being in community with such persons and speaking the truth about them. For example, we must prosecute those who torture others in the name of keeping our community "safe." There is no safety in a world in which such treason is passed over. Royce's philosophy in such situations comes down to having the courage to sacrifice one's own comfort, or freedom, or life in order to serve truth, for, in the end, there is no difference between the beloved community we seek and the *truth* about it. Speaking personally, I cannot serve traitors and I will not be silent, especially when they are supposed to be the *humble* incarnations of the ideals of freedom and individuality that we are supposed to be pursuing together. But I also want to call out the betrayers of freedom and the purveyors of greed, militarism, imperialism, racism, and the ruthless exercise of raw power for its own sake, in such terms as may make possible reconciliation and hope. That requires care as well as courage.

This book, and Royce's ethic, is such a care-taking mission, not itself a piece of activism so much as a platform for activism's intelligent success. Or so I hope. We cannot rectify the government sanctioned crime spree that characterized the first years of the twenty-first century without words of hope and respectful remembrance of the truth about what we have done. Tens of thousands, possibly hundreds of thousands of human beings have been killed for the gratification of power, greed, and fear in the last decade. It must be challenged, but in ways that open toward a better future. There is no good outcome to finger-pointing and name calling within our community. We all bear the guilt and the burden for reconciliation.

With that said, some other words of appreciation are due. Many thanks I offer to the Nevilles, to numerous students with whom I have discussed Royce in the last dozen years (made easier by the reprinting of *The Philosophy of Loyalty* by Vanderbilt University Press, and *Basic Writings of Josiah Royce* by Fordham University Press). In particular, among the students, I have to mention Dwayne A. Tunstall, who is now associate professor of philosophy at Grand Valley State University in Allendale, Michigan. I am quite certain I learned more from Dwayne than he ever learned from me. I appreciate his reading of much of this manuscript while I was writing it, and for his suggestions that have improved it. The manuscript was also read by my friends Jan Olof Bengtsson of Lund University in Sweden, and Jackie Kegley of California State University, Bakersfield; I thank them fondly for their friendship and help. The book has benefited greatly from their support and suggestions.

My colleagues in the Josiah Royce Society are a continuing source of conversation, illumination, and encouragement. The senior scholars among these, John McDermott, Frank Oppenheim, Jackie Kegley, John Lachs, John Clendenning, André De Tienne, and the late Peter Hare, have for many decades done so much to improve our historical and philosophical understanding of Royce, that nothing written on him in the present or future can estimate the debt. I will not attempt it. As portions of this book were presented as papers at professional conferences over the last several years, I benefited from commentaries and questions from numerous colleagues which led to needed revisions. In particular, Joanna Crosby of Morgan State University basically raked me over the coals regarding some parts of what became Chapter 10 (parts that are now gone of course), and I am glad she did so; that's what friends are for (just ask Royce and James). My friend John Fritzman of Lewis and Clark College was somewhat gentler but no less helpful regarding Chapter 4. And among my colleagues in the philosophy department at Southern Illinois University, Carbondale, I am especially grateful to Ken Stikkers and Doug Anderson.

My own Royce teacher, Charles M. Sherover, to whose fond memory this book is dedicated, passed away a few years ago. But his seminar on Royce at Emory University in 1988 was for me a redeeming experience. In the years that followed, I was able to argue Royce with Charles, sometimes for days on end, when I visited him in his retirement home in Santa Fe, New Mexico. Many people miss Charles, but perhaps I miss him more than most because I would have loved to hear his critique of this book, and in some ways I wrote it because it is supposed to be the book he himself always intended to write but never found the time. I take the views in this book to be largely in line with his interpretation of Royce, but since he published only a little on Royce, there is no way to decide that. Yet, the community of memory is as infinite as the community of hope. In our memories, our teachers are still interpreting us to ourselves, through what we imagine they might have said. I devoted the last chapter of this book to the teacher/student relationship because I am convinced of its sacred character. We teachers, or anyone who teaches anything to anyone (and that is all of us), would do well to remember the sacred character of learning and the required ethic of teaching when we are tired and irritable, but the student has one more question. That next question may be the one that changes one's own thinking in ways that will become of inestimable value. I am glad Charles Sherover never wearied of my questions and half-baked opinions, or if he did, I never knew it.

No one can do very much in life without the generous support of loved ones, and I am fortunate to have more than my share of support and love. In particular, I stand in reverent awe at the unselfishness, patience and appreciation, love and support that my spouse Gaye has freely offered for over a quarter of a century. No one with any power of circumspection can feel worthy of such support. Similar notes of gratitude must be added regarding my parents and parents-in-law.

This book was largely written during a sabbatical leave made possible by the institution I serve, Southern Illinois University, Carbondale. I was assisted by the staff of the Harvard Archives under the beneficent leadership of Megan Sniffin-Marinoff, the University Archivist. Harvard undertook, beginning in September, 2007, the complete reprocessing of the Royce papers, and the development of a new on-line finding aid, a project now completed. This was a first step toward the commencing of the massive project of creating a critical edition of the works of Josiah Royce. That project is much further along now, and my friends in the Royce Society have done me the honor of appointing me General Editor of this long term project. I hope I live to see it completed, but publication will commence in 2014 one way or another.

In this book, Chapters 1, 2, 3, 4, 5, 9 and 10 are based on materials that are published elsewhere, in different form from their presentation here. I have listed these other writings in the bibliography, but the material in this book supersedes these other writings. There are some slight modifications of interpretation, and some corrections and refinements, but with one exception (that I shall mention in the introduction) the views expressed here are supposed to be the same as those in my other published writings. The expressions and formulations are clearer and more integrated here. Surely many faults still remain in the book, and doubtless it could be improved if I spent another year researching and refining and correcting it. But it is time to let it go and ask forgiveness for the remaining flaws.

In addition to the Harvard Archives, I also need to thank the staffs of the Morris Library at SIUC for assistance and the Woodrow Wilson Presidential Library in Staunton, Virginia for their help.

Introduction

A new study of Royce in the light of time and distance from his day is desirable for its own sake, but that is only one aim of this book. I will discuss this scholarly aim in some detail later in this introduction.

Living Ideas

The other principal goal is to present some of Royce's best ideas in forms that will facilitate their active application to contemporary life and thought—living ideas. I take the term from the beginning of Alfred North Whitehead's *Aims of Education*,[1] where he rightly points out that only a teacher who has living ideas will succeed in teaching anything. I see Royce as an available teacher for our time and culture precisely because the works he left us are brimming with living ideas. The development of philosophical thinking in the Anglophone world has long been diverted from matters of vital relevance to the improvement of life, mainly by excursions into various formalistic and theoretical possibilities, grouped under the name "analytic philosophy." Philosophers have preferred to frame ideal languages, abstract theories of meaning and reference, and construct flawed solutions to other long-standing abstract puzzles, through close attention either to the use or to the structure of language. I am not especially appreciative of philosophy when it is reduced to the consideration of word puzzles or to dialectical word-play.

These recent philosophers generally have had a horror of "metaphysics" and have been convinced that philosophy could become *more* relevant to the task of *knowledge* by becoming more scientific and less metaphysical (as though "more scientific" *were* less metaphysical, when science is really deeply embedded in a questionable metaphysics, or several). I will explain the history and results of this widespread conviction in Chapter 10 of this book. As exciting and promising as these logical endeavors were at their beginning, in the early twentieth century, the result of the collective effort of four generations has not amounted to much. These days, many analytic philosophers, wearied by the endless and irresolvable pseudo-problems and barren debates that arose from their own narrow epistemological standpoint, have begun to return to pragmatism as a way of finding some practical point of departure from which to make evaluations of life. Philosophy has not become a science, as many vainly hoped, and it never will, and indeed, never should strive to be. But the re-emergence (and, if I read the winds aright, the impending dominance) of pragmatism requires both that we look forward and backward in time. Analytic philosophers are not good at that, but they should strive to become better.

Other philosophers, mainly on the continent of Europe (with many self-loathing American followers childishly tugging at their sleeves), have been so consumed with the *critical* task of philosophy as to leave themselves with little to say of a constructive nature, and they hold fast to this emphasis on critique for fear of falling back into a kind of dogmatic metaphysics which was rightly rejected and ridiculed by the philosophers of the early twentieth century, both on the Continent and in the Anglophone world. Whether metaphysics is synonymous with *bad* metaphysics is a question that has re-emerged among them in recent years (thanks in no small part to the influence of Gilles Deleuze, who was certainly a good metaphysician), but the over-arching suspicion against metaphysics is still alive and well. That habit of thinking will need to change. This book is designed to contribute to that process of change. Not all metaphysics is a mistake, and I encourage readers to check their prejudices at the door and pay special attention to the discussion of method in Chapter 2. This is *not* the metaphysics of our philosophical fore-parents, and while one can hardly be blamed for being suspicious, we will never build a vision of a better day on suspicion or critique alone. Metaphysics will be with us in all philosophies, whether implicit or explicit, and the question is not whether we will *do* metaphysics (we shall), but whether we will do it *well*. Metaphysics is difficult and requires patience, along with years of effort, to do well. It is time we made a start.

Royce said that we have to rewrite philosophy to make it relevant to the present. I am taking Royce at his word, and, in a very conscious sense, "rewriting" his ideas to make them relevant, to the best of my ability. I think this book contains some novel ideas, ones not found explicitly in the philosophy of Royce, ideas that I would call my own, insofar as I should take responsibility for stating them and the consequences of doing so, but no one's ideas are entirely his or her "own," as Royce so clearly shows. Many of these novel ideas are simply interpretive angles or ways of combining texts in ways Royce never thought about, although I hope he would welcome these novelties as faithful to his philosophical aims. Some of the novel ideas are ones that couldn't have occurred to Royce because subsequent developments in the sciences, in logic, in philosophical method, and in human culture, all provide perspectives that were unforeseeable in Royce's lifetime. Other novel ideas arise perhaps from my own way of thinking, which I hope is creative without being merely idiosyncratic. I have tried to be clear about when I speak with my own voice and when I intend to be explaining what I take to be Royce's views. The book is thus a mixture of old and new, but one hopes the confusion of the two is avoided or minimized.

Yet, philosophy has a special relationship to its own history. I do not think good philosophy often emerges from anything less than a thorough immersion in the thoughts of past philosophers, and Royce said as much in great detail many times, but especially in the Preface and First Lecture in *The Spirit of Modern Philosophy*. I agree whole-heartedly. Philosophers who neglect the history of thought will end up saying what has been said before, and almost always with less insight and excellence than the most gifted philosophers who went before. One can hardly think of a better example of this than Wittgenstein. From ignorance of the history of philosophy, and in spite of the cultish fascination with him among analytic philosophers, Wittgenstein's brilliance was largely wasted, since he shifted his basic views every time he deigned to read a classic philosopher. William James also suffered from an absence of philosophical training, but unlike Wittgenstein, he approached his lack of knowledge with humility and was conscious of the failing. It still resulted in shifts in his basic viewpoint (a mark of inadequate training) and inabilities that formal training and devoted study to the whole history of philosophy might have softened (I will demonstrate a particularly acute problem with James in Chapter 7). But humility saved James's genius, and he did not merely re-invent the wheel. Arrogance greatly reduced Wittgenstein's contribution relative to what it might have been, but I do not deny his genius, only his importance.

At the other end of the spectrum was Alfred North Whitehead, who read, not broadly, but deeply and repeatedly in some of the most crucial figures—Plato, Aristotle, Descartes, Locke, Hume, Kant, Bergson, and James. As a result of a lack of immersion in secondary literature, along with a peculiar talent for reading, Whitehead came up with a novel and fruitful philosophical method (extensive abstraction), a sound approach to inquiry (a novel version of radical empiricism, borrowed from

James), and managed to say valuable and creative things, among them, his original interpretations of the philosophers he *did* read—interpretations that were firmly rooted in the text and which emphasized different aspects of their thinking than the secondary traditions had emphasized. I would not say Whitehead was exactly "lucky"; after all, his character, humility, discipline and temperament produced exactly what they should have produced. But I will say that his peculiar combination of gifts was the exception to the rule when it comes to philosophers who have not read broadly in the history of philosophy. *We* are all *fortunate*, even if Whitehead was not exactly "lucky." Wittgenstein's genius was, if not quite misguided, inadequately guided, and his work was merely idiosyncratic and uninformed, where it might have been truly creative, which is terribly *un*fortunate. The lesson to be taken from this is that we are wise to read both broadly and deeply in the history of philosophy before forming our final judgments regarding its central questions. There is a good reason that philosophy throws almost no young turks up the pop charts—at least none whose early thought stands the test of time. Royce had the best combination: an excellent training in the history of philosophy (and he had few equals in his generation in the mastery of texts), a number of languages, wide travel and experience, along with a decisive sense of the problems of his own time. The balance is difficult to attain.

The Present State of Royce-Related Scholarship

If philosophy is to be a progressive effort of human self-understanding, only the most rigorous understanding of its past will serve adequately as a basis for the project. If one does not wish to re-invent the wheel, and to do so badly, squandering the effort already expended by abler laborers, one should become apprenticed to (not enslaved by) the philosophers of the past. Thus, this book is, in that sense, a thoroughly historical investigation into the history of philosophy—and specifically, the history of "American" philosophy.[2] The book contains new research and new arguments about the historical context and actual history of philosophy in the United States between 1875 and 1925, with some reference to developments since 1925. I have tended to leave aside the information that has already been widely understood, concentrating instead upon historical facts and interpretive approaches that have been neglected. Thus, there are detailed discussions of, for example, the roles of George Holmes Howison and William Ernest Hocking (Chapter 3), Borden Parker Bowne (Chapter 7) and James Edwin Creighton (Chapter 10), none of whom has received the attention that was due. I have also advanced a novel argument about William James in relation to Royce and the overall philosophical context of the fifty-year period in which I am historically interested. These are among the historical aspects of this book which highlight previously neglected matters.

I have adopted the practice of trying not to repeat the efforts of those who have gone before, and of not weighing down the text overmuch with simply hundreds of citations and quotations. I often make points that others have made, but I have not attempted to make note of every single point of agreement or indebtedness to others. Let readers assume that the large and rich scholarship has been incorporated into my analysis, and maintain their awareness that just because I say something without footnoting it does not mean I claim the idea is exclusively my own. Those who know the scholarship will notice what is specific or peculiar to my account, and most other readers do not need to be slowed down in their reading by the explicit marking of the fact. I am relying heavily upon the prior work of, especially, John Clendenning and Frank Oppenheim, with whose studies I am in sympathy, with only a few minor exceptions. My reading of Royce is perhaps closest to that of John J. McDermott, and shares his existential and concrete turn, but with the addition of a more systematic metaphysics than he customarily employs. I am also close to the reading of George Douglas Straton, whose work on Royce is not widely known, but perhaps should be consulted.[3] I am also in agreement with the interpretation of Royce by Cornel West, insofar as I have been able to learn what his views are, since his major work on Royce is not yet published.[4]

In many ways my book can (perhaps must) be read jointly with the recent books on Royce by Dwayne Tunstall and Jacquelyn Kegley.[5] The circumstance is pleasantly strange. Dwayne developed his book from a master's thesis I directed, but based in part on studies and conversations related to my already developed views, some of them forming early drafts of chapters for this book. Dwayne had his own ideas, and as we studied Royce together, I was encouraged by the amount of agreement we found on what were non-standard interpretations of the primary texts of Royce, especially regarding the issue of the unity of Royce's thought, his personalism, and his method. Dwayne took these ideas in his own directions (with objections to my versions!), added them to his own, and finished his book manuscript before I even formally started my own. Dwayne's manuscript was sent to Fordham University Press and accepted by, among others, Jackie Kegley, who read his book for Fordham. Meanwhile Jackie was laying out her own new book on Royce, and was aware that I was working on mine. When I finished the first version of my manuscript in May of 2007, I sent it to Jackie for her response, just as she was beginning the serious writing part of her book. She asked if I would read and comment on her chapters as they were finished, which I did, and I was thus able to incorporate some references to and ideas from her manuscript into the 2007 version of my own manuscript. But publication of my book was delayed, due to circumstances beyond my control. In the years(!) since I completed this manuscript, the books by Kegley and Tunstall have appeared, incorporating *their* references to *my* work in manuscript pages. But I am now able, in revising this manuscript in late 2010 and early 2011, to go back and fill in actual references to their books, and I have done so.

The three books are different, but they agree on a few crucial themes, particularly Royce's temporalism and the unity of his philosophical thought throughout his development. All three books provide developmental accounts of Royce's thought that, in different ways, demonstrate the presence very early on of all of his central philosophical ideas. I hope that together these three studies may accomplish what any one of them alone might not, which is to lay to rest, once and for all, the idea that Royce went through major reversals in his ideas. I also cannot help thinking that Royce himself would have smiled at the idea of three authors triadically puzzling through his work in a sort of exemplary "community of interpretation." That we three should represent different generations of scholars makes it all the more pleasant. At all events, that three major interpretive works should be appearing almost simultaneously from three separate publishers seems to buoy the idea that Royce is again surfacing for a new examination. I believe that the appearance of the critical edition of Royce's works will add steam to the growing interest in these ideas, but in the end, it is the excellence of the ideas themselves which will bring about a full renaissance in Royce studies.

Also of recent interest has been the flurry of attention devoted to questions surrounding Royce's views about race and European cultural supremacy. In a way, the issue had been warming for some time, with articles written and widely read by Jackie Kegley and Elizabeth Duquette, and then took off with the republication in 2009 of an expanded edition of Royce's *Race Questions, Provencialism, and Other American Problems*, edited by Scott Pratt and Shannon Sullivan. In addition to essays by Pratt and Sullivan, significant work, and controversy, has been added by Tommy J. Curry, Jackie Kegley, Dwayne Tunstall, Marilyn Fischer, and others. The exchanges have sometimes been intense, and if anything demonstrates that Royce's ideas are still alive and kicking, I can think of no better example.

My exposition is narrative in form and tells a story of ideas, but it also strives to be organically systematic. I mean by this that every portion of this text implies and depends upon every other, and the full *purpose* for the introducing of any one idea in its relation to the others becomes clear only as the book draws to a close. The order of the topics I have treated is determined not by my estimation of their chronology or philosophical importance, but of how a reader needs to follow the story of these ideas for maximum understanding of the whole. But this order of topics presupposes a willingness on the reader's part to bear in mind that there is always more to the "story" later in the book, and of course, the full story comes to more than I can tell in the scope of the book itself.

For example, I have provided no general exposition of Royce's concept of "loyalty," because this has been done very well by numerous other writers. But what others have *not* done, in my view, is to provide the *full* metaphysical underpinning of that important idea (to many, John E. Smith may seem to have done so, but I think this not true, as I will attempt to show in the next part of this Introduction). I also have *not* provided a thorough discussion of Royce's most important "living idea," the "community of interpretation," and its ideal in the "beloved community."[6] Yet, I have provided all of the pillars upon which these crucial ideas rest, something that no interpreter has yet done adequately, in my view. I have not explained the "social infinite" or the "community of interpretation" in detail because I am completely satisfied with Smith's explanation of these ideas in his 1950 book *Royce's Social Infinite*. With Smith, I happily grant that, together, "loyalty to loyalty" and "the social infinite" are the two most important ideas in Royce's philosophy. These ideas will come up often in this book, with only brief explanations, but I will direct readers to the work of other scholars for fuller treatments. The importance of these two ideas has been long recognized and that is why they have merited numerous books and articles of their own.

I have also left off a detailed treatment of *The Problem of Christianity* (1913) and *The Sources of Religious Insight* (1912) because not only Smith's book (and his other writings on Royce), but also Frank Oppenheim's three excellent books on Royce's mature thought, along with Straton's book, have said what needs to be said. Royce was better at the philosophy of religion, and more pre-occupied with it, than perhaps any other topic. My omission of a detailed discussion of his philosophy of religion as a whole should not be taken to indicate that I think it unnecessary for a full understanding of Royce. But I also think that the tendency among scholars of Royce, and even of those who read Royce more casually, to focus upon his philosophy of religion leads to a subtle distortion—an over-emphasis upon this topic, as though 1. it was all he did really well, or 2. one can approach his whole philosophy from the standpoint of his philosophy of religion and succeed in understanding what needs to be understood about the whole of it. I think this is a mistake.

In addition, Oppenheim's most recent and extensive book, *Reverence for the Relations of Life*, treats well nigh exhaustively Royce's philosophical relation to Peirce, James, and Dewey, and so what I will say of these relationships in this book is both dependent upon and supplemental to Oppenheim's treatment. I am more satisfied with his discussion of Peirce than with his (much longer) accounts of James and Dewey. I think Oppenheim is too deferential to James, and *far* too deferential to Dewey —perhaps bending over backwards to keep his more intuitive appreciation for Royce from becoming a bias in his book. I think he could afford to be less gentle with James and Dewey than he has been. In many ways they simply did not understand Royce (as Oppenheim notes), and they are very much responsible for the misconceptions they introduced into subsequent thinking by frequently unperceptive reading and listening, and indeed, stubborn intellectual thickness of the head when it comes to logic and metaphysics. But Oppenheim's thorough treatment of all three is indispensable for a full understanding of Royce's philosophical context. I will be less deferential to James and Dewey here, but I would point out that I hold their respective philosophies in great esteem, equal to my esteem for Royce. That I reject their readings of Royce does not imply that I reject their own philosophical perspectives, or that I automatically agree with Royce and disagree with James or Dewey when they part ways. Very often I side with James or Dewey on philosophical points, even if I do not think they have understood what Royce was arguing. In this book it may appear that I am a Royce-partisan when the fact is that I am only a defender of the proper understanding of Royce's genuine position. I would want that kept in mind by readers. My own philosophical commitments are not primarily under discussion here, but if they were, they would be closer to Whitehead than to Royce.

With all this scholarly work done on Royce, to date, no systematic treatment of Royce's entire philosophy has yet been attempted. With the exceptions noted above, and of one other crucial topic, this book is that attempt. I have provided, I hope, the basis for grasping not only Royce's thought, but also the other secondary texts and where they rightly fit in to the whole story. The other exception is Royce's logic. So intricate and complex is this logic that to attempt even a cursory exposition of it here would slow the progress of this book intolerably. I will make some very pointed claims about the role of logic in Royce's philosophy as a whole, and I have included an interpretation of his use of necessity in relation to negation, of the levels and functions of generalization in his thought, of the relational aspect of metaphysics, and of the role of universals in his method and his thinking. I have drawn upon his logic for these purposes, and these ideas are explained in some detail, with reference to his logic. But the logic proper I have not examined here. I have provided a presentation of my views of Royce's logic in some detail at the Summer Institute of the Society for the Advancement of American Philosophy (Boulder, Colorado), and at the second International Conference on American and European Values (Opole, Poland), both in the summer of 2008. Those who were present will have formed an idea of the work on logic I will eventually present, in a separate study.[7]

I am pleased that the collection of Royce scholars associated with Scott Pratt of the University of Oregon, including notably Brent Crouch and Kimberly Garchar (now of Kent State University), has been hard at work on this challenging topic of his logic, and I hope to influence their work through my discussions of method, here. They have combined their efforts with the Critical Edition, and I expect they will produce (independently or not of my views), in the near future, a whole series of studies of Royce's logic, in addition to their valuable work in assembling and organizing his unpublished logicalia, as a part of the critical edition of Royce's works. I will return to this topic when their work is substantially complete to compose an essay, or something longer, on the relation of logic to the central theses of this book, but to do so now would likely just produce an account I would need to revise in light of the results of Pratt's on-going work. I will await his (and their) results.

If I have executed adequately what I set out to do, the present book should be a self-sufficient introduction to and guide through Royce's entire philosophy. It will be easy, after reading this, to pick up the books on loyalty, religious insight, and Christianity, as well as all the others (except the symbolic logic, as opposed to the philosophical logic), and to read them with a full understanding of their assumptions and bases. Royce's philosophy is quite difficult and to learn it with any fair understanding of how each part relates to the others has, up to now, required a tremendous commitment of time and effort. I intend to save students and colleagues, as well as the interested public, some of that effort. There is no substitute for reading Royce's own works, of course. The issue is how to approach any part of his system with a sense of how it relates to the other parts; such is always the problem with organic philosophical systems. Until now, the only way to approach this great edifice of thought was to choose a book and work one's way slowly in every direction, modifying one's inferences about the starting place as the work proceeds. Most readers cannot stay with Royce long enough to prevent major distortions from creeping in and taking root. And most scholars in related areas –interpreters of Peirce, James, Dewey, and others—make the error of *believing* what their heroes have said about Royce, then reading Royce spottily, finding only the confirmation of those partial viewpoints in what little they actually read. The result is a hopeless swirl of contradictions and warring assertions about Royce's thought, made and traded by persons who really haven't read enough to form balanced judgments. This book should alleviate that situation, if those who ought to read it choose to do so.

The biographical information offered here is minimal (at least compared to its importance) and geared only to what is needed in order to understand the story of ideas that follows. But I should say that my biographical exposition contains a number of assertions no biographer has previously made. These are not factual assertions so much as assertions about intellectual influence and patterns evident in Royce's thought. I am not, however, even a true historian of *ideas*, let alone a historian of concrete fact. Factual assertions are usually drawn from either Clendenning or Oppenheim or both, sometimes also from Robert Hine or Vincent Buranelli. Rather than a historian, I aspire to be a responsible interpreter of historical data, and these data point in some definite directions that have not been noticed before. Thus, my historical claims may serve to open more questions than they (fully) answer. That is not a bad thing.

The *warrant* for these historical assertions is to be found in the *subsequent* exposition of ideas in this book, but the important aspect of the historical part of the argument is that it *justifies* (or aims to) a much more unified account of Royce's thought than is usually assumed. It has been widely held (with help from some of Royce's late autobiographical ponderings) that Royce went through some major changes in his thinking, abandoning previously held "mistakes" for better ideas he picked up from Peirce or someone else.[8] The historical record now available (but long suppressed by the Royce family, reportedly in keeping with Royce's own wishes), shows this idea of major shifts and very distinct periods to be effectively false. Royce's thought certainly *developed* in the sense of the continual enrichment and refinement of early insights and their greater articulation and concrete application, but there were no major shifts. One certainly *can*, as Oppenheim has done, document important insights that deepened Royce's understanding of his own earlier thinking, but one *cannot* show that these moments of insight, or of sudden clarity, resulted in any decision to drop his existing major doctrinal commitments and substitute for them ideas that were at odds with the earlier ones. Royce never changed his mind in any major way, and most particularly, he never "abandoned" the concept of the Absolute (the most egregious and oft-repeated error of fact and interpretation).

My own thesis about the essential unity of Royce's thought is supplemented by (and in some ways grounded on) the textual exposition done by Dwayne Tunstall in his book, which argues vigorously and convincingly for the unity of Royce's thought centered upon a single "ethico-religious insight." I am in substantial agreement with Tunstall, and I wish to draw upon his arguments in support of my own position. If a reader is unsatisfied that my exposition here demonstrates the essential unity of Royce's thought from beginning to end, I urge such a reader to suspend judgment until Tunstall's case has also been examined in conjunction with my own. Kegley's newest book adds still more evidence, and as I have said, the three of us are in essential agreement on matters of Royce's development.

If my case, taken as a whole (and that is how I hope it will be judged), *is* adequate to show the unity of Royce's thought, then it justifies also my decisions about how to treat the "living ideas" themselves, and my method of exposition. I did not attempt to arrange the exposition chronologically. After making the chronological development clear, I have chosen instead to move to whatever Royce text I believe is the clearest, most representative, and most perspicacious for telling the whole story. Thus, I will carry out and document my exposition of the living ideas from texts as far removed from one another in composition as nearly forty years. I have tried to be sensitive to the development of the ideas, but have stressed the essential unity of insight and viewpoint.

My use of quotations and endnotes even from the primary text, while extensive, is as sparing as I could manage. I have tried to choose only the most poignant and decisive extracts and to offer them at the points of discussion at which they are really necessary. The rest of the time I speak of Royce's views in a fairly general way, noting developments in his outlook only when needed. This makes for a more readable text, and I am confident that my generalizations can be confirmed by readers themselves when they read any text by Royce on the topics I have treated. Proving exhaustively and to the satisfaction of a devoted skeptic that I cannot *possibly* be wrong is not worth the effort. The litmus test will be Chapter 2, on ontology. While I believe that this thesis is wholly and exhaustively demonstrable on the basis of the text, and while I have offered sufficient textual support for the claim, readers who cannot suspend judgment long enough to consider the possibility that this account of Royce's method is correct would be wasting their time to read the rest of the book. If my account of Royce's method in Chapter 2 should prove substantially incorrect, the rest of the story would have to be told as if in a different (and foreign) country.

One final point should be made about the scholarly aspect of this book. I have become aware in the course of writing it that there are certain gaps in my own knowledge which may lead to certain problems in the text, and I would rather point them out myself than have anyone think I am pretending they don't exist, or am ignorant of my gaps—I may be ignorant of some gaps, but not of two of the most important. It is very clear to me that my reading in the nineteenth-century background of German philosophy has some weaknesses. I am well acquainted with Kant and Hegel, but not adequately versed in the later Schelling, the speculative theists (especially I.H. Fichte—J.G. Fichte's heir) and Rudolf Hermann Lotze. I have studied both Schelling and Lotze, but not enough. I will be relying on the excellent scholarship of Jan Olof Bengtsson to make up for this gap, and I am setting to work presently on improving my understanding of Schelling, but this book cannot wait forever, and remedying my weakness here will require some years.

Still weaker is my command of British idealism. I have read Bradley (mainly the logical writings), but not closely, and have barely at all examined Greene and Bosanquet. Discussions with Phil Ferreira of Kutztown University, and some reading of the scholarly writings of T.L.S. Sprigge, have made me acutely aware that I am in need of a serious course of study in these figures and their context. Discussions with John Shook of the Center for Inquiry in Amherst, New York and Washington D.C., along with material I found in the Harvard Archives and letters of Royce, have made me aware of the importance of F.C.S. Schiller, and of his disputes with the British idealists, for my clearer understanding also. I hope to have that better perspective in time.

The result of these two areas of weakness in my background could be that I tend to see the world through Royce-colored glasses. I may be apt to present an idea that was commonplace in these traditions in a tone suggesting that Royce came up with it first. For example, until recently, I harbored the impression that Royce's emphasis on "uniqueness" in his theory of individuality was his own innovation. I now know that he took much from Schelling in this area. Wherever I may leave the impression that Royce came up with something first, but in reality he did not, I regret that the finiteness of life and time has prevented my gaining the best available perch, and I am committed to improving the situation in the coming years. I am not, however, worried about this problem relative to Peirce and James (and Dewey is not crucial here). I have a thorough sense of their relationship to Royce and a scholarly command of Peirce and James (and Dewey), each in his own right. I know, as numerous scholars do not (because they have neglected the study of Royce), that in many,

many instances it is simply not possible to determine whether James or Peirce got an idea from Royce, or vice-versa. Oppenheim's most recent book, and my own, should be consulted for arguments about why the direction of influence is undecidable in many cases. But as examples that I will mention later, the theory of attention and the idea of the stream of consciousness attributed by almost everyone to James appeared over five years before the *Principles of Psychology* in Royce's writings.

The Prevailing Misconceptions

Readers who are not keenly interested in *details* of the way this book relates to the existing tradition of Royce scholarship should skip now to Chapter 1. I need to set out here where I depart principally from the 1950 book by John E. Smith, *Royce's Social Infinite*.[9] By the time I have said my piece, readers may form the impression that I mistrust or dislike Smith's book and do not have anything good to say about it. Nothing, and I mean *nothing*, could be further from the truth. For the purposes for which it was *intended*, Smith's book will never be surpassed in its excellence. Its intended purpose is to untangle what Smith rightly sees as Royce's most important idea—the way in which the sociality of our being gives finite beings access to what is actually infinite. Smith fearlessly confronts one of Royce's most difficult writings, the "Supplementary Essay" to the First Series of the Gifford Lectures, *The World and the Individual*, and successfully wrests from it the clearest possible analysis of the "actual infinite." He then traces this idea to its application in the "community of interpretation" in *The Problem of Christianity*. Smith's book is outstanding in numerous other ways as well—but its clarity and brevity are high among its chief virtues.

However, due to the lack of a systematic introduction to Royce's whole philosophy, scholars have been, for sixty years, relying upon Smith's sixty or so pages on the "background" of Royce's thought as their *introduction* to Royce. The book was never intended so to serve, and it is not adequate for that purpose—indeed, it is nowhere close to adequate. Dozens of times in the text Smith reminds the reader that he is providing something that is just a sketch sufficient for his main purpose, while pointing to other things that should be discussed at greater length. But readers have insisted upon and persisted in using the book as it was never intended, as their short-cut to a full understanding of Royce. And in spite of all the disclaimers and qualifiers, Smith accidentally encouraged readers to think this way at the end of his background chapter, saying: "The foregoing account of those elements in Royce's earlier thought which are necessary for the understanding of his community metaphysic contains implicitly the core of Royce's philosophy in all its aspects."[10] Read carelessly, this seems to say "I have given you everything you need." But that is not what Smith said. He only claims to have provided the elements needed for the community metaphysic (I think there are several more that were necessary, so I disagree with his judgment), but then goes on to point out that while these elements do *not* provide the full story, they *implicitly* point to it. The operative word is "implicitly." The explicit story has not been provided, not even the core ideas of the explicit story. Smith is careful about this, but his readers usually are not.

There is another peculiar fact that needs to be emphasized about Smith's place in the history of Royce scholarship. There is a strange historical bottleneck associated with his book. Much of the scholarship on Royce's work that was published during his own lifetime is collected in a three-volume set of books I edited.[11] These writings are generally known to Royce interpreters, and are regularly consulted. But there was also a good bit of writing on Royce from 1917 to 1950, as reflected in the bibliography of Smith's book. This scholarship is simply not read by most Royce scholars today. There is a tacit assumption that Smith's book adequately sums up the results of that scholarship and supersedes it. This is false and Smith makes no such claim. Some of these studies emphasize very different aspects of Royce's thought than Smith treats, and if anything, Smith is rendering his own account briefer by *not* repeating the results of others. Why Royce scholars themselves do not consult many of these books, dissertations and articles I do not really grasp.

The result, however, is that not only scholarship, but scholarly *consciousness* about Royce is formed by Smith's book. He set the agenda, and whatever happened to be absent from his book simply was not in the consciousness of Royce's subsequent interpreters. If Smith's book had been *intended* to be comprehensive, there might have been no problem. But it was not so intended. It was a specialized study of two major ideas. When one adds to this the fact that Smith wrote, as a young man, at a time when interest in Royce was declining, and that such interest did not begin to increase again until well after Smith's book came out (enjoying something of a peak between 1965 and 1972, and then declining again before its current re-emergence), there was a gap, between about 1935 and 1965, during which almost nothing apart from Smith's book was published on Royce, and after which scholars younger than Smith—who very much and for very good reason revered him both as a scholar and as a person—resumed the work of interpreting Royce. This is the bottleneck. Smith's book was almost alone in its generation.[12] As a result of it, Smith's points of emphasis became everyone's agenda, Smith's weaknesses became everyone's weaknesses, and what Smith left out just disappeared. These important ideas, notably his neglect of Royce's personalism and his decision to treat Royce's philosophy of time as something embedded in his philosophy of community (rather than a part of his entire method), were overlooked in Royce's text even by close readers. They did not notice what they were *not* looking for, and they were not looking for anything Smith left out. I revere Smith as well, and his recent death in 2009 was a great loss to philosophy, but the texts of Royce have some features he neglected, features essential to their proper understanding.

In what follows I will present, in turn, three related, general problems with Smith's account, many of which are traceable to bad habits by his readers, while others are due to a lack of available evidence when Smith wrote his book. These general problems have three specific adverse results which I will mention (although there are others). It seems a shame to focus so heavily upon what may be perceived as "faults" in so fine a piece of work. But I am weary of attempting to converse with scholars, especially scholars of James, Peirce, and Dewey, who have read Smith, and a little bit of Royce, and dogmatically conclude they have the right story and the full story (for Smith is not only a respected Royce scholar, but was and remains pre-eminent in almost every area of the history of American philosophy). Other scholars who read Smith often do not know what they are talking about, and due to Smith's (well deserved) standing as an authority who cannot be questioned, they doubt those of us who have done far more research than they have done themselves, and indeed, those of us who have been able to do more research on Royce than Smith himself could, due to the new materials available.

That Smith should have written a book that has stood for sixty years as an indisputable authority is very much to his credit. That whatever Smith left out, for the sake of streamlining his main discussion, should have then simply *ceased to exist* in the minds of scholars and the public, is not a very good testament to the independence of mind and reading habits of the scholarly community, or the wider community of American philosophers. The weaknesses in Smith's book, for reasons he often could not have prevented, have resulted in an occluded perception of Royce and has hindered the proper assimilation of his ideas. It needs to be corrected. I am doing my best to correct these problems herewith. I will present the problems in turn.

1. Peirce's Influence

Smith stresses, at numerous places in his text, Peirce's decisive influence upon Royce. This influence certainly occurred and was indeed decisive. But at the time Smith wrote his book, not much was known about the relationship between Peirce and Royce. Their letters had not been released for study, let alone published, and judging from the text and notes, it appears that Smith could do no archival research for his book, on Peirce's influence or any other question. He relied upon whatever Royce said about Peirce in print, and on what had appeared in the first six volumes of Peirce's *Collected Papers* (1931–1935) that seemed relevant. No biography of either man had been written, and the documentary evidence of their relationship, both philosophical and personal, was at that time suppressed (along with everything else). The Royce papers had been given to Harvard shortly after the death of his wife Katherine in 1944, but they were not processed or readily available for study in 1948-49. The inferences about Peirce and Royce that Smith drew from the available resources were mostly warranted at the time, but they turned out to be only a drop in the pond, if not the ocean, of what was the case. The extent of the issue becomes acutely obvious when one considers the following footnote from Smith:

> One wonders whether Royce was at this time [1908] acquainted with Peirce's article on this theme. (*Collected Papers*, V, 213ff.) Dewey believes that the influence of Peirce goes back to *The Religious Aspect of Philosophy* (*Papers in Honor of Josiah Royce*, p. 22 n. 2). Yet Royce spoke in *The Problem of Christianity* as if the ideas he discovered in Peirce came at a much later time and effected a change in his own thought. His remarks in *War and Insurance*, pp. 85-6, make this even more certain.[13]

Smith should have listened to Dewey, and even Dewey underestimated the matter. But Smith settled upon the idea that Peirce's thought came along late (1912) as a sort of semiotic savior for Royce, and he discounted Dewey's suggestion from 1915 that the influence of Peirce went as far back as 1885. Smith could have (and should have, I think) asked Dewey, or someone else, since there were others still alive by 1949 who could have prevented Smith from settling upon this erroneous judgment. Along with Dewey, Jacob Loewenberg, William Ernest Hocking, John Elof Boodin, and Daniel Robinson were still alive at the time. A little more digging might have turned up Peirce's *review* of *The Religious Aspect of Philosophy* (which Royce would certainly have read), or the published portions of the "Abbott Affair" in which Peirce played a role (1892), or Smith could have made the inference that Peirce and Royce must have known each other by the time they were both writing entries for Baldwin's *Encyclopedia* in the late 1890s, given the content of the articles each contributed. But Smith chose to trust an inference from an appearance in the texts of 1913-14. He was doing what he could, but it was incorrect.

The truth of the matter is that Royce was aware of Peirce, and was reading his writings and being profoundly influenced by them, by 1877, and possibly earlier. Royce was actively interacting with him no later than 1880 when he was invited by Peirce to send to Johns Hopkins, to the Baltimore version of the Metaphysical Club Peirce had started there, a paper for the group's critique and discussion. This paper, "On Purpose in Thought," already shows the decisive influence of Peirce (especially Peirce's seminal 1867-68 articles from the *Journal of Speculative Philosophy*), as well as a thorough-going commitment to what I call in this book Royce's "temporalism," and also, that paper shows the same idea of "purpose" I will be highlighting as one of my major themes here.[14] While only a portion of the subsequent correspondence between Peirce and Royce has been found, it is clear that their intellectual exchange was constant after 1880, that the influence was mutual, and that Royce often knew of Peirce's work *as* it was being written, before publication, and that he knew of much that was never published. Royce did not "find Peirce" in years afterwards. He looked upon Peirce as a teacher for almost 40 years, but the influence was clearly mutual. The fuller story, to the extent that it can be told in the present, is in Oppenheim's *Reverence for the Relations of Life*.

In a sense, our fuller understanding of the relationship makes Royce *more* rather than less philosophically dependent upon Peirce, even though the influence went both ways. But our recognition of the intense, constant and long-term character of their exchange also eliminates the supposition that Royce took a sudden turn in 1912. It not a "Peircean turn," due to some late discovery, it was an insight about how to *use* Peirce's theory of signs (which Royce had known for years) as a tool for the *application* of his own (long-held) triadic theory of community to historical and present and future communities. And the "Peircean insight" of 1912 was no more than that. Peirce did not "save" Royce from absolutism or turn him in any fundamentally new direction.

This historical mishap led to another unfortunate and entrenched habit of thinking about Peirce and Royce. As mentioned, Smith tended to emphasize Peirce's influence late in Royce's life (since that is where the preponderance of the published evidence lay), and thus to treat the relationship as one in which ideas flowed only from Peirce to Royce, and only a few key ideas, and only late in Royce's life. Thus, Peirce scholars (who are a breed unto themselves) have often carried away the impression, really a simple prejudice, all too readily confirmed in attending only to the positive instances, that all the important ideas were Peirce's, and these ideas were then generally botched by Royce (whose main defect was, apparently, that he was capable of finishing a book and holding down a job, "so he must not be as smart as Peirce . . ."). I realize that sounds petty, but being dismissed by Peirce scholars is a lot like being ignored by a finicky cat. It doesn't mean the cat is right or very smart, only that it is resolutely unaware of what it happens to be ignorant about.

It is true that, as brilliant as he was, Royce was not as smart, in terms of pure intellect, as Peirce. Almost no one in the Western world has ever been that smart—maybe Aristotle, Leibniz, and Whitehead. And Peirce had indeed been sharply critical of Royce in print—something Peirce scholars knew, even if Smith did not mention it or discover it. So the "Master" (Peirce) found Royce lacking in some ways, and his disciples believed it. Smith never says anything even remotely suggesting this sort of one-way influence, but since he was deprived of the detailed story, he presented what he had (which wasn't much), and since he was interested not in what influenced Peirce, but in understanding what influenced Royce, he presented only what apparently flowed from Peirce to Royce. This left the wrong impression, and most Peirceans have felt licensed to ignore Royce ever since. In fact, some of the really creative ideas in Peirce (as with James also) seem to have been Royce's, and Peirce scholars would do well to reassess their historical conclusions. They do themselves and their Master a disservice by setting Royce aside.[15]

2. Royce's Development

The problem with understanding Peirce's relation to Royce is only the most important illustration of an issue that haunts Smith's entire account —creating a perception among scholars of all sorts that persists and yet is simply indefensible. This is the idea, mentioned above, that Royce's thought went through major changes, divided into stages of development, usually accompanied by the judgment that he moved away from philosophical idealism and towards pragmatism, semiotics, and phenomenology (which is also usually seen as an improvement in his philosophy). In a telling way, Smith draws upon his conclusion about Peirce's influence and, in assessing his (overly epistemological) account of Royce's account of the Absolute; he says:

> The idea that absolute thought takes the form of a third or interpretant is of decisive importance in the complete formulation of the community metaphysic, but at this early stage Royce had not yet discovered the idea of mediation through interpretation; rather, he was thinking in terms of integration and intuition.[16]

It is true that only in 1912 did Royce come to grasp the Absolute as the interpretant. This was part and parcel of his "Peircean insight." But it is false to say that Royce had not discovered the idea of mediation through interpretation. Royce had read Peirce's "New List of Categories" (1867) no later than 1878, and was already using the idea of mediation through interpretation and a triadic theory of relations by 1880. I will offer instances of this from Royce's early thought in the following chapters. Smith is correct that the idea is of decisive importance in the community metaphysic, but that metaphysic was already in evidence by 1885, if not before. As I have said, what Royce discovered in 1912 was how to *use* the semiotic theory of Peirce, with which he had been working for years, to express the community metaphysic in a way that bridged his logic and metaphysics with human practice. Yet, the primacy of the concept of "communication" was present from the beginning of Royce's thought, and was well worked out in the Second Series of Gifford Lectures (1901). He knew all along that the link between his metaphysics and logic, on one side, and his account of practice on the other, was mediation by communication, and the idea of "interpretation" was always central to his ideas about communication. What he did not have was an adequately general *expression* of the communication process that would convert the norms of reflective life (including the norms governing good logic) into a seamless unity with his practical philosophy, the philosophy of loyalty. And Royce did not abandon thinking in terms of "integration and intuition" after he adopted the idea of the Absolute as interpretant. Rather, he found a general theory that described that very process in Peirce's semiotic.

But Smith continues (and here is where the damage was done):

> This last point [quoted above] is of the highest importance. Royce's thought exhibits a very definite development in the conception of the Absolute, and since the thesis that in the Absolute thought all ethical, religious, and philosophical problems are solved is central to his view, it is of some moment to be clear about this development. Speaking generally, the all-important change in Royce's conception of the Absolute consists in the shift from the idea that the Infinite thought is an all-embracing consciousness apprehending at a glance all truth and harmonizing at once all conflicts between [sic] the multiplicity of finite wills in existence, to the idea that the Infinite is actual as a well-ordered system (or ultimately, community) having a general triadic form and involving a type of cognition called interpretation.[17]

There is no such shift. First, Smith is correct to say that the ethical character of the Absolute is the governing idea for Royce, but he does not emphasize, as he should have, that this conviction of Royce's is the *ground of the unity of his thinking about the Absolute*. This unity is far more important to the overall understanding of Royce's development than the further (and subsequent) elaboration of the concept of the Absolute (here, I state in my own words, the conclusion of Tunstall's book). And so there *was no shift*; there were separate inquiries with their own requirements that led Royce to characterize the Whole (the Absolute) in one way or another. One can find the idea Smith identifies as "late" clearly present in Royce's earliest work, and throughout Royce's work (as I will show in later chapters), and one can find the idea Smith identifies as the "early," more epistemological view of the Absolute advocated in Royce's final course on Metaphysics, 1915–1916. As with the Peirce relationship, this evidence was not available to Smith, but it is available now.

I do not say that Smith drew an unreasonable inference from the evidence he had, but I will note that Royce says so many different things about the Whole or the Absolute in the course of his inquiries, characterizes it in so many different ways, that Smith was obliged to construct a simplified framework for interpreting Royce that highlighted only the main and most repeated views. Smith settled on three descriptions of the Absolute: (1) the Absolute thought; (2) Infinite system unified by a purpose; and, (3) the community of interpretation.[18] One could note that Royce *emphasized* these views successively, but the emphasis was governed by the requirements of whatever inquiry was at hand, not indicating a shift in his view. Royce must have used close to fifty different terms for the Absolute, depending on the context of inquiry. He makes no serious effort to justify the variety of expressions, but the variety, which is evident from 1884 onwards, is always grounded in the unity of his conception of the Absolute as an *ethical* idea (as Tunstall shows). Particularly, I would emphasize, that one major aspect of that ethical idea implies a norm for thinking *clearly* about the Whole in relation to its parts. To think clearly, for Royce, is an *ethical* requirement, an indispensable part of an ethical life. Thus, we can *call* the Absolute anything we like so long as we recognize that good reflective thinking requires a working conception of the Whole, and that this requirement is a *norm* that ties reflective life to practical decision-making.

If one thinks of the unity of the Absolute in, for example, purely epistemological terms (the logically necessary conditions of reflective thinking that ground knowledge), *without* its ethical ground, one thinks of a vacuous abstraction (again Tunstall's book should be consulted). Royce rejects such a vacuous conception of the Whole or the Absolute from the very beginning of his work and never changes his view. Smith's account invites us to think of Royce as having unwittingly allowed such a bloodless abstraction into his thinking until he was rescued from it by Peirce. This is just incorrect. Unfortunately, a majority of Royce's readers have simply misunderstood his view, attributing to him precisely the view he rejected. There will be detailed discussion of this issue in Chapter 5.

Further, the separate characterizations of the Absolute Smith chooses as his supposedly successive "stages" are *all* present *throughout* Royce's development, but the crucial characterization Smith omits from his account, and the one I will emphasize in Chapter 5, is, in my view, actually the key to understanding how Royce thinks of the Absolute. It is the *temporal* conception of the Absolute that depends for its demonstration upon the irrevocability of an individual deed, and the Whole to which that deed belongs. Royce says that the finite human *will*, our volitional power, unceasingly counsels irrevocable deeds, and that if we would have a practical proof of the reality of absoluteness, we should simply act and then try to undo the deed. This irrevocability of the act has to do with the character of the past, and it is our least mediated *experience* of the Absolute. Of course, the deed itself is always an ethically significant act, expressing a decision (of which we are not and cannot be conscious until after we have acted), and such an act, our most intimate access to the reality of the Absolute, is thoroughly ethical and active in character, not epistemic or even conscious. The metaphysical and logical characteristics of this encounter with the Absolute are generalized from the encounter itself and are subordinate to it. It is false to say that Royce ever "deduces" the meaning or ontological status of the individual act from the logical requirements of the Absolute. Rather, he generalizes the act in order to form differing conceptions of the Absolute or the Whole depending on what type of inquiry he is undertaking.

This point about allegedly successive conceptions of the Absolute in Royce, which Smith says is of the first importance, is just the most crucial instance of a way of understanding Royce that has subsequently pervaded all other aspects of his philosophy. People have tended to be dismissive of Royce's early work as if it were unformed and later superseded, and to see in his middle years a constellation of ideas whose main value was the way they foreshadowed his work after 1912. As a result, every assertion in Royce receives its assessment in light of Smith's thesis about Royce's development, and the entire philosophy has been gradually pigeon-holed by it. Because Royce's corpus is immense and difficult to master, even very conscientious scholars have taken Smith's framework into their own studies as a "field guide." This has been disastrous. There are no major shifts in Royce's development involving the abandonment of earlier positions and the adoption of new ones. There is an enrichment, and elaboration, and varying applications of the basic insights that unify his thought from the beginning. There is also no change in emphasis or successions of definitions in his major concepts.

3. Method

Smith's discussion of Royce's method is quite cursory. The issue arises only twice in his "Background" chapter, and the sparse subsequent mentions depend on the earlier discussion. Smith introduces the discussion of method saying that Royce "sought the Absolute, not as a mere ideal, but as an actuality."[19] I have gone to significant effort in Chapter 2 (and beyond) to show that this is a false dichotomy, between "actuality" and "mere ideal." Royce's hypothetical method, and the way he limits philosophical activity to a reflective exercise in service of moral insights ("philosophers are musicians of reflective thought"), together make this dividing of the (merely) ideal from the actual a philosophical impossibility for Royce. Indeed, Smith's own central thesis on the accessibility of the actual infinite to finite experiencers *through* the ideal of the beloved community should have led him to realize he had missed something in Royce's method. Obviously in this instance, Smith's own thesis shows that the ideal and the actual coincide, and if such a coincidence can be effected, what is a "mere" ideal? Royce speaks of and rejects "bare possibilities," but these are not ideals, they are empty abstractions (such as the ungrounded conception of the Absolute I mentioned above). There are no "mere" ideals for Royce—an ideal already has an indivisible relation to the actual. Not all *possibilities* we can think about have such a connection, however.

Smith goes on to say that Royce's method is the "method of doubt," and he means this in an un-Peircean sense. Smith asserts that:

> In this attempted elimination of all doubt, he [Royce] adopted a method which, although by no means original with him, he used with acuteness and with some somewhat surprising results. Royce proposes an analysis of doubt itself, and the presuppositions of the doubter, which he carried through in the ingenious section "The Possibility of Error" in *The Religious Aspect of Philosophy*.[20]

It has been common since Smith's book to treat this chapter from *The Religious Aspect of Philosophy* as Royce's "method." But this is not adequate. First, there is the problem that the best way to understand "doubt" in Royce's extended discussion of it, especially the result of it, is in terms of Peirce's famous articles of 1877–78, especially "The Fixation of Belief." Royce did in fact mean "genuine doubt" as Peirce had set it out. But Smith had decided that Peirce's influence did not go back to 1885, and so he took a different tack, treating Royce's method as more in line with the kind of dialectic and logic used by the British idealists. This is just incorrect, and Royce's common protest that he *was* a pragmatist (as Smith notes elsewhere) should have led Smith to be more careful about drawing this conclusion.[21] Second, the dialectic of doubt, even in the correct Peircean sense, is very far from being Royce's full or principal method of doing philosophy. I will set out in this book Royce's method, in full, its various levels and features, and the reasons for them. These should be substituted for Smith's version of Royce's method.

Third, Smith makes the fatal mistake of trusting Dewey's assessment of Royce's method. Smith rightly notices that appealing to the "whole," and the relation of part to whole, is a constant feature of Royce's method. But he thinks that for Royce, "method" is an epistemological device aimed at obtaining *truth* and *knowledge*, with *certainty*. This is incorrect. Royce's method is a hypothetical ontology on the basis of which various epistemological and other reflective thoughts are built. The method is not aimed primarily at securing certainty or knowledge, but rather at maintaining intellectual norms—a species of ethical norms—that govern clear thinking and facilitate intelligent practice and action. Paraphrasing Dewey, Smith says:

> The procedure adopted by Royce [in the "Possibility of Error" chapter in *The Religious Aspect of Philosophy*] in arriving at the metaphysical concept of absolute truth illustrates the method which he always sought to follow in his philosophy. He began with accepted fact and sought to show that its reality necessitates the reality of its conditions, etc., until the analysis finally results in the necessary recognition of the infinite or the absolute.[21]

It is not accurate to say that *every* analysis aimed at showing the necessity of the infinite or Absolute. This assertion misunderstands necessity, in Royce's sense, and the relation of necessity to what Royce means by "reality." Smith makes the matter appear as though Royce claimed ontological knowledge for his philosophical conclusions and used some conception of logical or epistemological necessity to ground such knowledge. But Royce had read Peirce's critique of this kind of necessity (Smith did not know this), and employs necessity in the same limited way that Peirce does, not as the British idealists did. What Royce *really* "always" did was take an accepted fact and show what was presupposed in taking that fact to have a *past* and a *future* as well as a *pres-*

ent, and then treating the *temporal* reality of the fact as furnishing a normative condition for thinking of it in relation to a whole. In this book I will explain in great detail how this temporalism functions in Royce's philosophy. For now, we should simply notice what Smith is claiming for Royce's "method": it is, for Smith, necessitarian, epistemological, and aims to capture the "real" with certainty. But Smith and Dewey only noticed, and *misunderstood*, a habit of Royce's, not a method. Royce's response to Dewey's misunderstanding is made explicit in Royce's 1911 Harrison Lectures. These have not been published, but hopefully will be soon. Smith trusted Dewey on the issue of method and Dewey was badly mistaken about Royce, in this case. Smith would have known not to trust Dewey had he been aware of the depth of Royce's familiarity with Peirce. So the error regarding the influence of Peirce affected the discussion of method.

In Royce's actual method, every version of the "whole" is hypothetical—in the sense that it is a possibility one can entertain, conceptualize in different ways for different types of reflective inquiries, and while no given conception of the whole can be known with certainty to be the correct conception, *some* concepts can be eliminated for philosophical purposes because of the nature, norms, scope, and limits of *philosophy*. Such eliminable conceptions are classed as "bare possibilities," once they have been analyzed, but they are never ideals. Even then, it is not that we *know* that such-and-such a conception of God or the Absolute or the whole cannot *be*, it is rather that we can see the disastrous results for our *thinking* (and our practical lives, which are not wholly separable from the processes and results of our thinking) if we adopt some views rather than others. Thus, Royce uses an ontology of possibility *in relation to time*, principally the future, to ground both epistemological and moral philosophical inquiries.

This is in fact not far from Dewey's method, except that Royce was far more adept at setting it forth and using it than Dewey was. Dewey's late ontology of the "situation," however sound, is thin by comparison, and his various references to "the whole" remain vague. And for lack of a metaphysical (or even logical) turn of mind, Dewey was never a reliable reader of anyone's texts at the level of metaphysics. This led to a narrowing in *his* ideas about *their* methods—e.g., Dewey had similar difficulties in understanding Peirce and Whitehead. Royce is no exception to Dewey's weaknesses in working with formalized kinds of thinking. His book on Leibniz exhibits the weakness abundantly, but I do believe Dewey got better as time went on at understanding formal thinking and using it in his own philosophy. But Royce was long gone before

Dewey really began to grasp these aspects of philosophy. Smith himself was somewhat better at formal philosophy, as his analysis of the actual infinite demonstrates, so it is more difficult to excuse Smith for these errors in reading Royce.

4. THE RESULT

Three results in Smith's account follow from the issues with Peirce, Royce's development, and method I have outlined above. All of these consequences have affected our understanding of Royce adversely.

First, Smith does not rightly distinguish between the "actual" and the "possible" in Royce's philosophy. I could give many instances of the looseness of this vocabulary in Smith's book (although his use of "mere ideals" as distinct from something actual in the previous section is one such example), but I will settle for one revealing instance and leave readers to verify my point for themselves. Smith says:

> Royce was perfectly aware of the fact that both the complexity of the community and the weakness of man in his tendency to place his own individual interest uppermost in his thoughts are factors which render any *actual* community far from perfect.[23]

Smith's entire book is aimed at showing that the "beloved community" *is* "actual," because *all* genuine ideals are actual, and the beloved community does not have this particular problem with being in any sense non-actual. Concretely, the actual (including actual communities) *includes* the possibilities that are ideal. In philosophical thinking, one deals *first* with possibilities (and it is difficult to distinguish ideals from bare possibilities, but that is what a good philosophical method accomplishes, by means of logic) hypothetically, and *then* interprets actualities from that standpoint. Smith does state this point correctly at one place:

> At any given moment our body of knowledge is incomplete because it falls short of the whole, but our recognition of it as incomplete is possible only upon the *assumption* [i.e., hypothesis] that there is a conspectus which possesses the truth in its completeness. The "whole of experience," [Royce] said, possesses the truth, but no single individual has direct access to such a whole; nevertheless, the *assumption* of its *actuality* is a necessary *condition* making *possible* any truth whatever.[24]

Here in a nutshell is a statement of Royce's true philosophical method, of what I call in Chapter 2 "fictional ontology," and the distinction is evident between the requirements for doing *philosophy* and other, non-philosophical types of knowledge (which derive from generalizing concrete experience, rather than from an hypothesis about the whole). But Smith fails to take his own advice about the distinction between the actual and the possible. Clearly, in the passage cited earlier, Smith means to say that any "concrete, community, considered in the mode of the present" is "far from perfect" due to the presence of narrow self-interest, but he does not use the proper vocabulary. He uses the term "actual" in a way that is inconsistent with Royce's sense of the term because it excludes the temporal possibilities for the community being discussed. That is exactly what *cannot* be excluded in any discussion of an "actual" community, for Royce. This sort of problem occurs throughout Smith's book, but is most apparent when Smith calls Royce's method "essentially the Platonic one of developing presuppositions in order to decide on their status and their justification on the basis of considerations relevant to such an inquiry. The 'deduction' of the good on this view consists in showing the actuality of what is assumed. . . ."[25] This is truly misleading to readers. Royce's conception of the philosophical primacy of possibility is in no sense Platonic, and his deductions in no sense establish the certainty of his conclusions. Royce is a temporalist. Plato (as received by tradition) is an Eternalist. The difference is as stark as that between Parmenides and Heraclitus. Of course there are commonalities, even between Heraclitus and Parmenides, as Plato showed, and Plato can also be read as a temporalist, but Smith is inviting readers to internalize a profound misunderstanding of Royce with such assertions.

In succeeding chapters I will explain in some detail the distinction between the actual and the possible in terms of Royce's temporalism, and readers who have gone through my analysis will easily recognize that Smith, although he noticed an important characteristic of Royce's use of terms and method, did not thematize it or see its role in Royce's method, with the result that Smith under-estimates the scope and importance of Royce's temporalism.[26]

Second, Smith does not distinguish properly between the concepts of "appreciation" and "description" in Royce's philosophy. Smith treats appreciation as private, subjective, intuitive, and individual, while treating "description" as public, objective, reflective, and social.[27] Smith infers the character of this (very subtle) distinction between appreciation and description from Royce's 1892 work *The Spirit of Modern Philosophy*, neglecting both the earlier treatments and later treatments, as well as the important interpretive work on it done by Gabriel Marcel—who gets the distinction right, in my view (and then takes issue with it, justly).²⁸ Read correctly, "appreciation" is just as public, objective, social, and communicable as description. Art and narrative are primary examples of the "world of appreciation," and their type of communication is more basic and more important to practical social life than are descriptive communications. We could have vital communities almost entirely without descriptive knowledge (including philosophy), but we could attain neither genuine community nor descriptive knowledge without building it up from the world of appreciation.²⁹

Appreciation may or may not have a "reflective" aspect—this is what Marcel was concerned about in Royce's philosophy. It is a debatable point.³⁰ I have tried to show, throughout this book, that the appreciative mode is the philosophical master of the descriptive mode, and to explain how it is every bit as social and public as description. I will not summarize those arguments here, but merely point out that I depart from Smith on this issue, and I would attribute his inadequate statement of the distinction to the issues of development and method, especially the idea that Royce had an epistemological method and conception of the Absolute at the time he distinguished between appreciation and description. But it is harder to understand why Smith did not take Marcel's interpretation of this distinction more seriously. The issue of how to deal with immediate experience from a Roycean perspective depends upon this discussion. I will address it in Chapter 3, more in terms of Hocking's critique than Marcel's, but the two are quite similar.

Third, and finally, Smith does not explicitly distinguish between "individual" and "person" in Royce's philosophy. There are numerous instances of this, but here is a clear one:

> The value of community in all its instances is twofold; by showing the individual a supreme value which introduces some harmony among his conflicting inclinations it helps him towards self-realization, and by interpreting all its members to all its other members through a common past and a common future it brings about a unity and harmony among persons such as would not otherwise be possible.³¹

Smith is entirely correct in his expression of the two-fold importance of community, and I have no qualms whatsoever about the exact wording of his point. The trouble is that there is a world of territory between the social character of human individuality and the work of community in nurturing *persons*. That world of territory is crucial for the proper interpretation of Royce, and Smith, while generally using the terms accurately, does not help his readers in any way to grasp that there is a difference between individuality and personhood. The distinction is altogether crucial, and if Smith has understood the difference (which he may have, given that he uses the terms correctly), he certainly overlooked its importance. Had he seen the importance of the matter, he surely would have helped his readers grasp it.

Smith was more attuned to pragmatism than to personalism in his work, which is understandable. But the scholarship prior to the "bottleneck" had been cognizant of the point that Royce was defending a kind of personalism (as Tunstall demonstrated, this being part and parcel of Royce's "ethico-religious insight"). After Smith, this personalist emphasis was somehow forgotten, in spite of the fact that it screams for recognition from almost every page of Royce's writing. I will attempt to bring this emphasis back to the fore of Royce interpretation because the proper understanding of both the conception of "will" and of "purpose" depends upon this.[32]

I believe that the three distinctions above that have been either misunderstood or under-emphasized by Smith: actual/possible, appreciation/description, and individual/person, are all of great significance. A more thorough grasp of Royce's method and development will open these distinctions up for consideration, and such consideration brings to light some very important and useful ideas. I will show this as the book unfolds. Now, however, I wish to conclude this discussion by reiterating my admiration for Smith's excellent book and the subsequent work he has written that builds upon it, although I admit the repetition of these same errors, perhaps especially in Smith's long introduction to the University of Chicago edition of *The Problem of Christianity*, the edition read by most of the scholars of my generation and the generation just before mine. It seems everyone I encountered for many years who read that edition carried around all of the misconceptions I have outlined in this section. It is time for these problems to be corrected.

[1]
Biography

My aim in the present chapter is not to provide any sort of extensive study of Royce's life. Outstanding studies already exist, not only of Royce's life as a whole but also numerous specific studies of episodes in his life.[1] I will draw upon those studies in my offerings here, but the purpose is to tell the story of Royce's life in a way that provides a biographical grounding for the philosophical and interpretive points I will make in later chapters. The present chapter is a way of narrating Royce's life for philosophical rather than historical purposes. Hence, each of the *sections* of this biographical sketch will bring out the philosophical points that are discussed in greater detail in a corresponding chapter. It would be premature for readers to form quick judgments about the textual evidence for my philosophical claims based upon this chapter alone. The textual support for my broad interpretive claims is to be found in the later chapters that expand upon and explain the points made in this sketch.

Biography and Philosophy

A general point should be made, at the outset, about the relationship of biography to philosophy (at least philosophy of a Roycean stripe). It is rarely appreciated in Royce studies the extent to which he followed closely and was influenced by the work of Nietzsche. All who read Royce extensively do eventually notice that Royce took Nietzsche very seriously, agreed with him on many points, and where he took issue with Nietzsche it was the kind of disagreement possible only for a philosopher who holds his counterpart in the highest respect. In many ways Royce and Nietzsche were Schopenhauer's two most ungrateful philosophical offspring, for having internalized the stubborn primacy of Will in the world, they each fought with all their might against

Schopenhauer's pessimistic (or as Nietzsche had it, "life-denying") conclusions. How can the primacy of Will, irrational and uncomprehending of itself, point to anything but pessimism? It was a soul-wrenching problem for both Royce and Nietzsche. And neither Nietzsche nor Royce would allow himself to accept evasions or easy answers to the challenge of Schopenhauer's pessimism. In a word, Royce and Nietzsche took Schopenhauer's philosophy "personally," as an affront to their own self-existence, and both responded to that affront with vigor.

While it was Nietzsche who proclaimed that a philosophical system can be true for its creator alone, that all philosophical arguments are really *ad hominem* attacks, and that therefore philosophy is a kind of autobiography veiled in generalizations and concepts, this perspective is more quietly and more carefully shared by Royce. There is no final separation for either thinker between the choices one makes in life and the philosophy one creates. John McDermott's writings on Royce, and his original writings in a Roycean vein, emphasize this aspect of Royce's philosophy, and I heartily agree that the best doorway to questions about the life of Royce is from his thought, and *vice versa*.

Yet I do not believe Royce would have accepted a formula like "philosophy just *is* autobiography," and indeed, I also don't believe it is true. Nietzsche was given to hyperbole. But the more carefully stated view that "no philosophy can avoid bearing the unmistakable stamp of its creator, and is, to that extent, revelatory in its way of a unique perspective, and of a life lived and hoped for" is true, in my view, and I think Royce would have agreed. Thus, philosophical ideas are never fully separable from their provenance, but that doesn't make them reducible to it. The key is to see the relation between the life and the ideas, to recognize the scope of the life in the ideas without exaggerating it. This is delicate and fallible work.

The second teacher, apart from Schopenhauer, shared by Nietzsche and Royce was Ralph Waldo Emerson. It would require a long inquiry to place this crucial mutual influence in its proper context. What can be said here is that for every analogy one can find between Royce and Nietzsche, including the voluntarism, one may find a solid source in Emerson. A future study should be devoted to Emerson as the intellectual progenitor of Royce and Nietzsche, but I will not attempt it here. The point is that understanding how Schopenhauer and Emerson overlap, and how they clash, is not a bad way to think through the relation of philosophy to life, and an interesting picture of Royce emerges from the effort.

An Initial Estimate of Royce's Achievement

Royce was among the most accomplished, ingenious, and original thinkers America has begotten, and he stands as an equal among its true giants. If he was somewhat less creative and intellectually brilliant than C.S. Peirce, the discrepancy was not great and was compensated for by an ability, which Peirce lacked, to see a project through to its conclusion, to teach effectively, and to struggle through disappointment and tragedy with his social circle still intact. Royce's sheer intellect certainly surpassed James, Dewey, and Santayana.

Royce had something of John Dewey's plodding dedication to practical philosophy and given a comparable life-span (Dewey lived thirty-one years longer) would have certainly produced a body of writings equally large, although Royce's output was prodigious for one who died comparatively young. Where Dewey, in his superannuated writings, surpassed Royce as a social and political thinker, and certainly as a public philosopher, Royce was a talented logician and metaphysician, capable of systematizing his thought (without losing his concrete bearings) in ways Dewey could not manage. Royce was a more creative and thorough moral philosopher than Dewey, both in terms of the full integration of his moral thought with his logic, epistemology and metaphysics, and also in the originality of his thinking up genuinely new moral concepts that ameliorated moral dilemmas. While Dewey's virtue ethics, excellent as it is, amounts to updating Aristotle, and is in some ways difficult to reconcile with his metaphysics and aesthetics, Royce's moral philosophy is wholly integrated with his full philosophy and genuinely novel, solving many problems that persist in Dewey's thought.

Perhaps Royce was not the equal of William James in collecting and categorizing massive amounts of data according to new insights and relations, but he did not give as much away to James in this respect as did Dewey and Peirce, who were far less patient with, for example, historical data than was Royce. Royce's ability in metaphysical, formal and systematic thinking certainly surpassed anything James could accomplish. I will treat this last point in some detail in Chapter 7. Unlike James, Royce was a careful and accurate interpreter of figures in the history of philosophy, and a reliable judge of their strengths and weaknesses. James could not be relied upon to interpret accurately even the living philosophers he knew personally, let alone those who were dead. For all his brilliance, this deficiency hindered James his whole life. A formal and serious education in philosophy was wanting, and it showed every time he attempted to report the views of another philosopher. The more subtle the philosopher, the more his views would be distorted in James's accounts. Royce had no such difficulties.

If Royce was not George Santayana's literary equal, and he was not, he exceeded Dewey and Peirce and was the equal of James as a writer—although both James and Royce were also capable of producing dry and uninteresting prose, as in Royce's perfectly awful literary performance in *The World and the Individual* and James's maddeningly tedious and pointless book *The Meaning of Truth*. Yet, at his best, and here I would especially point out *The Sources of Religious Insight* and *The Philosophy of Loyalty* (excepting the chapters on James!), Royce wrote as well as James ever did. Royce's command and understanding of the literary tradition itself surpasses all major American philosophers excepting Santayana and Emerson.

Royce was the best philosopher of religion America has ever produced and in this regard he has no serious rivals at all, at Harvard or anywhere else. William Ernest Hocking and Charles Hartshorne were certainly brilliant philosophers of religion, but they would have to be elevated far beyond their current status to be seen as rivals to Royce.

Students who studied at Harvard during the days in which these monumental figures (James, Royce, Santayana, and on sporadic occasions, Peirce) filled the lecture halls were especially careful not to try to choose a superior among them. Rather, the generation including figures such as Hocking, George Herbert Mead, Helen Keller, T.S. Eliot, Alain Locke, W.E.B. DuBois, and John Elof Boodin, to name but a few, went away with *several* masters and with the philosophical task of reconciling seemingly contrary truths that would absorb many of them for a lifetime. Royce's intellectual context was as complex as his thought, but the context must be grasped along with the ideas. If my initial estimate of Royce seems overly generous to some, I encourage them to return to it after having completed this book.

California

The specific relation of Royce's life to his thought is somewhat enigmatic, for the sweep of the ideas is grand and the particulars of his life explain the origins of his ideas less than might be hoped, but the particulars need to be included. Royce was born on 20th November 1855 in the town of Grass Valley, California. Royce died on 14th September 1916 in Cambridge, Massachusetts. He was the son of Josiah and Sarah Eleanor (Bayliss) Royce, whose own families were recent English emigrants, and prior to his birth, in 1849, Royce's parents sought their fortune in the westward movement of the American pioneers.

A narrative by Sarah Bayliss Royce of her family's passage over the plains and mountains, and of the early days in the mining camps in California, was culled from her 1849–1850 diary at the request of her only son (and later published in 1932).[2] All of Royce's biographers lay stress on his unusual upbringing in the unformed conditions of California, and they commonly assert that this experience exerted a profound influence upon the development of his philosophical ideas, particularly regarding community, which are among his most important contributions to philosophy. This is undoubtedly true, and it is demonstrable that he generalized from California communities to human communities. Yet, important as it is, I believe the "debt to California" is over-estimated, as I shall argue in the course of this chapter.[3]

The character of Royce's parents is also of crucial moment in the view of his numerous biographers. No doubt the general view is largely correct, as it would be safe to say the same thing of almost any human being. The mystical fervor of Royce's mother (some say that her pioneer narrative is really an argument with her son's heterodox religious views) may have motivated Royce's thorough critique of mysticism. His father was absent much of the time as Royce was growing up, trying to pull together various business endeavors, most of which failed. The father's absence, it has been suggested by some, including Frank Oppenheim, may have set Royce upon a lifelong quest for father figures (such as he found in William James) and might even have explained his fondness for the Absolute (just as surely as the over-bearing omnipresence of James's father led him to react *against* the Absolute, according to many of *his* biographers).[4]

There may be truth in this and other tempting connections that have been drawn regarding relations between Royce's life and his ideas. But it is difficult to turn such notions as these into reliable knowledge, since we are wisely dubious of such notions when they are pronounced regarding *living* persons of whom we could *ask* whether they might be true. Indeed, I think no one short of a guru can credibly claim to have *knowledge* of such questions regarding even himself or herself, let alone anyone else, and least of all the dead whom we have never personally known. And my expectation is that even a guru, having attained such self-knowledge, would not answer such questions at all as to whether his mysticism or philosophy issued from an unconscious response to a parent's habits. It is better to be cautious and to resist the urge to pretend that we have Royce on the therapist's couch.

At most such biographical notions are interesting suggestions that spur *our* thinking, not conclusions upon which we can safely lay our inquiries to rest, no matter how much they seem to explain. And indeed, the temptation is great to use such hypotheses as foundations for building the edifice of an interpretation, even if what is subsequently built can be no steadier than its doubtful footing. The temptation should be resisted, but hasn't been in many instances by Royce's (and James's and Peirce's and Dewey's) biographers. A good example of this danger is illustrated in the rather extensive differences between the first (1985) and second (1999) editions of John Clendenning's excellent biography of Royce. No one knows more about Royce's life than Clendenning, or ever will, but new evidence emerged between 1985 and 1999 that obliged the biographer to back away from many of the psychological hypotheses about Royce that had provided a net of motives in the earlier telling, especially regarding his home life. Clendenning is much more circumspect in the 1999 edition, for which he is to be thanked.

The fortunes of Royce's family were various in the rural mining camps, sometimes they had a nice house and plenty, sometimes they didn't fare as well, but by the time they moved to San Francisco in Royce's eleventh year, the family was very poor and would remain so until Royce was grown. I do think it is of crucial importance to bear in mind always that Royce knew poverty and hunger first-hand, but I will not use it as a building block. It is only good to keep in mind that real experience with hunger and want set him apart from James, Santayana, Peirce (until late in life), and even the more modest but still adequate means of the Deweys.[5]

When present, Royce's father was apparently an unrelenting disciplinarian and an enthusiastic Campbellite, a "restorationist." The emphasis among Campbellites upon what they call Pauline Christianity, rejecting all creeds, sects, and denominations while insisting upon the full sufficiency of the New Testament (and the individual's right interpretation thereof), may have something to do with Royce's later emphasis upon Paul in his own interpretation of Christianity. Indeed, Royce's *The Problem of Christianity* has very much a restorationist tone, without the historical realism of the Campbellites, and without their tendency to fetishize the early church (as they imagine it). But beyond the suggestion of a noticeable Pauline tenor to Royce's appropriation of Christianity, we should not venture a hypothesis. I will say that a general failure on the part of many interpreters of Royce to investigate the views of the Campbellites has led them to treat Royce's philosophy of religion as though it were more original than it is. Those who know something about the Campbellites have no difficulty fitting *The Problem of Christianity* into the "liberal" side of the Campbellite theological literature, while those who see in Royce a kind of Calvinism completely miss the mark. It was reforming Calvinism that gave the restorationists their impetus.

One might suppose that with two aggressively evangelistic parents, one a mystic and the other a Biblical literalist, there would be a clear reaction against either father or mother, or both, perhaps even an anti-religious bent, but it seems to me that Royce's own view of organized religion and religious experience was moderate and his non-participation more a matter of lack of inclination rather than a reaction. It appears now that the decision of Royce and his spouse Katherine to raise their three boys without any denominational or other organized affiliation, was more the decision of Katherine than of Royce himself. Yet, the importance of *agapic* love in Royce's philosophy is almost certainly rooted in his Christian upbringing, while his re-interpretation of its meaning in terms of a progressive and universal sense of "loyalty" seems not to be an idea one would be likely to find in the early California context. The interpretation of *agape* as "loyalty" appears to be Royce's own insight, or at least, no biographer or other researcher has identified a likely source up to now. But Royce's modernism and progressivism is not adequately explained by the openness and freedom of a California upbringing, for his type of modernism was more akin to the progressivism of the industrial East and far more at home there than in California.[6] Royce's love of Old World ideas, especially the German philosophy of the late eighteenth and nineteenth centuries, is also uncharacteristic of California, but was common in Boston and Baltimore where he later lived.

The efforts of some biographers, therefore, to grasp the roots of Royce's theory of community in terms of mining camps ring hollow in light of the fact that Royce struggled mightily from early in life to break free of the individualism and ethical egoism, the prevalence of naked self-interest and grasping greed, with which he had grown up in California, and he finally felt he had "succeeded" upon leaving the state in 1875. Royce never wanted to return to California for more than a visit, if he could manage it (although he was not to get his wish). While he loved the natural beauty of California and this may have had much to do with his later development of an idealistic environmental philosophy, he was equally happy with the New England countryside when closeness to nature was needed. Royce needed to *get out* of California. He missed his mother and sisters, but he did *not* miss California or its "communities." This fact needs to be set alongside the habitual emphasis on California that characterizes many biographical writings on Royce.

Studies

At the young "University of California" (first in Oakland and then moving to Berkeley during his matriculation), Royce studied classics, literature, physical sciences and mathematics, distinguishing himself as a student and elected to be one of four commencement speakers. There was no formal training in philosophy at Berkeley in those days, but he read Darwin, Mill, and Spencer under the watchful eye of the philosophically inclined geology professor Joseph Le Conte, leading Royce to a crisis of religious faith and a short bout with skepticism. Royce was an evolutionist from the earliest days of his higher education, but rejected Darwin's materialist interpretation, embracing instead a moderate personalistic naturalism like LeConte's.[7] At Berkeley Royce acquired Latin, Greek, and French, but apparently not German.

With the help of former Berkeley president Daniel C. Gilman, Royce studied in Germany in 1875–76 (and acquired German there, evidently, a language of which he would retain mastery for the rest of his life). At Leipzig he studied the history of philosophy with Wilhelm Windelband, Sanskrit with Heinrich Hubschmann, and physiological psychology with Wilhelm Wundt. At Göttingen Royce studied with Rudolf Hermann Lotze. If Royce had flirted with romantic philosophy early in his education, his experience in Germany turned him decidedly and permanently toward the strains of development in the Kantian philosophy that would inform his thought from that time forward. Royce was never in any serious way a follower of Hegel or himself a Hegelian philosopher, although a persistent (and forgivable) misunderstanding of his thought under this label emerged early and has endured in spite of Royce's own efforts and the efforts of subsequent interpreters to dispel it. Royce *loved* Hegel's philosophy, and he even proposed himself to the publishing firm Henry Holt as the first translator of *The Phenomenology of Spirit*, but he was not a *follower* of Hegel at any time in his life. It *is* possible to admire something one does not philosophically endorse. Royce's conceptions of the Absolute (and there are many different ones, as I said in the introduction) bear little resemblance to Hegel's idea.

Returning from Germany in 1876, Royce was offered a fellowship at the new Johns Hopkins University, where he continued studying classics, Sanskrit, Plato, and Aristotle. He systematically read

Spinoza, Hegel, Schopenhauer, and Kant, offering lecture courses of his own on the latter two. Royce's Schopenhauer seminar was apparently the first graduate course ever offered in the United States. William James lectured at Johns Hopkins during the spring of 1877, and Royce spent that following summer in his company in Boston. Although they had first met in 1875, this association of 1877 began in earnest a lifelong friendship and one of the most important philosophical exchanges in the history of American thought. Royce also may have met Peirce that spring or summer, although Peirce was in New York rather than Baltimore or Boston. It is nearly certain that spending this time in the orbit of James, Royce learned of Peirce and read his important philosophical essays.

Royce also read Kant and some of the neo-Kantians that summer and in the spring of the following year he defended his doctoral dissertation, a neo-Kantian investigation of the interdependence of the principles of knowledge. To state it in the words of one of Royce's biographers, "there is no shred of absolutism anywhere in the work."[8] I would stress the "ism" in that remark, since Royce was never given to absolut*ism*, if by that term one means a proponent of the final authority of unqualified philosophical knowledge over other kinds of knowledge or practice. His dissertation is now chief among the great unpublished works in his literary remains, and it is a fine contribution to Kantian thought. Royce was in a group of four who were the first to receive Ph.D.'s from Johns Hopkins.

Back to California

Following his graduate studies Royce reluctantly took a position teaching literature at the University of California and immediately set about trying to get another position back East. In spite of his position teaching literature he continued studying and writing in philosophy, publishing a number of articles and a "primer" that lay on the borders of philosophy, rhetoric, and grammar. He married Katherine Head, the daughter of a well-to-do Bay Area judge, in 1880. The first of their three sons, Christopher, was born while they were still in California, in 1882. Christopher's was a short, difficult, and tragic life (he died in 1910, having been institutionalized for two years), from which Royce learned much in the way of wisdom and compassion. Royce's most beautifully written work, *The Sources of Religious Insight* (1912), was a product of his grieving process for Christopher and for William James, who had also died less than a month earlier.

Temporalism

Among the important accomplishments of his final years in California was the development of Royce's temporalist philosophy. By the term "temporalism" I mean to indicate any philosophy that takes the fundamental character of time to be the key to effective and meaningful reflection on philosophical problems, as distinct from "spatialism," which seeks its primary orderings of "rationality" according to analogies with geometrical or other mathematical methods. Spatial philosophies, especially geometrical ones such as Spinoza's and Hobbes's, embody the Enlightenment conception of reason as a philosophical tool. Yet, any kind of reasoning that tends to set individuals in *permanent* relations to the whole of reality will be "spatial" in the relevant sense.

Rationalism and spatialism are about the same thing, historically, but the connection between the excellent use of reason and the spatialization of our thought is contingent rather than necessary. Temporalist philosophies have existed at least from the time of Heraclitus, but they began to become increasingly important through the nineteenth century (the rise of philosophies of historical consciousness from Vico to Hegel is an example of the growth of temporalism). In the twentieth century, temporalist philosophies became, in my view, the *only* viable philosophies, in the sense that only a temporalist philosophy can solve philosophical problems in a way that is plausible for the dominant ways of "fixing belief" (that is, resolving doubt) that have become prevalent in contemporary times. Spatialist philosophies and all those embracing an Enlightenment conception of reason have died very slowly, but they are dying no less for that, largely from their utter irrelevance to contemporary life.

"Rationality" of the sort that analytic philosophies of the twentieth century defended has never really existed and certainly solves no genuine human problems, philosophical or otherwise. The dominant philosophies of the mid-twentieth century were groundless fairy tales. We spatialize our problems only at the cost of rendering the world of thought virtual and fantastic. Genuine problem solving can *employ* spatializations of our thinking, but can never take such fantasies literally or think of them as "corresponding" with some state of affairs. Defenders of "correspondence" theories of truth need therapy for their superstitions more than anything else. Language simplifies our experience as it aids in spatialization—making the flow of experience stand still and stand in relations and categories. That is why language is so useful. Concrete states of affairs, on the other hand, are infinitely complex. No bit of language "corresponds" to a state of affairs in some necessary way, nor can it. Language is vague, the world is not, or at least not in the same way. No more need be said about it. Temporalist philosophies do not commit this error of imagining that the world must yield its secrets to the right magic words. We spatialize time at a cost to our act of knowing, rendering that act partial, incomplete, since infinitely many spaces are compatible, in thought, with any single concrete moment of duration. Royce not only knew this, but he assumed it was obvious to everyone else, as indeed it *is* to all but willfully ignorant intellectuals who have become invested in a contrary superstition, the myth of all-encompassing "reason."

Royce began the construction of his philosophical system by means of a critique of ontology, by which he meant the study of the form(s) of allegedly "independent" existences and their relations. In 1881, in an article published in the *Journal of Speculative Philosophy* and another in the British journal *Mind*, Royce examined the ontologies that were being defended in his day and argued that every ontology is a useful fiction at best. I will discuss this in more detail in the next chapter. According to Royce, we may *postulate* an ontology, make for ourselves a useful "myth," but *knowledge* in this domain is impossible. Royce also rejects ontological necessity here, embracing by implication a *descriptive* method in metaphysics.[9] The *present acts* by which we construct our *possible* future experience must be regarded as real, and these acts involve a temporal structure that is irreducibly three-fold. The past and present must be "acknowledged" and the future "anticipated" in every act.

Most striking in this early account is Royce's definition of the "present" as the *acknowledgment* of other conscious beings and *their* possible experience. The present, for the purposes of ontology, simply *is* the experience of others that I am *not* having, only acknowledging and interpreting. What he would later call "the community of interpretation" is therefore already present in his first efforts at systematic metaphysics, although the terminology was nascent. It is also notable that Royce resists, in this definition of the "present," a common rationalist tendency, beginning with Leibniz, to define the present as "simultaneity," or at-the-same-time-ness, and then to identify this simultaneity with "space." Royce's definition of the present embraces no such absoluteness or homogeneity of space, no such "slicing" of time. Instead, Royce chooses a phenomenologically sensitive description that will include overlapping durational time-spans and multiple "presents" for the beings whose durational spans are quite different from the range of human spans.

Also notable in these early articles is Royce's account of the future as holding the anticipated objects of *possible* experiences not yet had, the products of our "projections." Royce is already using the term "possibility" in a fairly consistent way to describe not only the existential mode of the future, but also the most basic modal idea of the present ("other *possible* experience"), as distinct from "necessity" (which receives a number of formulations in Royce, including "the irrevocability of the past," but all formulations involve *negation*, which requires a step *away* from concrete complexity, requires that something be *left out of account*). From this early date Royce recognized that the "myths" we tell ourselves in practicing ontology (including postulates about necessity, or *possible* necessities) should serve *moral* ends and aspirations. The maxim could be stated: "do not leave out (i.e., negate) whatever is morally required for practical action." All philosophy must simplify, must negate, must employ the vagaries of language and submit to the spatializations of thought, but philosophy must not do this without a thorough submission of its norms for postulating to defensible *purposes*. Thus "purposes," for Royce, as future plans, as *possibilities*, were indispensable to any philosophy, as he argued in 1880 in an unpublished essay "On Purpose in Thought."[10] This creative take on descriptive metaphysics, ontology, the sociality of present experience, and the relation of act to possibility, suffices to give Royce, along with Peirce, a claim to being the first full-fledged process philosopher in the U.S., and certainly a committed temporalist from at least 1880 forward.[11]

Many of Royce's interpreters have claimed that Royce's position on ontology changed in his first major work, *The Religious Aspect of Philosophy*. This is not obvious, although it is fair to say that Royce became increasingly convinced of the power of reflective reason to deliver truths which, if they should *fail* to hold in relation to the whole, would render the entire enterprise of knowing vain and pointless, and would undermine the moral purposes for which all persons live. This might be rephrased by saying that, by 1885, Royce had come to the conclusion that we have no choice but to *believe* the "myths" we construct for ourselves in reflection, and that there are decisive methods for judging among the competing myths (which he was already saying in 1881 as he showed how certain ontologies, even if they be taken as hypotheses, lead to contradiction).

Harvard

In 1882 William James arranged a temporary position for Royce at Harvard as a replacement for himself while he was on leave. Then came another temporary appointment in 1883–84 replacing George Herbert Palmer, who was on sabbatical, and finally a full-time appointment, split between philosophy and literature, beginning in the fall of 1884. Royce remained at Harvard until his death, taking important journeys, leaves, and sabbaticals along the way. In particular Royce took voyages to the South Seas and the Caribbean to restore his mental health during times when family life and professional pressures exhausted him.

No sooner had Royce arrived in Boston than he began to shake the dust of California from his sandals, in several important writings. While in the west Royce had struggled (albeit briefly) with skepticism about the knowability of the world in itself, with the ethical egoism of various thinkers, with individualism, romanticism, and with a full panoply of other fundamental philosophical (especially epistemological) orientations. California, then as now, certainly lent itself to free thinking, but the insight into the temporal interrelatedness of all genuine individuality seems to have come to Royce *alone*, among all the intelligent people from California, so one wonders what California as such might have had to do with the most basic insights, if its supposed communicative power was discernable to Royce alone among all of its sons and daughters. We are all the products of our places, but places only set our contexts. They do not cause insights or prevent them.

Royce's temporalist personal idealism was an answer, philosophically and religiously, to some of the very problems *posed* by the rise of California, holding, as it did, a "golden" opportunity either to achieve the beloved community, or to fail in the attempt, or to ignore the very possibility of community and fall into selfish and blind egoism. This situation was a problem for Royce precisely because Californians did not, on the whole, wish to *view* themselves critically and reflectively, especially in light of categories of moral consistency. The triumphal arrogance of the white Californians disgusted Royce, and he saw that, like all places, this place was complex.

The explicitly *moral* terms in which Royce wrote his history of California (from the safety of Boston) are based upon his moral insight about the individual's temporal relation to community; according to which each present act exemplifies a *social* consciousness with a past, a present, and a future. In assessing the actors in the historical narrative, he tacitly or explicitly asked at each turn the question whether each actor had allowed himself to be informed in his present by the immanence of a Kingdom of Ends, in which case he is a hero, or failed to recognize this reality, thus acting in service to an ultimately illusory self, in which case he is treated as a villain—and there were far more villains than heroes to be found in nineteenth-century California, by Royce's reckoning. In many ways Royce's *distance* from California is what is plainest in his history of it, as he self-consciously condemns the so-called "Bear Flag heroes" for having deceived themselves into thinking that the motives for conquest had anything to do with bringing the blessings of liberty to the Spanish, and how these false "heroes" can "show us what it is to have a national conscience sensitive enough to call loudly for elaborate and eloquent comfort in moments of doubt, and just stupid enough to be readily deluded by mock-eloquent cant."[12]

Praising the collective shame that was *eventually* widely felt at the immorality of American aggression in the Mexican War, Royce's distance from California translated into a somewhat rare sense of distance also from American nationalism and patriotic fervor. Royce concluded:

> It is to be hoped that this lesson [the immorality of the Mexican War and its clear implications for the immorality of the conquest of California], showing us as it does how much of conscience and even personal sincerity can coexist with a minimum of effective morality in international undertakings, will someday be once more remembered; so that when our nation is another time about to serve the devil, it will do so with more frankness and will deceive itself less by half-unconscious cant. For the rest, our mission in the cause of liberty is to be accomplished through a steadfast devotion to the cultivation of our own inner life, and not by going abroad as missionaries, as conquerors, or as marauders among weaker peoples.[13]

The most interesting feature of this anti-imperialist hope is the exclusion of missionaries. It is worth considering in that it shows that Royce was very far from being naive about the part played by religion in militarism and imperialism.[14] What the California experience and later reflection upon it provided for Royce was a poignant and personal example of the difference between what is ideally possible, its great distance from actual life, and how various ways of cultivating the inner life can either reveal that distance to us or lead us to conceal it from ourselves. It was the collection of solutions to these problems of self-deception, ignorance, and error that provided the impetus, the direction, and the goal of Royce's entire philosophy, in all of its particulars. The cultivation of the inner life in quest of community as a remedy to loneliness, isolation, fear, feelings of abandonment, depression, and despair was the human lot. Thus, the hypocrisies of California were as much a negative lesson as its free experimental communities were a positive influence on Royce's thinking. What these episodes indicate is not just an uncommon childhood resulting in an uncommon man, but also a child who was from the first uncommonly detached (as John Clendenning has effectively argued in his biography of Royce). Royce was better able than most to see his situation as a whole *while* he lived it, and better able to judge it as a whole when he left it behind.

Early Works

The years between 1882 and 1895 established Royce as one of the most eminent American philosophers. His publication in 1885 of *The Religious Aspect of Philosophy*, and in 1892 of *The Spirit of Modern Philosophy*, both based on Harvard lectures, secured his place in the philosophical world. The former of these contained a new "proof" for the existence of God based upon the reality of error, which drew much attention, perhaps too much. To be in error is to be in error in comparison to some total truth, Royce argued, and we must either hold ourselves infallible or accept that even our errors are evidence of a world of truth.[15] Having made it clear that idealism depends upon *postulates* and proceeds hypothetically, Royce defends the necessity of objective reference of our ideas to a universal whole within which they belong, for without these postulates, "both practical life and the commonest results of theory, from the simplest impressions to the most valuable beliefs, would be for most if not all of us utterly impossible."[16] Hence, the justification for idealistic postulates is *practical* and normative. Royce confronts the fact that he has not offered, and perhaps cannot offer, a complete or satisfactory account of "the relation of the individual minds to the all-embracing mind,"[17] but he pushes ahead in spite of this difficulty to offer the best account he can manage. This takes the form of an expression of his personalism:

> The ambiguous relation of the conscious individuals to the universal thought . . . will be decided in the sense of their inclusion, as elements in the universal thought. They will indeed not become 'things in the dream' of any other person than themselves, but their whole reality, just exactly as it is in them, will be found to be but a fragment of a higher reality. This reality will be no Power, nor will it produce the individuals by dreaming of them, but it will complete the existence that in them, as separate beings, has no rational completeness.[18]

This is an unavoidable hypothesis (and reading closely, it is clear that an hypothesis is *all* he is offering, a way of deciding how to *think about* an issue), and its moral and religious aspects point to an Absolute. The senses of "Absolute" Royce defended were quite different from the well-known ideas of Hegel and Bradley, as I have mentioned in the Introduction. Royce's Absolute is, among other things, the ground and originator of community, a personal, temporal being (later called the "interpreter spirit") who preserves the past in its entirety, sustains the full present by an act of interpretation, and anticipates every genuine possibility in the future, infusing these possibilities with value according to their relation to the ideal of community. The principal difference between Royce's Absolute and the similar idea held by other thinkers is its temporal and personal character, and its interpretive activity. This divine activity Royce increasingly came to see in terms of the notion suggested by Peirce of "agapasm," or "evolutionary love." Royce's Absolute is, among other things, a person in relation to which all persons exist as mutual interpreters. But its role in his philosophy is to provide a number of different conceptions of the "whole," so that the parts become interpretable in their temporal existence.

The Conception of God Debate

A benchmark in Royce's career and thought occurred when he returned to California to speak to the Philosophical Union at Berkeley, and ostensibly to defend his concept of God from the criticisms of George Holmes Howison, Joseph LeConte, and Sidney Mezes, a meeting the *New York Times* called "a battle of the giants." There Royce offered a new *modal* version of his proof for the reality of God based upon *ignorance* rather than *error*, based upon the fragmentariness of individual existence rather than its epistemological fallibility.[19] It is important to be aware that the apparent shift in the "proof" was really an adjustment for a different inquiry which was ontological more than epistemological.

Up to 1895, Royce had taken it as a given that one can have a fragmentary existence, as part of a whole, and still be a *person* in the full sense. The extract I offered above demonstrates his view of this question. Howison attacked Royce's epistemic doctrine of 1885 as having left no ontological standing for the individual over against the Absolute, and having therefore undermined individuality, Royce had also undermined personality, rendering Royce's idealism a kind of pernicious impersonalism. Royce never intended this result and responded to Howison's criticism first in a long supplementary essay to the debate (published in 1897), which made out his view of individuality, and then by developing the philosophy of the individual person in greater detail in his Gifford Lectures, published under the title *The World and the Individual* (1899,

1901).

Simultaneously Royce was enduring a resolute assault on his hypothetical metaphysics from James (who never quite grasped Royce's method and wrongly insisted it was an absolut*ism*). Royce later admitted that his engagement with the philosophy of Bradley may have led to a more vigorous waltz with an abstract Absolute than was warranted, and it might be added that his persistent reading of Spinoza and Hegel might have had similar effects. I do not think this is correct, however. Royce's regrets were more about the way he had expressed himself than about the conception of God or the Absolute. But the encounter with Howison was a sort of Waterloo for Royce, in my view, putting him on notice that his idealism required not only a clearer expression, but the full development of a theory of individuality in order to preserve the idea that persons are ontologically significant entities, and that one is obliged to postulate their coeval reality with the Whole. Some of that work on individuality is in the 1897 supplementary essay, but the full story comes out in his Gifford Lectures. The defense of a plurality of metaphysically real individuals as a requirement of good ontology also committed Royce to a type of metaphysical pluralism.

The World and the Individual

The First Series of Gifford Lectures (1899) made the case against three historical conceptions of being, called "realism," "mysticism," and "critical rationalism," by Royce, and defending a "Fourth Conception of Being." Realism, according to Royce, held that *to be is to be independent*, but the quest to demonstrate the independence of any existence involves unsolvable contradictions. Mysticism (in Royce's peculiar sense of it) and critical rationalism advanced other criteria for being. For mysticism, *to be was to be immediate*, for the mystic has come to recognize that if something exists, including mind, it is part of a total immediately related unity which cannot as a whole, become an object of knowledge.

For Royce, the contradictions in realism *drive* one to mysticism, if any conception of being is to be retained (skepticism is the other choice, of course). But mysticism depends upon a claim it cannot demonstrate, which renders its conception of being unstable and unsatisfactory, for as a *conception* of being, it is supposed to be a kind of philosophical knowledge, and philosophical knowledge is mediated rather than immediate. The idea of "immediate" philosophical knowledge is, according to the account of Peirce in 1868 (that Royce always followed), an untenable idea. One is driven therefore to making only qualified knowledge claims about being, and this is the essence of critical rationalism. For critical rationalism, having "objective validity" in one's ontological knowledge claims is the best one can do. Thus, being itself supports claims that identify *experience* with *existence* wherever objective validity can be demonstrated. This is recognizable as a "conception of being" particularly where a transcendental philosophy, such as Kant's, has replaced mysticism and realism. But critical rationalism, however much it may search for a formal criterion of objective validity, cannot find one that is adequately secure. As a result, its conception of being remains at best an ungrounded claim.

As hypotheses about the fundamental character of being, Royce shows by dialectical arguments that each of these conceptions of being is inadequate as an "account," and by *reductio* arguments he shows how the first two fall into contradiction. This effort occupies some 250 pages, but the succeeding 200 pages offers Royce's *hypothesis* that *to be is to be uniquely related to a whole*, which is one way to summarize his "Fourth Conception of Being." This formulation preserves all three crucial aspects of being, namely the Whole, the unique individual, and the relation that constitutes them. Where previously Royce's hypotheses about ontology had taken for granted that relations are discovered in the analysis of terms, here he moves to the recognition that terms are constituted *by* their relations. Insofar as terms are taken to refer to entities, as we must assume, we are obliged to think about individuals as *uniquely* constituted by a totality of relations to other individuals (and to the Whole) that are theirs alone. The relational logic employed in the Gifford Lectures is explicitly triadic; although Royce's ontology had been a temporalist triad all along (past, present, future), it seems fair to say that the formalization of this viewpoint in a logic of relations was probably due to the impact upon Royce of Peirce's 1898 lectures on logic at Harvard, and of Royce's subsequent "study" of logic with Peirce by correspondence. Not much survives of this correspondence, and it is difficult to know how extensively Royce did "study logic" with Peirce, but even if the minimum estimates of its extent are true, the effect on Royce was profound—possibly more profound than the "1912 Peircean insight," of which interpreters have made too much.

The first series of lectures was published with a lengthy "Supplementary Essay" of over 100 pages, in a small typeface, which was not a part of the original lectures. All Royce scholars regard this as an important writing. It treats the philosophy of Bradley, contrasting Royce's style of idealism with that system, but more important is the analysis of the relation of the infinite to the actual. John E. Smith has explained the importance of this essay to Royce's overall philosophy in *Royce's Social Infinite*, which I will not summarize here.

In the Second Series of Gifford Lectures Royce *temporalizes* these relations of Whole and individuals, showing that we learn to *think* about ideas like "succession" and "space" by noting differences and directionality within unified and variable "time spans," or qualitative, durational episodes of the "specious present." Royce explains, "our temporal form of experience is thus peculiarly the form of the Will as such."[20] Here Royce makes a crucial step in his struggle with Schopenhauer's pessimism by re-conceiving the "will" in relational terms, providing an orderly and logical (if not wholly rational) way of describing it. Hence, for Royce, the will reflects the inner dynamism that reaches beyond itself into a possible future and acts upon an acknowledged past. Space and the abstract descriptions that go with it are a falsification and negation of this dynamism, and metaphysical error; especially "realism," proceeds from taking these abstractions literally. Philosophy itself proceeds along descriptive lines, relying upon abstractions, and therefore must offer its ontology as a kind of fiction. But ideas, considered dynamically, temporally instead of spatially, in light of what they *do* in the world of practice and qualities, have temporal forms and are activities.

The *narrative* presentation of ideas, such as belongs to the "World of Appreciation," in Royce's terms, is "more easily effective than description . . . for space furnishes indeed the stage and the scenery of the universe, but the world's play occurs in time."[21] When time is conceived abstractly in the "World of Description," even though it can never be wholly spatialized, the conception provides us with an *idea* of eternity, as a time-inclusive (not static) "Whole," while lived time and concrete experience ground this description (and every other), historically, ethically, and aesthetically. Since philosophy proceeds descriptively rather than narratively, "the real world of our Idealism has to be viewed by us men as a temporal order," in which "purposes are fulfilled, or where finite internal meanings reach their final expression and attain unity with external meanings."[22] Hence, for Royce, an unavoidable limitation of conceptual thought obliges us to philosophize according to logic rather than integrating our psychological and "appreciated" experience wholly into our philosophical doctrines. In adopting this limitation as a cautionary note against taking our abstractions literally, Royce continues in his Peircean manner of treating the famous "Four Incapacities" and their consequences as his guidebook to philosophizing responsibly.

The fact that our conceptually mediated accounts of our activities are not wholly integrated with our immediate experience, or even our appreciated experience (which is socially mediated), is not a serious problem. There is ample evidence for supposing a solid parallelism between our conceptual and perceptual experiences (each can be interpreted in the terms of the other), and for using the former as a guide to the latter, according to Royce, particularly with regard to the way that the idealization of our inner purposes enables us to connect them with the purposes of others in a larger whole of which we all lack immediate experience. We can *appreciate* the sense of fulfillment we find in serving a larger whole and we do form our characters progressively upon the ways in which those experiences of fulfillment point us ever outwards, beyond the finite self, but we are not so constituted as to experience immediately the greater Whole to which our experiences belong. Limitation is our lot. Yet, we cannot help supposing that there is some experiencer within whose inner life the Whole exists, but only the inevitability of the assumption for reflective philosophical purposes, and *not* any experiential content, assures us of the reality of such an experiencer.

The Philosophy of Loyalty

This social metaphysics lays the groundwork for Royce's formal articulation of the philosophy of loyalty, although Royce had been concerned with the idea of loyalty and had been using the term in a philosophical sense from the very earliest of his works.[23] The famous book published in 1908 derived from lectures given at the Lowell Institute, at Yale, and at the University of Illinois in 1906–07. Here Royce set out one of the most original and important moral philosophies in the recent history of philosophy. His notion of "loyalty" was essentially a universalized and ecumenical interpretation of Christian *agapic* love.

Broadly speaking Royce's is a "virtue ethics" (as opposed to duty or consequentialist ethics) in which our loyalty to increasingly less immediate and more comprehensive ideals becomes the formative moral influence in our personal development. But this account incorporates both the imperatives of duty and the appreciation of elevated pleasures, such as service and social belonging. As persons become increasingly able to form loyalties mediated by their idealizations, they are able to achieve practical and on-going devotion to causes greater than themselves. As these loyalties become unifiable in actions serving the higher purposes of groups of persons over many generations, humanity is increasingly better able to recognize that the highest ideal is the creation of a perfected "beloved community" in which each and every person shares. Thus, a developing historical consciousness also informs Royce's ethics. The "beloved community," as an ideal experienced in our present acts of loyal service and mutual interpretation, integrates into Royce's moral philosophy a Kingdom of Ends, but construed as immanent and operative instead of transcendental and regulative.

While the *philosophical* status of this ideal of the beloved community remains hypothetical, the *living* of it, in the fulfillment of our finite purposes, concretizes it for each and every individual. Each of us, no matter how morally undeveloped we may be, has fulfilling and comparatively complete experiences that point to the reality of experience beyond what is given to us individually. This wider reality is exemplified most commonly by when we fall in love. Royce says:

> [The] spiritual union [of the lovers] also has a personal, a conscious existence, upon a higher than human level. An analogous unity of consciousness, an unity superhuman in grade, but intimately bound up with, and inclusive of, our separate personalities, must exist, *if* loyalty is well founded, wherever a real cause wins the true devotion of ourselves. Grant such *an hypothesis*, and then loyalty becomes no pathetic serving of a myth. The good which our cause possesses, then, also becomes a concrete fact for an experience of a higher than human level.[24]

This move illustrates what Royce calls his "absolute pragmatism," which is the claim that ideals, however comprehensive they may be, are thoroughly practical, and the more inclusive ideals are the maximally practical ones. The concretization of ideals cannot, therefore, be empirically doubted except at the cost of rendering our conscious life utterly inexplicable, leaving our evident capacity to appropriate the *possible* future experience and *possible* present experience of others a total mystery, since ideals exist *for us* only in the temporal mode of the possible. If we admit that the concretization of ideals genuinely occurs, Royce argues, then we are not only entitled but compelled to take seriously and regard as real in our philosophical thinking the larger intelligible structures within which those ideals exist, which is the purposive character of the divine Will.[25]

The way in which persons sort out higher and lower causes that they might serve is by examining whether one's active service to a given cause destroys the loyalty of *others*, which is an essentially social assessment. To tread upon the loyalty of others is to destroy what is best in them. But the condition of even such destruction is the reality of *other possible experience* than my own—i.e., the modality of *present possi-*

bility. Ultimately Royce makes his most controversial move when he concludes that personal character as a social development reaches its acme in the recognition that we serve best and grow morally most when we serve lost causes, through which we may learn that our ultimate loyalty is to loyalty itself.[26] His principal examples of a "lost cause" are the religion of the Jews after the diaspora (remembering that the modern state of Israel did not exist in 1908), and the situation of the disciples of Jesus after his crucifixion.

The Problem of Christianity

The final phase of Royce's thought involved the application and further illustration of the concepts he had defended since 1880. Some have seen here a fundamental shift in Royce's thinking in 1912, but the evidence for that view is far from conclusive. Royce's hypothetical ontology, temporalism, personalism, and his social metaphysics based on the Fourth Conception of Being remain unchanged throughout, along with the operation of *agapic* loyalty, and the unity of finite purposes in the ideal of the beloved community. There is no obvious shift in method and no overt move to abandon idealism after 1912. Royce himself declared the "successive expressions" of the philosophy of loyalty "form a consistent body of ethical as well as religious opinion and teaching, verifiable, in its main outlines, in terms of human experience, and capable of furnishing a foundation for a defensible form of metaphysical idealism."[27] Royce never was an absolutist (in the sense of giving to philosophical ideas an unconditioned authority over the conduct of life) in either method or ontology, but there were those among his peers (and subsequent interpreters) who only came to recognize this limitation on the authority of philosophy in his later thought.

Some of these peers and interpreters, seeing in his last works the relatively modest scope of philosophical authority and philosophical knowledge, believed Royce had changed his view in some fundamental way. I think this view is surely mistaken. Royce's ethics and religious philosophy certainly matured, but the basic philosophical framework did not shift. Having provided throughout his career an idealistic way of grasping the Will, in contrast to Schopenhauer's materialist and pessimistic treatment, it remained for Royce to rescue Pauline Christianity, in its universalized and modernized form, from the critique of Nietzsche and others who tended to understand will in terms of power and who had rightly observed that the historic doctrine of God was no longer believable to the modern mind. Here Royce says:

> For the highly trained modern agitator, or the plastic disciple of agitators, if both intelligent and orderly in habits, is intensely both an individualist and a man who needs the collective will. . . . The individualism of such a man wars with his own collectivism; while each, I insist, tends to inflame the other. As an agitator, the typically restless child of our age often insists upon heaping up new burdens of social control, —control that he indeed intends to have others feel rather than himself. As an individualist, longing to escape, perhaps from his economic cares, perhaps from the marriage bond, such a highly intelligent agitator may speak rebelliously of all restrictions, declare Nietzsche to be his prophet, and set out to be a Superman as if he were no social animal at all. Wretched man, by reason of his divided will, he is. . . .[28]

Hitler and Heidegger were both twenty-four and unknown to the world when Royce wrote this, although it seems so clearly to be about them. And Lenin and Stalin and Mao were equally obscure children of their age. But Royce was struggling against a heavy pressure in human history of which they were all a part, the same weighty development that Schopenhauer and Nietzsche were confronting variously. We might call it the onset of nihilism. Oswald Spengler was contemplating a huge book on the same subject in 1913, but it wouldn't take on its real form for him until after the reports of Guns of August 1914 echoed across the world. By 1913, Royce had been battling nihilism for almost forty years. He continues:

> But note: These are no mere accidents of our modern world. The division of the self thus determined, and thus increasing in our modern civilization, is not due to the chance defects of this or of that more or less degenerate individual. Nor is it due to man's more noxious instincts. This division is due to the very conditions to which the development of self-consciousness is subject, not only in the present social order, but in every civilization which has reached as high a grade of self-consciousness as that which Paul observed in himself and in his own civilization.[29]

The applicability of Pauline Christianity to the present nihilism derives not from a bloodless and abstract absolutism, but from a historical recognition that high civilization creates an alienated individuality. The restoration of wholeness to such individuals in Royce's time required only the adapting of the essential structures of Pauline Christianity to the historical particularities of the modern age—temporalism, and specifically historicism provided the required structures for adaptation, because Royce's age believed in history when it could no longer believe in myth.

Striking, then, in this work of Royce is the temporalist account of the Holy Spirit, the Holy Catholic Church, and the communion of saints as a universal *community*. This community is a temporal process of mutually interpretive activity which requires shared memory and shared hope. In seeking to show the reality of the invisible community, perhaps Royce was also personally seeking communion with his departed son Christopher and William James. But Royce kept these and other personal tragedies far from the text of his published work; the grieving certainly affected and deepened his insight and perhaps even exaggerated the quality of his own hope, in philosophical descriptions, at least. If his philosophy is hopeful in the end, and most would say it is, this is a contrast and counter-balance to his life, which was increasingly difficult for him to bear.

Royce continued teaching at Harvard until his death and spent his free time more and more on ships bound for tropical climes. Toward the end of his life as social and political conditions in the world deteriorated, Royce wrote furiously. At the outbreak of the First World War he argued that an international insurance corporation, administered by a corporation of nations, which would pay reparations to any nation that was the victim of aggression, would have the effect of securing world peace. This idea may be seen as an important presentiment of the League of Nations, although only in more recent times have financial institutions such as the World Bank and the International Monetary Fund undertaken anything similar to Royce's idea. Though he had become frail, Royce's bitter disappointment at the imperialist aggression of his beloved Germany may even have hastened his relatively early demise at age sixty, in the view of some biographers. One must grant that emotional upheaval can shorten life, but whether it did in Royce's case is impossible to know. After a few years of deteriorating health, a ruptured blood vessel in the brain caused his death.

Royce's life was a fully human life. Very little marks it off as extraordinary, and it was in almost every way conventional. He knew love, tragedy, success, and a bit of failure. He endured and he got through life without betraying his own fundamental loyalties, at least in the estimation of his biographers and those who knew him. He gave the world some amazingly creative ideas, ones that need reconsideration today as I will argue, but what is more important is that he left behind a good name.

[2]
Ontology

Having sketched in Chapter 1 some of the basics of my reading of Royce in the context of his life, I now want to examine the first of his "living" ideas, his "fictional" ontology. There are at least two reasons to look at this topic. First, the Royce scholars have not adequately understood, I believe, how Royce's ontology relates to his whole philosophy, and how it serves as the most conspicuous and general aspect of his philosophical method. I aim to convince the community of Royce interpreters that this is crucial to reading Royce properly and to explaining his philosophy.

But what is far more important is, second, I think Royce is *right* about ontology, and that it still ought to be done as he did it. This way of approaching ontology avoids the pretensions and excesses of Heideggerian "fundamental ontology," with all its need for hero worship, obscurantism, and the cults of personality that characterize so much contemporary Continental philosophy. On the other hand, it avoids the thin, unimaginative, tepid and timid approaches to ontology found in contemporary pragmatism. Here we find people either condemning all metaphysics or claiming that descriptive metaphysics means whatever Dewey said, and repeating it endlessly.

Yet, it must be admitted that both Dewey and Heidegger were on the right track, and this seems to be the verdict of history at this point, even if their followers have failed to take up and advance the standard. And in this regard, Royce combines much of what Dewey and Heidegger would later assert, individually. Many philosophical confusions simply disappear when philosophers understand that logic and reason do not have the power to close the gap between "knowing" and "being," or as I prefer to call it, "experience" and "existence." No philosophical method yet devised delivers "ontological knowledge," by which I mean unmediated or perfectly transparent knowledge of being in itself. Rather, good philosophy creates *philosophical* knowledge, the value of which we shall discuss in the last chapters of this book.

Philosophy is one among many human activities embedded in a finite but open mode of existing, and it articulates one aspect of the reflective life of the finite perspective. When philosophy attempts to do more than that, it goes astray, trades in vicious abstractions, sets itself upon a stolen throne. As humans, we can perhaps steal the fire from the gods, but philosophy is not in command of that expedition. Perhaps poetry, understood broadly as *poiesis*, or creativity, leads the quest for the divine fire, and certainly philosophy, when done well, is not wholly bereft of *poiesis*, but philosophy is not the sole ruler of the *poietic* kingdom. One thing that attracts me to Royce's philosophy is the poetry of it. He is himself the "musician of reflective thought" that he encouraged all philosophers to be—at least in my estimation. If Kant is the Mozart of reflective thought, and Hegel is its Beethoven, surely Royce gives nothing away to Brahms by analogy. One could do worse.

The Unholy Trinity

In what follows I will make the textual case for the claim that Royce always held that metaphysics is descriptive and hypothetical in character, and that philosophical hypotheses do not and cannot yield ontological knowledge. Again, by "ontological knowledge" I mean basically the set of characteristics Dewey would later associate with "the quest for certainty," and which I would summarize as an unholy trinity in which the necessitarian structure of abstract logic is used to close the concrete gap between knowing or (more broadly) *experiencing* something, on one side, and the being or *existence* of the thing known or experienced on the other side. This is a familiar philosophical distinction, of course.

The tradition of associating logical (or mathematical), psychological (or cognitive), and ontological *necessity* with one another, which I call the "unholy trinity," was the basis for claiming ontological knowledge from Aristotle up to the mid-nineteenth century. As the last 150 years have unfolded, the old assumptions about all types of necessity have come unraveled. All philosophy and most science that depends upon the iron association of logical, psychological-cognitive, and ontological necessity have become untenable. Hence, for example, as I suggested in Chapter 1, the conception of "rationality" used by nearly all analytic philosophies is dependent upon at least the association of logical and ontological necessity (this is the very meaning of "rationality" in the way they use the term), and to the extent that scientific conceptions of knowledge have moved beyond this out-dated idea of necessity, science rightly ignores the demands made by analytic philosophy that science should be or must be "rational."[1] Although most philosophy departments have not gotten the news, rationality today is based on the structure of possibility and probability, not on the structure of necessity, and knowledge today does not require necessity of any kind—logical, psychological-cognitive, or ontological.

Even the movements, following Royce's brilliant student C.I. Lewis, to reinvent logic so as to deal effectively with possibility, have been rendered largely pointless because they have clung to various modes of necessity to account for possibility, with each new version of modal logic interpreting possibility according to a slightly varied sense of necessity and its corresponding notion of validity. So long as necessity is taken to be the guarantor of rationality, the conception of rationality advocated will be as useless to science as it is to practical life. I will not here rehearse the sins of David Lewis's "modal realism," but will only make the point that realism in all of its forms, and with its narrow conception of rationality, has been left behind by any philosophy that has a genuine chance of living in the present century and beyond, just as it was left behind by science over a century ago. Royce's ontology presents living ideas precisely because it does not employ necessity of the indefensible kind for its ground (an interpretation of the sense of necessity Royce uses is in Chapter 5 and expanded in Chapter 6).[2] Royce's ontology is grounded in the assumed primacy of the possible, and whatever necessity may be, it is subordinate to possibility in our thinking and in every kind of knowledge we have, including logical knowledge (which is at bottom normative, as both Royce and Peirce always insisted).[3]

Royce never subscribed to the unholy trinity, which is why his ontology remains relevant today. But since there is an entrenched habit of reading Royce as though he embraced ontological necessity and associated it with logical necessity,[4] it is needful that we begin to modify that habit in order to show the relevance of Royce to our viable contemporary conceptions of knowledge, which are proposed and used almost exclusively *outside* of philosophy departments by people who rightly ignore what analytic philosophy talks about. It falls to me to make the textual case that Royce is relevant because he has been so often misread. It is ironic that if the standard readings of Royce were correct, he would satisfy the misguided requirements of "rationality" vainly imposed on all knowledge by analytic philosophers, and indeed, would qualify as far *more* rational than most of them. Yet, if this were the case, Royce's ideas would now be as dead as those of analytic philosophy itself, so it is fortunate that Royce has been misread. The reason, I suspect, for this narrow, rationalistic, necessitarian misinterpretation of Royce is that the misinterpreters, like Smith, were trying desperately to make Royce look like a respectable philosopher during the wasted years of professionalized philosophy from the 1930s to the 1990s. It is better to be out of fashion, however, than to be respectable to ineffectual and miseducated people who not only know nothing but also suspect nothing.

Beginning with the End

Let us begin with some autobiographical remarks from the end of Royce's life and then go back and examine the origins and progress of his basic ontological ideas. In January 1916, Royce said: "When I came to Harvard in 1882 to teach, I brought this: We are in a position of postulates, voluntary attitudes, will attitudes towards the world, and our purpose as philosophers is to reflect on these and to bring them into some kind of union and also to attach them to experience."[5] Note that Royce defines philosophy as a *reflective* activity and gives it the imperative, the duty, of unification *in reflection* of experiences had, both cognitive and non-cognitive, and the imperative to employ the results of reflection in practice. Postulates and hypotheses are the tools of philosophical reflection. Royce continues:

> But the difficulty is that your general opinions, the categories of your understanding, are useful to you so far as they give you views which you state in universal propositions. You want your postulates to tell you something universally true; but so far as you deal with particulars, your difficulty is to attach your postulates to your empirical data.[6]

Here Royce acknowledges a tension in the two tasks he assigns to philosophy. Universal propositions that neatly unify all reflection cannot be seamlessly applied to the particulars of experience. He then specifies a *norm*, which is the *way* Royce always resolves this conflict between the need to unify reflection and the need to act:

> The philosopher must be guided by postulates which he doesn't *attempt* to verify but only asserts, or which he verifies by verifications which are matters of the moment. A general truth is *never* illustrated by experience and must be defined in terms of a postulate. . . . we *never* get in experience a survey of the whole, the synoptic view which gives you necessary laws.[7]

Royce is not trying to dichotomize experience and reflection here, but rather to recognize something about *philosophical* inquiries which we might not wish to say about other cognitive (even reflective) activities. Philosophy is peculiarly reflective in that its general assertions are not ones we even *attempt* to verify. I will address whether this limitation upon philosophy prevents Royce from being a pragmatist in Chapter 4. For now, please note that reflection, as philosophy's characteristic cognitive mode, is removed from particular experience—it must work with generalizations and postulate universals.

Asserting things we will not even *attempt* to verify is a *norm* for philosophy, according to Royce, since philosophy must be carried on hypothetically, in his view, and a hypothesis is a generalization or a universal postulate that cannot be made wholly adequate to any particular experience—because particular experience is not exhaustible in words and propositions, or as he earlier called these "descriptions." Royce views this norm as a restriction upon the results and applicability of philosophical thinking first realized in Kant's thought. He sees it as a mark of permanent progress in human thought that we can now tell the difference between the types of thinking that are genuinely empirical ("appreciative" is his favored terms in *The World and the Individual* and also earlier) and those which are hypothetical and descriptive.

Royce adds that necessary laws belong to the province of reflection *alone*, not to empirical experience. Philosophers want the "right to assert something about the nature of the world. We are always left with postulates on our hands which are statements about what we are not now verifying in experience, and yet we want to verify them."[8] But philosophers, *qua* philosophers, will be doing no such verifications. That task (never to be completed) is for other kinds of thought and experimentation. Royce goes further to point out that ordinary people live on postulates all the time and that philosophers are no worse off than anyone else in the practical sphere. But what of science? Does it not provide us with more than postulates? Royce answers "I doubt not your right to your postulates in the laboratory, but what you don't see is that your scientific point of view is also a postulate."[9]

Royce goes on to describe how he departed from Kant's view of postulates because Kant thought postulates could be defined as permanent categories. Royce's move to *temporalize* all categories unseats this Kantian assumption and with it the idea that necessity reaches across the bounds of logic and into ontology. Necessity may be the mark of the *a priori*, but it is also the mark of the general, and generality is the mark of thinking, while universality is the principal tool of reflective thinking, and reflective thinking proceeds upon the weight of postulates it cannot verify in particulars, when such postulates are *philosophical*, we ought not even *attempt* to verify them. In a sense, Royce has already foreseen the failure of the verificationist dreams of the logical positivists who would not yet appear for several decades. And part of the reason that his ideas about ontology are important today is that they provide guidance about what to do when verificationism has failed. These ideas about ontology are still useful to contemporary philosophers who do not want to abandon the power of reason, but who cannot seem to find a philosophy of language or mind that overcomes the problems. Part of the answer is to adopt a new view of the limits of philosophy along with the corresponding norm Royce recommends.[10]

But if we cannot verify philosophical hypotheses, and ought not even attempt to, we can at least discover some of our philosophical mistakes, and it is the modality of error, not of truth, which enables us to begin to connect the hypothetical and general to the *real*, which is to say the relation of temporal existence to teleological purpose.[11] Hence, we frame hypotheses reflectively, treat them as generalizations which *might* apply to something that links the present to the future, and when our prediction fails (as it surely will at some point), we are obliged to reformulate our generalizations. The *universal* principles that ground our general hypotheses are what is meant by "ontology." No ontological principle or assumption is necessitated by experience itself, and infinitely many possible ontologies can be given to ground a conception of any single experience. What are these ontological hypotheses? Having examined some of Royce's last words on the subject, let us dig into some of Royce's earliest writings and see what he thought ontology was.[12]

Back to the Beginning

Royce's ideas about ontology were intertwined with his ideas about time from the very beginning. I have sketched in Chapter 1 the development of Royce's "temporalism" as a biographical matter. Here let us look more closely at the arguments of his early articles. As I have noted, Royce began the construction of his philosophical system by means of a critique of ontology, by which he meant the study of the form(s) of allegedly independent existences and their relations. In his 1881 articles for the *Journal of Speculative Philosophy* and *Mind*, Royce described the ontologies that were currently being defended and he argued that every ontology, from the advent of Modern thought forward, is inadequate.[13] A reform in ontology was needed.

Royce was confident that Kant's philosophy was a permanent gain in the progress of thought, and so asked, "what modification of the elaborate system of the *Kritik* is needed in order that we may substitute for these tumultuous assemblies of quarrelling ontologies, these famine-riots of hungry Being-hunters, an orderly organization of critical doctrines, related to one principle, and conscious both of their limits and of their attainments?"[14] Kant's mistake, according to Royce, was buying in to a doctrine of causal *necessity*, "the assertion that there are throughout experience cases of existences upon which certain other existences must always follow whenever the first occur."[15] As a generalization, however, this is assertion superfluous in the domain of reflective thinking (where logical necessity suffices) and unverifiable in the domain of particular experience without the aid of an unverified generalization. Kant's error, according to Royce, "lay . . . in supposing sense to be a datum wholly apart from the active setting of the house in order through the category."[16] To the extent that the datum was individual and independent, it was not *necessarily* in (causal) order, and to the extent it was included in our generalized thought (and the causal order, where that sort of necessity can be postulated), it was no longer individual and independent. The conundrum was maddening.

The clue to its solution lay in recognizing that not only all actual but all *possible* data exist in relation to one another (the actual and possible taken together effectively form what Royce means by the "real"), and the order we hypothesize for those relations is the universally mediating relation of time. The "possible" is associated with the future and the "actual" with the past, while the present moment is an indefinite duration that links what is actual to what is possible in overlapping (i.e., "social" in the most literal sense), nested hierarchies of time-spans. Necessity does not govern the present in any concrete way; rather, possibility is the most basic mode or presence (or present-ness), i.e., other *possible* experience (I will say more about this below and in subsequent chapters). The possible itself is not given in particular experience, but we are both practically and reflectively obliged to treat it as real.[17] To do otherwise paralyzes practical action and renders all philosophical speculation incoherent.

The power by which we reach beyond what is given in the present moment is called "thought," and it trades in generalities.[18] The propositions by which we describe the principles of general thought are ontologies, and these are *universal* (hence maximally abstract) hypothetical descriptions which, while they may prove false in experience, are never finally verified (indeed, we do not *seek* to verify them, insofar as we are philosophers). Such descriptive propositions are asserted for the purpose of unifying thought and rendering it *more* adequate to experience. Ontologies are ways of hooking the past to the future through what is both general and particular in the given present, or, more simply, of hooking what is actual to that which is possible, or in more phenomenological terms, hooking the concrete workings of the will to its own future purposes, by articulating those purposes in general terms and unifying the generalities by means of universal postulates.[19]

The idea of "cause" is *one way to attach the actual to the possible*, but it is not the only way or even the best way, since it conflates logical with existential necessity (hence the problem with generalizing existential quantifiers). Even Kant already knew that this path, using the concept of causation to attach the world of practical action to the world of causal laws was hopeless, since cause meant at least three fundamentally different and irreconcilable things. To express Royce's temporalist solution of the problem in his own words:

> . . . the whole of experience, except the meager little sense datum of this moment, is past. Hence, experience is possible as an object of knowledge only in and for the act by which the past is created, as it were, out of the material present data. This act of asserting more than our data can possibly contain, by projecting from the present moment the scheme of a well-filled actual past no longer existent or directly knowable . . . this act I call the act of *Acknowledgement of the Past*. But acknowledgement of a reality beyond the present data is not confined to the assertion of a past. Reference of present data to a future forms a second class of acts which may be called *Anticipations*. Reference of present data to external reality, in acknowledgement of other conscious beings besides ourselves as real, and of other experience besides our own as possible, in brief, *Acknowledgement of a Universe of Truth*, forms the third class of conscious acts by which present sense-data are transcended through reference of them to a reality of which in themselves they give, and can give, not the faintest evidence.[20]

The present does not actually evince the past or the future. Not even faintly. Let me say that again in different words. The present *qua* present has only a finite fragment of the actual and does not give, by itself, even the faintest evidence of the reality of a wider world. To move to that wider world requires that something somewhere be generalized, and that through generalization what is actually absent is treated as virtually present. The act by which this occurs is, by definition "thought" (i.e., any act by which something general comes into existence is "thought"—a view Royce shares with Peirce), and for "thought," both the actual and the possible are *virtual* (i.e., neither strictly possible nor strictly actual). Thought, as actually existing in the present, is *about* what is *not actually present, even when it deals with what actually **is** present* (i.e., thought treats what is present as if it *might not be present* had the past been different, and as what *will not be present* in the future). The alternative to such an hypothesis about thought is to admit that there is no truth, according to Royce.

I will explain later, in Chapter 5, how it is that while the fragment of actual experience we call the present seems concrete, while the act of thought by which it is apprehended seems abstract, the situation is in truth the reverse. The fragmentary experience is abstract and the generalization about it is the genuine act. If this sounds like Hegel to you, it should. Royce was not a follower of Hegel, but the lesson of concrete universals was not lost on him; it became in Royce's hands the reality of concrete generals. Royce avoided nominalism without giving way to Hegelian or Bradleyan absolutism, but gave the Hegelians their due by allowing that philosophy does and must trade in these kinds of universals. But, contrary to Hegel and Bradley, Royce does not accord to philosophy any kind of overall authority when it comes to acts of knowing.

The point for the present is that ontologies, as acts of thought, are hypothetical descriptions we have to postulate for both practical and philosophical purposes. As Royce says, "there is something dramatic, or often perhaps rather to be called romantic in an ontology."[21] We may postulate an ontology, make for ourselves a useful myth, but *knowledge* of precisely what to postulate in this domain is impossible for us. Such knowledge would require a view of the whole we don't possess. Royce actually uses the word "myth" to refer to the act of making an ontology in a letter to William James at the same time he was writing these articles. Referring to these articles he says:

> The sum of them all is that ontology, whereby I mean any positive theory of an external reality as such, is of necessity myth-making; that, however, such ontology may have enough moral worth to make it a proper object of effort so long as people know what they mean by it; that philosophy is reduced to the business of formulating the purposes, the structure and the inner significance of human thought and feeling; that an attempted ontology is good only in so far as it expresses clearly and simply the purposes of thought just as popular mythology is good in so far as it expresses the consciousness of a people; that the ideal of a truth-seeker is not the attainment of any agreement with an external reality, but the attainment of a perfect agreement among all truth-seeking beings; that the ethical philosophy is the highest philosophy. In the *Mind*-article I have sketched a little ontology, partly my

own, mostly very old; just to show what myths we can make if we choose. Then I tear up the myth and show how it was made.[22]

The key to rescuing this greatly restricted project of philosophy lies in the temporal structure of *moral* ontology (i.e., the relation of willing to purposing, about which I will have much to say in later chapters). The present acts by which we construct our possible future experience must be regarded as real, and these acts involve a temporal structure that is irreducibly three-fold. The past and present must be "acknowledged" and the future "anticipated" in every act. I have said in Chapter 1 that what I find most striking about Royce's comments in the Kant article is his definition of the "present" as the acknowledgement of other conscious beings and *their* possible experience. This establishes the sociality of all moral ontology as one of Royce's "universals," and he has already described it in 1881.

Thus, as I said in Chapter 1, what he would later call "the community of interpretation" is already present in his first efforts at systematic metaphysics, and already triadic, in spite of his later statement that it was a "Peircean" moment of insight.[23] It quite possibly was a Peircean insight, but it occurred over thirty years earlier. The universal hypothesis and its basic triadic structure were present in Royce's thinking all along. Peirce's semiotic later showed Royce *how to handle* the "present," the "Acknowledgement of a Universe of Truth," phenomenologically and semiotically *as* the will to interpret. This is a very important insight, but it is a means to systematizing and operationalizing something Royce already thought. The so-called Peircean insight of 1912 is not an altogether new insight or a shift in Royce's position. Royce's philosophy is undeniably triadic from the beginning, largely because it is temporalist from the beginning, and time comes in a triad of past, present and future. Had Royce not defined the "present" in terms of sociality from the outset, we might say that his 1912 insight was really a "breakthrough." But that view of Royce's development is simply and demonstrably incorrect.

Also notable is Royce's account of the future as holding the anticipated objects of experiences not yet had, the affordances of our "projections." From this early date (while Dewey was still teaching high school), Royce recognized that the dramatic stories we tell ourselves in practicing ontology should be informed by *moral* ends and aspirations. "For since the ultimate fact of the knowing consciousness is the active construction of a world of truth [the social world] from the data of sense, the ultimate justification of this activity must be found in the significance—in the moral worth—of this activity itself."[24] This is process philosophy, but it is closer to the process personalism of Borden Parker Bowne or Howison than to the aestheticized process philosophies later defended by Whitehead and Dewey. As I mentioned in the last chapter, one might give Royce the title of the first process philosopher, even over Peirce. In the same letter to James cited above, in which Royce described his "myth" making, he criticizes Peirce saying: "In one way he seems to regard reality as for us merely the representative of our determinations to act so and so and of our expectations that we shall succeed if we do not act so. For such a view the determination and the expectation would be everything. Instead of saying: there is reality and I must conform to it, we should say: there is in me this determination to act so and so, and this expectation of success. That is all."[25] Thus far Royce agrees, since this is the basic structure of temporalist moral ontology, the act (comprising the way the past exists in the present) and the anticipation. But he sees Peirce as hesitating to stop there. He continues to James:

> Yet Peirce is not content with this, but continually appeals to the transcendent reality as justifying our determination and our expectation. Now I want to be on this matter very explicit. I fear the ambiguity and the hesitation. For me the sentiment of reality, the determination to act thus and so, the expectation of certain results, all these facts of the active consciousness are together the whole truth. There is needed or known or conceivable above these facts of consciousness absolutely no transcendent reality.... And yet I am no subjective idealist of the old-fashioned sort. Not *myself* is the ultimate truth, but Consciousness as such.... [Consciousness] is given as a single act of submission to a conceived other consciousness about it."[26]

Here we see consciousness is already social for Royce and that to the extent Peirce is willing to embrace temporalist moral ontology and restrict philosophy's role to that, Royce agrees. To the extent Peirce falls back into asserting a reality beyond that, and using it as a ground of ontological knowledge, Royce disagrees. Hence, with the temporalist, hypothetical moral ontology and the sociality of consciousness as act and anticipation, Royce might also be the first panexperientialist in American thought, as well as the first process philosopher; Peirce (and James and Dewey) came around to this viewpoint later.

As I stated in Chapter 1, Royce's view of fictional ontology did not change in *The Religious Aspect of Philosophy*.[27] Not only is much of the material from these two early articles repeated verbatim in the book of 1885, but the overall viewpoint is deepened into a philosophical *method* in Chapter 9 of that book, which, as Tunstall has rightly pointed out, never changed.[28] Yet, Royce is not exactly happy about the way he feels obliged to limit philosophy: "We confess at once that we want something much better than a postulate as the basis of our religion, in case we can get it. If postulates are to have any part in our religion, we want them to be justified by some ultimate religious certainty that is more than a postulate."[29] But can we have more? The answer, as with all good philosophical questions is "yes and no." Royce says:

> But how is this postulating activity actually related to our knowledge of reality? Much more closely than one might suppose. Very much of our thought rests upon blind faith, or upon what many take to be blind faith; but this, when we reflect upon it with due attention to the office it fills, is transformed before our eyes into practically unavoidable postulates. Such are the assumptions upon which our science rests in forming its ideal of a "universal formula." There may indeed be some deeper basis for these postulates of science. But most men know nothing of its basis. And so, when we accepted in our last chapter these postulates, we had to admit that they are a kind of faith.[30]

His argument amounts to saying, "well, no, we don't get more than postulates, but don't underestimate postulates; that's how *all* our knowledge comes to us." At this point in *The Religious Aspect of Philosophy*, Royce can do no better than to point out that philosophy, like every other kind of human thought, thinks in generalities, and that the generalities are grounded in a kind of practical faith. That is why even philosophy has a "religious aspect"—a point that seems lost on most Royce interpreters, in spite of the fact that this point is important enough to *give the book its title. There is no philosophy without a kind of religious faith*, which is why it cannot proceed without postulates. But practical faith is also closely associated with thought. Royce is, after all, a pragmatist (see Chapter 4). By the end of his ninth chapter in RAP, Royce has decided, unhappily, to leave the postulates in place *as postulates*. He says: "Still we are seeking the eternal. Postulates about it we must indeed make, or else we shall do nothing. But can we not go beyond mere postulates? Is there no other road open to the heart of things?"[31] This lament is followed by a defense of philosophical idealism, and thoroughly hypothetical, which is to say, dependent upon postulates.

What has misled many interpreters of Royce, however, is that following the defense of idealism Royce launches into his "proof" for the existence of God based upon the *possibility* of error. What many interpreters overlook is the form of the argument. It treats the *possibility* of error as a reflective consideration prior to the experience of any actual error. In order to discuss the matter philosophically, one must have a *concept* of error, not just instances of errors, and the concept is already a generalization, a product of *thought,* now brought under a universal proposition for *reflective* consideration: error as such. This is wholly conscious on Royce's part. He undertakes the argument to see whether he can get beyond postulates, while understanding philosophy "with due attention to the office it fills," and declares:

> . . . it will indeed be well if we can get for ourselves something more and better than mere postulates. And if we cannot, we shall not seek to hide the fact. Better eternal despondency that a deliberate lie about our deepest thoughts and their meaning. If we are not honest, at least in our philosophy, then we are wholly base. To try once more is not dishonest.[32]

Obviously Royce is appealing not to the tools internal to philosophical reflection, but to the norm that governs philosophical activity, as a human activity with moral meaning. The proof for God from the *possibility* of error follows, an argument Royce himself describes as a "wilderness,"[33] and one assumes that the allusion here is either to Moses and the Israelites spending forty years looking for the Promised Land, or the temptation of Jesus in the wilderness, or *both*. It is in any case, not a pleasing prospect. The argument is a wilderness because most of the chapter is dedicated to finding *some* way to conceptualize "error" so as to provide Royce with a generalization that is susceptible of the universal proposition that an Omniscient Being exists. He tries one concept of error after another and discards them all as inadequate for the purpose, pronouncing his disappointment explicitly.[34] Given our inability so much as to make sense of the concept of error, as appropriated in the mode of its possibility, it begins to appear that error is *impossible*.[35]

Does the walk in the wilderness gain Royce more than postulates, now that we see his whole-hearted dedication to being honest about it? The crucial climax of the argument occurs when Royce, having failed in every effort to grasp how any class of errors can *possibly* be erroneous, says "error must be real, and yet, as common sense arranges these [supposedly erroneous] judgments and their relations to one another, error cannot be real. . . . In short, either no error at all is *possible*, or else there must be *possible* an infinite mass of error. For the *possibilities* of thought being infinite, either all thought is excluded once for all from the *possibility* of error, or else to every *possible* truth can be opposed an infinite mass of error."[36] I offer this passage to emphasize that the mode of Royce's argument is that of the possible, one of the key characteristics of his fictional ontology.

To find his way out of the wilderness, Royce confronts Kant's version of temporalism (which he had criticized in his 1881 article) with a problem:

> To explain the possibility of error about matters of fact seemed hard, because of the natural postulate that time is a pure succession of separate moments, so that the future is now as future non-existent, and so that judgments about the future lack real objects, capable of identification. Let us then *drop this natural postulate*, and declare *time* once and for all present in all its moments to an universal all inclusive *thought*. . . . Then all our puzzles will disappear at a stroke, and error will be possible, because any one finite thought, viewed in its relation to its own intent, may or may not be seen by this higher thought as successful and adequate in its intent.[37]

Royce's commitment to the postulate of the intentional structure of all reality is evident here, for thoughts are futural and do not wholly contain the objects of experience which they intend. Thus, they may err, because they are "incomplete thoughts."[38]

Is this "declaration" of an all-inclusive thought itself a postulate, but simply a different one than Kant's "natural" postulate about the succession of moments? It is. Royce directly confronts the claim that his all-knower is only a *possible* being, and confesses that this is the only objection he really fears.[39] He knows he needs a thinker and judger who is more than a "bare possibility."[40] He can demonstrate that *without* such a thinker, not only is error impossible for humans to conceive without contradiction, but intention is also impossible to conceive; Royce can show that giving up upon the all-embracing thought implies giving up all philosophical meaning, for it implies the unreality of every act of intending. And so Royce describes the All Knower: "The actual judge *must* be there; and for him the incomplete intention *must* be complete."[41] The "must" in this sentence is not a logical or ontological "must," it is a *moral* "must," governing the norms of philosophical thinking, since, as he says in this spot, "all this is, to the separate judgment as such, a mystery."[42] The "separate judgment as such" is the form of all human knowing and judging, including *philosophical* knowing. We must *choose* what we shall believe, but the choice is a moral one, for the merely *possible* God is also an option, one among many.

Royce summarizes his case, and makes as explicit as anyone can that it has been hypothetical:

> It will be seen that wherever we have dealt in the previous argument with the possibility of error as a mere possibility, we have had to use the result

of the previous chapter concerning the nature of possibility itself. The idea of the barely possible, in which there is no actuality, is an empty idea. *If* anything is possible, then, *when* we say so, we *postulate* something as actually existent in order to constitute this *possibility*. The conditions of possible error must be actual.[43]

And how do we assert this actuality? With a postulate: "And thus, the inclusive thought, which constitutes the error, must be *postulated* as actual."[44] Royce does not say the Absolute *must be* actual, he says it must be *postulated as actual*, and the "must" is a moral must, not a logical or ontological necessity. But the something actual we "must" *postulate*, so as to constitute the possibility we want to consider (in this case, error) does not *have* to be the All-Knower, it simply *should* be the All-Knower, because *good* philosophers, *honest* ones, will not choose a position that requires them to deny that time and intention and meaning are real, and that errors never occur.

In the foregoing section I have done nothing other than summarize Royce's most famous argument, taking no liberties at all. The fact that previous interpreters (apart from me and Tunstall) have never noticed it is hypothetical is puzzling to me, except that the length of the argument may make it difficult for some readers to trace the formal aspects. It might be said that the argument is difficult or convoluted, to which I can only answer that it seems pretty clear to me. Royce regularly summarizes his progress in the argument and orients the reader as to what has been accomplished and what remains to be done. If the temporalist and hypothetical character of the famous "argument from error" is not clear to readers, perhaps Royce just needs better readers.

Philosophy as a Moral Activity

The whole case above depends upon the existence of norms for guiding philosophical activity. These norms are stated reflectively and are themselves postulates of philosophy, but aimed at a deeper and presupposed activity of *philosophizing*. Why the moral bearing for all philosophy? We might call this "moral temporalism," as I have in chapter one, built upon temporalist moral ontology, albeit a fictional ontology, but its roots are in the philosophy of history, or at least of historical consciousness. It is in fact a kind of historicism (in the philosophical sense of the term, not the sense given it by historians), and it is good to remember at this point that Royce was a fine historian, and he was uncommonly aware of the interaction between the norms of reflection that govern philosophy with the reflective norms of other disciplines of knowing (such as history).[45]

As I have said in Chapter 1, and have shown by example, Royce's moral temporalism developed partly as an answer, philosophically and religiously, to moral problems posed by the annexation of California, and Royce was working on that history of California and this argument about error *at the same time*. Royce's history of California was an *application* of his dramatic or even romantic ontology to the problem of historiography.[46] What I asserted in Chapter 1 may now be better understood: it was the collection of solutions to these problems of self-deception, *ignorance*, and *error* that provided the impetus, the direction, and the goal of Royce's hypothetical or fictional ontology, in all of its particulars. The cultivation of the inner life he called for as a remedy to the misbehavior of the Bear Flag "heroes" is nothing other than the cultivation of the norms of reflection, especially as they bear upon practical life. The development of external boldness, decisiveness, cleverness, and all the virtues praised by the "mock eloquent cant" of the euphoric masses is meaningless without the firm association of these virtues with excellent reflection upon our experience, and such reflection begins with the idea that *we always could always be in error*. This is Royce's *fallibilism*. The fact that it has not been recognized in the literature on both Royce and the other pragmatists that his argument from error is a statement of Royce's commitment to fallibilism simply boggles my mind. What could be more obvious? And yet, supposedly intelligent people charge Royce with absolutism, in the very sense contradicted by his argument from error?

Ending in the Middle

Having dealt with the side of fictional ontology that treats "error," I should say a few words about "ignorance." I will confront the "Conception of God Debate" in more detail in the next chapter, but insofar as it bears upon the development of Royce's fictional ontology, I should address it here.

I have shown the presence of fictional ontology, and Royce's denial of the need for appeals to a transcendent reality, at both the very end and the very beginning of Royce's thought. I have explained how that ontology is structured around ethics as first philosophy and the norms of philosophical activity. Did Royce slip in the middle into some other stance, in which the Absolute became an ontological necessity? I do not think so. During the years between 1882 and 1895 Royce became a famous philosopher, so by 1895 he had become a tempting target, although he really did not realize it.

As I mentioned in Chapter 1, Royce came to Berkeley at the invitation of George Holmes Howison, whom he had known for over ten years, to revisit his alma mater and to see his family. He knew that Howison had been teaching *The Religious Aspect of Philosophy*, and that it would be discussed publicly in Berkeley. But Royce regarded the book as an inquiry long past, ten years old, by 1895, and had been reconfiguring his conception of the Whole for *different* inquiries in the intervening years. Royce was adapting his basic viewpoint about the norms of reflection to the history of philosophy, and to the various disciplines (especially science, education, and literature). Thus, we get an argument in 1895 that has certain crucial differences from the one we have rehearsed above.

How were they different? Important in this area of interpretation is Gary L. Cesarz's point about the difference between the formulation of the "proof" based on error in 1885 as contrasted with the 1895 formulation of the "proof" based on ignorance in *The Conception of God*.[47] Cesarz describes this as a greater break with the previous formulation than I would. I think that Royce realized by 1895 that his choice of the term "error" in 1885 was misleading people as to the status of his method and ontology, and he was simply correcting a misperception by refocusing the argument in more ontological and less epistemological vocabulary, which explains why he said in 1895 that the two arguments (from error and from ignorance), were "essentially the same."[48] Still Cesarz's subtle formulation of the argument in the terms of modal logic shows the great extent to which Royce was engaged with the idea of possibility and was attempting to fashion his logic to deal with it. Cesarz shows formally Royce's engagement with possibility, but does not associate possibility with futurity, nor does he connect it with the temporalist ontology. These omissions make Cesarz's formulation appear more like a claim of ontological knowledge on Royce's part than it really was. The philosophical aspect of the proof is driven by logic, but only in the sense that logic is normative for good, healthy thinking, and even at this, there is not a single logic to which thinking must submit, but logic is an on-going creative expression of many modes of thinking, not some settled affair.[49]

Admitting that his God is only a concept, Royce says from the outset what he plans to show: ". . . that the very nature of human ignorance is such that you cannot conceive or define it apart from the assertion that there is, in truth, at the heart of the world, an Absolute and Universal Intelligence, for which thought and experience, so divided in us, are in complete and harmonious unity." Tunstall, commenting on this passage, rightly says:

> [The above excerpt] makes it evident that Royce considers human ignorance to be the existential and ontological condition demonstrating that there is an omniscient Being at the heart of our world. He views human ignorance in this way because it discloses the liminal character of our actual, fleeting, and fragmentary present experience. Accordingly, he thinks that our ignorance of anything beyond our immediately present experience motivates us to construct ideals that organize our present experience in relation to an overarching ideal realm of experience, at least seen as being ideal from the vantage point of our present experience.[50]

The effect of this move from error to ignorance is to supplement the seemingly epistemological case from 1885 with an ontological version in 1895. It does not, however, alter the hypothetical character of the argument. In fact, to the contrary, Royce finds himself obliged in 1895 to allow that even *God* has to hypothesize:

> Ideas must always transcend content, even in Absolute Experience? Yes, as abstract or unreal ideas . . . No actual experience could adequately fulfil, or present contents adequately expressing, the infinite regress, the infinitely infinite groups of possible examples of every universal, whose abstract possibility a merely abstract thought demands. Ideas, then, must indeed in one sense transcend data even in Absolute Experience. But how? Answer: *As hypotheses contrary to fact*, not as expressions of genuine and unfulfilled truth.[51]

Royce is here hard up against a dilemma, one which he would later confront directly in the "Supplementary Essay" of *The World and the Individual*. If he says God experiences possibilities as unfulfilled truth or promise or purposes, then God's omniscience is lost. If he says God does not experience possibilities at all, he renders God effectively unconscious and impersonal (consciousness depends on there being more possibility that those possibilities that are actual; without possibility, there is nothing to be conscious of). Royce must keep alive the idea that God is an intentional being who can form purposes, yet, he cannot allow that God's experience of possibilities has any falsity, failure, or incompleteness, or even unfulfilled hopes.

Royce lands upon the idea that God can consider counter-factuals, just as humans can. God thinks of what *might have been* on the basis of what is, and in God's case, what "is" is all that was, is, and will be, a chronosynoptic experience. So God postulates, but does not "inquire," does not philosophize as we do, does not, by postulating, solve problems. Even God (so conceived by a finite philosopher) has an ontology, but where ours must be fictional, God's would not be, in such a conception. Obviously it is not easy to see why God would bother to *hypothesize*, given that no apparent addition to the Divine Self would result. So Royce continues:

> But what sort of Absolute Experience would that be, in which there were ideas present as hypotheses contrary to fact, as bare or unreal possibilities? I answer, it would be an experience of fact as individual cases, exemplifying universal types in such a fashion as to embody a knowledge of the essence both of these facts and of their types. So far, it would then be an experience of a concrete and individual fulfillment of all genuine ideas. On the other hand, this fulfilment would embody universals, not in all abstractly or barely possible cases, —since that would be, concretely speaking, impossible—but in contents sharply differentiated and thereby preserved from lapsing into the bare continuity which would link together the series of abstractly possible contents such as could be defined by mere ideas.[52]

In other words, to have meaningful concrete experience, God must know not only what each individual existence was, is, and will be, but must experience that existence in the mode of the possible as a *limitation* or *principle of individuation*, for otherwise the individual is *only* an idea in God's mind—and no genuine individual (which is in essence what Howison accused Royce of implying). So the way in which I, as an actual individual, am appropriated by the Absolute Experience is both as what I was, am, and will be, and as sharply individuated by God's immediate grasp of what I *might have been* and *might be*, but am *not*.[53]

I think I can agree with Royce that he is driven to having to admit that a God who is conceived as a conscious being, an experiencing being, could not coherently be conceived as lacking some modality of experiencing the *possible*, since possibility is a precondition not only of consciousness, but also of both will and purpose (i.e., intentional life construed as having a moral existence). While Royce does not explicitly make the obvious move in *The Conception of God* to theistic finitism, i.e., a God who is not omniscient nor omnipotent, he clearly should have made this move, and in other writings *of the same time*, arguably did make this move—as numerous process philosophers later did.[54]

In many ways, the issue of Royce's fictional ontology begins to coalesce around the ways in which he regards all philosophical activity as thoroughly mediated, as dealing with already formed generalizations and concepts. I will take up this issue of immediacy in the next chapter, and will argue that I do not think Royce satisfactorily resolves this problem. I will not take a stand in this book on the issue of whether philosophy, strictly speaking, *can* deal with immediate experience, but I will say that if phenomenology is a kind of philosophy (and for Royce it really is not), then philosophy *strives* to deal with immediate experience, whether it succeeds or not. This point will return when we examine the fate of James's personalism, as it is dashed on the rocks in its failed effort to articulate "pure experience," as discussed in Chapter 7.

But there is something important Royce realized in the course of these twists and turns regarding God, which is that he needed a better conception of the *individual* in order to make out his conception of the Whole with adequate clarity. I will treat Royce's important later works in subsequent chapters, but for now, I believe the issue is focused on how to deal, philosophically with "immediate experience," and when we have examined that issue, we can move on to the formulations of the Absolute and the individual without further obstacles. For now, the living idea that emerges from this chapter is that, at least where it is not confronting immediate experience, philosophical reflection should be fallibilist and its ontologies fictional. This is a requirement of temporalist philosophies that want to use possibility as the most basic modal notion, philosophies that seek to grapple with futurity as something ontologically more meaningful than the traditional "non-existent" label allows. The future exists in the mode of possibility, and if so, the will, purpose, and ideals, i.e., the intentional character of the *real*, are always understood in terms of temporality.

[3]
Immediacy and Mysticism

In the last chapter we left Royce in a bit of a bind. He has run up against a very serious dilemma. His commitment to defining philosophical activity as a reflective exercise in unifying general concepts by employing universal postulates denies to him the capacity to deal adequately with immediate experience, at least *within* the scope of what he defines as "philosophy." I will follow out the implications of this way of defining philosophy in the next chapter, but to prepare the way for that inquiry, we must examine the issue of immediacy, or immediate experience, as Royce and some of his critics confront it directly. This task is especially difficult because Royce wants to construe God as being simultaneously a willing, intending, purposing, personal being, *and* as maximally rational.[1]

The maximally rational God, with *immediate* access to all that was, is, and will be, seems *not* to be an experiencing, personal being. Recognition of this issue may have motivated Royce's effort to describe God as having an experiential modality that appropriates the possible as the counter-factual, as explained in the last chapter. It dawned on Royce, by the end of his supplementary essay in *The Conception of God* that if he is to reconcile these two demands, an intentional and personal being on the one hand and a maximally rational being on the other, the key is to develop a theory of divine experience in which the principal divine activity is that of individuation. I will address Royce's theory of individuality in Chapter 5, precisely because it is one of his "living ideas." But here we should pause to look at the issue of immediate experience.

In his book on Royce, Dwayne Tunstall makes the following observation about my own interpretation of Royce:

> While Auxier reads Royce's philosophy as an interrelated series of hypothetical postulates whose meaningfulness is ultimately determined by their

ethical import in our lives, I still yearn to read Royce's philosophy as one in which he advances philosophic propositions that actually describe some features of the world, as experienced by human persons, which substantiate his ethico-religious insight. I cling to this yearning despite the fact that I think that one can plausibly interpret Royce's philosophy in the way that Auxier does. Otherwise, I am not sure that anyone should spend time reading Royce beyond his later, fully-developed ethics, since one could read, say, William Ernest Hocking for the communitarian and religious dimensions of Royce's thought. Indeed, one would learn more from reading the insights Hocking has on the nature of religious and secular communities than from reading Royce as a hypothetical metaphysician.[2]

In a very real sense I agree with Tunstall about this, and later chapters in this book will attempt to meet the challenge of showing that Royce's philosophy does actually describe some features of the world. But I think Hocking's attempt to retrieve "mystical experience," which is one way of describing immediacy from the finite perspective, from Royce's critique of it in *The World and the Individual* was the correct move. I think Hocking is better at describing immediate experience than is Royce, and I agree that Hocking's theory of community adds to and fills out Royce's account in excellent and creative fashion. But I do not believe one can grasp the import of Hocking's theory without Royce, especially Royce's metaphysics, and I will show in this chapter why I take that to be the case. By the time I am finished, however, Hocking will be in no better condition than is Royce. But I believe there is a path out of the problem which will emerge at the end of Chapter 7, when I have examined James's struggle with immediacy and have shown Royce's resolution of the issue. The present excursion into immediacy requires us to resume the story of Royce's developing thought at the 1895 "Conception of God Debate," so as to grasp rightly the origins of his critique of mysticism (and immediacy) in *The World and the Individual*.

Royce in Subsequent Developments

In his 1968 book *Royce and Hocking: American Idealists*, Daniel S. Robinson noted the view shared by Hocking and Gabriel Marcel that "feeling is cognitive," and claims that this view is the "major insight that took [them] beyond Royce."[3] Depending upon what one means by "feeling" and "cognitive," this may also be understood as among the central insights of Whitehead and Hartshorne, and a view fundamental to all process philosophy. Indeed, like pragmatists, existentialists, and phenomenologists, process philosophers have never been entirely comfortable with claiming Royce as one of their own, which are issues I will address in subsequent chapters. Rather, all these movements tend to think of Royce as a thinker who expressed early on certain insights that came later to be seen as crucial to the development of process thought, or pragmatism, or phenomenology, or existentialism. But there are points in Royce's thinking from which the phenomenologists, existentialists, pragmatists and process philosophers all feel obliged to distance themselves. For these movements in twentieth-century thought, Royce's idealism generally—and especially his so-called absolutism—are unpalatable. But it cannot be the case that William Ernest Hocking was averse to Royce's *idealism*, and herein we find the value of his critique, since it takes Royce more upon his own terms than terms set by subsequent movements. And yet Hocking himself sees the insight about the cognitive value of feeling as the insight that took him beyond Royce.[4]

I will strive to explain how I think Hocking came to believe this insight about the cognitive value of feeling was an advance on Royce, and how Hocking believed this view about feeling can still be maintained within an idealistic framework. In short, Hocking attempts to solve the problem of "immediate experience" I have outlined in Chapter 2, while retaining a view of the scope and character of philosophy that is the same as Royce's view (idealistic process personalism). I will then criticize Hocking on this point by showing that, contrary to his intention, the sense of immediacy he defends points away from idealism *per se* and toward either process metaphysics or phenomenological ontology. I also wish to maintain that a consistent version of idealism *could* be given that accommodates Hocking's insight about the cognitive value of feeling. In all of this the issue of the fundamental nature of persons, particularly of individuality in the having of mystical experience, is the pivot, and a discussion of that issue must be our initial point of departure, although a full treatment of Royce's view of individuality will be forestalled until Chapter 5. In several ways, this chapter picks up where Stephen Tyman's essay, "Royce and the Destiny of Idealism" leaves off. Tyman says:

> The gap that emerges between the Hindu's subjective idealism [as a result of Royce's critique of mysticism as immediate experience] and Royce's concrete idealism comes later [after the Conception of God Debate, in *The World and the Indiviual*]. In particular, the gap pertains, in terms of the Gifford Lectures, to individuality. But in the actual course of Royce's thought, Royce himself is able to find a higher order of individuality in the consanguinity of the species, not just of the flesh, but of consciousness. This

may be Royce's greatest contribution. But how much does one hear of it in our time? How could this conception fail to have helped rather than hurt by a philosophical view in which the thinker is allowed to reach to an ideal as yet unsupported by a conceptual infrastructure seeming to suggest it as a necessity? But in order to achieve this, a rethinking of the category of the mystical would be necessary. This would be a worthy undertaking in the interests of securing for Royce his most salient thought, namely, the "general place of personality in the universe."[5]

In this chapter and the next (and indeed, also in Chapters 7 and 8), I will do my best to bring that "worthy undertaking" to some kind of fruition. What Tyman describes as perhaps Royce's "greatest contribution" is the temporalist-conceptualist solution to the problem of universals I explained in chapter two—I like the metaphor of the consanguinity of the species and flesh of consciousness. That strikes me as exactly the right image. And we don't hear of it in our times, times bereft as they are of learning and condemned to repeat the mistakes of the past.

The Royce-Howison Debate

When Royce spoke before the Philosophical Union at the University of California, Berkeley, in 1895, George Holmes Howison attacked him for propounding a version of absolutism that undermined the idea of personality in God and in individuals. Royce had always taken himself to be a personalist (although he did not use that term for it, see Chapter 7), at least as far as maintaining that God is a personal God, and that God's absolute character does not undermine the personal existence of individuals, and that the development of personality is the highest and most sacred moral and religious purpose. But Howison argued quite effectively that the doctrine Royce offered in *The Religious Aspect of Philosophy* (1885), and in the expanded doctrine of his paper on "The Conception of God," was incompatible with personalism and with pluralism. I have pointed out earlier that *all* personalists are metaphysical pluralists, for if God is the only complete person, and the rest of us are but fragments (and not full ontological individuals), this would be a kind of impersonalism.[6] The elevation of the personal mode of existing, ethically and ontologically, as the highest value is a communitarian principle, requiring indeed more than just intersubjectivity. This is not just *experience* of the other, it reaches into individual *existence*. One person alone is no person at all. This criticism by Howison was a great spur to Royce in the further development of his metaphysics, and in particular, the development of the doctrine of the four conceptions of being as presented in Royce's Gifford Lectures, *The World and the Individual*, First Series.[7]

Royce was having a similar debate with William James at the same time (see Chapters 5 and 7), and also with Thomas Davidson (see Chapter 7). But Howison's criticism is the only one of the three that could not be swept away in a cloud of arguments about philosophical methodology, since Howison largely shared Royce's dialectical method of eliminating conceptions that lead to contradictions (if not, however, Royce's fictional ontology) and also shared Royce's idealist assumptions. Howison's conception of philosophical reason (and its power to resolve questions about being) was a version of the "unholy trinity" I criticized in Chapter 2. This difference between Royce and Howison surely contributed to their problems in communicating with one another, but it had no great bearing upon the results of their debate. Howison remained an old-style idealist and Royce remained a fictional ontologist.[8]

After 1895, as before, Royce's development remained continuous, and one could fairly characterize it as a reconfiguration of hypothetical rationalism in a relationalist conception of being.[9] However, Howison advocated an extreme metaphysical pluralism which Royce could not endorse. To Royce it seemed that Howison's account of the individual was so rich that individuals became gods, and hence, Royce playfully charged Howison with being a polytheist.[10] If Royce's Absolute threatened the individual, Howison's extreme pluralism threatened the possibility of community and the unity of the ideal of community. Nevertheless, Royce's critique of *realistic* pluralism in WI1 contained a response not only to the pluralism of the coming new realists, but to that of James and Howison (which developed together, see Chapter 7). It seemed to Royce that any pluralist of the Howison sort must accept that real plurality implies "independent existence" for the real beings it alleges. But in so thinking, Royce failed to confront Howison's actual position—a point Howison complained about until Royce finally grew irritated with him.[11] While James was a realist of a sort (if not the worst sort), Howison was a personal idealist, and Royce's charges against realism do not well apply to his pluralistic idealism. The strongest reason to single out and examine Howison's critique closely is that he succeeds in showing the genuine fault lines in Royce's philosophy, while most critics simply fail to grasp Royce's actual position.

Contrary to Royce's summary, Howsion did not take himself to be advocating the extreme metaphysical independence of beings as Royce assumed realistic pluralists must. In his "Supplementary Essay" to *The Conception of God*, Royce had characterized the dispute between himself and Howison as an antinomy between the philosophical requirements of ethical individualism (a real variety of existing individuals), and the absolute nature of God (that all truth must be present to the unity of a single Absolute Consciousness).[12] Hence, Royce assumed that Howison was obliged to affirm both sides of the antinomy, and Royce proceeded then to resolve it. But in fact Howison had denied the claim that all truth must be present to the unity of a single Absolute Consciousness.[13] Howison's thesis is: "The world of Truth, including truths of fact and law as well as truths of value and conduct, springs, as a whole and in every part, from the world of self-active intelligences; presupposes, and in its wholeness *is* a Plurality of such strictly free minds, and cannot be contained in the unity of any Single Consciousness."[14] Howison characterizes Royce's position as: "The world of Truth, including truths of value and conduct as well as truths of fact and law, cannot spring, either as a whole or in any part, from a world of many self-active intelligences, but prohibits a Plurality of such strictly free minds, and cannot be contained in the unity of a single absolute consciousness."[15]

In thinking that Royce's absolutism rested first and foremost upon a *rejection* of metaphysical pluralism, understood in a certain light, due to its alleged logical flaws, Howison anticipates the criticism of Royce that Hocking and Marcel later made. And indeed, Howison's solution to this antinomy is akin to Hocking's, and remains clearly within the domain of idealistic philosophy, as we shall later see. Howison's solution is that the unity of the Absolute Royce thinks necessary to truth is *not necessary* because the required "unity" for truth is of the nature of "harmony," not the absolute unification of all experience in a single consciousness. Hocking, on the other hand, does not embrace harmony, insisting still on unity in the Absolute, but a unity of the "essence" or "heart of God," not requiring a strict unity with the whole of the world.

According to both Howison and Hocking, Royce has, in effect, substituted a hopelessly abstract conception of logical unity for the kind of concrete unity realized in every intelligent self that strives for and achieves, for its part, harmony in the universe. That is, while retaining the Roycean demand for a teleological order in nature and the purposive character of all Being, Howison believes he can also hold that the end of properly ordered free intelligences is a process of development, to be achieved in history through the harmonization of the wills of free individuals. It is clear how Howison's pluralism is friendlier to the maintenance of individual personality than Royce's alleged "monism" of 1895 (and remember, Howison did not see this "monism" as a postulate, he saw it as an ontological claim, and it is not perfectly clear that Royce was really a monist in anything like the sense Howison believed).

After Howison's criticism, but without admitting there was a weakness or a mistake in his thinking, Royce set to work on a more robust account of the individual (specifically the individual will) precisely in order to preserve personality in God and in individuals, and the requirements of *freedom* for individuals seem intimately related to the issue of their personhood, while also defending the claim that what was present to finite individuals only in mediated form was present to the Whole immediately. In a sense, Royce sought to articulate a modified or qualified pluralism.

I would characterize Royce's development after the "Conception of God" debate as a gradual evolution toward dealing increasingly well with the problems of individuality and immediate experience, but he remained idealistic.[16] Howison, upon reading *The Problem of Christianity*, commented that he feared Royce had left the fold of idealistic philosophy, which horrified Howison mainly because he had never grasped the difference between his own and Royce's methodologies.[17] Had he grasped the difference all along, he would have been horrified far earlier, for much earlier Royce had limited the scope of reason, philosophy, and reflection in such a way as to deny the possibility of ontological knowledge from any finite perspective, and had distinguished sharply between the finite perspective and the whole—i.e., reason could not bridge the gap, and philosophical knowledge was dependent upon hypotheses that were both unverified and unverifiable from any finite perspective. Reason could not provide unmediated knowledge (philosophical or otherwise) any more than mystical experiences could. What is important to note in both cases, Howison's as well as Royce's, is that personalism is among their prime motivations in avoiding a Hegelian or Bradleyan type of absolutism.

This disagreement Royce had with Howison over the metaphysical status of individual persons in relation to the person of God set the stage for Hocking's central insight that feeling is cognitive (the key to addressing immediate experience in an idealistic philosophy), but I must explain how this is so before moving to an assessment of Hocking's critique.

The Role of Method and Necessity in Nineteenth-Century Idealism

I have already mentioned the "unholy trinity" of gluing experience and existence together with one mode of necessity, i.e., the *logical* mode, writ large. This way of handling the problem of experience and existence was constantly being reformulated in the nineteenth century, because logic and mathematics, the paragons of "reason," were changing in fundamental ways (in the case of logic, this was the first real development since Aristotle). It is not surprising, therefore, that the relation of predication, of how subjects relate to predicates, for the purposes of metaphysics, was being overhauled. The way in which Hocking moved "beyond" Royce is something that cannot be well understood without this context. Hocking was, among other things, attempting to solve a *problem* in Royce's philosophy, and we must recount how he came to think of the problem he solved as a serious difficulty for Royce. Then we may grasp the solution and its importance.

There is a great deal in Royce's philosophy that Hocking's view assumes, but interestingly, Hocking really takes Royce's Gifford Lectures, particularly the four historical conceptions of being, as a starting place, instead of beginning with *The Religious Aspect of Philosophy* or *The Conception of God*, including Howison's criticisms. Hocking was well aware of these works and of Howison's critique, and acknowledged the strength of the critique.[18] But Hocking did not explicitly document the relationship between Howison's objections and Royce's effort to *reply* with a metaphysics of individual will (preserving the personhood of God and individuals, and hence the freedom of persons). Rather, Hocking took for granted the need for and importance of a metaphysics of individuality that preserved personhood and freedom, perhaps because these very issues had been stressed to Hocking by Royce himself. Hocking's tendency, therefore, was to *start* with the view Royce articulated in *The World and the Individual* and amend its weaknesses. This is quite understandable in light of the fact that Hocking was Royce's student between 1900 and 1904, when the Gifford Lectures were appearing, and hence, the state of Royce's thought when Hocking first encountered it was something he might be fairly expected to take for granted.[19]

Hocking strove to accommodate Royce's view in the Gifford Lectures to the genuine insights of the New Realists and "mysticism" (a term we shall need to spend time explaining later). The philosophical climate around Royce was changing and while Royce was able to adjust his view to the insights of the pragmatists (see Chapter 4), he was less able to deal constructively with the New Realists,[20] and still less with the way the world of ordinary religious believers was developing. Hocking was considerably more sensible of the way the philosophical and cultural winds were blowing, and what challenges to the assumptions of personal idealism these currents were bearing. The responsibility of the philosopher and theologian was changing, and Hocking expected of himself that he should answer those new demands.

Whether he realized it or not, Hocking was doing much the same thing as Howison, but for a new generation, and without the necessitarian "unholy trinity." If Hocking did realize this similarity, he would have seen that Royce's Gifford Lectures were already a response to the same metaphysical concerns Howison brought to the table, but a response that took its departure from *idealistic* versions of these criticisms, not realistic or mystical versions of pluralism, and still less from popular concerns about the standing of religious faith in the world of ordinary believers. With his thicker account of the individual in *The World and the Individual*, Royce was attempting to solve a problem internal to idealistic personalism, and not so much addressing the non-idealistic competitors, except as far as was necessary to explain how the non-idealistic views all fall into contradictions. Royce believed that the refinement of his system was best advanced by addressing and overcoming its idealistic competitors—particularly F.H. Bradley, whom Royce greatly admired (perhaps too much). This is partly why the "Supplementary Essay" to the First Series of Gifford Lectures takes on (and disposes of) Bradley's monism,[21] and the essay points up something characteristic in Royce's method that is worth noting here.

Like Bradley and most other nineteenth-century idealists, Royce tended to proceed dialectically by eliminating competing views through *reductio*, and then seeing what (idealistic) options were left once he had eliminated the ones that led to contradictions. This dialectical method, interestingly, tended to make his philosophy *seem* in the first place reactive rather than constructive, for the main justification for his view seems to be defended not first upon its merits, but upon its ability to *avoid* those contradictions to which the other views fell victim. With our earlier account of Royce's fictional ontology, and when we recall the strict limits he sets upon the "World of Description," while giving primacy to the "World of Appreciation," we can see that this is not quite the right way to understand Royce's *reductios* and dialectics, but it certainly *seems* right, and it is what Hocking took Royce to be doing. Logical contradiction has the force only of eliminating certain combinations of hypotheses, not of establishing that some particular and concrete state of affairs *cannot* exist. No description has that kind of power. When we encounter contradictions, in dialectical push and pull, or any other kind of reflective analysis, we have learned only that our descriptions are problematic in some combination.

Hocking's temperament was very different, taking its direction from a more intuitive sense of human experience that first affirms the validity of personal experience and only *then* seeks an account that will be a maximally consistent generalization of particular experience, and true of it, insofar as language and expression permit. Hocking does not give much clout to "universal postulates," or universals of any sort. And Hocking was less impressed with the *reductio*, even in its restricted form of eliminating hypotheses, since he was not inclined to give to abstract logic (whether dialectical or deductive) the pride of place in settling difficult philosophical issues.[22] Hocking's first appeal was to experience, while Royce's first thought, so far as philosophical reflection could bring order to our generalizations, was for employing reason, and his last test was logical coherence.[23] James and Hocking both complained that one might construct a perfectly consistent set of propositions that was still untrue of the world, the self or God. Royce could not accept that. Human reason develops and improves, with effort, and incoherence undiscoverable to us now might be discovered later, when our methods are improved; and indeed, such incoherence must at least be discoverable in principle to a consciousness sufficiently attuned to the relations of part and whole. An incoherence really *is* an incoherence, and sits there *being* incoherent. That makes it discoverable to any consciousness keen enough to see it as such.

In my view, this situation of believing that multiple complete, coherent but inconsistent descriptions of the world can be given eventually created problems for Hocking and James (for the latter, see Chapter 7). It would not have created problems for Hocking if he had not been attempting to articulate a type of personal idealism of his own in a context in which the fundamental assumptions of idealism were being brought seriously into question. Howison, twenty-one years Royce's senior, was like Royce in treating reflective reason as a power capable of settling *philosophical* dispute, although Howison defined philosophy broadly, while Royce defined it narrowly. But unlike Royce, who took the unity of God and of truth as a fundamental requirement of any viable philosophy, Howison's first gesture was always to treat the primacy of personhood as a matter of *logical* necessity, and then to assume that personhood would find its confirmation in every true account of experience. As with Royce, this position problematized the fundamental nature of persons for Howison, but rather than eliminating competing metaphysical positions to see what account could stand up to scrutiny, Howison started with a constructive metaphysical position that he built from the requirements of personal existence (God, freedom, and immortality), and then refuted competitors by *reductio* as they appeared.[24] Royce *seemed* to start, in *The World and the Individual*, with the critique of competitors and to arrive at his conclusions by elimination. But the method of *exposition* (for the sake of readers) should not be mistaken for the *philosophical* method; the former is a part of the latter.

This methodological difference is extremely important. Since scholars such as McLachlan and Cesarz have already well described Howison's method in other studies, I will simply use a contrasting analogy of temperaments: it is as if Howison began by getting together a baseball team in his hometown, with the players available there, and then fended off challengers as they appeared, insisting that no better team could be built anywhere else because no team had conquered his own. Royce, on the other hand, really began as a wanderer without a team, who postulated a series of ideal baseball teams in his mind ("Perhaps I'll build my team on the ideal of power, having McGraw for my coach, Wagner at short, Walter Johnson on the mound, . . ." etc.), and then challenged not the *actual* teams of others, but the *ideal* of those other teams, showing that they could not *possibly* be better than the team he was *thinking* about, owing to certain internal inconsistencies in the concepts upon which they were built (in this analogy, these would be ideals like speed, power-hitting, pitching, a deep bench, and the like—these concepts leading to implications, like "a speedy team will lack adequate power due to its slighter physical constitution," etc.). Royce also would not recognize as worth considering any concrete teams (such as the Red Sox or Yankees) that were not constantly in his view. Rather than scouting such teams, he would sooner ask what *kind* of team it was, and classify it according to his scheme. Unfortunately, this is how Royce handles mysticism, realism, and critical rationalism—less through the examination of the views of actual defenders of these positions than through the *idea* upon which *any* such view must be built.

Hocking was more the observer of how people "played ball" in the past, how they were playing it now, and what would be needed in terms of new ideals and adaptations to keep the game itself vital. Thus, Hocking would have made a better manager, working conceptually with the team he had rather than thinking about possible teams someone *might* have. This is James's robust influence on an otherwise idealistic thinker. But Hocking would not have attended many games; he would have read about them in the papers. James, on the contrary, would have been in the stands every day for years, keeping score, collecting stories and observations, reading every book ever written on the subject along the way, organizing the tidbits that seemed most significant, endlessly, and putting off his publishers until he could no longer bear to see another game or read another book. Then James would form a few astute provisional judgments about what a baseball is and has been, and leave the task for others to speculate about its ultimate meaning. After the book appeared it would occur to James to try playing the game himself. Dewey, by contrast, would play the game for years and then write an honest if uninteresting book, while Peirce would review all of the books critically, noting with devastating accuracy the genuine weaknesses of each of the approaches. He would then start his own book on the topic seven different times and never complete or publish any of them. Such is the rotisserie league of the classical American philosophers.

I believe Royce never over-indulged his tendency to judge the products of philosophical thinking based solely upon their avoidance of contradictions. Royce's faith in reason, and especially logic, was such as to lead him to think that whatever account of experience we may give, it could be neither true nor adequate if it fell short total logical consistency, but logical consistency was a litmus test of a philosophical ordering of general ideas, not the over-arching principle governing reality.[25] Royce did not presume that philosophical reflection could dictate to practice the final word on its "order." He really was more Kantian than Hegelian, i.e., a philosopher of limitation not an apologist of the Absolute. But he had learned from both Hegel and Schelling that the labor of the negative is not in vain.

This is all just a complicated way of pointing out that Royce and Howison shared the abstract, necessitarian *temperament* of nineteenth-century idealists, if in very different ways (necessity being subordinate to possibility in Royce's case), and Hocking did not have such a temperament at all. Hocking was a melioristic and descriptive metaphysician, as were Marcel, Dewey, and Whitehead after him. I would have said that nineteenth-century idealism had its back broken in the Great War, but the truth is that Hocking had seen the cracks in the façade before then, having published his masterpiece of twentieth-century (chastened) idealism in 1912. Here the aim was not to construct a logically self-consistent system so much as to provide an interesting and valuable generic description of being—a description that preserves and accounts for the meaning of experience and which places meaning above truth. This way of approaching metaphysical issues made a great difference to philosophy in the twentieth century. Here contingency replaces necessity as the more basic category of experience in metaphysics, whereas for Royce, possibility was more the operative category than contingency.

Royce's metaphysics can be made consistent with this "contingent" approach, once his fictional ontology is appreciated, although Royce himself felt defeated in the attempt to communicate what he was doing.²⁶ The reason behind Royce's sense of defeat is not hard to grasp. Strict idealists of the nineteenth century had taken the view that the very essence of idealism is the active view of mind, and that nothing real exists apart from this kind of activity. Further, the essence of the active mind was to be found in its rational ordering of the real. This rational ordering did not *result* in the rules of logic, but rather *presupposed* those rules as *a priori* laws of being. Thus, logic was not the *product* of mental activity for the nineteenth-century idealists; rather, logic was the *law* that made mental activity possible, and our advances in logic marked our increasing understanding of how "mind" worked, while "mind" was the highest and most crucial expression of becoming, and therefore made all being both possible and actual. There was, for such idealists (Hegel and the early Schelling being the two best examples) no difference between what *could be* thought and what *could be* actual (notice that this is a modal claim). Hence, the laws of logic governed possible mental activity, both human and divine, and served as a necessary link between the human and the divine. I emphasize that these laws were *necessary* laws, and without them, the mind could do nothing. Such was the view of *a prioristic idealists of the nineteenth century. Royce was not this kind of idealist*, but his peers, including James, kept responding to him as though he were—especially tagging him with the label "Hegelian." By 1913 Royce was simply fed up with this mistake and was despairing that his peers would ever grasp their error.²⁷

The melioristic and descriptive view, on the contrary, saw logic as the best articulation of the ordering activity of the mind, but was not inclined to give to any logic the status of the necessary lawgiver of the mind or as exhausting mind's possibilities. Even if it were perfectly understood, logic was not the governor of mind. Logic was rather a distilled *result* of the efforts of finite minds to grasp what they were already doing, and any account of the logic of mental activity would need to be revisable in light of a better understanding of the powers and limitations of finite minds, as well as descriptive of their on-going creative powers, which increased with human effort. This view was eventually espoused by Dewey, Cassirer, Whitehead, and others, and retained the active and dialectical view of mind, but rejected the hegemony of *a priori* reason and the unholy trinity.

In sum, as the project of self-knowledge proceeds in history and cumulative experience, we should expect to have to revise our understanding of logic. This view involves relinquishing the claim that any given logic is the foundation of all mental activity, possible or actual, and consequently, the necessity we discover in logical relations is a necessity internal to the account of logic and reason we have offered based on our reflection upon experience, understood historically, culturally, and symbolically. Logic provides norms for how we ought to think, seeing thinking as an action, not descriptions of how we actually do think. The feeling of necessity in our reasoning is a normative goad to the well trained mind, not the finite echoes of the infinite language of God or Nature. This is, in fact, Royce's view, as it is Peirce's. Both reject ontological necessity. But whereas Peirce's interpreters and even his foes recognize that he has done this, even Royce's fondest allies overlook it.

In Hocking we see his descriptive meliorism in the chapters from *The Meaning of God in Human Experience* in which he argues on the one side that feeling *always* tends to produce ideas, and ideas cannot exist alone but depend for their being upon feelings. Indeed, this is the meaning of his claim that "feeling is cognitive." The question that arises with the descriptive, melioristic view is whether it is still "idealism." Most philosophers think that granting an independent and foundational status to "ideas" is part and parcel of "idealism." I will confront that question in the next chapter, arguing for an idealistic strain of pragmatism, as distinct from the pragmatism of Dewey and James. With Hocking the case is less clear. If we allow that a psychological or phenomenological description of mental activity will suffice as an account of the fundamental character of mind (or consciousness), then an idealistic view *can* be maintained by those who abandon metaphysical and logical necessity, and perhaps Hocking has done that (at least Marcel thought he had). The main requirement of such an idealism is that it hold strictly that nothing really *makes sense* in reflection that is not intentional in structure, or as it would be better said, all things that can be conceived to exist derive their *meaning* from their personal (and hence conscious or volitional) modality (keeping in mind that "personal" is already and primarily a social, or more strictly a communal characteristic of ideas). Dewey, Cassirer, and Whitehead did not follow this path, leaving aside personalism as they left aside old-style idealism—perhaps to their detriment.

This more personalistic view, such as we find in Royce, Hocking, Marcel, Scheler, and Brightman, requires a broader account of the order created by mind or will than any version of "reason" had so far, up to Royce's time, been able to express. The term "experience" is better suited to the idealism of Hocking than "reason" in this light. The move to the primacy of experience over reason is found in Royce, as I will show in Chapter 4, but the full recognition of the importance of the move is clearer in Hocking. In general, however, the more *broadly* one conceives "reason," the better the personalists will like the account. But it would be a mistake to reduce knowledge or experience to reason, no matter how broadly construed, for no account of reason will capture the whole meaning of experience, since much experience is sub-rational, irrational, or supra-rational. At all events, Hocking's experientialist (and pragmatic) leanings made him readier than Royce to downplay the importance of reason in metaphysics, even if neither of them was a slave to reason.

Such caution with regard to the power of reason may give rise to a provisional idealism that waits upon increasingly better articulations of the *nature* of reason, and hence better knowledge, perhaps in the hope that a perfect articulation may be available in the infinitely distant future. This is Peirce's type of idealism. But one could go further and say that *no* account of reason can *ever* perfectly articulate the activity of mind (or volitional will) because reason is only one among many ordering principles that mind or will employ in creating the real, or responding to each other (as Howison and Hocking have it). If that means giving up the idea that God is maximally rational, then so be it, except that "maximally rational" can be interpreted, along lines analogous to those later defended by Hartshorne, to mean "more rational than any other actual or possible person." The maximally rational God is not the same idea as the omni-rational Absolute. Such is the nature of my own position, and of Hocking's, as I understand it, although I am not certain Hocking always truly maintains his "idealism" in following this path. In attempting to show how ideas are always already present in every feeling, and lead inexorably to thoughts, Hocking leaves us wondering what the *being* of feeling could be, apart from the experience of it. If the *being* of feeling is identical with the experience of it, then either Hocking is an ordinary idealist and ought to follow Royce or Howison, or if Hocking refuses the identity of feeling and its very being, he has a problem with immediacy and he must overcome Royce's critique of realism.[28]

Hocking sees *desire* at the bottom of all conscious activity (which agrees with Hegel, but Hocking's study of Eastern philosophy is also here in evidence), undergirding both thinking and feeling. But if desire is the *being* of feeling, what is the being of desire? If one states, experientially, that "desire happens," one may with justification ask "what does 'happens' mean here?" Is it the ideal order as already conceived in the mind of God that grounds the happening and being of desire, or is Hocking suggesting that desire is its own independent existential ground? Granting that desire is intentional in structure, and issues in feeling and then thought, why does desire exist rather than nothing? Granting that no one can honestly doubt that he or she experiences desire, what creates it? Is desire one or many, ultimately? Is its knowledge-content meaningful apart from each individual occurrence of each individual feeling-thought? If so, what validity accompanies the claim that desire is either one or many? The Buddhist schools and the vedic philosophies before them spent millennia on the same questions.

Royce's arguments against radical pluralism recommend themselves here. But it is important to note that unity is seen by melioristic, descriptive idealism only as a requirement of reason in its effort to comprehend concepts or generalizations that have already been formed, not a requirement of the *being* of mind or desire as such. Naturally our accounts of the activity of the mind and desire should strive for self-consistency, not because we *know* the order of the universe to be necessarily consistent *with itself* (in some sense of the term "consistent"), and not because we can eliminate all views that lead us to contradictions (indeed, we cannot philosophize at all without the spur of paradox), but because when we strive for maximum self-consistency in philosophical thinking, meaning is better preserved and propagated. Hocking was well on his way to such a view with the insight that "feeling is cognitive," but whether his historical and experiential method holds him within the idealistic fold is another question. Let us more fully understand his critique of Royce before pursuing that question.

Hocking's Critique of Royce

What, then, is the problem in Royce's thought that Hocking is attempting to solve? There are really two problems, one that belongs to the world of *thought* or philosophical reflection (description, in Royce's terms), and a second that belongs to the realm of individual religious experience (which is a part of the world of appreciation, in Royce's terms, though by no means the whole of that world). I will deal with each in turn. The problem Hocking sees within the domain of thought is little different from the problem Howison recognized, namely, that Royce's metaphysics, particularly his absolutist tendency, threatens the personal aspect of being. This comes clearly to the fore in Hocking's discussion of our knowledge of other minds in *The Meaning of God in Human Experience*. There he says:

> "Our fellows are known to be real," says Royce, "because they are for each of us the endless treasury of more ideas. . . . (They) furnish us with the constantly needed supplement to our own fragmentary meanings." To anything that appears in our life with the character of a *response*, we instinctively

attribute outer personality. . . . God is most real, undoubtedly, to that person who finds his prayers responded to; for, to paraphrase Royce's criterion, response is our best ground for believing the social object is real. Upon this way of reaching the Other Mind, we must make the following comment. That we are still left with only an inference of that Other; a faith and not a knowledge of experience. Even though we say, with Royce, that reality is nothing else than response (or fulfilling of meaning), we have not so far as this criterion goes, found that reality personal save by probability of high order. We can still speak only of "the source of our belief in the reality of our fellow men," not of an experience of that reality itself.[29]

This is the "immediacy problem." At bottom, Hocking cannot be satisfied with a merely inferential knowledge regarding the personal character of reality. There must be some *experience* of the other, and of the real, that serves as ground for the reality of persons.[30] He goes on to point out that Royce's "response" theory, true as far as it goes, has the difficulty that it presupposes the *idea* of the other mind, for without the presupposition, there can be nothing to respond *to*, and we could not distinguish our internal dialogue from our dialogue with the world and with others. One must *expect* the other mind in order to respond to it, or take it as having responded to oneself.

Hence, Hocking is feeling cramped by Royce's restriction of philosophy to a kind of reflection that is obliged to work with general ideas and descriptions, and not capable of creating them—ideas such as the idea of the other mind, in this case. If reality is social at bottom, as Royce holds, this restriction on philosophy portends a dilemma between the intentional character of all reality and the already accomplished and completed character of the Absolute experience which has immediate access to past, present and future (as I have explained in the previous chapter). This is precisely Howison's point as well. Hocking goes on to say that "I cannot doubt that the last mystery of mutual contact is contained in the will, rather than in the intellect; a thesis we shall have later to consider."[31] Howison had made this very point in suggesting that it was a harmonization of wills that unified God as the ideal of each individual being, and God is nothing other than this unified ideal. But for Howison, it was the rational will, whereas for Hocking the unification is prior to rationality.

Hocking's analysis and grasp of the problem goes further, since he is willing to place in question the assumptions of descriptive (as opposed to Howison-style necessitarian) idealism. He says:

> The ultimate difficulty in this matter is due, as I have come to think, to our over-dogmatic ideals of knowledge, and to the explanations we adopt of the

> knowing process. We take our knowledge of physical things as the type and ideal of all satisfactory knowledge, —and we find naturally enough that we have no such physical knowledge of fellow minds. We explain our knowledge of any object by a relation between object and subject, in which the object presumably produces some effect on the subject, —and we find naturally enough that anything which is intrinsically *subject* cannot become such an object. But if such were the true ideal and explanation of knowledge, we could not, of course, know ourselves any more than we could know others.[32]

We see here how Hocking has incorporated the existentialist and phenomenological insights associated with the paradox of subjectivity, and the reasons for the existentialist and phenomenological rejection of science and its brand of reason. This move amounts to favoring the primacy of Royce's "appreciative world" (which might as easily have been called the "life-world," for his configuration of that concept is quite similar to Husserl's later idea[33]), and it comes as little surprise that the problem of immediate experience also haunted Husserl. Hocking too recommends that the model for knowing physical objects we have imported from the physical sciences must be set aside in favor of a deeper way of probing into the presence of the other to the self, but it is not clear that he consistently maintains this stance, as I shall indicate in a moment, since he relies upon psychology (and indeed the social sciences in general) instead of natural science as his way of grounding our relation to the other in a kind of objective knowledge. Obviously this is the other trap that both Husserl and Royce tried to avoid.

It is worth remarking that Hocking's criticism of Royce, if it is correct, would undermine Royce's restrictions upon philosophical reflection, restoring the availability of immediate experience to philosophy, in a way Royce's critique of mysticism had precluded. This move also fails to respect Peirce's restrictions upon philosophical evidence in the 1868 articles that informed all of Royce's thought. And that restoration of immediacy to philosophical relevance is exactly what Hocking attempts. Yet, somehow, in Hocking's delicate handling of the problem, one is soothed into assuming that the problem is not so terrible for Royce. Howison, by contrast, was a bull in Royce's china shop, able to find the most expensive pieces and shatter them to bits. For those sympathetic to his project, Hocking is more like an entrepreneur in Royce's *mismanaged* china shop who sees the possibilities, buys the store and gently transforms it from bottom to top until it sells everyday dishes, which is what the people really needed. But to grasp fully what Hocking has done, we shall have to turn to his account of mysticism to see how he employs the notion of immediacy to restore our assurance that reality can be reflectively known to be personal, meaningful, and free, even in philosophical activity. Only then may we fairly ask "is this still idealism?"

The second and deeper motivation for Hocking's critique of Royce comes from his surveying the world he was living in and coming to the conclusion that religious *life* is in peril in the present civilization. He sees that the practice of worship has largely lost its meaning and that many "believers" have drifted toward a deeper trust of their ideas and moral convictions than of their direct religious experience. Worship no longer presents persons with the presence of God, but rather with a sort of numbingly dead sequence of rituals that offers no sustenance to the fundamental project of every human soul. The mediators of God to humanity—books, priests, saints, etc.—have taken the place of a sense of the reality of the divine that is external to us and yet immediately available. William James had complained of this in *The Varieties of Religious Experience*, and Royce, in spite of his stated intention (in *The Problem of Christianity*) to restore vitality to institutional and community faith, certainly was not helping the situation with his heretical intellectual reconstruction of Pauline Christianity. Hocking came to believe that if he could not help to preserve in individuals the willingness to trust in their direct experience of the divine, God would cease to have a meaning in the world for many people, and the world would not be better for it. The experience of the mystic is indispensable in this regard, and must be saved from Royce's attack on mysticism for the good of the world and the individual.

Thus, Hocking looks at Royce's philosophy and is impressed but sees deficiencies that can be reconstructed with the aid of psychology. Yet, what concerns him far more is how Royce's *theology*, the theology implied by his philosophy of religion, substitutes the reflective account of divine being for the sacramental life itself. Royce's theology is a supreme expression of what human thought can accomplish in ordering its speculations upon ultimacy, but in so doing creates only an abstract symbol of life as we experience it. This is what one would expect from the applications (theological and otherwise) of a philosophy that is restricted to the ordering of reflective concepts, a hangover of the Kantian idealism of limitation. The symbols applied to the domains of reflection are so thoroughly mediated by reason that one can scarcely recover the impulses (in this case, religious impulses) that must have once made the symbols seem important and vital.

Thus, in recovering a place for mystical experience, Hocking hopes to provide a ground for sacramental living, and to revitalize prayer, worship, and the other aspects of our habitual and instinctive lives that do not merely *remind* us of the reality of God, but assail us directly with an *immediate experience* of God. Royce had no interest in any such project. This is the crucial test case of the broader question of immediate experience. If we drift further into a faith in our *thoughts* and reflective moral convictions, we will not be inclined or even able to believe that our direct experiences of God are real or authoritative, or that experience of God can fix belief where doubt has irritated us and paralyzed activity. We would thus deny God when God appears (or anything else that we experience immediately). A culture or a people that has ceased to be able to believe in its God or gods is in very great peril, and the peril is not lessened when immediate experience is regarded as inadequate for fixing belief. Hocking cannot allow that to happen, if it is within his power to prevent it, and Royce is part of the problem, not part of the solution.[34] It is clear that Hocking's second criticism of Royce is motivated by his personal experience, and he makes clear that the fundamental concerns of *The Meaning of God in Human Experience* are in part autobiographical.[35]

Hocking sees every self-conscious finite soul, in virtue of its finitude, as being set upon an irresistible quest for greater nearness to the Absolute, and this he calls "the love of God." The soul cannot help loving God (think of Diotima's speech as recounted by Socrates in Plato's *Symposium*), but it may be at a loss as to how to achieve closer proximity. And here the mystic is needed as a guide.

Royce and Hocking on Mysticism

Royce's critique of mysticism in *The World and the Individual*[36] concerns itself almost exclusively with the type of *thought* to which mysticism leads, specifically, the type of speculative metaphysics it presupposes, viz., "the doctrine that reality is pure unity, the negation of all appearances and pluralities, immediate therefore, and ineffable."[37] Hocking is willing to accept as decisive Royce's critique of this type of *thought*,[38] but is unwilling to agree that mysticism is best understood in terms of this metaphysics, or indeed, even that mystical experience *always* leads to *this kind* of thought. As Hocking says, "unquestionably we restrict our view of historical mysticism in identifying it with this [speculative] result: mysticism has been a much broader thing than this type of metaphysics. Not all mystics have been independent speculators; not all speculators among the mystics have conformed to this type."[39] Instead, Hocking sees mysticism as rooted in the act of worship, which is a matter of voluntary will, concretely situated and historically enacted, before it can become a subject of reflective thought. Hocking's approach to mysticism is therefore more empirical and historical than Royce's, although perhaps we can excuse Royce when we remember that Hocking had access to James's brilliant empirical treatment of mysticism in *The Varieties of Religious Experience*, and Royce did *not* when he wrote *The World and the Individual*.

James's 1902 book really launched the discipline of the psychology of religion, and Hocking's *The Meaning of God in Human Experience* could not have been empirical in the way it is without that earlier work. James's efforts enabled Hocking to be concrete where Royce had been abstract, and indeed, it is not easy to decide whether Hocking's major book is really one we ought to class in the philosophy of religion or in the psychology of religion. I am inclined to believe it belongs with the latter (especially when compared with John Elof Boodin's efforts in the same vein, which treat exactly the same subjects in ways that are more clearly philosophical). This anticipates my criticism in the final section of this chapter, for if Hocking is an idealist, he is so as a matter of psychological conviction more than of metaphysical argument. An idealist metaphysics has a difficulty with immediate experience, and psychologism comes no closer to a solution than does naturalism. We will see the result of this conundrum in the next chapter.

Interestingly, however, this tendency to psychologize is precisely the problem Hocking finds in the history of mysticism that leads it into the bad metaphysics Royce attacks. The mystic has an experience that results in a kind of knowledge, but finds himself or herself unable to express or articulate this knowledge. "And as the mystic has been hard put to it to tell what it is that he knows, he has in our later and Western world had increasing recourse to reporting the *psychology* of his experience, in lieu of its cognitive contents. Indeed, he has not only used psychology, but has made it for his own purposes."[40] But here, rather than thinking it a fault to use psychology in expressing the mystical experience, Hocking questions the *quality* of the psychology the mystics used—as being too subjective and not as objective-minded as original religion itself must be. Religion does not produce its effects in history and society simply by creating a subjective satisfaction in those who experience the divine, it affects the world by convincing the believer that the meaning of and truth about the world is the same for others as for himself or herself. Religion seeks to give an *objective* account of the world, not merely a subjective sense of the worth of the individual soul.[41] And it is this objectivity that constitutes religion as a force in history and present society, with convinced believers acting in the world and changing it. Psychology, Hocking thinks, must study and also *follow* this objective gesture if it is to succeed in providing knowledge of mystical experience. So it is not the *use* of psychology that calls into question the accounts of mystical experience, but rather the fact that *bad* psychology is being used. As Hocking says, "unquestionably the reputation of mysticism in this world would have suffered less if our mystics could earlier and more completely have commanded this psychological mode of expression."[42]

What, then, is Hocking's account of mysticism, and how is it supposed to solve Royce's problems? Here we finally reach the heart of his claim that "feeling is cognitive." The validity of Hocking's entire philosophy may indeed turn upon his interpretation of mysticism, and more care is needed to bring out its subtleties than I can provide here. Still I shall endeavor to bring out its essential features in full recognition that convincing responses may be offered to the criticisms my brief sketch will raise.

First, then, in mystical experience Hocking seeks to maintain both the individuality of the experiencing person and the immediacy of the experience of the unity of all being. This is an experience in which the experiencer is led to think of this experience as an immediate unification of the self with the One, or God. But if all is One, how is the experiencer different from the experienced? In this light, the term "contrast" lends itself to Hocking. "If there were no contrast in reality between the one and the many, between the substance and its appearances, between the indescribable and its describable aspects, then an experience which was 'one, immediate and ineffable' would find simply nothing in the world to light upon. But he who would deny that such an experience can discover anything real must be prepared to abolish the reality of substance."[43]

Hocking takes it as obvious that one would not wish to destroy the reality of substance, and here he fails to anticipate what process philosophers, including his own student Hartshorne and his future friend and colleague Whitehead, would soon do. Indeed, when Hocking wrote *The Meaning of God*, Ernst Cassirer had recently (1910) published a critique of the idea of substance that would be decisive for many thinkers, and Einstein's general theory of relativity would within six more years revolutionize the common understanding of physical reality in ways that seemed to make the old idea of substance expendable in physical theory. And as a result of the increasing willingness to abolish the reality of substance, process philosophers would have a problem with the nature of the real as opposed to the ideal, coming down on the side of neither except insofar as they assert that process is the real, or that the real is in process. This problem will be taken up in Chapter 6, where I will discuss the temporal relation of the possible and the actual. But Hocking's metaphysics depends upon the assumption that we seek Substance, and with the decline of Substance metaphysics his philosophy is vulnerable to many questions he did not anticipate.

Hocking's point for now is that a contrast must be maintained between the experiencer and the thing experienced, and here he continues by saying that "the mystic cannot find the whole of reality, but he may find its center; he may find the only handle by which the whole can be held as a unity."[44] Thus, for Hocking, the experience of the mystic is our access to the unity of the whole of existence insofar as a finite mind may grasp it. As we have noted, this places much importance upon the character of mystical experience. And in this context we must reproduce in full a crucial passage:

> And this is the advantage of psychology in dealing with mysticism, that it is non-committal in regard to the cognitive or other possible importance of an experience, and may yet furnish the clue to such meaning. For where self-expression falters the signs of meaning may still be read in causes and effects. The immediacy of any experience must submit to the interpretation by what is outside it and related to it. The logic and the psychology of our experiences are so adjusted that what becomes invisible to one becomes visible to the other. It is possible that the thread of meaning, lost though it may be to the mystic himself in his ecstatic moment, may at that very moment appear, so to speak, on the reverse of the cloth, as something then and there happening to the substance of the mystic himself; justifying his sense of the "ontological importance" of that event. This implies, of course, that the "immediacy" of the mystic experience has its external relations; and this implication I fully accept and shall try to justify. Some part of the meaning of this experience is to be discovered in its external career. For which reason, not only the psychologist, but such other scientists as like him see mysticism in its outer bearings, the historian, the sociologist, have been quicker than the metaphysician to recognize its vital importance in religion.[45]

In this passage, Hocking is saying, in essence, that James had a far better account of the importance of mystical experience in religious life than Royce had. And this is correct. But said in his gentle way, one could almost miss the implication. And here we see that Hocking is committed to using the insights of psychology in his account of mysticism, not because it sees further into the soul; rather, Hocking uses it because it better takes account of the objective world than does the thought of the mystic which reflects upon his own experience. Yet, Hocking has been, prior to this point, no ardent defender of scientific or other external accounts of first person experience. He has made some assertions that would loosen the restrictions upon philosophical reflection introduced by Royce, but has simultaneously yielded both to psychologism and naturalism, the very assumptions that phenomenologists had been striving so ardently to bracket, under the (entirely correct) conviction that these assumptions actually *prevent* philosophers from giving adequate descriptions of immediate experience.

Why Hocking draws in empirical "science" (if indeed psychology is or can be or should be a science) at this point is not easy to understand. But his motive seems to be pragmatic at bottom: "Mysticism, then, we shall define not by its doctrine but by its deed, the deed of worship in its fully developed form. Nothing concerns us more than to know what that experience means, and what it may add to our knowledge of God: but we shall not foreclose these questions by taking a finished speculative system into our definition of mysticism."[46] Here Hocking is criticizing Royce without naming him, and calling attention to the fact that Royce could see in mysticism only what the system of thought Royce *brought* to the question *allowed* him to see.

Hocking was underestimating Royce, although it will require a good bit of analysis to show fully the extent of his error. It will be argued in Chapter 4 that Royce was a pragmatist of a stripe who could easily embrace what Hocking has just asserted. Hocking was claiming that Royce's account of mysticism was unempirical, while James had the better and admirably empirical alternative. In the next chapter I will explain why the description is correct, but perhaps not the conclusion. Remember, James was a *realist* and could afford in his metaphysics the assumption that experiences point to an independent reality. But his brand of realism is destined to be dashed on the very same rock—the question of immediate experience (see the end of Chapter 7). We shall also see how Royce accommodated the insights of psychology and what place he gave it in the philosophical domain in Chapter 5. Royce had destroyed the claim of immediacy as a *concept* of being, in the abstract, in *The World and the Individual*, and argued that only a fourth conception of being—to be is to be uniquely related to the whole—could avoid contradiction. The meaning of this fourth conception will require Chapters 5 through 7 to explain fully.

Can Hocking's idealism remain an idealism while preferring James's approach to mystical experience to Royce's, or in other words, is it, in Royce's terms, philosophy at all, or is it just a Jamesian conceptual mess? For now it will be sufficient to note that mystical experience as embodied in the act of the individual will which Hocking calls "worship" starts in feeling. But feeling of what? And what is the cognitive significance of this feeling? In this context I must reproduce another lengthy passage by Hocking, partly because no summary could equal its eloquence, and indeed, its eloquence is a great part of its persuasiveness:

> Worship may be regarded as an attempt to detach oneself from everything else in uniting with God. It seeks God first as an object, that Other of all worldly objects; and it seeks to join itself to that absolute other. The mystic proceeds by negation; this and that, he says, are not God: it is not these that I seek. The effort of worship measures the soul's *power of detachment*. And my power of detachment measures the whole of my freedom, the whole of my possibility of happiness, the whole of my possible originality, the whole depth and reach of my morality and of my human contribution. What the mystic reaches is, in terms of his world-conceptions, a zero: not indeed the whole of reality, but Substance, the heart of God. It is just such a zero as one encounters when he seeks his own soul behind the shifting content of his experience, or when he seeks the soul of another, in distinction from that other's various external expressions. This zero is not a place to stay in; but it may be pre-eminently a place to return to, and *to depart from*. In worship one touches the bottom of that bottomless pit of Self and perceives at hand the real Origin of things; gaining not the whole of any knowledge, but the beginning and measure of all knowledge. May not worship be described as the will to become, for a moment and within one's own measure, what existence is; or more simply, as the act of recalling oneself to *being*?[47]

Thus, mystical experience is an act of the will through which it detaches itself from the world (and the worldly self) by negating all particularity, and literally everything depends on this act—freedom, happiness, morality, originality, knowledge and creativity in the finite person. Note how the detachment from particularity, such as Hocking requires here, meshes with Royce's view, explained in the previous chapter about how and why all thought, especially philosophy, is obliged to deal with already formed generalities. But Hocking is saying, in essence, that in mystical experiences we have immediate experience of the universal, or at least the general.

The influence of Royce is also clearly seen here in Hocking's voluntarism, but we must recognize that this emphasis on the will, its employment in negating what is particular, is also in line with Kierkegaard and Nietzsche, so there is the existentialist tonality as well. But I am led to wonder if voluntarism is wholly appropriate to the phenomenon of mystical experience. Very often mystical experiences come to us unbidden and without any conscious act of willing, without preparation, and indeed without effort. Hocking seems not to account for these. He does acknowledge that in so willing the mystic mainly *prepares* for the experience rather than causing it. One can evoke but not command the mystical experience. There is still the sense in Hocking that some external agency has acted to lift us to that place and time wherein we experience union with the divine (and this would be in line with Kierkegaard, but not consistent with Nietzsche; for Royce the community is this agency). For Hocking, the individual will acts to negate the world in preparation for the work of an outside agency, and this outside agency may or may not appear in response to these preparations. When this external power chooses us, we can no more resist it with our wills than we can command it. As we will see in later chapters, this is not how Royce understands "will," and this move places Hocking more in the line of Kierkegaard, James, and Marcel with respect to the philosophy of the will.

It seems to me that process philosophers, such as Whitehead and Hartshorne, in speaking of "divine lure," are attempting to recognize that agency on both the side of the finite individual and the divine is required in the account. And indeed, Wesleyans have a religious doctrine of "prevenient grace" that does something similar, while Augustinians minimize (without eliminating) the power of the finite agent to a simple turning towards God, while God does the rest. Calvinists place total agency externally in God, and Lutherans tend in this direction, while post-millenialist Christian thinkers like Schleiermacher have a tendency to place a more robust responsibility for willing the Kingdom of God upon the agency of individual believers. This variety of accounts of agency and willing is repeated in all the other major world religions, and evinces Hocking's requirement of some sort of external agency in mystical experience. This renders the relation between the finite person and the external agency one of response, just as Royce had insisted—not a *concept* of response, but actual responses. But for Hocking, the finite will negates and detaches, the external agency acts positively to unify. I repeat, this is not Royce's view of will. For Hocking, there is immediate experience of that which is above the particular. The external agency is, as we have earlier indicated, what Hocking calls "the love of God" (which is interestingly ambiguous regarding the origin and destiny of the act of loving—whether it is God's agency and our patience, or the reverse). He says:

> We must not hesitate, therefore, to explain the love of God by what it is not, —the one by the many, the disinterested by the interested, the self-aban-

doning by the self seeking. We must assert that there is no love of God which is not at the same time an unlimited self-valuation; that there is always something self-seeking about worship and mysticism. . . . Perhaps this spark of ontological ambition which creative nature has deposited in the single self, is nature's own way of bringing the new to pass for the good of all creation.[48]

Thus, the concrete will of the finite soul opens itself to the action of the divine by self-interestedly negating the world and all the empirical aspects of its own experience, and in so negating itself seeks others and God, and even itself *as* substance (not mere experience).

The way in which Hocking attempts to solve Royce's problem of the independence of the personal individual is by placing upon that individual an infinite responsibility to act negatively, in self-negation, to seek God, compelled by its own infinite desire, by an effort of its own will. Without such action the self cannot be happy, free, moral or creative—and it cannot experience God. Hocking's God (apparently) does not visit the individual soul unbidden, and if the soul remains dissolute in its isolated condition, not seeking the divine, that soul will never find itself above particular experience, or others or the world either. This is a lost soul, trapped in the particularity of its individual experiences, untrusting of anything general, suspicious of everything substantial, miserable, and, in short, a nominalist. For that reason, the soul (the individual, the person) will remain isolated until it seeks the world, others and the divine by negating itself.

So, an effort of will is a necessary if insufficient condition for the immediate experience of God, others, and even ourselves. This view, if it is true, assures us of the individuality, and perhaps also the irreducible personhood, of the finite soul, so constituted by its evident proprietary control over its own will. We can render ourselves less personal and less individual by inactivity, particularly failing to act so as to seek immediate union with God. And indeed, this solution is not very much different from Royce's response to Howison's criticism (see Chapter 5). Royce turned also to the individual will as the bulwark of individuality itself, and as I will argue, defended it along two lines, one phenomenological and the other metaphysical. Here Hocking defends the view more empirically, more along the lines of James, and unlike Royce or James, adopts the insights of negative theology—instead of adopting argumentative dialectic to refute competitors, Hocking employs an experiential dialectic that negates the empirical world in its particularity so as to seek the "heart of God." This sounds more like mystical practice in world history than anything Royce mentions in his critique of mysticism.

Critique of Hocking

Even though they have differing fundamental ideas about the will, in both Royce and Hocking individual will comes to the fore as a solution to the problem of the One and the Many, and the problem of immediate experience, resulting in a modified metaphysical pluralism. Indeed, Howison also followed this avenue, but in a more radical way. Is Hocking's empirical or Jamesian emphasis on the will really a better solution to this problem than Royce's? I do not think it is, although I agree that Hocking's general tendency to criticize Royce for not being historical and experiential and empirical enough ought to be heeded.[49] Royce's "mysticism" is not mysticism, which is to say that Royce has prematurely attempted to set aside the issue of immediate experience by treating it under the unformed head of "mystical thought." He has also failed to address the question of the immediate experience of generals and universals—and this problem is the very one he addresses in his later semiotics. The doctrine of signs is a doctrine of immediate experience of generalities. It amazes me how often philosophers of all stripes focus on the functional aspects of semiotics without noticing, apparently, that the whole attraction of semiotics is its way of addressing the classical problems of universals by making out an account of the experience of generals (or even universals). An ontology is presupposed in Peircean semiotics which is neither realist or nominalist, in itself, but conceptualist. Royce and Peirce follow the same path, although Royce's version remains conceptualist throughout while Peirce presses on to realism.

I have noted along the way a number of places where Hocking's account of immediate experience of God is susceptible to criticism. Here, briefly, I will collect them. The first and most serious objection regards method. Hocking's method is not logically rigorous enough for the kind of philosophy he professes to be doing, mixing as it does the empirical and psychological (and social scientific) conception of experience with an ontological approach to generality and particularity. Most idealists adopt a dialectical logic, whether negatively using the reductio as Royce does, or positively constructing its edifice, as Howison does. Both begin with the reality of general ideas (or even universals in Howison's case), and both restrict themselves to this level of generality, realizing that to bring in particular experience is to raise the specter of immediate experience as a philosophical problem (as distinct from empirical or phenomenological—see the next chapter—problem). Royce's whole intent to follow Peirce limitations in the 1868 essays was to find a more defensible ground than Kant's for limiting the scope of *philosophical* evidence, while allowing that other sciences could work with first-order generalizations even if philosophy cannot. Hocking does not maintain this all-important separation of empirical versus philosophical reflection. His dialectic cuts across the limitations set out by Peirce and maintained by Royce.

Royce adds to Peirce's approach the method of fictional ontology, to support the dialectic with needed restrictions upon the scope of philosophical knowledge, once attained (although fictional ontology does more than just this). Hocking's method is, by contrast, empirical and historical. He relies upon psychology and the other social sciences to provide him with his empirical data, and trusts in their ability to attain objectivity. By analogy he points out that other social practices, such as religious worship, obtain objective effects in culture and history and thus have an objective side. One assumes that no one in particular needs to have thought out or reflectively organized, or indeed, to have consciously intended these effects for them to be relevant to philosophy. This is quite at odds with Royce's view of philosophy, and might be fine for a realist, but for an idealist it is a problem for several reasons.

First, the social sciences are not producers of objective knowledge unless they are guided by a rigorous methodology—whether that is cognitive psychology's obsession with modeling neural networks, or behaviorism's self-restriction to observable behavior, or Gestalt psychology's tireless recording of perceptual reports. Hocking submits philosophical evidence to no such methodological restrictions. He argues that religion is objective because it seeks the world and affects it profoundly in human history. The same may be said for the social sciences when they are properly done, he admonishes. But we can dispute whether this amounts to a level of objectivity sufficient to ground an idealistic metaphysics, and indeed, Hocking's sort of objectivity better accords with realism and its correspondence theory of truth, or with pragmatism and its theory of meaning than with idealism and its demand for coherence. But Hocking rejects full-fledged realism, and insists on maintaining a substance metaphysics anathema to pragmatic theories of meaning, which he regards as a purely negative theory of philosophical criticism. What is substance? Granting that Hocking declines to speak of substance beyond the experience of it, why even call the sought immediate unity "substance" unless it is taken to have a prior and external existence?

The fact is that Hocking *does* believe God has a prior and external existence, and acts from that external position upon the soul (the individual seeking person, who is apparently not "substance," but active will). He simply has a different version of Royce's problem of genuine individuality, and perhaps did not go as far as Royce did in overcoming the idea of substance, as I will argue in chapter six. Further, other minds, and even the deepest parts of the self, partake in Hocking's "metaphysical substance" by actively willing, in the same sense. Hocking offers no account—beyond the psychological *need* of it—that would ground his faith in substance, or the "being of infinite desire," or the "heart of God," or the "love of God," if we prefer. Hocking would have done better to move to a full temporalism, rejecting substance and couching the issue of immediacy in terms of the temporal relation of the actual and the possible.

I do not say that no answer can be made to these criticisms, but the most obvious answers are those that abandon idealism and seek a rigorous method elsewhere. Given Hocking's great sympathy with empirical methods, it would seem appropriate for him to have followed James further than he did, abandoning idealism and the Absolute.[50] Indeed, the problem of immediate experience led many pragmatists to abandon idealism. Marcel, with whom Hocking shared so much, also departed from idealism and followed a phenomenological and existential path, not the path of substance metaphysics. And finally, with the insight of the cognitive value of feeling, Hartshorne and Whitehead built systems of process metaphysics that also were non-idealistic. As for answering Howison's real criticism, it is not clear that either Royce or Hocking succeeded. We shall examine Royce's theory of the individual in chapter five to see. It is good to remember that the problem of how to treat immediate experience philosophically is, in a sense, created by Peirce's restrictions on introspection, intuition, and the power of thinking without signs, so the issue of immediacy is embedded in the soul of pragmatism. For now we are well situated to examine Royce's pragmatism, for there we shall find another living idea, the idealistic version of pragmatism.

[4]
Pragmatism

Royce needs a way to address the question of immediate experience, and I have argued that Hocking's way will not fill the need. This situation comes about in part because Hocking was not a pragmatist. Like Howison, Hocking was a personal idealist, and for him "idealism means, in name and in truth, the freedom in this universe of the thinker, the unlimited right of Idea in a world where nothing that is is ultimately irrational."[1] Like Howison's, Hocking's view of pragmatism was that it was useful for criticism and for the elimination of ideas that do not work, but in short, pragmatism bakes no bread.[2] Hocking is incorrect about this, and if he thought he was choosing Royce over James in taking this view of idealism over pragmatism (and that is what he thought), I think he was also mistaken about that. My admiration for Hocking's philosophy is great, and his thought deserves more attention than it receives, but he did not exceed his teachers in the most crucial respects. One need not choose between idealism and pragmatism, at least not if the type of idealism defended is Royce's type.

Any fair accounting of the early history of pragmatism needs to be broader than the standard stories one hears today. Of the many varieties of pragmatic theories of knowledge that were proposed between 1890 and 1920, the two dominant American pragmatic theories of knowledge can be classified as "radical empirical," defended by James and Dewey, and "idealistic," defended by Peirce and Royce. In this chapter, I argue that for both strands of pragmatism: 1. there is a commitment to the primacy of *experience* as both the source and the final test of the value of philosophical reflection; 2. that philosophical reflection is a kind of critical problem-solving activity that needs to take its impetus from genuine (as opposed to hyperbolic) doubt; 3. that truth is understood in light of the way it addresses actual problems and genuine doubt in practice; and 4. that practice and practical consequences are the measure of the value of philosophy, not *vice versa*. I also argue that the idealistic strand of pragmatism has a better answer for many of the problems pragmatic theories of knowledge face today, especially Rorty's nominalism.

Pragmatism in the Postmodern Hospital

Pragmatism provides a crucial aspect of addressing the relation of experience and existence, what I have earlier called the problem of immediate experience. Yet, James was utterly defeated by this problem, as I will argue in Chapter 7. Dewey initially handled the issue with a postulate, the "postulate of immediate empiricism," later realizing that a postulate was not rich or concrete enough for his philosophy. Having thoroughly botched the relation of experience and existence in his 1925 *Experience and Nature*, which in spite of its popularity is one of Dewey's worst and most confused books,[3] he rightly set out to address the problem of immediate experience in more promising ways. A series of essays in the early 1930s, "Qualitative Thought," "Time and Individuality," and "Experience and Existence," set Dewey on a much more promising course. Drawing on this work, his two best books, *Art as Experience* and *Logic: The Theory of Inquiry* handle the issue of immediate experience more adeptly.

There is little need, at this time in the history of philosophy, to argue that pragmatism is a living idea. It is widely studied and discussed. After a hiatus of a quarter-century, between the death of Dewey in 1952 and the publication of Richard Rorty's *Philosophy and the Mirror of Nature* in 1978, there has been a huge resurgence of interest in pragmatism.[4] But the gap in time had an effect, namely that of altering and narrowing our understanding of the idea so that, while it is definitely alive in the present, it is on philosophical life support, and the electro-encephalogram suggests to me that we would not be doing great damage to pull the plug on the emaciated patient Rorty calls "pragmatism," and what most people now understand by the term after he deflated it. But I think pragmatism is not quite brain-dead. I will address the narrowing of the life of pragmatism and do what I can to revive it (using Royce and some shock paddles) which means restoring to pragmatism a capacity to address immediate experience, to do respectable descriptive metaphysics, and to recognize its own children.

Royce not only regarded himself as a pragmatist (in a sense to be defined), in fact he *was* a pragmatist, and was so long before this approach to philosophy was called by that name. If we have made his problem with immediate experience pointed enough in the last chapter, we can also say without fear of contradiction that all pragmatists have had a difficult time dealing with immediacy. In some ways, this is their Hegelian hangover, for Hegel was the arch enemy of immediacy if ever there was one. The philosopher of mediation had good reason to deny the reality of immediate experience, since there is little hope of accurately calling it "rational," which is the only "real" for Hegel and his school. But pragmatists do not accept that the real is the rational; all of them allow that the real can be pre-rational, and that immediate experience occurs. To adopt a standpoint on philosophical thinking that sees *its* descriptions (rather than the experiences being described) as mediated, and to give philosophy no authority to claim ontological knowledge (this is the departure from Hegel) is to find oneself in possession of mediated descriptions whose relation to immediate experience is less than clear. I will have more to say of immediate experience in the chapters that follow, but for now it is sufficient to note that (initially at least) neither James nor Dewey had any clearer idea about how to handle the relation of existence and experience than did Royce. In fact, C.S. Peirce, among the pragmatists, probably has the best approach to immediate experience, in his phenomenology and theory of signs, but let us examine in a more general sense the legacy of pragmatism itself, and see where this leaves us relative to immediacy.

Our Faith in the Work of History

The term "pragmatism" encompasses a lot more historical territory than is often appreciated today in scholarly and philosophical circles. There is both an advantage and a danger in allowing the term to coalesce, as it has, around the meanings given to it by the thinkers whose ideas have stood the test of time; in this case, we speak mainly of James and Dewey, although Peirce has a very healthy following, and is even more influential in Europe and Latin America than in the United States.

The advantage of letting our present ideas about pragmatism suffice derives from our confidence that history sorts out for us the voices and ideas that are most worthy of our continued consideration. This confidence is often well placed. Those views do survive, most often, whose defenders have been the ablest, and in the case of "pragmatism," I do not dispute the judgment of history. Peirce, James, and Dewey represent three very different conceptions of philosophical pragmatism, all defensible today, all still very much a part of the on-going development of philosophical thinking, and all showing different excellences toward which pragmatic thinking can tend. Each of these conceptions of pragmatism continues to enrich us, and the interplay among these views remains a source of new variations in our thinking. We could say, over the objections of some, perhaps, that the thought of Hilary Putnam and Owen Flanagan nicely embodies and extends the spirit of James, while Richard Rorty has built upon Dewey's achievements (in controversial but fruitful ways), and Susan Haack builds upon Peirce's type of pragmatism.

As much as I admire all these contemporary philosophers, they are also the ones who put pragmatism in the hospital—which was better than letting it die in the gutter, frankly. But they are analytic philosophers, trained to believe that it is perfectly alright for a philosopher to lift whatever he or she likes and happens to agree with from any historical context, and use it for whatever purposes strike their present fancies. I suppose that would not be such a bad thing except that nearly all analytic philosophers (and here I do not include good philosophers like Putnam and Flanagan and Haack), from ignorance of history and the lack of an ethic of responsible scholarship (not to mention much pure laziness about reading closely and widely), end up reinventing the pragmatic wheel, and almost always either badly, or at least not as well as the wheels that were once in wider use. A mind is a terrible thing to waste; several generations of wasted minds is a travesty. No one will read anything written by any analytic philosopher in a hundred years, but people will still read Dewey, James, Peirce, and yes, probably Royce. It is simply better philosophy than anything produced in the second half of the twentieth century. I will dedicate my final chapter in this book to tracing the history of this problem and offering a solution.

One disadvantage of our blind faith in history comes in a small way from the possibility that genuinely valuable directions and meanings will come to be forgotten whenever history's judgment is imperfect, due to any of a thousand types of historical accidents of timing, trend, tides of popularity, and the like. But the greater disadvantage comes from our tendency toward an occluded view of the major trends themselves, in which we fail to understand fully the push and pull against which important ideas, like "pragmatism" were formed. We fail to understand fully the push and pull against which important ideas, like "pragmatism" were formed. Royce was very much at the center of the development of pragmatism, and although he criticized James's version of the idea, Royce regarded himself justly as a dedicated a pragmatist (and long before it had the name). This is little understood today.

Interpreters and defenders of James who have not closely studied Royce will remain blissfully ignorant of something they desperately need to understand. They will not grasp what motivates much of what

James says about pragmatism, why he makes the moves he makes, unless they see the extent to which Royce's criticisms are pressing James's thinking, placing before him alternatives, and forcing him in some cases either to choose or to shift ground. His journals clearly reveal the extent to which Royce's viewpoint pressed him. An important example of this will be examined at the end of chapter seven. Similar problems have marred the understanding of Peirce even by those interpreters most dedicated to his ideas—but not dedicated enough to read what Peirce read, which included nearly everything Royce wrote.

To give an example of an important but little known and underappreciated historical episode, when the Italian philosopher Giovanni Vailati met Royce in Heidelberg in 1908, Vailati was favorably impressed with Royce's work in formalizing the logic of relations and he was well aware of Royce's call for an "absolute pragmatism."[5] Vailati also had meetings with James and was among the first to call attention to the differences between the types of pragmatism that James and Peirce were pursuing, but he believed both could contribute to the guiding of science. Indeed, in telling the story of ideas leading up to the present pragmatism, Vailati usually mentioned not the standard sources so familiar to Americans when they tell their own story, but a story beginning with Socrates and/or Plato, running through Berkeley, Hume, and John Stuart Mill. It is a narrative no one in the USA would even consider, but the story is defensible.[6] Contemporary Italian philosophers who are interested in pragmatism take Vailati's version of its origins as a historical given. The point is that many stories can be told that differently inform our present sense of what we mean by "pragmatism." I believe we are not currently working with the best stories, as measured by our own purposes. My purpose, among others, is to breathe some life into pragmatism by restoring to is a healthy sense of the place of responsible idealism and personalism in its discussions.

Long before this tendency in philosophy had the name "pragmatism," Royce was among the small handful of eminent philosophers working to develop it. For Royce, as for some of the others of that generation, such as Borden Parker Bowne, the arrival of the *label* "pragmatism" was not an event of any remarkable moment. Insofar as the label designated something worth considering (a practical turn in philosophy that recognizes the role of practical consequences in the further conduct of philosophical thinking), it was something they had embraced many years before.[7] The label itself was rather more like the advent of a new *problem* in philosophical nomenclature than the sudden birth of a new trend in thinking (the subtitle of James's 1907 *Pragmatism* indicates as much: "A New Name for Some Old Ways of Thinking").[8] And the problem with nomenclature became a serious distraction from the genuine issues at stake.

The popularity of the label itself, early on, presented a temptation among philosophers to climb aboard the bandwagon without waiting to sort out the precise role of this tendency in philosophical thinking. In this case, the bandwagon itself certainly belonged to James, and Peirce rather quickly decided he did not want to ride, renaming his own approach "pragmaticism" as is well known. Dewey stayed aboard James's wagon a while longer, and when James died, Dewey seems to have taken the reins. In the first and second decades of the twentieth century, so much was written about pragmatism, both pro and con, that it became impossible to tell who was on whose wagon, and how many wagons there were, and who was driving any of them. A.O. Lovejoy's summary indictment of the movement in his "Thirteen Pragmatisms" nicely depicts the confusion.[9]

In the chaos, numerous important voices were lost to subsequent thinkers and scholars, including Royce's and two of his better students, Hocking and John Elof Boodin.[10] Our understanding of pragmatism has been grievously diminished by this loss of memory, by the accidents of history, and by the fickleness of philosophical fashion. But my aim in the present chapter is not to exhibit Royce's pragmatism in detail or to scold philosophers for being narrow, willful, and forgetful (at least, no further than I already have). My aim, rather, is to sketch in outline two different pragmatic temperaments and to recommend the restoration of the one now missing from contemporary pragmatism. I take very seriously and wholly agree with James's claim in "The Sentiment of Rationality" that a philosopher's temperament is simply crucial to grasping his or her thought, and to its formation.

Frank Oppenheim, associating the pragmatism of Royce with that of Peirce in his magisterial study, *Reverence for the Relations of Life*, chooses the term "prophetic pragmatism" to describe something of the approach I will take in this chapter. I believe this is an appropriate label for the type of pragmatism I want to advocate, but my own efforts will be a bit more modest. I will attempt to fill out and supplement what Oppenheim has done. I believe pragmatism *should* be prophetic, and to this extent I find myself in sympathy also with the efforts of Cornel West, who has chosen the same moniker for his thought. But for my present purposes, if I can succeed in staking out the importance to pragmatism of developing adequate ways of treating *ideals*, then I will be content. If that manner of handling ideals should turn out to be "prophetic," so much the better. But a great part of pragmatism's difficulty with immediate experience is in knowing what to do with ideals, because ideals depend upon possibilities that they think are not immediately given.[11]

It may seem odd that the most abstract notions, such as ideals, would pose problems for pragmatists, when it is immediate experience, the most concrete mode of being, they struggle most to describe. But the two are connected. Pragmatism commits itself to dwelling in a human-sized world, leaving aside both the fundamental character of immediate experience and the scope and necessity of abstract claims about the necessary characteristics of Being. Yet, even the mid-world has connections to all existence, and it is in the concept of existence that the ideals and the immediacies are joined. Immediate experience and ideals both point us toward *not* what is actually experienced, but toward what is *possible* for experience. Pragmatists want no part of transcendental arguments about possibility, but they cannot help employing *both* descriptions of immediate experience (mediated first by the descriptions themselves, and then by reflection upon those descriptions), *and* ideals, which unify the ends of practical action. In short, even a pragmatist needs ways of dealing philosophically with possibility, and possibility resides in existence, both the immediate and the ideal aspects of experience, and how these point toward the open universe of possibility.

Royce's Pragmatic Temper

While Royce uses fictional ontology and descriptive metaphysics to deal with the question of *existence*, he employs pragmatism to address the issue of *experience*. For our purposes, pragmatism can be summarized as involving the following key ideas:

1. a commitment to the primacy of *experience* as both the source and the final test of the value of philosophical reflection;

2. that philosophical reflection is a kind of critical problem-solving activity that needs to take its impetus from genuine (as opposed to hyperbolic) doubt;

3. that truth is understood in light of the way it addresses actual problems and genuine doubt in practice;

4. that practice and practical consequences are the measure of the value of philosophy, not vice-versa.

We must add to this characterization the restrictions on philosophical thought found in the four incapacities and their consequences analyzed by Peirce, and also the critique of ontological necessity offered by Peirce and adopted by all pragmatists, including the recent schools. This is admittedly over-simplified, but it is enough to help us grasp Royce's pragmatic temper, and to grasp how it differs from the strains of pragmatic thinking currently dominant. The treatment of these themes will be taken up further in subsequent chapters of this book, so the sketch that follows is not intended to be complete, but rather, will find whatever completion it has in subsequent discussion.

Generalizing Experience: Two Territories

Regarding the first of these characteristics of pragmatism, consider the following from Royce's 1895 address "The Conception of God" (before pragmatism was called by its present name):

> All that we know or can know . . . must first be indicated to us through our experience. Without experience, without the element of brute fact thrust upon us in immediate feeling, there is no knowledge. . . . I absolutely accept this view. This is true and there is no escape from the fact. Apart from—that is, in divorce from—experience, there is no knowledge. And we come to know only what experience has first indicated to us. I willingly insist that philosophy and life must join hands in asserting this truth.[12]

The primacy of experience does not, for Royce, mean simply, as with Kant, that we cannot philosophize in the absence of experience *in general*. Royce insists rather that *particular* experience is the source of all knowing (one of the key principles of James's radical empiricism), and that what is known is never without its contextual dependence upon particular experience. There *is* no "experience in general," although we do experience generalities or general ideas, but only as the further clarification of practical, particular experiences that accumulate as the history of the individual truly grows. Royce means by "experience" approximately what Dewey and James mean by it, and all of them are in some way or another beholden to Peirce's articulation of the question. The primacy of immediate feeling and the elucidation or generalization of feeling into concept is the shared conviction of pragmatists, including Royce, although James alone among the pragmatists yields almost wholly to nominalism.[13] In other words, the idea that Hocking believed took him beyond Royce, the cognitive value of feeling, is in fact common to all pragmatists. Hocking did not recognize this idea as a pragmatic one.

Differences among the early pragmatists begin to appear when we consider both *how* feeling becomes concept, becomes generalized, and in the *extent* to which the resultant concepts can be trusted in terms of warranting our conclusions, especially our *philosophical* conclusions. In this domain, we can think of Royce as the most sanguine of the pragmatists, the one who places the greatest confidence in the scope of philosophical conclusions to provide us with a sort of warrant that justifies our claim to possess philosophical "knowledge," although Peirce is plenty optimistic, Dewey less so, and James might be thought of as allowing to philosophy the slightest degree of generalization of its conclusions.

The continuum of views here reflects not only of the temperaments of each thinker, and perhaps also the degree of their commitment to radical empiricism (and Royce simply is not a radical empiricist, Peirce more so if not much, Dewey is thoroughly empirical but still allows for an occasional flirtation with idealistic conceptions of the "whole," while James is simply horrified by any such move), but also the extent of their respective commitments to the role and function of the a priori in addressing the practical life (which is the functional inverse of radical empiricism). The more a thinker tends to focus upon the peculiarities and accompanying complexities of a particular problem in relation to its own context, the less likely he is to give broad scope to any generalization of its solution to other contexts. Also the degree of genuine doubt, in response to a problem, becomes a measure of the importance of the problem itself—the more pressing the doubt, the greater the problem. And here differences in temperament begin to become differences in the estimation of the power and value of pragmatism and of philosophical knowledge itself.

Pragmatists agree that the type of thinking called forth by practical problems is a substitute for direct action, and that when action is taken, reflective thinking has been completed. All pragmatists agree that where the action taken proves inadequate to solving the problem, we will withhold our affirmation that a "true" solution has been found. But regarding the relationship between *action* and *thinking* there is a world of *territory*—the place where psychology (or phenomenology) and philosophy meet (and where the problem of immediacy is posed). Alternatively, where the solution proposed by our thinking *succeeds*, there is another wide range of possibilities for its generalization, and this is a second *territory*.

But these two territories, these types of pragmatism, fare differently in the hands of the dominant pragmatists. Where psychology (or phenomenology) and reflective philosophy meet, where the task is to explain in empirically responsible ways the process by which feeling or immediate experience becomes concept, Dewey and James have held a great advantage in the judgment of history. Not only were both of them more accomplished psychologists than Peirce and Royce (which is not to say the latter two were unaccomplished[14]), but the growing tendency in the twentieth century to place greater confidence in this psychological aspect of knowing (precisely because it was more easily studied by scientific and other empirical methods than the second territory, i.e., how to generalize successful hypotheses, and here we see also the reflection of Hocking's confidence which I explained in the last chapter) has tended to elevate the Dewey-James type of pragmatism to the place of honor. The task has been to fill out this psychology with a descriptive phenomenology that will translate empirical claims into concepts that can be used by reflective philosophy, by attending carefully to the active contribution of consciousness to the immediate givenness of the object of experience. Indeed, the James-Dewey brand of pragmatism has effectively crowded out all other senses of the term. This result is not entirely to be despised, because after all, the process by which our concrete problems become our conceptual problems bears mightily upon our prospects both for understanding them and solving them.

But our historical emphasis upon this psychological territory, while it has yielded increasingly refined ideas about social epistemology and social psychology, has distracted us from the second territory, our norms regarding the generalization of philosophical results for practical purposes, and has occluded our sense of the full range of "philosophical" responsibility. For it is in this second territory, the effort to understand the relationship between a successful course of action and its proper generalization to other contexts, that issues of value, imagination, vision, and ideals resides. In this territory one needs a keen sense of logic, the capacity to create formalisms that permit proper generalization, that do not encourage illicit generalizations, and that can handle the functional role of universals as guides and limits to thinking. Peirce and Royce are very good at the creative formalization of thought, which for the purposes of pragmatism means the invention of restraints on inference that *prevent* the transformation of maxims drawn from particular experiences into bloodless abstractions.[115] Such a logic adopts the norm of distinguishing logical possibility (in which necessity plays a crucial role) from temporal possibility wherein no necessity is operative (whether in the form of causal laws or dogmatic metaphysical claims).

The Dewey-James pragmatism is notoriously weak in dealing with this side of the matter, while this is the very strength of the Royce-Peirce variety of pragmatism. Indeed, Dewey and James, not possessing the needed gifts for this kind of thinking, tended to be suspicious of any activity of this sort. Dewey was far better at creating formalisms than was James, but Dewey only achieved a fair competence with it after reading through Peirce's *Collected Papers*, between 1931 and 1934. By his own admission, Dewey spent a lifetime failing to understand how and why Peirce was doing what he did, until the light went on around 1934, and was able thereafter to achieve some good results in logic, even if his results were quite modest compared to the logic of Royce and Peirce.

I am willing to call the Royce-Peirce temper (and talent) in this second territory "idealistic pragmatism," not only because Royce and Peirce each used the term "idealism" to describe what was being done, but also because I hope we are, in the present time, mature enough to be aware that the horror of idealism, warranted as it was by the excesses of that school in the nineteenth century, was an unfortunate over-reaction. It is difficult, if not impossible, to carry out any serious philosophy without at least *postulating* some conception of the Whole (that is, considering a *possible* Whole), for the purposes at hand.[16] And as I have argued earlier in this book, such a postulate does not entail the assertion of it as an ontological truth. Thus, Royce and Peirce have significant commerce with the Whole, and even if they do call their systems versions of idealism, I think it is probably safe to set aside the term "idealism" and simply use the adjective "idealistic," to describe the philosophic temper of their versions of pragmatism. Let us pause over consideration of these idealis*tic* versions of pragmatism to understand better how they operate.

Idealistic and Radical-Empirical Pragmatism

The difference between the radical-empirical pragmatism and the more idealistic pragmatism emerges most pointedly from cases in which the "problem" is primarily *intellectual* from the start, and the genuine doubt it inspires is *intellectual* doubt (and note that not all intellectual doubt is necessarily hyperbolic or Cartesian doubt; there are genuine intellectual problems). Here, Peirce and Royce will freely employ a priori thinking, especially the *reductio ad absurdum*, and without hesitation *carefully* generalize the results to other *intellectual* problems, especially philosophical problems. Success in addressing an intellectual problem gets the advantage of having used intellectual tools (logic, mathematics, dialectic), and since these intellectual tools are *already* conceptual, their proper adaptation to other intellectual contexts is something that can be safeguarded by a thorough grasp of method and the proper employment and limitations upon logic. So long as one does not enter a hypothesis that works *formally* at cross purposes with some other generalization previously made, and so long as one discharges all hypotheses before hopping from one level of abstraction to another, the results of a good deductive argument can be employed in new intellectual contexts. Logic thus serves as a collection of *norms* for moving from a successful use of concepts, a successful inquiry, to different contexts.[17]

Dewey and James are quite hesitant about the employment of logical tools across contexts, especially where universals are employed, not wanting to distinguish among generalizations in any way that requires final commitment to a distinction between intellectual and practical problems. They do not accept the finality of a pure *reductio* (the sort that formulates propositions in universal terms, excluding the middle) as eliminating concepts from consideration in a given inquiry. This certainly protects them from making illicit moves in dealing with intellectual problems, but it also commits them to reinventing and re-justifying all their conceptual tools for the purposes of each new problem. Naturally they are willing to begin with generalizations carried over from previous inquiries, but these are ventured hypothetically and adapted to the particularities of the inquiry at hand. This means that even intellectual problems are treated in their particularity first, and their generality only later. In other words, the Dewey-James pragmatism is ponderous and unwieldy in dealing with very abstract problems, such as those one would associate with metaphysics *and its ideals*. And, the Dewey-James pragmatism also offers almost no hope for intellectual advance in such subjects as pure logic or in any domain of thinking that requires the development of new logical tools for handling other types of intellectual problems (beyond philosophy itself). Dewey professes this limitation on logic as a virtue, beginning with his 1903 *Studies in Logical Theory*, and continuing through his subsequent work in logic up until his epiphany with Peirce's *Collected Papers*. In 1903 Peirce assailed Dewey for this "genetic" principle in logic, which is utterly reductionist in the most narrow-minded sense—to reduce logic to the history of practical problems it has solved in the past, blocking the road of inquiry. Dewey was simply too slow-witted even to grasp what he had done that set Peirce off on scolding tirade.[18]

So while Royce and Peirce were hard at work on the logic of relations, Dewey and James remained fairly silent. This silence is not so great a problem until one enters the domain of pragmatic metaphysics, a domain in which even radical-empirical pragmatists need some footing in order to offer some account of the value and role of ideals and the Whole in setting out an ethics and a political philosophy. Here, Peirce and Royce have far better tools, and idealistic pragmatism has better metaphysics largely because it has better logic. With a solid metaphysics in place, something James never achieved at all,[19] and Dewey's work is partial and inferior (which is why Rorty cast it off, perhaps[20]), ethics and political philosophy become more manageable, less *ad hoc*, and more inspiring. That Dewey was good at ethics is undeniable, but how his virtue ethics exemplifies or connects to his muddled metaphysics will always remain unclear. Dewey's ethics does fold in nicely with his social epistemology, the first "territory" above, of which we may fairly proclaim him prince. But his metaphysics is a morass, amounting to not much more than lists of generic traits of existence with almost no analysis of how these generalizations are interrelated. Royce, by contrast, is, in my view, the best ethicist America has ever produced, and that is not surprising when one grasps how integrated his moral philosophy is with a clear, well-constrained hypothetical ontology and a developing modal logic of possibility. In short, Royce knows how to handle ideals and their relation to possibility.

So the principal pragmatists begin to diverge over the *relative* independence of intellectual problems from practical ones (none suggests a complete independence of course), and the fruit of this divergence is harvested in how to handle problems that require some independence from present context (the problematic situation, concretely experienced), especially the role and existence of *ideals* in informing our present problems. This divergence results in differing conceptions of the scope of philosophy itself. We come here to our second point in my sketch above of the essentials of pragmatism, that philosophy is a kind of criticism that solves problems raised by genuine doubt. Royce is quite explicit about this point. For instance he says "I am a student of philosophy. My principal business has always been criticism."[21]

But, while all the combatants seem to agree that philosophy is critical reflection, the view that it has some independence, its own problems and qualities of genuine doubt, was attacked by James and Dewey as "intellectualism." This is a true misunderstanding of Royce's position. In 1911, when Royce was called upon to make a response to Dewey's critique of absolute truth, he made the following remark:

> I have earnestly asserted for many years that the so-called "pure intellect" is a myth. I believe, and so far quite in harmony with recent pragmatism,

that all our human thinking is a part of our conduct, that the life of the intellect is always a constructive process, an activity, a fashioning of ideas, a committing of ourselves to assertions and denials, and adjustment of ourselves to our situation—in brief, I believe that our intellectual life is a part of the expression of our will. I decline then from the start to be classified with the so-called intellectualists. And now this position of mine is no recent concession of a half-repentant absolutist to the novel contentions of the popularly triumphant pragmatists. I expressed in print this general view about the relation of thought to activity more than twenty-five years ago. My own form of philosophical idealism has ever since been based upon it.[22]

This is illuminating with regard to what Royce means by "will," i.e., the term for conceiving of thought as a kind of conduct, commitment, and adjustment to the "situation," and it is worth noting that Dewey did not fully articulate his own conception of the "situation" as the bridge of experience and existence until nineteen years had elapsed from the time Royce said this. But we will take up Royce's view of will in later chapters. For now it is enough to be aware that restricting philosophy to reflective activity and granting to it a type of problematic situation that is intellectual in nature, does not necessarily imply intellectualism. The issue turns upon the relation of will to thinking. Here Dewey takes the view that reflection is a break in the continuity of action, a pause for secondary activity upon the materials of primary experience. Royce is arguing for nothing more than this, although there may be room for disagreement about what instruments are appropriate to such reflective activity and their proper scope.

Philosophy as Critical Reflection (with a Small Diatribe)

While Peirce and Royce see *philosophy* as a fairly restricted kind of reflection upon certain kinds of problems that are *already* conceptual in character, Dewey and James want to include the process of conceptualizing the problem as one of the practical aspects of philosophy itself. While Royce and Peirce will insist that the philosophical problem already comes in conceptual terms, and that philosophy can assist us in re-conceptualizing it, and that this work is as much a priori as empirical, Dewey and James are leery of this move. Effectively, Dewey and James wonder whether *genuine* doubt can be inspired by a problem that is primarily (or even purely) intellectual. Is a primarily intellectual problem really a problem? Is it preventing us from acting? This depends upon whether thinking is a practical activity, since an intellectual problem can certainly inhibit the flow of our thinking. If thinking is an act, then its inhibition by an intellectual problem can create genuine doubt. By 1938, Dewey was willing to say that a primarily intellectual problem can inspire genuine doubt, but James never came to the point of admitting it. How, after all, could one distinguish *hyperbolic* doubt from *genuine* doubt if one allows that "purely" intellectual problems do inspire genuine doubt? This seems like inviting Descartes (and all that is wrong with a priorism and dualism) back into one's philosophical tent.

But in some sense, Descartes is already *there*, in the tent, like an ill-behaved adolescent who must be disciplined. Dewey and James essentially put him in the "time-out" corner, which is ineffective with adolescents. It is not as if Dewey's *postulate* of immediate empiricism seriously confronts the mind-body problem (and one might as well call this the "time-space" problem, since that is what it became, or the existence-experience problem, or the problem of immediacy), especially when one has no logic adequate for explaining the status of a *postulate*. Dewey accomplishes nothing more with his postulate than Locke accomplished by saying that we only know our own ideas, yet there must be *something* beyond them, some *je ne sais quoi*. Dewey's approach essentially says "Let's just pretend the object of experience just *is* (i.e., exists as) the thing it seems to be," and he goes along his merry way for another three decades. The denotative method of *Experience and Nature* reworks this postulate into a simplistic theory of reference, but it remains simply an *ad hoc* device for avoiding tough questions.[23] No wonder people dismissed pragmatism for so long, if that is all there is to pragmatism. Fortunately Dewey got better in the 1930s. And as damning as Dewey's sins are, they seem venal compared to those of James. Peirce complained about James's kidnapping of pragmatism very loudly, and with justice. Neither James nor Dewey is left with any serious, reflective tool for addressing the issue of immediate experience—just a handful of ungrounded postulates or denotative references. And what is worse, each of them has, in his way, created a stumbling block to the development of solid phenomenology, by psychologizing or naturalizing (or both) the concept of experience.

But there are (at least) two ways to deal with this difficulty. One can peremptorily preclude as "intellectualism" all discussion of problems that does not answer to an empirical, practical problematic situation, as James and Dewey do, *or* one can restrict the role and authority of philosophical reflection itself to problems that have already received conceptual formulation, as Royce and Peirce do.[24] These two ways of conceiving of the scope of philosophy are a further way of grasping the difference between our two "territories" described earlier. Unfortunately, each approach has a difficulty. The Dewey-James approach decapitates philosophy, forbidding it fully to use its powers of abstraction, for fear that it will put the head before the embodied heart and neglect or try to tyrannize the "problems of men," in Dewey's phrase, with "the abstractions of philosophers." Given the excesses of rationalistic philosophy in its history in the West, this is certainly a legitimate fear. Royce and Peirce, on the other hand, cut off philosophy at the knees, giving it scope and applicability only within the domain of human cognitive endeavors, and so they are obliged to introduce phenomenology and semiotics as, strictly speaking, *extra*-philosophical descriptive activities that enable us to give our problems an initial conceptualization. Then, and only then, can critical philosophical reflection deal with such problems according to its own proper methods.

In the end, however, the Peirce-Royce approach makes for better pragmatism. The reason is that phenomenology was, then, and remains the better horse to bet on than the nominalist nightmare of depriving philosophy of its functional universals, although it would have been difficult to know that at the time Peirce and Royce were restricting "philosophy" to reflective consideration of already conceptualized problems.[25] In Peirce's theory of signs and Royce's theory of interpretation, we find significant progress toward providing philosophical reflection with a concrete footing. The "thirdness" of our being-in-the-world is interpretive existing, one phase of which creates concepts.[26] This, of course, is what phenomenology means for Peirce and Royce, and its interpretations are *required* for philosophy, although not properly speaking a *part* of philosophy. It turned out, as we know, that phenomenological description can be done in extremely productive ways, and (apparently) infinitely many conceptualizations of immediate experience can be accomplished through phenomenological description, by those with the talent for it, in ways that do not produce simplistic abstractions, and without giving in to rationalism, psychologism or an over-stretched naturalism. Peirce and Royce had *some* talent in creating such descriptions, as did Dewey and James, but none of them had the talent of later phenomenologists, particularly Marcel (in the Roycean strain and temper[27]), the later Husserl (in the Jamesian temper[28]) and Merleau-Ponty (in the Deweyan temper[29]).

It may be argued that phenomenology ought to be classified as "philosophy" proper, although there is little question that Royce (and sometimes Peirce) denied to it that classification, but I do not think the issue is much more than a quibble. If phenomenology is not "philosophy" proper, it is certainly "philosophical." Many phenomenologists have claimed, on the contrary, that philosophy simply *is* phenomenology, but that is a hopelessly parochial view. Such phenomenologists spent a century pretending to be allergic to metaphysics and logic for fear that *all* metaphysics is *bad* metaphysics (again the heritage of rationalism's excesses), while they claim all pure logic is empty formalism. Phenomenologists heaved a collective sigh of relief when Husserl abandoned his approach in the *Logical Investigations* and moved on to *Ideas*; serious logic never returned to phenomenology, giving the phenomenologists an excuse not to learn it (and with a few notable exceptions such as J.N. Mohanty, they haven't). But in recent decades it has become clear, I think, that these phenomenologists were mistaken. Phenomenologists have slowly begun the process of reclaiming metaphysics, and logic will soon follow. It always does. One cannot do philosophy without both metaphysics and its normative complement, logic.

While phenomenology has developed (whether it is a part of "philosophy" or not), and has restored the "legs" of philosophy as conceived by Peirce and Royce, enabling it to walk around (and providing it with a philosophical—as opposed to psychological or reductive naturalistic—path through the first territory), no complementary development has occurred in Deweyan-Jamesian pragmatism to restore to it the "head" it cut off, the capacity to do metaphysics and logic. This inability to deal with abstract thinking is most keenly problematic when Dewey and James (and their contemporary proponents, Rorty and Putnam) are obliged to confront *ideals*. Clearly Putnam, for example, does not want to concede that pragmatism must be nominalistic, and he wants to hold on to universals—even cultural universals, which are surely the most unpopular strain. But Putnam has not yet incorporated Royce and Peirce into his defense of universals. Until he does, he will be susceptible to Rortyan criticisms. It might be fair to say that neo-pragmatism is what happens to pragmatism when it refuses to deal with, formally and logically, the reality of ideals, or denies that ideals have any reality (and so embraces nominalism, willy nilly).

Unfortunately, this refusal to become adept with ideals reduces pragmatism to an unending series of edifying dialogues, an exchange of opinions and efforts to communicate private vocabularies, the effect of which on the world and the academy is *most* unpragmatic. Philosophy becomes an irrelevant chatter among eggheads. And that is what neo-pragmatism has become, except in the very few cases in which a contemporary pragmatist has broken the mold and dared to speak of ideals. Here, Cornel West comes to mind, as one who, in spite of what he sometimes says, is much more in the line and temper of Royce than of Dewey.[30] Perhaps this is why West is presently writing a book on Royce.[31]

While ideals are therefore treated as concrete concepts by Royce and Peirce, available for the work of philosophical reflection, they are bloodless abstractions in James's estimation, and at most promissory notes in Dewey's view. One will not be able to keep a philosophy in play for very long without learning to work with ideals, and *that* requires a mastery of logic and metaphysics. In short, pragmatists in the James-Dewey temper will have to learn how to do *difficult* philosophy, something they have successfully avoided doing for about three generations, through disinclination, dullness of mind, and uninformed superstitions about the role of reason in philosophy. The inheritors of the James and Dewey temper, however, are such as to believe, quite dogmatically, that *all* metaphysics is *bad* metaphysics—and here we have nice examples among them of the methods of tenacity, authority and the a priori method, which is what they have done in fixing their beliefs about the matter. Hence, they neither read nor understand Royce, nor Whitehead, nor anyone else who is difficult to understand, and they often dislike Peirce and do not understand him, even though they have developed a conscience about forcing themselves to read him, once. Asking contemporary pragmatists to reconsider metaphysics is received as though one had asked them to go to church to get a little religion, an affront to any respectable intellectual these days, especially the followers of Dewey and James. They would rather go to hell than learn logic and try some metaphysics. But most of them already have done some metaphysics badly, and fail to grasp the situation, until they feel Rorty's pointy nominalistic trident poking their collective behind.

I have shown in an earlier chapter that not all metaphysics has to be bad metaphysics; some approaches avoid the unholy trinity. Here I will content myself in noting that dogmatism is unbecoming of a pragmatist, as is ignorance of historical context. James and Dewey read Royce and did not sniff at him with superior dismissal. I do not see why a good pragmatist today who takes himself or herself to be developing the pragmatic line of thinking would imagine it is alright to dismiss what the progenitors of their movement thoroughly respected. If that is the attitude to be taken, pragmatists might as well become analytic philosophers, where it is regarded as praiseworthy to remain largely ignorant of what one is studying. If philosophy is critical reflection, it would seem that being self-critical is required. That requirement reaches to a reconsideration of the prevailing attitudes about metaphysics and logic.

Truth in Philosophy and in Life (with a Further Diatribe)

So the question comes down, finally, to whether a pragmatist can afford to entertain ideals, and reason upon them in metaphysical and logical fashion, without ceasing thereby to be a pragmatist. Naturally, all pragmatists, no matter how nominalistic, retain *some* place for ideals in their philosophies (even Rorty has goals for public discourse), but there is great disagreement about how binding our reasoning upon ideals is, how determinate they are, how concrete. And thus we arrive at the third of my points in the initial sketch, namely, what makes a concept "true." Royce tends to follow Peirce in his estimation of what makes a concept "true," and it involves giving philosophy a broad authority to make judgments upon various formulations of ideals, and the formation of purposes, using a priori methods.[32] The justification for this view is that philosophy is a kind of social *practice*, and the ideas it endorses in one phase have practical consequences in later phases. There is such a thing as a *true* philosophical idea because a *true* one solves a *genuine* philosophical problem, and that is a very *practical* matter *for a philosopher*. Royce and Peirce do not think everyone should strive to be a philosopher, but for those who are, intellectual problems that have already received conceptual formulations inspire genuine doubt—even if they may not inspire genuine doubt in persons who are *not* philosophers. Royce is forever saying that one need not accept *his* philosophy or *any* philosophy to appreciate and affirm the practical point he is making here or there, and when he says this sort of thing (in his lectures this type of remark occurs about every twenty pages), he is reaffirming his idea that philosophy is a fairly limited activity.

It is certainly important to the human community that *some* persons should be philosophers, and should contribute to our common life the benefits of that activity—conceptual clarity, tools for analysis and synthesis of concepts, teaching, and most importantly, the clear statement of *ideals* as possibilities for human living in the future. The pragmatic *truth* of philosophical ideas thus depends upon *how* those ideas resolve, for better or worse, *philosophical* problems. The result of a "true" philosophical idea is philosophical knowledge, the resolution of a philosophical doubt (which is the same thing). Philosophical knowledge can be contributed to the community in the form of clear and important words and actions (and asserting a proposition is an action) that demonstrate the reality of ideals as future possibilities for our common life, which is another word for "teaching" in the broadest sense (the topic I will revisit in the final chapter). This is a kind of "possibilist" teleology, which is to say, it is *not* the ontological assertion of antecedently existing "fixed ends," but the recognition and excellent handling of the reality of ideals as future possibilities—without which we simply cannot plan our lives. Thus, Peirce and Royce are not only not averse to teleological philosophy (in this possibilist sense), they think it a strict requirement of doing *good* philosophy, a norm we really *must* adopt (and this is a moral not a logical "must"). Without it, speaking of ideals and possibilities becomes only a way of edifying our present selves, not planning for our future selves. It is not worth doing.

The Peirce and Royce type of pragmatism will go further, granting to philosophy an authority to determine, through argumentation, which ways of conceptualizing ideals are hopelessly unclear, contradictory, incoherent, irrational. Ideals that cannot be clearly explained, fitted within a system of ideals, related to one another in methodical ways, cannot be wholly dismissed, but must be reformulated until they become practicable contributors to an overall philosophical worldview, which is to say, these ideas are reworked until they are "true." In short, philosophy has authority over the ordering of ideals, assuming that reflection has been undertaken "scientifically," in the broad sense in which Peirce uses that term.

Dewey and James allow philosophy no such authority, even over its *own* problems, and will not embrace teleological language in any but the most provisional ways. Life, in their view, exercises judgment on philosophical truth, either by "growing" or failing to grow beyond generalizations that are no longer effective, or simply out-growing earlier statements of philosophical problems. In emphasizing such notions as "growth," Dewey is smuggling ideals into his valuational scheme, but do not ask him, or any Deweyan, to explain their philosophical meaning. One simply receives an analogy or metaphor to biological flourishing, followed by the point that we *are* biological beings, as though that were an argument. It is as if Dewey's followers believe it is fine to hop back and forth from the biological to the moral domain of discourse without remainder. Since the philosophical question concerns "growth" as a *moral* ideal, one cannot answer it with a biological analogy unless one is prepared either to reduce morality to biology, or to discuss also the formal *dis*analogies between moral growth and biological growth. The analogy falls short. Many people do a great deal of moral growing in the process of biological dying, for example. This latter is a discussion most Deweyans are ill-prepared to have, since they are often (not always) untalented or untrained in logic and logical relations, of which analogical reasoning is a subset.

Humans are certainly biological beings, and biological beings "grow." Humans are also moral beings, and seem to "grow" in some sense there. But the nutrition that fuels biological growth seems to be made of matter, while the nutrition that "feeds" moral growth seems to involve teaching and learning ideals. It would make as much sense to learn how to understand and teach ideals as to learn how to cook, if one wishes to "grow."

Cashing In (See Endnotes for Other Diatribes)

We are now ready for a brief consideration of the last of my four points about the essentials of pragmatism. What is the "cash value" of this difference between the Dewey-James type and the Royce-Peirce type of pragmatism, for *life*? Whether today one ought to favor the radical-empirical pragmatism to the exclusion of the idealistic type in matters of value remains a bit unclear, but certainly we are aware, with this much time and distance from the initial discussions among these four pragmatists, that the inability of the radical-empirical pragmatism in its current popular manifestations to articulate a vision of ideals, one that inspires the moral admiration of philosophers and ordinary people, is one of the red marks on its side of the philosophical ledger of the twentieth century—and things are not looking any better for the twenty-first unless something changes.

The idealistic sort of pragmatism has not really had its "audit" at this point, for it has passed into trust without ever having its capital spent. Royce's nascent re-emergence into philosophical prominence may provide that opportunity for entrepreneurs who are willing to risk the investment, or perhaps it will remain in trust until another generation is heir to it. Much of what needs a new consideration, in my view, is contained in this book, but readers should be aware that there is far more in Royce than my treatment contains. But Royce is a pragmatist. And what can be said with a fair confidence is that the cash value of radical-empirical pragmatism is seriously occluded by its habit of ignoring the resources with which it might learn to handle ideals. I will have more to say about how pragmatists can employ ideals in the service of both philosophy and the world in my last four chapters.

[5]
Individuality

Following the distinction set out in Chapter 4, between the idealistic type of pragmatism and its phenomenological grounding, we should now examine the extent to which Royce has provided an account of each. Being a pragmatist, even of the idealistic stripe, Royce does not neglect practical arguments in giving his account of the relation between existence and experience. Recalling that immediate experience remains an issue for Royce, as it does for all pragmatists, we must examine what he does do, both within and beyond "philosophy" as he conceives it, to address the problem. To examine this requires that we grasp his theory of individuality and how "individuals" both experience and exist. His theory of individuality is more complex and nuanced than has been understood in the interpretive literature.

There are three levels to Royce's theory of individuality, which may be rightly denominated the "psychological," the "phenomenological" and the "metaphysical" aspects. The psychological description Royce provides is intended to be empirical, and to follow the norms adopted by science. It is outside of philosophy, as Royce defines it, and should be judged by the standards of empirical evidence, like any other scientific description. The type of "phenomenology" Royce gives us, while it is itself a philosophical description, treats phenomena that fall within what he denominated the "world of appreciation." It is a part of his "philosophy" *in form only*, which is to say that Royce treats philosophically the concepts of the appreciated world and the experiences that populate it, but these concepts are products of reflection, not appreciation as such. The content of these concepts is "appreciated" content—pre-discursive, but no less social than the world of description.[1]

Royce's phenomenology does not quite fit within what has been later called phenomenology by subsequent philosophers, since it is at once "descriptive" in the sense Royce uses the term (recalling that the whole world of knowledge is descriptive for Royce, including philosophical knowledge), and yet treats as its *content*, the type of experience that is "appreciative," i.e., quite beyond describing. Phenomenology is a hybrid activity, describing what cannot quite be described, making experiences into concepts. But unlike the most popular types of later phenomenology, Royce does not seek to integrate the descriptive requirements of the phenomenological task to the forms of givenness of the object to consciousness. In this sense, Royce's phenomenology seems crude or at least "free form" compared to Husserl's, but it does bear a striking resemblance to less formal types of phenomenology, such as Merleau-Ponty's. However, Royce's description does not attempt to bring a phenomenological method, such as it is, to bear upon *immediate* experience, but rather deals with experience *in general*, or generalizations about experience discoverable in psychology. Yet, it is still phenomenology of a sort, and I maintain that the phenomenological account of individuality remains one of Royce's "living" ideas by nearly anyone's standards.

Whether the psychological and phenomenological descriptions need to be, or even *can* be, reconciled with Royce's metaphysical account of individuality is what I will examine in this chapter. I believe the three aspects not only can be reconciled, I think they ought to be, for the reason that another of Royce's "living" ideas emerges from the effort, and that is his "Fourth Conception of Being"—*to be is to be uniquely related to a whole*. Having the full account of individuality is required for grasping the term "unique" in this Fourth Conception of Being. We cannot wholly neglect in this chapter the concepts of "whole" and "related," but their primary treatment will be taken up in Chapter 6.

I think that *any* viable metaphysics in the present will be some formulation of this Fourth Conception of Being, for this conception epitomizes temporalism in metaphysics. The effort to bring into relation the psychological, phenomenological and metaphysical levels of individuality requires us to understand the Absolute in Royce's thinking, at least insofar as the idea is required for his living ideas about individuality. Royce says hundreds of different things about the Absolute in his corpus, but I will settle upon one constant feature of his account which connects the Absolute to each level of individuality and does so by appealing to temporality. One must have some idea of the conception of the "whole" with which one is working before the parts, the individuals, can be situated. Thus we begin with a discussion of the Absolute.

Wrestling with God

We have seen in earlier chapters that Royce's efforts to answer the challenge of Howison brought him to the point of recognizing that he needed a thoroughly worked out theory of individuality in order to maintain, on one side, God's intentional, willing, experiencing, and personal character, and, on the other side, God's rationality. The individuality of God is the prime case of individuality and much depends on finding a way of conceiving God that preserves both sides. More will be said of this tension in the next chapter, but I have suggested that the right course for Royce, and the course I think he eventually adopts in *The Problem of Christianity*, is a kind of "theistic finitism," which essentially involves letting go of God's omnipotence and omniscience (as an outmoded conception of rationality) in favor of a process account of God's interpretive activity in pursuit of ideals—and such an account does not imply abandoning the concept of the Absolute, as I will show). Yet, Royce is already dealing with the finite-infinite relation as a temporal process long before 1913. As early as 1897 Royce already thinks of God's experience as a "process," and note that, if it is the same process as our own, only "generalised," it is also a social process:

> To the Absolute Experience, then, we should attribute just such a generalised form of the process that in us appears, clouded by countless psychological accidents, as the process of attention; just such an individuation of its contents, just such an attentive precision, whereby its universal types get discrete expression . . . This generalised form of attention, which we attribute to the Absolute Experience, is now conceived by us as that aspect of the Absolute which, in the total movement of the world's unity, determines the ideas to find this concrete realisation which they do find.[2]

If this passage is held in mind as we pass through this chapter, and perhaps consulted again by the reader at the end, it will be clear that God's experience is being described here at two of the three levels of individuality, the phenomenological and metaphysical—i.e., God is an individual. The psychological level is being clarified and set to one side. The two psychological laws that I will discuss, the keys to Royce's whole psychology, do not exactly apply to God. God has a temporal history of willing (this will be examined in the next chapter), but it would be difficult to apply Royce's ideas about "imitation" to God. The activity of individuation Royce speaks of above he would later call "the will to interpret." The bottom line is that God doesn't have particular experience, for Royce, only generalized experience.

That is also true, however, of our own experience *insofar as we can make sense of it*. Even the act of willing is general, in us as in God, to the extent that it can be *understood*.

We shall have more to say of God as a process in Chapter 6, but two things are lost if we skip too quickly past *The World and the Individual* and look to *The Problem of Christianity*, so as to bask prematurely in the more popular light of Royce's mature view. The first is that we miss the importance of Royce's theory of individuality, in its metaphysical, phenomenological, and psychological formulations. The result of leaving this aside is that we risk reading Royce's triadic theory of interpretation (which is already at work in *The World and the Individual*) without a proper appreciation of how the activity of interpretation *individualizes*. The second thing we miss is that, with a wave of the hand, we may conclude that Royce's "Absolute" was a mistaken idea, which is to say that we grant James a complete victory in the battle of the Absolute. James may or may not have "won" the battle, but he never properly understood Royce's view (see Chapter 7). As I have stressed, Royce does not mean by "the Absolute" what Hegel or Bradley meant. The hypothetical character of his ontology is one clue to this, but there is much more.

Royce's Absolute is not primarily an abstract placeholder for the conception of the "Whole" in any given inquiry. Royce is actually speaking of God.[3] It is important to wrestle seriously with Royce's Absolute because such an idea of God not only *can* remain operative in the world of religious experience, it *should* remain operative. Human beings are going to be religious. The issue is not *whether* human beings will believe in God (they will), but rather how they will conceptualize that belief. It is irresponsible of philosophers in the academy to think themselves above taking "God" seriously. If anything is clear in the present century, it is that the world's troubles are greatly tied to how persons (beyond the academy) are at one another's throats over how rightly to think about God, and many are willing to kill and die for one concept rather than another. To treat this struggle as sub-philosophical is to abdicate the responsibility of philosophy to the world. And many, probably most academic philosophers have abdicated. It is treason against philosophy and a betrayal of the wider world to refuse to engage the issues that divide the world. Whether academic philosophers approve or not, ideas about God and their proper meaning will be fought over for the foreseeable future. Our task is to do whatever we can to promote sane and peaceful dialogue about such ideas, and the more difficult the idea, the greater is the challenge. It is difficult to imagine a more challenging task than to help in bringing about a better understanding of the idea of God in the present. We can do better.

The Will and the Absolute

The key to understanding the relation of the Absolute to the individual in Royce lies in his view of the will, and as I have previously mentioned in Chapter 4, the will has, for Royce, both a practical and an intellectual character. But the intellectual aspect is derivative of the practical experience of activity. "Will" is Royce's most general term for the *intentional* character of all experience, and insofar as experience touches existence itself, for all existence. I call this Royce's "intentional stance," i.e., the claim that all reality, so far as philosophy conceives it, has the character of intending. That the will seeks an object—principally a *purpose*—is an indispensable aspect of Royce's thought. If the term "will" seems old fashioned, substitute for it whatever term you prefer, so long as it is temporal in form and aims at a future in a normative way. If there is a way to address the immediacy problem within Royce's philosophy, it is associated with "will," but we should always bear in mind that for Royce there is a difference between will as experienced and *concepts* of the will, generalizations with which philosophy works. We may safely say that the concrete universe is at least not hostile to the existence of will, since will pervades all of our experience, or more generally, we might say that whether or not the universe is characterized by an all-pervading will, it certainly does not forbid the existence of will.

Here the philosophical question shifts *away from* whether the universe is or is not intentional in structure, and shifts *toward* the norms by which finite human beings *ought* to think about it; this is the question not of the structure of the universe *an sich*, but of what Royce calls "the real" or "reality." Reality is a philosophical idea that includes and is based upon norms. The understanding of reality is the primary aim of philosophical reflection. In regard to this norm, Royce thinks that we are obliged to think about the universe in terms of its intentional character, because, practically, and therefore metaphysically, the presence of intention or will is an inescapable condition for thinking about anything. To assume that the conditions of our own thinking are exceptions or peculiarities in the order of the universe is to conceive to the universe in an overly abstract way, and to render the conditions of our own thinking mysterious or problematic in ways that are not only unnecessary, but also unwise. His use of the term "Absolute," and his defense of the idea follow this norm for thinking to its logical conclusion in the domain of metaphysics, but one can accept his practical (phenomenological) description of will without becoming a philosophical idealist, as Royce often points out.

Truth, Will, and the Absolute

The description of the *practical* character of the will is a phenomenological exercise, while the philosophical description of the *intellectual* character of the will is called metaphysics and is governed by logic. I will focus this distinction by examining Royce's summaries of his own view of will in 1911, when he approaches the issue as part of a defense of "absolute truth." From there we can move to more specific consideration of his psychological, phenomenological, and metaphysical descriptions of the activity of will as the creator of individuality.

One needs to be aware that, for Royce, "absolute truth" and its relation to the Absolute should be distinguished from other similar ideas in the history of philosophy, as for example, the claim that an assertion is "certain" or "self-evident." Absolute truth is not certainty or a self-evident assertion. As Royce says, "Certainty is a predicate applicable to propositions so far as the mind of some human being has feelings of assurance when he considers his own views about that proposition . . . no assertion that is true, even absolutely true, need appear certain to any individual man . . . and no false statement can be found so absurd that some human being may not feel perfectly certain of its truth."[4] Certainty is psychological, not logical or ontological. It has no philosophical value. Absolute truth also has no sense of the "self-evident." As Royce says, "if any proposition about any topic in heaven or earth seems to you 'self-evident', or 'immediately certain', you may regard such self evidence as an excellent ground for the presumption that you do not understand the so-called self-evident proposition, and do not comprehend the matter that is in question, and do not yet know whether or why that proposition is true."[5] Royce is no friend of certainty in 1911, and he never was.

Rather, for Royce, truth has an *intentional* structure: "our assertions are bits of conduct . . . they are part of our effort to comprehend, to make clear, to define our situation," which is to say, for Royce, that "some sort of will is expressed."[6] He continues, "our assertions and denials are acts of accepting or of rejecting some characterization or classification, or *acknowledgment* or *prediction* of objects. In general, they are *acceptances or rejections of some interpretation of our experience*."[7] We see Royce's theory of interpretation is at work here, just as interpretation was already at work in his understanding of the will in his earliest published works. But what is more important is the employment of the word "acknowledgment," for if we recall the argument of Chapter 2, this is the term for our basic intentional stance toward the past (both our own past and the past world beyond our own experience), and toward the present, which is the "acknowledgement of a world of truth." "Acknowledgement" means for Royce that we form our own activities of willing (and ultimately our "purposes," which as we shall see, are the fully formed intentional objects of the will) only in the presence of others, i.e., *others* are the world of truth, and truth, in Royce's sense, cannot be conceived except where the willing and purposing of others is actively occurring. To have a world of truth is to form our purposes socially, and the social formation of the purposes of others is prior to the development of individuality itself, in any single instance.

Royce follows the term "acknowledgement" with the term "prediction," which indicates that he is thinking temporally about what he has called "anticipation" in *The Religious Aspect of Philosophy*. I make this point in order to stress that for Royce, truth is about the intentional relationship between our thinking-conduct and our adjustment to the temporal and social situatedness of practical action. And even with this thoroughly pragmatic account, Royce thinks there is "absolute truth." Clearly he does not mean by this phrase what most of us are accustomed to associate with it.

Royce further connects this thinking-conduct with problem-solving:

> When you assert or deny that things are or that they are so and so, you are endeavoring to solve a problem that is never one of the mere copying of an indifferent fact, or a mere repetition of a world of fact which you conceive to be independent of all your purposeful relations to it. Purely theoretical truth, that is, truth having no bearing upon conceived modes of conduct, is as much an impossibility, a contradiction in terms, as is the so-called pure intellect.[8]

What then is "absolute truth"? How does it reveal to us the reality of "the Absolute"? Royce offers this general characterization of truth, pointing out near this passage that it is entirely in keeping with the views he had expressed from 1885 onwards:

> Any assertion that you please, if it is somebody's sincere effort to tell the truth, is *an act which selects its own object, and which expresses, as far as it goes, its own intentions about that object, and which also determines, from the point of view of the one who asserts, precisely the sort of correspondence with its object that is in question and that is intended.*[9]

Royce refuses to remove perspective from his notion of truth, but unlike Nietzsche's perspectival account of truth, Royce's theory is not only social, but as we shall see, individuality is at every level a *product* of the social process, i.e., individuality (and perspective) is not a condition for truth but one of the more valuable *results* of the reality of truth. It is not the case that there is truth *for* an individual, idiosyncratic and inscrutable, but rather that because there is a social "world of truth," individual perspectives become intelligible through their *acknowledgment* of that social world. In some ways, this view seems to render the concept of the "Absolute" utterly without a function, and that all we require for truth is a social setting, and indeed, this may be all that is required for practical warrant. But the *irreducibility* of the *social* character of truth, and its *intentional* character, are ineliminable conditions of truth, and *that much* is "absolute." Even practical warrant emerges from a past and intends a future, and a provisional ontology of that as a "situation" does not explain the situation *of the situation itself*. For the situation of the situation, we have to conceive of the whole in some way, however provisional our conception may be. So also irreducible in truth is its *temporal* character. To review, then, truth for Royce is irreducibly social, intentional, and temporal.

Thus Royce does not think we can, in metaphysics, simply postulate a situation, draw lines around a limited time-span, and pass over the rest of the relations that constitute the problem. All problems are some person's problem, at some time, and problematic situations belong to a whole, as parts. Phenomenology can afford to take the individual perspective as a given starting place (and this assumption is part of the reason it is not quite "philosophy," which cannot, for Royce, assume the prior reality of the individual at the outset), but metaphysics must account for the possibility *and* actuality of individual perspective. If we are not to assume the individual as an ultimate category—which Royce (rightly) rejects—we are posed with a problem, which is "how can one judge the precise intentions of another when an assertion is made?" If my truth depends upon the willing and the purposes of others, how can I learn their wills and purposes?

Royce is acutely aware that the act of judgment must be possible in order to retain both the perspectival and the social character of truth. If I cannot learn the intentions of others, then I cannot know truth. As he says, "nobody can set the truth standard for another man *unless*—and here is precisely the centrally important condition of all fair criticism—unless the critic fully shares, fully takes over, and assumes, the precise intentions of the thinker who is criticized."[10] The kind of judgment involved here is what Kant had called "reflective judgment," as distinct from the judgments of reason or understanding that determine their objects, and reflective judgment depends on sympathy, Kant believed.[11] Royce is following this idea through to the irreducibility of our sociality.

Such judgments are always temporal as well. It is impossible, Royce argues, to possess even an individual intention without connecting it to a possible future to which it might or might not correspond when acted upon. The prediction, or the future, is experienced as an ideal, an unactualized possibility, with some measure of determinate structure, and that structure is experienced as a working solution to the problem an individual intends to solve. But ideals, i.e., comprehensive, organized possibilities, do not exist in blissful metaphysical isolation, floating around in some noumenal beyond; they are intended from a concrete present in a concrete social situation of which the individual is already a part. That individual is not isolated from others, and that individual's ideals are not isolated from other ideals, whether these be ideals of his or her own, or the ideals and purposes of others. To intend a single act, as the solution to a single problem, is to intend a world in which both the concrete individual and the ideals he or she intends exist within a larger context, a "world." They require a whole to which they belong. Further, once acted upon, the concretized ideal previously intended becomes "irrevocable," it cannot be undone and thus becomes a part of what has to be "acknowledged" in the past, and not just for the individual who has so acted—as Royce puts it, "once done," your individual deeds "are yours no longer."[12]

The *acknowledgment* of the past act of a given individual is now obligatory for all of us, nay, more than obligatory, it is Absolute. This is not to say we are yet in a position to judge how *well* the act answered the problem it intended to solve or address. That judgment requires that we take the position of the actor and grasp the actions in relation to those purposes and intentions, i.e., the perspective. Our whole worry is how this position of judging may be achieved. But for the moment, the act, undertaken as a part of the social world of truth, no matter how it is judged or interpreted, has now become an irrevocable aspect of *everyone's* "situation." All acts of purposing also *fail* to intend their *own* ideal future object in crucial ways if they fail to acknowledge the irrevocable acts belonging to our own histories and the histories of others. Thus we learn that acknowledgment of past and present are reflective intensional judgments that presuppose a world of truth. Anticipation is a determinate judgment, but it determines only an individual act.

But it is worth pausing at this point, having encountered the Absolute, in the form of the irrevocable act, to reiterate that Royce is *not* claiming to possess ontological knowledge. I have taken some care in chapter two to explain how Royce does hypothetical or "fictional" ontology, and this includes his concept of the Absolute. Immediately upon pointing out the irrevocability and sociality of the past deed, Royce says:

> I assert this principle [of the irrevocability of the past deed], at present, not as a self-evident principle which I at this point require you to accept as itself absolutely certain. I only point out that the ideal postulate according to which this is the real nature of action, is a postulate in terms of which action itself gets for us some of its deepest values.[13]

I have indicated that ethics is "First Philosophy" for Royce, and metaphysics is a derivative branch of the analysis of values, proceeding on the basis of postulates. Metaphysics cannot discharge these postulates; that work depends upon moral philosophy, which is through and through practical. The case for the Absolute cannot be made *without* metaphysics, but also cannot be completed *by* metaphysics. Royce proceeds to a practical and moral justification for accepting the irrevocability of the past, saying that "no view of life is more practically useful, for people who have wills at all, than just this belief in the absolutely irrevocable nature of all our deeds."[14] And here Royce moves on to what was later named by Whitehead "the objective immortality of the past":

> When we act we believe that we get deeds done; and that is why we can be content to sleep a little when this day's work is over, because our little accomplishments of the day are in any case safe. So much is completed. We can never have the trouble and responsibility of doing this day's work over again. This we can recall, and sleep. And if the sleep is death, still life itself has been, as we conceive, an indestructible accomplishment of deeds. Now, as we thus naturally view our voluntary life [i.e., the history of willing], no truth can be mentioned that seems to us more absolute, than in this supposed truth that deeds once done cannot be undone. In any case, whether rightly or wrongly, we all do conceive that in reality our life is of this character; and so to conceive life is useful for the formation of every clear sense of personal dignity, responsibility, and effectiveness.[15]

Even having offered the practical, moral argument for the Absolute, in the irrevocability of the past deed, Royce still does not claim ontological knowledge. Rather, he says, in effect, you would not change this characteristic of experience even if you could, for to do so would remove you from seeing your own life, and that of others, as real. The consequences would be both impractical and immoral. Royce uses the irrevocability of the act as his principal argument for the Absolute from 1885 until the end of his career (here we see it in 1911, but the famous phrase the "hell of the irrevocable" in *The Problem of Christianity* aims at the same insight). It is a normative argument, at bottom, each time it is offered. If any of the many things Royce says about the Absolute ties all the others together, it is this argument. There is more reason to note the unity of his thought in this thread than to concentrate on the shifts in his descriptions in the Absolute, as Smith and so many scholars who follow him, have done (see the Introduction). Royce's discussion of the Absolute is always adapted to the inquiry at hand, but the argument I have given here *is* his constant argument for the Absolute and his practical and moral motive for proffering it as an unavoidable philosophical hypothesis.

Thus, although Royce says more about the Absolute than that it is the irrevocability of the past, in my view, his case for the Absolute always depends upon this argument. I have chosen the 1911 "defense" for its poignancy and compactness, for its direct address to pragmatism and especially Dewey, for its place in Royce's maturity, and for its place before the so-called Peircean insight of 1912. The most significant result of the defense of the Absolute in Royce is the way it focuses our attention on the question of forming judgments about one another's intentions and purposes in asserting that anything is "true." Royce has pointedly defended that truth is perspectival, and he thinks of the perspectives thus involved as those of fully developed "individuals"—but his individuals are not monads or independent atoms. Yet, these individuals are such strong loci for purposing and willing that we may be tempted to see them as something close to absolute breaks in nature—an issue we will discuss in greater detail in Chapter 7.

It is also significant that the account of the Absolute has been couched in thoroughly temporalist terms—that the Absolute is the irrevocable past in relation to an acknowledged social present and an anticipated future. I will take up Royce's temporalism in the next chapter, but for now, we should seek to understand the sense of the "present," the "world of truth" in Royce's metaphysics, for it is this account which grounds the sociality of truth, the emergence of the individual through the history of its actions, and the reasons why it is possible to learn the intentions and purposes of another with sufficient clarity to make assertions about their "truth."

A Further Refinement of Royce's Method

In the beginning was the act, or activity. The will, as experienced, is *derivative* of activity and the ways in which activity accumulates, which is to say, the ways in which the past is objectively immortal in each succeeding present and in every possible future. In presenting Royce's psychology of the will, I will draw upon both his 1903 *Outlines of Psychology*; for the phenomenology of the will I will use his 1885 *The Religious Aspect of Philosophy*. The former book, unduly neglected by Royce scholars,[16] takes the individual as empirically given, since it is psychology, but it presents an important supplement to the account of the formation of individuality in the earlier work. In *Religious Aspect*, Royce's treatment of the activities by which wills are formed, and subsequently individuals, is not intended to be empirically adequate. Even as phenomenology it is hypothetical, a starting place for a metaphysics. The *Outlines*, on the other hand, is intended to be an empirical work that culminates in a phenomenology of the individual will. Thus, in spite of chronology, the descriptions of 1885 are based upon those of 1903, at least insofar as the former can be given an empirical basis outside of philosophy.

We should note, however, the refinement of method that is evident in these levels of description. We cannot here enter into Royce's philosophy of science, and the place of psychology as a science. But methodologically philosophy requires generalized concepts with which to work, and science provides many such concepts. Yet, there is a great difference between taking a generalization in its scientific sense and treating the same generalization philosophically. The sciences are in no position to offer ontologies, for the sciences assume situated methods and values, as well as certain aspects of the phenomena under consideration (e.g., biology takes life for granted, not asking whether there is life or what it is, but rather, given that life exists, how does it change?). Philosophy has assumptions and postulates also, but these are taken in the mode of possibility rather than actuality. Thus, Royce's psychology begins with actual individuals and asks how they do what they do. In moving to phenomenology, he begins to open up possibility in certain of its modalities, although he does not make possibility the basis of actuality in this exercise, or vice-versa; they are treated on more or less equal footing. When he moves to the consideration of metaphysical individuality, part of philosophy proper, possibility will be the primary category (the same would be true if Royce were considering ethical individuality). But all three levels involve both possibility and actuality. The difference involves their priority and relation.

In reference to the categories of analysis set out in Chapter 4, there is nothing un-pragmatic in recognizing that, at *any* level of analysis, empirical, phenomenological, or metaphysical, *some* conception of the "whole" is presupposed. What is terribly un-pragmatic is to neglect to do the difficult work of articulating the character of that whole at each level—and James and Dewey are largely guilty of this neglect. One may or may not accept Royce's way of providing an account of the whole, both its distinctions and its continuities, but one is vulnerable to nominalism without having done this difficult work. Royce's account of the whole is both systematic and adapted to the needs of the various levels of analysis. The constant in his articulation of the whole is the reality of time, as expressed in the relations of actuality and possibility. This may not be the only way to connect the various levels of analysis, but I think it is the best way, and one that is in keeping with the requirements of pragmatism.

Let me be as explicit as possible about this refinement of Royce's method, for it acknowledges what Dewey had rightly observed in his assessment of Royce's method and corrects its narrowness. Dewey had said, in essence, that Royce "began with an accepted fact and sought to show that reality necessitates the reality of its conditions, etc., until the analysis finally results in the necessary recognition of the infinite or absolute."[17] Dewey rightly observed that there is an empirical aspect to Royce's method, but he did not understand how the idea of the "real" is normative for Royce and how the value of that idea is judged by its capacity to preserve meaning, and how the norms of our thinking are a part of the norms for acting, since thinking *is* acting. Dewey also mistakes ontological necessity as being the principle that governs and grounds empirical observation for Royce, when in fact necessity, considered metaphysically is, as I shall show, simply a formalization of the activity of the exclusion of possibilities. I introduced the tension between phenomenology and philosophy in the last chapter, and in Chapter 2 I argued that there is a difference in function between generalizations and universal propositions in Royce's ontology, the latter being the philosophical reflection upon and the arrangement of the former. But we can now see very clearly a three-fold schema in Royce's habits of inquiry (and his habits of inquiry are part and parcel of his method). Let me restate, then, in a more refined and corrected fashion, Dewey's point about Royce's method.

First is particular experience, generally had, and then described in its positive (i.e., inclusive) mode, and this is the "empirical" and the lowest level of generalization. Royce's psychology is an example, but the same applies to all sciences. This most empirical level of inquiry is, however, general, for all thinking requires generalization, but these are only generalizations about what is *actual*, or positively present in our experience.

Second, we consider the more general conditions under which the positive description comes to have just the structure and regularity it exhibits, and we do so by considering the edges or periphery of our experience, the relation between what is clearly present and what is only vaguely present to us, or what might be absent in some sense and present in another (e.g., since we do not actively "attend to" all that we "sense," which is Royce's point in his account of attention in *The Religious Aspect of Philosophy*). Hence, at the second level, we consider *possibilities* under the restriction of their being concrete conditions for the positive phenomena before us. This level of generalization and can rightly be called "phenomenology" in Royce's sense. Such generalization clearly involves reflection upon and seeking order among generalizations we already possess, although Royce speaks of it as a "practical" kind of reflection and does not think it requires one to subscribe to any particular "philosophy," especially not to "idealism." He thinks that all we need do when he is making a "practical" (i.e., phenomenological) argument is to consult our own experience and verify for ourselves that the phenomena and generalizations have this or that character, and that reasoning upon this character can proceed well enough without reference to any scheme of metaphysics.

The third level of generalization, philosophy proper, requires us to place the possible before the actual, which is to say, we consider the actual as an instance of what is possible, and to do so, we hypothesize in the mode of the possible using universal propositions. "The Absolute" is an example of such a universal hypothesis, as is any philosophical conception of the Whole, and any part of that Whole which is fitted to a conception of the Whole for a particular philosophical inquiry. Readers will be able to confirm for themselves that in every place where Royce is doing "philosophy," i.e., employing a fictional ontology that places the possible before the actual, his statements about the Absolute are ways of formulating a *possible* conception of the Whole, as suited to the demands of the philosophical inquiry at hand. Where that inquiry is epistemological, he will speak of absolute knowledge; where it is logical, he will speak of absolute truth, and so forth.

Royce is already thinking in this way about the various levels of method and philosophical discourse as early as 1880. He says:

> To study the purposes of human thought is impossible unless we know something of the structure of thought. My effort at teleological analysis depends, therefore, in some wise upon both the previously mentioned kinds of thought-analysis [psychology and logic]. Yet psychology and logic fur-

nish rather statements of the problem than solutions thereof. Though nothing can be more fundamental *in its sphere* than exhaustive logical analysis of the principles, assumptions, and methods, and great results of thought, yet it is possible to go further than this analysis by viewing the whole material in a new light, and by asking new questions about it. Though, on the other hand, no mental fact lies outside of the province of psychology, yet psychology seeks mainly to give a history of the evolution of mental processes, not an analysis of their significance in view of any end. And furthermore, as psychology is in the widest sense of the term, a physical science, that is, a science of explanation of effects by causes and of facts by laws, psychology is itself logically dependent upon the results of philosophical analysis of knowledge, and therefore, cannot supersede either the analysis of thought-principles or the study of thought purposes.[18]

This is not Royce's fully developed scheme, since he is here conflating what I call psychology with phenomenology, but the point is that Royce began his career by defining the scope and reach of various types of generalizations, and he refined but never fundamentally changed his view of their levels and functions. Logic never became the autonomous arbiter of knowledge, ethics remained first philosophy, and the sciences supplied generalizations for our thinking. The development of his conception of phenomenology in the years between 1880 and 1885 placed and intermediary kind of appreciative description between science and philosophy proper.

Royce certainly also believed he could provide a phenomenological and simultaneously empirical account of the Absolute, and he does so in characterizing it as the irrevocability of the past. He also thinks that the Absolute is empirically given in the forms our wills take, but he was not very successful in explaining either the empirical or the phenomenological (i.e., practical) descriptions he offered at these levels. Most of his readers and listeners were unconvinced. Only idealists, of one stripe or another, were inclined to buy into the "philosophical" defense of this idea of the Absolute. The concept of the "individual" in Royce's philosophy is far more convincing, empirically, phenomenologically, and philosophically, than the idea of the Absolute. Yet, I have come to believe that the fate of this conception of the individual, the only one I have ever found compelling, is tied in some less than comfortable ways, to the success or failure of the defense of the Absolute. I will try to make out, in the final section of this chapter, the character of that interdependence of individual and absolute.

But what is at stake is this: Royce's account of individuality is nearly the only one I have encountered in post-Kantian philosophy that satisfies the dual demands of avoiding nominalism and also not obliterating the individual in a sea of abstractions and universals run amuck (i.e., various forms of neo-Platonism and Platonic realism, and Absolute idealism in the objectionable sense that Howison charged Royce with defending). Because Royce's metaphysics is hypothetical, and since he claims no ontological knowledge can result from metaphysical inquiry (he is a fallibilist), and because, in the face of these demands, he still manages to avoid nominalism (in my view), his ideas and his philosophical method remain viable. I am convinced that nominalism at various levels is one of the diseases of our age, and that the James-Dewey style of pragmatism cannot avoid it. I also think that there is a way out of nominalism without doing bad metaphysics, and it does not involve asserting the reality of timeless universals that exist in some Platonic heaven. Rather, the key to avoiding nominalism is to allow that possibility has a mode of existing that is related to actuality, but not reducible to or fully estimable from the standpoint of any given actual situation.

All temporalist philosophies allot to possibility such a standing, and most often they associate the mode of existence the "possible" has with "futurity." All temporalist philosophies subordinate necessity to possibility, and Royce is no exception. We will take up these concerns in detail in the next chapter, but for now what needs to be noted is that the empirical, phenomenological (or practical) and philosophical levels of thinking constitute three different levels of generalization and treat possibility differently as the level of generalization becomes more abstract. Thus, empirical individuality, phenomenological individuality, and metaphysical (or ontological) individuality represent the same idea treated at different levels of generalization, and therefore, according to different rules of description and analysis.

Psychological Individuality[19]

Whether one would today judge Royce's psychology to be empirically adequate is an open question, but I will say that Royce builds his entire psychology upon two key ideas, that of "imitation" and what he calls the "law of docility." Regarding imitation (especially imitation as an "instinct," which is how Royce characterizes it), the theory was long out of favor among psychologists, especially in the USA, but it has made an impressive return in recent years due to the discovery by neuroscientists of "mirror neurons."[20] I will not here examine those findings except to say that they seem to confirm Royce's assertion that activity, for human beings, is imitative *before* it can be "willed," and that it is connected with the emotions; current work seems to confirm his claim that we first experience ourselves *acting*, and only then learn how to "will" that action.[21] We might say today (although I dislike the metaphor intensely), that we are "hard-wired" to imitate. Treating the will as derivative of activity (imitative or otherwise) saves Royce from having to assert or postulate the will as an ontological "given." This is a feature of Royce's thought that is often overlooked—that his *voluntarism*, while often stated as a fundamental postulate when he does metaphysics, is based upon an empirical psychology. The generalization of that psychology in normative terms is served by the metaphysical postulate of "will," and the value of his metaphysics must be judged in terms of its contribution to that normative project.

When I first began to recognize how much Royce's empirical account of the development of the will (and the resulting individual) depended upon this claim about imitation, and because I had studied at least some contemporary and twentieth-century psychology, I was disappointed that Royce had given so much weight to this claim about imitation. I looked for ways to rescue his more generalized phenomenology of the will as not depending upon his empirical hypotheses about imitation. Now I find that it was I, not Royce, who had been misled by popular trends in empirical research in developmental psychology and biology. It would appear that Royce's psychology is "back in the game," so to speak, and with it, his phenomenology of the will. My estimation of the viability of Royce's psychology, made here without detailed argument, is that it is perhaps more relevant to contemporary discussions in empirical psychology than is James's, which is still widely studied. If our brains are hard-wired to imitate, and only from acting imitatively may we learn to "will," can empirical psychology not frame a conception of "will" that is testable? More important, can psychology afford to overlook the social character of imitation? Royce's psychology poses (and suggests answers to) some very important problems.

What has not been properly appreciated in contemporary discussions is that, if, as Royce claims, imitation precedes both will and individuality (and I believe it does), then both will and individuality are *social* achievements. Part of what had been frustrating, for me, in Royce's psychology is that his claim about the sociality of the will depended upon this claim about imitation, and overly so in my former estimation. I now think Royce was prescient in approaching the subject as he did, and that he was wise to have trusted his observations of infants and their imitative activity. Thus, imitation remains crucial to Royce's psychology, and to his phenomenology of willing, being the empirical basis of his claim that will is socially constituted.

Regarding the "law of docility," in Royce's psychology, it amounts to, in Royce's words: "the capacity shown in [an animal's] acts to adjust these acts not merely to a present situation, but to the relation between this present situation and what has occurred in the former life of this organism."[22] I cannot see that this "law" is in any serious empirical trouble even after over a century of further developments in empirical psychology, but its formulation by Royce is dependent upon wider features of his temporalism (see Chapter 6), and upon his account of individuality (which we take up now). Given these matters, "docility," or in terms appropriate to our earlier discussions "acknowledgement of the past," remains an empirically viable and needed hypothesis for psychology. That our acts constitute a "history" or historical thread, and that each new act "adjusts itself" or is "docile" to a history of previous acts, is a crucial feature of empirical living and conceptions we form of it.

It may readily be seen that the irrevocability of the act is presupposed by the law of docility. If I need not act in ways that acknowledge my own past acts, then it means almost nothing to say that my past act is "irrevocable," since we need not acknowledge it as making any contribution to the present act. Speaking empirically, docility points to temporalism, and speaking philosophically, temporalism presupposes a concept of docility to the past. We would not have a "history" of action if such were not the case. The act is irrevocable; it becomes a part of my history, independent of my willing or choosing that it be so, and all future acts will adjust themselves to that history whether I choose it or not. Royce cannot prove, empirically, phenomenologically, or metaphysically that the universe necessitates such a continuity of acts and their associated individuals, but he can (and often does) point out that our lives cannot be conceived as having meaning and moral purpose without such an assumption. Thus, the empirical "law of docility" depends on the experience of the Absolute in the irrevocability of the deed, as a meaning-preserving norm for our thinking. It is not the case that the irrevocability of the deed is the ontological ground for the law of docility, but rather that the irrevocability of the deed is a warranted postulate in metaphysics due to the warrant of the generalization about the docility of the present will to its own past.

It must be noted that the ideas of "imitation" and "docility," upon which Royce builds his psychology are principles of "inclusion." That is to say, they are hypotheses about how the activity and consciousness of animals, including humans, come to have the positive characteristics they possess, by "including" their own actual past. This inclusive stance is warranted in empirical and phenomenological inquiries; we shall see that exclusion (of what an individual *might have been* but *is not*) is an increasingly important feature of Royce's method as he moves to phenomenology and then metaphysics, for it is exclusion the evokes the possible. But empirically, if we observe an active being, we are struck first by what it *is*, and we tend to ask only later what relation this positive existence and activity may have to what it *is not*. This is only to say, as I have said earlier, that in empirical inquiries, we privilege the actual over the possible. When we move to phenomenological description, in the sense Royce does it, we seek the general relations between the actual and the possible in relation to experience. When we move to metaphysics, the possible takes precedence over the actual, which is why metaphysics is hypothetical.

This account of psychological individuality, in light of imitation and docility, is obviously only a sketch. I have here indicated that the description of individuality at the empirical level is the function of those two standards, imitation and docility. When these two are combined, activity acquires an interpretable history, and the continued activity in light of its history provides the empirical ground of our common sense individuality. It is derivative of the social situation, but individuals are very real, on account of their different histories. As the songwriter Jim Croce once put it, "After all, it's what we've done that makes us what we are." The sociality of imitation and the individuating consequences of docility are the key points for our purposes. A more thorough investigation of Royce's psychology ought to be undertaken, but to do so here is beyond the scope of my aims in this book.

Phenomenological Individuality

Let us then, begin the phenomenological account of individuality with the end of *Outlines*, for its conclusions provide the phenomenological ground for the discussion of 1885. I have already noted what needs to be said relative to the empirical description, but let us take up the point about imitation and docility as positive or inclusive principles, applying them to what is positively before us in an animal. The law of imitation is treated more or less as a synchronic, empirical marker, which is to say, we can use it as a working definition of what we mean by "animal." Wherever something imitates, we can say there is *experience* in some degree. This functional marker helps us select our phenomena, although it is not itself a metaphysical or phenomenological category; imitation is a *sign* of the *existence* of *experience*. Imitation may prove to be an inadequate marker in some domains, but for the purposes of empirical psychology, it enables us to recognize the animals we want to describe and provides us with a solid and reliable general trait we may look for. If we were to find a human being or even an invertebrate with *no* imitative behaviors, we would be at a loss as to how to understand it as an experiencing being, at least in the current state of our science. That such non-imitative animals might exist is something we need not rule out, once and for all, but we are not studying these, if there are any.

Docility, on the other hand, is a diachronic, empirical principle of continuity and, if you will, of functional "identity." Docility does not attempt to explain *why* an individual organism tends to retain its past activities as "experiences" to be drawn upon as a repertoire for meeting its present challenges and problems, or why it does so by sacrificing some portion of present possibility to past patterns of activity. Docility, as a marker or sign, simply notes that there is, more or less (mainly more), a reliable general tendency in animals to adjust themselves to their own past acts. For whatever reason, then, experience accumulates and animals learn. We need not express this as some eternal or necessary law. The point is that it happens. This is a functional principle of continuity and of conservation, but it conserves individuals (and we shall see in Chapter 8 that there are many levels of individuality).

The law of docility does not claim that nothing is ever lost to an organism's history, only that something important is always conserved, and that which is conserved remains functionally present. This is a temporal principle as well, since its general character has to do with the relation of the past to the present, and sees the present animal as obedient or "docile" to its own past experiences. We do not say the animal either chooses or doesn't choose this obedience, and so we do not know, then, at this stage, whether things *must* be this way, only that they show this reliable and general tendency. Indeed, empirically, we treat only as "individuals" those things in our experience that are docile to their past deeds. In the case of inanimate objects, continuity of past and present seems unproblematic (at least until we reach the quantum level), whether one estimates them according to the statistical probabilities of their swirling sub-particles or their practical givenness as chairs or rocks or tables. There may be a "deed" involved in simply repeating in the present moment what the object already was in the past (the chair keeps on "chairing"), as Whitehead holds, and that seems a fair criterion for individuality even in supposedly "inanimate" societies of actual entities, but here we will reserve the term "docility" for the type of continuity that evinces learning. It is good to be aware that Royce doesn't think anything in nature is inanimate, as I will discuss later.

The case of animals is, of course, more complicated than such things as chairs and rocks. Given their penchant for adjustment to novel situations, docility must include not just simple repetition of the past in the present, but rather selective repetitions of some portion of an acknowledged past as it is needed or valued in the present context. This suppleness of selection and acknowledgement of the past could be called "memory," without too much distortion of the term. We reserve the term "individual," in the sense psychology intends it, for those existences that apparently select and grow from having selected from among possible ways of repeating themselves. In a limited sense, then, a tree is an "individual" for such psychology, but a chair is not. Animals learn by actively imitating what they attend to, by positively experiencing their own bodies in those acts, and by retaining or remembering what it was like to undertake those movements, or by being docile to the past, in Royce's terms. These are individuals in the sense relevant to psychology.

Thus, these are the positive generalizations from psychology we were seeking, but what of their phenomenological meaning? To bring out this level, we must now consider not just what is positively included in experience, but also what was *excluded* from it (which *might have been* included, selected, enacted, but was not), and how, and what the meaning is.

The *Outlines of Psychology* concludes with a phenomenology of attention, in full agreement with the phenomenology of attention Royce had offered (without the empirical underpinnings) eighteen years earlier in *The Religious Aspect of Philosophy* (Chapter 9). I will take up in Chapter 7 some of the historical points about the relationship between James's theory of attention in *The Principles of Psychology* (1890) and Royce's account (published five years earlier), but I am not interested in assigning final credit for the theory of attention; I am just interested in the theory itself. As I have said, for Royce, in the beginning was the act, or activity, and the activity that concerns us here is "attention," for it is the condition for "attentive guidance of our conduct." This is what Royce calls "Will in the narrower sense."[23] We shall see what is meant by will in the broader sense shortly, but for now, the empirical experience of attention for the formation of practical action is what we will consider phenomenologically.

Empirically, we experience our own activity positively, and this experience includes an emotional aspect, leading us to either satisfaction or dissatisfaction as a dominant quality of the activity itself. The satisfaction of the activity (whether it is a thinking act or a physical movement of some kind) "expresses our desires," successfully, in Royce's terms.[24] But it is being *dissatisfied* that interests us more, for it is dissatisfaction that leads us to form plans for future activity. To form some positive plan is to select some available experience at the expense of other available experience, and the phenomenological question is how does that act of selection occur, and how is it carried out in the efforts of a dissatisfied animal?

Here is where Royce enters upon the phenomenology of the will. He says:

> We not only observe and feel our own doings and attitudes or tendencies as a mass of inner facts, viewed altogether, but in particular, *we attend to them with greater or less care,* SELECTING *now these, now those tendencies to action as the central objects in our experience of our own desires.* For the process of attention often has as its objects not only external facts, or facts of sense perception, but also desires, actions, inhibitions, tendencies to action, concerns, feelings, passions—in brief, whatever constitutes the active side of our nature.[25]

There is, in selection, a synthesis of inner experience and available sense experience, the result of which is "perception." We select some tendencies of activity to stand in relief from others, and what is crucial about this selection is that it proceeds first by a selection of some available experience for the sake of some plan—a plan built upon addressing our dissatisfaction with the results, both inner and outer, of our previous activity. This is an encounter with possibility, for not all available experience (whether this is desire for something beyond our bodies or what our bodies sense) can be chosen. Some possibilities are left aside, or left vague. This activity of forming plans of action by leaving aside of other available lines of activity is, for Royce "will" in the broader sense, or "*the attentive furthering of our interest in one act or desire as against another.*"[26] He continues, "actually to will a given act is *to think attentively of that act to the exclusion or neglect of the representation or imagining of any and all other acts.*"[27] Neglect is perhaps the better term at the phenomenological level, for "exclusion" characterizes more accurately the fully formed will, but the terms should be employed carefully, for neglecting available experience, allowing it to remain vague, is one mode of encountering the possible, while exclusion, as we shall see, is more definite, both as a concept and an activity.

In other words, the term "will," considered phenomenologically, is a threshold concept—all attention involves selection, but when attention rises to the level of excluding *all* other options, the activity has been "willed" in the "broad" sense. Among the *possibilities* for attention (from both perception of the environment and the emotions), some tendencies to action have been selected, and then as attention rises in intensity, other possible combinations of inner and outer experience are neglected. When that occurs, we may say at the phenomenological level that we have "willed" something. We have selected and placed in the foreground a possibility as a plan of action (which will, of course, leave us either satisfied or dissatisfied, or both in various ways).

One might suppose from this account that "will" precedes activity for Royce, but the opposite is the case. Willing, in both the narrower and the broader senses, is dependent upon docility entirely, which is to say "*we can never consciously and directly will any really novel course of action. We can directly will an act only when we have before done that act, and have so experienced the nature of it.*"[28] It is not the case that will creates plans of action; it rather forms plans on the basis of past experience. The experiences then *had* in acting upon the plan are the sources of novelty and learning, as we become docile to them. One can will oneself to step out of an airplane, to skydive for the first time, not because one already knows how to skydive, but because one knows how to take a step; one can will oneself to attempt to make a sound on a trumpet because one already knows how to blow air through one's lips so as to make them vibrate, but adjustment to the experiences had in acting are the subsequent sources of the refinements of future willing. These refinements are further attentive selections. As a result, the "will" is a derivative product of activity, and dependent upon the docility of the present self to the past self; or phenomenologically phrased, willing in the narrow sense is an act of memory, or of "recognition" in Royce's terms.

Oddly, imitation is the source of novelty in empirical experience, and hence in phenomenological descriptions of selection, we have to mention imitation. When we see or hear another moving his or her body in a way we have not previously moved our own bodies, phenomenologically this is experienced in the mode of positive possibility. We see it is possible for another to move in this way or that (and here, listening to another person sing or play an instrument still involves bodily movement in the relevant sense). Our empirical imitation will generally be notable for the fact that what novelty it contains derives from failure to reproduce the action precisely. But there is tremendous novelty generated in the experience of feeling our own bodies move in new ways. Much of the value of novelty is phenomenological, a level at which no act of imitation is "mere" imitation. What is new *to me*, in activity, is as new as anything in the universe.

Therefore, when we tally these insights, we conclude, with Royce, that we are not born with a will. We acquire it by imitation and a certain kind of rich, selective docility. Indeed, we must even learn to *attend* by learning to select available experience (all but the mother's breast perhaps), and only as past activity accumulates, and we acknowledge (are docile to) the past, or, only as we remember it, does the will come into existence. As Royce says: "Before we can come to possess a will, we must first perform numerous and complex acts by virtue of the inherited tendencies of the brain. Such original tendencies of the brain are the source of human instincts."[29] Here Royce agrees with contemporary neuroscience. Whatever we mean by "instincts," we are really appealing to something about the way our brains and nervous systems function. We select some available experience and do not select other available experience (i.e., we allow it to remain vague) in order to attend sharply to what was selected Attending is activity, and the activity provides either a satisfied or dissatisfied quality to our on-going experience; we subsequently refine attention in the presence of *dis*satisfaction by neglecting more and more possibilities or candidates for our attention. In time we learn to exclude all possibilities excepting one unified group, and we may then "will" that group in the sense of acting upon it *as if* it were a future possibility foreseen in a plan of action—the "willed" group is already possessed by our acknowledgement of a past in the present, but is not a present actuality.

One could easily imagine from the foregoing account that the development of a "will" is an *individual* achievement. One would, however, imagine wrongly, if one did. There is no "individual" at this stage. Rather, individuality is the gradual *achievement* of the enacted will, not one of its conditions. Not only is imitation social, and the crucial empirical ground for the development of the will, but learning to attend to some group of inner and outer available contents of experience, to the level of excluding all others, is also a social achievement. And this is something we enact and experience before we have learned to will it. In short, we must learn to exercise our wills in order to *have* wills. Individuals in the relevant sense are centers the kind of activity marked by willing.

Attention, Recognition, and Construction

Phenomenologically, the act of willing for Royce has three basic aspects: attention, recognition, and construction. These correspond of course to present, past and future, respectively. Attention we have already discussed, but in *The Religious Aspect of Philosophy* Royce provides some excellent examples of attention that serve to distinguish it from perception, showing how we actively attend, serially, to varying available contents in our sensory and affective present experience, excluding now this and now that from the center of attention, pushing the excluded content to the periphery, and how we are capable of modifying the quality and intensity of what we have selected.[30] There is no sense in which any of this attending activity alone amounts to "will," even though the modifications of quality and intensity are actively undertaken. Attention is, in this phase, only sorting among the possibilities for willing, not coming quite to the point of excluding all but one grouping.[31] As Royce says, "attention, in its most elementary forms, is the same activity that in a more developed shape we commonly called will."[32] The "more developed shape" adds to attention "recognition" and "construction." A good amount of this exclusionary activity is just simplification of the experienced content or "field," according to Royce, and we can attribute the simplification to attention itself;[33] fully formed, it is the exclusion of actualities in our experience, but willing requires that we also exclude possibilities, and to exclude possibilities for action requires a more expanded temporal awareness than the present. The expanded temporal awareness that combines what is possible with what is actual is a condition for willing, because willing requires that we join what is present to us with what is not present, from both past and future.

But focusing for now on the phenomenological description, Royce says, "attention never works alone, but always in company with the active process of *recognizing* the present as in some way familiar, and of *constructing* in the present ideas of what is not present."[34] It is the "not present" part that engages attention with the vaguely *possible* rather than the actual. We can distinguish recognition from attention because it "completes what attention begins." In recognition, we make past experience a part of present experience, and the latter is mediated by the former. Interestingly, and this bears upon the problem of immediate experience we have introduced in Chapter 3, for Royce, "recognition is not found apart from attention, though attention may exist more or less completely without recognition."[35] This is attention unmediated by recognition is something akin to "pure experience" in James, an issue I will address (and I boldly claim to lay to the issue to rest) in Chapter 7. Here Royce says "attention without recognition implies wonder, curiosity, perplexity, perhaps terror."[36] To attend to something with no recognition at all is unsettling, to say the least.

We get no more here from Royce about pure attention or immediacy, but the point is that, phenomenologically considered, the act of willing involves the active completion (recognition being one aspect of completion) of the Gestalt to which we are presently attending, and such completion requires *making present* what is *not* present but already past, i.e., dealing with the "possible" (not present) in the mode of past experience we "acknowledge." This is an attenuated mode of possibility because the familiarity of the object of attention can be recognized only upon the basis of what has already been actual in our experience, i.e., the possibility of *again making present* what was once actual. To the extent an object of attention is recognized, whatever is novel in it is sacrificed, set aside even if not wholly negated.

Recognition still involves an engagement with possibility, for there are many different ways of recognizing an object of attention, and these options must be sifted and culled until we feel we have recognized the object of attention in the desired modes. We cannot "recognize" and "complete" something utterly unlike our previous experiences, but at the very least, completion occurs according to some sort of temporal form, so having an experience *utterly* unlike anything we have previously experienced is uncommon (although mystical experiences may come close). Still, we have many past experiences that may be drawn upon in recognizing what is before us at any given time. Thus, we also have many past experiences which we *do not* actively employ in a given act of recognition, in favor of those we *do* employ, so that recognition involves engaging the "not present" alternatives among past experience, and the selection of some and not other possibilities (in this limited sense of possibility).

In completing the object of attention in one way rather than another, we modify its quality, make it our own, appropriate it by employing one possible way of completing it, to the neglect of other ways, even though we may pause for some time over how to complete it (some will, after all, be satisfactory, while others are not). The process of recognition will, however, come to complete the object in some single way before we can *will* an action regarding it, but notice that we are *acting* on the object of attention already in *recognizing* it (and such action may be as much physical as mental), we simply are not yet willing anything in the full sense. Recognition is the phenomenological version of the empirical law of docility (and Royce calls it a "law" but not in the sense of an inviolable cause, just in the sense of an empirically exceptionless generalization), which is as follows: "The alterations of the data of sense in the moment of recognition are alterations in the direction of simplicity and definiteness of consciousness. The present is assimilated to the past; the new is made to seem as familiar as possible."[37]

To have an object of one's will in the full sense is also to "construct." As Royce puts it, "out of what from moment to moment comes to us, we are building up our ideas of past and future, and of the world of reality," which is to say, this reality includes a *possible* world, not actually present in full. This act of completion (attention plus recognition and construction) includes the futurity and direction of activity for the attended to and recognized object. This further act of construction is "possibility" in a less restricted sense, the more open possibility of a plan of action, and the object cannot become something regarding which we have a "will" until possibility in this more open sense is taken into its construction. "Mere dead impressions are given. We turn them by our own act into *symbols* of a *real* universe."[38]

For Royce the "real" includes the actual and the possible, and neither can be regarded as "real" without the other. Bare possibilities he will not consider (hence, his postulates and metaphysical hypotheses are not bare possibilities), and bare actuality without the possible (its past and future) is, he says, dead, which leaves one to think that whatever Royce meant by pure attention still involves activity. But what is crucial for Royce in this is not, at this point, the definition of the "real," but it is the recognition that the threshold for willing, in the phenomenological sense, operates on *symbols* it has created. The completed object, attended, recognized, and constructed is a symbol (please note that he said this in 1885, long before his so-called "Peircean insight"). A symbol is a unification of the actual and the possible that refers to this broader temporal reality, including both what is present and what is not present, i.e., the actual and the possible. This is still not possibility in the metaphysical sense of the word, but positive future possibilities, as expressed in plans of action, are not dependent upon specific past actualities for their existence *as* possibilities. Such possibilities as are symbolized can be shared precisely because the planned acts to which they give structure are not yet either mine or yours. We can share symbols in a way that we cannot quite share individualizing acts.

And here we discover the *social* ground of the will at the phenomenological level of generalization. Just as *imitation* was the empirical ground of the sociality of will, *symbolization* is the phenomenological ground of the sociality of will, because symbols are inherently social. I cannot use symbols to point to a future that is mine alone, and thus I cannot grasp, phenomenologically, what it would mean to have an exclusively individual future. Thus, it is not that we privately fashion symbols in preparing ourselves to will something the view here is that we learn to exclude content and supply missing possibility until we have something that *makes sense* to us, i.e., a symbol. That which makes sense to us may be a perspective on that wider reality, but the entire exercise in valuing the broader reality, so as to symbolize it, is one we learn from others. It is true that psychology takes the individual as a given for empirical descriptions, and equally true that phenomenology takes the individual as given at a different level of generality. Yet the individual is not a primitive given; it is a temporally formed and constituted process, and is itself a symbol every time we make sense of ourselves. In short, to have a self, we must interpret the symbols we have made for that purpose.

It does not follow from the assumption of individuality in psychology and phenomenology that the requirements of our descriptions of the world are identical with conditions of the coming-to-be of what we are describing. Yes, individuals symbolize, but as a matter of fact, the principal symbol with which the "individual" operates is the symbol of the *individual self*. The given individual in psychology and phenomenology is *already* a symbol, that is, a description when handled as a concept, and an appreciated fact when handled in more artistic and emotive ways, and this is so whether we are interpreting ourselves to ourselves, or interpreting others to ourselves, or being interpreted by others. At the very least, individuality requires that past activities be recognized and constructed under the general idea of "mine," and "mine" is a socially learned symbol. As Royce later puts it, even in the most private experience, the present self interprets the past self to the future self. But at the phenomenological level, this is a matter of attending to the present in light of the past and the future, and the individual is the most important produced symbol of such activity.

It is true that "perspective" is presupposed in all this activity; both the empirical and the phenomenological accounts require perspective. Having a perspective is a condition for being an individual, but being an individual does not follow inexorably from having a perspective. Individuality is an achievement of *meaningful* perspective, and it cannot be accomplished without symbols, at least for human beings.

Thus, we have described the social basis of both the empirical and the phenomenological levels of "will." It is also significant that at each level we have seen how the activity of imitation and symbolization proceeds first by exclusion, or more precisely (so far as we have come), by the neglecting of possibilities, and only *then* by inclusion. At bottom, these are acts of "exclusion" and "inclusion," to give their universal and philosophical names. These acts, considered philosophically, are *conditions* of thinking of an act as "willing"—which is to say that without symbolization, there is no willing, as far as we know, and without imitation and docility, there is no symbolization. But even taken together, these conditions are not sufficient for a fully developed act of willing in the sense of having an individual will. The activity of exclusion and inclusion, of culling the selected relations of the actual to the possible, has, at the level of a fully formed symbol, still not quite produced "will," and certainly has not produced individuality, but it has created the symbol of the real, which is what the will requires in order to form a *purpose*.

A purpose is more than a possible plan of action, as we shall see, but in order to move to the exercise of the will, and to see how its exercise creates individuals, in Royce's sense, we have to move beyond phenomenological description (or more precisely, the philosophical description of our practical action). The phenomenological level of description is practical for Royce, as I have suggested, and it will take most people far enough to conceptualize whatever they do to negotiate their daily needs. Philosophy is a more specialized kind of reflection, however, suited for dealing with reflective generalizations in the light of universal hypotheses. We must move into metaphysics.

Metaphysical Individuality

Obviously Royce was already interested in the issue of "individuality" and the "individual" when he wrote *The Religious Aspect of Philosophy*, but since his first sustained treatment of the topic as a part of metaphysics comes in his "Supplementary Essay" to *The Conception of God* (1897), I take this to be evidence that Howison's criticisms of 1895 led Royce to recognize that his phenomenology of the individual was not robust enough to carry the burden of metaphysical individuality. Immediately following that debate, Royce seems to have undertaken a survey of the historical theories of "individuals," and he found to his surprise that little had been done with the idea since the high middle-ages.

One of the first insights Royce gleaned from his study is that individuality cannot be fully captured by a philosophical theory, although it can be the *subject* of such a theory. The significance of our lives, as symbolized to ourselves for our appreciation and practical action, is far richer than any descriptive theory, whether philosophical or scientific, can convey. Individuality belongs to this appreciated, practical world as an ethical idea, in the first instance, not as a metaphysical idea in the world of description. Ethics is first philosophy for Royce and is supported by metaphysics, not the other way around.[39] Thus, the metaphysical theory of individuality is not only shot through with values, it is framed for the sake of moral activity. As Royce puts it, in the domain of appreciation:

Individuality is like a ferment. Introduce the germ of it into your world of knowledge, and the universe soon swarms as with yeast, and individuality bubbles out everywhere. For in relation to any one individual, you can define countless other individuals. But the first individual you can know only by breathing the breath of a new life into the otherwise dead and stubbornly universal categories of merely abstract theory. Man individuates the objects of his knowledge because he is an ethical being.[40]

Note that individuation applies to all things we know—to know something is to bring to bear on it the individuating process, the morally charged symbolization mentioned earlier. One might assume that the first individual we know is ourselves. And one would be wrong. We know another before we know or even *have* selves, or can discover our own wills, and that other becomes for us, as Royce calls it, "the exclusive object of interest." This exclusive object of interest becomes the meaning of the term "will" in its metaphysical sense, but it is phenomenologically operative in finite human beings as "love," which is to say that this act of existential exclusion is something of which we have a profound experience. Newborn infants do not possess the power to love, for they have not learned how to exclude the content of their experience, both felt and perceived, to the level of symbolization. Among those who symbolize some may not yet love, even if they know what the word means and can use it in a sentence and envision it as a plan of action. As Royce says, "such power comes only late," after attention and symbolizing.[41]

Royce uses the example of a toy that the child comes to "love" and for which no substitute, however similar, will be accepted. It is in rejecting the substitute, this act of exclusion, that the child moves toward having genuine individuals in his world. "Now, at this moment, I say, when the child rejects the other object—the other that pretends to be an apt appeal to his exclusive love for the broken toy—at this very moment he *consciously individuates the toy*. And he does this with an exclusive love that *permits no other*."[42] This act of willing is not planned, it is enacted, a "reflex of his nature," in Royce's terms, but it has both wonderful and terrible consequences. This act of exclusion happens because "his exclusive interest, as such, is instinctively so set that it declines to recognise, in any unity of consciousness, the presence of two or more equally acceptable cases of the type defined by this love,"[43] i.e., this act of exclusionary will. Royce continues, "the rival being excluded, one stands in the presence of an object concerning which one simply feels that '*there shall be no other*' of this particular value."[44] With each such act of symbolization, we build up our mere perspective into a stronger and more unified willing. Perspective becomes standpoint, and finally place.

The result of this cumulative effort is that we gradually discover our own wills, essentially by loving what we love to the exclusion of all else. "With such exclusive interests one learns to love each of one's more permanent possessions —one's home, books, trinkets; one's children and all other members of one's family; one's country, business, life; . . . one's friends."[45] The most crucial individuating moment in childhood is the phenomenon of mother love: "the mother's love, for this infant, is exclusive, and so individuates both mother and child."[46] For our adolescent lives, the crucial episode is falling in love with another, which is neither planned nor willed (until it is too late). "The love for one beloved, and one only, is an accident which for the first time individuates both lover and beloved."[47] Later we will choose devotion to a cause, and if our service continues to individuate us, eventually we will be able to fall in love with the world. Many shocks and tragedies stand between mother love and loving the world, however.

The difference in the cases of the child-mother and the adolescent first love is crucial for grasping our experiential process, for we are genuine, irreplaceable, unique individuals for another (the mother is crucial, but so are others for whom we arrive on the scene "unique") before we can learn to individualize others. That is, we are already loved before we can learn to love, are already individuals to others *before* we come to see ourselves as individuals. There is every reason to think that the emergence of our own individuality is encouraged and facilitated, indeed, one could fairly say "caused," by this exclusionary act exercised by others toward us, in which we are loved by them as something unique and irreplaceable. Then, later, when we fall in love as adolescents, we take the first hesitating steps in learning to give this gift of individuation to another first, and find ourselves as stronger individuals in its reciprocation, or more tragically, sometimes in the absence of reciprocation. Unrequited love is effectively reactive individuation, in that I individuate without being positively individuated in return, by indifference—active hatred is a kind of positive individuation—so I simply end up taking as my own gift the negation of whatever I have given, and am individuated as unworthy of exactly those positive gifts I have given.

Our capacity to individuate others lags far behind our being individuated *by* others. But gradually, as the world values us more and more—for the persons we have become and for what we have accomplished, for the service we have rendered to others (and it is important to remember that even punishing us for our crimes acknowledges our value)—we learn to generalize our own valuing of the world into an appropriate self-love. For Royce, appropriate self-love is what makes it possible to fall in love with the world, and in a sense, his famous conception of "loyalty to loyalty" is just that. There is a reason that Royce identified the concept of "loyalty" he defended as the same thing Paul spoke about so poetically in 1 Corinthians 13, and one might add that the sense of "for God so loved the world" and "no greater love has a man than to lay down his life for his friends" in John's Gospel, love in the mode of loyal self-sacrifice is also operative here. For the love that gives to the other the social (and indeed metaphysical) grounding for individuality is never selfish, always kind, believes all things, hopes all things and endures all things, and never ends. We can see that, for example, St. Francis loved the world. Gandhi loved the world. Martin Luther King, Jr., loved the world. This is the act of strong and fully formed individuals in the fullest (i.e., ethical) sense.

Perhaps God also did or does love the world. I do not know. Some people think so. Royce and James thought so, and they loved each other and were very smart and very wise and had time to discuss it. If any such matter is to be decided as difficult as whether God loves the world, it will surely be decided among such friends in such discussions as James and Royce had, and until we become such individuals and such friends, we probably will not be able to appreciate the answers they reach. We will not become such friends unless we make it our purpose to become so, and thus many of us will never know. I do not think either Royce or James was ever quite able to fall in love with the world, but I believe they knew it was possible and wanted to do so. But much has been written about this friendship and we need not rehearse it here. This account of individuality is, as an ethical reality, in any case, a living idea (if any idea is).

What is crucial for our purposes is two-fold. First, that developing our wills to such a level of exclusion as to individuate the other is thoroughly social, both tragic and life-giving in its consequences. The process is primarily ethical and can be experienced but not theoretically explained. The metaphysical account of this process of individuation as exclusion and inclusion is an elaboration of the ethical being of individuals, but the metaphysics is not the foundation of ethical individuality. Metaphysical individuality is a derivative and abstract *description* of real individuality. The tragedy is that in excluding all else to the point of making unique whatever is our exclusive interest, we lose all competing possibilities and discover our finitude; but more tragic still is that we must inevitably either lose or be lost to, irreplaceably, those who have given us this gift of individuality and those to whom we have given it.

Second, we discover our own wills and become individuals only as a result of this activity of *exclusion*. There is no verb in English for "making unique," which is an interesting lacuna in itself. Although the word is horrible, we could call the kind of will that individuates "uniquifying" will, meaning that by excluding all else, such that there shall be no other, I make the object of my will, of my love, unique. This is to say that my activity of attending to what I love moves beyond being a symbol to me of *a* real world and becomes something without which I cannot become who *I* plan to become, and without which I cannot even easily remain what I *have* been.[48] This individuating love is not a mere symbol to be mulled over in generalities, this is the symbol becoming fully concrete, pointing not to a real world in general, but to *my* real world in particular and not in its mere being or existence, but in its meaning.

The act of exclusion will be *formalized* in our subsequent discussion, which is what identifies it as belonging to the level of metaphysics, as Royce understands it, and not just phenomenology. But I must reiterate that the formalization of metaphysical individuality, as described above, is meant to serve this ethical and even religious character of individuality, to clarify its structures and to help us grasp reflectively what we have already experienced in our ethical lives. No formalization of any idea in Royce's philosophy does more than this. If there is ontological knowledge in Royce's philosophy, it is love's knowledge, knowledge of who we are and where we belong—and reciprocally, who we are not and where we do not belong—not some sort of abstract, metaphysical necessity.

The *meaning* of *my* world is the means by which I can appropriate its being, as an abstract correlate of my concrete willing. Such is the activity of metaphysics, the effort to appropriate the being of the world *through its meaning*. It is hard to imagine that anyone who has never fallen in love and been sensible of how he is loved irreplaceably could be very adept at Roycean metaphysics. And yet, historically, metaphysicians are often loners not lovers, from Plato to Aquinas to Schopenhauer to Nietzsche to Heidegger. That they were loved as unique individuals one cannot doubt; that they learned how to love others in the fullest sense is more dubious. Buddha and Socrates and Jesus and Muhammed and Gandhi were better at Royce's type of metaphysics than Plato.

Traditional, bad metaphysics depends upon a willingness to treat individuals *as they are not*, to handle them roughly, replaceably, *systematically*. If there is one thing a genuine "individual" is *not* and can never be, it is the value of a bound variable or a truth preserving substitute, or a logical atom. These ideas of the meaning of being and individuality, when asserted as the rational and necessary ground of knowing or experience, are not just wrong, they are pathological and immoral. Individuals are not, metaphysically, "types," but rather are the ethical ground of types. Individuals are also not particulars, even though they may be treated in their particularity for logical and metaphysical purposes. If we could have convinced Bertrand Russell to love even a single one of his logical atoms, irreplaceably, he might have become a little more capable of intimacy in practical life, having as much compassion for those who loved him irreplaceably as he had in the abstract for "humanity." Royce's metaphysics is so far from the monstrous concession to abstraction and intellectualism that he has been charged with that it is offensive even to hear the charge repeated. But ignorance must be forgiven. It is the human lot.

I have to think that both loving other individuals in the sense of "appreciation" Royce defends, and becoming an individual through the gift of being loved *by* those others, often disinclines a person even to do metaphysics and logic. Unless, perhaps, one has trouble in loving oneself *as* the individual one is becoming, resists seeing oneself in the unique light that only appropriate self-love can offer, striving to be instead what others expect one to be, what they have made of one in giving their love, rather than what one is for oneself. That situation could prevent a person from falling in love with the world, for that wondrous act of the will requires a very strong individual. Inappropriate self-love, arrogance, and self-certainty, then, are actually modes of self-hatred, of closing out the world and one's debt to others, withholding the only gift any of us can give the world, which is our individuating love.

Metaphysical individuality has its basis in this thoroughly social structure of will, and the theories we may offer from this principle of individuality are various, but all viable theories have certain features, and one important consequence. The features are relationalism, temporalism, sociality, the primacy of value, and the intentional stance. The consequence is that purposes or ideals are real, not in the abstract, but concretely, as a matter of the meaning of the world. Royce's numerous efforts to convince his readers and hearers that the sum of individual wills must form a whole and be experienced by that whole, a world will, have usually failed. People are not idealists (in any sense) these days. They fail to see how the very idea of individuality Royce so forcefully explained implies a larger reality to which those individual wills belong, through which they communicate, and a larger whole which has its own purposes for them. So be it. I will not here attempt to repeat Royce's arguments. I am convinced of their possibility and coherence as a metaphysical hypothesis, and I will accept the Absolute up through the acknowledgment of the irrevocability of the past. Beyond that, I am also not wholly compelled by the argument, but I also cannot dismiss the fact that it points to a possibility which follows from all I do accept in this case. I can also see that metaphysics depends upon a willingness to arrange generalities with the aid of universal propositions. Without logic, more specifically, a logic of relatives and of possibility, metaphysics is just the *ad hoc* rearranging and listing of generic traits of existences, such as Dewey offers. That may be metaphysics, but it is not *good* metaphysics. Rather, I think that the upshot of Royce's account of individuality is the way it allows him to articulate and to ground his "Fourth Conception of Being."

The Fourth Conception of Being

I think Royce would say that the account of individuality and absoluteness I have culled from his works does not provide us either with the Absolute or the Individual in the full and required sense for metaphysics. One cannot have the fully differentiated Individual, the "genuine individual" without a World Will that individuates fully what the human community can accomplish only in part. The question does not, for metaphysics, turn on whether we can prove that such an Absolute and such an Individual exists. The question turns on what is required for a complete account, in terms of the principles of order and the norms adopted for the philosophical undertaking. I have declined thus far to employ the universals Royce uses, in light of which the generalities may be metaphysically ordered. I actually do not deny Royce's point, however. Methodologically, his course is sound. We do need universal propositions for metaphysics, as all process philosophers assert (even Dewey). And I agree with the relevant propositions Royce uses in this case, namely inclusion/exclusion, and part/whole, the employment of which amounts to no less than an effort to address the problem of the One and the Many, and that of the World and the Individual as willed by the time-inclusive or "chronosynoptic"Absolute. Those are the propositions we should employ, since the norms of excellent philosophical reflection demand it. And doing so in no way implies that we claim for ourselves ontological knowledge, only philosophical knowledge.

As I have emphasized, Royce holds that ethics is First Philosophy and that metaphysics serves it. He also holds that the concept of the "individual" is, in essence, an ethical idea.[49] The issue is not, therefore, whether I have followed through the metaphysics to its completion, but whether enough has been said to serve ethics. In this case, I think we can leave the metaphysics somewhat unfinished and work for practical and ethical purposes with the individual as socially constituted. I do not think any individual leads a full life, even in community, without wrestling with the essentially religious questions about ultimate meaning that Royce associates with a completed metaphysics. If full individuality is achieved, surely it is achieved in light of that struggle, and depends upon the outcome of the same. But my aim has not been to wrest God from Royce's metaphysics and implant the Divine Will in the community. If there is a God, I am sure "his" powers are sufficient to accomplish that without the aid of arguments from me—or Royce (as Royce would doubtless agree). I prefer that philosophy not have too much intercourse with theology, which has entirely different aims than the capturing of human truths for human purposes.[50]

Rather, my aim has been to draw a line from the defense of absoluteness in experience to individuality, and to show how individuality, however conceived, presupposes perspective, temporality, and the intentional structure of the real (in this case, in the form of the "will" as the most general category of intending, but not the origin of it). But the will, as a *product* of social experience, has to be considered in order to show how perspective becomes concrete, active, and the origin of purposes. And a condition for the concrete, active will that forms purposes is "uniqueness," or the product of exclusion taken to its extreme. The will cannot operate except within its own interpretive context, including the modes of value to which it attends, the degree and forms of docility it exhibits to its past, the way in which it acknowledges a world of truth (the experience of others), and its exercise of its powers of exclusion. No two such interpretive contexts are identical, but each and every one depends upon a common world, a world shared with others from the outset. These points would make a better set of ideas for defining a "situation" than those later offered by Dewey, and would be of service to contemporary pragmatism. The situation is a way the World is had, a way-station of the World appreciated, described, and reflected upon. That World has its own past to be collectively acknowledged (Royce calls this the community of memory, later), a World of possibilities and purposes (the community of hope) and an on-going "will to interpret," which is another name for the "World of truth." In this domain, not only is the achievement of individuality a requirement, both practically (i.e., ethically) and philosophically, but "uniqueness" is also required. "Uniqueness" is metaphysical perspective grasped in terms that may be used in ethical thinking.

In addition to uniqueness, however, one needs a conception of the "whole." It might be argued that in setting aside Royce's God, and all that goes with it, I have denuded the whole of its ethical usefulness.

Royce might well say this. The formulation of his Fourth Conception of Being, that *to be is to be uniquely related to a whole*, requires as robust a whole as it requires fully unique individuals. I would counter that I have not left the whole short, for I have embraced the "real," in Royce's terms, and have indicated that I regard it as the combination of the possible and the actual. Possibility is in some senses a wider category than actuality, since some possibilities never become actual as a result of the exclusionary activity of finite wills, and I cannot accept that even Royce's God experiences "might-have-beens" in just the same way as actualities are experienced by that same God. Even God would have to acknowledge a distinction between the possible and the actual, and to affirm that possibility in some sense exists, even if it is not wholly separable from actuality. In short, even if God is conceived as wholly actual (and I think that is a bad idea), there must be some modality within that actuality that we call "the possible," and when we use that term to include all the actualities of past, present, and future, as well as the unactualized ones (the actuality of them *as* possibilities), we are referring to the whole. Thus, if the real world is the actual and the possible, as I am willing to affirm, that is the functional idea of the whole, regardless of whether one dwells upon the actuality of the possibilities or allows, as I prefer, that possibilities exist without necessary dependence on actualities.

To be, then, is to be uniquely related to that whole, no matter how it is approached, metaphysically. We have discussed uniqueness, as individuality of a certain ethical kind, and to some degree we have treated the "Whole," as the Absolute. The third term in this Fourth Conception is the word "related." In the next chapter I will take up what that term means, but it can be said now that "time is the possibility of relation." This is my assertion, not Royce's, but I will show that he adheres to this view. There are philosophers who have expressed the Fourth Conception of Being with greater adeptness than Royce did. Alfred North Whitehead is probably the best representative, for his Ontological Principle, in its numerous and precise formulations, simply is a statement of the Fourth Conception, and he adheres to it more faithfully than Royce. Heidegger's idea that Being is always already a question for Dasein is another version of the Fourth Conception, stated in an indiosyncratic kind of phenomenological (rather than metaphysical) terms. But my point will have been made if I have here shown why uniqueness is a requirement. In the next chapter I will give more attention to the whole and to relation, but I do so because I aim to assert that not only is the Fourth Conception of Being a living idea, it is the only viable way of doing metaphysics in the present and for the foreseeable future.

[6]
Temporalism

Up to now I have stressed the importance of time in Royce's thought. This aspect of his philosophy has not been well understood in the literature, and it is the key unifying thread in all that he does philosophically. The reality of time is what connects his empirical, phenomenological, and metaphysical levels of generalization. Nearly everyone who examines Royce's theory of time takes as the central text his chapter on "The Temporal and the Eternal" in the Second Series of his Gifford Lectures, *The World and the Individual*.[1] To do so has become almost customary, but the result has been unsatisfactory, and for good reason. In that chapter Royce is really doing "metaphysics," in the most general and abstract sense, which is to say that the propositions are offered hypothetically in the form of universals and are being employed to organize other generalities into a complete system. In the same way that Royce's fully developed account of the Absolute fails to convince, in the minds of many or most readers, and to connect to his practical sense of the Absolute (and to his phenomenological grounding of it), his "temporalism" as expressed in "The Temporal and the Eternal," leaves many or most readers with the impression that Royce really is an "eternalist." The argument that God is "time-inclusive" or chronosynoptic rather than atemporal seems like semantics rather than an important distinction, if one begins with Royce's metaphysics. I can confess that my first reading of that chapter many years ago led me to the common conclusion that the time-inclusive Absolute by any other name still smells of stasis. Now I do not believe that is the correct conclusion, but I certainly understand why it has been widely held.

Only closer consideration of some of Royce's other articulations of his temporalism, coupled with a better grasp of where the chapter from *The World and the Individual* fits with the rest of his thought, has led me to alter the judgment I once held that Royce is at least a closet eternalist, if not an outright apologist of stasis. I will attempt to set out a line of reasoning and reading that better situates Royce's most abstract statement of his view of time in what follows. My view of Royce's temporalism has come to be in parallel with the account of individuality and the Absolute I have offered in the previous chapter, which is to say that if one distinguishes clearly the levels of discourse, i.e., the empirical description, the phenomenological description, the practical and ethical description, the general reflective and philosophical description, and the most abstract metaphysics (guided by universals and logical necessity), then Royce's temporalism falls into a more comprehensible and persuasive order. The time-inclusive Absolute is a concept one must employ in the mode of a universal hypothesis in order to bring the idealistic system into complete coherence. This does not mean it is a claim of ontological knowledge, only that anyone who wishes to have a robust, consistent, conceptual account of "the Whole" to which "the Individual" uniquely belongs and to which it contributes, will require the hypothesis of a time-inclusive Absolute. Royce insists that such a hypothesis does not eliminate the reality of time, does not imply static eternalism, but most of his readers have remained unconvinced.

In my judgment, a more convincing case both for Royce's commitment to temporalism and the viability of the idea itself, should be drawn from other writings—phenomenological, practical-ethical, and general philosophy (not specifically the most abstract metaphysics). Royce wrote little on the empirical level about the subject of time—by which I mean that there is not much physics, but the subject of empirical time is crucial to his understanding of evolution and his psychology. I will pass over the full treatment of evolutionary and psychological time, but I can recommend that readers examine these empirical aspects of Royce's thought to fill in the gap, and I will offer a review.[2] Such a review will supply generalizations analogous with those about the individual in the previous chapter.

In this chapter I will first revisit the phenomenological account of individuality in the previous chapter, but now I will draw out its specific applications to the question of temporalism. Second, I will generalize the phenomenological description into the level of practical ethics, in which the fully developed will is operative. Third, I will move to the general philosophical account of time, showing the nature of the concepts with which philosophy deals in considering time. Fourth, I will examine these concepts especially as related to possibility, actuality, and the principles of continuity and discontinuity. Finally I will examine Royce's account of "relation." I will show that *time is the possibility of relation* for Royce, even though he never quite formulated the idea in just this way. All of these considerations culminate in Royce's practical ethical position, and philosophical conviction that "time is the form of the will." The formation of future purposes, and the causes one may serve, is the "end," or "that for the sake of which" temporalism is adopted as part of a philosophy. Royce is certainly convinced of the "reality" of time, but the source of this conviction is not derived from his metaphysics; it comes from his ethics and is *served* by his metaphysics. One could hold that the metaphysics, as stated, does not serve this ethical viewpoint well, or even adequately, without thereby damaging the general philosophical account, the practical ethics, or the phenomenology. Rather, the result of adjudging the metaphysics lacking would be to take on the task of providing a more adequate metaphysical description (perhaps eschewing universal propositions altogether, or relying upon different hypotheses).

Phenomenological and Practical Temporalism

It is important to be aware Royce's full view of temporality, and a statement of his temporalism in the language of fictional ontology, is in place *before* he arrived at Harvard. In 1880, Royce wrote:

> To sum up, from this point of view the end of thought appears to be: That experience past and future, *should be conceived* as one whole with a necessary connection of parts; that the present and immediately given content of consciousness *should be found*, not alone significant nor enough, but a moment in a world of life; that the *relations* conceived as necessary for one part of the time-stream *should be conceived* as necessary for the whole time-stream. And the end of thought is realized in the act of *constructing the image* of *possible* experience. For by experience, we mean, in addition to what is given, that which *is conceived as* past and future.[3]

I have emphasized the language in this passage which makes it clear that Royce is speaking hypothetically and employing intellectual *norms*. Also, please note the role of "image construction" in light of the phenomenology of the previous chapter. This view never changed, although the idea that only the present is immediately given, while the work of thought is to unify it with past and future, is what created the problem of immediacy for Royce, as discussed in Chapter 3. I will take up that problem again in Chapter 7, and attempt to "solve" it.

Earlier in this book I have emphasized Royce's account of "acknowledgement of the past," the "acknowledgement of a world of truth," and the "anticipation of the future." The principal description of this schema occurs in *The Religious Aspect of Philosophy*, and while there are modifications in Royce's vocabulary in the course of his career, the basic experience he is describing as "acknowledgment" and "anticipation" remains constant.[4] The intentional stance he adopts—and we have noted now that the concept of "will" is his broadest term for it—requires phenomenological temporalism, at the least. Under the more general heading of "intentionality," we have discovered, in Chapter 5, the pre-volitional elements of *activity, attention, recognition, construction,* and *perspective*, which, under the proper circumstances, produce "will," but it should be stressed that "activity," "attention," and "perspective," etc., as *concepts*, are a part of the philosophical effort to reflect upon the structure of experience. These concepts *describe* pre-volitional experience, but they are nevertheless concepts, i.e., generalizations with which we can or should work in providing a philosophical account of experience. Hence, these concepts are not intended to exhaust immediate experience, but rather to generalize it by means of phenomenology, and as generalizations these concepts are *post*-volitional, even if the experiences they describe are pre-volitional, by which I mean that the concepts are *products* of the will (already dedicated to a well-formed purpose and its norms, that of philosophizing well), even if the phenomena so generalized are treated as conditions for the development of the will.

Charles M. Sherover has provided a good account of Royce's "intentional stance," and its relation to sociality and temporality, and I do not intend to repeat that work here. Sherover's result is that:

> Royce saw that what we now term systematic phenomenological questioning provides not only categorial ways in which to comprehend existential situations—which Heidegger developed in many ways beyond what Royce had done; he also has shown that an at-least speculative metaphysics cannot be dispensed with—that serious questioning rather requires and leads to a metaphysic which, though it must remain speculative instead of dogmatically cognitive, is yet requisite to sustaining and undergirding the pluralistic community of the whole of being in which we participate.[5]

What is missing from Sherover's account, however, is the explicit connection of the intentional stance to the will. But Sherover is right, in my view, to recognize the "at-least" speculative metaphysics required by temporalism and the intentional stance, and that some conception of "the whole of being in which we participate" is needed for such "at-least" metaphysics. Thus, I take Sherover, also, to want to draw the line somewhere short of the Absolute as a universal proposition and to want to employ the idea of the Absolute (and other such ideas) as a working hypothesis about the whole to which experience belongs. I think Sherover was inclined to play down the scope and importance of Royce's voluntarism because he was making links to German (and especially Heideggerian) phenomenology.

The concept of the "will" that Royce works with is so thoroughly associated with Schopenhauer and Nietzsche in German thought as to distract attention of readers from its character *as* intentional. It is not necessary to see these differing levels of emphasis, on the will as opposed to other intentional concepts (like consciousness or *Dasein*), as creating a tension between the Royce's thought and more recent phenomenology, however, because the derivative or socially produced character of will, in Royce (as opposed to Nietzsche and Schopenhauer, where will serves as an ontological primitive) is not at odds with the more basic "pre-volitional" ideas of activity, attention and perspective. The issue regarding which Royce may part company with European phenomenology has more to do with the claim that ethics is First Philosophy—that is, that the phenomenological description is undertaken for the *purpose* of grounding an ethical will, and is wholly in service of that aim. Even here, however, Royce is in line with such German phenomenologists as Scheler and his school. The at-least speculative metaphysics serves the same ethical end. European phenomenology has shied away from both of these extra-phenomenological, but clearly philosophical, tasks, creating in Heidegger studies, especially, a lot of issues with "praxis." There is growing recognition, over the past decade, that such extra-phenomenological accounts of ethical existence are needed, and these seem to require something like an "at-least" speculative metaphysics, often with religious content reminiscent of Royce. The growing importance of Lévinas (stressed by Tunstall in his book *Yes, but Not Quite*) and the phenomenology of Jean-Luc Marion come to mind as examples.

One of the key differences between phenomenological description and reflective philosophy (as Royce understands it, recalling that he does not regard phenomenology as part of philosophy, see Chapter 4), is that phenomenology takes "experience" to be, in the primordial sense, "activity," while ethical philosophy, First Philosophy, regards it as "action." I have been using the terms "action" and "activity" in distinct senses throughout this book, but I am only now making the difference explicit. The first result of activity is perspective, which indicates that individuation is occurring, but individuality is not yet achieved until those who have been individualized by the love of others begin to reciprocate. But "action," meaning action upon a plan which is willed, *when generalized* into a concept for "at-least" metaphysics, becomes "actuality," and actuality is what serves the will in forming its *purposes*. Purposes are more than plans of action, as I will explain more completely in Chapter 8. Where plans of action are thoroughly social and have ethical import, and where the concept of a plan of action suffices for phenomenological description, metaphysics requires a more generalized, perhaps even universal formulation. "Purpose" is such a formulation for Royce. Thus, the ascent from immediate experience to phenomenological description is a first level of generalization, from immediate experience to descriptive concepts like "activity," while the move from phenomenology to ethics is a generalization of ideas like "activity" to that of "action," while a still broader generalization transforms "action" into "actuality." Royce is quite consistent in using the terms in this way.

Applying this point to temporalism, for phenomenology one can say that "the present is the only real," while "the future and past are shadows both," but one cannot move to philosophical reflection without recognizing that "without the shadows, the real has *for us* neither life nor value."[6] The key phrase "for us" here indicates that we intend not only to describe experience as activity, but, in the words Royce uses here, to "contemplate" it, to consider it philosophically, not just phenomenologically. The term "life" is one Royce uses interchangeably with "will," and the term "value" points to the primacy of ethical norms in both practical action and in philosophizing. In short, one will need to generalize ideas like activity into action and then to actuality, and perspective into individuation and then individuality, and attending into valuing, and then into reflecting or contemplating before anything will have *philosophical* meaning. This stops short of Will, Individuality, and the Whole (and we may reserve the capitalized terms to designate concepts operating under the universal mode, the most abstract level of metaphysics—Royce does tend to capitalize when he is speaking in this mode, although I would not claim he does so either consciously or consistently, yet the habit is fairly consistent).

These connections among and between the levels of Royce's discourse have been noted by his interpreters before, although they have not been, in my view, satisfactorily understood. For example, John E. Smith notes "the necessary connection between a concept, a belief, and an action."[7] Here the *mode* of necessity makes all the difference.[8] There is a sort of necessity in the immediacy of determinate judgment, of making sense of one's experience in light of the way the body functions, and the fact that it cannot operate in just any fashion it chooses (and here the law of docility applies, among others, as discussed in chapter five) is an articulation of the temporality of activity, perspective, and attention. There are also the practical necessities that accompany willing, which involve a broader appreciation of our temporal existence, including the "acknowledgements" of the past and a world of truth, and the anticipation of the future; and then there is the dialectical necessity accompanying any clear philosophical reflection in accordance with *its* norms (to do philosophy well) and for *its* purposes, and of course the logical necessity that accompanies abstract metaphysics.

There is no good reason to assume that the type of dialectical necessity that accompanies philosophy in general is anything other than a *freely* adopted norm for the sake of doing philosophy well. One serves philosophy by choosing to follow its norms, and the sort of necessity that accompanies dialectical thinking is such a norm, not (as far as we know) an ontological feature of the universe in itself (i.e., Hegel is being rejected). Philosophical dialectic, and its type of necessity, is a generalized schema of considering alternative definitions and arrangements of concepts whose structure does not apply as a set of inflexible rules throughout all experience; the conceptual arrangements arrived at dialectically are fallible and revisable. To think as if experience can be or must be made to conform with norms of philosophical reflection is the foolish error that has been made by most of Western philosophy. Royce does not err in this way. Ideas such as logical necessity are also distilled products *of philosophical* experience created for very specific ends (in this case, reflecting in a still *more* orderly fashion so as to support a broader philosophical worldview than dialectic can offer).

For Royce, the *experience* of necessity, for example, such as we find at a practical level in the irrevocability of the acts counseled by the will, or at the psychological level of description in the law of docility, or at the phenomenological level in the requirement of selection for attention, is *derivative* of both temporality and freedom as concretely experienced. We do find "musts" in our experience, but each must or experience of necessity is accompanied by a type of freedom. There is no particular reason to think that *logical* necessity of the sort we employ in our most abstract metaphysics would even be required of non-temporal beings, if any such beings existed, for logical necessity derives from a practical norm associated with a certain kind of *thinking* –a kind we need not even choose to do (thinking philosophically is not a requirement of living a good life). Thinking is a temporal process. The philosophies of non-temporal beings, if they had any, would probably require a different kind of order. Necessity, as *experienced*, for Royce, is an *effect* of temporal existence, from immediate experience all the way up to metaphysics, but it has to be thoroughly understood, for the roots of necessity run deep in our experience, and our sense of freedom and possibility are poorly understood without appreciating the ground of necessity in experience.

We have seen in Chapter 5 how the emergence of individuality depends upon, at the phenomenological level, the way that activity expresses perspective in attending, while attending requires selection, and selection implies that we neglect that which might have been the focus of attention, but is not. The combination of what we have selected with what we have *not* selected constitutes the phenomenological field of *possibility*, and the activity of attending creates for us a foreground and a background, a periphery and a center. Royce is very clear in stating that the background or fringes of attention are not entirely lost, not entirely excluded in the act of selecting a center for attention. He says:

> . . . the boundaries of our consciousness are crowded with unknown impressions –unknown, because not attended to; but yet in some inexplicable way a part of our consciousness, since an effort of attention serves to bring them, any one of them, clearly into mental vision. At this instant you are looking at something. Now, without moving your eyes, try, by merely attending to your visual impressions, to say what is now in the field of vision, and where is the boundary line of the field of vision. The experiment is a little hard, because our eyes, condensed embodiments as they are of tireless curiosity, are always restless, and rebel when you try to hold them fast. But conquer them for an instant, and watch the result. As your attention roams the artificially fixed field, you will at first, indeed, be confused by the vagueness of all but the centre; but soon you will find, to your surprise, that there are more different impressions in the field than you at first can distinguish. One after another, many various impressions will appear. But notice: you can keep your attention fixed on only a portion of the field at a time. The rest of the field is always lost in a dim haze. You must be receiving impressions all the time from all points of the field. But all of these, except the few to which you pay attention, nearly or quite disappear in the dim thickets that seem to surround the little forest-clearing made by our attentive consciousness. A like experiment can be tried with the sense of hearing.[9]

Our first experience of necessity is not pure negation or total exclusion, but of a kind of limit to our selective capacity—try as I might, from the available phenomenal field, I cannot select for attention the whole of it. Hence, to put the point in Kantian language, even determinate judgment depends on attention; the entire sensuous manifold is not synthesized in the "I think," but rather, only the portion to which we attend. It is very important to note that, experientially, in the phenomenological sense, the whole field is *positively* available to me, as a field of *possible* attention, and that my first experience of "negation" (really of necessity as limitation) comes in the form of the limits implied by the effort of selection. A more experienced, mature person can attend with greater perspicacity, and also more broadly, to the phenomenal field than can, for instance, a child. Yet, for all my experience, I cannot select the whole field; yet I am experiencing it.

We have already discussed how recognition and construction fill out and temporalize the phenomenal field, bringing to it *not* only what is only vaguely present, but even what is entirely absent, i.e., the past and the future of the selected portion of the field, which now becomes an "object" of attention. But temporality is already at work in the selective activity of attention itself because whatever it selects becomes for it a center that may *become* an "object," while what is not selected is temporally *deferred* in the mode of *possible* centers not selected (or neglected). The experience of *limit* in expanding the center of attention toward the full phenomenal field is the primordial experience of necessity, or as I would call it, the "impossible-to-include," which is derivative of the possible. There is variation, from one individual to the next, in the modalities and extent of exclusion. The highly refined proprioperception and exteroception of the NFL quarterback or the powerful act of "seeing" the chessboard by a master, as opposed to the broad and supple (and hence inclusive) range of the meditating guru are among thousands of examples that might be given. This order of possibility and impossibility, the priority of the former over the latter, has to be preserved at all levels of generalization, up to and including universal postulates. To do otherwise is to treat negation and necessity as though they preceded positive experience (the possibilities combined with the actualities), which they never do.

Once the will begins to employ the *recognized* and *constructed* objects of our attention for the formation of plans of action, the limitation we experience in selection comes to be expressed as "doubt," for Royce. Doubt is an affliction of the will, not of the phenomenological level of experience (which would be dissatisfaction), and doubt depends upon freedom as much as selection depends on it—we need not complete the objects of attention we have before us in just the way we have done, and we can alter those objects with different activities of recognition and construction, and by attending to the phenomenal field differently. We may ask ourselves: "Is the object upon which I plan to act, in this way rather than that way, the object I need or want?" Perhaps so, perhaps not. We will not know with any assurance until the action has been (irrevocably) performed. Facing this doubt requires that we form postulates, according to Royce, which is not first and foremost an intellectual act, but is rather a volitional task for dealing with the possibilities for action that have been *excluded*. He says:

> Postulates are not blind faith. Postulates are voluntary assumptions of a risk, for the sake of a higher end. Passive faith dares not face doubt. The postulate faces doubt, and says: "So long as thou canst not make thyself an absolute and certain negative, I propose to act as if thou wert worthless, although I do well see thy force." . . . The postulate is deliberate and courageous volition.[10]

Postulating is a deliberate act of the will that is at bottom a moral activity. It counters doubt. One notes that the willed plan and the unwilled possibility converse in the mode of intimacy, the address of "Thou." This exclusion, this negation of living possibilities, is undertaken freely and in intimate awareness of the real possibilities of alternative courses of action and ways of constructing the object of attention. Unchosen (and therefore unwilled) possibilities will be transformed into "might-have-beens," irrevocably, as soon as action is taken, but they are excluded reverently, by the prior and deliberate act of the will in the presence of doubt.

The will uses postulates to create a plan of action. Here the experience of necessity is a practical necessity; we cannot pursue every available course of action. Some plans we might have formed will be left undone, and there is risk, and with the risk comes the doubt about whether we have proceeded adeptly. Genuine doubt confronts genuine risk in dealing contingently, but irrevocably, with possibilities for action. To fail to confront the reality of possibilities, especially positive possibilities, as unchosen plans of action, is to act in "blind faith," to behave as though one had only one available course of action to which one was inexorably compelled. It treats necessity as the dominant mode, places it over possibility, and refuses to take responsibility for its own valuations and willing. "Blind faith is emotion, and often cowardly emotion."[11]

At the level of practical action, to temporalize our concept of experience is not only to treat the future as "real," it is to *risk* the future and take responsibility for its form, as only one possibility freely chosen and willed from among many available plans. Necessity here is the intimate experience of nodding to the unwilled and unchosen possibilities as they pass into might-have-beens. To choose one's bride or groom is to forsake all others, even if the principal act of choosing is positive and actual. There is no point on pretending otherwise. If selection is the "cost" of embodiment, doubt is the "cost" of willing a plan of action, and each is experienced in the mode of a kind of necessity that is derivative of possibility. The reward for this cost is, in attending, the formation of a definite and clear consciousness, a consciousness that has an object, at the level of action. The reward, then, is individuation, and when willing rises to the level of exclusion that is associated with uniqueness, the reward is *full* ethical individuality (if not quite Individuality), that is, bearing a unique relation to the whole—*regardless* of what the whole is (perhaps including the Whole).

Here, then, we discover the experiential roots, both phenomenological and practical (i.e., moral), of possibility and its *derivative*, necessity, as expressions of the Fourth Conception of Being. For Royce, these levels of the experience of possibility depend on the act—activity, action, and finally actuality—but he has detached the experience and the existence of necessity from the act and the actual, and has relocated it in the possible as one mode of possibility. Necessity is, for Royce, and for all serious temporalists, a possibility, not *vice versa*. We come to be uniquely related to the whole (however it is conceived) by forming our own objects of attention and adopting our own plans of action relative to those objects. At every level, *to be is to be related to a whole*, but when the will is planning, in certain instances only one possible object will suffice, and when all others are deliberately excluded, i.e., when we love that one object, uniqueness is in evidence, which carries with it an imperative that we experience as *necessity*. It always means something like "I cannot be the individual I am without this object" and of course, where the will is mature, the unique object is always another person or other persons (and here, the term "person" includes communities, as explained in Chapters 8 and 9).

Yet, the choice of that one object and the acceptance of no substitute remains a choice, and one for which we are responsible. The ground of necessity is an unwillingness to act otherwise, even though we technically could. This kind of relation may be raised to still another level, when those other irreplaceable persons are united by a cause, an ideal which they serve in common, but for now the point is that the experienced necessity carries a strong feeling of negation, that none other shall be acceptable, which wholly negates other genuine possibilities by means of the maximum effort of the fully formed will. Having chosen to eat it, I cannot still have my cake, one might say.

What moves our account forward is the recognition that the priority of possibility to necessity is not in the least a static relation; it is entirely temporal. It would be tempting to cast possibility strictly in the role of futural time, but that would not be accurate, either as a reading of Royce, or in our experience. Possibility, for Royce, pervades the present as well, in the reality of a "world of truth," or other *possible* plans of action than my own, as willed by others with other experience than my own, as I stressed in Chapter 2. The reality of the present and future, whether understood as the field of possible selection for attention, or the field of possible actions, or as the similar activity and, eventually, the *purposes* of others, is in all cases regarded as real. Even the past is experienced as much in the mode of possibility as actuality, for recognition, whereby we complete whatever has our attention, and is not entirely spontaneous or immediate. It allows for adjustment as we attend and consider such mundane matters as "is this thing at my feet a snake or a stick?" From the resources of recognition, there are always many possibilities.

This detachment of necessity from actuality, and grounding necessity in choice and the feeling of negation it brings, is the central move of temporalist philosophies. One finds varied accounts of possibility, but the demotion of necessity to a mode of the possible is universal among temporalists. To move beyond the priority of the possible in the domain of phenomenology and practical action, one needs to examine Royce's "at-least" speculative metaphysics. That is, without needing to drag ourselves through the chapter on "The Temporal and the Eternal," there is a level of general philosophical description that is sufficient to mark out Royce's commitment to temporalism, and to show what type he defends and the extent to which it is, for him and for us, a living idea, regardless of whether we ascend beyond dialectical thinking to the metaphysics governed by logical necessity.

Metaphysical Temporalism

The aim of this section is to show how the possible and the actual are related in Royce's philosophy. We will discover that the issues of continuity and discontinuity complement the account of individuality we have already provided, and end by raising the question of "personality" in Royce. I will argue in the next chapter that Royce's idea of personality is crucial to the formation of "purposes," which will be taken up in Chapter 8. Getting to the heart of these important, living ideas requires that we grasp possibility in a fuller sense than we have, as yet. For these purposes, and more generally, I regard Royce's expression in the 1906 essay "Immortality" as the best general account of his temporalism.[12] When "The Temporal and the Eternal" is read immediately after the essay on "Immortality," the two form a natural movement from the less to the more (or most) general level of metaphysical thinking, from dialectical necessity to logical necessity.

Making the move from the practical and phenomenological account of Royce's temporalism to the more dialectical level of metaphysics requires a bit of care. Where mistakes have been made in interpreting Royce, very often they have been made because readers failed to recognize the ways in which generalization occurs. Royce begins his account of time in "Immortality" with a return to and a repeat of his intentional stance, as expressed in the account of "will":

> Time, to my mind, is an essential practical aspect of reality, which derives its whole meaning from the nature and life of the will. Take away from your conception of the world the idea of a being who has a will, who has a practical relation to facts, take away the idea of a being who looks before and after, who strives, seeks, hopes, pursues, records, reports, promises, accomplishes; take away, I say, every idea of such a being from your world, and whatever then remains in your conceived world gives you no right to a conception of time as any real aspect of things.[13]

Here, not only does Royce make clear the scope of what he means by "the life of the will," which is inclusive of *all intentional modalities*, but also draws upon a dialectical sense of negation, the hypothetical operation of exclusion—take away *this* (hypothetically) and your are not entitled to *that* (hypothetically), which is the form of this argument, a common form in Royce's dialectical thinking. But now the discourse operates at the level of excluding *concepts* from an account, for thinking is itself also an intentional activity of the life of the will, but it includes and excludes concepts dialectically by means of hypotheses.

The manner of generalization is excluding possible concepts and settling upon others for the purpose of creating an account, in this case, a *philosophical* account, but generalization proceeds along similar paths for scientific or historical or other types of accounts, according to different rules and for different purposes (and with different norms). The cost of excluding the intentional stance would be to render the resulting concept static, atemporal, and that is unwise in philosophy. In every case, whether historical or scientific or philosophical, we are deciding what to *think*—which is also an instance of deciding what to *do* (since thinking is an act). Royce continues saying that "the time regions [past. present and future] get their distinct types of reality solely from their diverse relations to a finite will, and, for us, to our own finite will."[14] Royce makes explicit here a generalization from the individual perspective and experience to a generalized conception of "will," although this is still not Will in the sense of a universal proposition. He proceeds to a demonstration of how any finite will must come to terms with past, present and future, concluding that "in terms, then, of my attitude of will, and only in such terms, can I define time, and its regions, distinctions, and reality."[15]

Having so stated, dialectically, the practical requirements of our concept of the will, and restricting it in this way, Royce then moves to generalize his account in the direction of metaphysics, after which he asserts his general dialectical principle:

> Time then is, I should say, a peculiarly obvious instance of the necessity for defining the universe in idealistic terms—that is, in terms of life, of will, of conscious meaning.... we are prone to forget that it is the human will itself which defines for us all such concepts, which abstracts them from life, and which then often bows to them as if they were indeed mere fate. If you look beneath the abstractions, you find that time is in essence the form of the finite will, and that when I acknowledge one universal world time, I do so only by extending the conception of the will to the whole world.[16]

This is actually pragmatism, of the idealistic type explained in Chapter 4, stating the instrumental character of conceptions and definitions, and with a voluntarism of a kind that is akin to James's. It would be nearly impossible to place too much emphasis on this brief passage for the understanding of Royce's philosophy as a whole, and for his temporalism in particular. Here he has indicated the mode of necessity we are to use, the dialectical sense which the practical, temporal conception of the will requires for its generalization, embedded in the intentional stance, and a rejection of the over-arching necessity associated with "fate," i.e., treating the resulting concept as though it were the necessary ground of the process which has produced it. In short, he rejects what James calls the philosopher's fallacy and Whitehead calls vacuous abstraction with misplaced concreteness.

Here Royce notes the process of forming concepts is itself a temporal act of will, that these concepts are taken from a broader and richer "life" for certain purposes (following their own norms—what Dewey would call "ends in view"), and then the statement of a general dialectical principle (not a universal proposition, at this point) that time is the form of the *finite* will. If, subsequently, there is to be a *concept* of an Infinite Will, we also have to conceive of *it* in temporal terms. And this will be accomplished by first *acknowledging* a universal world time—by which he means a shared past, a shared present, and a shared future, in which my deeds are not first and foremost my own but first are contributions to the shared reality, and secondarily contribute to the development of my individuality—and then extending, i.e., generalizing, my *conception* of the will to the whole world. A will that is *no one's* will at *no* time is not a "will" at all. It might be a dead concept or a blind force, but it is not a will.

Should I generalize everything I understand and *can* understand about time in such a way as to *avoid* the result that the world will has as *its* form of *our* common time? To do so is to negate the intentional stance, to use the will to negate its own form. Royce cannot see the justification for negating the intentional stance at this level of abstraction, since only the intentional stance provides us with the means of generalization that take us to this point. Why follow the path of will, and its structure, up to the very brink of a metaphysical concept and then drop it? If time is the form of the finite will, and the dialectical account carries dialectical necessity, why would we frame a universal proposition about the world which is ungrounded in a further generalization of that kind of necessity? And why would we refuse to acknowledge that the most abstract sense of necessity, logical necessity, is derivative of dialectical necessity and its temporal presuppositions? To assert that there is a world, but that it has no will is to deny that it is a temporal world in any sense we can genuinely understand. One certainly can assert such a thing (Royce cites Münsterberg as someone who has made this error), but why would one violate a norm of proper generalization merely to avoid a certain result—in this case that the world has a will whose form is our common or shared time?

Ironically, James really had it right when, on a walk with John Elof Boodin down Commonwealth Avenue in 1896, James said: "If there is an absolute, he must be just like Royce, a great metaphysician with a great stack of books under his arm and knowing everything."[17] In form, James has this exactly right—that the Absolute must be conceived on some such model if it is to be an operative philosophical concept. It is not crude anthropomorphism, it is rather an effort to retain the consistency of one's generalization process.

But what is perhaps of the greatest importance in the above passage, and its analysis, is the way it illustrates the principle of *continuity* in Royce's thought. The maxim we can extract from this movement of generalization from psychological and empirical, to practical, to dialectical, to logical, is that one should retain, as a norm in philosophizing, a continuity of *meaning* through the process of generalizing, while the forms (relations of possibility and many derivative modes of necessity) are refined, from selection, to valuing, to choosing, to excluding objects, to excluding concepts, to deducing logical consequences. A second maxim is that one should not take the derivative results of a generalization process to be the ontological or necessary ground of a lower stage of generalization.[18] And because, in this instance, the aim is to grasp the sense in which experienced time, in the dialectically generalized sense, is continuous with the experience of time for the *non*-finite will, and we are given only one option, according to Royce, for its proper (in the normative sense) generalization: the employment of the intentional stance, or "extending the *conception* of the will to the whole world." We see here a crucial case of generalization constrained by varying levels of ever-tightening necessity, the type of tightening that eventually produces our ideas about logical necessity. *If* we would conceive of time at all, as something shared, we *must* generalize it as the form of the will. To do otherwise leaves us without a ground, in Royce's view.

Now that we have grasped this movement of generalization in thought, with regard to the proper generalization of time, other continuities will appear. In particular, I will point out the senses in which activity, action, and actuality form a continuous chain of generalization of the experience of the act, and also how positive possibilities in embodied experience become possible actions, and possible actions become plans, and eventually, plans can become "purposes," when undertaken socially by individuals capable of love (and at the highest level loving the world). These are further continuities that arise from the proper generalization of our temporal experience.

This leaves the issue of sociality for us to consider, or re-consider, at this level of generalization. Yet, we have also traced continuity in generalization without noting the *limits* of continuity, for clearly there is individuality, which is to say discreteness, or a crucial mode of *discontinuity*, in experience. We have treated individuality as a product, an outcome of certain kinds of continuous social experience. But continuity is itself a *concept*, valued for certain purposes while remaining an obstacle to other purposes. To grasp the limits of continuity, as both a dialectical principle and correlatively as a rule of sound generalization (for something is excluded every time we generalize, as the gradations of tightening necessity show), we should consider the limits of continuity. Interestingly, the limits of continuity are discovered in our social existence itself. What is discontinuous with us is what Royce calls, the non-Ego, or what we would now call, following Hegel, the Other and its otherness. Royce says:

> The only possible way to get at the existence of the finite non-Ego is through some form of social consciousness. What a finite non-Ego is, your

> fellow teaches you when he communicates to you the fact that he has inner experience, and is the same object, however many finite observers view him. Now, if his continuity with the phenomenal nature of whose processes his observed expressive movements are an inseparable and continuous part [including his role in shared or world time], impels you to say that if he is real his whole body, and so, in the end, the whole nature of which that whole body is an inseparable part and an evolutionary product, is also real, in an inner and finite sense, then the only possible way to interpret this relation is to say: "Nature, by itself, is a system of finite experience which, on occasion, and by means of perfectly continuous evolutionary processes, passes over into, or differentiates from its own organization, the communicative form of socially intelligible experience that you and I call human."[19]

Thus, we see that the continuity we embrace is for the sake of selecting and attending to, in the phenomenal world, those parts continuous with it, that communicate to us inner lives of their own. To have the other before me, as communicative, is at a minimum to attend to an embodied other with whom I crucially share a world of truth, a present, and a shared past and anticipated future, all of which are real. The application of continuity in generalization is also for the sake of communicating my thinking (and the reality of my inner life, especially my will) to another. My thinking, inner life, and will, is part of the phenomenal experience of others, and the constraints to which it submits are governed by the requirements of communication, making my inner experience intelligible to another by yielding to the continuities we find in the system of nature. But is that continuity absolute? Not at all. Royce continues:

> The force of this proof is limited, of course, by the fact that it is precisely an argument from continuity. It is capable of endless development and illustration; and I take it to be the only possible proof that nature exists in any way beyond the actual range of our more or less similar human experiences of nature's observable facts. Yet no argument from any continuity of apparent processes has absolute force. It does not follow that every hypothetical conception which you and I now form of this or that natural process, e.g., of the atoms or of gravitation, corresponds to any distinct form of the inner-nature experience.[20]

I do not know your inner experience, as a possible object of attention or will, and you do not know mine, except as communication reveals these aspects of reality. Communication can be more or less effective, but the continuity of shared time, in the sense of a world of nature, and the sense in which that world supports shared memory, shared truth, and shared hope, to that same extent we bow to the constraints of continuity. It is a choice about how to frame hypotheses based on a norm.

We may think as chaotically as we wish, compartmentalize our consciousness, but communication will suffer, as will memory, truth and hope. Continuity is not an absolute, for Royce, which is why it was always unjust and incorrect for James to characterize his philosophy as monistic. Royce was probably as pluralistic as James himself, but unlike James, Royce had a robust account of individuality that could be defended philosophically. Continuity is, however, a dialectically required hypothesis for philosophical reflection. When we consider, i.e., *think about*, a shared world, we adopt time as its broadest possible principle of continuity, and we imagine "a vast system of finite experience, real as our socially communicative fellows are real, and manifesting its existence to us just as they do, viz., through phenomena which appear to our sense through material movements in space and time."[21] Hence, we start our generalizations with phenomenology because the phenomenal field is the communicative aspect of our embodied experience, and we attend not just to what we privately or capriciously select, but rather, we *select* what *communicates*, and only then do we begin to generalize our "facts" in accordance with our plans, and eventually, our purposes. This generalization depends not only on continuities, but on distinctions, discontinuities, leaving some possibilities out. As Royce says:

> Most clearly this correlation of facts and purposes appears in all our Classifications. To classify is to regard certain facts as different (just because we find that to us certain differences are important), and certain objects as in a specific sense alike (because our interest in their likeness predominates over our interest in making certain possible sunderings). *What* classes your acknowledged world of fact contains, your own interest in classification obviously co-operates in determining. Hence the possibility of the well-known and endless disputes over whether our classifications in science stand for the truth of things, over whether our general Ideas represent "external realities," and over the historically significant problems of the theory of Universals. From our own point of view, these controversies get a very simple solution. Of course all classification is relative to the point of view, varies with that point of view, and has value only as fulfilling the purpose of whoever classifies. And, nevertheless, the question *How ought I to classify?* has an objective meaning in precisely the sense in which any question about facts in the world has meaning . . . [which] involves emphasizing certain presented or conceived differences, and regarding as equivalent certain facts that, from another point of view, could be subdivided or contrasted.[22]

Classification in this passage is an instance of generalization, and here Royce describes its dialectical workings. Even Universals are concepts taken in a particular way and subordinated to certain purposes, in this case, philosophical purposes and the norms it adopts for the broader practical ends that it serves. They continue to exhibit our interests in classifying, no matter how abstract they become.

Whatever we may now say about possibility and actuality, in general, depends upon the way in which we generalize the intentional character of experience, employing both continuities and discontinuities (or exclusions or negations) to serve the norm of communicating philosophical thoughts *philosophically*, and whatever dialectical necessity we may find depends upon the way in which selection becomes voluntary exclusion in the face of doubt, whether doubt about action, or that important type of action called thinking (thinking in general is an activity, but philosophical reflection, as carried out under the norms of excellent philosophical reflection, is voluntary at a higher level—more than an activity, it is an action). To understand Royce's temporalism on any other basis than as the normed generalization of the temporal form of the will is to misunderstand it entirely. Therefore, the relation of possibility and actuality I will now explain is to be understood as deriving its definition and its necessity from the process of generalizing time as the form of the will.

Possibility and Actuality

I have shown how the various modes of possibility are prior to all that is "necessary" in the activities and actions with which they are associated (attention presupposes neglect; the plan of action presupposes exclusion; postulation presupposes and risks doubt), and have argued that possibility in the sense of the *possible experience* belonging to others is a condition for individuation and individuality, for the development of a fully operational "will." I have shown how possibility is to be found in all three temporal regions, past (as negation), present (from selection to exclusion), and future (from anticipation to plan of action). But now it is crucial to recognize that, for Royce, this priority of possibility to necessity, cannot safely be raised to a higher level of generalization without asserting its irreducible connection to intentional perspective, or the intentional stance as a principle of continuity, which is what "actuality" means in metaphysics. The principle (and it is a hypothesis, not a bit of ontological knowledge) is that every experience we can treat as "possible" from a *finite* perspective must be actual from *some* perspective. When the other perspective from which a possible experience that is not my own is treated as the actual perspective of another finite experiencer, we have no serious problem about the relation of possible and actual. My merely possible experience as I consider your viewpoint, is, presumably, your actual experience, and these "possibilities," past, present, or future, are grounded in something actual. The fact that I may be mistaken doesn't change the fact that, with correction, what is merely possible experience to me is actual experience to you or someone else.

The problem arises when we consider genuine possibilities for experience that do not, apparently, belong to *any* finite experiencer. To treat such possibilities as real, we must ground them in the intentional perspective of *some* experiencer, which is to say, even the most abstract possibilities have *some* actual existence. To sever possibilities from all actual perspective is to deny the intentional stance, and that opens the door to vicious abstractions, or "bare possibilities" in Royce's vocabulary, which leads us to assert metaphysical concepts that are not grounded in experience. The only option Royce can see is to hypothesize a being whose experience encompasses the shared or common temporal system we call "nature." Given that no *finite* experiencer possesses, actually, all of the phenomenal world, we must ground all genuine experiential possibilities in some actual perspective, and this is what he variously calls the Absolute or the World Will, or any of a number of other names, but all of these designations come down to "the perspective from which all genuine possibilities are actual." That perspective is both temporal and eternal for Royce, in different senses.

Yet, here we meet with the central problem that challenges all viable temporalist philosophies. All temporalists are experientialists of some sort, and all begin with the "act." All experiential temporalists construe the act as, in the immediate instance, the free act of the finite experiencer, rejecting mechanistic and deterministic and substance metaphysics. The commitment to some degree of freedom in the finite act places possibility at the center of concern, for to act with some degree of freedom is to possess a perspective from which possible acts *not followed* still have some genuine existence. But what is the mode of existence of the possibility not chosen? No temporalist philosopher is willing to grant complete independence of possibility from actuality, and Royce is no exception.

But different temporalist philosophers handle the problem of the unchosen possibilities in different ways. In the case of Heidegger, for example, we find the difficult problem of the relation of beings to Being. In Peirce, while he is willing to grant to possibility a degree independence when it is considered mathematically (he calls mathematics the science of possibility, and says that when a mathematician is considering possibilities, *qua* mathematician, he cares not a straw for existences), he is unwilling to allow that the actual is cancelled thereby; the mathematician is still an actual, finite thinker who has chosen not to consider possibilities in light of their actuality. And he separates mathematics from logic precisely because the norms that govern the consideration of mathematical possibilities are really a subset of broader norms that cannot be ignored. For Whitehead, his Ontological Principle, that the actual world is always the actual world of one actual entity, insures that bare or mere possibilities will not be considered in independence of some perspective on them. Similar points can be made regarding other temporalist philosophies.

What remains, then, unresolved is the question of the "absolute relation" (for lack of a better term) between actuality and possibility. In substance metaphysics, actuality was always given primacy, whatever was actual was wholly necessary, could not be otherwise and could not fail to be, and finite perspective was understood as a deficiency of full actuality. Since what was fully actual could not be otherwise, and hence necessity was given priority over possibility. This rendered freedom metaphysically problematic, and also reduced possibility to potency, at least insofar as possibility was understood as having any role in the temporal world (viz., the world of appearances, the world of experiences that at least *seem like* they might be otherwise than they are).

And yet, early on, logical *possibility* was recognized as having a certain scope that seemed to rival that of logical *necessity*. As it came to be increasingly recognized that logic was normative, a study not of how we *do* think, but of how we *ought to* think, it became increasingly difficult to deny to logical possibilities a primary role in experience. Phenomenological considerations of the act, especially the activity of being conscious (but really the intentional stance in any form), began to reveal perspective, valuation, and the presence of possibility as a constitutive aspect of every finite experience, and necessity began to look less and less primary, or more and more derivative. Necessity came gradually to be recognized as a great distorter of philosophical understanding, by the time Peirce lived. Yet, this development (from eternalist to temporalist philosophies) did not displace the primacy of the act, at least in experience. And the act came to be understood as the intentional act, first and foremost. Not only those we call phenomenologists, but all pragmatists, all process philosophers, most personalists, and many idealists, adopted the finite act as the grounding and basis for philosophical activity.

Royce was all of these: phenomenologist, pragmatist, process philosopher, and personalist. He was unwilling to sunder possibility from actuality, or to subordinate the possible wholly to the actual, and he knew he had defined actuality in terms of the finite act. This was his commitment to the primacy of particular experience. This starting point precludes, or seems to, any serious consideration, in metaphysics, of the absolute relation of actuality and possibility, except under a hypothetical mode. In some sense, what a philosopher must consider in confronting the question is whether possibility itself "existed" before *anything* was actual, or whether all the possibilities that exist for (his or her purposes) are rooted in some prior actuality. Obviously, if possibility is conceived as ontologically prior, it is difficult to imagine how anything ever became actual. If actuality is conceived as wholly prior, it is hard to see how possibility is anything other than potentiality for that fundamental actuality (whether it be God or some impersonal will, or Being).

Unsurprisingly, temporalist philosophers came increasingly to emphasize "creativity" in response to this problem. Creativity seems to preserve the ideas of freedom, act, and possibility, all in one very powerful idea. Royce did not follow this route, although Peirce, James, Dewey, Whitehead, and many others did. I have discussed earlier how Royce handles the issue of novelty, that what is new for me (or any finite experiencer) is new in every sense we can seriously consider in philosophical reflection. It would make for an interesting study to explore why, among process philosophers, some (such as Royce, Borden Parker Bowne, and Robert C. Neville, for instance) take a route leading away from the philosophy of creativity.

Royce decided to hedge his bets by keeping metaphysics hypothetical, and then asserted that actuality is prior to possibility. In his view, anything possible from any finite perspective must be actual from *some other* perspective, whether finite or infinite. This view comes out most clearly when Royce is considering world time, or commonly shared time, or time that characterizes the system of nature, making possible such communicative expressions of time as we find in calendars and clocks. Imagining not a mechanical clock, but a living, developing process of duration in nature which can be mechanically represented by clocks, Royce says:

> Suppose that the clock as it is in the hypothetical consciousness endures for a considerable time, and is called the real clock. Then when I shut my eyes or go away or die, there exists still in the real clock, i.e., the clock in the hypothetical consciousness. Though all my fellows die, there is still the real

clock, independent of our consciousness. The clock may for a time go on running; that is, in the hypothetical consciousness there may be a rhythm of sensible events, corresponding to what, for me, *were I present, would be* the rhythm of the pendulum-beats and the movement of the hands.[23]

I stress the subjunctive as well as the hypothetical here. The hypothetical voice is the indicator that we are doing fictional ontology, but the subjunctive mood indicates that we are addressing ourselves to the relation of time and possibility, or "possible time," not actual time as finitely experienced. Royce continues:

> Now suppose this hypothetical consciousness extended, so that it contains facts corresponding to my ideas of the ether-vibrations that fall upon or that are reflected from the face of this clock [we would now say "photons," of course]. Suppose that it further contains facts corresponding to each of my ideas of the relative position of this clock and of other objects. Suppose at last that this hypothetical consciousness is extended to all the facts of what I call my universe of actual and of possible sensation. Suppose that each possible or actual experience of each moment in my life or in the life of any other animal is represented by some actual momentarily present fact in the hypothetical consciousness. Then consider the hypothetical consciousness at any moment, and see what it will contain. Every material atom, every wave of ether, every point of space, every configuration of material bodies, every possible geometrical relation, will be represented in the hypothetical consciousness by some definite fact.[24]

We see that Royce has committed himself, hypothetically, to the view that everything genuinely possible is from some viewpoint actual, or a definite fact. The telling part of the list is the inclusion of "every possible geometrical relation," for it is that inclusion (and Royce never departs from this) that indicates his unwillingness to entertain any serious degree of ontological independence for even mathematical possibilities. With Peirce, Royce rejects the independence of logical possibility outright. Logic is normative for Royce, an activity of finite consciousness, so far as we know. Thus, we arrive at the hypothetical status of continuity in Royce's philosophy, and not just his dialectical thought, but his full-fledged metaphysics. It is that actuality is to be construed as continuous, and the presence of possibility is the mark of finitude and the basis of discontinuity and individuality. Wherever, for Royce, we encounter genuine possibility, we have finitude and discreteness, the difference between my actuality and yours just *is* possibility, as experienced. Royce continues, now becoming more explicit about "relation":

> The relations of these facts will be in nature and in complexity similar to the relations among the facts of my actual and possible sensations. On the other hand, the limits of my possible consciousness at any moment will be determined by the actual consciousness of this supposed universal Knowing One. What it actually knows, I conceivably might now know. If it is conscious of a certain series of facts, then I might be conscious, were I now on the other side of the moon, of living creatures there. If the hypothetical consciousness contains another set of facts, then I might be unable to find such living beings were I there. And so with all facts of possible experience.[25]

What is crucial for our purposes is not whether Royce is right or wrong about this proposed solution. We need to recognize what his options are, given temporalism, given the problematic relation between finite actual experience and genuine possibility, and given the limitations of philosophical knowledge (that it ought to move hypothetically).

To allow that there are possibilities that are not the possibilities of-and-for some consciousness is the denial of the intentional stance, or so Royce thinks. He cannot see how to frame an experientialist philosophy that starts from the ontological irreducibility of possibility, but he also cannot see how having an analysis of the primacy of the finite act entitles him to assert a fully actual God, for even God has a "will," for Royce, i.e., is a personal being with purposes. It would seem that the above implies (and indeed Royce says so elsewhere) that the experience of the hypothesized Knowing One will be similar in nature and complexity to my own experience of the actual and possible (the continuity of methodological generalization for which I have been arguing, should also be noted here, for this is a fine example of that method). This "similarity" in nature and complexity implies an experiencing God, a temporal God. But Royce does not want to allow that his God's experience of the possible is really the "possible" in just the same sense as our finite experience of the possible. God's experience is fully actual—perhaps the divine experience of possibility is of the actuality of these possibilities *qua* possible (if we assume, as Royce does, that whatever exists is actual in some sense, so that even possibilities are in some sense actual). Yet, Royce's God is also an Individual, and that implies exclusion, uniqueness, and the rest. It would seem that Royce's God does need to experience possibility and negation in close to the same sense that we experience them. If so, then it simply does not follow that Royce's God must be wholly actual, which is another way of asserting theistic finitism. Royce's God *can* be frustrated in achieving "his" purposes, can suffer, can need, can lack, and can *create* in response. In what sense is such a God wholly actual?

When speaking in the theological mode, Royce seems fairly content with theistic finitism. But when he moves to metaphysics of the universal kind, he subordinates possibility to actuality and discontinuity to continuity, hypothetically (which, it should be recalled, is a mode of possibility, so under the auspices of the possible in the broadest sense, actuality is *conceived as* primary). Naturally, this problem was addressed differently by later temporalists, and differently by some philosophers in Royce's own proximity, such as Peirce, James, and Bowne (see the next chapter). I see this tension in Royce's metaphysics most clearly in the chapter on "The Temporal and the Eternal," and I regard it as a genuine tension in Royce's thought. I think Royce should have allowed that, although experientialist philosophies will have to maintain the intentional stance, and although possibility can never be dissociated from the finite act without introducing vicious abstractions, nevertheless, we may maintain that possibilities exist, for us and for God, that really are not actual in *any* experience. It is enough for a possibility to have a mode of existence that it *should have been* a *possibility* for *some* finite being, including God, at *some* point in the past, present or future, and that this, combined with whatever is actual, is what we mean by "reality."

Whether this *definition* of the possible exhausts the *whole* of possibility itself, we do not know. No matter how we define possibility, some possibilities may really exist that do not conform to any current account of it we can give. We also cannot claim that there *are no* possibilities that have never been possibilities for *some* finite being. Perhaps some such possibilities would have no meaning *for us*, but there is no evidence upon which to rule them out of existence or to decide in advance what forms of experience and action are possible for beings with which we have no current acquaintance. We also cannot claim that there is *no being* for whom all possibilities are experienced as actualities. We have no idea. Such claims as these require that we presume our omniscience, at least in form or in principle, and that presumption is never wise or justified. What we *do* know is that such beings and such possibilities are beyond the reach of responsible philosophy, philosophy that takes experience as its starting point, and hence, such beings would be beyond the reach of temporalism as it conditions human experience. It is also fair to say that we do not safely *call* a hypothesized infinite being "God," or those possibilities that are not the possibilities of any finite (temporal) beings "possible." To use the words "God" and "possible" in this way is to risk using them equivocally or in no determinate sense at all, which is irresponsible in metaphysics.

Yet, if I am correct in seeing a tension in Royce between the fully actual God for whom all my possibilities (and everyone else's) are actual and the finitude of God implied by intention, will, individuality, interpretation, and purpose, then, in a sense, we have to choose, for the sake of having an adequate philosophical conception, between that fully actual God and the finite God who wills, who loves, who has a purpose. We will never "know" one way or the other which idea, if either, is true of the universe. The question is: which is the better hypothesis? Which is the clearest conception? I think that, throughout his corpus, Royce divides his time about equally between defenses of the fully actual Absolute, and the finite, experiencing God. I think that readers who have sympathy for his profound articulations of theistic finitism, especially in *The Sources of Religious Insight* and *The Problem of Christianity*, have naturally wanted to distance themselves from the Absolute as an actual infinite, and to read Royce as having outgrown the idea. Royce did not outgrow the idea. He defended not only the Absolute to the very end, but also the idea that possibilities for finite actual experiencers are actual experiences from the standpoint of the whole. The second idea (so popular with so many readers) is not philosophically separable from the first. If you have bought in to the idea of the "beloved community" in Royce you already took the Absolute home with you too, in the relevant sense.

But after all, when brought explicitly into the context of the Fourth Conception of Being, we are here attempting to understand the words "related to" and the word "whole," and to do so in such a way as to maintain the modality of uniqueness. We might ask, so if God is the Absolute, how is God "uniquely" related to the whole, since God *is* the Whole? It seems like sophistry to answer "God is uniquely self-related." But that is not sophistry, in any obvious sense; on the contrary, that is trinitarian metaphysics. If sophistical, it has been widely accepted as the contrary of that. Perhaps God may be simultaneously the whole and a unique individual, just as a set may have itself as a member. This issue arises when we consider the negative formulation, whether God or the Absolute is also a member of the set of finite things, or more clearly, if the set of all finite things is an infinite set (and Royce's view seems to imply this), then is the set a member of itself (as he seems to want God to be, both the set of all sets, and a member of all possible sets). The paradox is well known, and we will examine Royce's solution directly. If we have clarified the possible and the actual, a word about Royce's view of the reality of relations is needed before we begin to draw out the living consequences of his temporalism.

Relation

Clearly we have shown that continuity is the methodologically dominant relation, and especially the continuity of inner experience with the social and natural worlds, but also continuity of generalization. That supposition of continuity is grounded in Royce's insistence that individually experienced time is continuous with, and indeed a *product* of social time, since time is the form of the will and will is derivative of social reality, which must be regarded as real if anything is. The idea that nature forms an extended social system is also shown by its temporal continuity in the combining of "my time," with "your time," with "her time," with "his time," and all other possible times, and recognizing that implied in all of these, when combined, is a common time that is *more than* the combination of all finite perspectives. Thus, continuity for Royce is, at its root, *temporal* continuity. The continuity of generalization adopted in philosophical thinking, as a norm, is an application of the existence of temporal continuity to the experience of thinking.[26]

The principles of discontinuity associated with perspective, and then attention up through full blown individuality, and the modes of limitation, negation, and necessity show us possibility *as distinct from* actuality, but are also temporal; yet, the over-riding assumption, or hypothesis, is that discontinuities are differentiations within wider continuities. This apparently is not full-fledged pluralism, then; it seems rather like a modified pluralism, with discreteness and individuality made as strong as they can be without the sacrifice of unity (and continuity). But that is just an appearance. The pluralism is modified, but not attenuated or half-hearted. Continuity is not the same as unity. Plural continuity is easily conceived. Unity is simply one way of expressing the whole as the logical implication of continuity, but not the only way of expressing the whole. The issue of pluralism here hinges on whether there can be more than one account of the Whole and whether inconsistent accounts shall be allowed. For Royce, such inconsistent accounts of the whole are allowed, but in philosophical reflection they constitute a weakness and a task to be confronted. Even James can do no better without abandoning the idea that philosophical reflection ought to be done well, to the extent that it can be managed. Radical pluralism does not sanction intellectual anarchy.

Thus, if we are to understand why continuity is apparently the favored mode of relation, we need to understand what *relation* is, for Royce. Any astute reader can discern that Royce has *apparently* favored internal relations over external relations. He is, after all, an idealist. Yet, as the story goes, if he allows that internal relations are more "real" than external relations, it will be clear why Howison's critique, that Royce has sacrificed the individual to the Absolute, holds. It will be asserted that there must be true externality and an external mode of relatedness equiprimordial with internal relatedness that holds, for otherwise, the individuals that are "uniquely related to the whole" become emanations of the One, or nodes of the One, or Loci, or expressions, or as Spinoza said, "modes."

But this is the wrong story, entirely. It is simply incorrect to say that Royce has favored internal relations over external relations. The fact is that he has in every case favored *triadic* relations over dyadic relations, such as "internal vs. external." The dialectical necessity associated with comparing concepts, rejecting some possibilities and retaining others, is not accomplished by the rigid application of excluded middle or non-contradiction, or any other dyadic (i.e., subject-predicate) logical law. The process of thinking things through is moved forward by obtaining a third standpoint from which the internalities and externalities of any two objects or terms are grasped from a distance. Royce employed the triadic theory of relations in his earliest published writings, and there is no reason to think he ever seriously entertained another view. Whether he settled on the triadic theory as a result of early readings of Peirce is less clear—even though it is clear that he had read the "New List of Categories" of 1867 no later than 1880 (probably earlier, in 1877), but he might have just as easily gleaned his own version of the triadic theory from Hegel's *Logic* as from Peirce. The source is less important than the recognition that this is a constant feature of Royce's thought. It goes with his temporalism, since any temporalist philosopher is constantly balancing not two but three aspects of time, past, present, and future. None of these aspects can be made sense of without both of the others, and as a result, the fundamental structure of relation for temporalists is triadic.

Another common misperception is that Royce only truly recognized after 1912 that the third term relevant to interpreting and two terms is "mind." This is incorrect. However we might understand Royce's self-described Peircean insight, he had been using "mind," or more specifically, the intentional stance, for the third in his theory of relations since 1885, as I showed in the last chapter. A very clear example is in *The World and the Individual*, Second Series, in the chapter entitled "The Linkage of Facts." Attending to any two objects so as to sort their differences and likenesses is a process that implies a relation *between* them, he explains, and "in order to estimate more carefully the meaning and universality of such processes, we next need a *generalization of the relation expressed by the word between*."[27] As tempting as it is to rehearse

Royce's entire solution to the problem of the "between," I will restrict myself to a brief summary, but note that the difference between geometrical relations and logical relations is the key to the argument, that geometrical points have certain set-theoretical functions.[28] When logic, which is normative, is brought to bear on the issue of the existence of some third point being "between" any two points, the result is a re-assertion of the intentional standpoint. Royce says:

> Generalizing . . . one may go quite beyond . . . [these] instances of the classes and points and say, Let there be any system or collection of objects, such that, if they are really different, these objects can be discriminated by an attention once properly directed. Let it be also possible for a given intelligence *not* to discriminate two objects belonging to that collection. Or again, let it also be possible for this intelligence, although discriminating them, still to regard two of them at will as "equivalent," that is, such that their difference does not count for a given purpose. Then let an object m of the system in question be so related to a and to b that *if* you, either by inattention, neglect, or deliberate choice, disregard their difference, so that in any way they blend or become equivalent, m thereupon of necessity blends with both. In this case we shall say that, in the generalized sense, m is such a member of the system in question as to lie *between a* and *b*.[29]

In this case, m might be treated either as an object or a relation, but the point is that if you want to know a relation, you must attend to it, discriminate it; failure to notice it does not imply its unreality, and neither does deliberately ignoring it. If no act of attention from any intelligence suffices to find some m between a and b, we could then say that a is b, but from the standpoint of finite intelligence, such statements are hypothetical at best. To return to our paradox above, the issue of God's self-relatedness becomes, *for philosophy*, triadic, which is to say that if there is a self and a relation, there must already be a third. Whether that third is the world-that-is-not-God, or the individuals in that world, is not here the point. The point is that some discriminating intelligence must seek a standpoint from which to discriminate the Divine Self (call it a) and whatever it is to be distinguished from (call it b) and that some m is the relation the two bear to one another. The relation m is the *result* of the act of discriminating, and not separable from that act. The intelligence that so discriminates could be in error, but the triadic form would hold whether the specific instance was or was not an error. Perhaps God is One in the most self-identical, totally actual way, but such a God would not be available as an object of thought for finite intelligence (e.g., there would be no "experience" of such a God). Such a God would have a most paradoxical relation to time, and the consideration of the temporality of such a God would lead to a choice between the unreality or time or the unreality of God. But that is a false dilemma, generated by the application of a dyadic logic to the terms of time and God, and ignoring the role of the finite intelligence that is attempting to grasp the relation.

Royce continues by pointing out that "the advantage of this formal generalization" in which we can make m disappear or appear depending on our acts of attention,

> . . . is the power that it here gives us of facing an important logical aspect of all discrimination, comparison, and differentiation. . . . The generalization . . . will show us that contrast and comparison involve, in general, a relation of at least *three* objects, viz. a and b, and something else that *helps us to keep them apart*. . . . In other words, it is what one may technically name a *triadic* relation. The possibility of observing this relation is due to the fact that, since our discriminating attention is a voluntary act, possessed of its own internal meaning, we are able to see, by reflection, how one discrimination follows from another.[30]

At this point it should be very clear how the generalization from attention up through the most universal features of logical relation has been undertaken by way of continuity. The intentional stance, that attention, will, and intelligence or mind, is operative at every stage is the source of the continuity. But the source of continuity is also the source of discreteness and discontinuity—the act of attention is voluntary, and possessed of its own inner meaning, i.e., it is a distinct perspective, nay, under more developed conditions, a *unique relation* to the whole. The relations are generalizable, under the condition of negating, i.e., choosing to ignore certain differences and similarities, to exclude differences, to say that they do not count *for some purpose*. That is, the intelligence that considers relations logically is responsible for both the continuities and the discontinuities in the generalizations, and must justify them in accordance with some purpose—e.g., some valued plan of action.

Here we come round full circle, recognizing that to have a valued plan is to acknowledge a past and a present and to anticipate a future, all of which are regarded as real, i.e., a relation of what is actual to what is possible, related by the actuality of will in the *form* of time. In short, time is the possibility of relation, but now we see that the relevant relations are always intentional relations, and all possibilities are possibilities for some intentional being, and all such beings are temporal beings. It does not seem to me that Royce's understanding of generalization, discontinuity and continuity, triadic relation, and temporal reality has been presented in Royce scholarship in such a way as to silence the din of Jamesian and Deweyan voices calling Royce a monist. To be as committed as Royce was to triadic relations and still supposedly a monist seems more than unlikely.

Personality

There are purposes for which we treat persons the same and purposes for which we attend to their differences. *Philosophical* purposes are a subset of practical and ethical purposes, and are guided by various logical norms at various levels of generalization. If, for example, we attend to the *concept* of God as an over-arching fully actual unified being, and in this sense "eternal" or "time-inclusive," we do so voluntarily (i.e., it is an act of will), and we come to this way of thinking by ignoring differences, pluralities, and choices among our own possibilities for so conceiving the Divine. We do the same thing when we attend to the *hypothetical unity* of any finite individual, for we may *feel* certain that there *is* a unified will before us, in the presence of another person, or that any other given object is adequately individual for us to form at least a plan of action relative to it. It does not follow that any object or any person just *is* such a unity. For other purposes, both philosophical and practical, we may attend to differences and relations, voluntarily take them into account. When we conceive of the Divine as temporal, as possessing a will, as an intentional being, we attend to these differences, these discontinuities, this plurality for other purposes.[31]

The issue we confront here, then, for the first time, is the fundamental character of *purposes*, their formation and their meaning. I can say in advance of the analysis that, because, for Royce, ethics is first philosophy, purposes are more basic to its proper practice than are the results of the most abstract metaphysical speculations. When we act on a purpose we have formed, and our purpose is to possess a metaphysical description of some kind—say, a description of the world, or God, or the self—we do adopt logical norms so as to have a *good* description, but the description serves the broader purpose of having a good philosophy, and a good philosophy is a philosophy that well serves the moral lives of finite intelligent, individual persons, adding wisdom, understanding, patience, forbearance, and resolution, to the other purposes upon which we act. Human beings philosophize for the same reasons that they write poetry, study nature, create societies and governments, dance, sing, and do anything else beyond what is required for physical survival. Whitehead said it well, in asserting that the function of reason is to live, to live well, and to live better. Philosophy, as the highest expression of human reason (and it *is* that), serves the one sacrament of living, which is expression.

Because the sub-region of philosophical activity called metaphysics is subordinate to the ethical whole of philosophy, the descriptions metaphysics produces that focus upon such concerns as unity, full actuality, the eternal, the Absolute, and bare possibility are less important than the descriptions that focus upon plurality, difference, and temporality. The inversion of these priorities in substance metaphysics, effectively subordinating ethics to metaphysics, has been the corruption of philosophy itself. The re-instatement of the priority of the ethical, and the subordination of logic and metaphysics to the wider aims, is the needed correction. This is what Royce, and all temporalists, have done. Unsurprisingly, when metaphysics and logic were restricted to their proper roles in philosophy, certain basic ethical notions, such as the idea of personality, began to resurface, historically. Not all temporalists became personalists, which is to say that not all temporalist philosophers were willing to take personality as an irreducible aspect of philosophical description. But Royce was one who did so take it. We will examine the historical context more thoroughly in chapter seven, but for now, I will bring Royce's personalism into relation with his temporalism because for, him, the Fourth Conception of Being implies personalism.

It is worth remarking, however, that Royce's development of temporalist ideas contains most of the seeds of both the later non-personalist and personalist developments in temporalist philosophies. On the non-personalist side, we see, for example, in Royce's willingness to treat canyons and rivers and trees as experiencers, an anticipation of the Whiteheadian non-personalist strain of temporalist philosophy. The non-personalists are not impersonalists, by any means, but rather they tend to restrict the idea of "person" to a characteristic feature of the higher phases of experience, and to read "experience" itself in terms of "feeling" or *aesthesis*. Such philosophers usually see moral value as a further development of aesthetic or feeling value. Following Royce's phenomenological descriptions all the way up through his philosophy of nature, he could be read in this way, and his "world of appreciation" could be seen as the domain of aesthetic valuation, broadly understood. This approach makes Royce seem a lot like Whitehead.

This is not, however, the right way to read Royce. There is little question, indeed, there is no question at all, that for Royce moral value is *philosophically* prior to aesthetic value, even if feeling might be conceived as being experienced before there is a purposing social will with its judgments—as indeed Peirce conceives it. Yet, for Royce, it is for the sake of such a will that feeling has any cumulative or temporal value. Peirce's (and Whitehead's) emphasis on the primacy of feeling has the advantage of asserting the intentional stance as broadly as Royce has done, but the disadvantage of employing a mere concept (i.e., the concept of feeling) to serve as a conduit for all immediacy. This occludes subsequent philosophical thinking, since fundamental and irreducible modes of relation that are independent of feeling may be part of immediacy. To postulate a concept of feeling as the basis of all intention is to court a case of misplaced concreteness.

In the order of human experience, feeling apparently comes first, but in the order of action (including thinking), moral purpose is the condition of meaning. Far from being built out of feelings, moral purposes can be contrary to all human feeling. Among temporalist philosophers, this is the view commonly held by the personalists.[32] They draw the result that the personal mode of existence (and the intentional stance) is presupposed in all philosophizing, and therefore an irreducible element in philosophy itself, however hypothetical and fallible it may be. The non-personalists, including for example Dewey and Whitehead, tend to think of "experience" as involving pre-personal acts of valuation, and that the philosophical consideration of these acts is best carried out with the "personal" or higher phases of the development of consciousness, as one of the contingent outcomes of the process of experiencing. In a sense, Royce joins with both camps, being willing to consider both aesthetic or feeling value and natural processes as "experience" that is proto-personal. But his subordination of metaphysics, aesthetics, philosophy of nature, and logic to ethics, and his elevation of personality to the highest ethical value, is what marks him as a personalist. He is a naturalist or aestheticist only within specialized inquiries, but is an ethicist in his approach to all actual and possible philosophy, since he recognizes the norms of philosophizing as a sub-species of practical norms for all living.

A curiosity in the history of Royce interpretation is that for some reason many of his interpreters after 1950 did not emphasize, or apparently even notice his personalism (see my Introduction for a suggested reason). This curiosity may be associated with the general decline of idealism in the academy, both in the United States and eslewhere, and with the (accurate) association of personalism with idealism. It stands to reason that if one wishes to offer up a thinker such as Royce as having something important to say in the context hostile to all idealism, establishing a distance between his ideas and his idealism was a sensible goal, for that time (1950–1980). But by the time another generation of Royce interpreters came of age (such as McDermott, Clendenning, Kegley, and Oppenheim), the new group was not simply creating a distance between Royce and the personalist tradition, but was in fact largely *unaware* of the personalist tradition. As a result, there was a tendency to overlook the rather obvious importance of the concept of "person" in Royce's philosophy. This is quite understandable, but it has been a continuing obstacle to the proper understanding of Royce, one which I am attempting to correct here.

On the other side of the scholarship, personalists themselves (few in number but contributing enough in scholarly output), have always recognized that Royce was a personalist, but have been deeply suspicious of his defense of the Absolute. Personalists oppose Absolute idealism about as vigorously as they opposed mechanistic and materialist philosophies, since the most representative versions of Absolute idealism belong to impersonalist philosophers, especially Hegel and Bradley. In short, personalists have taken Howison's critique of Royce to be well placed and decisive, and personalists were largely unsatisfied with Royce's heroic effort to defend individuality in the face of such a critique. Howison was, after all, among the most important founders of American personalism. Royce's own two-step with Bradley, in the "Supplementary Essay" to the First Series of *The World and the Individual* (and Bradley is the most offensive impersonalist of all the Absolute idealists) seemed only to confirm these suspicions, although some personalists express greater sympathy for Royce's final works, and are motivated to read them as though the combined efforts of Howison, James, and others finally led Royce to abandon his Absolutism. This is incorrect, but what has been missing from the personalists' understanding of Royce is what I have attempted to provide in the last two chapters—in short, that Royce's account of individuality and time really does support a kind of idealism which, if not quite acceptable to all personalists, does not fall far short of their standard temporalist, pluralist fare.

With the availability now of Jan Olof Bengtsson's magisterial work in intellectual history *The Worldview of Personalism: Origins and Early Development*, a tremendous gap in our understanding of the relationship between German idealism and American personalism is now filled, and it is possible to see the extent to which a thinker such as Royce is indebted to personalistic strains and themes in the "less objectionable" Absolute idealists, especially Schelling. The American development itself has been well documented by both Albert C. Knudson and (more recently) Rufus Burrow, Jr., and with the welcome addition of

Bengtsson's work, it is now possible to piece together something like the "whole story." Royce fares far better as a personalist for one who has digested this whole account given by Bengtsson. But that history is not our concern here. I will draw on it in the next chapter in more detail.

What is "person" for Royce? He discusses the matter in numerous places, and employs the ideas and results in every part of his philosophy (and indeed, beyond philosophy in his literary criticism, histories, and fiction). I think the clearest statement of his view of "person" is coupled with the defense of his temporalism in the essay we explored at the beginning of this chapter, entitled "Immortality." We begin with the familiar (and now I hope clearer) situation of God, as related to time. Royce says:

> We are simply different modes of willing, continuously related to one another and to the total world will which throbs and strives in all of us alike, but which . . . does not deprive us of individuality. It needs our variety and our freedom. And we need its unity and its inexhaustibility of suggestion.[33]

With this restatement of relation (mutual dependence, mutual immanence), continuity, and individuality in place, Royce indicates that he means "by the term 'God' the totality of the expressions and life of the world will, *when considered in its conscious unity*."[34] Royce is not identifying God with unity, but is rather voluntarily ignoring the differences between the world will and finite wills *for a purpose*, i.e., to get a working concept of unity; in short, he is triangulating a relation for use as a concept, and this one is God as wholly actual and time-inclusive, without possibility and negation. It does not follow that there is no possibility or negation "in God," only that we are not *considering* it here. Royce then continues: "God is immanent in the finite, because nothing is which is not a part of his total self expression. He is transcendent of all finitude, because the totality of finite processes is before him at once, while nothing finite possesses true totality."[35] That sounds like the standard "scary stuff" people don't like in Royce. But Royce immediately then shifts perspectives:

> If one hereupon asks, Why should there be finitude, variety, imperfection, temporal sequence at all? —we can only answer: Not otherwise can true and concrete perfection be expressed than through the overcoming of imperfections. . . . Not otherwise can absolute personality exist than as mediated through the unification of the lives of imperfect and finite personalities. . . .[36]

There are several other "not otherwise" statements in this list, which are negations based on possibilities, but the one Royce then develops is the one concerning the requirements of personal existence, and in this case, the sternest necessity is invoked, the "not otherwise" of impossibility. The employment of this kind of necessity indicates to us that the logic of triadic relatives is governing the metaphysics. And in this case, the point is that for God to be a person, there have to be other persons, indeed, finite and imperfect persons, so we are not here considering the persons of the Trinity. Immanence in finite persons is the source of suffering in God, and the suffering is the source of God's achieved perfection. All moral and religious experience teaches us the truth of this law of suffering, Royce asserts. But having made this point about divine personality, Royce explicitly shifts away from the most abstract metaphysics: "So much, then, for some hint as to how the temporal is, to my mind, related to the eternal."[37] After this remark, he considers, dialectically, and far less abstractly, how we should understand human personality.

> A human personality has many aspects, psychological, physical, social, ethical. But a man is a significant being by virtue not of his body, or his feelings, or his fortunes, or his social status, but by virtue of his will. The concept of personality is an ethical concept. . . . All else about him besides his will, his purpose, his life plan, his ideal, his deed, his volitional expression —all else than this, I say, is mere material for manhood, mere clothing, mere environment, or mere fortune.[38]

It is certainly worth noting that, just as Royce identified the idea of individuality as an ethical idea, he here associates the idea of personality with the same level of discourse, namely, ethics or first philosophy. But we have here also a helpful constellation of associated ideas, especially "purpose" and "ideal." Where personality is lacking, do we conclude that personality does not exist? Royce forbids this:

> . . . if one who appears in the outer form of man shows no sign as yet of having any personal ideal, or life plan, or purpose, *or individual will at all*, then one can only say, "Since here we find a seemingly blind expression of the world will, but not an expression that *as yet* gives an account of itself, *we must indeed suppose that some form of personality is here*, in this *fragment of the time process*, latent, but we simply cannot tell what form." In such a case we indeed call the being whom we know in our human relations a person, but he *so far* appears as a person by courtesy. An explicit personality is one which shows itself through deeds that embody a coherent ideal—an ideal—an ideal which need not be abstractly formulated, but which must be practically active, recognizably significant, consciously in need *of further temporal expression*.[39]

I have emphasized in this passage the terms that mark it as being a temporalized description, and the adoption of the characteristic "what should we say?" and "we can only say this . . ." is a reliable indicator in Royce's writings that he is speaking dialectically, at the level of general philosophical discourse, not abstract metaphysics.[40] This is one of the marks of his method in ethical philosophy. And at this level, his "musts" have the necessity of the practical requirements for significant action (in this case, the action at stake is that of thinking properly about the idea of "person"), not the systematic and complete exclusion of every alternative conceptual formulation.

Much more can be said (and indeed much more will be said) about Royce's personalism, but for now the point has been to show its relation to his temporalism, and we are now in a position to draw the needed conclusion. Even in the most abstract formulation of metaphysics, the world will or God cannot be personal *in any possible* way except through the mediation of finite persons. This is an abstract but necessary conclusion, Royce holds. At the level of ethics or first philosophy, the imperative is both that we must have purposes in order to become persons, and that the absence of these purposes (in short, the absence of communication) cannot be taken to indicate the absence of will, or the personal mode of existing, only of its undeveloped condition, i.e., there are for Royce, in addition to actual persons, also *possible* persons.

It should be pointed out also that although this example is concerned with human personality, for Royce, the human and divine persons are not the only persons, either actual or possible. We will examine the issue of communities as persons in chapter eight, but for now, we have shown temporal personalism for Royce in both the case of the abstract metaphysics and as his general philosophical position (ethical philosophy). We might put a good deal more energy into demonstrating how his personalism and his temporalism imply one another, for I have only shown his personalism as an instance or application of his temporalism. But a deeper consideration of the role of will in Royce's temporalism, and his association here of will with the task of becoming personal, should suffice to indicate to any reader that it is not just that Royce is a personalist "by courtesy," and a voluntarist overall; rather, Royce's voluntarism is part and parcel of his personalism. In the next chapter we shall take up some of the unanswered historical questions associated with Royce's personalism, and we shall discover that the issues of continuity and discontinuity, of temporalism, and of immediate experience, have some surprising implications.

[7]
Personalism

The last two chapters have, I hope, brought us to the point of recognizing the importance of the ideas of will, individuality, and person in Royce's philosophy, and for our present philosophical context. It is necessary here, however, to interrupt the progress of our philosophical story in order to get a better grasp of Royce's context, and to examine more closely the idea of "person" and the personalism that was a prominent feature of that context. I have already done something similar in Chapter 3, with the investigation of Howison's and Hocking's assessments of Royce, and indeed, in Chapter 10 I will present another comparative analysis with J.E. Creighton and the development of the American Philosophical Association. A part of what enables us to appropriate living ideas in our own context is the possession of an adequate understanding of what the ideas meant in their own contexts. In a sense, living ideas are the gifts left to us by prior generations, but their adequate understanding is a gift we give to ourselves. Without this slight detour, we will deprive ourselves of that gift.

Therefore, I will approach this chapter somewhat differently. There is no need here to make the full textual case that Royce was a philosophical personalist, and was so in every relevant and meaningful sense of the term. Dwayne A. Tunstall has done this work as well as anyone could wish in Part I of his book *Yes, but Not Quite: Encountering Josiah Royce's Ethico-Religious Insight.* But something crucial about Royce's personalism remains to be done, which is to fill in an account of the origins of personalism in Royce's thought, mainly with the aim of understanding more thoroughly his concept of person so that we may, in Chapter 8, begin to grasp how "person" is both the product of will, or of intentional life (and not only for human beings), but also how such a conception of person is the ground of "purpose," in Royce's sense of the term. This idea of "purpose" is and remains one of Royce's living ideas, but without a fairly complete grasp of his concept of "person," the idea of purpose would be misunderstood as an overly teleological expression of an abstract idealist metaphysics. It can be understood at that level, but there is no good reason to think of this abstract aspect as either the most important or fruitful or definitive part of Royce's concept of purpose. Thus, we examine "person" with an eye to showing its role in the idea of purpose, for we have now understood something about time, and about will (or at least about Royce's conception of them).

Borden Parker Bowne (1847–1910), who is commonly called the father of American personalism, was in Royce's intellectual proximity, across the Charles River at Boston University, from the time of Royce's arrival at Harvard in 1882 (Bowne had come to Boston University in 1877) until Bowne's death. Royce knew Bowne personally and knew his work, although how closely either studied the other is difficult to say. It is also clear that Bowne's ideas are implicated in the "Battle of the Absolute" between James and Royce. When James substituted for Royce in his famed Metaphysics course in the spring of 1899 (Royce was in Scotland delivering his Gifford Lectures), James chose to teach three books as a way of striking a definitive blow against the philosophies of the Absolute: Bradley's *Appearance and Reality*, Royce's (and Howison's) *The Conception of God*, and Bowne's *The Philosophy of Theism*.[1] Bowne and his ideas were mixed in with Royce's context because Bowne was friends with James, and of course James was Royce's intimate friend. It would seem that there was some personal warmth between Bowne and Royce, but whether they knew each other well is hard to determine. James was most likely the intermediary between Bowne and Royce.

Yet, Royce was aware that there was something worth understanding in the relationship between Bowne's philosophy and his own. When Edgar Sheffield Brightman wrote to Royce in 1913 asking his estimation of (the recently departed) Bowne, Royce responded "I wish somebody would tell me what my precise relation to Bowne is. I suppose that our arguments were rather on the increase towards the end of his work. I always prized him much; but each of us had many irons in the fire. I ought to have come closer to him before he left us."[2]

It is too late to tell Royce personally what his precise relation to Bowne is, but it remains for "somebody" to tell those who study Royce. Interestingly, however, it is not Royce's personalism upon which the story depends, it is James's personalism. The reason that the story must go this way, in my view, is that I think Royce probably learned his "personalism" from Lotze, as Bowne did, but refined it in his interactions with Howison and James. But James and Howison each had in common a close *philosophical* relationship with Bowne (and both knew him well personally also). I have already examined Royce's confrontation with Howison in some detail, and I do not believe it is claiming too much to say that Howison awakened Royce to the threat of impersonalism in his metaphysics and to what appeared to be a pernicious strain of Absolutism. As I have shown, Howison was probably wrong to think that Royce intended to be advocating either impersonalism or the pernicious sort of Absolutism, but he helped Royce realize that a stronger account of individuality and person was needed. Howison did not understand how Royce's method of fictional ontology protected him from these problems, but many others have misunderstood this both during and since Royce's life. James and Howison were also friends, and together with Bowne and Thomas Davidson, they should be regarded also the founders of philosophical pluralism in the United States. The relationships and issues are complex. In this chapter I will devote myself primarily to showing the Bowne-James relation and will draw my conclusions about Royce as the account proceeds.

This undertaking is also desirable because the proponents of James have been, in the last fifty years, parochial regarding Royce—reading him not at all or piecemeal at most, and actually *believing* and parroting what James says about Royce. It is perfectly obvious to anyone with even the slightest bit of initiative that James did not *understand* Royce's philosophy in numerous important ways, which he freely admitted, and that James is thus not to be relied upon as the sole competent critic of its weaknesses. Yet, while all Royce scholars read James thoroughly and closely, James scholars rarely return the courtesy. It is clear that James's followers nearly always lack the temper for wading through systematic thought like Royce's. Royce is difficult, after all, too difficult for James himself. The regrettable result, however, is that, among the many things current James scholars do not know, is the fact that James was a personalist (which does seem forgivable in light of the same failing among Royce scholars, who not only do not know James was a personalist, but commonly do not even know that Royce was). Indeed, the interpreters of James often do not know even know what personalism is.[3] As I will show, personalism turns out to be fairly important in grasping James's philosophy. This leaves James's proponents with a noticeable inability to see what James took himself to be attempting. In describing his philosophy as a whole, James said:

> It means individualism, personalism: that the prototype of reality is the here & now; that there is genuine novelty; that order is being won—incidentally

reaped. that the more universal is the more abstract[;] that the smaller & more intimate is the truer. The man more than the home, the home more than the state, or the church. Anti-slavery. It means tolerance and respect.[4]

I will organize this chapter around two initial questions: one historical, one thematic. The historical question is: "What did James know of the philosophy of personalism?" The thematic question is "where does the idea of the person fit in throughout James's corpus and how does it develop, if at all?" I will address these in turn. A third and *philosophical* question is, "what does radical empiricism, and more specifically, descriptive metaphysics modeled on the idea of pure experience, require us to say about the ontological status of the person?" This third question will serve to rejoin the argument of this chapter with those of previous chapters, addressing the issues of immediate experience, the scope of philosophy, the role of fictional ontology, the roles of will and time, and establishing the basis for the idea of purpose within its course. From this standpoint we can say some plausible things about Royce's personalism that supplement the account given by Tunstall in his book, and what has been indicated at the end of the last chapter.

The Historical Question

Let us begin with a brief survey of personalists in William James's life and reading, and move to a thesis about the extent of James's commitment to philosophical personalism, and the questions that follow from it. The next sections are sketchy and they feel forced, and that is because they are edited to a very specific purpose. To write these sections out in more readable and convincing prose would require many pages, and I will forgo that here for the sake of brevity.

Personalists in James's Philosophical and Biographical Context

First, it is important to be aware that personalism was not *called* "personalism" until around 1903,[5] but James knew a lot of personalists long before that time. I will discuss only three, but I would point out that, importantly, James knew Whitman, DuBois, Renouvier, and Hocking among those I will not discuss.[6]

James was reading the writings of both Borden Parker Bowne and George Holmes Howison from well before the time when he began writing philosophy himself. He rightly regarded them as thinkers who were ahead of him in their understanding of and facility with philosophy, and he did not mind playing the role of "student" to Bowne, and to an extent also to Howison, insofar as he believed Howison had a better command especially of Hegel and other "objectionable" German idealists than he possessed himself. James was not willing to adopt the role of student with Royce, however. But James did regard Royce as having the better intellect—better than almost anyone's, including his own, and excepting perhaps Peirce's—than any of the other philosophers, let alone personalists, he knew. James respected Bowne immensely and they were friends of a formal sort. James knew Howison more personally and their friendship had achieved a greater degree of informality. Let us rehearse some of the philosophically relevant facts regarding these friends, each in his turn. I will spend the most time on Bowne because I find that almost nothing has been written on this relationship. Even the careful Ralph Barton Perry takes only slight note of it, but it turns out to be quite important in understanding James's philosophy, I believe.

BOWNE

James was aware of and looked favorably upon Bowne's work from at least 1878,[7] at which point Bowne had published only one book *The Philosophy of Herbert Spencer*[8] but he had by then published some thirty articles in philosophy. I find subsequent references in James's books and letters to almost all of Bowne's books up through *Personalism* in 1908 (more on this below), and each of the books has at least one reference that indicates not only familiarity with the existence of the book, but with its contents. In the case of over half of these books, there is indication or strong reason to think James read the whole book, and of course, he taught *The Philosophy of Theism* in 1899. He reports a consistent familiarity with Bowne's views from 1878 onward, and uniformly uses and summarizes these views in an *approving* way.

In *Principles of Psychology*,[9] for example, James excerpted a large passage from the first edition of Bowne's *Metaphysics*,[10] and the use of it is favorable. James corresponded familiarly with Bowne, asking for books from him at times, expressing admiration for each as he read them. James reported at least one dinner with Bowne in 1888,[11] and there were probably other occasions for dinner, given the formal but familiar tone of the existing letters, which cover only the years 1895–1909 (there were certainly more letters, but they have not emerged). For those who know Bowne's life, it is easy to imagine a genuinely warm, if formal, friendship because apparently Bowne was never informal with *anyone*, even his wife (who called him "Mr. Bowne")—the very picture of an upright Victorian gentleman. There was a time when James tried to get Bowne a visiting appointment to do a course at Harvard in 1895, although the plan fell through.[12] Bowne and James corresponded regarding James's interpretation of Bowne in *Varieties of Religious Experience*,[13] and James wrote a fairly intimate note of moral support when Bowne was being tried for heresy by the Methodist Church.[14] They died the same year and corresponded until close to the end, but Bowne died first and James sent a letter of sympathy to Mrs. Bowne which, while it is typical of James's tone in such letters, is still revealing of their relationship. This is the letter in full:

Lamb House, Rye, Sussex. April 14, 1910

Dear Mrs. Bowne,

The news of your husband's sudden removal from this life, which has only just reached me, has been a great shock to me, and I cannot help sending you some expression of my sorrow and sympathy. Would that I might go myself as suddenly! But he went before his time—for his very best work in my opinion was his latest work—and high as his place was in American philosophy, it would probably have been higher still, had he been spared to do more writing in the future. He had a sarcastic pen which made strangers think him scornful, but when one knew him well, one saw how much of it was humorous good nature. He was brief, clear and pithy in an extraordinary degree, and less and less technical as he grew older, which in my eyes is a mighty merit. I have always regretted that our Harvard philosophical department saw so little of him. We see indeed but little of one another, and my very bad health in the past years kept me very unenterprising socially. I wanted a month ago, to come and dine on lunch with Prof. Boutroux, the French philosopher, who, with his wife, was staying with us while lecturing, but B. was in such a bad state of fatigue at the time that I didn't dare to increase his complications. I shall never cease to regret this failure to act, on my part; nor cease to deplore the absence from our philosophical arena, of the valiant fighter for truth now taken from your side.

Pray, dear Mrs. Bowne, do not think any reply to these words necessary. They are only the voluntary expressions of my sympathy—and my wife's too—in your sorrow. We are stopping with my brother Henry for a while on our way to Nauheim for a part of the summer. Believe me, with sympathy and sorrow,

Very sincerely yours,

Wm James[15]

James was one of the greatest letter-writers of his generation, if not one of the best in history. A part of what made his letters so endearing to those who received them (and they were countless), was the tone of intimacy he adopted, out of keeping with the Gilded Age. James used familiarity to flatter people, and also wrote in keen awareness that his letters would be saved and probably published. Thus, it is easy to over-emphasize the level of intimacy he may have actually shared with his recipients. James had thousands of friends and at least feigned intimacy with most. But in this case there is a little something more. Mrs. Bowne has just lost her life partner. James refers to that event as his "removal from this life" and actually expresses *envy* at the suddenness *to Mrs. Bowne*. James could be insensitive, but there is wry humor in this expression of sympathy. The most likely explanation of the tone is that James and Mrs. Bowne know one another well enough that there is no need for James to follow the customs surrounding such notes of condolence, because each shares the conviction that death is not the end of personal existence, and that Bowne remains with them. In the circumstances, this is either a very odd letter (and James wrote some odd ones), or it indicates a shared context of understanding, unstated, that enables James to approach someone who is grieving with a dash of humor.

How many personal meetings James and Bowne may have had over the years cannot be guessed, but James reports that Bowne and Howison were both members of "a little philosophical club that used to meet every fortnight at [Thomas Davidson's] rooms in Temple Street in Boston."[16] This gathering was something of a successor to The Metaphysical Club; it would seem. James went regularly, and evidently came to know Bowne and his views well. Their correspondence has the familiarity of persons who do not need to stand on ceremony and who can speak in a kind of shorthand to each other. James and Bowne shared a deep admiration for the philosophy of Lotze and both reported his pluralism and empirical turn as constant influences in their thinking. Like Royce, Bowne was student of Lotze. In 1908 Bowne published *Personalism* and James read it. James's remarks about the book will be taken up later, thematically.

Howison

James had known Howison from the days when the latter taught at MIT, through the 1870s, and was familiar with his philosophical views from the time well predating his own appointment as a professor of philosophy in 1880. In 1879 Howison wrote a review of one of the elder Henry James's books that led to a public exchange between Howison and the elder James over whether the book did or did not lead towards idealism —an exchange that embarrassed Howison for a long time afterwards.[17]

Indeed, James later had to make the difficult decision whether to back Howison or Royce for a faculty position at Harvard in 1882, to replace himself for a leave, and (due in great part to James's support) Royce was chosen for the interim position that later led to a regular appointment at Harvard, while Howison was banished to the (then) backwater of Northern California for the rest of his career. James's estimate of Royce as the more original and promising mind, proved, of course, to be entirely correct. Howison remained a presence in James's universe until James's death (Howison, although older, died later, in 1916). However, we will not look in detail at their philosophical relationship here, partly because James placed Howison in a "Hegelian box" early on in their relationship, and never really woke up to anything the two really had in common philosophically, apart from one important area of agreement.

This most important thing they held in common was not in their views of "person," since Howison's views would have been far more dependent upon a kind of moral logicism than James could have tolerated (essentially the same qualms James had about the rationalism of Renouvier's later thought). Rather, the thing James and Howison shared was a commitment to metaphysical pluralism, and indeed, it would be interesting at some point to explore the extent to which Howison's (and Renouvier's) continual lobbying for pluralism might have influenced James's thought. James tended to think of both Howison and Renouvier as being *too* pluralistic, to the point of being even atomistic, but where Renouvier had clearly given way to atomism, Howison never did, keeping his view close to James's.[18] Howison and James were aware they shared a common metaphysic of pluralism, but Howison managed to argue over their agreement in 1904 by charging James with placing pluralism in danger by professing irrationalism.[19] The relationship was a close one in many ways, but it is a difficult one to study because, as Perry points out, Howison published little and his writings had "exerted no influence at all comparable with that of his character and spoken word."[20] A serious investigation of the sources of pluralism in American philosophy would need to look closely at this relationship.[21] That is not, however, our task here.

Royce

Obviously the most persistent personalist voice in James's ear was Royce, but whether Royce became a personalist through the influence of James, or James together with Howison, or from Lotze, or Schelling, or whether he was in some sense a personalist independent of these influences, is less clear. His tendency to emphasize the idea of "person" in his philosophy noticeably increased after he came to Harvard. We have already seen that Royce and James were divided on the issue of the Absolute, although perhaps that division is now seen as less important than it has often been thought to be, for James's version of the Absolute in Royce was not sensitive to the various levels of generalization and the limits upon ontological knowledge that Royce always respected. And I have argued that Royce was a modified pluralist—at least once he became aware, thanks to Howison's spurs in his flanks, that his theory of individuality was insufficient for a personalist. And indeed, even James was a modified pluralist compared to Howison.

The relationship between James and Royce has been closely studied and written on and need not be rehearsed here.[22] All serious Royce interpreters end up addressing this relationship. Most James scholars tend to acknowledge Royce's continual influence on James and then move to other topics as quickly as their mental legs will carry them, without investigating it further.[23] One can scarcely blame them. The ideas are complicated and the story is a long one, requiring more effort than most scholars of any temper can reasonably devote to it. But even among Royce scholars, who presumably have more time for James than James scholars have for Royce (due to the asymmetry of their unequal historical importance), precious little in the literature raises or treats the issue of the "person" in James, and I have found not a single comparative discussion of the idea of the person in James and Royce. This has largely to do with the fact that, ironically, most who write on Royce are not interested in his personalism—indeed, many Royce scholars are not even aware of it, as I explained in the Introduction—and those who write on James are even less aware of the presence or importance of a distinction between the idea of "self" and the idea of "person" in his thought. This becomes a complex interpretive issue quickly, partly because Royce does not refer to himself as a personalist, even though James does. Yet, James would never have accepted the label of "personal idealist," and for many this is the same as "personalism."

In later generations it became clear that "personal idealism" was not just a label for Howison's philosophy, but a whole movement in American philosophy, of which Howison, Bowne, and Royce were the most prominent leaders. There were a lot of lesser lights around, such as Hocking, J.E. Creighton, and Ralph Tyler Flewelling. Apart from Tunstall's book, others have elsewhere addressed some of the issues with correcting the standard interpretations of Royce and understanding properly how he was a thorough-going personalist.[24] Indeed, his confrontations with Howison can only be understood properly against the backdrop of the assumed commitment to personalism Royce defended (if not under that later moniker). However, comparing James's understanding of the idea of "person" with Royce's is not the best path. It would require two very complex tasks—first explaining and defending Royce's personalism in order then to explain James's personalism. This might be historically backwards, since Royce's sense of the term "person" may have come from James (and Howison and Bowne). There is much to be said about how Royce's way of using the idea of "person" and how James's use of it is related. Let me simply summarize by saying that this is not the same idea as "self," which is a psychological and epistemic idea for both James and Royce.[25] The idea of "person" is an ontological notion, for both, and for Royce this means, of course, a postulate, but one whose more basic, actual meaning is ethical. But person is ontological in the sense that both James and Royce embrace ontology. The idea of "person" in both James and Royce is akin more closely to "individual" than to "self" (apart from what has been said earlier in Chapter 5, more on this will be said later in this chapter). This point has importance for James scholars as much as for Royce scholars.

This is all I will say about the historical matters at present, although other important historical information will appear in the rest of this chapter. For now it will be easier to move into our thematic question by noting the important relationship between James and Royce, but *studying* the relation between James and Bowne. I do want to point out, however, that James regarded Royce from the beginning as one who overstepped the commonsense boundaries of thinking, wandering into the land of dangerous abstractions, and that James *explicitly* distinguished Royce from Bowne in this respect.[26] James believed that Royce was going further in embracing the Absolute than Bowne would ever go, but he did see both of them as rationalists in a problematic sense.

James and the Idea of the Person: Starting at the End

The aim of this section is to draw attention to what James means when he uses the terms "person" and "personal" and even "personality," and to compare this with personalist views of those same ideas in his intellectual context. It is my contention that from *Principles of Psychology* forward, the idea of "person" in James's writings and thinking is sharply distinguished from the substantialist idea of "self," and that James treats "person" as a *mode of ontological relation* from the very start; he never saw "person" as a substance in the Cartesian sense. Some interpreters have confused the views of self he later modified with the rejection of "person" in the sense it was used in *Principles*. That James modified his view of the "self" is clear, but self is not "person" even in *Principles*. To establish *prima facie* that James not only understands the "person" this way, as a mode of ontological relation, but also saw himself retrospectively as having always held this view, I would like to begin with a passage from a letter he wrote to Bowne in 1908, after reading *Personalism*. James remarked:

> It seemed to me a very weighty pronouncement, and form and matter taken together a splendid addition to American philosophy. . . . It seems to me that you and I are now aiming at exactly the same end, though, owing to our different past, from which each retains special verbal habits, we often express ourselves so differently. It seemed to me over and over again that you were planting your feet identically in footprints which my feet were accustomed to—quite independently, of course, of my example, which was what made the coincidences so gratifying. The common foe of us both is the dogmatist-rationalist-abstractionist. *Our common desire is to redeem the concrete personal life which wells up in us from moment to moment,* from fastidious (and really preposterous) dialectic contradictions, impossibilities and vetoes, but whereas your "transcendental empiricism" assumes that the essential discontinuity of the sensible flux has to be overcome by high intellectual operation on it . . . my "radical" empiricism denies the flux's discontinuity, making conjunctive relations essential members of it as given, and charging the conceptual function with being the creator of factitious incoherencies. You don't stop with the abstract syntheses of the intellect, however; you restore concreteness by the "will," etc.; *whereas I keep the full personal concreteness which I find in time and the immediate particulars that fill it.* I have been tremendously confirmed in my radical empiricism, and emancipated, by Bergson's writings. He treats (as you probably know) the whole intellectual function as being primarily practical. By it we jump or fly over the surface of experience and perch on distant spots conceptually, for our advantage here and now, instead of wading through the intervening concrete particulars, as animals without intellect have to do [e.g., ants and arthropods, and other invertebrates[27]]. New values, indeed, arise by the use of the intellectual function, but it gives no insight into forces of activities, which must be lived directly or represented sympathetically, not *conceived*. All this is entirely congruent with your scheme; so I think we fight in exactly the same cause, the reinstatement of the fullness of practical life after the treatment of it by so much past philosophy as spectral. I personally prefer my own director [sic.] method, but so far has the thinking (at any rate the "academic") mind been warped away from directness by school traditions, that I have no doubt your more complex treatment will prove by far the more effective in the philosophy market. . . . But the essential thing is not

these differences, it is that our emphatic footsteps fall on the *same spot*. You, starting near the rationalist pole and boxing the compass, and I traversing the diameter from the empiricist pole, reach practically very similar positions and attitudes.[28]

I first want to alert the reader that James is often effusive in his praise of books he has just read when in correspondence with authors. This is not a singular letter, and many such letters could be examined today with some warranted skepticism about how much of the praise they contain was simple flattery. James praises clearly second-rate work as though it were world class and of permanent significance. I don't think that this general truth about James affects the importance of this particular letter, however, because James knew the recipient was not one who would respond to flattery. James means what he says here, and for the most part he is also correct in his assessment. There are many things to note in this long passage, not the least of which is the suggestion of pragmatism throughout.[29] For now, but only in passing, I would call attention also to James's clear use of ontological language (we will return to this matter at the close of this chapter), and his complete comfort with discussing the redemption of the concrete personal life in terms of the flux, relations, and the issue of continuity. These aspects should resonate and clarify some of what has been discussed above in the chapters on fictional ontology, individuality and temporalism. And this issue of how James confronts continuity will become important in the next section of this chapter. With these ideas in mind, it may be advisable at this point to reread the letter.

I also want to note in passing that James sees the difference between himself and Bowne as one partly of verbal habit and background, partly of method. James misunderstands Bowne's method, however, in thinking that Bowne's persistent demands for conceptual clarity and Bowne's insistence that conceptual confusion is a kind of intellectual suicide, are part and parcel of his method, amounting to the claim that the power of the intellect to transcend the concrete would entitle Bowne to something like ontological knowledge (or at least a pragmatic a priori). Here James is incorrect. Bowne is not claiming ontological knowledge, or even a pragmatic a priori. Like Royce, Bowne has a narrow conception of what philosophy can do, and he agrees (with the idealistic pragmatists) that philosophy is critical reflection and that it can work only with generalities that have already been formed. James does not recognize that feature of Bowne's thought, the curtailment of the scope and authority of philosophical reflection.[30]

Bowne is framing a fallibilist descriptive method in metaphysics that is closer to phenomenology than to the familiar logic of the older idealism. Bowne's insistence that logical rigor be applied to avoid confusion and obscurity within the descriptions offered is akin to Husserl's early use of so-called pure logic in his descriptive method, but far less formalistic, and not far at all from Royce's movement from selection to voluntary exclusion, to conceptual dialectic. Bowne simply wants clarity, and he does not seek pure structures or a priori, universal principles. James does not understand this, but Bowne is really very clear and consistent on the matter. The role of conceptual clarity is to avoid confusion within our (highly general but not *universal*, and here Bowne is closer to James than to Peirce and Royce) descriptions of experience. Proper logical rigor and conceptual clarity cannot guarantee us access to any sort of ontological order, for Bowne, but failures of clarity can certainly render our efforts to describe experience worthless.[31] Thus, James is wrong in thinking that Bowne's use of conceptual and intellectual ideas is less empirical than his own method, but he is correct in recognizing that Bowne's treatment of the issues certainly is far more sophisticated than his own. (We can allow ourselves now a bit of a smile at the suggestion that Bowne's version of things would have greater appeal in the philosophical marketplace.) Bowne's method is not less "direct" than James's for being more sophisticated, it is simply more thorough, more intellectually patient, and more critically engaged with the genuine alternatives. And a case could be made that Bowne was a type of radical empiricist—something that could not be said for Royce.

Yet, James had greater empirical patience than Bowne, exhibited in a willingness that Bowne lacked to wade through endless reports and accounts to compile his books. But Bowne had greater patience for the demands of conceptual organization, clarification, and systematization. In the point of conclusions, James is correct that there is no important difference, pragmatically, in the two views. He does not realize that there is also no important difference methodologically. We will return to metaphysical and methodological issues in the next section. Here, with these points in mind, the letter above bears yet another reading.

For now I want to call attention to James's comfort and facility with the idea of "person" in this letter, and how one could never substitute the word "self" in these passages in a way that would be consistent with James's philosophy. The idea of "person" is different from the idea of "self" for James. We cannot exhaustively survey every occurrence of "person" in James's corpus, but let me offer a few passages, traversing his career, to show that he customarily thinks of the idea of person as an existential or ontological modality of relation—a *way* of being, not a kind of being.

James and the Person: Putting the Beginning in the Middle

Let us begin tracing the theme of person with a crucial passage from *The Principles of Psychology*, in the famous discussion of the stream of thought (although I should note that Royce was using the idea of "person" in precisely this way in *The Religious Aspect of Philosophy*, five years before James's *Principles* appeared). James confronts there the issue of whether consciousness implies the personal modality. Having just made the point that we cannot assume an "I" to accompany each or every act of thinking, and asserting that instead we ought to say "thought goes on," James then says:

> How does it [thought] go on? We notice immediately five important characteristics in the process . . .
>
> 1. Every thought tends to be part of a personal consciousness.
>
> 2. Within each personal consciousness thought is always changing.
>
> 3. Within each personal consciousness thought is sensibly continuous.
>
> 4. It always appears to deal with objects independent of itself.
>
> 5. It is interested in some parts of these objects to the exclusion of others, and welcomes or rejects—chooses from among them, in a word—all the while.[32]

One can see in outline here, the account of individuality (rising from selective attention), the stream of thought, the conjunctive principle of temporal continuity, the theory of the will, and the theory of attention itself. All of these are cast in the modality of person (and each of these key ideas occurs earlier, in similar words, in Royce's 1885 book—indeed this could be a summary of Royce's view). James then continues in more detail regarding what he means in saying consciousness "tends" to the personal form. He remarks, alluding to St. Augustine's famous remark about time, that "personal consciousness" is one of those terms whose meaning we know so long as no one asks us to define it, and he finds such definition among the most difficult philosophic tasks.

Preliminarily James offers the following bit of ontology, and I ask readers to note that his discussion deals with the *forms or modes of exis-*

tence thoughts may take, not *how* they are given or known or *what* we know on account of them:

> In this room—this lecture room, say—there are a multitude of thoughts, yours and mine, some of which cohere mutually, and some not. They are as little each-for-itself and reciprocally independent as they are all belonging together. They are neither: no one of them is separate, but each belongs with certain others and with none beside. My thought belongs with my other thoughts, and your thought with your other thoughts. Whether anywhere in the room there be a mere thought, which is nobody's thought, we have no means of ascertaining, for we have no experience of its like. The only states of consciousness that we naturally deal with are found in personal consciousnesses, minds, selves, concrete particular I's and you's.[33]

Note here the similarity of the language from James's 1908 letter to Bowne in which he claims that his desire all along has been to redeem the concrete particular personal life from abstraction. He does use the term "self" as synonymous with "person" here, but that sense of the term "self" is the one he later rejected. The issue here is not the existence of consciousness, but its tendency to appear *only* in personal form. This is a discussion of the forms and modes of *existence*, with explicit recognition that when *all* our experience comes only in a single form, the personal, we are hard pressed to suppose, within the limits of radical empiricism, that such experience *ever* takes another form. We may suppose that experience *could* be impersonal, but where is the evidence of it? When we encounter a "mere thought" that is not conformed to the personal mode, then we can worry about it, but James does not see it as a likely encounter. Further, the generalized tendency of consciousness to come only in personal form is consistent with pluralism. Indeed, one reliable indicator that James is thinking about the question of the person in metaphysical or ontological terms is his invocation of pluralism in this passage, but in case there is any doubt about this in the passage cited above, James proceeds in the next paragraph to make it quite explicit:

> Each of these minds keeps its own thoughts to itself. There is no giving or bartering between them. . . . Absolute insulation, irreducible pluralism, is the law . . . Neither contemporaneity, nor proximity in space, nor similarity of quality and content are able to fuse thoughts together which are sundered by this barrier belonging to different personal minds. The breaches between such thoughts are the most absolute breaches in nature.[34]

Here we have an extra-ordinary admission for James (and a clear case of his kinship to Howison's brand of pluralism). As an apologist of ontological continuity, he confesses that the *personal* boundary, nay "barrier," is the closest thing to "absolute" discontinuity we find in nature. Although his aversion grew over the years, James was never fond of the term "absolute," but that is the term he chooses here, twice. Notice also that in this important context, the term "personal" is used, as it has been throughout, in the adjectival form. It may modify "self" (at this stage of James' career), or "thought" or "consciousness" or "mind," but in every case "person" is a modality of the *existing* of these other phenomena, not itself a phenomenon on the same level, not a thing or a substance, a relational modality, defining both the continuity of my thoughts with one another, and the discontinuity of my thoughts with yours or anyone else's.

James finishes off any doubt by continuing: "Everyone will recognize this [barrier] to be true, so long as the existence of *something* corresponding to the term 'personal mind' is all that is insisted on, without any particular view of its nature being implied."[35] Therefore, the idea of "person" comes into James' thought and vocabulary as an existential modality which may be further qualified by particular views, but the affirmation of this modality, the "personal," is a requirement of ontological pluralism, and "irreducible pluralism is the law." The implications for our discussions of Royce in the preceding chapters on individuality and temporalism should be clear, but they will become clearer still.

James then proceeds to distinguish the "personification" of the modality of consciousness from anthropomorphism (as Bowne often did). James points out that even the phenomena that are normally classed "unconscious" are nevertheless "parts of *secondary personal selves*," which have poor communication with the primary personal self, but are nevertheless personal, continuing: "although the size of a secondary self thus formed will depend on the number of thoughts thus split-off from the main consciousness, the *form* of it tends to personality . . ."[36]

More can be said regarding the specifics of James's concept of the personal, but my purpose here is to establish the early use of the idea in accordance with the personalist principle that "person" is an ontological or existential *relation* that conditions, at the very least, the interpretation of experience, contributing its ontological functional *form* to every interpretation of experience. In James's case, a stronger claim is in effect: it is not simply by the mediation of the personal that we know or understand experience; rather, "personified" is the way *all* experience comes, so far as we know or can *imagine* knowing. The softer phenomenological or epistemological personalism that adopts the idea of person as a descriptive category for convenience is not James's type of personalism. James affirms the personal mode of existence as an ontological fact (albeit revisable, if ever a contrary form should appear), as part and parcel of pluralism itself, and indeed, arguably, the very basis of metaphysical pluralism, since the personal modality either creates or exceptionlessly characterizes *the* barrier between and among the plural existences that populate all experience. This is a strong form of personalism, and it is significant that at the crucial point in this discussion in *Principles*, the only thinker James cites for support of his view is Borden Parker Bowne. This is something that simply has not been noticed in the James literature.

James and the Person: Ending with the Middle

If I have established the early presence of the personalist theme with this discussion from the *Principles*, and the late view by bringing in James's remarks on Bowne's book *Personalism*, let me simply shore up the middle of James's publishing career by calling attention to his use of the idea of the person in *The Varieties of Religious Experience*. This serves two purposes. Up to now, I have shown that James does use the adjectival form "personal," the participle "personified" and the noun "personality" in the existential/ontological mode, at least prior to his explicit use of the actual term "personalism" in 1903 to describe his philosophy (which I quoted near the beginning of this chapter). These uses are very clear from the discussion I have cited from James's *Principles*. But what of "person"? Is "person" not simply another word for "self"? We know that the self "vanishes" in James's middle period, at least the substantial self, and indeed, so does "consciousness," in the substantial sense.[37] These supposed "things" become processes for James. One might claim that with the disappearance of the substantial entities goes also their personal modality, but if one claimed that, one would be terribly wrong. Person was *always* a process for James, and his view and use of the idea does not change or disappear because he never understood it as anything other than a process or governing relation.

First of all, it should be noted that James associated Bowne's work, along with Lotze's, with an attack on "being," by which he meant that Bowne and Lotze attack static or unchanging substance. James was aware that Bowne had replaced the idea of "being" with the idea of "process" as early as 1884.[38] Aside from this, however, we should look at the idea of "person," as distinct from the personal (adjectival use), in these middle years. In this regard, James said in his 1902 "Philosophy of Nature Syllabus" how we should think of this constellation of ideas he defends: "Tychism, essentially pluralistic, goes with empiricism, personalism, democracy and freedom. It believes that unity is in process of being genuinely won. . . . Tychism and 'external relation' stand or fall together. They mean genuine individuality, something to *respect* in each thing, something sacred from without. . . ."[39] It should be clear that James here echoes Royce's theory of individuality (although without the benefit of the triadic theory of relations), and we find thus associated the ideas of person, process, pluralism, individuality, with genuine externality (James has argued against "independent existence" just a page earlier, just as Royce had in *The World and the Individual*, First Series), and here asserts the connection of tychism, i.e., ontological contingency, with the reality of external relations. One wonders whether radical empiricism, as popularly understood, is not closer to idealistic pragmatism than the history of interpretation allows. We will see in the next section how these associated ideas "cash out" in the encounter with immediacy in the idea of "pure experience," and how James proposes a radical empiricist should deal with the issue.

Presently I will focus on some passages from *The Varieties of Religious Experience*. My point here is to try to make readers aware that the idea of person, in the most characteristic sense used by personalists, is not only present in James's thought all along, but emphatically present and repeatedly affirmed. And there is a reason for this, as I will show. Even if there should prove to be exceptions to this usage of the term "person" in James's corpus, I think the idea of person as an ontological relation or existential modality is one that any follower of James has to confront in grasping his ontology and his account of relations. To be a follower of James implies ontological personalism just as surely as it implies ontological pluralism, and to view the matter otherwise is to risk a vicious abstractionism, and to fail to be a radical empiricist—i.e., pluralism without personalism has no concrete grounding, at least for James.

Turning then to *The Varieties*, let me note a very important adjectival use of "personal" in this work. In addressing the issue of religious conversion James is considering how to handle the appearance of such grand scale discontinuity in one's entire outlook and behavior as "conversion" implies, and here he settles upon the image of a "center" and a "margin" in each person's psychological make up. We can recall that Royce uses the same image in chapter nine of *The Religious Aspect of Philosophy*, and repeatedly thereafter. This idea is also is not new to

James's thought by any means, but is here invoked in a revealing way. Groups and clusters of thoughts and desires and interests exist either closer to the center of one's conscious life, or further away from it, at the margins. The talk of margin and center is more than psychological for James, it is ontological, as will be shown later. With this image in place James discusses how, over time, the center can shift without the awareness of the person in whom the shift is occurring. It is here that James offers the following description:

> Let us hereafter, in speaking of the hot place in a man's consciousness, the group of ideas to which he devotes himself, and from which he works, call it *the habitual centre of his personal energy*. It makes a great difference to a man whether one set of his ideas, or another, be the centre of his energy ... To say a man is "converted" means, in these terms, that religious ideas, previously peripheral in his consciousness, now take a central place, and religious aims form the habitual centre of his energy.[40]

Of the many things we might note about this passage, the main importance for us here is the idea of "personal energy," and that it is a field or ontological region that is in process. Indeed, I want to suggest that this idea of "personal energy" is the very meaning of the term "person" in James's usage, and it is associated with the *ideas* "to which he devotes himself," not just the desires upon which the will acts, or the objects to which perception attends. Rather, there is the formation of, at the very least, a *plan of action* (if not a full-fledged purpose) as the object of the will, but since the context is the religious life of the individual, it is even fair to say that devotion to a set of ideas in the sense James uses it here refers to *purposes* (in the sense I will define in Chapter 8).

I will venture the following preliminary formulation, then, of James's idea of "person": For James, "person" is the disjunctive process of temporal becoming in which all philosophy is interested, and this disjunctive process provides the *form* of externality, for it is also the limit of internality—that which determines what belongs to me and what does not (and recall that James has said that my unconscious thoughts are personal, and "mine"). It will take some time to make this clear, but a part of that story lies in noticing the choice of the term "energy" to describe the shifting center of action, and the term "personal" to qualify its modality. Some future scholar should explain James's use of the term "energy" in his mature philosophy. I will not attempt that here.[41] Note also that this phrase, "habitual centre of personal energy" draws importantly also on James's idea of habit. Much time might profitably be spent in discussing every term in the phrase, but for my purposes it is enough if we notice that it is an ontological phrase, not simply a psychological or epistemological one. James uses this phrase "habitual center of personal energy" often in the remaining three hundred pages of the book. Sometimes he does drop the qualifier "personal" in the phrase, which is interesting, but it always comes back later, so I take his occasional omissions of it to indicate a kind of shorthand, not a philosophical distinction.

I would remind readers also that early in *Varieties* James, in circumscribing the topic, distinguished the "personal" form of religious experience from the "institutional" or "ecclesiastical," or even "social" forms, devoting his study wholly to the former.[42] His justification for this focus, given later in the work, offered in an Emersonian outburst, is that the persons who regard their *own* religious experience as authoritative are the real source of subsequent religious practice in the world, and they will necessarily experience persecution for following the affordances of those personal insights. Such persons are shunned, labeled heretics, and finally persecuted, but if the content of their message persists and survives this persecution, it comes to be an orthodoxy of its own, at which point James laments the original insight has lost all of its "energy." This sort of heat-death of first-hand experience is the very origin of institutional religious practice, and all such practice is second-hand experience and not greatly to be credited, according to James. Here James and Royce disagree, profoundly—indeed, it is the true source of most differences between them, in my opinion. For Royce, communities and institutions are not only *higher* concrete historical embodiments of purpose, socially directed will, these institutions and communities are in fact "persons" in a *fuller* sense than are particular biological individuals. We will take up this crucial issue in Chapter 8, but it is good to recall here that Royce took his two mature works on religious experience, *The Sources of Religious Insight* and *The Problem of Christianity* to be correctives of James's overly narrow focus on individual experience.

James wants to treat communities and institutions as abstractions in the domain of religious experience. For him, the religious experience that is philosophically and humanly important can only be had at first hand, and only, so far as we know, by human individuals. Hence, his devotion of the study to the individual mode of religious experiencing, to the exclusion of social and institutional forms, is not undertaken simply to save space, or to keep psychology from traversing where its methods are not suited to go. For James this is an expression of his conception of the person as an ontological modality and process. The social process is not personal for James. Royce, recognizing this imbalance in James, explicitly sought to make his *The Problem of Christianity* a companion volume to James's *Varieties*, by adding in what James had left out of account, and correcting what Royce calls his "profound and momentous error" of imagining that institutional religious experience could be only "conventional" and "lacking in depth and in sincerity."[43] If future interpreters want to focus on the *genuine* battle between James and Royce that is actually important, they should concentrate on their differing ways of conceiving the personal mode of existing. For Royce it is social at every level, and its sociality is a hypothesis that must be treated, in philosophical reflection, as having priority. For James the idea of the personal is a functional disjunction between internal and external modalities. This battle makes an actual difference in the world. The so-called "battle of the Absolute" is at most an internecine dispute among philosophers about how to handle universals and negation.

The circumscription of the topic by James is based on a philosophical conviction about the way that experience coagulates and crusts over as it becomes social and historical. Communities cannot be "genuine individuals" for James as they can be for Royce. Indeed, personalists have often disagreed on this point, as can be seen for example in the disagreements between Edgar S. Brightman and Walter G. Muelder in the middle of the twentieth century.[44] But in the case of James, this insistence upon the particularity and primacy of personal experience is not simply caving in to nominalism, it is also James's most Emersonian moment (and Emerson was no nominalist), i.e., James's nod to the claim upon us that our original relation to the universe ought to have, if we would truly attend to the authority of first-hand experience, as both radical empiricism and pragmatism require. And this particularity of experience also raises the issue of immediacy, as we shall see.

Within this framework, let us move on to the idea of "person" in James's *Varieties*. Here the discussion that interests us most is the lecture on "The Divided Self." James has described the sick soul and its desultory mode of existing, and has identified a movement deep within such a soul which is a yearning for unity. In defining the divided self James makes it very clear that this duality or heterogeneity of self is a matter of degree and is consistent with an active and profitable life, whether the inconsistency in the self is merely an "amiable weakness" or makes "havoc of the subject's life."[45] Here James describes the process that *is* the person: "Now in all of us, however constituted, but to a degree greater in proportion as we are intense and sensitive . . . does the normal evolution of character chiefly consist in the straightening out and unifying of the inner self."[46] The evolution of character is the person for James. Consistently within this discussion and throughout the book, James uses the word "person" to describe the overall aggregate being in which this process of unification takes place. I believe he uses the term "soul" interchangeably with person for the same process, but chooses "soul" only so as to establish the analogy between what traditional religious language uses for this idea and the term James prefers, which is "person." The point is that the *self* cannot be the same as the *person* or soul for James because the "self" may be greatly divided in the *same person*. Rather, the "self" is a sub-process in the overall process of the person.

I have hinted at this earlier, but I will say it explicitly now. James not only uses the terms "person" and now "soul" to refer to this ontological process, he uses the term "individual" interchangeably with these two. For James, the ontological modality of individuality *is* personal existing. In this usage he *follows* Royce, but *without* the nuanced metaphysics of the individual Royce had so painstakingly articulated (see Chapter 5). But Royce distinguishes "individual" from "person." Individuality is the product of the well-developed will, but personality is its *ideal* form, fully temporalized and adopted as a *purpose* (this will be fully discussed in Chapter 8). On the issues of will and time (see Chapters 5 and 6), James and Royce have the *same* theory of individuality, at the phenomenological level, and it is a *personalist* theory as far as it goes. Differences begin to appear in their ethical conceptions of individuality, and these result in metaphysical differences. (Remember, metaphysics is a descriptive elaboration of ethical existence and experience, not the foundation of it.)

Much effort has been utterly wasted by James scholars who are worried about his so-called "individualism." They cannot seem to reconcile his (merely apparent) social atomism with the rest of his thought. The resolution is not terribly difficult, for it requires only that one confront the fuller theory of individuality as socially produced, but this solution would require something almost no follower of James has either the temperament or patience for, which is that one would have to read Royce—really read him, and come to terms, eventually, with the issue of whether *communities* are persons, in relation to will, purpose and temporality, and also according to the requirements of fictional ontology and the problem of immediacy. James's employment of the term "individual" more or less interchangeably with "person" is a conflation that can be corrected, but not without a better metaphysics. In short, James is an "individualist" only because he has so little idea of what an individual is.

As I have shown, Royce's use of the term "individual," laid out in excruciating detail in *The Religious Aspect of Philosophy*, *The Conception of God*, and *The World and the Individual*, just *is* a way of dealing in descriptive metaphysics with the idea of the person and how the existence of the individual person may be reconciled with the reality of the temporal whole within which it exists, without reducing either the person to the whole or the whole to the person. Royce's formulation here, as I have argued, is "to be is to be uniquely related to a whole," and whatever is so related is an individual, i.e., as an actual or *possible* person. This is a simultaneous affirmation of pluralism and the Absolute. As far as I can discern, James has no problem with the account of individuality Royce offers, nor with selective attention, the exclusionary function of will, or the uniqueness that results. Even the prior sociality of the individual (if the term is used in *Royce's* restricted sense of it) seems quite clearly in keeping with James's position. His problems are with the whole, and especially with attributing, even hypothetically, personhood to any unit larger than the human individual. But what does radical empiricism require? We shall see.

For James, the "individual" is his Roycean term and "person" is his Bownean term for one and the same idea, which is the (temporal) process within which the fragmentary "self" seeks its unification. James was not a heroic individualist of the sort Thomas Davidson was, he is a broader sort of "individualist," i.e., a metaphysical pluralist who recognizes the "person" (as pointed out above in his *Psychology*) or the "individual" (used in *Varieties* and everywhere else interchangeably with "person") as *the* ontological boundary that constitutes a processive pattern or center of relation to the "more," or the "unseen" (if not the Whole or the Absolute, as in Royce, at his most abstract). James stakes his ontological viability on the use of the idea of "person" or "individual" to provide him with "habitual centers" from which to venture out into the "more." This is simply the structure of James's descriptive metaphysics, as far as he takes it. There is abundant and clear evidence that James became aware of the problem with his account of individuality in the notebooks he kept between 1905 and 1908 (which we shall take up shortly), and that he was aware that his view was not consistent with his own statement of radical empiricism.

For now, we may see that for James there needs to be a *conjunctive* principle to insure continuity, and a *disjunctive* principle to insure individuality. The principle of conjunction for James is *time* (and here he follows Royce); the principle of disjunction is *person*. I will repeat James's words quoted earlier:

> Absolute insulation, irreducible pluralism, is the law . . . Neither contemporaneity, nor proximity in space, nor similarity of quality and content are

able to fuse thoughts together which are sundered by this barrier belonging to different personal minds. The breaches between such thoughts are the most absolute breaches in nature.[47]

Person is the disjunctive principle. In order to remain a pluralist, James must place the principle of person, or, for him, "individual," on a level with the principle of time or continuity, and then confront the immediacy in which they become distinguishable in experience as continuity and discreteness. A newborn baby has not acted in enough successive accumulations to have any great separation between time and person, which is why James says a baby's experience approximates "pure experience." But is pure experience perfectly conjoined? If so, whence disjunction? Whence comes the person?

James scholars who have worried about the atomistic individualism, of the commoner sort, in James's thought, continue to fret because they are not attending to the work being done in James's ontology by the idea of the "individual," and they fail to recognize this work because they are unaware of the relation between "individual" and "person" in James's background and influences, and they fail to be aware of the conflation of these ideas and the alternatives to that conflation. They tend to be unaware of these ideas partly because they do not study Royce and Bowne in conjunction with James. James was, however, perfectly willing to study such philosophy. So, James is not an individualist of the pernicious and worrisome sort, he is worried about postulating higher than human persons, whereas Royce and Bowne not only posit superhuman persons, each posits subhuman persons as well.[48]

Concluding the thematic part of this discussion, I claim, the key to understanding the idea of person in James' thought depends upon knowing what an individual is, for him. The full story would require a book of its own, but I will indicate some of the particulars of that account in what follows. I have shown some of the "Bowne" side of James here (and I am not claiming James got everything from Bowne, but he definitely had many of the same ideas and was continuously reading Bowne). The Roycean aspect has emerged throughout this book, and more will become clear as we move toward the conclusion.

Radical Empiricism and the Person

In the 1908 letter to Bowne James identified what he believed was a methodological difference between his philosophy and Bowne's, and I have suggested he misunderstood Bowne's descriptive method. I have set out an interpretation of Bowne's descriptive method in metaphysics elsewhere, but I did not there claim that Bowne is a radical empiricist (that requires a separate study), and indeed, the philosophical issue that lies behind all this activity is actually closely related to this matter: "can there be an experience of the impersonal?"[49] This is the confrontation with *immediacy* phrased in different words, words that more closely approximate the problem James discovers with his conjunctive account of time and disjunctive account of person. A radical empiricist must face this issue of immediacy in determining whether the pervasive presence of a certain modality of relation in all *particular* experience, that of the personal modality, is evidence for the objective, general or universal character of that same modality.

Obviously Kantians have no qualms at all about treating universal categories as transcendental conditions for the possibility of experience. Royce approaches that level of commitment, but his ontology is fictional and his critique of Kant's view of temporality is clear. Hypothetically, Royce will postulate a Universal Person. But personalists do not treat logic or any structural feature of the act of knowing or cognition, especially the most abstract ones, as having a conditioning power or authority, an ontological necessity, and certainly not as providing ontological knowledge. Time and person are the required categories of clear reflection, and one assumes, as a result, only that the universe is not altogether hostile to temporality and person. Yet time and person seem so general in all experience as to suggest themselves as universals, and therefore "necessary" to philosophizing, if not to all existing. Bowne and Royce take the suggestion, in slightly different ways—Bowne more cautiously, treating time as phenomenal and person as transcendental; Royce less cautiously, treating time as the possibility of relation, and person as the condition of the reality of purpose.

The next move, for Royce, would seem to require us to say that, as such a crucial universal, the personal either *does* exist or *must* exist. But for Royce, this proposition is not ontological knowledge. It is undeniable in practice, and an unavoidable postulate for philosophy, but not more. The empirical personalist will say only that the personal surely does exist, but not that it *must*. This is Bowne's position, and it is James's. Bowne goes further to say that the consequences of treating the impersonal as something real are very bad for philosophy and for clear thinking. Royce holds that the personal *must* exist, in the sense that it is a universal hypothesis with which we unify generalities for philosophical purposes, and saying so is a moral norm of philosophizing well. Herein Royce differs from Bowne and James.

A radical empiricist, however, is entitled to the following ontological stance: that which presents itself as a feature or modality in *all* experience, such as the person, is empirically entitled to be thought of as really existing, but not as having a necessary existence. "Person" exists as a governing modality of temporal processes as experienced, and whatever the further structure of the real may be, that structure is ontologically compatible with the real existence of persons. This is not to say that the real is logically or epistemologically compatible with some *particular* version of what the person is (as James noted in the *Principles*), only that existence is a temporal process that affords the personal form, whatever else it may do.[50] Another way to put this point is "experience is not illusory." Since experience comes only, so far as we know, in the personal form, the suggestion that experience might not *have* to be personal is an allowable speculative hypothesis, but should not, for James, be treated as a universal proposition, for that way of approaching the "personal" has no demonstrable pragmatic or practical value.

Examining my earlier chapter on pragmatism, the reader will note that I think James is wrong to exclude universals from having practical value. I can here add that leaving *open* the idea that experience need not or sometimes does not come in the personal form, apart from being unempirical, is the commonest instance of the philosopher's fallacy, and leads to reductive materialism on one side or the pernicious type of absolute idealism on the other, both of which destroy the plurality of individuals upon which James bases his metaphysics. A radical empiricist is disposed to personalism as both a matter of practical honesty and metaphysical self-consistency. We are actually debating how far we are obliged to generalize that requirement in *philosophy*, not about whether we should make the assumption.

The phenomenological version of the same issue is "can we actually succeed in giving a wholly impersonal description of anything that exists?" to which the answer is clearly "no," for James. No impersonal description will be able to avoid vicious abstractionism. There is a good reason that all phenomenologists are personalistic philosophers, and many, such as Marcel and Scheler, are professing personalists. The epistemological version of the same question is "assuming something impersonal exists, could the encounter of a personal being with that existence have any meaning or make any sense?" Bowne and Royce answer this question in the negative. Here it seems James would have to remain agnostic, and to inquire whether the allegedly impersonal character of what has been encountered *as existing* could really be held apart from its personal character *as experienced*, or to phrase it in ontological terms: could the conjunctive principle (temporal process) be made intelligible and meaningful without the disjunctive principle (personal process)?

This actually raises the question of pure experience in James, to which we will turn shortly, but for the moment it is worth noting that the problems of alterity that have emerged in Continental epistemology and ethics in the twentieth century do confront this very issue. Scheler, for example, answered, in effect, that the impersonal could exist and could be experienced, and indeed, this is what is meant by something like "the otherness" of the other, or even the objectivity of the real, or the formalization of any personal existence.[51] We can objectify ourselves and experience the impersonal *as* the formal, and we can also formalize others and render them impersonal thereby—which may be alright for scientific purposes, but it undermines all ethics and value to formalize others ontologically. We cannot, however, make full sense of that impersonal otherness and cannot know it in the way we know more concrete things, like other persons and God, but there is a type of knowing that is always approaching the impersonal, and that is the act of *formal* knowing itself.

The formal type of knowing is terribly misdirected if it is employed to tyrannize the domain of moral action or the meaning of existence, for Scheler, and Marcel, and Levinas (which is why the critique of technology is often central to their thinking), since it concretizes the impersonal in the life-world and comes to mediate too heavily our encounters with the other as "person." It is not, however, an altogether useless thing to have formal knowing, or to seek an encounter (mediated though it is) with the in-itself, such as when we want to do science, for example. To be sure, this formal knowing is an inferior and derivative mode of knowing that tends toward what is impersonal, and to that degree, it is ultimately incomprehensible in our experience (or comprehensible only in terms of a deeper personalism). This is a phenomenological version of Royce's own restrictions upon the process of generalization. Like James, then, Scheler, Marcel, Levinas, Bowne, and Royce, all affirm the priority of personal forms of knowing and experiencing over scientific forms, or any other forms, and the experience of the person (or individual for James, at this point) is just what "experience" means.

Alterity remains a problem, of course, but only a "formal" problem, in the sense that *whenever* we attempt to know anything by formalizing it, we *introduce* in the very same act an otherness or alterity that is "impersonal" and thereby problematize the concrete value of whatever we are attempting to "know" in this way. Garden variety realists, such as one finds everywhere these days, simply will not admit that abstracting away from the personal modality is a loss of any significant kind (indeed, they see it as a gain, as an achievement of neutrality, and they foolishly deny the role of *perspective* in knowing—fortunately, quantum physics seems to have challenged this utterly naive assertion and brighter philosophers, such as Hilary Putnam are insisting upon a difference between objectivity—which is important—and value-neutrality, which is a pernicious fiction).

It is not often appreciated, however, that this matter of formal knowing is an epistemological problem with ethical (i.e., formal, legal, political) consequences, not primarily a metaphysical or ontological problem. Relationalism of the sort that all these personalist thinkers affirm will fall into vicious abstractionism the instant that one allows formal knowing to hold an equal or superior place to personal experiencing. The fundamental gesture of all *viable* philosophy in the twentieth century (i.e., temporalist and personalist), in my view, was the recognition of the derivative character of abstract and formal knowing, and the affirmation of the primacy of the personal form. Versions of realism that treat the abstract and impersonal products of cognition as ontologically prior to the experience of them have no living account. Their ideas will be swallowed up in subsequent history, and that cannot happen soon enough for me. The fears of academic philosophers and political neo-conservatives that we will all become subjective irrationalists are themselves the truly irrational fears. The checks upon our experience that come from its prior sociality and its derivative individuality are quite enough to prevent our floating off into a solipsistic dreamland of our own fancies and vices.

The question here has been whether radical empiricism requires the general (or even universal) affirmation of the primacy of the personal modality of existing in order to be radically empirical. My view is that not only does radical empiricism require a personalist stance, but also that James himself was well aware of this. What experience has any of us ever had that was not first in the personal form? If we have had nonesuch, then why do we refuse to acknowledge the pervasive presence of this modality in our experience? Why would we choose to tyrannize our own experience with an impersonal modality, when to do so is among the most unempirical things we can do? Why would it be philosophically dangerous (as these contemporary rationalists hold) to generalize this fundamental *personal* aspect of experience, this disjunctive complement to temporal continuity? Is the phobia of subjectivism so controlling that we cannot bear to allow the personal its rightful place in our empiricism? Concrete relations, insofar as the may be experienced and described, always come in the personal form, according to James, and to anyone else who has ever thought about it honestly. If we cannot generalize a modality so very pervasive in experience, what *can* we safely generalize? Overcoming idiosyncratic subjectivity, which is desirable, is not the same thing as overcoming the personal form of experiencing—in fact, these are opposites. The overcoming of merely subjective experiencing is precisely the achievement of a meaningful personal mode of existing.

But the recognition of this personal principle, as one to be affirmed with the broadest generality, requires a thorough account of individuality. Radical empiricists may be able to take perspective as immediately given, but individuality is *socially* achieved, on any viable account. The issue requires the acceptance of a wider-than-individual consciousness, or what is sometimes poorly called "the compounding of consciousness." James was more than wary of this idea, but his wariness was caused by his habit of taking the compounding of consciousness as a *consequence* of, rather than a hypothetical condition for, a certain account of individuality. I will address this below.

Radical Empiricism and the Miller-Bode Objections

There is no *immediate* experience of impersonal matter, nor of the pure in-itself, nor of any impersonal Absolute, nor of an impersonal logical structure, nor of an impersonal physical law. The *im*personal is a later abstraction. Relations, principles, and existences, *qua* experienced, presuppose and imply the personal mode of existence, for James, which he takes to be the same as the individual mode. Whether all such existences *must* come that way, James does not know, and neither do I (and Royce never claims they must). Wondering whether impersonal relations *may* exist beyond the centers of experience with which we are obliged to deal is akin to wondering whether there might be a "mere thought" in this room that is nobody's thought, and while it may be so, we will have no commerce with such a thought, as indeed, we will have no worries about such relations, since it is hard to see how a "mere thought" can *do* anything. These would all be differences that make no difference. Posit, if you like, all the noumenal relations you fancy, and make them personal or impersonal as it suits you, you will still be talking about nothing that can possibly make a difference in action, as far as our experience goes. The relations that matter are all personalized in the act of our experiencing them, as individuals or persons (recalling that "individual" and "person" are the same for James, but different for Royce).

In this regard, therefore, I should recall two important passages in James's corpus. I aim to be a radical empiricist in my own thinking and I freely subscribe to the formulation of radical empiricism James offers. Radical empiricism is a living idea. As a philosopher I am convinced that any responsible radical empiricist will come to a personalist stance unless seduced from that path by a solicitous abstraction prowling the streets of the philosophical red light district. I am less assured of James's description of pure experience, however, and I believe that there are better methods of to describing the way in which experience contains its relations, for the purposes of philosophical description and understanding (the right kind of temporalism, as described in Chapter 6). I hold that the two general or universal markers of all "experience" (and I mean "existence" here also) are 1. its temporal character; and 2. its personal character. I have argued elsewhere that indeed, the temporal and personal aspects of existence imply one another, although they are not identical.[52] In this I agree with Heidegger, Whitehead, Hartshorne, and most others among the *viable* philosophers of the twentieth century.

The personal and temporal character of all existence is what radical empiricism requires us to accept as a starting point for philosophy, especially for metaphysics, and James certainly defended the requirement of the "person." Accepting "person" as the pivotal ethical (and hence ontological) idea requires us to accept the combination of "will" and "purpose," as the correlated pair of generalities that fill out what is meant by "freedom," which is another word for describing the intentional character of the universe, insofar as it can be made sense of in philosophical reflection. Yet, an account of "will" requires a description of individuality that underpins the *meaning* of personal mode of existing, for while it may be that "person" can exist without individuality (we cannot be certain), person seems to be individualized in all experience, and then given *meaning* as a temporal ideal.

Obviously James is a temporalist, as are all radical empiricists, and others have defended his temporalism;[53] the claim I make regarding its pervasiveness and role in James's thought is not controversial, although James scholars will sometimes disagree over how to characterize his temporalism. Some see his temporalism as pragmatic, others as an ontological description of experience, others as an existential starting point, others as an indication of a broader metaphysics that James never fully developed, and still others understand it as something connected foremost to radical empiricism. I will not enter into this discussion here except to note that I take the latter two points as my own view, along with such scholars as William J. Gavin, but I see all of these interpretations as being viable in different ways.[54] The point is that for James, two "principles,"[55] time and person, are so pervasive in experience as to warrant, not an a priori standing in our "categories" (since we will have no a priori categories), but a presumptive role in the description of every experience. The account of pure experience James provides should, itself therefore, be understood as qualified by temporal and personal relations, in the sense that all relations that can make a difference in experience have these features, at least in every instance we know.

It follows that what James says about "pure experience" needs to be read in light of these findings about the characteristics of "radical empiricism." We err if we try to use the passages on "pure experience" as a guide to radical empiricism. Rather, radical empiricism presupposes time and person. The *concept* of pure experience (we always must remember that we are dealing here with a concept) is one of the results of taking the orientation in philosophy of radical empiricism. The concept of pure experience is not the starting place of radical empiricism.

Let us look now at James's use of the temporal principle in radical empiricism and move from there to the principle of person. I offer the following passage: "You also see that it [radical empiricism] stands or falls with the notion I have taken such pains to defend, of the through-and-through union of adjacent minima of experience, of the confluence of every passing moment of concretely felt experience with its immediately next neighbors."[56] Whitehead could not have said this better, but in his case, the modality is not personal until it achieves higher phases of neighborliness. Not so with James. Here James is affirming the temporality of all relations, the conjunctive principle or his version of ontological continuity. For the affirmation of the personal character of all relations, let us look at his definition of radical empiricism, now with more educated eyes:

> Radical empiricism consists first of a postulate, next of a statement of fact, and finally of a generalized conclusion. The postulate is that the only things that shall be debatable among philosophers shall be things definable in terms from experience. The statement of fact is that relations between things, conjunctive as well as disjunctive, are *just matters of particular experience*, neither more nor less so than the things themselves. The generalized conclusion is that therefore the parts of experience hold together from next to next by relations that are themselves parts of experience. The directly apprehended universe needs, in short, no extraneous trans-empiri-

cal connective support, but possesses in its own right a concatenated or continuous structure.⁵⁷

Not only does James begin with a *postulate* (and he certainly knows how postulates operate in philosophy from arguing with Royce for twenty years), and that postulate is a *norm* for good philosophizing—here we see the familiar structure of Royce's fictional ontology, along with the affirmation that philosophy needs to proceed on the basis of a norm—but his *norm* is exactly the same as Royce's in affirming the authority of experience. Royce and James are both pragmatists, after all (see Chapter 4). But then James moves to state a point of what he takes to be disagreement with Royce, a statement of fact: that *particular* experience, not generalizations, are the "things" with which philosophy works. Yet, in stating the *fact*, James builds in the conjunctive *and* disjunctive relations, i.e., time and person, as matters of *particular* experience. Royce would say we have an entirely particular experience of generalizations, but James would call that sophistry. I don't think it is sophistry. But, granting James his point for the sake of argument, then and only then does he generalize, and his generalization is an ontological principle: both relations and individuals are experienced, concatenated (individuals) and continuous (time). That is as far as James will go. He will not postulate a Whole.

James's philosophy supplies only a norm, a fact, and a generalization: time and person, as particularly experienced (conjunctions and disjunctions), with all their relations. That is radical empiricism. That leaves us two questions, at least: 1. whence time and person from immediacy? and 2. how do we properly create the generalities with which we philosophize?

Here we need only recall the way James uses the idea of concrete and particular experience, and then recall that for him all experience is *someone's* experience (the conflation of individual and person), so far as we can say or know anything about it, and we should have our grounding in the meaning and extent of James' personalism, but also his problem with immediacy. His commitment to personalism is very broad, as are its implications. Reminding each of us how this stance affects, for example, James' moral philosophy: "According to empirical philosophy . . . all ideals are matters of relation."⁵⁸

The unseen, the more, the vague, the things beyond current reach, the future, these are the sources of life's deepest meanings, in their vital relation to the present. The puzzle about ideals and life's moral meaning depends upon our ability to answer questions 1. and 2. above, and those depend upon understanding the conjunctive and disjunctive principles, and their relations. What joins us to what is beyond our present moment, and what sunders us from the things we are obliged to believe by means of percepts and concepts although they are not "ours" properly speaking? The relations that take us to these concerns are all personalized *as they are experienced*, and radical empiricism not only does not require us deny this, it requires us to recognize it.

The concept of pure experience, as James describes it, seeks to do justice (as radical empiricism requires) both to continuity (or conjunctive experience), and discontinuity (or disjunctive experience). The very key to understanding how both sorts of relations can be done justice is to recognize that the boundary between the conjunctive and disjunctive type of experience is the personal, since the personal principle is temporal, but its individual will and purposes are the *only* source of generality, and hence of *ideals* (or more clearly, "purposes"), that James allows. Interpreters of James rarely grasp this simple point. But Mark Moller understands it. In his article, "James, Perception, and the Miller-Bode Objections," he traces James's struggle to reconcile James's radical empiricism with his doctrine of pure experience.[59] I will not summarize Moller's entire case here, but a few of the points and the result are crucial for moving from where we are in our present analysis to a point of clarity about James's and Royce's personalism and its role in grasping purpose, or "ideals."

Moller points out that in the account of pure experience that James had provided he could not explain the sense in which an object experienced by two individuals was "the same" object. Pure experience, as a concept with authoritative scope, did not allow individual perspectives to be something apart from the pure immediacy itself. I have called this the problem of disjunction in James. As Moller summarizes it:

> . . . at the level of immediate experience none of the individuals are [sic] aware that others are perceiving the same pen [the object James uses as an example is a pen]. If any ever do [sic] become aware of it, it is only after each has a subsequent experience that enables him to reflect on and differentiate his immediate experience. But if this is so, and an experience is as it is experienced to be, James cannot say that the individuals immediately experienced the same pen. None of them ever immediately experiences the pen as being the same, and thus it cannot be said to be the same.[60]

After struggling with this issue for some time, James began to become aware that he had no solution. He considered several solutions, such as the collection of all the individual experiences taken together, but this was unsatisfactory for James, as indeed it had been for Royce. James stated his conundrum in this way:

> But how, when all is simultaneous, can the parts *equate* to the whole, and yet the whole be experienced as such, when each part only experiences that part. Either no whole is experienced here; or, if experienced, it must be by a more inclusive experient. But can the pure experience theory furnish such a simultaneous experient?[61]

Clearly James is hard up against Royce's long-standing point about experience belonging to a more inclusive experience, and he realizes it. Another problem he is dealing with is that time is here being neutralized by the concept of "simultaneity." James continues:

> The difficulty for me here is the same that I lay so much stress on in my criticism of Royce's Absolute, only it is inverted. If the whole is all that is experienced, how can the parts be experienced otherwise than as it experiences them? That is Royce's difficulty. *My* difficulty is the opposite: if the parts are all the experience there is, how can the whole be experienced otherwise than as any of them experiences it?[62]

I hope I have shown that what James takes to be Royce's problem here is due to a misunderstanding of Royce's theory of individuality and his temporalism. The effort to deal with immediate experience always produces such problems, as we have seen in my third chapter. It is completely understandable how Royce shields himself from the problem of immediacy by limiting philosophy to dealing with already formed generalities. He then supplements this with an extra-philosophical phenomenology and psychology, as I have argued. James gives to philosophy a somewhat broader scope, but does in some sense accept Royce's "fictional" starting place by introducing radical empiricism with a "postulate" about the norms of philosophizing. Yet, here James confronts the issue of how he may have an adequately robust particularity (his "fact" in the radical empiricism triumvirate) in the face of a requirement that pure experience is serving as his functional "whole" to which the parts, i.e., individuals, are uniquely related. James considers several solutions, including the *correct* solution, which was Royce's solution, although neither James nor Moller recognizes this as Royce's solution. As Moller says:

> One possibility that James considers here makes use of his notion of virtual or possible existence. He suggests there might be two realms of experience where one would consist of actual experiences had by an individual, while the other would consist of all the "virtual" or possible experiences that are available to him, but are not, as yet, actual. The realm of possible experience in this case would be more inclusive than the realm of actual experience: "in

particular and at any moment what I do concretely experience may be less than my possible experience." It would also be what fixes the identity of the pen when it is experienced. The relation that allows for the individual's actual experience of the pen would be just one of the virtual relations that the pen stands in.[63]

This description should connect quite clearly with what I have argued in Chapters 5 and 6. It employs the same ideas about possibility and actuality, i.e., Royce's ideas. To deal with individuals as temporal experiencers, one cannot well avoid the issue of temporality, itself, and in dealing with temporality, one confronts the actual and the possible. But James is thinking of these as *distinct* realms, and it is true that no amount of dyadic fretting over how actuality and possibility are related will bring a solution. They are not separate realms, and the triadic theory of relations is needed. James lacks this theory, and he is also untalented at metaphysics, even if he has good instincts about it. After *almost* seeing the right answer, which would have led him to understand what Royce had been trying to tell him for over twenty years, James apparently gave up, or so Moller thinks (and I see no reason to disagree). Of his suppositions on actuality and possibility, James rightly judged, "this is obscure groping on my part."[64] Indeed, it might be groping for James, but for someone with a more subtle metaphysics, such as Royce or Bowne, this is not groping, it is all in a day's work. In elaborating on James's dissatisfaction with his "groping," Moller says:

> James offers no reason for why this solution [distinguishing the possible and the actual] proves unsatisfactory. Consider all the questions it raises: What really is the status of virtual experience? Is it real in the same sense as actual experience? If the answer is yes, as it seems it must be if virtual experience is to be what fixes the identity of the object experienced, whose experience is virtual experience prior to its becoming actual? If anything, the suggestion of a realm of virtual experience does more to hurt than help James's radical empiricism. It does exactly what James most wants to avoid doing, namely, underline[s] the need for an Absolute to solve his problem.[65]

These are, of course, the very questions Royce answered, as I have carefully traced earlier in this book. It is true that James wants to avoid the Absolute, but it is not true that this solution to his problem hurts his radical empiricism very much. Indeed, I think Moller has overlooked James's solution, by not attending closely enough to James's actual statement of pure experience, as I will show in a moment. I also think that one may solve James's problem without positing Royce's *most abstract* version of the Absolute. The sociality of consciousness provides an adequately general, dialectical solution to the issue, but one has to prioritize temporality and accept that sociality is intentional, is "alive," and is prior to individual experience (i.e., prior to the process of individuation, as in Chapter 5). Almost as if by magic, that is the very solution James adopts, although Moller equates the solution with "panpsychism," rather than simply allowing the priority of sociality as an experienced fact. I think Moller errs in this assessment, but he is certainly correct in claiming that James did not recognize he had stumbled on Royce's own conclusion. But that radical empiricism *requires* the priority of social to individual experience is the result I wish to emphasize. The individual is not an originary "given" in temporal experience, it is an achievement, an outcome of activity and action. Once individuality is present in some measure, then we may begin to ask after personality—although we cannot rule personality out where it is not communicative, and although we recognize that the personal mode of existing is a governing disjunctive assumption in all theorizing (which works with already generalized descriptions).

We seek the *meaning* of the personal mode of existence in the encounter of *purposes* of the other. That is what a thorough-going temporalism requires, not an Absolute. This is an important (and living) idea.

If we ask which of these two principles, the personal or the temporal, is the more basic, the answer is neither; all relations bear both marks: continuity and discontinuity, or conjunctive and disjunctive, as indeed pluralism requires. The assertion of the personal to the exclusion of time leads to atomism (and to a confusion of individuality and person); the discussion of temporality to the exclusion of person leads to total continuity, i.e., absolutism or materialism, and thus impersonalism. It sounds more familiar, however, simply to say that over-emphasis of continuity leads to dogmatic abstractionism and over-emphasis of discontinuity leads to dogmatic atomism, neither one being empirical enough to satisfy philosophy's deepest normative requirement (James's "postulate"). With this much said we can venture a look at the structure of pure experience as James describes it. After criticizing philosophies throughout history that posit or assert "subject and object" as "absolutely discontinuous entities" (this is the same as Royce's critique of realism), James says:

> All the while, in the very bosom of finite experience, every conjunction required to make the relation [of subject and object] intelligible is given in full. Either the knower and the known are:

(1) the self-same piece of experience taken twice over in different contexts; or they are

(2) two pieces of *actual* experience belonging to the same subject, with definite tracts of conjunctive transitional experience between them; or

(3) the known is a *possible* experience either of that subject or another, to which the said conjunctive relations would lead, if sufficiently prolonged.[66]

James associates (1) with perception, (2) with conception, and (3) is, of course, the key to everything, because it raises the question of the possible (i.e., the future and other possible experience in the present), and its prolongation (the infinitely distant future in Peirce's terms, or the social infinite in Royce's—concepts James lacks). The entire scheme depends upon the disjunctive principle: that we are *entitled* to ask after the origin of generalities from immediate experience from the standpoint of *individuals* or *persons* (i.e., particular experience, his "statement of fact")—that is what James's radical empiricism has put in place. The conjunctive principle, temporality, is employed here to provide continuity in all three, perception, conception, and possible experience. Before we discuss (3), something must be said about discontinuity.

There has been something approaching unanimity among James scholars that he is at bottom an apologist of continuity, and that discontinuity comes about at the conceptual phase, (2) above. Indeed, James says almost this very thing in his 1908 letter to Bowne cited near the beginning of this chapter. This widely held opinion is incorrect; James allows discontinuity at the pre-conceptual level, in the form of the *possible* experience of others; and the widely held view is not only incorrect, this view is responsible for the conundrums associated with James's account of pure experience, and for the general feeling among most scholars that he has failed in articulating it defensibly. Part of the reason for this error on the part of nearly all James interpreters is that they have failed to understand James's personalism and his account of individuality as an ontological principle on a par with his account of temporality and continuity. But part of the problem, as far as I can tell, is the selective attention in their own reading of James that follows from neglecting his account of individuality in relation to Royce, Bowne, Howison and others. It is not as if James does not *say* what I am asserting here. Just prior to the passage cited above, James says:

> Radical empiricism, on the contrary [as opposed to rationalism], is fair both to the unity and the disconnection. It finds no reason for treating either as illusory. It allots to each its definite sphere of description, and agrees that

there appear to be actual forces at work which tend, as time goes on, to make the unity greater.[67]

Here, James is not only acknowledges Peirce's description of the growth of mind, from a discontinuous and chaotic state toward greater unity, but he requires this sort of description to ground what he has asserted in (3), which echoes the Peircean theory of truth. The disjunctive principle is a problem, and it is being overcome as the universe advances into the future, into the possible. For an account of this ideal community in which the source of disjunction is *no longer* the individual human being, but is still a "person" and becomes the social mind, or the beloved community, one needs Royce and the superhuman person. We will take up this point in the next chapter, but for now, it is sufficient to read the overcoming of finitude or fragmentary experience as the *purpose* that informs (or is willed by) social process (and we may also say "progress," in light of the meaning of that term I will explain in Chapter 9).

But Peirce's "Mind" is crystalline, unchanging, and I might add *dead*. Fortunately, such Mind is never fully actual for Peirce. Royce's social infinite is both actual and living. This difference between Peirce and Royce is mainly verbal, but it has different practical consequences in limited cases. Yet, for both, mapping the advance of the disjunctive principle toward unification requires that *higher persons* be *possible*, for us now, and something toward which we are at least striving. We might say that we want to be *more than* individual, but it does not follow from this that we purpose to be *more than* personal; rather, the overcoming of that finitude or fragmentariness that is the tragedy of our individuality, of the selection, exclusion and negation of genuine possibilities, *overcoming that* does not make us *more than* personal, it makes us *more personal*. But overcoming that tragedy does render us more than individual, in the human, biological sense of the individual. Thus, constricted (if full) individuality is the price we pay for learning our own wills, and, having achieved the possession of active wills, we may become *persons* by willing ideals or purposes. One of the purposes we choose or will is that the cost of individuality should be less tragic, if we can make it so, that finitude should find redemption, and that we may grow into more personal beings. That is a purpose that a personal being *ought* to will. We will take up this question in some detail in my next chapter, on Community.

For now it is sufficient to recognize that radical empiricism is the basis of this description of pure experience, and radical empiricism treats the disjunctive principle of person or individual as coeval with conjunction or continuity. There is no question that James is making a case for continuity, but that is because both empiricists and rationalists have so often tried to discredit continuity, arguing for the very sorts of "realism, or "independent existence" that Royce attacks. How to have a principle of discontinuity that does not succumb to a hyspostatization is James's concern, which would be another way of saying, how can one adopt a principle of discontinuity as coeval with continuity and not succumb to one of the three conceptions of being that Royce criticizes so effectively? The Fourth Conception of Being is the correct answer, even if James does not quite realize that this is the answer he is giving. We can be rescued from this hypostasized discontinuity, James says,

> ... by a couple of simple reflections: first, that conjunctions and separations are, at all events, co-ordinate phenomena which, if we take experiences at their face value, must be accounted equally real; and second, that if we insist on treating things as really separate when they are given as continuously joined, invoking, when union is required, transcendental principles to overcome the separateness we have assumed, then we ought to stand ready to perform the converse act. We ought to invoke higher principles of *dis*union, also, to make our merely experienced *dis*junctions more truly real. Failing thus, we ought to let the originally given continuities stand on their own bottom. We have no right to be lopsided or to blow capriciously hot and cold.[68]

I do not know what could be clearer than this. To read James as an apologist for the primacy of continuity is to be lopsided in just the way James forbids. Is it an accident that the very next thing James does in the text is to describe immediate experience as I have quoted above, as actual and possible? Or is it *more* reasonable to suppose that the disjunctive principle is very much in James's mind in his description of pure experience, and is on equal footing with the conjunctive principle? Thus, James *does not privilege continuity* in his ontology; rather, only James *interpreters* do that. It is demonstrably incorrect in the text, and more importantly, it is inconsistent with radical empiricism, to privilege continuity over discontinuity. The followers of Dewey could stand to learn this lesson as well.

We are now properly equipped to say something about (3) in James's schema of immediate experience. It is incorrect to associate all discontinuity with conceptualization, and James is at pains to point out its continuity, via time, in (2). He then says "Type 3 can always *formally and hypothetically* be reduced to Type 2."[69] This only means that possible experience will have to be discussed by *philosophy* (recall the postulate with which James begins the statement of what radical empiricism is) under the same conjunctive and disjunctive principles (i.e., time and person, although we now see it is not precisely person, but "individuality") as conceptual experience. James gives an example of imagining something he *might* do and then *actually* doing it, so as to fill out the purpose he has formed with a percept that satisfies that imagined possibility, however imperfectly. Then he makes the same point Royce makes, rejecting "bare possibilities" (as Royce does in *The Religious Aspect of Philosophy*), which is that if you are imagining a possibility for which no experience did, can, or could furnish a percept, you are thinking about no genuine possibility at all. Where Royce and James part ways is on the question of *whose* percept we can draw upon to fulfill a future possibility. James does not want to go beyond the sphere of action of the individual human being, but does allow a division of labor—so long as *someone* can get such a percept, we may include it in our conception of possible experience. Royce is willing to say that the "experience" had by institutions and trees and canyons, and the Absolute, will fulfill James's requirement of providing an actual experiencer. Both of them reject bare possibility.

But Royce does not think an adequate philosophy can be built upon the idea that will and purpose are solely the office of *human* persons. On the positive side, institutions and families do *will* and *purpose* and *take action* and achieve those purposes, and on the negative side, to limit the conjunctive principle to purposes that can be formed and later perceived only by *human* persons makes history and culture miraculous—just the haphazard collection of persons picking up the projects of others, and there is no historical continuity or even objectivity beyond the scope of human mortality. Purposes would die when the human persons who have willed them die. But they do not, or at least not entirely. I am living the life my great grandparents purposed in deciding to have a family, even if I am doing it in a way that could only be vaguely purposed by them, and in a highly general way. Purposes endure for generations and millennia. To suggest otherwise is an inadequate account of our own present social and temporal experience. We will examine a more adequate version in Chapter 8.

Conclusion

Interpreters of James have struggled for decades with how to understand his radical empiricism and his forays into the idea of pure experience. They have done so with little success. Most of them have assumed that the best way to get a handle on these ideas is to ransack James's notes and letters and unpublished manuscripts for tidbits that will illuminate his concerns. I do not wholly disagree with this approach. It had to be done. But I will confidently claim that the best understanding of these ideas is the one presented in this chapter, and in the context of this book; it requires that one investigate closely the other thinkers with whom James was in meaningful dialogue (and of course, I have only looked at a few), no matter how temperamentally averse to them James's contemporary followers may be. These thinkers include Royce, Bowne, and Howison, at a minimum. It is close to shameful that it should come as news to anyone that James's theory of individuality is adapted to and from Royce's, and is a *personalist* theory, or that James's radical empiricism is a *postulate* in Royce's sense, proposing a norm for philosophy and a way of grasping the personal principle and the temporal principle without allowing overly abstract universals, and that the problem of immediacy is the same as the problem of pure experience, treating discontinuity on a par with continuity. But that is how the best account goes, or so I claim.[70]

[8]
Community and Purpose

In Chapter 7 it became clear that one of the most pointed differences between Royce and James concerns whether there are "superhuman" persons. I do not care for this term, but since it is the one Royce uses, it is appropriate to alert the reader to it. A more careful and appropriate label for the idea is that of "wider or more generalized personal existence beyond the level of individual biological humans." This is, however, too clumsy, and so I will occasionally use Royce's term, with this caveat: it need not refer to anything supernatural for Royce, and does not for me. The category of the supernatural has no serious relevance for personalists.[1] If person is not a natural kind, nothing is, and the idea that there is an utterly impersonal nature somewhere "out there" beyond our experience of it, as I have said earlier, is at least as superstitious as supernaturalism. Nature, like God, is a *concept*. It ceases being useful when it constricts our thinking and imagining, and I suggest that those who are in the habit of bludgeoning one another with these allegedly opposed concepts of God and nature need to grow up and recognize that this is a child's dispute unfit for mature people. People like that are more alike than they could ever stand to admit.

The point of difference between Royce and James, where James clearly expressed his own problem as the opposite of Royce's (in the previous chapter), is a *version* of the venerable problem of the One and the Many, a problem every philosopher confronts sooner or later, and not childish at all. In James's formulation, Royce had to explain how not to absorb the many in the one, while he had to find some unity in the many. It is a metaphysical problem, of course, but its most important ethical dimension—indeed, the very reason philosophers must deal with the question at all—is due to its implications for the relations between individuals and their communities. Where ethics is first philosophy, the metaphysical consideration of the relation of parts and wholes serves, first and foremost, the *clarification* of our thinking about the relation of the individual and the community. I will move to the issue of superhuman personal existence in this chapter, but first, a taking-stock of what has been learned, and a contextualizing of it, is needed.

The so-called battle between James and Royce is characteristic of the sorts of arguments that have gone on within the personalist fold for as long as there have been personalists—essentially since the end of the eighteenth century. The general problem is really a very simple one, and quite familiar to all students of philosophy. To over-stress unity, or the One, or Monism, is to render precarious or illusory the ontological status of the Many or the individuals. That is the line Royce is trying to negotiate. To over-stress plurality is to move toward atomism and to be left with no good explanation of experienced unity, whether that unity be that of felt-experience, of the feelings of community with others, of the bond of love between spouses, or parents and children, of thought or truth, the supposed laws of nature, or, most importantly, to account for the unity evident in the capacity to act (whether with one's whole being, or at least the preponderance of one's individuality). And indeed, as a subset of this last category, it seems to us that communities are certainly capable of unified action. Whence the unity? The personalistic pluralist must have an answer.

But James and Royce are negotiating the issue as personalists, not just as philosophers in general, which is to say that both are regarding personality as the aspect of reality that cannot be sacrificed—it is not an impersonal One or an impersonal swirl of atoms they seek to hold in relation, it is rather the personal mode of existing in both cases that is the clue to the solution of the problem, if indeed it has a solution. James was hard up against this latter issue of over-pluralizing, at every level. He wanted to pluralize without atomizing, and to regard the personal mode of existing as experientially pervasive, while also using it as the principle of disjunction, coeval with the principle of conjunction or continuity, which for him was time. Meanwhile, Royce wanted to unify (or account for the experience of unity) without losing genuine individuality, specifically the ethical meaning and relation of person to purpose (as I shall explain later in this chapter). The two have in common the idea that practical action is ontologically prior to the unification of our thought, but they have different senses of the scope of philosophy (not to mention different talents and temperaments).

It is generally not recognized either by the interpreters of Royce or those of James that their "battle" was not primarily the confrontation of pragmatism with Absolute idealism. Those who continue to try to explain the battle in these terms are constantly obliged to ignore or deny Royce's pragmatism, and to minimize or dismiss the pervasive idealistic elements in James's philosophy, or both. This is not only an inadequate interpretation of either philosopher, but it tends to reduce their conflict to temperament and to a caricature of the movements of both pragmatism and personalism in the development of twentieth century philosophy. In short, we fail to appreciate the greatest gifts Royce and James gave us, and at the same time do not give ourselves the gift of rich historical perspective and thorough self-understanding, when we read them this way.

The struggle between Royce and James, and the configuration of the problem they faced with the One and the Many, is just one interesting episode in the more general internecine struggle of personalists to confront their true historical enemy, which is pantheism.[2] Personalists regard pantheism not only as the source of impersonalist Absolute idealism, but as the source of all the forms of materialism and naturalism that, in numerous ways, eliminate uniqueness and genuine individuality, and thereby personality and freedom, from philosophy. It is easy to document the turn from Hegelian pantheism (and whether this is the best way to understand Hegel is dubious, but that he has been widely read in this way is undeniable) to dialectical materialism. The progression from Feuerbach to Marx has been widely discussed.[3] From a personalist standpoint, if Right Hegelians were one sort of pantheists, Left Hegelians were the opposite sort of pantheists, i.e., materialist pantheists. In all such cases it is the person as a unique individual that disappears, and whether one places matter or Absolute spirit at the most basic metaphysical level makes little difference. The individual is metaphysically eliminated either way, and with that, the purposes of the person.

To put the point in another way, there are many ways to kill the personality of God—Enlightenment rationalism, Absolute idealism, dialectical materialism, evolutionary naturalism, psychoanalytic reductionism, and so on—and once one has killed the personality of God, the sacredness, dignity, and value of human personality becomes tenuous, which is to say it lacks an ontological ground. Pantheism makes possible *all* of these strategies for killing God by making the surprising move of universalizing *certain* aspects of God's existence (such as unity, simplicity, immutability, causal power), by means of reason, to the exclusion of others (primarily the intentional aspects, willing, loving, even thinking). Enlightenment reason has difficulty with personality, and personality was one of the early victims of such universalization, most clearly evident in Spinoza, but also in the deists and many other developments during the seventeenth and eighteenth centuries.

Thus, materialists, absolutists, positivists, many types of humanists (we might call them modernist Protagorean humanisms for their reduction of all to the human measure, or Promethean humanisms for their tendency to heroize the peculiarly human type of personality), and non-theistic naturalists are all dependent upon a move made by Enlightenment rationalism to eliminate, by means of reason, the personal aspects of the divine. That is one short step from full elimination of the divine. And anyone can see that once reason has been so employed as the knife that kills God (or as the anesthesia that renders God unconscious), there is little to prevent its similar use upon the *human* personality. Indeed, this is what happened. The totalitarian systems that emerged in the nineteenth century and nearly destroyed the world in the twentieth are all forms of impersonalism, and all made possible by turning the knife that killed God towards human personality, serving some abstraction in its stead (whether Spirit, material conditions, or a narrow scientism). Pantheism made all this possible. That is why personalists attack pantheism.

Personalists do not try to revive classical theism or anthropomorphic conceptions of God. They try instead to place personality on firmer ontological footing without rejecting Enlightenment reason. To continue the simile, is it possible, personalists wonder, to place that very sharp knife of reason in a sheath and carry it at our side, using it wisely and only when necessary? The move to rein in the scope of philosophy that we find in Royce and Bowne is related to their effort at describing the circumstances under which the knife is (and is not) to be used. When James attempted something similar he was accused of irrationalism (the equivalent of saying the knife has no real use or can only be misused), but Royce's commitment to reason was such that none would charge him with such a crime. Yet, contrary to the standard readings of Royce, in which "the logical situation controls the existential conditions,"[4] Royce was in fact doing exactly the converse—and he was trying to prevent the logical situation from controlling the existential conditions, for his entire career. That meant either limiting the authority of reason in its universal form (i.e., reining in philosophy), or increasing the scope of the personal, the existential modality that logic was created to serve. Royce took both paths. It is simply incorrect to read him as a rationalist. He is far closer to being an existentialist.

In addition, Royce was dedicated to re-conceiving God in a way that preserved the value of the concept of God without returning to classical theism or yielding to pantheism and atheism (which amount to the same thing—anyone prepared to identify everything with God hardly has need of God when "everything" will suffice). It is no easy task to work out a new conception of God that is faithful to religious tradition (preserving its value) and also faithful to the changing requirements of the existential conditions in which Royce was living. He tended to sacrifice tradition whenever he could not find a way to rescue it from its eternalism, and as a pragmatist, he gave the greater weight to the present existential conditions. Personalistic theism is quite different from classical theism—being process oriented, pragmatic, and based on a more contemporary conception of "person" than one finds in the history of that concept. Personalists in general do usually sacrifice tradition to the existential conditions when they are obliged to choose, which is to say they are progressives (even if also often conservatives, a point we shall take up in the next chapter). Not all personalists are theists, although Royce and James certainly were; most are, but their common aim is not the revival of God. They aim at securing the dignity and worth of personality against totalitarian and impersonalist consequences of Enlightenment reason.

The trouble with the pantheistic turn from Spinoza to Hegel and Fichte, among others, is that its ethics and political theory were anti-democratic from the start, and they spawned modern totalitarianism, which was foreseeable and was foreseen. It was evident from very early on, well before Royce's time, that this totalitarian impulse in Enlightenment reason was a danger. From F.H. Jacobi and the later Schelling, the attempt to counter this growing threat was to develop and defend the philosophy of personalism, and indeed, personalism has been at the very forefront of the fight against totalitarianism, both in philosophy and in the practical world, from the beginning of the totalitarian disaster. And personalism remains a great force to be reckoned with in the world; it was not an accident that philosophical personalists were the key leaders who brought down racial segregation in the United States and communism in the Eastern world—almost bloodlessly. There is much to be said about this, some of which has been said very well already by other scholars. Personalism originated and remains a friend of a certain conception of progressive democracy, a communitarian conception. My present point is that if the tension between James and Royce is not recognized as a struggle *within* the ranks of personalism, and a quite characteristic struggle at that, it will be misunderstood (as indeed it widely has been). Sorting out the actual history is not my task, however.

Groundwork of the Metaphysics of Community: Person and Time

The historical account I have given, cursory as it is, has been aimed at showing what *is* different and important about the ways in which James and Royce engaged the problems that *all* personalists face, but if it is not understood that these *are* personalists, and what that means, one cannot even begin to grasp what was actually at stake in their disagreement. There is nothing unusual in the least about the shared voluntarism in James and Royce. Among personalists, the two most prevalent strands are voluntarists, on one side, and what might be called "consciousness theorists" on the other side. Personalists who hold consciousness to be the seat of the personal mode of existing (such as Brightman or Marcel) develop their thought either in the direction of idealism or phenomenology, in which the act of thinking, of being conscious of an object, is the philosophical starting point. Voluntarists (such as James and Royce and Bowne) tend to see practical action as the starting point, and to account for thinking as a kind of action, predominantly practical. All sides agree that "in the beginning (of philosophy) is the (concept of the) act," but disagree about whether the act is best characterized, for philosophy, as an act of thinking or of willing. Most personalists agree that the "act" is the *finite* act. There is no question that both James and Royce belong to the voluntarist side of this distinction. Personalists such as Hartshorne and Hocking tend to construe the act as "feeling" rather than willing, but whether "feeling" is further elaborated in terms of consciousness or practical action varies. But in all cases the act is *intentional* in structure. Obviously, voluntarists give thorough accounts of consciousness (such as we see in the theories of attention and concept formation held by James and Royce), while consciousness theorists often give thorough accounts of the "will," as Brightman and Scheler do, for example. This is not a dichotomy; it is a matter of methodological emphasis.

Some professing personalists have seemed to go the entire distance toward unity, embracing ontological absolutism, as is often said of Royce, but incorrectly in my view. Closer to this view would be Andrew Seth Pringle-Pattison, but even that characterization can be and has been questioned. Absolute personalists are not so very absolutist, by Bradleyan standards.[5] While Royce came close to favoring unity too much, he did not go the entire way. Other personalists have gone the full distance towards radical pluralism, or atomism, such as J.M.E. McTaggart (and Howison could be said to take only a slightly less dramatic route), but James did not go the full way, although he went most of the way. Some sensibility, some intuition, held Royce and James back (perhaps it was even their friendship and respect for one another), and I would suggest the intuition involved their jointly held conviction of the *reality* of time *as experienced*. Perhaps the most balanced (in terms of unity and plurality, and consciousness and will) personalist philosophy that has ever been fully developed was Bowne's, but Bowne sacrificed the reality of time in so doing, treating it as phenomenal only. Bowne employed a methodological device that kept his philosophy *consistent* with temporalism, but did not embrace temporalism as basic to his philosophical system, as I have elsewhere explained.[6] To the extent that Bowne sacrificed the reality of time from the scope and reach of *philosophical* thought, Royce and James would say he sacrificed the continuity of experience with the "real." I think this would be a just criticism of Bowne. Berkeley's phenomenalism is evident in Bowne, but rightly rejected by James and Royce. Giving the reality of time its full due is a vexing stance; it gives rise to new versions of all the oldest philosophical questions, such as the One and the Many, and the problem of Universals.

In noting that the key difference between James and Royce is a methodological orientation toward either unity or plurality, we come closer to what is genuinely important and original in their exchange. Taking the estimate of what philosophy can and cannot accomplish, they differ, and their methods correspond to this difference. The way Royce prevents the One from over-running the Many is by limiting the scope and reach of philosophy, relegating it to working reflectively with already generalized hypotheses, of ever-increasing generality, as fictions, and leaving for practical action the broad field of experience. But Royce will not, like Bowne, so restrict philosophy's scope as to exclude from it the *full* consideration of practical action. Bowne thought that when it came time to act practically, philosophy sort of disappears.[7] For Royce, we might say that metaphysics and logic take a "back seat" in the domain of practical action, but they are still in the philosophical automobile; they simply aren't licensed to drive.[8] Thus, philosophizing, which is a type of thinking, becomes an important *kind of experience*, for Royce, valuable to the guiding of practical action because of its role in unifying purposes (which are reflectively unified and freely chosen plans of life). I will have more to say about this process later in this chapter.

For James, philosophy can reach into immediate experience and is responsible for explaining the *presence* of generalities in experience, *how* they come to exist and what they mean (phenomenology), as well as for carefully arranging those generalities in ways that are of aid to practical action, i.e., that have concrete consequences. And James had a great talent for the first of these tasks, the phenomenological task, while Royce's great talent was for the second, the careful (systematic) arrangement of generalities. However, Royce was a better phenomenologist than James was a metaphysician (and Royce was also a better dialectical philosopher, which is why his ethical thought is also far superior to

James's). This is to say, Royce was perhaps not as accomplished at doing what James was *best* at, but in fact Royce was still quite good at it. James was not very good at doing, or even understanding, what Royce did best, when matters moved beyond the phenomenological level, into the statement of general principles in light of the description of experience. Even when James was genuinely making progress toward the kind of solution Royce had been defending all along, the temporalist solution, i.e., the recognition of the relations of possibility and actuality as a valuable philosophical tool, James thought he was himself merely "groping." And indeed he was. He was out of his depth.

Without the triadic theory of relations, with all the logical questions it raises (and which I have admittedly not discussed in sufficient detail here), the treatment of possibility and actuality becomes just so much endless academic dispute. Genuine temporalism must *begin* with a triadic relation, and that first triadic relation will be "time" itself, past, present, and future. By no means does this temporalist move *solve* the problem of the One and the Many. Rather, it replaces the static monistic and (boringly) dualistic versions of that problem with temporal versions of the same, so that we may now argue over, for example, whether the world will, which is temporal, *is* God, who is time-inclusive, rather than whether God bears a "real relation" to the world, as classical theism and philosophy have done. The same sorts of questions appear at the level of individuals—whether in thinking of an individual we mean to include possible experience along with actual experience as an individuating power. This replaces the discussion of individuality in terms of universals, particulars, and singular terms, from Plato to Duns Scotus to Leibniz. The move to possibility, the reality of time as experienced, and the triadic theory of relations is what distinguishes temporalist philosophy from substance philosophy.[9]

In the case of Royce, explicitly, and James more implicitly, the incorporation of temporal *possibility* (mainly the present and future in Royce) into the theory of the individual is a distinctive move, and it is also a constructive move (not simply a shunning of other philosophical paths). The theory of negation and necessity as grounded in the irrevocability of the act (i.e., lost possibilities, so that now necessity is derivative of possibility), and the exclusionary activity of selection and action of willing, is a way of concretizing temporal experience in philosophical description that has great promise, and which has been developing (sometimes in the spotlight but more often in the wings, in the last sixty years) for about two centuries. The move that has been poorly understood, but is altogether crucial, in Royce's philosophy, is the association of *present possibility* with a *world of truth*, and with the *experience of others*. Many philosophers, at least from Vico forward, have embraced the priority of social consciousness over individual consciousness, or the priority of sociality over individuality more generally (beyond just consciousness). Many have also embraced *history* as the relevant type of temporality with which to account for the priority of social consciousness or sociality, but history, while indispensable, is insufficient as a temporal framework, in my view and in Royce's. History is only *one way* in which temporal experience is appropriated. At the least one also needs an account of evolution (or growth) and physical time, in addition to historical time.

Less common among personalists is the idea that individual will is a *product* of our sociality, but this view is also not unique to Royce, among personalists (for example, Lotze held this view before Royce, and Hocking held it after Royce). But for Royce, everything depends upon what we *do* with the association of *possibility* with the *experience of others*, and with treating the reality of this concept of possibility as the *ground of truth*. This is why Royce's theory of *community* is so essential to his philosophy: We get truth from others. The theory of community is what we *do* with the reality of truth, in the face of the fact that we do not each possess more than a fragment of that truth, and are prone both to error and to ignorance. We depend upon community for access to truth, and it must be *community*, not mere sociality, as I will show.

Metaphysics of Community: From Will to Purpose

Mere sociality is not a ground for truth, any more than mere *individual* willing (or the intentional stance by itself) is a ground for a purpose. At most, an individual will can hatch a plan of action. It cannot supply the *meaning* of that plan without access to the ground of truth, or *other possible experience*. The *social* will of individuals provides the *context* for plans of action, but it cannot provide the grounds for unifying plural plans of action into purposes without developing something idealized into its own future social experience. "Community," for Royce, is a way of understanding how a *social* group can learn its own social will by freely and jointly willing idealized purposes. A purpose can provide a concrete ideal and actual unity that is only *wished for* in the action of social willing. But at the level of purpose—or idealization—we discover *more* than human individuality, and more than social will: in their unification, we discover the unfolding of personality or personhood, or more accurately, the development and growth of the personal mode of existing, which only happens, as far as our experience goes, when the social will and the wills of finite individuals within that social group come to be unified under an ideal, a purpose.

We know of no other way to develop personality than through the unification of plural wills in unified purposes. A social group that desires to *have* a common will must also have already achieved some individuality of its own—which is to say, as Royce often does, that social groups can become *individuals*, still finite, but not in the same sense as the human individuals who contribute to them. But to have a *purpose*, i.e., to act meaningfully on its social will, to turn a plurality of willed plans of action into a community effort, a social group also begins to develop a personality, a simultaneous growth within itself and among its finite members, and to build itself into a kind of person. The unification in light of purpose is what Royce calls a "cause," in his technical sense of the word. Royce says, "A cause, we said, is a possible object of loyalty only in case it is such as to join many persons into the unity of a single life. Such a cause, we said, must therefore be at once personal, and, for one who defines personality from a purely human point of view, superpersonal."[10] To the extent that a social group achieves a personality, to that same extent it becomes a *genuine* community. A social group may not develop into a community, but it *can*, and usually it *should*, in Royce's view (groups can develop defective personalities just as individuals can, depending not only upon the content of its purposes, but also upon whether the forms of those purposes treat personality as the highest ideal).

Why should social groups strive to become "persons"? The reason might be summed up in the fundamental hypothesis, or conviction (both moral and philosophical) of all personalists, which was well stated by Copleston: "one of the basic factors in personal idealism is a judgment of value, namely that personality represents the highest value within the field of experience."[11] This is wholly correct, and it should be noted that it is a value judgment to be weighed against the *meaning* of reality as *experienced*. But Copleston also says that "the basic principle of personalism has been stated as the principle that reality has no meaning except in relation to persons," taking this to be a restatement of the above.[12] But note the subtle shift in this characterization. The first is a constructive claim, an assertion of the value of personality *as experienced* and its meaning for what we treat as real. The second is a negative claim, that *nothing else* can have meaning *except* in the personal mode. This latter claim is not the view of either Royce or James. They do not know or *claim* to know whether the personal mode of existing exhausts the meaning of the universe, or whether there can be meaning apart from it.

The issue for Royce and James is whether finite human beings can gain any *philosophical* ground by engaging the question of the meaning of the real in non-personal or impersonal terms. Actually, *some* ground can be thus gained. In metaphysics, Royce would say that something can be learned by pressing the edges of the impersonal (not in the Absolute, but in the employment of logic and universals, which abstract away from the personal aspect of existing so as to characterize it in its necessary, i.e. negative, interrelations). To return to our earlier simile, Royce is willing to *use* the knife that killed the classical God, Enlightenment reason. Whitehead also takes this idea very far indeed, without becoming an *im*personalist thereby (he is a non-personalist), choosing to modify the character of Enlightenment reason by both definition and method: the function of reason is to live, to live well, to live better.[13] But for Royce, unlike Whitehead, this logical move is in service of the constructive, ethical judgment about the value and dignity of personality. James is suspicious whether anything good can come from such a logical exercise, but neither he nor Royce will make the move to ontological exclusion implied by Copleston's second formulation. It is one thing to assert that personality is the highest value we experience and that we cannot, apparently, get meaningful lives without making of it an ideal. It is quite another thing to claim that *no* value or meaning is *possible* apart from personality. This second claim amounts to claiming ontological knowledge—and that is a mistake, because it is far easier to know that something exists and has value (in this case personality), than to know that something does not exist and/or has no value. The first claim requires only positive finite experience. The second requires God-like knowledge.

Copleston immediately proceeds from this second, negative claim, to equate both claims with the following: "that the real is *only* in, of or for persons. In other words, reality consists of persons and their creations."[14] If Copleston were correct in supposing that all personalists hold these positions, and he is not, James and Royce would be something other than personalists, and they are not.[15] It is true that some personalists, notably Brightman, would equate all of Copleston's statements.[16] But Royce and James would not. Copleston's first statement is indeed a judgment of value, and the meaning of experience is what is at stake. To understand what is distinct about Royce's (and to some extent James's) theory of the person depends upon grasping that it is a modality of existing that *ought* to be idealized, and that such idealization depends upon the social will of a group that has become a community, and in concert with its parts, has formed a purpose that each should become persons, while the community itself also strives to become more personal. Whatever is an aid to this purpose is to be judiciously employed in service of this purpose. This purpose itself does not depend upon having the correct metaphysics, or religion, or adopting any other specific doctrine, dogma or practice. But aiming at such a purpose in the right form and with the proper content is greatly aided by having a clear philosophy. Idealizing community without the proper emphasis upon the personal mode of existing is exactly what both fascists and communists do. They may not *intend* to obliterate the person, but they do so nevertheless, as the history of the twentieth century so painfully demonstrates. As a result, the communities so purposed by well-meaning materialists, naturalists, absolutists, and the like, become pathological and impersonal collectives; in truth, these communities are defective persons. The existence of such communities is adequate proof that the abstract (i.e., impersonal) universal can exist concretely, but it is monstrous and horrible.

Back to Radical Empiricism

Yet, James is surely a radical empiricist and Royce surely is not.[17] How are we to understand and adapt the radical empiricist orientation in philosophy—a viewpoint I do wish to endorse and defend—to all this discussion of communities as persons, the priority of social will, and the other idealistic elements of Royce's theory of community? Sean Lipham has argued that one of the features of James's personalism has to do with conceiving God as "Thou," and if he is correct (which I think he is), then it is clear that James could not actually forsake the idea of our being *immediately* related to persons, both conjunctively and disjunctively, who are non-human.[18] In the case of the Divine, one would certainly invoke the metaphor of height, which is to say that such a personal being as God is certainly "higher" than human. Whether an analogous relation with subhuman persons could be attributed to James is unclear, but it is worth noting that he took seriously the possibility of communicative relations with the dead, which one assumes are either non-human or at least post-human persons.[19]

Radical empiricism requires not only that we not hypostatize our concepts, but also that we take seriously whatever seems to be experienced by anyone anywhere, and that requires at least investigating carefully whatever people *report* experiencing. Hence, James along with Royce, Frances Ellingwood Abbott, and others formed a committee to investigate paranormal phenomena, for example.[20] It is certainly fair to say that this group (with the exception of James, who was closer to being lukewarm) was skeptical about what they were investigating, and were far from eager to venture the notion that there are post-human persons, but it was not a notion they wholly dismissed. My point is that for a radical empiricist, non-human personal existing is no more ruled out than is the existence of impersonal meaning (as we saw in the previous section). Radical empiricists leave these questions open, which is not to say that they would all agree on the relative importance of the questions themselves. James thought the questions about post-human persons, personal survival of death, the existence of God (or a divine person) were all important enough to devote serious time to each. It does not seem to me to be consistent with radical empiricism to assert a final rule on the *non*-existence of anything, whether it is the possibility of "impersonal meaning" or ghosts.

But the case of non-human persons is clearer when it comes to Royce (as with other personalists, such as Bowne[21] and later Hartshorne[22] and Brightman[23]). There is nothing unusual among personalists in attributing the fundamental existential modality of "person" to non-human beings, especially God, but also to animals, and to fail to do so would be unusual for a personalist. To assume there are nonesuch apart from humans requires that we ignore a lot of reported experience, and that is unempirical. To be extremely cautious about how to approach the personhood of non-humans is also the norm among personalists. One must be careful to avoid anthropomorphism, the mere projection of human experiences, and to avoid simple personification. Equally important is recognizing the *difference* between those characteristics of personal existing that can reliably be postulated for non-human experience—such as temporality, sociality, communication, and specifically the intentional structure of experiencing, willing, purposing, valuing—and those which *cannot* be as reliably assumed, such as symbolizing, self-consciousness, and reflecting.

How properly to generalize the personal mode of existing is a matter regarding which many personalists part company. James is far more cautious than Royce in making such generalizations. Indeed, apart from Hartshorne, Royce may be the *least* cautious generalizer of the personal mode of existing, which is to say that Royce is ready, without hesitation, to attribute possible personhood *wherever* he finds temporality—and that is pretty much everything that exists, so far as philosophy is able to form reflective postulates about our experience. This is to say that "person" (and here we include the structure of willing, purposing, attending, and valuing), along with "time," is a methodological universal for Royce, i.e., a postulate that is employed to organize the other generalities with which philosophy deals. Royce regards this association of time and the intentional stance (and hence the personal mode of existing) as an *empirical* requirement of doing philosophy well.[24]

Panexperientialism

To delve deeper into this issue we must broaden the context and ask precisely what "experience" means for Royce. If one's empiricism is to answer to experience of all kinds, leaving none out, then it matters deeply what we say about the concept of "experience" itself. In employing this universal postulate of person, along with time, Royce becomes aware, for example, that everything in the natural world is to be thought of as "living," as having an *inner* life, by which he means an immanent temporal dynamic. He says:

> . . . Scattered sensory states are mere abstractions, just as the atoms of physics are. There is no evidence for the reality of nature-facts which is not defined for us by the very categories of the social consciousness. No evidence, then, can indicate nature's inner reality without also indicating that this reality is, like that of our own experience, conscious, organic, full of clear contrasts, rational, definite. We ought not to speak of dead nature. We have only a right to speak of uncommunicative nature. Natural objects, if they are real at all, are prima facie simply other finite beings, who are, so to speak, not in our own social set, and who communicate to us, not their mind, but their presence. For, I repeat, a real being can only mean to me other experience than mine; and other experience does not mean deadness, unconsciousness, disorganization, but presence, life, inner light.[25]

Many people, especially philosophers, begin to shift in their seats when anyone speaks this way. There are whispers of "panpsychism" and the like. But before anyone has a chance to whisper, I want to call attention to the fact that Royce is being very explicit about saying that this is a limitation we humans *bring to* the situation, as a result of the way *we* experience things. He is leaving entirely open, as Hartshorne, for example, does *not*, the question of whether nature *an sich* (if there is any such thing) is or is not conscious or alive. Philosophy makes terrible mistakes when it attempts to use the tools of reflection to close the gap between experience and existence *an sich*. That is where bad ontology and bad metaphysics resides, what I have called the "unholy trinity" in Chapter 2. All Royce is saying here is that the personal mode of existing is presupposed in everything *we can call real*, philosophically. To *suppose* that there are real things devoid of immanent temporality, of an inner life, is abstractionism, positing something to which temporality makes no inner difference, something that can only change by being affected externally, with no internal *dynamis* (a word which might be rendered with the English activity, action, actuality, or dynamism) by which it comes to be altered as a result of its own coming-to-be or concrescence. This is not a claim of ontological knowledge by Royce, it is recognition of how philosophical reflection operates, which is by and for persons who form a purpose to think philosophically and communicate their thoughts (and then do so).

Perhaps some will say, "alright, living things have 'experience' in some sense, and insofar as they do, perhaps some even exist personally (horses and dogs and porpoises and chimpanzees), but *some* living things, like paramecia, just are not persons, and certainly there are non-living things that exist non-personally." Not only is this "concession" a misreading of Royce's claim (and pretty much all personalists, including James[26]), for it still assumes that Royce is making a claim about *natural organisms* when he is in fact making a claim about the conditions of doing *good* philosophy, but the position taken by the supposed objector is demonstrably incorrect.

In order to allot personhood to some things and deny it to others requires that we operate at two different levels of abstraction, without acknowledging we are doing so. One can abstract the personhood from all things and speak of them *as if* they were constituted by external relations alone, *as though* any change in them were caused or brought about through forces external to their own mode of becoming. The mechanistic worldview does this consistently, which is to say that at least mechanists operate at the same level of abstraction regarding all that exists (including humans), but of course this leaves half of the phenomena of change and process out of account, and there would never be any justification for claiming pure and total externality as some kind of ontological knowledge, any more than there would be justification for claiming that internal relations and immanence are the only reality.

The other consistent view, besides mechanism, is the one Royce—and all pragmatists and all personalists—adopt, which is to recognize that the most concrete account we can offer, philosophically, of time and change, is one that treats all phenomena in light of the primacy of experience, since experience (at the very least our *own*) is presupposed even in the mechanistic account as well as in all other accounts. The issue is whether, in order to avoid vicious abstractions, we are obliged to generalize "experience" itself to all descriptions of existence, and the answer given by Royce, and all pragmatists and all process philosophers, and all personalists, is "yes." *How* to generalize experience is a point of contention, but not whether experience is a functional universal. It is.

If by "panexperientialism" one means only that experience is the touchstone of all philosophizing, and the form of experiencing must in some way be generalized and never left wholly out of account (just for philosophy, that is—there is no serious reason to consider the form and content of experiencing in, say, fluid mechanics or differential geometry), then one can safely say all pragmatists, process philosophers, and personalists are panexperientialists. If one means by the term "panexperientialism" the claim that experience is *all that exists*, and nothing else, and that this is an ontological certainty, nearly all of the above, including Royce, drop out of the picture. Hartshorne and Brightman, for example, make a qualified version of this claim for experience, which calls into question not their status as process philosophers, but it casts into serious doubt whether we should call them pragmatists or personalists (since it is a relapse towards "pantheism" in the sense I have described in the first section of this chapter). Pragmatists operate on fallible postulates, while personalists cannot afford to suppose that there is *not* impersonal meaning in the universe, and must carefully qualify the use of philosophical reason (not making claims of ontological knowledge). Royce is a pragmatist, as well as a personalist and a process philosopher. His position on panexperientialism is as strongly stated as a pragmatist can allow, which is to say that he holds experience to be a universal postulate. James allows no universal postulates, at least not formally, but as we have seen, his conjunctive and disjunctive principles (time and person) approach the status of Royce's universals, in function if not in name.

For those who are uncomfortable with Royce's universal claim above, about the character of experience as a functional universal in philosophy, the question that needs to be considered (and this is how Royce would put it) is not whether he is generalizing experience too much, but whether one can do adequate philosophy without some universal principles. And it can easily be argued, and convincingly, that both James and Dewey smuggle such universal principles into their philosophies—especially principles of continuity—without providing an adequate logical and metaphysical grounding for their functioning. One need not choose specifically "continuity" or "experience" or "will" or "purpose" or "person," but one needs universals in order to have a functioning logic and a grounded metaphysics. Dewey finally understood this and allowed for universals in his 1938 *Logic*, after he had grasped why Peirce was criticizing him for blocking the road of inquiry.[27] This is another reason to treat Dewey's *Experience and Nature* as Dewey himself did, as a provisional attempt at metaphysics, at most, and an unsatisfactory attempt at that. Dewey was clearly unsatisfied with the book, and his disciples would do well to heed their master in this regard (see chapter four). The greatest generality *Experience and Nature* allows for is "generic traits of existence," and that is insufficiently general to be supported by any serious logic; it cannot deal even with the existence of mathematical knowledge, which, as Peirce rightly says, is the science of possibility *qua* possible.

Dewey and James are far more comfortable with "middle-sized" generalizations, ones that can be traced down to the concrete experience of human persons, persons who could, at least in principle, so situate their bodies as to fulfill in perception whatever possibility has been conceived or imagined. Dewey was clearly more adept at metaphysics than James, but neither was especially good at it. When generalizations begin to look impossible for humans to perceive, James and Dewey become hesitant. Peirce, Royce, Whitehead, and others are more confident, and unsurprisingly, this confidence flows from a great facility with logic and mathematics, and a clear grasp of their limitations. Dewey and James, whose talents were more limited in this domain, are unsure of the status of generals and universals; unaccustomed to the multiple crossing modes of generalization that can be safely organized by universal assumptions and propositions without giving up the grounding of concrete experience.

There is no reason to take seriously the hesitations of thinkers who simply do not know how to handle abstractions without becoming lost. James and Dewey are truly gifted generalizers and organizers of generalities. But they are limited in ways Royce, Peirce, and Whitehead are not. The fact that James could not do what Whitehead did hardly means, however, that James was a radical empiricist, while Whitehead was not.[28] To think that James is a radical empiricist while someone with a method of extensive abstraction, such as Whitehead's, cannot be, is to mistake what is accidental in James's thought (and its limitations) for what is essential to the kind of philosophy he frames. Whitehead (to take as an example a thinker more aggressive with abstract reasoning than even Royce) certainly is both a radical empiricist and a panexperientialist. He just happens to be better at logic and mathematical thinking than James, and so can move more freely and creatively with its available tools. But Whitehead's statement of how radical empiricism deals with experience is perhaps even more poignant than the statements from James we have examined in the last chapter:

> In order to discover some of the major categories under which we can classify the infinitely various components of experience, we must appeal to evidence relating to every variety of occasion. Nothing can be omitted, experience drunk and experience sober, experience sleeping and experience waking, experience drowsy and experience wide awake, experience self-conscious and experience self-forgetful, experience intellectual and experience physical, experience religious and experience sceptical, experience anxious and experience care-free, experience anticipatory and experience retrospective, experience happy and experience grieving, experience dominated by emotion and experience under self-restraint, experience in the light and experience in the dark, experience normal and experience abnormal.[29]

Whitehead, like James, hypothesizes that we should think of events as drops of experience. For James, this is a generalization, and one of the more adventurous ones he makes. For Whitehead this is a universal hypothesis, which, once we have adopted it as an assumption, we may follow out, without ever asserting that experience *actually* exists *only* in drops.[30] Royce is making a similar point. If we begin with experience, we have to be prepared to see that the philosophical norm of remaining at the same level of abstraction or generality, or to move among levels of abstraction only by the vehicle of explicitly introduced assumptions and their subsequent discharging, requires us to recognize the experiential aspect of everything we are describing. That is the character of Royce's panexperientialism.

This issue is important because it bears upon the issue of humans' being-in-community with non-human persons. All of nature we are obliged to conceive as "existing experiences." Some of these existences are within our "social set" and hence "communicative"—e.g., humans, horses, dogs, and chimpanzees. Other things with which we are in community are present but not as communicative relative to us, such as paramecia, trees, and canyons. These things are not necessarily "dead"; we could not even *know* them to be dead, if indeed they were. We could *suppose* them to be dead by abstracting from their internal temporality, their inner lives. We can do that just as easily with human beings—that is what makes possible the dehumanization and depersonalization of others. But the act of so abstracting requires a decision. We are in the habit of affirming, by hypothesis, the inner life of most other humans and perhaps some animals because they are in our social set, i.e., communicative of their inner lives to us, but there is no absolute or necessitated obligation to treat this habit as the law of the universe. We choose both the habit and the maxim it suggests—to treat all humans as having an inner life. Indeed, learning to communicate with what has been previously uncommunicative is *the same as* moral and intellectual growth, and cutting off the possibility of communication is very close to making ignorance something we honor rather than attempt to overcome.

The rule or norm for philosophical generalization is as simple as this: do not generalize so as to render inexplicable or incomprehensible key aspects of experience. For mechanistic ontologies, experiences of consciousness, will, hope, attention, life, value, person, time, purpose, and unrealized possibilities are all inexplicable—as is anything else that communicates an internal dynamic or an inner life. It is probably, therefore, unwise to generalize the concept of "causation" very much, if by "cause" one means efficient causal laws. To universalize efficient causal laws in this sense is intellectual suicide. One does better to generalize causal will, but that has limits as well, which is why Royce treats will as an outcome of activity, instead of, with Nietzsche, making will the originary principle.[31]

To generalize the *personal* mode of existing is obligatory for all philosophy because philosophy involves, in essential ways, internal dynamics, such as consciousness, will, hope, attention, life, value, time, purpose, and unrealized possibilities. And as far as we know, to put it in James's terms, all of these experienced phenomena "tend to the personal form." It is impossible, as far as we know, to do any philosophy without actively employing these intentional features of experience. To employ philosophical reflection to explain away these aspects of experience (instead of trying to understand them) is simply bad philosophy. And that is all Royce is saying in universalizing experience. Experience is always, as far as we know, *someone's* experience (recall James' point about this rehearsed in the last chapter). That is to say, experience exists, as far as we know, in the intentional mode, and philosophy assumes a norm of treating "person" as one of the experienced values in the experiential field. Personalism treats it as the highest, but no philosophical endeavor can safely ignore it. Thus, the squeamish but demonstrably incorrect objector above may not like it, but this means that not only biological organisms are in some sense to be treated as personal, but so are, for example, geological formations and astronomical motions, according to Royce:

> [T]he actually fluent inner experience, which our hypothesis attributes to inorganic Nature, would be a finite experience of an extremely august

temporal span, so that a material region of the inorganic world would be to us the phenomenal sign of the presence of at least one fellow creature who took, perhaps a billion years to complete a moment of his consciousness, so that where we saw, in the signs given us of his presence, only monotonous permanence of fact, he, in his inner life, faced momentarily significant change.[32]

Here, in order to generalize inner temporality (and the intentional stance) in an appropriately concrete way, we are obliged to acknowledge that whatever exists in our present (remember that Royce calls this "the acknowledgement of a World of Truth," which he defines as "other *possible* experience," see Chapters 2 and 7), has a past and a future, and its "experience" has to do with how these time-spans, variable and overlapping, are ordered and achieved. The canyon or the moon *experiences us*, we are obliged to assume, although there is no evidence for supposing we make much difference to the moon—whatever communication is possible for a "fellow creature" whose experiential "moments" cover billions of our years is certainly not a kind of communication we know much about. I would point out, however, that since Royce's time we have learned a few things that might be relevant to having a "conversation" with the moon, even on *its* terms. If we devise a missile that would or might alter the moon's orbit (and that would be a pretty stupid thing to do), we might be able to introduce a discontinuity in the lunar inner dynamic that would constitute for it the end of one moment and the beginning of another, i.e., a serious disruption in its temporal continuity. That would be an act of communication from our time-spans to its time spans, perhaps. But the point is not whether we can do this or something analogous in the cases of other "uncommunicative" existences, the question concerns how we ought to think about aspects of our experience and generalize consistently in so doing.

We do not know much about the inner life of natural things when they require billions of years for single experiences, but the idea that such objects of our attention, will and purposes *have* inner lives, of a sort that *can* be interpreted by us, is not insane—the entire field of study now goes under a host of scientific names, such as general systems theory, or information theory, or complexity theory, or any other means we may devise of studying what we loosely refer to as self-organizing processes (which I might add, implies a "self," in some sense). I cannot at present think of any reason that the scientists and engineers at NASA should worry about the inner life of the moon, since the purposes they form regarding it can safely assume the regularity of the moon's temporal continuities ("repetitions" to us, a monotonous permanence of fact, in which it is functionally continuous in every "now" we designate), when those repetitions are measured in durational spans that make sense to *us*, e.g., years or hours or centuries. But it is also clear that the moon "communicates," in some safely general sense of that term, with, for example, the tides, earth's gravity, the sun, and other natural phenomena whose internal dynamics are more closely attuned, temporally, to the duration of moon "experience." Thus, there is no reason to deny that the moon and earth and sun are in a social set and that they interpret one another—for all we know, a solar system may even be a community. The issue is not what scientists at NASA need to assume so as to adopt a reliable set of abstractions for their plans of action and purposes, the issue is what philosophers need to say in order to apply the same type of generalization across the events *they* wish to describe.

Thus, although it has a metaphorical aspect, it is not simply a metaphor to suggest that human and non-human persons can *communicate* with one another, that this communication is related to the durational character of their experience, and that the communication is the ground of their "community." To approach the issue otherwise is to assume that time makes no difference to some parts of nature while it does make a difference to other parts. Such an assumption needs a ground. We have no such ground to assume, let alone assert, such a fundamental temporal discontinuity, and we have no evidence for the discontinuity. It is true that we also have little evidence in favor of the temporal continuity we assume (ours with the canyons and stars, at some level of generality –that it's all still "time," and we aren't equivocating on that word), when it comes to entities profoundly unlike us, but there is ample evidence that time makes a difference, externally, to everything in nature. It is also good to remember that we *require* such continuity to ground such scientific hypotheses as the evolution of what we call "living" from what we call "non-living," and that here we face two choices for the form of our generalization: the discontinuity of life and non-life, rendering life a mystery; or the continuity that leaves somewhat mysterious the character of the inner life of natural processes we do not currently grasp.

Royce chooses the latter, and it is clearly the more empirically warranted option, since it permits the following elucidation: Wherever the duration of events, i.e., the basic scope of time-spans, endures for similar lengths as our own, as with horses and dogs and chimpanzees, more of the inner life of the other is communicable. Where the inner life of the other is easier to interpret, the overlapping of will and purpose is available in a more nuanced form. Communicative intermediaries are more available, and shared memory, hope, and interpretation are available. We see how the past experience of the other contributes both to what is willed and what is purposed, and how the purpose makes sense in light of the past experience and present context of the willing individual. Where time-spans vary greatly, our challenge is one of learning to communicate.

Whether we are indeed required to postulate an *all-inclusive* experience can be debated. Obviously Royce thinks that maximally good philosophy does require this postulate. Postulating the "whole" is a requirement for the most lucid examination of relations among the parts, whether by logic or mathematics or systematic ontology or even metaphor and narrative. Supposing this whole to be an "experience" is simply a consistent application of the pragmatic principle that experience is where we begin and end our philosophical activity, regardless of whether that term, "experience" includes or excludes, for "philosophy," *immediate* experience (which can also be debated). Royce does not expect to communicate with the Absolute—any more than he expects to communicate with the moon. He wants, rather, to adopt the best norm for philosophizing and to stick to it.

Hocking, as we have seen, regards both the exclusion of immediate experience (the cognitive value of feeling) and the absence of an expectation of communication with God (such as we find in worship or mystical experience) to be weaknesses in Royce's philosophy. Perhaps they are. Hocking's suggestions about *how* to communicate with the Absolute are, however, not very promising. Royce's supposition that we are interpreted by an all-embracing Interpreter Spirit, whether or not we can finitely grasp it, is just as cogent as anything Hocking offers. Indeed, we *could* frame as a norm that "it is better to be interpreted than to interpret," as the counterbalance of "it is better to give than to receive." For, to be interpreted *by* another is a prerequisite of giving anything meaningful *to* another, in Royce's view. This is just another way of saying, as Royce so consistently does, that we are social before we are individual. We should say, philosophically speaking, that we are in a social relation *with* nature and nature *is* social. This is not a metaphor, it is a postulate required by any philosophy that keeps its abstractions properly arranged. Community requires more than sociality, however.

The purpose of this foray into nature and panexperientialism has been to show what it means to say that animals and canyons and stars have "experience," and hence why it should be said to exist in the personal mode, even if the experients have not attained any personality *we* can discern. With this we prepare the way for what many will find a far more difficult idea, which is the idea that institutions are persons.

Community Persons

This brings us to what I regard as Royce's most important living idea—that communities, and specifically institutions, should be philosophically conceived as communal persons. But before I can say what I have to say about institutions, I need to discuss communities. Clearly there is a relationship between institutions and communities, but how best to think about that relation, philosophically, is what I eventually want to describe. Most of us share an intuition that it is one thing to say that dogs (and perhaps rivers) are persons with whom we are or can be in community, and quite another to say that institutions are persons. Yet, if it is crucial to admit that, for philosophy, nature ought to be conceived as personal, and that to say so is simply recognition that we are social (with nature as with other humans) before we are individual, then it will be even harder to deny that institutions are to be thought of as persons in some sense. There can be little doubt that most of what is significant in human individuality depends upon the on-going activity of institutions, for institutions are interpreting us long before we can meaningfully return the kindness. We are obliged, practically, to treat institutions as persons *in order to interpret ourselves*. One could almost dismiss or ignore this implication of Royce's position; although it is present throughout his philosophy, he is not perfectly explicit about it until near the end of his life. In Chapter 9 I will examine his early essay "The Nature of Voluntary Progress," from which it will be evident that Royce regarded institutions as persons from the beginning.

Royce explains in a number of places why we resist the idea that in our sociality we are "members of one another," and this is connected to the way in which we hold as "decisively authoritative" a "principle of individuation" which "keeps selves apart, and forbids us to regard their various lives merely as incidents, or as undivided phases of a common life."[33] We have seen the upshot of Royce's own theory of individuation in Chapter 5, and it will be evident why he rejects the commonly held account of individuation, which, while he calls it a "stubborn pluralism," is actually objectionable because it is a kind of atomism and commits the errors of realism (i.e., independent existence).

Royce characterizes this atomistic view by noting three facts that seem to support it. 1. "We appear, then, to be individuated by the diversity and separateness of our streams of immediate feeling."[34] Here we have seen in earlier chapters how the problem of immediate experience, radical empiricism, and the disjunctive principle of person make this assumption problematic. It is a philosophically non-viable approach to individuation. 2. "We are individuated by the law that our trains of conscious thought and purpose are mutually inaccessible through any mode of direct intuition."[35] This assumption is dashed on the rocks because we do not have such direct intuitions of even *our own* thoughts and purposes, except as socially mediated, and this includes the active mediation of the "persons" in nature with which we communicate, whether they be animal, vegetable or mineral, and even our own natural bodies, as persons of this sort. To discover my own plan or purpose, or the simplest meaning of my thoughts, I must be interpreted by another. Finally, 3. "We . . . seem to be individuated by our deeds."[36] My actions are mine and yours are yours, it is commonly supposed. Yet, in order for any act to find its place in a wider context, without which it has no meaning (and is thus neither anyone's will nor anyone's purpose), my act must serve (or disserve) a cause *we* serve, or an ideal of some kind, and the *creation* of such a cause is the peculiar domain of communities. In short, persons are irreducibly social in every respect, including their individuality. It is simply not the case that my deed rests only upon my peculiar soul, beyond the reach of effect upon or atonement by a community, or that it originates in me alone from some primal will. If deeds are not essentially social, community cannot exist, because it cannot will, purpose, or attain any meaning (i.e., it cannot act). This kind of "hard bed pluralism," that insists upon the originary power of the individual will, to which Royce is opposed, is atomistic and it contradicts the existence of community as a philosophical idea, let alone a socially desirable ideal. James flirts with this kind of view, but does not submit to it. We will have more to say about such atomism in the next chapter, for it is not a true form of pluralism. One may get a "crowd" from this atomistic description (to use Royce's term), but never a community.

It is unsurprising that Royce seeks to define community, not first in terms of the dyadic relation of Individual and Community, but with reference to a triadic temporal process (since this is how Royce defines every philosophical concept). To say that anything exists as *real* is, for Royce, to say it has a past, a present, and a future. A community has a past, which we call its memory, and "the wealthier the memory of a community is, and the vaster the historical processes which it regards as belonging to its life, the richer—other things being equal—is its consciousness that it *is* a community."[37] The other things that need to be "equal" are, of course, the community's vital present and future hope.

The key to a vital present is that we accept as truth, and as our own, some portion of the communal memory, and share some portion of the same hope, and acknowledge that others have possible experience of the same.

And here Royce makes a crucial point: "The rule that time is needed for the formation of a conscious community is a rule which finds its extremely familiar analogy within the life of every human self . . . [M]y idea of myself is an interpretation of my past,—linked also with an interpretation of my hopes and intentions as to my future."[38] Notice that the community is the base term of the analogy, the starting place, and that the individual is explained by means of the community, not vice versa. The community's memories, its hopes, and its vital, present self-interpretation and truth, are the social ground upon which I build my self-interpretation, and upon that interpretation rests the development of the person that I have been, am, and purpose to become. And when matters are understood in this order of priority, Royce has no difficulty with the term "pluralism": when the "interests of each self lead it to accept any part or item of the same past or the same future which another self accepts as its own, —then pluralism of the selves is perfectly consistent with their forming a community, either or of memory or of hope."[39] Royce summarizes: "The concept of community, as thus analyzed, stands in the closest relation to the whole nature of the time-process."[40]

As a temporal process that coheres meaningfully, the community has *experience*. This is not a mere metaphor to human perceptual or conceptual or immediate experience, it is employed in the same sense we have explained in discussing panexperientialism above—for we should think of dogs and horses as time-processes in no fundamentally different sense than are rivers and moons, and human persons. What varies is the duration of an event or an experience. Communities, even strictly human ones, experience events in a broader durational span than do individual humans; yet communities do have experience. As Royce phrases it, "for our purposes, the community is a being that attempts to accomplish something in time through the deeds of its members."[41]

But we must not atomize the deeds of the members of a community. They do not act for themselves, at least not primarily: "It is, in fact, the ideally extended self, and not, in general, the momentary self, whose life is worth living . . . The genuine person lives in the far-off past and the future as well as in the present."[42] I can never over-emphasize the importance of Royce's use of the term "person" in such contexts, for person is a modality not in the least bounded by the extremes of biological birth and death. The genuine person is a hoped-for *possibility* in the community before he or she is *acknowledged* as a present part of the World of

Truth, of "other possible experience." And persons are *remembered* by the community after physically leaving it, whether by death or departure, not only in the individual memories of those who happen to have known or heard about the individual, but also in the present configuration and hopes for the future that exist in his or her community as a result of his or her past deeds. This is not just a concept, it literally happens, and philosophical concepts need to reflect this experience.

The modality of personal existing is simply more broadly extended in time than physical life. The community remembers each of us not by having a brain that processes sense impressions and retains traces and engrams thereof, but by existing itself in a particular meaningful, interpretable way, just *this* way and not some other, because you and I have uniquely acted so as to own a part of our community's memory and so as to accomplish some portion of its hopes and expectations. Communities *do* remember and they *do* hope. And they act; they will and they purpose. Royce says:

> As an essentially social being, man lives in communities, and . . . his communities . . . have a sort of organic life of their own, so that we can compare a highly developed community, such as a state, either to the soul of a man or to a living animal. A community is not a mere collection of individuals. It is a sort of live unit, that has organs, as the body of an individual has organs. A community grows or decays, is healthy or diseased, is young or aged, much as any individual member of the community possesses such characters. Each of the two, the community or the individual member, is as much a live creature as the other. Not only does the community live, it has a mind of its own, —a mind whose psychology is not the same as the psychology of an individual human being.[43]

The thesis of the experience of a social mind is far more worked out in Royce's unpublished writings than in his published work, but there is no reason to be hesitant about seeing this as his view, whether late or early in his thought. But the point for the present is that we see evidence in social groups, due to their memories, their hopes, and most importantly, their capacity to unify plans of action into joint action itself, the evidence of the personal mode of existing at the level of community. And in this regard I am obliged to reproduce in full a lengthy passage from Royce, which I think of as the master key to his whole philosophy and his most important living idea, the idea for which I have been setting the stage for the whole of this book. Thus, it will be important for the reader to note the presence of the central themes of my foregoing analysis, especially time, will and purpose, but also individuality, his method of postulates, and the idea of ethics as first philosophy. Royce begins:

> So far, then, I have merely sketched what, in another context, will hereafter concern us at much more length. For in later lectures we shall have to study the metaphysical problems which we here first touch. A community can be seen as a real unity. So far we have seen, and so far only we have yet gone.[44]

In this book, I have reversed the order of treatment. We have already dealt with the metaphysical problems associated with what follows, and in more detail and with a greater degree of synthesis, I hope, than Royce does in the remainder of *The Problem of Christianity*, although we are not yet to the point of being able to appreciate fully the implications of things he says later in this masterwork. Royce continues:

> But we have now to indicate why this conception, whether metaphysically sound or not, is a conception that can be ethical in its purposes. And here again, only the most elementary and fundamental aspects of our topic can be, in this wholly preparatory statement, mentioned. To all these problems we shall have later to return.
>
> We have said that a community can behave like a unit; we have now to point out that an individual member of a community can find numerous very human motives for behaving towards his community as if it were not only an unit, but a very precious and worthy being. In particular he—the individual member—may love his community as if it were a person, may be devoted to it as if it were his friend or father, may serve it, may live and die for it, and may do all this, not because philosophers tell him to do so, but because it is his own heart's desire to act thus.
>
> Of such active attitudes of love and devotion towards a community, on the part of an individual member of that community, history and daily life presents countless instances. One's family, one's circle of personal friends, one's home, one's village community, one's clan, or even one's country may be the object of such an active disposition to love and to serve the community as an unit, to treat the community as if it were a sort of super-personal being, and as if it could, in its turn, possess the value of a person on some higher level. One who thus loves a community, regards its type of life, its form of being, as essentially more worthy than his own. He becomes devoted to its interests as to something that by its very nature is nobler than himself. In such a case, he may find, in his devotion to his community, his fulfillment and his moral destiny. In order to view a community in this way it is, again I insist, not necessary to be a mystic. It is only necessary to be a hearty friend, or a good citizen, or a home-loving being.[45]

We cannot prove that the community *is* a person, but we can certainly show that persons behave *as if* they believe it is—indeed, they stake their whole lives upon it. The type of experience and life that a community has is temporal, consists in a kind of memory, hope, and action *analogous* to the type found in its individuals, but the personhood of community, for philosophy, depends upon our willingness to (and adeptness at) generalizing these aspects of personality in ways that reflect their concrete presence in our social experience. Whether community is actually conscious, or actually possesses a will, is not a question we have to settle once and for all, but upon these additional suppositions rests the issue of whether the community has a *purpose*. The evidence of "community will" is found in its capacity to unify plans of action and to achieve outcomes. Whether these outcomes have any *moral* meaning depends upon our willingness to understand them as *purposes*.

Whether this difficult constellation of ideas—amounting to conceiving the community as a kind of person—has *metaphysical* meaning depends upon whether it has *moral* meaning, since the former exists only to serve the latter. Royce's point is that the norms we accept in philosophizing require us to attend to experience as it is had by those who philosophize. That experience includes this devotion to community as if it were a kind of person, a more-than-human person. To leave this out of account is to fail to be an empiricist, or an experientialist, or a pragmatist (or a personalist). To include it does not require mysticism (or philosophical idealism), only the concrete experience of life in community, especially of love, which acts to make the community we serve unique, irreplaceable, the exclusive object of our will, and an individual in its own right—one from which we derive our own individuality. It is not simply the case that we love our communities and so render them persons; rather, we are first loved *by* our communities and learn, in time, through making them the exclusive object of our interest, to return the gift. But we are individuated before we individuate.

In addition, it is not simple affection and attention we receive *from* our communities, it is the instilling of the purposes *of* our communities as possibilities *for* our future lives of service. We may be raised in better or worse communities, but so long as our community is more than a mere crowd, a disorganized social group, there will be purposes and in light of their influence, we become not just individuals, but persons. Social groups that are not communities can still individuate us (we can discover our own wills, form plans of action, without genuine community, but this is little more than a Hobbesian state of nature), but only communities can personalize us. If this is mystical, then we are all mystics, excepting perhaps those among us who are sociopaths. But this possibility of sociopathy warrants further consideration.

Defective Community Persons

The problem of the sociopath is precisely the failure to credit the *value* of the possible experience of others, and the metaphysics that follows from such a condition fails to credit the possible *reality* of the same. Only with such a perverse move can there be a "problem of other minds," and "personal identity," and other like pseudo-problems with which twentieth-century philosophy so often occupied itself. The real issue is not the reality of other minds, but the tendency among some to trust ungrounded abstractions above concrete experience, which we might dub "the problem of the problem of other minds," or more broadly and congenially, "the philosopher's fallacy," as James and Dewey called it. More pointedly, we might simply note that all forms of abstractionism and reductionism are sociopathic, and we might with justice lament that this is the current state of professional philosophy and a great deal of science, both social and natural.

It is even more tragic that education has been largely unable to escape the same trap. But even the most dedicated reductionist, from LaPlace to Comte to Churchland, probably loved someone—a spouse, children, perhaps even a community or a nation—and made himself thereby a walking contradiction: a "mystic" in life, a reductionist and abstractionist in thinking. That is a sad way to live, especially when it requires only that one give due credit to one's most intimate and trustworthy experiences to avoid it. And yet, the likes of Richard Dawkins, and E.O. Wilson, and Daniel Dennett, and other vicious abstractionists, did not create themselves as the intellectual sociopaths they ultimately became (I have no notion of their private lives, I speak here of their sociopathic theories). They developed in that direction in service of defective purposes, which they learned and adopted from defective scholarly communities. The academic institutions which provided these abstractionists with their ideals about what is and is not "knowledge" have poor memories and dim prospects, but they also participate in a wider community of communities, institutions dedicated primarily to economic or political or legal or scientific or religious purposes that provide the educational institutions with their own personalities. We should not be surprised when, for example, our economic institutions teach us that we are "consumers" and nothing more, that this will have an effect upon our educational institutions (and upon how they frame and pursue their own purposes). Thus, one could encounter a student who understands himself as a "consumer" of educational goods and services.

Analogously, if one has legal or political institutions that encourage people to see themselves as "having more rights than duties," as Royce phrases it, one can hardly be surprised when the legal system is choked by people seeking advantages at all levels and treating the law as an instrumentality for gaining them, and politics is packed with pundits and opportunists. The Supreme Court decision in the USA that gives to corporations, which are almost always defective communities, the same political standing as persons attributed to biological individuals is a fine case study. The travesty here is not treating corporations as persons (they *are* persons), it is treating our *current* profit-driven corporations as anything short of the criminally defective communities they are. Giving them political influence is like offering firearms to a person who is insane.

Similarly, if the scientific community is bent either toward the purpose of serving the bottom line or securing the military might of a nation, we should not be surprised when it begins to generate the kind of "knowledge" that serves those ends. Academic institutions are not, alone and of their own wills, defective. They grow to be defective by being valued inappropriately in the wider community of institutions, just as biological individuals can become dysfunctional from abuse or neglect or from having their lower qualities (such as physical attractiveness) exploited. The same is the case for economic, military, legal and political institutions. Such institutions do not *have* to behave sociopathically, but they often do. A government that misuses its military, as the United States does, inevitably warps its military.[46] The human being who strives to be a person by serving institutions that have been warped risks taking into himself or herself the defects of purpose and memory that are immanent in the activities of the institutions themselves—what they attend to and ignore, what they include and exclude, and how they treat possibilities and truth.

Thus, one can, under the right circumstances, get individuals such as Hitler, who *thinks* he is serving the genuine purposes of the Fatherland by purposing policies that destroy the very cause he sought to advance, or one can get scientists such as Dawkins and Wilson, or philosophers such as Dennett, these little fascists of the intellect ensconced within their tiny domains of thought (for such is reductionism in all its forms, as the *Endlösung* of scientific thinking), who are engaged in the academic and educational equivalent, cleansing the Reich of human thought of whatever strikes them as impure. They tell human beings, without apparent shame and without any hint of humility, that we are nothing more than our "biology" or our "physical aspects," or whatever the Zyklon B of their pet theories happens to be, and often this is not even recognized as a fundamental assault upon human dignity and the full range of human experience. No doubt, such persons see themselves as serving a noble cause, but it would be interesting to hear them explain what a cause could possibly *be*, if not an ideal purpose which, according to their fanciful stories, is not the sort of thing that ought to be regarded as "real." I would personally rather confront fundamentalists, since at least they *know* they are superstitious, and at least they are afraid of their own God.

Defective institutions grow sociopathic over long spans of time, and the individuals who come to be persons within the shorter time-spans they contain have difficulty in discerning the ways in which they have been degraded by their own sociopathic institutions. Unfortunately such sociopathic institutions are common these days (as happens in aging civilizations). But even Wal-Mart was not always sociopathic, as hard as that is to believe nowadays.

Institutional Persons

Yet, we are hesitant, and with ample reason, to look upon institutions as persons at all. Let us look more closely at the idea. Recently Nir Eisikovits, a personalist philosopher, has explained that a great harm has been done, historically, by bestowing upon corporations the legal status of persons. He shows how the theories of personal identity in Locke and Hume have been assumed in the history of legal rulings that gradually extended to corporations the same Constitutional rights enjoyed by human individuals, and he questions whether the Lockean and Humean theories are really adequate for grounding an account of personhood that will balance properly the issues of rights and responsibilities. He does not argue, however, that corporations are not persons, but rather shows the sense in which they have been *treated as* persons in U.S. legal history and finds it wanting. I agree with Eisikovits, and I think he is correct to have noticed that both the Lockean and Humean accounts of personal identity show a dependence upon *memory* that they cannot well explain. Royce's account is stronger in proportion to the adequacy of his accounts of memory, truth and hope (or past present and future, in the relevant, i.e., personal, sense).[47]

Extending Eisikovits's analysis into our own context, we can see that such a move as defining the corporation legally as a person can be and has been ill-used to excuse executives and leaders and workers associated with corporations from moral and individual responsibility for the consequences of their actions, yet their moral holiday does not follow inexorably from the status of corporate legal personhood—it is rather an abuse and a systematic undermining of that very status. It is easier to make the point if we consider a historical institution that comes as close as any to being treated as if it were a person by the majority of its members, and in this I mean the church. It is not an accident that Royce focused upon this very institution, with an eye to discovering its personal mode of existence and meaning in *The Problem of Christianity*. The general philosophical view is set forth in *The Philosophy of Loyalty*, and Royce is very clear that the situation in historical Christianity treated in the later book is an *application* of that broader philosophy of loyalty.[48]

There are other reasons to consider the example of the church, apart from the devotion and exclusive love felt by billions of people for their religious communities. In the case of Christianity, there has been the historical practice of conceiving of the institution itself as the incarnate body of the person of Christ. I am uninterested, here at least, in the dogma associated with this history, but the idea that the church is the body of Christ is of heuristic value, for it illustrates the personalization of community. One can certainly find analogies in other religious traditions—the body of the god as the community of the people is an idea that goes back as far as human history and predates that history by thousands of years. I choose the Christian tradition because Royce chooses it.

It is worth noting that the term "corporation" and its infinitive "to incorporate" mean "body" and "to embody." We reserve "incarnation" for religious contexts, but the wisdom of words is evident in treating a corporation as a legal person. I want to make it clear, however, that in all these cases, whether church, corporation, or any institution, *personalizing* the community is a *response* to the community's *prior* personalization of the members of that community. It is not the case that we merely project our own personalities upon an institution and so personify them. We can treat institutions as if they are persons precisely because they treat us as if we were persons before we actually attain any significant individuality and form plans which can become purposes in the community setting. Because the community has a body, and its body is already an incorporation or embodiment of the achievement of not just its will, but its purposes, the community is a person before we respond to it as such. Institutions, whether they be legal, educational, or religious, protect and nourish and *intend* our personhood before we have it, and the deeds of these institutions, including their memory, their hope, and their truth, constitute something akin to the soul or personality of any community in which deeds are enacted. One can wreck the physical places, displace, oppress, and dehumanize the people, and inflict all manner of havoc upon them, but so long as their institutions survive, the community lives. I suppose that the continued existence of Judaism through two thousand years of diaspora is an obvious enough example, but there are countless others. It does seem to me that if a community has a single essential feature in the collection of institutions that constitute its personality, its religion would probably be that feature.

Commercial institutions are also capable of this sort of personalizing of their servants, through the achieved personality of the commercial institution itself, but having become, under corporate capitalism, deeply sinful institutions (in a sense I will explain), commercial institutions more often destroy our personhood instead of teaching us the true meaning of finding a calling in life to serve. The dialectic of labor and management in the late nineteenth and early twentieth century was evidence of dysfunction, a growing sociopathy, in commercial institutions, the result of which was the depersonalization of both labor and management (a fine example of what Royce calls a "dangerous dyad" or "dangerous pair"), resulting in the inability of either to conceive of its own commercial enterprise as a unified person worthy of love, devotion, or service. But if labor and management struggles have abused the personhood of commercial institutions, multi-national corporate capitalism has sold them into prostitution—it is not unlike offering one's own mother for sale to the john who will pay her the least and treat her the worst. After a few years, the commercial institution has been so depersonalized as to become a mere shell, no longer recognizable to those who once loved it. But now such corporations, so reduced and debauched, are the dominant donors to American political parties which have pimped the legislative and executive powers, and now the elections themselves, to the corporate johns who shell out the most cash for attack ads. What, for example, would Sam Walton say about Wal-Mart today? I am certain he truly loved this institution. I doubt he would have made it into what it has become, which is the most frightening, exploitative, diabolical, and utterly sociopathic institutional person on earth since the Nazi state fell. Unfortunately, it has many siblings.

The church, among all of these institutions, has been explicitly proclaimed a person. It is not surprising that the church both brings out what is highest in us, and in its own sinfulness, destroys most thoroughly the same delicate and precious relations. There is simply nothing in human experience, even Wal-Mart, that damages persons more deeply than the betrayal of its members by the person of the church—although nation states have gone very far in their desire to compete with the church for inflicting maximal damage on the human personality, and commercial institutions are today doing their utmost to compete. We will have more to say about this political dimension of institutional personhood in the next chapter. For now we can simply remark that nations have deeply damaged the individuals who were devoted to them as surely as the church has. And there is a way of understanding this outcome, and perhaps even of avoiding it. We can certainly understand that the ardent nationalism of, for example, the Second Reich, was not set upon the purpose of destroying the loyalty of its citizens, or its own institutions, or itself. The aim, the co-ordinate will and the purpose of its actions was explicitly the opposite of this, and indeed, the same might be said of the Third Reich, Stalinist Russia, Maoist China, or indeed, neo-conservative America. But all of these political institutions, and countless others, have made a similar error, which is to have conceived of their ideals and visions and purposes in *im*personal terms, sometimes without *intending* to do so. It matters little whether the impersonal force through which the nation, or any historical institution, is conceived is a World Spirit, a folkish spirit, a dialectically driven material or economic necessity, a national manifest destiny, or any other kind of similar vision. What all of them neglect is to ground the devotion of their individuals in a purpose to make their institutions better *persons*, i.e., more rather than less socially adept at negotiating the possible experiences and the world of truth beyond their own social experience.[49]

The church, on the other hand, perhaps because it adopted the dogma of conceiving of itself as a person, cannot so easily embrace, consciously or unconsciously, a similar impersonal stance. This is something Royce understood, and he asked himself which among the many essential features of historical Christianity was most needful in maintaining the restraint from abstractionism and sociopathy and encouraging the development of personhood in its history. He decided upon three central ideas: Community, the Lost Individual (or State), and Atonement (or Divine Grace). Much excellent interpretation has been written about this application of the philosophy of loyalty, and I will not repeat it here.[50] Much more can be said about these living ideas. But my point for the purposes of this chapter is (at this stage) a simpler one.

Where an institution is conceived in personal and temporal terms, with due weight given to the most intimate aspects of individual experience, one has a built-in check upon the tendency of allowing it to become a force in history that depersonalizes both its own individual servants and those who serve other institutions. This has kept the Christian church from becoming utterly sociopathic, as a whole, even when it has descended into the most sinful depths in given places and times. We see, for example, that when faced with whether to treat "savages" as persons or not, the Roman Catholic Church, not without difficulty, decided to save the souls of the savages (or African slaves, or its own bitterest enemies) before exploiting them. In time, such decisions bear fruit; they have taken the savages or slaves or enemies into the body of the church, and the body is a person—the savage or slave or enemy is a "person," and therefore the mistreatment of him or her instills a contradiction into the heart of the community. Paul says to them that the eye is not supposed to despise the ear or the foot, for the body is one. In time, the community experiences this contradiction of mistreating its own as "sin," and confesses, and seeks atonement.

The check against depersonalization in the church is, however, insufficient in the short-run, and much damage has been done, and may be done, during phases in which the servants of the church (or any institutional person) have seen it as a vehicle for the establishment of power, wealth and secular glory in the short-term. Such persons blind themselves to the sins of this institution and also to its own need for atonement, even while they are employing it as a means rather than as an end in itself. And the confession and atonement may be insufficient to secure a healthy community of memory.

Reinhold Niebuhr famously observed that we tolerate behavior from groups, notably institutions such as nations and churches, behavior of a sort we would never condone from human individuals. He believed that nothing could be done about this—groups are incorrigible, and individuals, through the prophetic stance, would always need to set themselves against the immoral behavior of groups.[51] This is a bleak perspective, but unfortunately well warranted by the facts of history and the realistic expectations we might form in the present. Yet, although he was a thorough-going personalist with regard to human individuals, Niebuhr took an impersonalist view of institutions as the impersonal products of a dialectical history.[52] He had read Royce and, I think, should have known better than to adopt this methodological approach and to allow it to dictate to him such a hopeless, indeed, almost nihilistic conclusion.

The development of social groups toward realized community, institutions that serve humbly and deepen personhood for themselves and for all, is something the individual members of the group desire in concert. They almost never intend anything other than the achievement of these worthy and valuable ends (even Wal-Mart consciously aims to serve and uplift the thousands of communities it effectively rapes and murders, and the millions of workers it exploits and depersonalizes in the process, using them as instruments for the destruction of other precious, unique and irreplaceable institutional persons—and if this is not the community equivalent of rape and murder, I don't know what is). Wal-Mart does not aim at being a retro-virus in the communities it infects. The question is whether individual members of the Wal-Mart "team" can learn adequately to pursue the nobler aims. Those who do will leave the corporation. How do we learn to form purposes for our communities, that nurture their development *as* persons by serving our institutions, and how do we judge those purposes as either contributing to or detracting from progress toward that end?

This is a very difficult question, and partly for the same reasons we find trouble individually in attempting to discern for ourselves a life-plan that will lead to the development of these same values in ourselves. It is tough to commit oneself to a life-plan when one cannot adequately foresee the *outcome*, i.e., the "person" that results from the "purpose." That is, we cannot know in advance which purposes we may idealize and pursue that will, in the end, be detrimental or beneficial to our own developing personhood. For example, one might fall in love with someone who, in the end, is either self-destructive or is set upon the destruction of what is best in oneself. One might, analogously, advocate and approve a purpose for one's community—from building a Wal-Mart outside of town to expanding one's national territory, a commitment to manifest destiny or *Lebensraum*—that in the end destroys the very "person" one sought to develop, i.e., the community. And there seems to be no failsafe check upon misguided or misplaced loyalty. Under such circumstances, Niebuhr's bleak assessment seems inescapable. This is, indeed, the story of history, and part of the reason that the account of community in Royce is incomplete without the discussion of the Lost Individual (or State), and Atonement (or Divine Grace). However, even if there are no guarantees about what genuinely will nourish the development of institutional persons, there are some things we can recognize and adopt. We fall in love with a life-plan that we make our "purpose" in a way similar to falling in love with a human individual, and as the exclusive object of our will, it becomes the purpose from which we develop our own personhood.

It is difficult to avoid falling in love with the "wrong" person, and perhaps even more difficult to avoid falling in love with the "wrong" life-plan and making it one's purpose. Royce counsels falling in love with the *world* as a safeguard, but falling in love with the world will not happen until one has betrayed one's own cause, and has endured the consequences of having done so. Nothing can be more painful, and yet, nothing seems more inevitable, for according to Royce, the successful community creates a strong individual, and a strong individual resists the bonds of even an excellent community. He calls this "original sin." The relation of the community person to the individual person is unstable; it is only a question of time before the break occurs. Thus, the Prodigal Son leaves his father's house not because it was dysfunctional, but precisely because it was an excellent "person," a fine institution. Progress is possible, but it is very painful. One cannot simply choose to fall in love with the world until one has learned both the meaning of service to and betrayal of one's own community—and that means first becoming a servant of an institution. Progress can and does occur (we will see how in the next chapter). The key to it is the careful generalization of the relation between temporality and personality, to the extent we do understand it, to the institutions we serve, and from which we receive, as a return for our service, personal growth of our own.

Recommendations

While I do not know of any failsafe formula for the careful generalization from the personhood of individual humans to the personhood of institutions, in our *thinking* (for the process operates in the other direction in practice, i.e., our personhood is a concentration in individualized form of the community's interpretive activity), yet I do believe that some guidelines are available and reliable.

First, it is unwise to embrace a short-term view in one's individual life, and given that institutional persons experience temporal durations much longer than our own, it is proportionately more unwise to take a short-term view relative to institutional purposes. The churches have done fairly well at taking the longer view, adjusting themselves slowly to changing conditions and waiting to see the meaning of the changes before choosing its best course of adaptation. For example, it has been wise, in my judgment, for the Roman Catholics to regard the revelation of God's will for the church to be a matter that is on-going in history, and has been incredibly unwise—one is tempted to say idiotic—for certain Protestant denominations to declare miracles at an end and the revelation complete. I have no idea whether miracles occur, but it seems to be common sense to recognize that an institution which depends upon the reality of such events might not want to isolate itself from all possibility of their recurrence. Building in an on-going channel of communication that corresponds to the durational epochs of one's institution is needful. The process of amendment for the Constitution of the United States, along with staggered election cycles, provides for an epochal assessment of the national person.

Another guideline is evident in the recognition that institutions can be better and worse persons, but they are not disconnected from the moral character of their servants. That is to say, for example, if one were to designate an institution as having the legal status of personhood, such a designation should be so configured as to *strengthen* rather than weaken the level of responsibility borne by its individual servants. Personhood among corporations ought to be *earned* through service to others within and beyond its own membership, and corporate success should be measured in the moral development of its servants, not by its bottom line.

Wouldn't it be interesting if the right to move from private to publicly traded corporations were made by the Securities and Exchange Commission based upon the moral rather than the financial development of the company? And what if the privilege of trading on Wall Street depended not upon one's financial resources, but upon one's moral character? To some that may sound crazy, but it is not. If the legal status of personhood among corporations were something corporations could attain by selfless service rather than by self-serving financial success, the legal standing itself would perhaps be unproblematic, and there would be no temptation to use the "personhood" status as a substitute for individual responsibility among the leaders or workers. Morally developed servants of a genuine business community are prepared to risk their well-being on the destiny of that business, and I see no reason why that risk should be merely financial; it is a moral risk, and failure in the behavior of the institution should carry moral consequences for those who have served it (e.g., loss of individual freedom or incarceration). But as things stand, the goals of these individual servants are purely material in nature, e.g., power and gain, in which case, we cannot be surprised that these individuals are under-developed condensations of the corporation and its greed, and both corporation and individual servant are likely to behave in sociopathic ways, as for instance Wal-Mart now does, but did not always do. This outcome is avoidable, if difficult to avoid.

A third guideline is to recognize that no institution can afford to lock itself in its own closely held story about who and what it is. Without other institutions, and their experience, the story a "closed" institution tells itself about itself has no access to the world of truth. It lives on "bread alone," so to speak, having no ears for the words that come from the mouths of others. Such an institution may try to use force to get others to accept its private version of its identity or reality, it may close its borders to others, persecute those who will not accept the exclusive right of the keepers-of-the-story to control all its details. This is like trying to have a conversation with someone who will not credit what you say unless you first grant him absolute authority over the meanings of all of his words as well as all of yours. The United States has been behaving this way in recent decades, but it is neither a new phenomenon in history (see Royce's account of the conquest of California), nor the exclusive possession of one political party or nation.

Much that is pathological in the Roman Catholic Church, for example, derives from its unwillingness to be interpreted by anyone outside of its own ranks—when it credits external interpretations, it is healthier, when it denies the value and reality of such external viewpoints, it falls into sin. The Protestant Reformation is a fair example of how this sickness within the historical Roman Church can give rise to a response that damages everyone, and especially thwarts the "person" the church wishes to be. If the Church is the Body of Christ, what must Christ have felt during the Thirty Years' War? The simple point is that the interpretations of other institutions are crucial to the truth about the ones we individually serve, and any institution that is fundamentally closed to such interpretive activity will eventually behave sociopathically—or *is* behaving sociopathically—and cannot be long for this world. Institutional persons cannot grow in the achievement of their purposes without acknowledging the reality of other possible experience and its perspective upon truth.

A similar point might be made regarding history. An institution that covers up its past misdeeds, its betrayals of its own best purposes in the past, of its servants, and of others beyond its fold, cannot develop beyond a certain point. It is hard to know the exact degree to which the intense desire to forget our personal misdeeds, sins, and betrayals in the past occludes our capacity for hope and vital community in the present, but the point that Royce makes is that we can receive no atonement until such betrayals are allowed to become a vital part of the memory of our communities. To turn our historical backs upon, taking the U.S. as an example, the sin of slavery or the genocide of Native peoples in the Americas, is a nearly certain way to ensure that those who still endure the lingering effects of those sins are forced to choose between a truth they know immediately and a participation in social life which forbids the explicit speaking of their concrete perspectives. W.E.B. DuBois called this phenomenon "double consciousness." This is not terribly different from a person who carries around the memory (and consequences) of having committed a terrible sin which no one ever learns about, because he holds the secret too closely, perhaps not even letting himself be conscious of it. The outcome is a divided and desperate personality. The plays of Ibsen come to mind as repeated examples of this dynamic. The community of memory is the basis of present truth, if present truth is to be inclusive.

I know of many institutions that suffer from such afflictions of memory. Unsurprisingly, the persons who serve them often display the characteristics. Not being able to admit a mistake is bad enough, and common, but not being able to own a betrayal of one's own best purposes, such as, for example the second Bush administration did in creating a war in Iraq, damages an institution permanently. Atonement is not possible without owning the betrayal. When, for example, is the U.S. likely to admit to the world its betrayal of its own intentions to serve freedom? Ask the people of Iraq for forgiveness, and the world for help in atoning for the betrayal? I cite Royce again, in a passage I used early in the book, but now, perhaps, it may be read with greater understanding:

> It is to be hoped that this lesson [the immorality of the Mexican War and its clear implications for the immorality of the conquest of California], showing us as it does how much of conscience and even personal sincerity can coexist with a minimum of effective morality in international undertakings, will someday be once more remembered; so that when our nation is another time about to serve the devil, it will do so with more frankness and will deceive itself less by half-unconscious cant. For the rest, our mission in the cause of liberty is to be accomplished through a steadfast devotion to the cultivation of our own inner life, and not by going abroad as missionaries, as conquerors, or as marauders among weaker peoples.[53]

Other guidelines could be listed (and perhaps should be), but all of them are really just common sense recognition of a very basic insight: that our own personhood is an ideal that depends upon our temporal relation to community life, and that where there is civilization, that community life is governed by institutions.[54] Institutions might be, and might remain, defective persons—certainly the church is among the greatest of sinners, which seems to be contrary to the claim that Christ lived a sinless life. If the Church is the Body of Christ, in more than the ideal sense surrounding a hope for the eventual Kingdom of God, then

"Christ" is not doing very well in head, heart or body, although perhaps better now than he was doing in the Thirty Years' War. Yet, for all our failures, and with no guarantees of success, it is better to recognize that "person" and "purpose" are temporally bound together, and that wherever purposes are corrupted, persons will suffer beyond what is avoidable. We do have the option of forming purposes that at least prevent the foreseeable effects of depersonalization, but we can never accomplish this, in my view, without recognizing that idealized temporal purposes should guide both social and individual will, and that personality is the highest value in the field of experience, so far as we know.

[9]
Conservatism and Progress

In a sense we have completed the process of setting out the central themes of this book—especially time, will, and purpose, but also individuality, pragmatism, ontology, method, personalism, and others. I am hopeful that something has been learned in this process, not only about how to understand Royce, but how to use in our own day the living ideas I have tried to highlight and explain. What remains to be done is to apply these ideas in ways that will not only fill out some further aspects of Royce's life and development, but also show the way to put his ideas to work in our own time and place. There are many possible applications one could choose, apart from the political (this chapter) and the educational (the next chapter) domains I have settled upon. I choose these partly because they are of pressing interest to many people, and to me. I also choose them because less work has been done in these areas by other Royce scholars. Incredibly valuable applications of Royce's moral philosophy have been done by, for example, Jacquelyn Kegley, Griffin Trotter, Jason M. Bell, Mary Briody Mahowald, Marc Anderson, and others. I will not try to cover ground that has already been thoroughly explored.

Yet, while interpreters of the philosophy of Royce have been able to come to terms fairly well with his progressivism and his relational theory of community—indeed, the subsequent literature on his theory of community would fill a large bookshelf—one subject that continues to vex interpreters is, for lack of a better word, Royce's "conservatism." Nearly all of Royce's interpreters have been what we would, in today's political parlance, broadly label as "liberals," which really means progressive humanitarians and humanists, not so much members of the Democrat party in the US, or persons committed to the program of the Enlightenment and classical theories of individual rights and liberties that came to be embodied in the US Constitution. It is not an accident that Royce attracts persons whose views are, in this sense "liberal." He was a broad-minded and far-thinking person—liberal in the best sense. But the term "liberal" is vague in contemporary usage, and it is not a term Royce would quickly (or ever) apply to himself, in our present sense of it, were he to inhabit our troubled times. It is also clear that the term "conservative" suffers from the same vagueness, or perhaps even perversion, in the present day. Yet, that is the right term, in a certain sense, that best applies to Royce's political thought, and as we shall see, it is the term that best accords with his ontology. The aim of this chapter is to provide an account of his conservatism, to explain what it means and why he cannot be seen as an heir to classical liberalism.

Taken in strictly historical terms, this question of Royce's "conservatism" is really of interest to only the community of Royce scholars, but there are reasons beyond this limited sphere to investigate this question. Something of its more current interest becomes clearer when we consider the following: Martin Luther King's interpretation of "the beloved community" as a racially integrated society has had a great impact upon human life both within and beyond the United States, and what I have to say here affects also our understanding of King's thought and his legacy, for, if I am right, King was also a progressive conservative in nearly the same sense as Royce.[1] Indeed, the progressive conservative voice in the history of American political thought has been a poorly understood, but always vital, influence upon the development of democracy in the US and throughout the world. But since the days of King, this type of voice has been increasingly rare in US politics—one can barely point to a single clear example today—and the absence has been and remains a problem. The better we understand the progressive conservative, the better we may understand why the absence of its voice in the present is a great loss for civil discourse and contemporary political thought in the US. Thus, I am suggesting a return to Royce's political views as one purpose we might choose, and thereby revitalize our social groups in the direction of genuine communities. It is certainly a robust perspective, contrasting profoundly with the anemic politics of the present.

Metaphysics

It is generally taken for granted that when we speak of American democracy we mean by this something like "liberal democracy," i.e., democracy in the general tradition of Locke and Montesquieu, as read through the thinking, writing and action of the framers of American democracy, especially Jefferson, Hamilton, and Madison. We might add to these Enlightenment influences, the serious influence of classical (especially

Roman Republican) political thought.[2] There is little question that this liberalism is the dominant *intellectual* strand in the development of American political thought, and I see no reason to question that. But it is not the whole story, and indeed, progressive movements in American democracy, from the American Revolution to the Civil Rights Movement, have always been accompanied by, and perhaps even partly *driven* by, a different way of thinking than the hybrid Lockean-classical liberalism. That engine of change is conservative progressivism, and it is the viewpoint of many key political and intellectual leaders.[3] Royce is exemplary among these, and I will explain what this means and why we should continue to think of Royce as a conservative progressive, and why this is not a contradiction in terms. It will become gradually clear how this position relates to the accounts of time, will, and purpose explained in the foregoing chapters.

In making my case I wish to draw upon work by Aaron G. Fortune, who has articulated a useful conceptual framework for discussing issues of American political thought along the following lines: Fortune defines political positions as falling along three axes, each with its own structure.[4] Political thinkers may differ in 1. metaphysical presuppositions, depending upon whether they are *atomists* or *relationalists*; 2. they may differ methodologically, and here Fortune describes thinkers as endorsing either *liberal method* or *conservative method*; and 3. they may differ regarding the issue of social inclusion, in which case they are, in Fortune's terms, either *parochial* or *progressive*.

Any of these positions, in metaphysics, method, and inclusion, is compatible with any of the others from a different level of discourse, or generalization. Hence, a single thinker might be, for instance, an "atomistic liberal parochial," or an "atomistic conservative progressive," or a "relational liberal progressive," and so forth. Fortune does not discuss Royce, but in his terms, Royce would be a "relational conservative progressive." But what does this mean? And what is learned from such thinking? I would point out that the only universal in this schema is at the level of metaphysics, which is to say it is treated as a hypothesis that has a universal form and a logic appropriate to it. The entire schema is normative in character—a guide to how we *ought* to think about these issues, not a description of how we do think about them. The matter of method in the schema operates at a highly general and dialectical level, but as will be seen, it is the ethical level. The level of social inclusion is general, but less so, and subject to significant historical and contextual variation. All three levels are to be taken as applications of temporalist thinking.

Fortune argues that metaphysics, for the purposes of political thought, is really the metaphysics of *person*—one might say "personal identity," but that turns the question toward epistemology in a way that is not altogether necessary. He makes this case without attempting to set out a complete account of "person," but it will be clear at this point why I would see this distinction as congenial to the interpretation of Royce I have been providing. Clearly I think that the concept of "person," as the highest value in the field of experience, is the ideal for the sake of which one undertakes ontology or metaphysics at all. And we have now available, in the present work and in Dwayne Tunstall's book, a considerable and detailed account of the idea of person in Royce.

Fortune's basic point in distinguishing "atomism" from "relationalism" in the metaphysics of person is that, on the one hand, we may think of the individual, or person, as a self-sufficient being whose metaphysical status is *not* essentially *dependent* upon relations to other persons for its mode of existence. This is atomism. For an atomist, the isolated individual would have the necessary resources to be a person without a community, and as a result, for atomists, communities are really constituted by already (potentially) self-sufficient persons creating among themselves external relations (e.g., a social contract) whereby a community or civil society is created. An extreme and absurd version of such a view would be the romantic individualism of Ayn Rand and her cultic following. But the view is more often believed than seriously defended (it being nearly impossible to defend in any thorough-going way). Lockean individualism is often functionally treated in such a fashion.

It is possible to be both an atomist and a personalist at the same time, as I have pointed out in Chapter 7, although the position is not a common one. The relation between individuality and personality may also, in contrast, follow a developmental course for atomists, one consummate, functionally, with accounts like Royce's, that culminate in the temporal purpose of creating genuine communities that protect and nurture personality. But the social groups created by such individuals are derivative of the rational will (e.g., Locke) or irrational will (e.g., Hobbes) of those who create them. Thus, there is (or can be) rich common ground between atomists and relationalists in terms of practical life, plans of action, and even purposes. Communitarian conservative progressives don't have too much trouble making common cause with some sorts of Leftist individualists, such as committed civil libertarians. But for an atomist, the individual is given, irreducible, and hence the rationale for community originates in the choices of individuals.

Thus, an atomist, no matter how community-minded, will see political arrangements and social groupings of all kinds as an external addition to individuality, and individuality as ontologically prior to sociality, at least in terms of how best to *think* about social and political order. Civil libertarians begin with the Bill of Rights rather than asking after the ground of such. The functional universal of atomist metaphysics is the independent individual. Many atomists take this starting place to be more than a hypothesis—it is commonly claimed to be a bit of ontological knowledge. Whether an atomist proceeds hypothetically or in accord with the "unholy trinity" (see Chapter 2) matters little for our present purposes. The universal functions the same in this kind of thinking about political and ethical life in either case.

A relationalist, on the contrary, will hold that personhood (and thus meaningful individuality) exists only in community, and that no individual has, unto himself or herself, the needed resources for full personhood, or in Royce's case, even individuality, without the essential contributions of others. Thus, for relationalists, civil societies are expressions of interdependent communal beings, and *personal* existence is a product of an ideal or aim of life in community. Here meaningful individuality in political association is the great work of the relational community itself, not an external construction from which communities are formed. Sociality (as a mode of relation) is given, individuality emerges, and personality is an ideal social achievement, when individuality is adequately facilitated with a life plan that makes moral sense. Thus, for relationalists, the functional universal is relation, not independent individuality. In the case of Royce, that fundamental relation is to be understood as having a temporal structure, but as we have seen, what brings relation to have any concrete meaning is that temporality is social, since it is understood as the form of the "will" or the intentional stance, and the will is the outcome of social-temporal relatedness.

With that said, it should be clear why Royce is a relationalist in metaphysics, according to Fortune's schema. For Royce we do not even have individual selves, let alone attain personhood, until we learn what we are from others.[5] What is given for Royce is a perspective that does not know itself, and through action the will discovers itself as the relation of irrevocable past action to present truth; the will individualizes us by an act of exclusion, the first example of which is loving another in such a way as to make that other irreplaceable and unique.[6] Only after this act of exclusion by the will does a genuine individual begin to take shape, to discover reflectively what it has already willed. Only when the will is guided by a moral purpose, a plan of life, does a full person begin to emerge, the product of a community of interpretation. Thus, for Royce, personhood is a relational phenomenon and the *conception* of person as a self-sufficient atom is, from his viewpoint, a vicious abstraction. Royce is a relationalist in the metaphysics of person.

Social and Political Inclusion

Royce is also a progressive, and in Fortune's terms, this means someone who favors the on-going expansion of who counts as a citizen. While "parochials" tend to rely upon fixed traditional or transcendental criteria regarding who "counts," progressives are constantly pressing the boundaries of inclusion, expanding the sphere of moral and political concern so as to take into the political community those who may have been excluded for some reason.[7] Royce explicitly defines "progress" in the sense it is meant here as early as 1880, saying that it is "the way in which human purposes and desires modify the institutions and growth of society."[8] Royce counsels that we ought to embrace progress in this sense, and in his writings he argues for not only increasing social inclusion, but for total social inclusion, which culminates in loyalty to loyalty and the ideal of a beloved community.

The ideal of the beloved community includes all and any who share a community of memory, a community of hope, and an on-going will to interpret one another, and this is the practical expression of his temporalism. Not only are all persons included, but all who can *become* persons. There certainly are instances in which both progress and loyalty to loyalty demand the *exclusion* of some persons from community from the local, general, or world community.[9] Royce's criteria for such exclusion are clear enough. It is only through betrayal of the ideal of community and progress that persons (including communities, institutions and political bodies such as states, since, as we saw in Chapter 8, Royce regarded these collective entities as persons in the relevant sense) exclude *themselves* from the beloved community, the progressive realization of which simply *is* the only comprehensive moral imperative. There are numerous examples in Royce's writings of individual persons choosing such exclusion, through betrayals and rebellions of various types, and of the atonement which is available when such persons become aware of the atoning activity of the community itself. The same process applies to, for example, nation states that exclude themselves from the beloved community, and it is also the case that atonement for these rebellions depends not upon anything these nations can do for themselves, but upon allowing their betrayals to be atoned for by the other nations of the world.

Germany, for example, cannot undo its own misdeeds in the Nazi times, its own betrayals of everything the world holds dear. But other nations can work, and have worked, to bring Germany back into a more wholesome relationship with the beloved community. Who will do this, eventually, for the sins and betrayals of the United States is less clear, since the United States has always been loathe to admit a mistake. No atonement can come when a person (whether human or institutional) cannot own a betrayal of its own ideals.

Of course Royce defended causes that were "progressive" by the standards of his own day, such as the education of women, the inclusion in meaningful community of non-white races (by assimilation, which many see as problematic, but it is intended as inclusion), and many others. In Royce's defense, he does allow that whatever the dominant local culture may be, the wise provincial assimilates the foreigner to that dominant culture, and presumably the same would be the case whether one was assimilating an Anglo to an Africana local culture or vice-versa, or any other assimilation of the new comer to the dominant group. Our sensibilities about this sort of thing are different at different times in history. Fortune points out that what is *progressive* at one time may seem *parochial* at another. I have no doubt that Royce's "defense" of the black race, for instance, is unacceptably parochial by today's standards, but by the standard of his own day, it was quite progressive.[10] And Royce's conception of community, being an all-inclusive ideal, is essentially progressive in the relevant sense, by the standard of any time in history, regardless of whether his applications of it in his own time would be called progressive today. Thus, Royce is not only a relationalist in the metaphysics of person, but also a progressive in the domain of social inclusion.

Methodological Conservatism

This brings us to the question of conservatism. Royce's most extensive, explicit discussion of conservatism is in his 1880 essay, "The Nature of Voluntary Progress," but there is no reason to think he changed his view of it in subsequent writings. The fact that this view is so clearly expressed in Royce's early writings lends further credence to treating his views on community as more or less continuous in the development, and not best understood as a break with former views following his so-called "Peircean insight" of 1912. It is simply and demonstrably incorrect to understand Royce's mature account of community as anything except the further clarification of views he held all of his adult life. Tunstall has argued for the unity and continuity of Royce's thought based upon his "ethico-religious insight," but that thesis can be extended to most other areas of Royce's thought.

Royce's conservatism is not settled or even clarified by examining his political commitments during his lifetime. It appears that he may have been a Republican more than a Democrat, but he thought and voted independently, and for example, had no admiration for McKinley and Roosevelt, who were Republicans, and greatly admired Woodrow Wilson, who was a Democrat. There is simply no point in trying to grasp Royce's conservatism through a survey of his opinions about individual candidates or political parties in his day. But there are three senses in which Royce certainly was a conservative. I designate these as methodological, social, and ontological conservatism. Based on Fortune's schema, I will take each in its turn, moving beyond his schema and into the fundamental themes of this book.

Fortune argues that the term "conservatism" *most properly* designates a *refusal* at the level of methodology in social thought *to separate ethics and politics*. The methodological liberal distinguishes ethics from politics and pursues politics as either a morally neutral, rational endeavor, or if it is informed by ethical judgments, at the very least, the *account* of those judgments requires a separate inquiry with its own methods and questions. Whether ethical reason and political reason constitute separate types of reason is really the issue. Hence, for liberal methodology in political theory, the question of the good life and the question of the best state can certainly be related, but are studied separately. While we can see the beginnings of this distinction in Aristotle, in which the ethical inquiry is undertaken prior to and for the sake of a broader and more concrete political inquiry, the true break in method begins with Machiavelli, in whose hands questions of political expedience may be studied in isolation of their ethical character.[11]

Liberal methodology holds that political power can be grasped and understood in its own right and that it has an intelligible and rational character that does not depend for its success or failure upon its moral goodness. Hence, the political philosophy of Thomas Hobbes would be a clear example of liberal method, but any thinker who brackets the question of the "good" in order to understand the workings of political power would be adopting liberal method. One can also see in Madison's "Federalist 10" the strong desire to understand political power in connection with the good, but he proceeds with his analysis upon the lamentable necessity of treating the dialectics of faction without the benefit of moral ideals, substituting an ideal of a balance of power, and an assumption that people and parties will, with the best of intentions, pursue what is in their interest and find ways to *call* it the good. The mature work of John Rawls, seeking to avoid "comprehensive moral claims," is treated under this heading by Fortune in some detail, and clearly Richard Rorty also falls into this category. These are all examples of methodological liberalism.

One can generally see methodological liberals as taking a view of reason that treats it as objective and morally neutral—something that can be used for good or bad ends. This is certainly a persuasive approach to reason, since clearly it can be and has been used in the service of ends that most of us would condemn, and in the service of the opposite ends most of us would endorse. Most liberals in methodology give great importance to ethical questions, and most will certainly endorse that the best political order will beget the most ethical citizens, but they are hard-nosed realists about the workings and analysis of political power. They do not believe that the good *must* triumph and that the evil state *must* fall. They also tend to treat reason as something historically comprehensible independent of the will or desire of individuals, and to associate reason with a check upon desire and a guide to the will.

Certainly we can say that reason functions in such a way, but the issue is about its independence of the will, or at least the character of its sovereignty over the will. Methodological liberals usually treat desire and will as individualized or atomized, and reason as universal, hence giving reason an independence of individual will that grounds its authority or sovereignty—all legitimate government derives from the (rational) consent of the governed. Not surprising, then, is the difficulty for methodological liberals that arises from assaults upon the universality of reason—such as arguments that characterize all forms of reason as culturally embedded. Methodological liberals also have problems when desires become generalized and a whole group begins to pursue a plan of action that is clearly immoral, self-destructive and irrational, but more problematic still is when reason provides not only no check upon such behavior, but becomes a tool in the service of such mass desire. If it were unconditionally true that reason were universal and available to all as a check upon individual desires, then how could reason be used so effectively in forming plans of action that lead to the self-destruction of entire groups, like the Second and Third German Reich, which supposedly has a full command of reason in its highest forms? Methodological liberals have trouble with such questions.

Methodological conservatives, on the other hand, refuse to grant a distinction between ethics and politics, their ends, their descriptions, their results, or how we should judge them. For conservatives of this type, ethics is *the* general field of inquiry, and politics is one special application of its results. No grasp of political power is conceivable or existentially possible except upon the basis of some idea or ideal of the Good. For conservative method, the pursuit of political order, including political power, presupposes some notion of the Good, even if that notion is nothing more developed than naked self interest. Methodological conservatives also do not think that good must triumph and evil must fall, but they cannot imagine an intelligible account of power that is not rooted in some idea of the Good—so in their view, even Machiavelli's followers must assume something like "power" is the Good in order to be understood. Methodological conservatives try to absorb the descriptions of methodological liberals by couching their claims about political order in a broader conception of the Good. In distinguishing the analysis of power from its connection to ethical judgment, liberal methodology leaves aside an essential component of the phenomenon it is seeking to understand, according to methodological conservatives. But methodological conservatives have difficulty in dealing with the analysis of political power available to those in the Machiavellian tradition—wherever power is sought for its own sake, methodological conservatives are in a quandary as to whether to reach for their guns (in defensive or offensive mode), or to resist passively, or to try to shame the power seekers, or to try to persuade them of the irrationality and indefensibility of treating power as having its own rationality.

As a consequence of the conviction that all political reason has to be situated within a broader conception of the Good, methodological conservatives do not separate will from reason—reason simply is the formation of a rational plan and then willing it as one's ideal purpose. Methodological conservatives can be either atomistic or relationalist in their understanding of this joining of ethical and political will—it may be that the central task is the development of individual ethical wills (so that the proper externally created forms of political order) will be the morally best ones. This would be an example of methodological conservatism in, say, contractarian political order. Here we might list Woodrow Wilson as a good example of someone who was a thorough-going individualist, and also held that the political order can be no better than the moral development of the individuals who establish it.[12] Fortune treats the philosophies of Ralph Waldo Emerson, Margaret Fuller, Martin Luther King, Jr., and Malcolm X as examples of methodological conservatism, and I think he is correct to do so. They vary in their progressivism and metaphysics of person, but all are methodological conservatives.

Methodological conservatives have often also been parochial rather than progressive in their interpretations of social inclusion—we might even say that this is the commonest and most tragic pitfall of methodological conservatives, but it occurs in two different ways. The parochial methodological conservative may tend to insist on the moral character of all political relations and hence will become a moralizing fuddy duddy, resisting all progress because it might lead to our moral decline—and such people cannot see the difference between expanding the circle of inclusion and moral decline. In recent times, William F. Buckley would fit this description. The other (and until the twentieth century less common) form of parochial methodological conservative is the one who politicizes all ethical relations. Hitler is only the most frightening example of someone for whom the issue of social inclusion was conflated with the politicized ethical ("spirit" in fascist terms) vision of his regime. There is almost no limit to the damage that can be done by a methodological conservative who takes a parochial view of social inclusion and politicizes ethical relations. And in the case of someone like Hitler, rather than attempting to raise the political aspect of life to a higher moral vision, he inverted the order so as to politicize all moral possibilities. That drags moral life into the mire of political association rather than allowing political association to be only one of many institutional contributors to a broader moral development of persons.

In spite of these very tangible weaknesses in methodological conservatism (i.e., that it is susceptible to parochialism and to the subversion of the moral life to merely political or other forms of social order by a willful and indefensible reductionism), it is also the account that, in my view, can do the most good in the world. I regard the atomistic version of methodological conservatism as capable of doing *some* good, so long as it is not parochial, but the relationalist version is the better of the two, for it is this relationalist account that provides for us the vision of a beloved community and all other worthy ideals. The atomistic version, even where it is most progressive, ends in an enlightened kind of ethical egoism that is powerless to account for, or even describe the genuine spirit of community. Relational, progressive, methodological conservatism is also empirically superior to atomistic progressive methodological liberalism because there is very little reason, empirically, to treat individuality (and individualistic personhood) as metaphysical givens. We deprive ourselves of deep self-understanding when we assume that individuals are just utility maximizers or just the seat of all political rights. The most valuable self-understanding includes a viable sense of the origins of individuality. Clearly the individual develops over time (isn't just *given*), as the product of a social process, and clearly individual persons are more than just *affected* by institutions, they are *products of*, and simultaneously, *unique perspectives upon* those institutional structures. I have argued this case in Chapter 8.

Royce nicely conforms to what I have described as a relational, progressive, methodological conservatism, and thus, exemplifies what I regard as the best political philosophy. For him, ethics is first philosophy because the intentional stance (not the individual) is the primary given, and it is social from the outset, while discovery of the will is the result of temporal activity, and no individual or group can act effectively in the "world" except by forming plans of action, while these plans of action can be meaningfully judged only as communal moral purposes. In forming purposes, the will, whether it is that of a group or an individual, simultaneously individuates itself and pursues its own ideals. There are no morally neutral purposes because the *formation* of a purpose requires the exclusion of all other available purposes that could have been willed, and the person (whether an individual or group) who acts upon a purpose is judged not only by what has been purposed, but also by what might have been purposed but was not. All such judgment requires the assumption of the free dedication of the person to a cause.

It is tragic, for Royce, that the will can only value its own purposes by leaving aside others that might be worthy of pursuit. The cost of finitude is the permanent loss of valuable purposes that are excluded, but the compensation for such activity is the gradual formation of the individual person in community as a concrete and practical reality, and the gradual personalizing of the community itself. As I pointed out in an earlier chapter, Royce says, "the concept of the individual, in its primary and original sense, is a distinctly ethical concept, and that is so whether you speak in terms of knowledge or in terms of being."[13] It will be recalled that he says the same of the idea of "person," and we have now traced the temporal relation of the move from individuality to personhood through the free choice of purposes. Thus, for Royce, all will is social, all the purposes it forms are social, and all its resultant individuation is social. The application of Royce's relational theory of the person to the question of value is thus followed out in a view in which the entire universe is conceived as a social order of willing, and a social order of willing *is* a moral order, if it is to have any meaning at all.

For Royce there is no such thing as power, even in God, which is not at bottom the activity of some will pursuing its plans of action as a part of a community's purposes. Therefore, political power, for Royce, is the pursuit of ethical purposes by means of one type of social order as opposed to another. To treat political power as though it were intelligible and capable of being grasped on its own terms, independent of ethics, would be, for Royce, to pretend that it sought no purposes and implied no act of will (whether individual or social). The full separation of ethics from politics, or political rationality from ethical rationality, is nonsense. "Realpolitik" is neither real nor politics. It is foolish, myopic activity, and devoid of all wisdom and any but negative values. Even its successes are tainted and the world would be better off were they failures. Royce would have none of it. Thus, in this restricted sense, Royce is certainly a methodological conservative, according to Fortune's schema and my application of it. And I think Royce is correct about occupying this position about the relation of ethics to politics.

Social Conservatism

But Royce's conservatism goes further. One may, without threatening relational metaphysics of the person and progressivism, take conservatism beyond just the methodological variety. Yes, Royce will not allow a strong methodological distinction between ethical and political rationality. But he is also a *social* conservative, although the sense he gives to this idea is not a thoroughly familiar one. His case is, as usual, a temporalist description that turns upon the empirical observation that social *conditions* change more quickly than do social *forms of life* and *practice.* Here I continue to summarize the case he presents in the 1880 essay "The Nature of Voluntary Progress."

We create social forms voluntarily (and among these social forms are political institutions), Royce says, as ways of preserving the value of past experiences and providing present and future purposive frames for the activities of social groups, for their possibilities, and in the highest instance, these social forms are built-in channels for the development of personality in both human individuals and communities through the founding of institutions (including political institutions). We train individuals for loyal service to the causes they have freely chosen by sanctioning the causes we may choose and serve, setting them in stable social forms, including the state, but also any organization, or even other persons (one can go "into service" as the British used to call it), that can be loyally served in any way, such as a church, a club, a marriage, a family, a business, a school, an army, or a labor union. Any social form, including institutions, can be served as a cause and can be the object of devotion by which a human individual or an institution comes to find his or her or its place in a larger community. Naturally, social *forms* do change and evolve, but they do not change as quickly as do social *conditions*, needs and demands—which is part of the reason we create social forms. We want stability amidst the changing conditions.

Here Royce proposes a law of social conservatism (and this is an empirical generalization, on a par with his "law of docility," discussed in Chapter 5, but here we find the sociological equivalent to that psychological "law"[14]): people will generally attempt to use the existing (past) social forms to organize present and future social experience, or where the forms are inadequate, to change them as little as possible in order to accommodate new social experience and changing conditions. This is done because the overall effort of (social and individual) will is to expend as little energy as possible in adapting to change, and in this way *all* (social and individual) wills seeks to be progressive. Replacing our existing social forms with new ones, or even changing them in major ways, requires enormous energy, and we will avoid it where we can, Royce observes. Even when radical innovation of new social forms is required in order to accommodate novel social conditions (say, the Industrial Revolution, or the military occupation of Judea by the Romans, or any of a million other examples), the change will still be undertaken in such a way as to conserve energy and to simplify to the greatest extent those new social forms, and to adapt them to existing forms. This is why attempts by the United States to build Western-style democracies in places like Afghanistan and Iraq do not succeed. Groups will not replace their existing social structures with very different ones when it requires less energy simply to fight. When fighting requires more energy, gradual adaptations will begin to occur.

Indeed, we do not change our most stable and comprehensive social forms at all until they simply cannot accommodate current social conditions and experience without greater expenditure of energy and effort than would be required to replace them. Thus, as a social conservative, Royce looks to the *differential* between the energy required to adapt existing social forms and that required to create new ones as the measure of and justification for the widespread habit of social conservatism, and how progress shall be accomplished given this empirical law. Conservation is the condition of sustainable progress. That the will (whether social or individual) seeks to be *progressive* is a given, for Royce, and thus the conservation of social forms is not an impediment to progress, but a necessary condition for progress.[15]

The preservation of political forms, such as states and their governments, is simply a special case of the comprehensive social forms one might serve and *con*serve. Royce notes that even the radical and the revolutionary will betray something of the conservative spirit in attempting to justify the huge amount of effort required in replacing the present social forms by connecting the new, proposed forms either to some idealized past form of human life, or some idealized future hope of life which would be *in itself* worthy of conservation (perhaps Trotsky's theory of permanent revolution would be the most widely known counter-example to Royce's view, but this would simply mark out Trotsky as a self-consistent radical at the proper logical extreme of his own principles). No radical or revolutionary, Royce thinks (even Trotsky), can afford to call for a wholesale change of existing social forms without offering some alternative vision of society which would require less energy to create and conserve than is required by those which he or she attempts to displace. For Royce, both social conservatives and radicals seek progress; they simply disagree on whether to adapt the existing social forms to the new conditions, or create new social forms. Thus we see the structure of Royce's "social conservatism" and its law.

This sort of social conservatism does dovetail with a part of what has often been associated with the conservatism of thinkers like Edmund Burke and David Hume, for it is thoroughly communitarian, and endorses the idea that gradual change, or the idea that the "evolution" of social forms is generally to be preferred over revolutionary actions. But Royce's social conservatism, at the level thus articulated, is less a moral judgment about how persons can live best than a description of how they do in fact live. Thus, where Burke or Hume might try to convince us of the superiority of social conservatism over liberalism, Royce would adopt as his own norm whatever facilitates the progress of the ideal of the beloved community. His law of social conservatism amounts to following wise advice about how, generally but not universally, such progress is most likely to occur. Sometimes our institutions do become shackles upon our freedom to pursue higher ideals, and when that does occur, it may require less energy to replace an institution than to reform or adapt it. In such cases, one may revolt, indeed, one should. And in any case, some will do so.

One feature of Royce's account of community that is needed in the present, but missing from other accounts, is Royce's observation that strong, well-developed communities do create powerful genuine individuals who inevitably come to experience their own communities as an unwanted type of limitation upon moral vision. The more a community succeeds in creating strong persons, the more it insures the appearance of individuals who will question its own habitual processes, customs, and comprehensive social forms. Royce calls this dynamic of individuals and their communities "original sin" in *The Problem of Christianity*, but it is the tension of a community that is succeeding, not one that is failing. A failing community either never produces strong persons or spits out those who show signs of such development. As Reinhold Niebuhr once put it, an immoral society unknowingly crucifies upon the same Golgotha the criminals that fall below its moral standards and the prophets who rise above them. But communities that are succeeding and growing morally do so at the cost of a powerful tension between their social forms and their best individuals. One wonders whether traditional social conservatives, such as Hume and Burke, ever noticed the price of success in a community's moral endeavors. The creative tension thus built-in to Royce's social conservatism is a permanent hedge against utopian thinking of all kinds, which the old style conservatives would appreciate.

Ontological Conservatism

Yet, this social conservatism, vast as it is, does not ground the matter fully for Royce, because beneath the observation about the tension between rapidly changing social conditions and more ponderous progress of social forms (really an empirical generalization) lies a more basic observation, which is that the forms and habits of our individual thought and action change more slowly than does our concrete experience. Present experience moves very quickly, and to connect it to a past and a future requires habit (recall the discussion of the Law of Docility in Chapter 5), along with plans of action that are projected into possible experience not yet had and the possible experience of others. The entire effort of life, whether individual or social, can be cumulative and progressive *only* because a habit of action or form of thought, once attained by learning and experience, can be readily adapted to further experience.[16]

Thus, the process by which we become individuals is a social process of acquiring adaptable but stable forms of thought and habits of action, and all habits of action are social forms. Our repertoire of individual habits is sort of like an operational analogue of social institutions within the human individual. For example, if Jack is a musician, his musical habits (past training, current abilities, future musical actions) are the "Jack School of Music," and Jill's political history, present opinions and future hopes are her own purposed "Constitution for the State of Jill," and so on. Royce believes that individuals, once they have acquired such forms of thought and habits (such as are required to adapt to the rapid changes in their experience), will always attempt to adapt what habits they already possess to new experiences rather than alter the basic forms of their thinking and action, so long as the energy required to adapt is less than the energy required to develop a new way of thinking or acting. If Jack wants to learn a new instrument, he'll adapt what is already held and practiced in the Jack School of Music to that purpose. Indeed, according to Royce, as we have seen in Chapter 5, genuinely novel actions are not really possible for us.

This may sound like a psychological observation, rather than an ontological one, but for Royce, this is an ontological postulate.[17] What warrants it as an ontological postulate (a functional universal in his metaphysics) is the observation that the universe, whether understood as the activity of will, or as a scientific description of physical processes, *conserves* energy, and the energy conserved in forms of thought and human action is "energy" as truly as is the energy conserved in a scientifically described physical process. We do not speak equivocally of "energy" here, since even in physics this is "the power to do work," and we all know how much "work" it is to adapt our existing ways of making sense of our experience to the rapidly changing experiences we are having. We also know how much work and energy it requires to acquire new ways of thinking or replace old ways of thinking with different ones. Think of learning a new language. When human individuals attempt to learn new languages later in life, they have difficulty "thinking" in the new language without translating it in their heads. This is a conservation issue. They will exert enormous energy translating in their heads until it becomes impracticable, at which point they will either press forward without understanding, or break through to a new (if adapted) set of habits of thinking. At the social level, institutions with long histories (and tremendous social inertia), such as Oxford University or the Roman Catholic Church, have difficulty in pursuing new purposes except in light of their historic missions.

Anywhere there is activity, there is a balance of retaining existing forms of thought and action and accommodating novelty in experience, and whether this is a case of, say, the absorption of new energy by an extant physical system, or just you trying to eat your morning cereal left-handed (or right-handed, for the other ten percent of you), or in my trying to learn Italian, or the Roman Catholic Church trying to find a suitable role for the women who serve it, the tendency is everywhere the same, according to Royce. Everything that changes (and that is everything we know about) will attempt to adapt existing forms to new conditions or to change the forms themselves with the least expenditure of energy possible—at least everything *progressive* will proceed in this way, which is everything valuable for Royce. But this type of ontological conservatism is about conserving the *form* of experience at the expense of at least some its content, which is to say that it is *exclusionary* in the senses we have studied in the preceding chapters, so as to make the purposes already embraced capable of further pursuit. It is a trade-off and a balancing act for the sake of progress, and success is never guaranteed, in Royce's view. That we might have richer present experience were we able to "be in the moment" is hard to doubt, but that this richness would come at the cost of plans of action, and ultimately purposes we embrace as ideals, is also hard to deny.

Thus, we can see that not only a social but an ontological conservatism collects around something like, for instance, the Constitution of the United States. It is at this point almost unthinkable to most people that we should discard the whole thing and start over. Things would have to become very bad indeed before such a change would begin to make sense, for the expenditure of energy at every level to be more "conservative" in changing the political and social institutions and individual habits associated with them than in retaining and adapting the current forms. And hence, when a reformer like Martin Luther King, Jr., calls for major reform, he says things like "all we are asking is that you be true to what you said on paper," referring to the promises of equality of life, liberty, and the pursuit of happiness, and equal protection under the law. This call comes in the form of conservatism which is profoundly consistent with the idea of keeping our existing social forms, our existing forms of thought, and our moral purposes already willed, and the conviction that these forms *can* be adapted to changing conditions with less effort than would be required to change the forms themselves.

An Assessment

If Royce is right, everyone is an ontological conservative (which is why he offers conservatism as an ontological postulate in his metaphysics). And if Royce is right, the vast majority of people are social conservatives, at least in the sense he uses the term. But what makes Fortune's categories and analysis interesting for my purposes is that he places a finger upon what makes for a *political* conservative, in Royce's general account among many others, which is a process of following the general tendency of willing through from the order of the cosmos (in metaphysics of the person) all the way down to your next individual choice, and a continuity from the moral aspect of the purposing down to the political implications of the purpose. If the political is only one expression of the general structure of ethical willing, as it clearly is for Royce, then there would be no basis for treating inquiry into political order as different in kind from inquiries into any other moral or ethical order. Ethics does not, for a methodological conservative, pick up where politics leaves off, does not attempt to cultivate private virtue within the general framework of a public state (Rorty is, as he rightly says, a liberal). Rather, for methodological conservatives, there can *be* no state without its own purpose, and its purpose must be an expression of the ethical character and moral development of its citizens and their institutions (especially local government and culture), and of its relations to other states.

So where the methodologically liberal viewpoint might say that a just and equitable political order leaves its citizens free to pursue a variety of ethical ends privately, according to their best lights, a conservative will say that the state can be nothing other than the generalized expression of the moral development of its citizens as a community, and their community is a "person" among other communities. The freedom of persons in community is not, for a conservative such as Royce, what is "left to their own private pursuit," but rather whatever freedom they have acquired by choosing and pursuing a plan of life within a community that itself *has* a moral purpose, and converts the individual plans of action into ideal purposes that individuals may serve. If we would have a better state, we must become better persons and together direct our corporate will toward higher purposes, the ideal of which is the beloved community—and there is no other road, according to progressive relational conservatives.

How, such a conservative will ask, could you create a state that was better than the collective wisdom of its citizens can imagine and will for themselves? And how can citizens imagine and will for themselves what is beyond the comprehension of their own moral attainment? We all know that groups tend to behave worse than individuals do, as Reinhold Niebuhr pointed out so long ago[18] (and as I discussed in Chapter 8), and that we tolerate from groups behavior we would not accept from individuals. We should not, therefore, expect the state, or any other group, to rise above the moral development of its citizens taken as a group, and we can reliably measure the development of personality in their institutions by examining how it forms its purposes and how its servants pursue those ends. There will always be tension. But what we can expect is for the most developed *among* the citizens of a state, or any political order, to articulate the ideals that seem attainable if its members have only the resolve and the moral tenacity to bring themselves collectively up to that level. That is progress, for Royce. It is thoroughly voluntary.

It is quite close to what Cornel West has called "prophetic pragmatism."

Hence, we might note, a missing voice in contemporary political parlance, both in the US and elsewhere, and a voice that was once common at least in American political discourse, is the one that says: the state will become better when it learns to imagine its own best ideals as being pursued by the strenuous effort of its citizens to adapt the existing forms to the social changes that are upon us, and to be loyal to the development of personality in the world community of states. There are such voices in the present, and Cornel West is an excellent example of such a viewpoint, although perhaps he would label himself a "liberal," I do not think he is a liberal in methodology, being reluctant as he is to separate ethical from political purposes in his thinking. I also note that West is a personalist and relationalist in his metaphysics, whether he realizes it or not, and certainly a progressive. His views are quite close to Royce's as he has said himself.

To give but one example of how such a progressive, relational conservative voice might speak in the face of present fears about for example, terrorism, a state might use its military power to attempt to smash its enemies (perceived or real), or it might strive to become the kind of nation that no one wants to attack. The latter course costs less effort in the long run, since forming a purpose to smash one's enemies contributes nothing to the moral development of the state that acts on such a plan (as King so forcefully argued), especially when it looks to be neither necessary nor achievable. The US has increasingly relied upon its power to force other peoples and nations to *call* it "good," instead of seeking to become morally better so that no one will be surprised by how well the military and economic power of the US can be adapted to the moral demands placed upon it by bearing the burden of world leadership in the form of world service. This is to say nothing of how militarism contributes nothing to the moral development of the peoples who are smashed by it.

To use military or economic power in ways that betray our best purposes is the betrayal of those purposes themselves. When such betrayals take the form of political policies, such as those of the most recent Bush administration, the proper word is "treason" to the purposes and ideals of that nation. Those who argue that to punish such traitors under the laws of the nation will damage the nation only show their inability to grasp the rule of law as an ideal that a free nation must maintain. But political treason, whether it is that of George W. Bush or Adolf Hitler or Julius Caesar, is just one type of moral betrayal, for a methodological conservative, and while punishment may be a needed part of the remedy, what is called for is atonement, not simple punishment. When the misdeeds of misguided servants of the state are taken in the context of the community of nations, the atonement has to be carried out by other nations, not only by the nation that has betrayed the cause of humanity, as the United States has often done. But atonement is not an option until the betrayal has been recognized by the betrayers. Dogged insistence that betrayals are actually acts of loyal service locks a nation in the "hell of the irrevocable," which is where the US currently lives. I am confident that this is the proper application of Royce's philosophy to the present world, and anyone who doubts that should re-read his assessment of the conquest of California, especially the paragraph I have quoted twice in this book about how we ought at least to be honest with ourselves the next time we choose to "serve the devil." If a nation wishes to avoid terrorism, it might not go marauding among weaker peoples with its songs and slogans of liberation.

But the solution is not on the current horizon. So long as the American Left thinks of ethics as a private affair of pursuing private ends by our private lights, it will remain morally impotent. So long as the American Right acts as if might makes right while proclaiming that right makes might, it will remain morally self-undermining. None of this is conservative in any defensible sense of the term. The missing voice is, I think, that of relational progressive conservatism, a voice of loyalty which calls us to a higher standard in moral attainment, of communities that are in community with other communities, and only then looks for an improvement in its political institutions. The cultivation of the inner life of our communities, as of ourselves as individuals, is at the heart of voluntary progress. Such progress is slow, but it does not happen at all unless we set a purpose for ourselves and exercise our wills upon its attainment.

In fairness, the relational, progressive, conservative voice is not altogether absent from contemporary political opinion, but it is scattered and disorganized. Wherever one finds individuals who treat ideals as more real than individuals (not because they know this to be ontologically true, but because hope and memory depend upon it), one will hear echoes of that voice. I find those echoes in some strange places; in political organizations as disparate as the environmental movement and Green Party, on one side, and Pat Buchanan's magazine *The American Conservative* on the other side—which had the honesty to call out the Bush administration for its immorality and to ask about ideals when others grew cynical and lazy. There are many sane, progressive people of every shade in between, but they often fail to recognize their kinship, often because their shared intuition that politics is really just morality by a specific means does not guarantee anything close to similar moral judgments. Some relational progressive conservatives (those mainly on the Left) are inclined to ground their value judgments in a secular humanism that refuses to recognize the vital role played by religious devotion in public life. These people often trust science more than they should, in spite of their recognition that it can be and has been corrupted and misused by the greedy and power-hungry Machiavellians who would corporatize and commodify all human endeavors. But without religion, science is their best hope. Their fear of religious excesses prevents them, often, from being in community with those whose practical judgments would lead to almost the same policies and purposes as their own. I have noticed, for example, how odd it has been to both radical environmentalists and very traditional Mennonites to discover that they have so much in common and how easily they can work together. It would be nice if such discoveries did not come as a surprise. Many radical environmentalists are relationalist progressive conservatives, but lack a clear concept of their own view.

On the other side, the relationalist, progressive conservatives (mainly of the Right) tend to jeopardize their own progressive hopes by failing to recognize that increasing social inclusion is the only viable road to an increasingly moral society. They mistake expanded social inclusion for moral relativism, imagining that immigration, gay marriage, or the legalization of recreational drugs, will lead to the moral decline of their societies, when in truth these are all simply modes of expanding the circle of who counts and taking responsibility for our own. It seems not to occur to them that moderating the negative influences of these practices they adjudge detrimental, such as drug addiction, *depends* upon being in community with those who pursue those practices. If you want to get an addict off crack, passing a law that makes his addiction illegal and locking him up for years is not a very promising way of being in community with him. Moral community is hard work, and it requires an on-going *will to interpret*, in Royce's terms. That will to interpret is not going to exist where the possibility of shared community is cut off in advance. No "war on drugs" or Constitutional amendment banning gay marriage can have a good effect upon the development of any nation. It is parochial, which is a fancy way of saying that it is simple ignorance. The same is true of the use of political power to forbid people to speak or write in certain ways on college campuses, or to "atomize" the bodies of women who seek abortions as though the community has no stake at all in their decisions, which is just the very same mistake made by those on the Left. "My body, my choice" is atomism. It is unwise and just as morally under-developed as the attempt to impose a wholly external standard on an individual.

Nor are religious institutions, whether on the Right or the Left, themselves well served and strengthened by refusing to be in community with those whose basic values differ with their own. To have any sort of constructive effect upon those who hold contrary value judgments, the social groups must first be committed to mutual interpretation, to the possibility of a *acknowledging* a world of truth that includes the memories, plans and hopes of those whose memories, plans and hopes are different from one's own. Far from being relativism, this it simply moral common sense applied to shared political life, and common sense may allow perspective as a given, but an informed and valuable *point of view* on social reality is one of its products, not its cause.

[10]
Teaching

There have not been many times in human history during which teachers of philosophy have been comfortably ensconced in prestigious institutions and well rewarded for their work. Even rarer is the circumstance prevailing in the last century (and into the present one) that largely protects their free expression of ideas. Royce along with a small group of other philosophers played a crucial role in creating the opportunity in the United States for such comfortable and protected lives for those who love philosophy. In a sense, Socrates's suggestion, in his trial, that Athens ought to give him a pension for asking them such uncomfortable questions has not only come to pass in the present, but "professional" philosophers get more than a simple pension these days. In my judgment, this opportunity has not been put to very good use, and the prospects for change and improvement are not promising. But if we would serve the cause of philosophy as a communal purpose, we must try. My sense is that with the decline in the willingness of the public to use taxes to support institutions of higher learning (and in a time in which this is only one of many symptoms of the decline in public mindedness), it is only a matter of time before the institution of tenure and the ideal of academic freedom disappear.[1] People will marvel, a thousand years from now, that for a hundred years academics were actually pretty well protected (if not perfectly) from reprisal for expressing the truth as they saw it. This is almost unprecedented in human history.

It is tempting, on the other side, to observe that, in wasting this rare opportunity, professional philosophers, along with academic types more generally, have been "bought off" by the powers in business and government with a deal that goes something like this (if you can imagine the powers speaking): "We will give you a living wage, all the academic titles you want, job security for life, a little time to write articles and books for one another, and our own young people for a short time (when they reach an age at which their hormones are raging, their diligence and attention are at a minimum, they are totally ungovernable, and we have no idea what else to do with them); we'll also invite you to some of our parties so we can feel culturally aware and smart, and we'll pretend to listen and take you seriously, sometimes; in return, you academics will not cause trouble for us as we make all the real decisions and run the world." It sounds cynical, I realize.

But what is even more disheartening is my suspicion that even if the offer had been made this bluntly, it still might have worked. There would have been many takers. But nothing this calculated had to be done. In fact, all that had to be done was to ensure that the tendencies *already present* in people who love ideas and books and the life of study were tapped into, and that institutional structures were created which adequately facilitated and perpetuated both the appearance (illusion?) of success and endless internecine squabbles, and then the real holders of power could be assured of an increasingly detached, distracted, irrelevant and even lethargic intelligentsia that would be governed largely by its fear of losing a comfortable situation.

It has worked. Professors are, in public and institutional matters, largely like sheep, and they hire other sheep to keep them company, and they run off anyone who makes them feel insecure. They worry about *following* the rules more than do those who *make* the rules. A clever and worldly person could easily run the whole herd of academics off a cliff like lemmings. They would conform and conform and conform as they imperceptibly lost everything while constantly fearing they might lose something. When the real powers that be slash the classics department, the foreign language department is just glad it wasn't them; when they come for the foreign language department, the English department just breathes a sigh of relief it wasn't them. And so on. Sheep. Meanwhile, academics facilitate their own marginalization and dissipate their energies in disputes with one another, and in the bigger and more prestigious universities, they ignore their students to the extent they can (and that is a great extent indeed), allowing themselves to imagine that their "work" (by which they mean the article they are working on this year, which, if published, will be read by four people, maybe five) is the most important thing they do. Almost everyone in the big schools tends to regard extra teaching and keeping office hours as a kind of subtle punishment. Their colleagues in the "teaching schools" (regional colleges and universities, less well-to-do private liberals arts colleges, community colleges, etc.) are treated as second or third class citizens. The experience of graduate school at one of these bigger schools breeds within the professors at the "teaching schools" an intense desire to "rise" to a research position, and to feel a certain inferiority about devoting their lives and energies to teaching.

Professionalization of the professoriate, partly facilitated through the activities of their own scholarly societies, has certainly rendered the lovers of ideas effectively loyal (and often blind) servants of a multinational, corporate, and political machinery that now rules the world. The situation is probably sustainable for some time to come. It is also not altogether bad. The "bad" lies not so much in what is done, but in what is not done that could be done with such an historically precious opportunity, especially for those who call themselves "philosophers" these days, as well as for all the other teachers who enjoy these protections of their "academic freedom." What *could be* made of the situation, ideally, and what *is* being done with it, are things wide asunder. One is tempted to say the same about the great experiment in democracy that is the United States of America: Freedom wasted on the pursuit and attainment of material comfort, to the point of using military power to ensure a standard of living beyond our genuine means.[2]

One cannot help wondering whether human philosophical activity can really flourish where it has become so thoroughly devoid of risk, as it now is. When philosophers have been purveyors of dangerous ideas, were the ideas themselves better for the risks that had to be accepted in order to express them? When philosophy has been institutionalized, has it suffered in quality? The opinions that could be expressed on this subject cover a broad spectrum. Clearly a part of the role and purpose of philosophy, as a human endeavor, is also to ask *what* philosophy is, and what makes it better or worse. As a purely human endeavor, philosophy is in no danger of disappearing. People will always philosophize, and some will do it well, and if need be, they will do it without the institutional structures that facilitate philosophizing on a mass scale. Those who seem born to it, just like those who are born to poetry and painting and acting and inventing, will pursue philosophy with or without encouragement, and in spite of risk and poverty, even in spite of persecution and death. We always have. I see no historical evidence that the quality of philosophical thought necessarily *suffers* for want of institutional support. It occurs to me that at least half of the Western philosophers we still study today pursued wisdom as "amateurs," i.e., those who do something for the love of it. Spinoza and Locke and Hume and Rousseau and Kierkegaard had no chairs in philosophy, but they were not exactly "hacks." Some couldn't get teaching positions while others wouldn't take them when they were offered. Whether *anything* improves, over the long term, *with* institutional support could also provoke a very long discussion. But my point is that there is no good reason to associate in any strict way the *quality* of philosophizing with the presence of the institutional structures that now support it on a mass scale.

We need not fret over the destiny of philosophy, in any case. It will survive. It always has. But the social group I am most concerned with presently is that of university teachers, specifically, those who teach "philosophy" as it is presently defined. No such group need necessarily exist, but such a group does now exist. They are actually college and university teachers, by profession, but they like to call themselves "philosophers." This label they choose for themselves has generally been either accepted or ignored by the public, which seems to have reached consensus that it has no serious stake in this matter of nomenclature.

This social group, professional "philosophers," can be (and here *will* be) studied as a microcosm of other larger social groups in contemporary society, and even of the state, for none of these institutions was anything other than a result of the "voluntary progress" of the sort discussed in the last chapter, i.e., contingently created stable social structures that were intended to foster genuine community and to serve ideals of some sort, while preserving memory and connecting the ideals with the memories in an on-going will to interpret. And what has happened within the discipline of philosophy has been repeated, with slight variations, in many other social groups, and not just within the present educational institutions. There was a time, for example, when the local Chamber of Commerce was more than the local right-wing "Center for Marketing, Tourism, and Spin," and the local Lions Club was more than a weekly meeting of retired people. A stultification of institutional life has surely set in, in the US and elsewhere, and this was something Royce saw coming as early as 1908.[3] It must either be counteracted, or our gradual decline is assured—and has perhaps already gone so far as to be irreversible in the US. The proper way to counteract such a tendency is to adapt the existing structures to our current experiential conditions with as little energy as possible. I actually think there is something that can be done that requires very little adaptation, and which could revitalize not only our educational institutions and our professional organizations, but also our corporations, our local communities and perhaps even the nation state.

I will speak here of philosophy in the universities, from many years of experience of my own, but also because Royce was, after all, a philosophy teacher in a university that was emerging as the most important seat of learning in the US, due in some part to his own efforts. This topic of *teaching* was of great significance to him, and arguably it is the primary *cause* to which he devoted his own life. Royce taught a course load that we would currently associate with community college teachers, and he *did* complain about it occasionally, in much the way we hear from those with heavy course loads today. The idea of a two-course per semester load would surely have held some appeal for Royce just as it does for us today. The two-course load is quite a privilege.

Recalling, in my own experience, the years during which I, like Royce (and so many others) taught a 4/4 load, with four preparations every semester (i.e., no repeated material), I remember thinking not so much that I couldn't get much writing done, but rather that I couldn't do as good a job with my teaching itself doing four different courses as I might have done with three. That is, with the heavier load, it is not so much that publishing suffers as that *teaching* suffers. Many teachers deal with this by regularizing and polishing a small group of syllabi and teaching the same basic courses over and over. It is not necessarily a bad thing, but it can become a bad habit. I can't imagine that is a good plan for one's life or for one's students, but it is easy to understand why so many people do this. I mean, no one setting out on a career would say to himself "I want to teach just these three courses, Introductory Philosophy, Introductory Ethics, and Elementary Logic, and I want to do them every fall and every spring for forty years, until I retire, and that is my life plan." But it happens a lot. The people who polish and repeat may have ambitions for rich lives beyond just their labors for daily bread. They often want to raise and enjoy and serve families and their communities, to read and travel and write and gather with friends to discuss topics of mutual interest. It is easy to cut corners in one's teaching duties in light of such attractions, but to polish and repeat minimizes the damage to the students, even if it tends to mechanize one of the least mechanical of human relations—teaching. When teaching works best, it is because the encounter of teacher and student is a unique connection that brings the teacher's history into interpretive contact with the student's history. There is no standardized test for this encounter, and it is labor intensive on all sides.

Somehow Royce managed both an enormous out-pouring of written work and to be a good teacher, a good friend, a world traveler, an attentive parent and spouse, and a growing mind. As one of his former students, not a philosopher, said:

> It was when he got away from the great philosophic structure with which he was so much occupied that he revealed the personal qualities by which

he is remembered. He enjoyed knowing about many things. The Faculty Minute on his life said that few men knew so much about so many matters, and that his knowledge was so thorough that even specialists respected him. He was gravely conscientious. When a colleague at Harvard wrote to him from Switzerland for some information about kleptomaniacs, Royce misread the signature and thought the man a stranger, but he wrote him in detail nonetheless. He had convictions. He had courage. He had fidelity.[4]

Upon hearing Royce speak while a graduate student at Johns Hopkins, Woodrow Wilson wrote:

> I wish that I could live with Dr. Royce for a few months. He is one of the rarest spirits I have met. His is one of those very rare minds which exists in a perfectly lucid atmosphere of thought, having never a cloud on its horizon, seeing everything with a clear and unerring vision. He talked to us the other night at the Seminary, and the dullest fellow at the board listened with delight—I don't mean myself!—because he has the faculty of bringing masses of detail into a single luminous picture where they are grouped with a perfection of perspective and a skill of harmonious arrangement which fill the novice, the would-be historical painter, with despair.[5]

The point here is not whether Wilson is right or wrong about Royce, but the effect Royce had upon him—and apparently many others. Undoubtedly one could find some whose reports would glow, and some whose views would differ. That Royce was an effective and dedicated teacher and a well-developed person is, however, beyond dispute. I think much can be revealed about Royce, about how he put his philosophy into practice, by examining this topic of his teaching, but my purpose here is historical only insofar as it contributes to the community of memory in the present world of truth, and assists the living in forming communities capable of serving ideal purposes. Insofar as I can contribute to the social group with which I am personally most engaged, "professional philosophers" (God help me), the living ideas I have tried to articulate in this book should find their concrete applications most appropriately in the activity of teaching philosophy itself.

"Philosophers"

Royce said in 1913: "The philosophers differ sadly amongst themselves. They do not at present form a literal human community of mutual enlightenment and of growth in knowledge to any such extent as do the workers in the field of any one of natural sciences. The philosophers are thus far individuals rather than consciously members of one another. The charity of mutual interpretation is ill developed amongst them."[6] The more things change, the more they stay the same, it seems. Recently Doug Anderson has written:

> Royce faced a culture on the verge of social fragmentation; the avenue to his philosophical outlook was through a landscape littered with radically isolated and fragmented individuals adrift in a wilderness of finitude. Though we may whistle well in the dark, I don't see that we are in a much improved state. This is true, I think, of American culture at large, and also, more specifically of philosophers in America. As philosophers we are not so much a "community" as an aggregate of folks collected under the title of a profession. In some ways, I think, we have created an even more entangling and bewildering wilderness than the American pioneers faced. This is not to say that we live with the same physical stress and precariousness. Our wilderness is one in which we may find our own social and soulful identities seriously adrift. We have a wealth of life options, but little on which to take our bearings.[7]

Examining the efforts, historically, of the philosophers in America to form a community, or rather, examining the several (largely dysfunctional) social groups they did in fact form, none of which can be called a "community," in the sense of the term I have explained in this book, we learn something crucial, I believe, about ourselves. By the time Royce said what he did in 1913, he had already been president of the American Philosophical Association (APA), which was the brainchild primarily of James Edwin Creighton (there were others, but I contend that this was mainly Creighton's doing, and was largely done in his way). In 1901, Creighton wrote the following letter to Royce:

Ithaca, NY, Oct. 11, 1901

Dear Professor Royce:

You know, I think, that for some time there has been discussion of the advisability of starting a Philosophical Assn. In the meantime the philosophical sections of the Psych. Assn. has [sic] given an opportunity for philosophical papers and discussions. Just now however, the universities seem to be setting aside the first week of the year for Assn. meetings, and it seems a fitting time to decide what can be done in this way for the interests of philosophy.

Professor [J.G.] Hibben of Princeton have [sic] therefore taken the responsibility of asking a number of men to meet in New York on Saturday, Nov. 2nd to discuss the matter. We hope that you will be able to be present at this conference and will help us to some wise decision. The place of meeting Hibben promised to arrange later.

I have not heard any news of Professor James since his return, but sincerely hope he is going to be fit again. If you think he would be interested in our philosophical conference, will you tell him that he should have the chief seat at the table if he comes.

We are looking forward with interest to the publication of your second volume of Gifford Lectures. The first volume we discussed in my seminary last year with great profit and interest.

With kindest regards

Yours Sincerely,

J.E. Creighton[8]

Professor James did not come,[9] nor did Professor Royce, although Royce sent a letter of endorsement. When offered the honor of being the first president of the APA, James refused. He did not like the drift of thinking that was taking shape among his colleagues. In a letter to Creighton, James said "I don't foresee much good from a philosophical Society. Philosophical discussion proper only succeeds between intimates who have learned how to converse by months of weary trials and failure. The philosoph[er] is a lone beast dwelling in his individual burrow. —Count me *out*."[10] History has confirmed his misgivings about the association, I think, but perhaps not his assessment of philosophers as lone beasts. James attacked the gesture toward the "professionalizing" of philosophy, which he detected in the idea of the APA, in an essay called "The Ph.D. Octopus."[11] But James did eventually join and even became president of the APA for the 1906–07 academic year. By that time there was no stopping the movement in any case. The question was no longer *whether* philosophy in America would be professionalized, but *how*.

The founding of the APA did not occur in a vacuum, however. It arose locally from tensions that had been brewing in the American Psychological Association (founded 1892) between experimentalists on one side, and philosophical psychology on the other side. Both James and Royce had been president of this older group, and James had shown significant enthusiasm for its formation. James Campbell notes that "from James's response [to Gardiner and Creighton above], it appears that there was a significant difference between his approaches to the disciplines of psychology and philosophy . . . We can only guess that, for James, psychology benefits from the sort of interaction and co-operation that a professional association facilitates, whereas philosophy is for the most part the work of 'lone beasts'."[12] Apart from the tension developing in the psychological association, more globally, the university itself was changing. There is little doubt that philosophers who wanted to serve institutions in such a way as to serve philosophy itself had to consider with great seriousness how they would attempt to act in concert, and what role they would play in both the modern universities and their broader role in society. The older and the newer organizations (both designated the APA, but Campbell handily adopts the convention of designating the older group the AΨA) met together several times in the early years, but the permanent separation came within five years or so of the founding of the APA. This represented a growing and broad trend toward a new idea of the university and the professoriate. One could either join the professionalizing parade or be left out of the rewards that awaited the participants.

Royce, although he did not attend the initial organizing meeting (see Creighton's invitation above), accepted the role of being the third president of the APA, after Creighton had filled the "chief seat" himself in the first year, and Alexander Thomas Ormond of Princeton served the second year. There is more than one way to understand what happened with the APA,[13] but in light of what I have to say in this chapter, it is important to note that Royce said that philosophers "do not at present form a literal human community of mutual enlightenment and of growth in knowledge" over a decade later.

A clear example of the sort of problems Royce was witnessing is documented in his article "On Definitions and Debates," based on an address Royce presented at the APA meeting in December of 1911.[14] On this occasion, Royce takes apart and criticizes, in tremendous detail, the procedures the APA had adopted to ensure "fruitful debate." As absurd as this sounds today, the APA had decided to appoint a "Committee on Definitions" to specify the meanings of terms like "object" and "real object" and "perceived object," and mandating that discussants could use such terms *only* in the specified senses during debate. Always a willing experimentalist, Royce regarded this as an idea that might be worth trying, but its execution in this case had, in fact, *excluded* almost every interesting philosophical viewpoint from the debate, as he demonstrates. The Executive Committee and Committee on Definitions intended good but brought about the reverse. Those who snicker at the idea that professional associations might specify their definitions in advance and forcibly restrict "legitimate debate" to those meanings might wish to study the sad history of the Diagnostic and Statistical Manual of the American Psychological Association. Psychology is still pretending to be a science, and part of the way that profession creates and enforces the illusion is by means similar to those I am describing here.

In Royce's estimation, the APA had, up to that point (1912 or 1913), failed in its aim, and it was often taking the wrong road. It was showing signs of an affinity for sterile debate about abstract definitions and not much interest in concrete problems. I believe I know the main reason it failed, but I will refrain from making it explicit until we have examined a number of things the APA *did* succeed in doing, *how* it succeeded and *why* these standards and practices became what we see today.

Creighton and these other philosophers, including Royce, really *wanted* to be a community, purposed to be, willed it, and struggled mightily with what it meant, how best to form such a purpose. As Creighton stated in the first presidential address, "the insufficiency of the isolated individual and the consequent necessity of co-operation have not been so clearly realized by philosophers as by workers in almost every other department of knowledge," while philosophy is "that which demands, in order to be fruitfully prosecuted, the closest and most intimate intellectual relations between a number of minds."[15] Here we can see that Creighton is allowing James's point about the required intimacy while rejecting, just as Royce did, his view about "lone beasts" in their burrows. While a number of the early presidents of the APA devoted their presidential addresses to the purpose and meaning of philosophy or to the purposes of the Association, James and Royce did not. One wishes that perhaps they had,[16] although what James would have said on the topic I can't quite imagine—perhaps "back to your burrows!" Still his skepticism about the "profession," because he was so well respected, might have curbed, in desirable ways, some of the enthusiasm for the formalization of all philosophical relationships. Alas, he did not use his influence in this way.

Unhappily, the philosophers of Creighton's generation created a social order that so subverted the cause they loved as to render it, over time (several generations—and it is crucial to what I will say later that it here be noted that *time* is a crucial player in what has happened, and that *time* is here spread over a span that exceeds the lifetime of any single individual), something that would be *as* unrecognizable to *them* (Creighton, James, Royce) as the current Christian churches would be to Jesus or Paul. Then the philosophers passed this increasingly monstrous institution on to their students, who passed it on to their students and so on. For the sake of *desiring* a vital community *without* sufficient wisdom to create it, they betrayed philosophy, although they never intended to do that.[17] Their most ardent wish was to serve it well. I am not claiming I could have done any better, but I do wish to understand why I cannot now, in good conscience, serve the APA as a cause befitting a morally developed human being, and why so many of our institutions have gone the same way.[18] This deterioration of "institutional persons" into sociopathy is certainly not new in human history—one finds evidence of the same process of decline in the institutions of the earliest recorded civilizations of ancient Mesopotamia and the Old Kingdoms of Egypt. But for all that, continuing service to any community as something beloved by its servants depends upon addressing and redressing what goes wrong.

To put it in the terms of this book, the APA was supposed to become a person, and as an institutional person it was supposed serve the ideal of philosophy itself, by serving the institutional communities of Harvard and Cornell and Johns Hopkins and the like, where philosophy would be taught to those who would in turn teach it everywhere else. These more developed institutions in which philosophers would serve, I mean the universities *and* the colleges, had within their own powers of imagination the ideal of a broader community, a community of students, teachers, scholars, and researchers who could serve the infinite ideal of the pursuit of wisdom, knowledge and moral development by forming living human communities. The philosophers of Royce's day were searching for, one is tempted to say "fumbling around for," their proper place of service in that wider purpose. Royce summed it up, as he attempted to correct the course of the APA, to save it from those who meant to serve it, but were doing so in a misguided way:

> The issue involved is not as to their unquestionable sincerity and devotion, but as to the future policy of the Association, and as to the best way of securing, in the discussions at our meetings, the right sort of philosophical communion and community amongst our members. Our committees consist of valued and honored friends. But the Association itself is the "greater friend." We all wish it to find the best way of doing its work. We hope that it will long outlive our own generation. We want to initiate methods of co-operation which, as they come to be improved by experience, will continue to grow more and more effective as the years go on. To this end, we must be ready to criticize freely the first efforts to organize such methods of co-operation.[19]

But the APA was founded as much on defensive principles as upon hopes and ideals, as much upon the fear of philosophers' losing their place in the universities as of finding ways to advance the ideals of their own institutions and of philosophy itself. The philosophers were worried that they would be left behind by the modern university, would be misunderstood and thought useless, and they wanted to avoid the perception that they were a part of the "old order" of theological training, having no part in the new purposes.[20] Whether rightly or not, the philosophers of that generation, Creighton's cohort, felt that the public did not show the same respect and deference to philosophers as was willingly shown to "scientific workers" in other fields, and that the absence of public deference to their expertise was a threat to the future of the discipline as a vital part of the university. The APA was, simultaneously, an offense and a defense. The offense was probably largely successful in the early years, as James Campbell has documented, but the defense brought with it tremendous costs that are still being borne by their children's children's children's children.

Let us try to understand what sort of "person" or "greater friend" the APA was supposed to be, and how philosophy eventually came to be reduced to the sort of overlooked and puzzling parasite it now is, in the most revered American institutions. Let us do this for the sake of understanding how some of us might both become more than individual philosophers in our own burrows, learning also to serve philosophy itself as a cause worthy of actual devotion and idealization, and failing that, serving it as a lost cause whose "might have been" is more powerful in us than its "might be." There is a way so to serve philosophy and to do it well, and it will not be different for psychology or art or literature or religion. It involves, as one might expect, "training for loyalty," to use Royce's phrase. It is in examining training for loyalty, as applied in the teaching of philosophy that we land upon points that can and should be generalized to institutional life, to the lives of all institutions-as-persons, in the relevant sense.

Assessments of Academic Philosophy in the USA

Small decisions early in the lives of institutions can have their effects amplified over time in surprising and unforeseeable ways. Anyone who observes academic philosophy as practiced in the American universities of today would be justified in wondering how it came to be defined and practiced as it is, to do what it does, and to perceive itself as it does. Whatever is good or bad in academic philosophy today is the long-term result of decisions, trends, practices that started somewhere at some time, which came to be sanctioned and widely imitated. In the not too distant past, John McCumber defended the thesis that the current practice of philosophy in America was greatly influenced by the McCarthy era, and that the rise and flourishing, and eventual near hegemony of analytic philosophy, with its lofty disdain for social and political commitments, is explained by the fear and purges of philosophers who dared to speak out during that time.[21]

I am not an analytic philosopher and I do not think the culture of analytic philosophy has done much good for philosophy, but I am not convinced that McCumber has offered anything more than a small part of the story. And indeed, if I had to choose between the cluelessness, general ignorance, and laziness of analytic philosophers and the gossiping, sycophantic loyalty games of American philosophers who study French and German philosophy, I certainly prefer cluelessness, even willful cluelessness. I can barely imagine what Royce and James would say about our current profession, but I can't think they would be proud. But as important and timely as McCumber's book is, he attacks the culture of analytic philosophy as a partisan Continental philosopher (one relegated to a position in the German Language department at his university, presumably due to the clannishness of analytic philosophers). Frankly I doubt that the enthusiasts of Continental thought would have handled the development of the profession any better, had they been in charge.

A question McCumber does not ask, that I think we *should* ask, is how the institutional practices and forms of association came to be what they are, and since he argues that philosophy was proportionately harder hit by the anti-communist purges than any other discipline (and this appears to be true), why was this so, and why did the spaces created by the fear and the purges get taken up by analytic philosophers with a certain peculiar and narrow conception of the discipline? What ideals, if any, informed the practices that were exploited by these odd posers, the spiritual grandchildren of the "Committee on Definitions" Royce was chastening? Why are their Ph.D.-granting programs so powerful and why are they all so similar?[22] Why does the curriculum look as it does, and perhaps most importantly, why does the APA look as it does? McCumber addresses these matters in part, but the story goes further back than he traces it—it goes back to Creighton, Royce, James, and the generation of philosophers who created the purpose, the ideal of the APA.

In particular I want to address these questions by saying something about the paradoxical figure and self-conception of the academic philosopher, as he or she (usually he, usually white and *petit bour-*

geois—I do not except myself of course) presently exists. The paradox involves at least two difficult-to-grasp ideas. The first is the way in which academic philosophers conceive of themselves as being always about the (self-)important business of criticizing and interpreting the latest science, and that as the (self-)appointed critics and interpreters, they think themselves important laborers in the domain of professional scientific inquiry, and in service of the ideal of creating new knowledge. In this role they think they are contributing members of a wider community of inquirers and should be respected and included in the scientific endeavors of the universities, in spite of the fact that practicing scientists pay almost no attention at all to what the analytic philosophers say (nor should they). A similar story might be told about our so-called expertise in ethics in relation to all conceivable facets of practical human endeavor. The endeavors seem to proceed in blissful independence of the pronouncements of the professional philosophers, and without noticeably suffering for the lack of them.

On the other side, academic philosophers also like to see themselves as solitary thinkers, deeply absorbed in their difficult and profound and important contemplations, which no one else can really understand or appreciate fully, and as such, they ought not be judged by the standards of experimental productivity, success, and failure that are used in evaluating the work of scientists (such as, for example citation rates). While other empirical laborers are expected to pay their own salaries with grants, and to have their careers stand or fall on the results they can show, philosophers want to be *revered with* them, but not *measured like* them.

To illustrate this common attitude, in his book *Fashionable Nihilism*, Bruce Wilshire reports the following conversation overheard at an APA meeting:

#1: ... So did the interview go just as well?
#2: No. It really didn't go well at all. It was very odd. [*puzzled look*]
#1: How so?
#2: Well, for example, they asked me what I would like to teach and I talked about my philosophy of mind course, you know, and one of them cut in and asked me if I would have my students read William James and ...
#1: William James? The Pragmatist? [*said in disbelief*]
#2: Yes, yes, and so I told them of course not. Can you imagine?
#1: Good. What did they say?
#2: They said, "Why not?"
#1: What did you say?

#2: I said I never read anyone who takes philosophy personally [*look of great distaste*] or confuses philosophy with things that matter in their little lives.

#1: Right. If they want to talk about philosophy as if it matters personally, they need to get out of the profession or at least go back to school. Yeah—maybe we [Princeton] could get together with Pittsburgh and Rutgers and offer some regional post-doctoral remedial programs for those kinds of people.[23]

Here is the full paradox. In a sense these interlocutors are *having* a philosophical conversation in which the way "philosophy" is conceived very much matters to their personal lives—not only in the way that it affects their job prospects and their personal investment in the particulars about *which norms* are practiced in the discipline, but also in the sense of a firmly held *personal* ethic about what philosophy *is* and how it *ought to be* practiced. The fact that they *are* philosophizing poorly, dogmatically, even sociopathically, is not a fine testament to the quality of their Princeton educations. The *content* of their personally held ethic is that philosophy should be practiced impersonally. Their objection to James is that he took the practice of philosophy to be something personally significant. This is accompanied by the ethical judgment that each professional philosopher must (this is a stringent moral "must") hold the *same* ethic, and that enforcing this norm is something that requires a plan of action to remediate, should it slip (which obviously it has, if an interview committee could seriously ask about teaching James, who, in spite of the judgment of these sociopaths, is quite possibly the best philosopher America ever produced).

The implicit *ideal* in the anecdote (and I wish it were rare, but it is not), and whether these arrogant young men know it or not (probably the latter; they are just aping what they've seen) is that we must *all* uphold this "impersonal standard," or more accurately, this contradictory facade, because this little lie is what ensures our standing in the universities, and it is also what protects our autonomy from the encroachments of allegedly sub-philosophical (i.e., personal) criticisms. Professional philosophy has become a scam and must not be discovered as such, and its current practice entails a paradoxical pose, the "lone wolf, profound, inscrutable interpreter of science," which is now so often imitated that the swindlers themselves no longer realize they participate in a great confidence game.[24] We "professional philosophers" have a fear, mostly unconscious I think, that others will recognize how unsure of ourselves we are and will realize we are bluffing in the modern university, actually having very little criticism or knowledge of an *impersonal* sort to offer.

If we should ever slip and allow our peers to see that we pursue a kind of wisdom or peace of mind that cannot be perfectly attained or measured by impersonal standards, they might run us out of the academy, which would rob us of our comfort, not to mention our prestige, and might force us back into (gasp) the *agora*. It is safer not to pursue anything personal at all, and to ridicule any among our number who does. Where did this charade of professionalism get started and why?

The key player in trying to understand this facade that is the APA is J.E. Creighton. It is also terribly unfair to Creighton to focus as much upon him as I will, because he was an excellent philosopher, a true servant of its highest ideals, and someone who deserved a better community than was attained. There were many other views expressed in the early days of the APA, and there is no reason to think that Creighton's stated views were credited *more* than the contrary views of others, but there was something in the way his practice and views, both defensive and offensive, coalesced that was crucial to the development of the sociopathy displayed by today's APA (and the APA is no better or worse than five hundred other similar organizations). We have to understand the problem before we can examine the proposed solution, drawn from Royce.

Creighton's Paradoxical Impact

James Edwin Creighton was born in Nova Scotia in 1861, grew up on his parents' farm and taught school in Nova Scotia up to the age of twenty-two. Creighton went to Dalhousie College in 1883 and studied philosophy with Jacob Gould Schurman, who was to become his lifelong friend and patron. At about the time Creighton met Schurman, the latter was the favored choice of Charles W. Eliot for the Chair that Royce took at Harvard that next year, Eliot having been convinced by James to favor Royce. Quite possibly many lives would now be very different had Eliot hired Schurman instead of Royce, for reasons that will soon become clear. Instead of Harvard, Schurman went to the new school being founded in Ithaca, New York, with a land grant and the money of Ezra Cornell. Creighton later followed Schurman to Cornell University in 1887, and received the Ph.D. there in 1892. As was customary in that age, Creighton spent 1889–90 studying in Germany at Leipzig and Berlin, returning to Cornell to defend his thesis and then remaining there for the rest of his career in several different positions, including Dean of the Graduate School from 1914 until 1923.

More than his written work it was Creighton's ideas concerning how to *live* the philosophical life, and his manner of implementing those ideas, that has left a lasting mark on philosophy in North America. This contribution is filled with paradoxes, however—startlingly familiar ones. There was probably not another single individual as important as Creighton in establishing the *form* and *expectations* of the modern "profession" of philosophy, its role in contemporary universities, its characteristic curriculum, its professional organizations, and its forms and styles of publication. The professionalization of philosophy bears the mark of Creighton's vision at every turn. Yet, one could hardly find a philosopher who conceived of the philosophical *life* in *less* professionalized terms. The philosophical life was, for Creighton, the life of leisure—disciplined and properly employed leisure—for the development of the mind and of character, for the formation of small groups of excellent minds who press themselves and one another for the genuine attainment of ideals. This view is something close to Aristotle's notion of the "divine life," apolitical and contemplative, and nearly the opposite of the "engaged professional."[25] For both better and worse, and without clear intent, Creighton defined not only the *role* of the engaged professional philosopher for the twentieth century, but also the *image* of the philosopher as unengaged and contemplative.

The Philosophical Life?

Creighton's conception of the philosophical life was that of the humanistic scholar who uses leisure for the improvement of the mind. An excellent mind was marked by its clarity, measured by its capacity for rigorous argumentation. The best way to attain this clarity and skill is through the study of the history of philosophy, Creighton thought. Broad questions and questions of principle are the philosopher's province. An *ethos* of intellectual honesty, forthrightness, and sharp criticism of oneself and one's fellows was to be cultivated in this "society of minds." Creighton urged that his apprentices to the philosophical life trust their intuitions and discipline those intuitions by means of logic. Agreement upon a final set of ideas or a system was not the aim of the philosophical life; rather the end was the cultivation of excellent and clear thinking about philosophical issues among individuals committed to the life of the mind.

The measure of philosophical excellence was as much to be gleaned from one's capacity to carry on conversation, dialectic in the Platonic sense, as from one's capacity to write. Creighton advocated high academic standards throughout his life. Originality in philosophical ideas was neither especially to be sought nor likely to be attained. As a result of this ideal of the philosophical life, Creighton published comparatively little himself. However, he actually *lived* the life he envisioned, and by living it concretized the ideal of the philosophical life he advocated. As a colleague described him, "he rarely left Ithaca, took little exercise, and spent most of his life in the library."[26] He studied, he read, he taught his graduate students, he gathered with them and they challenged one another sharply, and they cultivated themselves together.

Creighton was not a solitary, he was an Epicurean in his Ithaca garden. This ideal of the philosophic life does accord nicely with the aim and purpose of living in a community—the academic philosopher is not quite a lone beast in his burrow, but is at his or her (and Creighton emphatically *included* women) best when in a community of interpretation. This is the main source of the image of the philosopher as an inscrutable contemplative, as we shall see when we look at how Creighton's influence spread, but the image was certainly reinforced by many others who operated quite independently of Creighton. It is important to note that the image of the philosopher as the socially engaged "public intellectual" is the main alternative, exemplified by people such as Royce, Dewey, and to a lesser extent James.

Cornell University and the Sage School of Philosophy

Understanding Creighton's ideas about the philosophical life and his ability to realize them requires some grasp of the animating ideals and resources of Cornell University. Cornell was the result of a collaboration between the controversial academician Andrew Dickson White and the wealthy Ezra Cornell. It started as an experimental way to take advantage of the Morrill Land Grant Act of 1862. The public and private colleges of the US had been plagued by sectarian religious strife and Cornell and White set out to show that a non-sectarian Christian institution, promoting both the liberal arts and the natural and applied sciences, especially at the graduate level, was the idea of the future. Cornell opened in 1868 and in many ways was the epicenter of the cultural forces that developed both the modern university and the liberal Protestant consensus in the US in the twentieth century, the latter being a tacit agreement among mainline denominations to strive for public unity by emphasizing points of agreement while privatizing points of sectarian difference. In this sort of space grew the secular pluralistic American ideal in both higher education and the nation. Cornell University was progressive from the beginning, becoming co-educational by 1872, awarding degrees in new fields such as journalism and veterinary medicine, pioneering the ideas of the lending library and the university press. The available resources were marvelous, and they were put to wonderful use.

Among the many experiments tried at Cornell was The Sage School of Philosophy. Creighton's mentor Schurman was made President of Cornell University in 1892, and he immediately appointed Creighton to the chair in "Logic and Metaphysics." Together they established The Sage School, and quickly began to create the institutional structures required to realize their ideal of the philosophical life. The idea of The Sage School was to be a center for all sorts of philosophical activities, but most of all for the formation of a society of minds devoted to the pursuit of philosophy both for its own intrinsic worth and for the betterment of their own character. The Sage School included, in addition to graduate and undergraduate education in the history of philosophy, colloquia and gatherings at which ideas were to be presented and debated in formal papers, a published journal, a philosophy club, and formal and informal ties to other centers of philosophy in the US and abroad. In effect, the pursuit of graduate education at Cornell in the 1890s set the pattern easily recognized in most every American graduate school of philosophy today. When we ask ourselves "why did we do the things we did in graduate school, and why did we think we *should* do them?" the answer is "Creighton," or "Creighton and Schurman." I will explain, at least in part, why this model prevailed, for there were certainly other models. Let us begin with the written record.

Publishing: *The Philosophical Review* and *Kant-Studien*

These days it is typical for universities that grant graduate degrees in philosophy to house a journal or a book series, or to have a liaison with a university press, or all of these. That a graduate program *should* house a journal seems so obvious to us today that it barely requires an explanation. Clearly the journals tend to reflect the philosophical priorities of the departments that publish them, and the prestige of the journal is often a reflection of the prestige of the department that publishes it. But this arrangement had never been a standard one before Creighton's model took over.

Among the first institutions created in The Sage School was Schurman's *Philosophical Review* (founded 1892), of which Creighton became co-editor in 1896, and Editor-in-Chief in 1902, a position he held until his death. Creighton also served as American Editor of *Kant-Studien* from 1896 until his death. These roles not only established the form in which professional philosophy would be published in the US, but made Creighton the principal gatekeeper and the setter of publishing standards. It also placed him in the role of the US philosopher who presented ideas to the German-speaking academies for their publication. Plenty of American philosophers had ties to Germany, but Creighton was sending them the material for publication. Naturally there were other alternatives in the publication of professional philosophy in the US, having followed a more humanistic model in W.T. Harris's *Journal of Speculative Philosophy*, begun right after the Civil War ended, and an interdisciplinary model in *The Journal of Philosophy, Psychology, and Scientific Methods* (later just the *Journal of Philosophy*) beginning in 1904. But the *Philosophical Review* quickly offered to publish the proceedings of the APA, so that one reinforced the other. The association of the journal and the new professional organization was an important one for the setting of standards in the subsequent profession, so that whatever happened with the Sage School at Cornell would have an effect on the APA.

Creighton and Schurman followed the European forms of professional publication in most ways, but it should be recalled that among earlier American journals, Harris's had conceived of philosophy as a *public* discussion, that philosophy can and should be published and discussed at a high level beyond the academies, and Royce's *International Journal of Ethics* proceeded along the same lines, as did some other early journals such as *The Personalist*, which also published poetry and fiction that had philosophical content, along with thoughtful essays on philosophical topics by all sorts of people. Many of the early contributors to such humanistic journals were not professors of philosophy. But the *Philosophical Review* published academic philosophers and tacitly (and perhaps unconsciously) advocated an exclusively academic idea of philosophical rigor, form and scholarship.

The great success of *The Philosophical Review* slowly (and perhaps without conscious intent) squeezed out high-level philosophical discussion among thinkers beyond the academy, or at least obliterated the awareness of any such discussion on the part of the academic philosophers. Gradually the other journals began to copy its forms and standards. It is therefore not really accurate to suggest, as McCumber has done, that the retreat into purely academic discussion of philosophy, by and for academics, occurred in the McCarthy era. It had begun long before that time, although certainly the McCarthy Era scare may have been the last nail in the coffin. The paradox involved is that Creighton's high professional standards for the journal also functioned as barriers to those who had not been enculturated to academic styles and forms of philosophical discourse. To participate in the "important" discussions, one would have to adopt its rules, and to adopt the rules one would need to study philosophy formally in the academy. In short, one had to conform to the dictates of the Committee on Definitions, in practice if not in policy.

As a result and over time, it was not easy for academics themselves to distinguish between, on one side, worthy ideas that were in non-standard forms, and on the other side, poor thinking. Gradually the effect of this practice of expecting standard forms to be observed was that the professional journals would sooner publish poor and trivial thinking that followed the sanctioned professional *form* than publish valuable ideas that did not. The same has come to be the case for the sterile and pointless papers accepted at APA meetings today. So while Creighton was a great champion of free expression, especially open criticism, his philosophical style contributed much to the segregation of public and academic philosophical discourse, in the US and to a lesser extent, even abroad.[27]

Apart from the two journals, a third way in which Creighton played a significant role in creating the public face of professional philosophy was through his contribution of twenty-six articles to the new *Encyclopedia Americana*, ensuring that students around America would be consulting Creighton's interpretations of major figures and movements in philosophy. The list of his contributions is telling. He wrote articles on Aristotle, Descartes, Kant, Schopenhauer, and Spinoza, among the figures, and Bergsonism, Cartesianism, Determinism, Empiricism, Idealism, Materialism, Pluralism, Pragmatism, Rationalism, Realism, and other movements. Creighton was sharply critical of many of these perspectives and movements, and to have *him* defining their basic principles and arguments for students everywhere placed him in a position of great persuasiveness, for encyclopedias were then fewer in number and held greater authority than they do today, and while other important encyclopedias and dictionaries of philosophy were published back then (notably Baldwin's), the *Americana* is still around and the others are not. Its continued existence is evidence of the influence it *has* had. In these and other writings Creighton was the consummate commentator on the philosophical developments of his time, a sort of journalist of the highest stripe.

The Curriculum

Creighton exerted great influence over how philosophy came to contribute to the overall curriculum of American universities. Prior to the development of Cornell's school of philosophy—although there were a few other universities working out other models, such as Harvard, Boston University, and The Johns Hopkins University—"moral philosophy" was commonly taught by the college president, usually an ordained minister, to seniors before they were graduated. The old idea was to impart to students a sense of the responsibility to God (and perhaps country) of the educated class. Commonly "natural philosophy" was taught by a practicing physicist, and particularly was dominated by the study of optics and electricity, during the nineteenth century. "Mental philosophy" was often associated with rhetoric and elocution. The coming of the modern, non-sectarian university, exemplified by Cornell, signaled an opportunity for philosophy to separate itself from religious commitments, sectarian and non-sectarian, and to redefine its role in the academy. The idea of a "philosophy department" was in the air, but the form it eventually took was greatly shaped by The Sage School under Schurman and Creighton.

Harvard really followed rather than led regarding the development of philosophy as a university discipline. President Charles W. Eliot, a chemist, regarded philosophy as a luxury in the university and had to be convinced, slowly, that it could contribute much to the university. Many of the arguments made by James and Royce to their own administration during the 1880s and 1890s had to do with convincing Eliot that philosophy was something more than a luxury, and this argument was made constantly by both of them for many years. In spite of his respect for James especially, it was unclear to Eliot precisely what philosophers were supposed to do in a university. In time, it was more the public success of James, Royce, and Santayana, in the estimation of both the public and the academic world, and the administrative influence of George Herbert Palmer (who was apparently very good at schmoozing with the powerful) that shaped the Harvard philosophy program. It was then and continues to be built on the personalities, writings, and public perceptions of the professors it hires, more than upon the Cornell model.

Harvard's "model" of graduate education, if it can really be called a "model," depended then, as now, so much upon the collection of personalities it gathered that it cannot easily be imitated. Yet, at several Ivy League schools (Yale, Princeton, and Columbia), there has been some effort to imitate it. Arguably, Yale succeeded and eventually exceeded Harvard in this model between 1950 and 1970, and Columbia has been a close competitor using the same model since the beginning, as has Princeton, with less success. I think most contemporary philosophy professors who currently work under the Cornell model in other universities would aspire to be parts of these "Harvard-type" schools if they could, but the model is limited by its nature. One has to *be* Harvard or Yale or Columbia to get away with the pretense of pre-eminence. Sometimes the model really is fulfilled in the grand efforts of its personalities, but more often it offers up a mere shadow of what it pretends to be, and the public has difficulty telling the difference.

At Johns Hopkins, being modeled upon the German university, President Daniel C. Gilman had decided that there should be *at most* one chair in philosophy, and proceeded to set G.S. Morris (a philosophical idealist and historian of philosophy), C.S. Peirce (a logician and experienced practitioner of several applied sciences), and G.S. Hall (an experimental psychologist) effectively into competition for the *philosophy* chair, giving them each lectureships to see how matters developed.[28] At stake was just about everything associated with how philosophy would play a role in the modern university. This diversity of instructors shows just how wide open the *idea* of academic philosophy was at that time in the US, but it still represents only a small window on all the activities that went under the name "philosophy" in American higher education at that time. Hall won the "competition" (the beneficiary of some decidedly non-intellectual intrigue), while Peirce was (unjustly) dismissed for moral turpitude, and Morris returned to a more secure place in the far provinces, at the University of Michigan (whence he had come).

At Johns Hopkins, philosophy became, predictably, psychology—an important early "loss" for the "philosophers," but it has to be remembered that philosophy and psychology were not, in 1884, regarded as separate disciplines. Hall was as much a "philosopher" as Peirce or Morris in the sense of the term used in that day. One wonders how academic philosophy in the US might have evolved differently if Peirce had been retained and had gone on to realize his promise as both a teacher and researcher. It is quite possible that the Johns Hopkins model would have prevailed, in philosophical studies. We might now have fewer doctoral programs in philosophy, since the Johns Hopkins model could be imitated only with a serious investment of institutional resources. Indeed, had even Morris collected the Chair at Johns Hopkins, the profession might today be quite other than it is. The Johns Hopkins model has been tried again subsequently, since that time, notably at Clark University and more recently with the New School for Social Research in New York City. But the model has always gravitated inexorably back toward the Cornell model. Hence, philosophy at Johns Hopkins today, and at the New School, is not far removed from the Cornell model, and has ceased to exist as a graduate level pursuit at Clark.

At Boston University, which was and remains a religiously affiliated university, the dean of the graduate school, none other than Borden Parker Bowne (see Chapter 7), was an ordained minister, and here the dying model of philosophy conjoined to theology (the old "moral philosophy taught by the minister-president" approach), as deeply modified by the growth of the universities themselves, prevailed there for another three generations. This model of philosophy as the religiously sympathetic capstone of a moral education only gradually waned, and it still survives in a few sectarian universities, such as Liberty University in Virginia, and in some graduate programs in Roman Catholic universities that remain dominated, administratively, by the adherents of various Catholic orders (although this is becoming rarer all the time). For the most part, the more successful a given university of this type has been, the greater has been the pressure upon it to succumb to the Cornell model in philosophy. Thus, hardly anyone takes Liberty University seriously as a place to study philosophy, but Baylor, which is also Southern Baptist but more humanistic, is closer to the Cornell model, and is taken seriously. Many successful universities, such as Vanderbilt, or the University of Southern California, or Syracuse University, or Loyola University in Chicago, either disaffiliated with a religious sect, or so greatly informalized the affiliation as to leave the philosophy programs to choose their own missions, and they all drifted toward the Cornell model.

In any case, the Harvard, the Cornell, the Johns Hopkins, and the Boston University, were the primary early models for graduate education in philosophy. The Cornell model set the standard in the long run, and the Cornell model was Creighton's. Creighton had a different idea from Harvard, Boston, and Johns Hopkins. His department would teach the history of philosophy and rational psychology, but not empirical psychology; it would teach no rhetoric or elocution; it would teach logic but not grammar (many thousands of philosophers would report relief that the English departments of America got stuck with the "burden" of teaching writing); it would teach foundations of the objective world in metaphysics and epistemology, but not the natural sciences. Creighton held that it was the job of philosophy to "interpret" the sciences and to examine their assumptions critically.

The centerpiece of philosophy's contribution to the university or college would be logic on Creighton's model. Certainly there were in 1898 plenty of logic texts available for colleges—the famous texts of Whewell, Jevons, Coppens, and even Royce's 1881 *Primer of Logical Analysis* (which still integrated logic with grammar and writing, and if *it* had become popular, those "relieved" philosophers might now have much for which to blame Royce). But it was Creighton's own textbook, *An Introductory Logic* (1898, rev. 1900, 1909, 1920, and revised again by Harold Smart in 1932) that established the subject of logic as philosophy's principal contribution to the curriculum. This textbook was still in print as late as 1947, giving it a half-century of influence during the formative period of the modern American university. Creighton succeeded. Philosophers would teach logic in the modern university. It did not *have* to be that way, but that is how the story went.

The paradox (or perhaps merely irony) arising here is that Creighton's ideas about logic were not even close to the formal discipline logic became during the revolt against idealism between 1910 and 1930. Creighton conceived of logic in humanistic terms, with little formalization. Defining the role of logic in philosophy was, for Creighton, something closely akin to defining what philosophy itself is, grasping what it can and cannot do. Logic was the tool philosophers use to *do* philosophy, and logic is not much more than that in his view. The *effect* of Creighton's view of the *role* of logic in the university became far more influential than his conception of logic itself. As logic became formalized and increasingly mathematical during Creighton's lifetime, he nevertheless held fast to his idea that the teaching and development of logic is the contribution philosophy makes to the advancement, interpretation and clarification of knowledge. Of course, there were many emerging models of how to formalize logic, with Peirce and Royce both developing systems that were more mathematical than Creighton's, but more humanistic than the models of Frege, Whitehead, and Russell that eventually took over.

If universities were founded for the creation and advancement of new *knowledge*, especially technical knowledge, as they were claiming to be, then philosophy must have a role in this project, Creighton believed. It is not insignificant that Creighton taught at one of the early land-grant colleges. He was in a position to see what was developing in the land-grant colleges (such as Iowa State, Kansas State, and Michigan State, which pre-dated Cornell), that the federal government was interested in technologies relating to industry and agriculture (and military science), and little interested in either pure science or the liberal arts (although these were not excluded). There was then, as now, a worry among humanists that the ideal of a liberal education would simply pass into the history of American education rather than be a part of its future. Creighton, with the help of a philosopher president in Schurman, thus created the institutional space in a land grant school for formal logic to become the center of attention in the liberal arts, shielding by its rigor and intellectual prowess a place where the history of philosophy would be taught and learned, and welded together by a crucial role for the critique of science. Logic was the scientific-looking camouflage, the technical tool that philosophers could learn and teach to which no other discipline had laid a definite claim. Clearly the mathematicians and the pure scientists might easily have made a play for control of logic—indeed, had Peirce succeeded at Johns Hopkins, it is anything but clear where control of logic might have ended up, since Peirce was about equal parts pure scientist, applied scientist, mathematician, and historian of philosophy.

Creighton did not contribute anything significant to the creation of formal logic itself; nor would Creighton have approved of the complete formalization of logic. However, Creighton should be recognized as the one who saw that philosophy would have to redefine itself in light of the way universities were evolving. As he observed, "in many colleges and universities the place of philosophy is only grudgingly conceded. It is regarded as a more or less useful handmaid to theology, or perhaps education, but its scientific status as a real and independent subject of investigation is tacitly or explicitly denied."[29] He saw how this problem could be overcome by allying philosophy to the sciences, in the way I have described (which should sound eerily familiar to those in the profession). The plan was successful. Without Creighton's foresight, philosophy as a discipline might have met the same fate in the university as elocution, since, as Creighton noted, "it does not seem too much to say that philosophy does not enjoy the general recognition, even among educated men, that is accorded to many of the other sciences, nor is the philosophical teacher and writer universally conceded to be a specially trained scholar whose opinions in his own field are as much entitled to respect as those of the physicist or biologist in his special domain."[30]

The American Philosophical Association

The preceding prepares us for understanding what the APA is and why it exists as it does. Why did the Cornell model prevail? How did it prevail? This raises the question of how Creighton managed to implement his ideas about philosophy. As I have mentioned, Creighton was among a small group of philosophy professors who founded the American Philosophical Association and he was elected its first president in 1901. While the APA was preceded by the Western Philosophical Association by a year, the idea was much circulated during the progressive era that respectable disciplines should form professional organizations for education, intellectual exchange and for setting the standards of their disciplines. While the first president of the Western Philosophical Association, Frank Thilly of the University of Missouri, used his presidential address to discuss the theory of interaction, Creighton used his address to present a manifesto on the purposes of the association, subsequently published in his own *The Philosophical Review*. But Creighton also was publishing the important papers given at the annual meetings of the Western Philosophical Association, while serving as the guardian angel of the APA. The connection of the APA with *The Philosophical Review* was one factor that led to the gradual dominance of Creighton's association over the WPA as well. But the publishing connection is not the full story. The "driving force" (to use Campbell's phrase) behind the organization of the Western Philosophical Association, and the WPA's first president, Frank Thilly, had been among the first "fellows" appointed to the Sage School of Philosophy at Cornell, in 1891, as soon as Thilly returned to the US from completing his doctoral studies in Germany. In other words, Thilly was one of the founders of the Sage School, was there when the Cornell model was designed, and took those ideas in 1894 to the University of Missouri, and to the WPA as its founder and leader. At the same time Creighton was pressing for the creation of the APA, Thilly was succeeding in creating the same structure in what we now call the Midwestern U.S. (then called simply the west). This gave the Cornell model a leg up, and Creighton's conception of the study of philosophy had now two strong pillars of support, with his journal being the organ of both.

To learn more about this model, we should examine Creighton's presidential address; it is quite informative. The American Philosophical Association today very much bears the forms and self-concept that Creighton espoused in his presidential address, making that piece perhaps Creighton's most influential and important writing. The address makes clear that philosophers themselves are not altogether certain why an association is needed or what it should try to do. Eschewing the idea that the association should gather for the edification of its members, and rejecting the idea that the association could solve every problem philosophers face, Creighton sought to define the scope and purposes of the APA by noting that "all modern scientific work" has the "striking characteristic" of "conscious co-operation among a number of individuals." The old notion of the philosopher as a "man of leisure," eccentric, alone in his contemplations and scribblings, was not to be perpetuated in the coming age—at least not by the APA. The philosopher was, for

Creighton's APA, a kind of co-operative scientist. This is, of course, the very opposite of his own practice at Cornell. The term "science" was meant in the broad sense of *Wissenschaft*, an ordered and systematic kind of study leading to knowledge, in the broadest sense, and not limited by the narrow definition of "natural science" such as is common today. The strategic advantage of having allied philosophy with science at the beginning became clear as the growing prestige of the sciences pressed hard against the humanities in the twentieth century. Creighton had no desire to be a scientist, but he could see the advantage of being perceived by others as one engaged in a scientific, that is to say, *wissenschaftlich* activity.

In spite of Creighton's broad sense of "science," ideas about what renders a discipline "scientific" later narrowed and formalized with the increasing success of quantitative methods. The paradox of the American Philosophical Association is that its initial vision as "scientific" and devoted to "research" was articulated by a thorough going humanist who would not recognize the largely anti-humanistic and impersonal association it eventually became. Unhappily, the same can be said of many other similar organizations that were overtaken by scientism in the twentieth century.

Second, in spite of his own devotion to the history of philosophy, and the role he gave it in graduate study at Cornell (and Cornell remains a historical program in reputation, even if now mainly consisting in narrow *uses* of historical ideas, and its university press one of the most important publishers of historical philosophy), Creighton did not project the study or discussion of the history of philosophy as being of central importance to the association. "The history of philosophy is only intelligible when read in light of present day problems," he said, and the activity of the association "is likely to be centered in the actual problems of the present time." Thus, the history of philosophy is not nothing, for the new organization, but it isn't much. The APA has taken Creighton at his word in this regard. The promotion of scholarship and research was the sole purpose of the association.[31] Harry Norman Gardiner, in his 1926 history of the APA's first twenty-five years, mentioned the failed "incidental activities" of the APA, such as the failed committee on the history of American philosophy and the failed Committee on International Co-operation, but in his history, "the main thing, of course, that concerns us in this retrospect of twenty-five years is the *work proper* of the Association as exhibited in the papers read and discussed at our meetings."[32]

That's it? That's what we do? Write papers and read them to each other and discuss them? The rest is "incidental"? It could be difficult to build a genuine community around an institution that serves such a cause, if indeed this is a cause at all. But it fairly describes the APA then as now; a bunch of white men, possessed of marginal social skills, yacking at each other. If this is our "work proper," we had best not let the deans of our universities or the public find out about it. Note that this situation was already well in place, and sanctified by decades of repetition and practice, before analytic philosophy became prominent, and long before the McCarthy era came along.

Third, and here is the key to the whole business, although Creighton was a legendary and influential teacher himself, one who served his students faithfully, he said *and meant* the following astonishing thing:

> I have said that the promotion of philosophical scholarship and research is the *only object capable of affording a purpose* common to all the members of the Association, and an interest which is likely to be serious and lasting. And in this connection I should like to express my opinion that it would be a mistake to make the discussion of methods of teaching philosophy a coordinate purpose, or even to introduce papers on this subject into the programme of the meetings. Even if the membership of the Association were composed wholly of teachers of philosophy, which will never be, I hope, the case, the meetings should not, it seems to me, be occupied with the consideration of such secondary and subordinate topics. This opinion is based not merely on the personal feeling that the discussion of methods of teaching philosophy is in itself a rather stupid way of wasting time, but on the conviction that even in our capacity as teachers it is courage and inspiration to attack problems for ourselves, to go to firsthand sources and so actually discover by our own efforts what we teach to students, that is the one thing needful.[33]

Surely Creighton is correct to say that one needs to be doing philosophy oneself in order to teach anyone else to do it. He has said this right after remarking what an onerous thing to have to teach so much and still have to publish, but that "does not entirely excuse us from producing something." He has just said, "the majority of the members of this Association are teachers, who can undoubtedly plead as an excuse for unproductiveness the demands of what one of our German colleagues has happily characterized as, *die zeitraubende und kraftsabsorbindere academische Lehrthätigkeit.*"[34] Campbell translates this phrase as "the time-stealing and strength-sapping busy-work," but that is not quite what it says. The last word is "teaching task." Creighton's audience knew full well what he was saying, and while he probably meant to be expressing exasperation at institutionalized life at the colleges, what he went after as the real obstacle to our "work" was teaching.

This is offensive. Creighton has literally suggested that the one thing philosophers do that has anything like the status of "sacred" in human culture, in the whole field of human relations, i.e., teaching, takes us away from our "work," which in his view amounts to devising arguments we scribble down and then gabbing with one another about them. I would think that the latter of these has been proven a "rather stupid way of wasting time" while the former, which we are not even supposed to discuss, is actually the "*only object capable of affording a purpose* common to all the members of the Association." The APA did not have to obey Creighton's wishes, but it did. Yes, there were desultory efforts made along the way at making "teaching" one among the failed "incidental" activities of the Association, but yacking and gabbing about nothing is what prevailed as our "work proper." There is revealed in this a weakness of the will in philosophers, a certain laziness, a preference for the Epicurean garden above the vicissitudes of the world.

This pathetic situation is why, as Royce points out in 1913, philosophers have not formed a community. We are lazy and weak-willed, and bought off by the powers that be, and taught to think of teaching as a strength-sapping and time-stealing burden. The philosophers here in the US chose what was, arguably, the most *trivial* among their many activities and made it their very purpose. I wish that philosophers were the only ones who did this, but many others disciplines, especially in the humanities, made the same choice. They wanted their meetings to be vacations to yack at each other, not purposes worthy of serious service. They convinced one another of the importance of this yacking, created the outward appearances of importance, and managed to foist the illusion on their deans and administrations. The public never quite bought the illusion. They have preferred professional sports to invest their energies in, and the powers that be are more than happy to allow them to dissipate their vital energies on something, that as Chomsky observes, is of no importance whatsoever (and here I want to say that I accept this only with qualifications; Nietzsche had some good things to say about the value of sports to a civilized society that need to be considered).

Of course, the students of these lazy and weak-willed philosophers have been paying the price ever since Creighton's time, just as the public has paid the price in scandal and corruption for allowing its attention to be diverted from the activities of its most powerful citizens. I love baseball, but I hope I never come to the point of thinking of it as the epitome of America's ideals regarding freedom, and I hope that "keeping my eye on the ball" really means something like "the price of freedom is eternal vigilance." And Creighton loved philosophy, and he wanted to gather with his friends and chat about it. The APA was the camouflage, and the less it actually does, the more it must try to *appear* "professional." If the organization actually accomplished anything meaningful, it would not matter as much how it *looks* to people.

It is not actually even partly true that philosophers dislike teaching. Even those sociopathic Princetonians in the anecdote above expected to teach, and quite possibly to enjoy it. I would not be surprised if more than three-quarters of professional philosophers prefer their teaching to their writing duties, but those are not generally the persons occupying places in the powerful institutions. And for some unaccountable reason, even those who *know* better, who *know* that there is nothing especially admirable about a philosophical life that eschews teaching, still admire the chosen few at the "top," read their books and even teach them, like a bunch of idiotic sheep. They allow those few at the "top" to define the vocabulary of professional philosophy, then imitate their attitudes toward the history of philosophy, learn to parrot what's "in" and what's "out" of fashion, ape the self-seriousness and self-importance of this "research" and publishing activity, and even go so far as to expel even from teaching institutions their very own colleagues for failing to publish enough drivel that no one will ever read anyway. With a stiff upper lip and a mild expression of sympathetic regret, they send their very own friends away forever, jobless and exiled, no matter how well those banished persons have taught and served their institutions. These same people then return from APA meetings to their teaching campuses, where presumably many received tenure by the skin of their teeth (having produced just enough ink on paper to survive), and then act as caring and generous teachers and self-sacrificing campus citizens. This is not just a paradox, it is perfectly absurd. It cannot and should not continue.

We have noted how deep imitation goes in the human species, in Chapter 5. The APA's ambivalence regarding teaching and promoting the teaching of philosophy takes its impetus in part from Creighton's vision, but in greater part from our own moral weakness. There is one further piece in the historical puzzle, i.e., the community of memory, that needs to be mentioned before we move to the Roycean point.

Creighton's Students

All of Creighton's experiments and ideas, along with their paradoxes, might have failed to take hold were it not for the number and subsequent influence of his students. Cornell was among only a few institutions producing Ph.D.'s in philosophy at a time when the modern university was forming. These students were devoted to Creighton and convinced by his model—indeed, academics of all stripes, within and beyond the humanities, commonly carry with them the model of their own graduate educations as a sort of operative "super-ego" ever afterwards. Creighton's students, of course, had not been educated at Harvard or Johns Hopkins or Boston University. They were educated at Cornell and they carried on Creighton's legacy and ideals, the wholesome ones and the absurd ones, with all the paradoxes I have mentioned, in numerous places around the country, implementing versions of his ideal in schools nearly everywhere. And here is the number you really need to know: Twelve of Creighton's students became presidents of either the APA, or the WPA, or one of the three divisions of the APA after the merger. This presidential number included two women, Grace Andrus de Laguna and Katherine Everett Gilbert, during the days when the professional barriers for women were enormous.

Creighton had not brainwashed his students or tried to make disciples of them, but the Creighton students were a close-knit group with a common experience. It would have been anathema to Creighton's style or thinking to expect his students to follow his own personal ideals or his philosophical viewpoint. As a teacher he insisted only upon clear thinking and expression, and that his students think for themselves. But his vision of the philosophy profession and the philosophical life was freely and eagerly propagated by his students. So the Creighton model spread, although largely without being credited to its visionary founder. Ironically Creighton's own philosophy did not meet with similar influence, which attests to the autonomy of thinking he encouraged in his students. Creighton's students never distinguished themselves as philosophers in any lasting way, but many were prominent as leaders of the profession and many lived fulfilling philosophical lives.

Speculative Idealism

In many ways, the two young fellows from Princeton in the conversation overheard at the APA, and reproduced in Wilshire's book, are living examples of the paradox of image and reality in philosophy, although they would be horrified to learn that the assumptions behind their ridiculous self-importance is a kind of "speculative idealism," which is the philosophy Creighton defended, come home to roost in their own attitudes about the norms of the "profession." There were three basic touchstones of Creighton's view: 1. that philosophy is a social activity; 2. the history of philosophy is central to philosophy itself; and 3. speculative idealism defines *the* philosophical attitude. The social activity of philosophy is exemplified in the APA and the professional activities of philosophy departments, attempting to concretize Creighton's "society of minds." In its corrupted form, this becomes an inbred society of mutual admiration and endless chatter about nothing. The history of philosophy, in its corrupted form, just means that there are problems and figures no one else talks about, and while we philosophers need not study them with any great seriousness, they are ours and no one else can have them. You all know the canonical list of figures, who's in and who's out. You are always free to talk about Kant and Aristotle and Plato, or views *like* theirs if you are too lazy to read them, but Thucydides and Demosthenes and Quintillian, and apparently William James, are "not philosophers." Academic philosophers today treat their own history in about the way real estate developers treat land they have bought near an interstate, but it's theirs to ignore, exploit, rape or sell as they choose. But in what way are those two young men from Princeton speculative idealists?

The term "speculative" does not imply, as Creighton's former student Katherine Gilbert puts it, "the roaming fancy or any character that conflicts with strict logical procedure."[35] The speculative and idealist posture meant, for Creighton, taking a certain approach to any and every objective and changing problem in the world, a commitment to reflective and critical engagement with any subject matter at all, in a word, what the current culture of analytic philosophy calls "reason" and "rational." This is a kind of idealism because this approach assumes that reflective processes have final authority over unreflective ones, in making determinations of knowledge (what Whitehead called misplaced concreteness, without which fallacy, no analytic philosophy can be done). Idealism could not be subjective, Creighton argued, because the world itself, objectively existing, changing and rational, was the reference point without which thought itself is impossible. The *philosophical attitude*, therefore, does not possess a peculiar subject matter. Rather, as Gilbert summarizes it, "the business of the philosopher is not to do some one thing co-ordinate with the work of the natural scientist or of the man of practice, but sympathetically and intelligently to penetrate the work of all classes of men and to help them become intellectually self-conscious and mutually respectful."[36]

This is, of course, a Socratic conception of the place of the philosopher in the *agora*. In the university, such engagement would mainly be with students (if engagement with students were not so very strength-sapping and time-stealing). Many readers have commented on how much Creighton's idealism resembles the very pragmatism of which he was so critical, but one might say the same for Socrates, and it was Socrates of whom Creighton was fondest. It is hard to believe that someone who would rather die than stop teaching philosophy, for free, has any relation to the present practice of philosophy, but often we most admire (and even identify with) those persons from whose moral development we most depart.

In the end it seems that the Socratic ideal is the notion that relieves some of the tensions in Creighton's simultaneous professionalization of philosophy and his humanistic concept of the philosophical life. He wanted to see himself as a sort of exemplar of the examined life; he made no bones about that. His intellectual progeny have followed him. They do see themselves that way, even today and even though they have never heard Creighton's name. Perhaps this Socratic self-conception relieves some of the psychological tension created by the gulf between what those young Princeton philosophers expect from others in terms of recognition of their professional standing and expertise, and what they actually do, regarding which they want no interference and no judges beyond their small circle of friends. But the incoherence of this view appears when we remember that they do want money for what they are doing—and they don't really want to be paid for teaching, which would be beneath their dignity and a kind of sophistry or intellectual prostitution; they want to be paid for thinking. They are quite certain that everyone is better off when they are left to their profound and inscrutable cogitations. Who knows? Maybe everyone actually *is* better off that way, given their twisted norms.

Maybe the mistake they made in Athens was not buying off Socrates with the pension he demanded. But then, Socrates was pretty adamant about going forth into the marketplace with his questions and putterings, and clear about saying that he would not cease or desist; our profession today is notoriously reticent about the marketplace of ideas, as McCumber has rightly observed. But our reticence predates by many decades the McCarthy scare. The function of graduate schools of philosophy seems to be something other than to insure that the marketplace would always have an ample supply of gadflies, and our practices in graduate schools of philosophy serve something quite apart from the creation of morally sturdy teachers. But the graduate programs seem rather adept at producing speculative idealists of Creighton's variety, even if they do not see themselves as such.

The Sanity of the APA

Creighton says that "to be insane in the full sense of the word is just to lose connection with one's fellows, to fall away from the objective and rational order of things, and to be possessed of subjective fancies and illusions."[37] In Royce's terminology this insanity is the equivalent of failing to acknowledge a "world of truth" based in other possible experience, and this can happen as surely to institutions as to human individuals. Institutions can go insane. Sanity in the world of truth, in my view, includes recognizing that if philosophers are not teachers, they are not anything much. The stated APA purpose of reading papers to one another and chatting about them, and perhaps finding ways to publish them, is not defensible as a purpose. It is not work, it is not service, and it is not a fit life for a mature human being. There is nothing here to serve. To pursue this is to fall away from the objective and rational order of things. In short, the activities cultivated insanity and gradually achieved it.

In Chapter 8 I emphasized that for any institution, *personalizing* the community is a *response* to the community's *prior* personalization of the members of that community. If an institution does not do the interpretive work of personalizing its members, they do not become persons relative to that institution. The same is the case of teacher-student relationships. As we can see, Creighton's actual style of teaching philosophy involved creating a community and a format for graduate and undergraduate study that would do the interpretive work of personalizing all of its members. That he found teaching onerous work did not, apparently, prevent him from performing the task well. Since Creighton's model is the dominant one (almost the only one) for graduate education in philosophy, and since its various activities should do the proper work, why has the "profession" become so very impersonal? What failure of interpretation on the part of institutions has led to such a sad failure of community? In a word, the failure derived from the selected purpose. We decided to teach our graduate students not how to become good philosophers, but how to play a sociopathic game of self-advancement.

Many philosophers become good teachers in spite of their educations, but it does not prevent them from internalizing the idea that teaching gets in the way of their "work." The failure of hospitality in the "profession" toward those who are leaving graduate school and seeking to become professional philosophers is one of the more notable features of the APA as it exists today. It is hard to imagine how anyone might develop a loyalty to an organization that brings them into its ranks through the incredibly impersonal and uncaring process that characterizes present APA meetings. No wonder that many who succeed in getting positions never attend another meeting, or attend only when they have no choice. All the while our young professors are taught in word and deed that to settle on a life-plan of *teaching* is to accept second class status.

The Value of Philosophy

The study of philosophy is not a requirement for living a full life, but like so many other things in human life, such as poetry, music, science, and history, there is a widely and firmly held conviction—a warranted conviction—that philosophical activity can add something worthwhile to living. Like anything else that we have created for the enhancement of living, philosophy can be done either well or poorly. Hardly any of us would long remain at a concert in which the music was being played poorly, or one in which the musicians did not play in such a way as to add some value to our own experience as a result of the effort we make in listening. One thing that has been lost in professionalized philosophy is the sense that it exists to enhance the experience of those who take the trouble to listen, to read, to learn to speak and think according to its patterns of order. This value can only find a measure in the way that thinking philosophically alters both the life that is (the sense of how the life that has been lived is to be grasped in light of what it might have been but was not), and how the life to come could be.

We must *use* our philosophical insight, or we gain nothing valuable from it. Even the walking contradictions one finds at the APA are probably trying to get some use from their study of philosophy. Unfortunately, it would seem that it has come to be used more for mercenary ends than for the ends of personal moral development and the development of vital communities. And this brings me to a thought experiment. I pondered what sacrifices I might make for the sake of the continued work of the various philosophical and academic institutions I serve or have served. It dawned on me, as it might dawn on you, regardless of what sort of life you lead, that there is precious little I would sacrifice for most of them.

For example, I have a hard time even sacrificing my *dues* for membership in the APA. For that amount of money I could get a couple of pretty good books. If the APA were about to be financially ruined tomorrow, and would have to close its doors, I would not spend a penny or a minute of my time to prevent that from happening. I am sure that the employees of the APA feel a different sort of loyalty to it, and perhaps they see their self-absorbed and self-important charges, the "philosophers," as those whose ends they serve. I am sure they are fond of us in some ways and exasperated by us in other ways. I wish we gave them something worthier to serve than facilitating our incessant yacking three times a year, and our traumatizing of young people who want to be just like us.

Yet, like many of you, within and beyond the academy, I belong to various smaller organizations, and to them I gladly pay dues, gladly attend meetings, gladly devote time and effort. But would I sacrifice, say, my career or even my present job for the continuance of any of them, their missions, their "work"? If I take, from among their number, say, the one organization I value the most, what would I sacrifice to forestall its dissolution? Not to be crass about it, but in terms of time and money, would I part with a thousand dollars? Two thousand? Would I spend two full weeks working, without pay, in its service? Two months? Two years? These are not great sacrifices in the service of something one truly values—such as one's family, marriage, home, perhaps nation. I know that for my friends who belong to some of these groups, I would make greater sacrifices, but this is because they are friends, not because they serve the same organization or institution. I am afraid I would not sacrifice very much to keep any one of those organizations alive, even the one I cherish most. I will work, but not sacrifice. Would you?

And thinking of the universities from which I have drawn my education and my living, what would I sacrifice for those? Here things come a little closer to home, for many of us. I would not want the institutions that educated me to close, and I intensely want them to thrive, but I will sooner part with money than time to help them. Regarding those at which I have taught, the arrangement is even less personal. So long as I can find an adequate position somewhere else, while I wish no ill to any institution where I have taught, and while I can enthusiastically endorse their missions (when those missions are actually pursued, which is the exception rather than the rule), I don't suppose I would sacrifice anything of great value for the sake of those institutions. I suspect many others among you are similar. People occasionally take risks at today's universities to maintain a principle, but even that seems more often an act of simple defiance than of service to higher ideals.

But what of philosophy, itself? What if I were told tomorrow that I could not read or discuss philosophy? I am certain I would do it anyway. At what risk? Quite possibly at great risk. And what sacrifice would I be willing to make to secure a covert conversation partner or a forbidden book in philosophy? That is difficult to say, of course, but I think many of us might make considerable sacrifices. Philosophy is basic in us just as poetry is basic in the poet. Am I to stop thinking? No, never that. So here we have something that seems like a starting place, something of value, for many persons at least. I would probably risk my life before I would consent to stop thinking philosophically. But how does one make a life plan from that, or, in community, a purpose?

Time, Will, and Purpose

Throughout this book I have steered away, as much as I could, from Royce's term "loyalty." It is not clear to me that Royce made the best terminological choice when he settled upon it. Yet, the idea, as he defines it, is his most important idea, I believe. Of his 1913 book, he wrote:

> This book, if it is nothing else, is at least one more effort to tell what loyalty is. I also want to put loyalty—this love of the individual for the community—where it actually belongs, not only at the heart of the virtues, not only at the summit of the mountains which the human spirit must climb if man is really to be saved, but also (where it equally belongs) at the turning point of human history . . . that homeland of the human spirit "which eager hearts expect," was first introduced as a vision, as a hope, as a conscious longing to mankind. I want to show what loyalty is and all that is true of the loyal spirit.[38]

Royce makes clear that what he is trying to explain with the term loyalty is in fact what is meant by Christian love, by *agape*. He wants to provide an account that is in no way dependent upon the actual history of the Christian movement or church, but he certainly holds that, while we might have learned about loyalty in this sense from any number of sources, the Christian tradition is the one he thinks really made this ideal of loyalty immanent in history. I do not necessarily agree with this appraisal of history, but it matters little for my own purposes. Loving one's community, making of the community an exclusive, irreplaceable, and unique purpose, as a personal mode of existence, requires thoroughgoing and practical devotion to that community as an idealized and freely chosen "cause." I do not believe I can adopt such a posture at all toward the APA –I would not choose it, would not serve it, and would have serious doubts about the judgment of anyone else who did so. I regret that cannot do much better in adopting this loving posture toward the universities that educated me and those in which I have worked. I see that in all of these places, some others do serve them with great devotion, and without that service and that devotion, surely the institutions would wither. But such is not my cause. These institutions, at their best, do serve worthy ideals, but while my efforts for them are practical, freely chosen, and diligently undertaken, they are not the source of meaning in the purposes I have set for myself. I assume that many others find themselves in a similar circumstance, and not just those in academia, but, for example, those who are civil servants and trying not to be cynical about the politics around them.

And yet there is something in philosophy itself I would not give up, even under severe threat. There is some ideal embedded in the quest for what is good and what is beautiful through a dedication to truth. I suppose a true philosopher can tell a lie for love of a cause, or where enough depends upon it—and here I obviously depart from Kant—but I do not see how a philosopher can *serve* a lie, or a falsehood, even for love of another. There is something in loyalty, as love, as *agape*, that demands its unity with the world of truth, which means the full acknowledgement of other possible experience. The other experience that is relevant in this service is not just that of other certified professional philosophers, it is first and foremost the experience of students. But the expansion of time dilutes the presence of purpose and weakens the will. That is, when teaching becomes a routine and an institutionalized act of repetition, stretched over years and even decades, it is easy to forget that the world of truth one inhabits in the classroom is not composed of students *in the abstract*, but of persons groping for their own purposes, and their own improvement in grasping the world of truth.

Thus when, in my case, the state of Illinois employs me, in spite of what the measures for promotion and tenure may be, I know that I am not really being rewarded for placing articles in journals that no one reads. My "work" is to encounter that kid from the south side of Chicago or west of Centralia, who, at nineteen years old, has come to the vague and unsupported conviction that "justice is the advantage of the stronger," and to say to that kid "maybe so, but you'll not leave this room without listening to me—and Socrates—and someday when you say that, or behave as if, might makes right, you may remember how easily you could be wrong." I don't know that Socrates is right, but I know how to bring such a student to acknowledge that he or she can't prove the alternative. That is what I learned to do by studying philosophy, and so did every one of my peers in the "profession." That challenge to ideology and to mental lethargy opens up the student's "world of truth" to other possible experience. In many cases, the philosophy teacher is the one and only fully developed philosophical mind our students ever encounter—other philosophical people, of course, are not uncommon, but those who have had the privilege of becoming trained to a fine edge in just this sort of relationship are not common. That, my friends, is our "work." To suggest anything else is a betrayal of philosophy and a betrayal of truth. To serve anything else, as a philosopher, is to serve a lie, which, I suppose, may be the reason that so few of us love the APA or the poor excuse for a community it facilitates.

And yet, if the argument of Chapter 9 is correct, the smallest adaptive change is called for. Why should we not learn to think of ourselves as teachers of a certain kind? Why should we not simply admit to ourselves and to our deans and department chairs, that our publishing and conference presentations are not important? Why should we not treat those among us who are most devoted to teaching, and who are best at it, as our best representatives and as the best among us? Why should the best teacher among us not be the APA President? Why should we not present ourselves to our institutions, whether they are big research universities or community colleges, as persons excellently suited to teach? And why should we not remember, and encourage one another through our "professional" gathering, to bear always in mind that the labors we expend in opening up the minds of young people to the possibilities of the experience of others is our most vital contribution to our institutions and to our nations? The change required is actually not great, since it primarily begins with a confession of our collective sin, and moves constructively from there to our various organizations. We don't have to change very much of what we do, only the way we habitually think of it.

In the terms of this book, the writing of which is an act of disciplined leisure, not my "work," I have tried to explain, to the extent that I can, the temporal relation of will and purpose. This temporal relation of will and purpose is, in my understanding of Royce, the key to "loyalty." I have avoided the word because perhaps it is not the best word for the idea. But a person who chooses the path of philosophy chooses to *serve* what is Good and what is Beautiful through his or her service to Truth. This is the freely chosen purpose that unites us in the domain of philosophy, and in every other humanistic field of study. To the extent that yacking with one another may further that service, by all means, let us yack. But anything that takes away from our primary encounter with students, or which dilutes it, is contrary to our purpose and to our cause.

Loyalty

On April 16th, 2007, a teacher of fluid and solid mechanics at Virginia Tech University named Liviu Librescu sacrificed his own life protecting his students from another student who had snapped and gone on a shooting rampage. Blocking the door with his body and instructing his students to hurry out of the windows, while suffering five gunshots, Librescu managed to save all of his twenty-three students, except one.

I do not know how well Professor Librescu may have known his students that semester, probably not very well, but I am confident he was not saving his "friends"; he was saving his *students*. Librescu was responding to their general mode of being—one protects one's students, precisely because that is what teachers who are mature and well-developed persons do. The act of generalized loyalty is an exemplar. Professor Librescu might well have saved other people who weren't his students, under other circumstances, but in this case, it was *his* classroom, the door to it was *his* door, and the students were *his* students. Something profound about this student-teacher relationship, and the love appropriate to it, is revealed in his act.

I have no idea whether Professor Librescu might have occasionally complained that his teaching duties were getting in the way of his "work" (the complaint is so very common, but there are some who never, ever say this), but I do know that when forced to decide, having only a few seconds, he chose the survival of his students not only over his "work," but over his own life. The students who survived learned far more than solid mechanics from Professor Librescu, as have we all, as witnesses of this act of loyalty. And yet, are there not many among us who would, if we had to choose, do the same thing? Professor Librescu had clearly spent a lifetime crafting the kind of character capable of such a decision and of such service. But time, the temporal circumstances of that day, compressed, for him, into only a few seconds, the kind of decisions teachers make every day, for each time we address a student, there is an analogous continuity and discontinuity—we share the time, as possibility, but not the same perspectives and personal modalities. There is a reason that the teacher is the teacher and the student is the student, and there is the possibility of community. It is not enough to *intend* the community of teacher and student, and it must not only be firmly willed, it must be the shared purpose of those who would have it.

Teaching is not simply a serious undertaking, it is a sacred purpose. Its temporal expanse, spread over semesters and years of intermittent contact, can weaken the will and skew the purpose, but that is precisely what has to be resisted. When such resistance to the forces that weaken our resolve succeeds, community coalesces around ideals worth serving. But teaching is the one thing philosophers can surely do that shows a result. If a teacher of fluid and solid mechanics can serve so well the purposes of hope and memory and truth, it seems clearly within the reach of other teachers, but how can one atone for failing to form such a purpose among those who claim to serve truth? Let Professor Librescu's selfless act remind us of how much can really be at stake when a student is at the office door or sitting before us in class. If our educational institutions and our professional organizations do not credit the sacred value of that relationship, do not credit it far above the next journal article or book we may publish, then it is time to find other communities more worthy of service, or to change our own purposes within the institutions we serve.

Notes

PREFACE

[1] Charles P. Pierce, *Moving the Chains: Tom Brady and the Pursuit of Everything* (New York: Farrar, Straus, and Giroux, 2006), 159–164. My suspicion is that Charlie Pierce would be gratified if someone were to point him toward Royce's essay on athletic training and his essay "Football and Ideals" written in 1908, available now in Josiah Royce, *Race Questions, Provincialism, and Other American Problems*, expanded edition, eds. Scott L. Pratt and Shannon Sullivan (New York: Fordham University Press, 2010).

[2] Jacquelyn Kegley devotes a long chapter to showing the relevance of Royce's ideas to all sorts of contemporary issues in her *Josiah Royce in Focus* (Bloomington: Indiana University Press, 2008), 136–162.

[3] For a good and uncanny summary of how similar are our own times to those of Royce, I recommend H.W. Brands, *American Colossus: The Triumph of Capitalism 1865–1900* (New York: Doubleday, 2010).

INTRODUCTION

[1] See Alfred North Whitehead, *The Aims of Education and Other Essays* (New York: Free Press, 1929), 1–2. Whitehead distinguishes living ideas from "inert ideas," which are learned without ever being utilized or put into practice.

[2] I am well aware that the term "American" philosophy is unfortunate, when what is really meant is philosophy in the United States. I cannot reform the linguistic residue of an imperialist and colonialist past in one book, and while I do not wish to contribute further to those habits, I will for convenience here refer to USA philosophy as "American" philosophy.

[3] See George Douglas Straton, *Theistic Faith for Our Time: An Introduction to the Process Philosophies of Royce and Whitehead* (Washington, D.C.: University Press of America, 1979). Straton uses Royce as a way of introducing Whitehead because, difficult as Royce is, he is much more accessible than Whitehead. This is a book that, had Straton not already written it, I would have been tempted to write. But there is little or no evidence of any serious influence of Royce on Whitehead, so the connections are philosophical rather than historical. One major difference between my study and Straton's is that while Straton does aim to "introduce" Royce, he concentrates on two

principal texts, the Gifford Lectures and *The Problem of Christianity*, and while I think he draws from these defensible conclusions, this is neither broad nor detailed enough to suffice. He focuses on central ideas—i.e., being, self, God, ethics and knowledge—and in each case uses Royce as a warm-up for Whitehead (which is what the book is really about). Royce has to have his own book, not determined by which among his ideas are best suited to finding paths into the labyrinth of Whitehead. I make this remark as one more thoroughly devoted to the philosophy of Whitehead than even to that of Royce. But Royce has a superior moral philosophy, and moral philosophy is more important than metaphysics, or any other kind of philosophy.

[4] I had heard rumors for some years that West was at work on Royce, and some rumors of what his focus was. In the collection *The Cornel West Reader* (New York: Basic Civitas Books, 1999), West says in the header for his essay "Pragmatism and the Sense of the Tragic" that he had been working on a book on Royce since 1990, and that the essay was a part of that effort. It doesn't give a clear sense of his overall approach to Royce, although it is a helpful and accurate comparison of Dewey and Royce. I was able to learn more about West's reading of Royce in May of 2007 when West spoke at the James-Royce Conference at Harvard. It was very clear from his address and from his active participation that he has indeed been hard at work on Royce's philosophy, and I found everything he said congenial to the views I have been working out for some years. This address was published in *James and Royce Reconsidered: Reflections on the Centenary of Pragmatism*, ed. David Lamberth (Cambridge: Harvard Divinity School, 2008). I look forward with great eagerness to the publication of some more of West's thoughts on Royce. I have no doubt that they have been slow to appear because learning Royce thoroughly requires a serious commitment of time, and West has been very much in demand.

[5] Jacquelyn A.K. Kegley, *Josiah Royce in Focus* (Indiana University Press, 2008); Dwayne A. Tunstall, *Yes, but Not Quite: Encountering Josiah Royce's Ethico-religious Insight* (Fordham University Press, 2009).

[6] I would call attention to two recent writings on the beloved community that I regard as very important. First is Rufus Burrow Jr.'s discussion of Royce's ideas in relation to Martin Luther King, Jr.'s use of the idea of "the beloved community in *God and Human Dignity: The Personalism, Theology, and Ethics of Martin Luther King, Jr.* (Notre Dame: University of Notre Dame Press, 2008); and Gary L. Herstein, "The Roycean Roots of the Beloved Community," in *The Pluralist* 4:2 (Summer 2009), 91–107.

[7] This study is now available as "Complex Negation, Necessity, and Logical Magic," in The Relevance of Royce, eds. Kelly A. Parker and Jason M. Bell (New York: Fordham University Press, 2013), 89–131.

[8] In particular I am modifying considerably the view developed by Frank Oppenhein in all of his books, but building on his earlier article, "Josiah Royce's Intellectual Development: An Hypothesis," in *Idealistic Studies* 6 (1976), 85-102.

[9] John E. Smith, *Royce's Social Infinite: The Community of Interpretation* (New York: Liberal Arts Press, 1950). In some ways Smith's book is an application and test of a prominent thesis of Herbert W. Schneider about the development of idealism in the history of American philosophy (Smith was Schneider's student); see Smith, 13 n.3. I will take issue with Smith's application, but in general I agree with Schneider's thesis.10

[10] Ibid., 62–63.1

[11] See Randall E. Auxier, ed., *Critical Responses to Royce*, 3 vols. (Bristol: Thoemmes, 2000); vol. 2 is a reprint of the 1916 *Papers in Honor of Josiah Royce* pub-

lished by the *Philosophical Review*. Hereafter this collection will be cited as CR, followed by the volume number and page number.

[12] The exception is an excellent book by James Harry Cotton, *Royce on the Human Self* (Cambridge: Harvard University Press, 1954). This book never got the attention it deserved. If people had used Cotton as their introduction to Royce, many of the problems I describe in this section would never have arisen—in particular the problems about the Royce-Peirce relation, since Cotton rightly concluded from the evidence that "whenever their personal acquaintance began, they must have read each other's articles from an early date" (217). Cotton proposes January 21st 1884 as the likely date, since that is when Royce gave his first lecture at Johns Hopkins that overlapped with Peirce's time there (216). As we will see, their acquaintance pre-dates that meeting by at least four years. Cotton also challenges Smith's interpretation (see 321, n.40).

[13] Smith, *Royce's Social Infinite*, 37–38n.

[14] This paper was published in *Fugitive Essays*, ed. Jacob Loewenberg (Cambridge: Harvard University Press, 1920), 219–260. Thus, Smith did have access to it.

[15] I am profoundly encouraged by the recent work of André De Tienne, the General Editor of the Chronological Edition of the Works of Peirce, who, having discovered what I am reporting here, has set out to correct the perception of the Peirce community. I believe that none of this work is yet published, but I expect it will have the needed effect. Also a recent essay by David E. Pfeifer documents Royce's influence on Peirce. I look forward to its appearance in print.

[16] Smith, *Royce's Social Infinite*, 13.

[17] Ibid., 13–14.

[18] See ibid., 34.

[19] Ibid., 12.

[20] Ibid.

[21] Doug Anderson attempts to work out the meaning of Royce's claim to be a pragmatist, and in a way that would be more or less consistent with Smith's reading of Royce in "Who's a Pragmatist: Royce and Peirce at the Turn of the Century," in *Transactions of the Charles S. Peirce Society* 41:3 (Summer 2005), 467–481. Anderson seems to have taken the impetus for this paper from reading (and reviewing) Oppenheim's *Reverence for the Relations of Life*. Anderson's article is packed with good information, but he has been misled by Smith's (frankly awful) assessment of the role of the Absolute in Royce's philosophy, and as a result Anderson's effort to sort out the meaning of the claim from Royce's end fails. Anderson also overlooks the all important exchange between Royce and Dewey in 1910–11 (cited in my chapter on pragmatism below) which, to my mind, is crucial to the question. This essay is revised and reprinted as ch. 2 of *Conversations on Peirce: Reals and Ideals* (New York: Fordham University Press, 2013), 16–43. Anderson repeats throughout the book that Royce's is a "closed" system of thought. Perhaps this is how Peirce saw it, but if so, Peirce was quite wrong.

[22] Ibid., 18. Smith cites Dewey's paper from the 1916 *Papers in Honor of Josiah Royce*, CR2, 26.

[23] Ibid., 76.

[24] Ibid., 57.

[25] Ibid., 46.

[26] Smith gives plenty of attention to Royce's temporalism, but his presentation of it leads readers to conclude that it is a prominent feature only of his last years. See ibid.,

68–69, 83–85. Temporalism had been an indispensable feature of Royce's method and philosophical outlook for his entire career.

[27] Ibid., 16.

[28] See Marcel, *Royce's Metaphysics*, trans. Virginia and Gordon Ringer (Chicago: Regnery, 1956), 95–106. I do not know whether Smith could read French (this work was first translated in 1956, after Smith's book was published, but I was fairly astonished to note that Smith was perhaps not even aware of Marcel's work, which is, even today, perhaps the most important work ever written on Royce. And given that Marcel was deservedly very famous when Smith wrote his first book, it seems hard to understand why he would not know about it, and if he knew about it, would not at least draw upon English or German responses to it.

[29] James Harry Cotton noticed this same weakness in Smith's account and pointed it out long ago—see *Royce on the Human Self*, 321, n.40. Unfortunately, Smith's indefensible way of presenting this distinction has become common in discussions of Royce, especially among those partisans of James, Dewey, or Peirce who have not read Royce closely. Unlike Smith, Cotton had read Marcel's work on Royce.

[30] In many ways this issue is parallel with the issue of whether Bergson's way of conceptualizing "intuition" does or does not have a reflective aspect. Since the debate over this issue has received no serious attention since the days of Marcel and Hocking, it is instructive to consult the special focus section in the case of Bergson in *Process Studies*, "Bergson and Whitehead," 28:3–4 (Fall–Winter 1999), 267–345. Pete A.Y. Gunter argues there, decisively to my mind, that Bergson's concept of intuition includes reflection. The entire issue regarding how to deal with immediate experience in both Bergson and Royce depends upon this discussion about the fundamental character of reflection. Cotton also noticed that this issue was connected with Royce's reading of Bergson (see *Royce on the Human Self*, 321 n.40).

[31] Smith, *Royce's Social Infinite*, 9–10.

[32] This same tendency to cover over the distinction between "individual" and "person" is evident in Smith's much more widely read *The Spirit of American Philosophy*, in which he adopts a tone of almost apologizing for Royce's method and his idealism, and nearly begging readers to take Royce seriously in spite of everything. Regarding the issue of individuality Smith says: that "no matter how much [Royce] stressed the idea of absolute truth or the ideal of a perfect knowledge, in the end he maintained that it is the purpose embodied in our will that makes us genuine individuals." This is technically correct, but it encourages readers to connect will and individuality with purpose *without* going through the conception of person Royce carefully defended. See Smith, *The Spirit of American Philosophy*, revised edition (Albany: SUNY Press, 1983), 82–83; cf. 93. The term "person" occurs several times in this chapter by Smith, and in each case it is used correctly, but the term "individual" and the term "self" are both used too broadly.

CHAPTER 1. BIOGRAPHY

[1] In this chapter I have used especially the biographical writings by John Clendenning, Frank M. Oppenheim, and Robert V. Hine, which are listed in the bibliography.

[2] Sarah Royce, *A Frontier Lady: Recollections of the Gold Rush and Early California*, ed. Ralph Henry Gabriel (New Haven: Yale University Press, 1932).

³ See my essay "Josiah Royce: In and of Grass Valley, California," in *Bulletin of the Nevada County Historical Society* 67:3 (July 2013), 1–6.

⁴ See my "A Mystery about History," the Afterword of *Pussy Blackie's Travels*, the book Royce wrote as a child, eds. Randall E. Auxier and Robin Wallace (Penn Valley, CA: Artemis Books, 2013, 49–59. I explore here the relationship between the young Royce and his father.

⁵ Peirce knew poverty and even hunger late in life, but was raised in comparative privilege.

⁶ The one caveat I would suggest is that the Empire Mine, Grass Valley's principal economic industry, was organized along amazingly progressive lines, with cutting edge technology and nearly utopian labor arrangements. But it is difficult to know whether Royce understood any of this, at such a young age.

⁷ Royce's relationship with LeConte is more complex and possibly profound than has been recognized by previous interpreters, but has been recently studied in some detail by Tommy J. Curry in his "On the Dark Arts: Problematizing Royce's Assimilative Arts as a Response to LeConte's 'Southern Problems'," an unpublished manuscript presented to the Josiah Royce Society, at the annual meeting of the Central Division of the American Philosophical Association, February 19th, 2010. Curry is engaged in a book-length project related to LeConte and Royce, as examples of how the white academy shifted ground from biological to cultural theories about supposed "racial backwardness." What I have seen of Curry's research convinces me of both his general thesis about the academy at that time (something also documented well by other researchers, such as John Haller), and also of Royce's specific complicity in that unfortunate academic trend. Curry hypothesizes that LeConte's very problematic work "Southern Problems" informs more of Royce's own work than has been recognized by Royce scholars. I need to give the matter more attention before stating my own views, but Curry's line of argument strikes me as regrettably astute and correct.

⁸ John Clendenning, *The Life and Thought of Josiah Royce*, revised and expanded ed. (Nashville: Vanderbilt University Press, 1999), 70.

⁹ Royce came to *call* metaphysics "descriptive" explicitly later, especially in *The World and the Individual*, Second Series (see p. ix–x for example), but he adopted the viewpoint well before he solidified the terminology.

¹⁰ The importance of this essay in laying bare Royce's early debt to Peirce is inestimable. It wasn't published until after Royce's death, but it is the most pivotal document in rightly interpreting Royce's development. It went unnoticed perhaps because it seems to be a specialized treatment of Hodgson's philosophy, when in fact it is an exposition *for* Peirce, requested *by* Peirce, demonstrating Royce's (impressive) command of Peirce's critical limitations on philosophical evidence (no intuition, no introspection, no power of thought without signs) set out in the articles Peirce wrote for the *Journal of Speculative Philosophy* in 1868. See *Fugitive Essays*, ed. Jacob Loewenberg (Cambridge: Harvard University Press, 1920), 219–260. The influential Peirce articles are, "On a New List of Categories," and "Questions Concerning Certain Faculties Claimed for Man," and "Some Consequences of Four Incapacities," all available in their definitive versions in *The Writings of Charles S. Peirce: A Chronological Edition*, vol. 2, eds. Edward C. Moore, et al. (Bloomington: Indiana University Press, 1984), 49–58, 193–241.

¹¹ One might even give Royce this title alone, as I will argue in Chapter 2.

¹² Josiah Royce, *California: From the Conquest in 1846 to the Second Vigilance Committee in San Francisco* (New York: Alfred A. Knopf, 1948 [1886]), 122–23.

[13] Ibid., 123.

[14] Royce's opposition to imperialism, vociferous as it was in some cases, was not consistent. The habit in Royce literature has been to depict him as anti-imperialist through and through, but Tommy J. Curry's work in counterpoint to this habit should bring about a more balanced view. See Curry's "Royce, Racism, and the Colonial Ideal: White Supremacy and the Illusion of Civilization in Josiah Royce's Account of the White Man's Burden," in *The Pluralist*, 4:3 (Fall 2009), 10–25; and "On the Dark Arts: Problematizing Royce's Assimilative Arts as a Response to LeConte's 'Southern Problems'," an unpublished manuscript presented to the Josiah Royce Society, at the annual meeting of the Central Division of the American Philosophical Association, February 19th, 2010.

[15] See Royce, *The Religious Aspect of Philosophy* (Boston: Houghton, Mifflin, 1885), chs. 9–10 (hereafter, RAP).

[16] Royce, RAP, 324.

[17] Royce, RAP, 371.

[18] Royce, RAP, 380–81. Royce's "personalism," like every other respectable version of philosophical personalism, explicitly rejects crude anthropocentrism. Royce actually uses the term "anthropocentrism" in rejecting the idea (WI1, 416–17), which may surprise readers who assume that the word is relatively recent in the philosophical lexicon.

[19] For a thorough analysis of the difference between these two "proofs," see Gary L. Cesarz, "A World of Difference: The Royce-Howison Debate on the Conception of God," in *The Personalist Forum*, 15:1 (spring 1999), 84–128.

[20] Josiah Royce, *The World and the Individual*, First and Second Series (New York: Macmillan, 1899, 1901), Second Series, 124. Hereafter "WI1" and WI2."

[21] Royce, WI2, 124–25.

[22] Ibid., 134. Here Royce draws upon a long argument about the internal and external meaning of ideas from WI1, 265ff.

[23] The basic outlines of the philosophy of loyalty are clearly present in the story he wrote as a boy, *Pussy Blackie's Travels*, cited above.

[24] Royce, *The Philosophy of Loyalty* (New York: Macmillan, 1908), 311.

[25] Dwayne A. Tunstall has argued in a recent article that this feature of Royce's philosophical system renders God "only a concept," not a living person. I agree that Royce qualifies our capacity to give an account of God by holding it within the limits of reflection, and reflection works, for Royce, with already formed "concepts," as I will argue in chapter four. As Royce says, "philosophy turns altogether upon trying to find out what our ideas mean," that is, the ideas we already *have*. Royce, *The Conception of Immortality* (Boston: Houghton, Mifflin, 1900), 3. Tunstall, in another extended work (his dissertation of 2007), has recommended that Gabriel Marcel's account of secondary reflection may allow us to overcome this restricting of philosophical accounts to the limitations imposed on us by reflective thinking that takes already formed ideas as its object of study, but even at that Tunstall grants that such a move is a "teleological suspension of philosophy," which is to say, we are not, strictly speaking, doing philosophy when we employ secondary reflection to supply us with material for our descriptions of God. Thus, I think I may agree with Tunstall about his reading of Royce, but I am disinclined to see the restriction on philosophy as any great weakness in Royce's thought. Philosophy is an important human activity, but it is inadequate not only to the experience of God, if there is a God, but to any and every concrete experience. See Tunstall, "Concerning the God that Is only a Concept: A Marcellian Critique of Royce's God," in

Transactions of the Charles S. Peirce Society, 42:3 (Summer 2006), 394–416; and *Doing Philosophy Personally* (New York: Fordham University Press (2013))..

[26] See Royce, *The Philosophy of Loyalty*, 276–286. Some are inclined to see in Royce's invoking of "lost causes" a sympathy for the famous "lost cause" of the Confederacy. Royce does use the Confederacy as an example of a lost cause, in the context of addressing a Southern audience and trying to explain his own much broader conception of lost causes. I see no evidence that Royce was in sympathy with the cause of the Confederacy except insofar as he recognized that all human beings eventually learn to serve causes that are lost, and this is not a sympathy for what was evil and destructive in the Confederate cause. Furthermore, I do not think that either history or philosophy is well served by the unqualified vilification of some particular causes at some particular time. Even Nazis, however misguided, *intended* at least some good by their service to the Third Reich. The evilness of the cause does not, for Royce, wholly destroy the quality of the service that is devoted to it. There are no "good Nazis," in an unqualified sense, but there certainly were selfless acts of devoted service to the Reich, to that cause, which elevated those who performed them. Life is ambiguous and tragic, and we do not learn our lessons by pretending that any person or community is wholly, irredeemably, unambiguously evil. This is true of the slave-holding South, and if Royce appeared to have sympathy with the South on some occasions, he certainly qualified that sympathy with a clear recognition of its profound injustices.

[27] Royce, *The Problem of Christianity*, 2 vols. (New York: Macmillan, 1913), vol. 1, ix. Hereafter "PC1" and PC2."

[28] Royce, PC1, 154–55.

[29] Ibid., 155.

CHAPTER 2. ONTOLOGY

[1] There is no reason to multiply sources here, but for those unfamiliar with such a claim, a good overarching critique of the failed project of analytic philosophy is Nicholas Capaldi, *The Enlightenment Project in the Analytic Conversation* (Dordrecht: Kluwer, 1998). For an accessible account of the end of necessitarian science, see Ilya Prigogine and Isabelle Stengers, *Order out of Chaos* (New York: Bantam, 1984). In the last decade, even the linear development associated with Darwinian evolution has begun to crumble. See the last-ditch effort of Stephen J. Gould to save it in *The Structure of Evolutionary Theory* (Cambridge: Belknap. 2002). I have examined this issue in some detail in my essay "The Death of Darwinism and the Limits of Evolution," in *Philo* 9:2 (Fall–Winter 2006), 193–220. Part of the philosophical background for this work is in Pete A.Y. Gunter's recent work in the philosophy of science, especially "Darwinism: Six Scientific Alternatives," in *The Pluralist* 1:1 (Spring 2006), 13–30.

[2] Not a great deal has been written on Royce's critique of necessity, especially when compared with Peirce's similar critique, and it is not claiming too much to say that even many of Royce's admirers seem unaware of his position. Fortunately an article by Michael Futch addresses this situation. See his "The Dogma of Necessity: Royce on Nature and Scientific Law," in *The Pluralist*, 7:1 (Winter 2012), 54–71. See also my "Complex Negation, Necessity, and Logical Magic."

[3] Peirce followed Kant in making logic normative for our thinking only. For Royce, thinking and action are so closely related that logic is normative for practice as well as thinking.

⁴ There are numerous examples of this habit throughout the history of Royce scholarship, stemming principally from those in the classical tradition of American pragmatism who *believe* the interpretations of Royce (and criticisms) given by William James and John Dewey. Harvey Cormier has provided a fair example of this habit in his plenary address to the Relevance of Royce Conference, "Royce, James, and Logic," April 9th, 2005 at Vanderbilt University, which has since appeared in *The Journal of Speculative Philosophy* 19:4, 201–214. This is a reading of Royce often given by both supporters and critics, and defended as his position. See the Introduction to this book for a discussion of the problems traceable to things Royce himself said about his reading of Peirce in 1912 and the way these remarks have come to be treated as canonical in Royce scholarship since John E. Smith's book, *Royce's Social Infinite: The Community of Interpretation* (New York: Liberal Arts Press, 1950), esp. pp. 11–63. The essential problem with Douglas Anderson's otherwise interesting work on Royce also lies here. Not having grasped the character of Royce's ontology, Anderson attributes to Royce a necessitarian viewpoint, which he says Peirce backed away from. This is incorrect, and it distorts the rest of Anderson's argument about whom and how to count the pragmatists, a view I will attempt to correct in Chapter 4. See Anderson, "Who's a Pragmatist: Royce and Peirce at the Turn of the Century," in *Transactions of the Charles S. Peirce Society* 41:3 (Summer 2005), 467–481.

To be fully honest, however, the view I am setting out in this chapter represents a slight departure also from my own earlier interpretation of Royce in "Mysticism and the Immediacy of God: Howison's and Hocking's Critique of Royce," *Personalist Forum* 15:1 (Spring 1999), 59–83, but now rewritten as Chapter 3 of this book in a form I can still endorse. I had advanced a line like Smith's there, partly because it was the standard reading and I saw little reason to question such revered authorities. Further research into the early Royce occasioned by the commission to write the Royce entry for John Shook's four-volume *Dictionary of Modern American Philosophers* (Bristol: Thoemmes, 2005), along with extensive conversations with Dwayne A. Tunstall, with whom I was privileged to work for four years, have modified my view. Chapter 5 of Tunstall's book on Royce treats this same issue of fictional ontology in some detail, and I agree with his conclusions, although he finds fictional ontology unsatisfying while I find it adequate. See Tunstall, *Yes, but Not Quite*, 85–95, and there is a longer version of the same argument in his "Concerning the God that Is Only a Concept: A Marcellian Critique of Royce's God," in *Transactions of the Charles S. Peirce Society* 42:3 (Summer 2006), 394–416.

⁵ Josiah Royce, *Metaphysics: His Philosophy 9 Course of 1915–1916, as Stenographically Recorded by Ralph W. Brown and Complemented by Notes from Byron F. Underwood*, eds. William Ernest Hocking, Richard Hocking, and Frank M. Oppenheim (Albany: SUNY Press, 1998), 82; hereafter cited as *Metaphysics*.

⁶ Ibid.

⁷ Ibid., my emphasis.

⁸ Ibid.

⁹ Ibid. It is worth adding to this remark by Royce the following:

> [Science] is abstraction that simplifies, and abstraction is invaluable to science. But he who returns from science to life is a poor pupil if he has not learned the art of forgetting his formulas at the right moment, and of loving the live thing more than the describable type.... Yet, on the other hand, it makes a great difference to you whether you possess the science that you can be wise enough to forget. Ignorance is one thing; the power voluntarily to ignore is quite

another thing. The former is a weakness; the latter a high spiritual power. Universally valid your "system" can never be; therefore hold it not as a system. But universally significant your scientific insight may become to you, if you once possess it, and can bear in mind that it is after all abstract, and yet noteworthy as an abstraction.

Josiah Royce, "Is There a Science of Education," in *Educational Review* 1:1 (1891), 22–23. Note how Royce uses the term "universal" in this passage, and that he is denying to science any hope of ontological knowledge.

[10] Such views are sometimes called "deflationary" accounts of philosophy, and are associated with defeatism, Rorty, and all things weak. I prefer to see such views as being responsible, sober, and lacking the arrogance and pretenses of the academy. It would be more accurate to describe the received (but dying) views of the twentieth century as inflated views of the authority, scope, and importance of philosophy.

[11] See Royce, *Metaphysics*, 78–79.

[12] For those who might be inclined to say that my interpretation of late Royce relies on unpublished writings and student notes, and that *The Problem of Christianity* replaces hypothesis with interpretation, I offer the following. Royce says:

> We have no ground for believing that there is any sort of real world except the ground furnished by our experience, and by the fact that, in addition to our perceptions and conceptions, we have problems upon our hands which need interpretation. Our fundamental **postulate** is: *The world is the interpretation of the problem which it presents* . . . Our Doctrine of Signs extends to the whole of the world the same fundamental principle. The World is the Community. The world contains its own interpreter. Its processes are infinite in their temporal varieties. But their interpreter, the spirit of this universal community, —compares and, through a real life, interprets them all. (*Problem of Christianity*, vol. 2, 61–61, bold typeface is my addition)

As Tunstall rightly says when he cites this passage:

> This means that even in *The Problem of Christianity* we are still left with a philosophical conception of God that is articulated in hypothetical and conceptual terms. And this is problematic given that our philosophic conception of God cannot denote something actually existing [in its bare particularity] due to the fact that (a) we construct philosophic concepts only out of what we can experience and (b) we cannot experience God directly for Royce." (Tunstall, *Yes, but Not Quite*, 94-95)

I will have more to say below about why Royce thinks this way, and why, in my opinion, it is not bad news (as Tunstall thinks it is), but for now the point is that Royce's method, the method of postulates, is clearly in evidence on the most important point in *The Problem of Christianity*.

[13] Josiah Royce, "Kant's Relation to Modern Philosophic Progress," in *Journal of Speculative Philosophy* 15 (1881), 360–381 (cited hereafter as "Kant's Relation"); and "'Mind-Stuff' and Reality," in *Mind* 6 (1881), 365–377 (cited hereafter as "Mind-Stuff"). It should be noted that the critique of ontology is repeated in refined fashion in *The Spirit of Modern Philosophy* (1892), and culminates in the critique of the three conceptions of being, realism, mysticism, and critical rationalism, in the First Series of the Gifford Lectures (1899). It is crucial for understanding these books, and the continuity of Royce's thought and projects, to be aware that the critique of currently accepted ontologies was a constant from 1880 until it was essentially completed in 1899.

[14] Royce, "Kant's Relation," 372.

[15] Ibid., 373.

[16] Ibid., 375.

[17] I should here register my disagreement with Royce on this point. I think the better hypothesis is that possibility is immediately given, and I defend elsewhere a Whiteheadian description of the ingression of possibilities in everything actual. But this is a book on Royce, and he denied that possibilities are immediately given. See Chapter 3 for a discussion of the problem of immediacy in Royce.

[18] For Royce, imagination is a kind of thought, and I believe he could well use a better account of imagination than he has in his philosophy.

[19] Some readers will recognize all of these moves. This is a kind of conceptualist solution to the old problem of universals, except that the relevant mediating *concept* is time (which is less common traditionally than other ideas, such as divine will), and *as concept*, time is not strictly "defined" in the traditional sense of definition. This is definitely post-Kantian philosophy.

[20] Ibid., 377–78.

[21] Ibid., 361.

[22] See *The Letters of Josiah Royce*, ed. John Clendenning (Chicago: University of Chicago Press, 1970), 106–07 (cited hereafter as *Letters*). My attention was drawn to this letter by Lucio Privitello's outstanding paper at the Vanderbilt Relevance of Royce Conference, "Josiah Royce and the Problem of Philosophical Pedagogy."

[23] See Josiah Royce, *A Collection of Unpublished and Scattered Works*, ed. Frank M. Oppenheim, S.J., 2 vols. (Bristol: Thoemmes, 2001), vol. 1, 19.

[24] Royce, "Kant's Relation," 380.

[25] Royce, *Letters*, 108. Had Smith been given access to such letters as old as 1880, the entire history of Royce interpretation would now be very different. See my Introduction to this book.

[26] Ibid. Of course, this "conceived other consciousness" is called the Absolute, in Royce's writings of the next five years. It is not quite correct to say that Royce became an apologist of the Absolute in *The Religious Aspect of Philosophy* (1885), for he was already using the same basic argument and point about the Whole here in 1880. It is more appropriate to say that he began to *call* this idea "the Absolute" in the book of 1885.

[27] Josiah Royce, *The Religious Aspect of Philosophy* (New York: Houghton, Mifflin, 1885); cited hereafter as RAP

[28] See Tunstall, *Yes, but Not Quite* (New York: Fordham University Press, 2009), Chapter 5. The irony of writing a book on Royce simultaneously with my friend and then student (now *former* student) Dwayne Tunstall, although from differing tempers and points of view, has created an odd situation for cross-referencing. Much of what I will say below about RAP draws on Tunstall's fifth chapter, including the passages he emphasizes from RAP Chapter 9. In turn, much of what appears in his Chapter 9 was earlier emphasized in my sessions on RAP in my graduate seminar on Royce at Southern Illinois University, Carbondale, in the fall of 2005. But I have spent so much time with Dwayne discussing Royce in recent years that I no longer know who said what first. I do know that Dwayne's thorough research for his Chapter 5 preceded what I will say next (although much of what is written in this chapter was written before Dwayne's fifth chapter), and he has saved me some effort, since I could not have done this better than he did.

[29] Royce, RAP, 300.

[30] Ibid., 299.

[31] Ibid., 333.

32 Ibid., 385.
33 Ibid., 390.
34 Ibid., 417.
35 Ibid., 420.
36 Ibid., 421–422; my emphasis.
37 Ibid., 422–423; my emphasis.
38 Ibid., 425.
39 Ibid, 426. Royce's fears come true in Dwayne Tunstall's article "Concerning the God that Is Only a Concept: A Marcellian Critique of Royce's God," *Transactions of the Charles S. Peirce Society: A Quarterly Journal in American Philosophy* 42.3 (Summer 2006), 394–416.
40 Royce, RAP, 427.
41 Ibid., 428.
42 Ibid.
43 Ibid., 429–430.
44 Ibid., 430; my emphasis.
45 A good text to examine in this light is Royce's use of Dilthey's historicism in "Is There a Science of Education," cited above, in which he approvingly summarizes Dilthey's historicist account of education, but expresses reservations about the extent of Dilthey's biologism, approving instead the historicism without so much biology. It is clear in the account that Royce fears the use of biology as a necessitarian ontology.
46 Josiah Royce, *California: From the Conquest in 1846 to the Second Vigilance Committee in San Francisco* (New York: Knopf, 1948 [1886]). Cited hereafter as *California*.
47 Gary L. Cesarz, "A World of Difference," in The Personalist Forum 15:1 (Spring 1999), 84–128. See *The Conception of God*, ed. George Holmes Howison (New York: Macmillan, 1897), 44–50; hereafter cited as CG. The proceedings of the debate were initially published in 1895 by the University of California, but we shall refer to the later publication because it contains Royce's important "Supplementary Essay," responding in writing to his critics of 1895.
48 Royce, CG, 45.
49 See my "Complex Negation, Necessity, and Logical Magic," for a fuller discussion.
50 Tunstall, *Yes, but Not Quite*, 91.
51 Royce, CG, 198-199; emphasis in the original.
52 Ibid., 199.
53 This is the very issue that separates Whitehead and Hartshorne in their conceptions of God, for while Whitehead will evidently allow that there is "negative prehension" in God, Hartshorne denies it. I have co-authored with Gary Herstein a work entitled *The Quantum of Explanation: Whitehead's Radical Empiricism*, treating in great detail the issue of negative prehension in process thought. The problem of possibility is addressed there.
54 Royce was writing "The Problem of Job" for the Augustus Graham Lectures of 1896 (HARP Boxes 52 and 78) at the same time as the "Supplementary Essay" for *The Conception of God*. The essay on Job appeared in *The New World*, 6 (1897), 261–281, and was reprinted as the lead essay the next year in *Studies of Good and Evil* (New York: Appleton, 1898). The simultaneous projects shows how conscious Royce was of the problem with his conception of God.

CHAPTER 3. IMMEDIACY AND MYSTICISM

[1] See Royce, *The Conception of God*, 201–02, for the statement of these contrary aims together (hereafter cited as CG).

[2] See Dwayne A. Tunstall, *Yes, but Not Quite* (New York: Fordham University Press, 2009), xi. Tunstall seeks to address this difficulty with Royce by tracing a line from Royce's ethico-religious concerns into Marcel's phenomenology. This is a promising course to follow, because Marcel's phenomenology does not preclude metaphysics, as do so many other approaches to phenomenology. On a larger scale, Tunstall seeks to rehabilitate the use of transcendental arguments, if it can be done, as a way of making phenomenology more responsive to metaphysical questions. This is an ambitious undertaking, and I doubt it can succeed without a fully developed metaphysics of possibility, that rests upon a very well articulated logic of relations. Tunstall holds that C.S. Peirce is probably the best source to draw upon for this effort. I agree, but would add that Royce's logic, along with Whitehead's metaphysics and Hartshorne's theory of internal and external relations, will be needed tools in articulating the account of possibility that can ground the rehabilitation of transcendental arguments without taking on the necessitarian character of Kantian and neo-Kantian transcendental argumentation.

[3] Daniel S. Robinson, *Royce and Hocking: American Idealists* (Boston: Christopher, 1968), 72.

[4] W.E. Hocking, "Preface" to Gabriel Marcel's *Royce's Metaphysics*, trans. Virginia and Gordon Ringer (Chicago: Regnery, 1956), viii.

[5] Stephen Tyman, "Royce and the Destiny of Idealism," in *The Personalist Forum* 15:1 (Spring 1999), 58. The quotation from Royce at the end of this passage is from *The World and the Individual*, Second Series, 418.

[6] See my extended discussion of this issue in Appendices 4 and 6 of *Hartshorne and Brightman on God, Process, and Persons*, eds. Randall E. Auxier and Mark Y.A. Davies (Nashville: Vanderbilt University Press, 2001), 100–120, 132–154.

[7] Josiah Royce, *The World and the Individual*, First Series and Second Series (New York: Macmillan, 1899, 1901); cited hereafter as "WI1" and "WI2." That Howison was such a "spur" in Royce's side is hard to deny, in light of the amount of effort Royce expended on the theory of "individuals" in the "Supplementary Essay" for *The Conception of God*. It appears that Howison's critique sent Royce back through the entire history of philosophy, especially to the medievals, to find out exactly what an "individual" is.

[8] Royce was conscious of this methodological difference between himself and Howison. He set it out explicitly in *Metaphysics*, eds. W.E. Hocking, et al. (Albany: State University of New York Press, 1998), 132–33, and criticized it. This is also a good passage for confirming that Royce rejected what I call the "unholy trinity." Howison did not grasp the meaning of this methodological difference between Royce and himself.

[9] As Hocking points out, Royce remarked that if he had the chance to rewrite his Gifford Lectures, he would call them "The World, the Community, and the Individual." This emphasis on community, as a third in a triadic relation, is part and parcel of what I mean by "relationalism." Peirce must be credited, of course, for bringing Royce around to recognizing how to use triadic relations to articulate this theory of community. See Hocking, "On Royce's Empiricism," *The Journal of Philosophy* 52:3 (1956), 58.

[10] See Royce's letter to Howison of October 5, 1897 in *The Letters of Josiah Royce*, ed. John Clendenning (Chicago: University of Chicago Press, 1970), 360–61; cited hereafter as *Letters*.

[11] Due to Royce's unwillingness to confront Howison's actual criticism, at least in Howison's view, Howison continually carped at Royce in letters, from the preface and footnotes of *The Conception of God*—and in this instance Howison really abused his position as editor in my view, constantly disputing and "correcting" Royce's remarks about him in Royce's "Supplementary Essay" (see CG, 181, 271, 321, 332, 333). Unsatisfied with the reviews the book received, he published "The Real Issue" in 1898 (cited below). Royce apparently remained untroubled by all this, and when I think of what *my* reaction would be if I were in Royce's shoes, I am amazed by his forbearance (although Royce was not always forbearant, as his behavior in the Abbott affair shows). But Royce's patience with Howison was not infinite. When he was preparing to return to California in the summer of 1902 to teach summer school, Howison wanted a "rematch" of the 1895 debate, and announced the rematch without first securing Royce's agreement. Royce wrote Howison a scolding letter and informed him that he intended to make no answer to Howison's criticisms, saying "I hope that you will expect no more than a passive, and perfectly cheerful acquiesence, on my part, in your right and duty to set forth to your students exactly what you think proper. For my part, I shall try to confine myself to telling my own story, without joining any public issue of any sort with you" (*Letters*, 432–33). The point was moot since Howison was too ill that summer even to teach and left Berkeley to convalesce at Shasta Springs. But Royce felt justified in not responding to Howison's view. Royce believed Howison had not made available a full articulation of Howison's own position, a position Howison claimed was a "Fifth Conception of Being," beyond the four Royce had addressed in WI1. I cannot help wondering if Howison's siege of Royce might have taken some of its impetus from the fact that Howison felt under-appreciated by the philosophical establishment in Boston. Indeed, Royce was selected for the position at Harvard in 1882 over Howison, taking Royce from the backwater of Berkeley to the greatest center of philosophy in America, while Howison was obliged to make the reverse trip, from Boston to Berkeley, in order to have his career. Howison's students, especially Arthur O. Lovejoy and John Wright Buckham, kept up the siege against Royce long after both Royce and Howison died, evidently inspired at least in part by Howison's sense that Royce had never answered him. See John Clendenning's account of these matters in *The Life and Thought of Josiah Royce*, second ed. (Nashville: Vanderbilt University Press, 1999), 196–204, and Buckham's account in *George Holmes Howison: Philosopher and Teacher*, ed. John Wright Buckham and George Malcom Stratton (Berkeley: University of California Press, 1934), 72–86. See also John J. McDermott's interesting summary of the debate in "The Confrontation between Royce and Howison," *Transactions of the Charles S. Peirce Society* 30:4 (Fall 1994), 779–790.2

[12] For a good summary and analysis of this part of the debate, see James McLachlan, "George Holmes Howison's 'The City of God and the True God as Its Head': The Royce-Howison Debate over the Idealist Conception of God," in *The Personalist Forum* 15:1 (Spring 1999), 5–27; and Gary L. Cesarz, "Howison's Pluralistic Idealism: A Fifth Conception of Being?" in the same issue of *The Personalist Forum*, 28–44. For a more thorough summary of Howison's "actual position" see James McLachlan, "George Holmes Howison: The Conception of God Debate and the Beginnings of Personal Idealism," in *The Personalist Forum* 11:1 (Spring 1995), 1–13; and my own "George Holmes Howison" in *The Dictionary of Modern American Philosophers*, General Editor John Shook (Bristol: Thoemmes, 2005), vol. 2, 1179–1185.

[13] Howison took special pains to point this out in his 1898 article "The Real Issue in *The Conception of God*," reprinted in *Critical Responses to Royce*, ed. Randall E. Auxier, vol. 2 (Bristol: Thoemmes, 2000), 24–28.

[14] Howison, "The Real Issue," 27.

[15] Ibid.

[16] This represents a change in my interpretation of Royce over the last seven years. Initially I agreed with Howison, and many other interpreters, that Royce ceased being an idealist after his Peircean insight of 1912. I now think that is incorrect. Closer study has shown me that Royce never was an idealist in the sense that most interpreters claim (since no previous interpreter has rightly grasped the method of fictional ontology), and therefore, there was no serious change in Royce's position. He was very clear in stating that he took himself to be an idealist after 1912, and given how he understood "idealism" in light of fictional ontology, I see no reason to doubt his claim. When my study of immediacy in Royce was first published, I still accepted the standard view. This chapter is a modification of that study in light of this change of viewpoint, and as adapted to the progress of this book.

[17] See Howison's "Introduction" to *Papers in Honor of Josiah Royce* (1916), reprinted in my *Critical Responses to Royce*, vol. 3 (Bristol: Thoemmes, 2000), 9–13.

[18] See William Ernest Hocking, *The Meaning of God in Human Experience* (New Haven: Yale University Press, 1912), 290; cited hereafter as MG. Hocking had been Howison's colleague at the University of California, Berkeley, from 1906 to 1908, and the effects of this exposure to Howison are evident in Hocking's critique of Royce. Also, Hocking and Howison take almost the same view of pragmatism as having critical but not constructive value.

[19] Hocking went to Harvard to study with James, having read *The Principles of Psychology*, but he did not know Royce's thought until he arrived (and James was away, but Royce was present). See my "William Ernest Hocking," in *The Dictionary of Modern American Philosophers*, General Editor John Shook (Bristol: Thoemmes, 2005), vol. 2, 1128–1135.

[20] See Dwayne Tunstall, "Josiah Royce and the New Realists: Seeing Their Metaphysical Differences Up-Close," in *The Relevance of Royce*, eds. Kelly A. Parker and Jason M. Bell (New York: Fordham University Press, forthcoming).

[21] See Joseph P. McGinn, "The Power to Will: Refiguring Selfhood in Royce's Philosophy," in *The Personalist Forum* 15:1 (Spring 1999), 143–152.

[22] There are many examples of this in Hocking's writing; see MG, 409n. for a clear statement.

[23] Charles Hartshorne went into some detail about this, seeing it as Royce's greatest flaw. See Hartshorne's "Royce's Mistake—And Achievement," in *Journal of Philosophy* 53:3 (February 2nd, 1956), 123–130. But Hartshorne was not reading Royce as a fictional ontologist, and I am confident Hartshorne would have rejected "fictional ontology" as perfectly absurd. Hartshorne sought ontological knowledge of the sort I have criticized in this book, and in some of my published writings on Hartshorne.

[24] My sense of Howison's view may differ slightly from the account given by Gary Cesarz in "Howison's Pluralistic Idealism" (cited above), but perhaps not. Cesarz rightly notes that Howison uses *reductio* to eliminate his competitors, just as I have said Royce does, and I agree that Howison also uses *reductio*. The issue is whether Howison uses *reductio* before or after he asserts the logical and metaphysical primacy of personhood, and builds his constructive view upon that basis. My view is that even though Howison

was slow to *publish* this constructive view, he held the view *before* he started reducing his competitors to absurdity, and indeed, I think it was Howison's conviction about the logical and metaphysical primacy of persons that *disposed* him to refute monists and absolutists. This is already evident in Howison's assertion of "the Personal Principle" in his 1885 lecture and essay on "Modern Science and Pantheism" (see Buckham's *George Holmes Howison: Philosopher and Teacher*, 218), before he had ever read Royce's *Religious Aspect of Philosophy*. It is possible that Howison's personalism predates even this. There is nothing in Cesarz's account that would contradict this refinement of the interpretation of Howison's method.

[25] On Royce's sense of his own failure, see Hocking, "On Royce's Empiricism," 57–58.

[26] Royce sets out very clearly the relation between logic and life in his unpublished "Introductory Statement at the Philosophy Conference of October 19th, 1903," in HARP, Box 73.

[27] See Royce, "Author's Preface," in *The Problem of Christianity* (Washington, DC: Catholic University of America Press, 2001 [1913]), 39.

[28] Hocking promised but never really wrote the systematic metaphysics required to defend his position. The closest he came was an article that announced a bold program he never finished, largely due to its unfortunate timing (December of 1941, just as the Second World War commenced and attention was diverted for many years from such undertakings). See Hocking's "Ten Theses Establishing Metaphysical Idealism by Another Route," in *Journal of Philosophy*, December 4th, 1941. John Elof Boodin did carry out the task Hocking never managed, although it is not clear he did so in precisely the fashion Hocking would have. See Boodin, *Truth and Reality* (New York: Macmillan, 1911); *A Realistic Universe* (New York: Macmillan, 1916); *Cosmic Evolution* (New York: Macmillan, 1925); *God* (New York: Macmillan, 1934); *Three Interpretations of the Universe* (New York: Macmillan, 1934) and *The Social Mind* (New York: Macmillan, 1939). Boodin referred to his synthesis of Royce and James as "pragmatic realism and cosmic idealism," and it depended heavily upon an articulation of the idea of "emergence" with and an interpretation of "creativity" that would have been congenial to Hocking's metaphysical outlook.

[29] Hocking, MG 248–249; the Royce extracts are from WI2, 168–174, and 168 respectively.

[30] Charles Hartshorne (who was Hocking's student) and Edgar Sheffield Brightman carried out exactly the same debate in the middle of the century, with Hartshorne insisting upon the "literal participation" of selves in other selves, a doctrine of mutual immanence. Brightman took the line of treating the conscious self as an immediate datum, while knowledge of others, God, and even our own bodies is inferential. Obviously Royce rejects the view of the "self" as an immediate conscious datum," but in other ways his view of the individuating will of the divine is similar to Brightman's. See *Hartshorne and Brightman on God, Process, and Persons: The Correspondence*, eds. Randall E. Auxier and Mark Y.A. Davies (Nashville: Vanderbilt University Press, 2000), and my essay "Immediacy and Purpose in Brightman's Philosophy" in the same volume.

[31] Hocking, MG 250. Here Hocking includes a footnote directing the reader to his chapter on mysticism in MG. Hocking amplifies this assertion later when he says "So the vision of, or unity with, the Real, is difficult and exceptional; but, if the mystic is right, it is an experience which satisfies both the intellect and the will," *Types of Philosophy*, revised ed. (New York: Scribner's, 1939), 453.

[32] Hocking, MG 251–52.

³³ The connection to Husserl might be more historical than merely philosophical. Winthrop Bell was a student of Royce at Harvard who went to study with Husserl for the Ph.D. and introduced Husserl to Royce's philosophy. How extensively Husserl knew Royce's thought is still being investigated, but the evidence that Husserl did know it is considerable. It is not out of the realm of possibility that Royce's idea of the "World of Appreciation" is one of the principal sources for Husserl's concept of the "life-world." See Jason M. Bell, "The German Translation of Royce's Epistemology by Husserl's Student Winthrop Bell: A Neglected Bridge of Pragmatic-Phenomenological Interpretation?" in *The Pluralist* 6:1 (Winter 2011), 46–62. Winthrop Bell's dissertation was on Royce's philosophy and directed by Husserl. The dissertation is being translated into English by Jason Bell presently. It is my understanding that there is some evidence that Royce's influence may have been decisive in Husserl's move to his *Ideas* period.

³⁴ Royce was not a member of a church during his professional life and not someone who attended church at all. His biographers usually explain this as a reaction against his parent's fundamentalism, although as I have argued in Chapter 1, I do not find that convincing. Hocking, on the contrary, was a faithful member of the Episcopal Church for his entire married life, having chosen the Episcopal faith as a compromise between his own Methodist upbringing and his wife's Catholicism. Perhaps regular church attendance would have kept Royce closer to a sense of the value of worship, prayer, and the sacramental life.

³⁵ See the "Preface" to the 1963 edition of MG, and Daniel S. Robinson, "Hocking's Contribution to Metaphysical Idealism" in *Royce and Hocking: American Idealists*, 87–90.

³⁶ Royce, WI1, Lectures II, IV and V.37

³⁷ Hocking, MG 351; cf. Royce, WI1 79–80.

³⁸ For a more detailed summary of Royce's critique of mysticism, see section three of Tyman's "Royce and the Destiny of Idealism."

³⁹ Hocking, MG 351.

⁴⁰ Ibid., 353.

⁴¹ Ibid., 54ff.

⁴² Ibid., 353.

⁴³ Ibid., 354.

⁴⁴ Ibid.

⁴⁵ Ibid., 354–55.

⁴⁶ Ibid., 355.

⁴⁷ Ibid., 365–66.

⁴⁸ Ibid., 367.

⁴⁹ See John E. Smith's similar judgment in *Royce's Social Infinite: The Community of Interpretation* (New York: Liberal Arts Press, 1950), 119–123.

⁵⁰ Hocking kept the Absolute: "We could not live without the Absolute, nor without our idea of the Absolute. I do not say that the Absolute is equivalent to God; I say that God, whatever else he may be, must needs also be the Absolute" (MG 206). It seems that if Royce's and James's "battle of the Absolute" were to be judged solely on the basis of who won Hocking's soul, Royce is the victor, except that Hocking has gone further than even Royce would recommend, beyond the *idea* of the Absolute to the Absolute itself.

CHAPTER 4. PRAGMATISM

¹ William Ernest Hocking, *The Meaning of God in Human Experience* (New Haven: Yale University Press, 1912), xxii; cited hereafter as MG.

² Hocking, MG xxiii.

³ This is why he rewrote the methodological part of the book almost immediately—compare the differences between the 1925 and 1929 versions of the book in *Later Works of John Dewey*, ed. Jo Ann Boydston, vol. 1 (Carbondale: Southern Illinois University Press, 1981); and note that Dewey was still trying to rewrite the same parts shortly before his death. The book simply did not accomplish what Dewey wanted to accomplish in his own judgment, an opinion with which I concur.

⁴ To be clearer about this, I should note that the Harvard philosophy department continued the work of pragmatism during this time, although they rarely used the name "pragmatism" to describe their efforts. There is little question that the giants of the Harvard department in the second half of the twentieth century were mostly pragmatists, and carried on in the tradition of C.I. Lewis, who had been the brilliant student of James and Royce, and who worked Royce's logical ideas into the first systems of modal logic. Thus, W.V. Quine, Nelson Goodman, Stanley Cavell, and Hilary Putnam have all been pragmatists of one sort or another, and it is not quite correct to date the end of "pragmatism" with the death of Dewey. But there certainly was a change in emphasis. I have treated this question, in part, in "The Decline of Evolutionary Naturalism in Later Pragmatism," in *Pragmatism: From Progressivism to Postmodernism*, eds. David DePew and Robert Hollinger (New York: Praeger, 1995), 180–207.

⁵ See Giovanni Vailati, *Gli Instrumenti della ragione*, ed. Mario Quaranta (Padua: Il Poligrafo casa editrice, 2003), 235.

⁶ See ibid., 270–276, 285–297.

⁷ There is no reason here to make the historical case that Royce was a pragmatist. This case has been made many times, and is now definitively documented beyond any disputing in Frank M. Oppenheim's most recent historical study, *Reverence for the Relations of Life: Re-imagining Pragmatism via Josiah Royce's Interactions with Peirce, James and Dewey* (Notre Dame: University of Notre Dame Press, 2004). Anyone who at this point persists in saying "Royce was not a pragmatist" is being willful and showing a narrowness of thinking and historical grasp both of the term "pragmatism" and of Royce's thought.

⁸ Important essays in this debate over nomenclature and the pragmatic movement is John Elof Boodin's "What Pragmatism Is and Is Not," *Journal of Philosophy, Psychology, and Scientific Methods* 6:23 (November 11th, 1909), 627–635.

⁹ See Arthur O. Lovejoy, "Thirteen Pragmatisms," in *Journal of Philosophy, Psychology and Scientific Methods* 5:1–2 (January 1908), 5–12, 29–39.

¹⁰ For a summary of Boodin's thought and a working bibliography, see my "John Elof Boodin," in *The Dictionary of Modern American Philosophers*, General Editor John Shook (Bristol: Thoemmes, 2005), vol. 1, 283–88.

¹¹ I should repeat here that in my view, possibilities are immediately given—indeed, it is actuality that is always thoroughly mediated, and possibility that is experienced immediately. Possibilities are transformed into the actual world of a conscious or sentient being by a process of semiotic and symbolic mediation. This is not, however, the view of Royce or of any other philosopher I have ever read. In this book I will press Royce's thought gently in the direction of recognizing that immediacy is possibility, and that the mode of existence possibilities have is indeed the place where existence and experience coincide, and that understanding "time" is the key to this relation. In my view, Royce was on the threshold of seeing this, but he did not quite get to it. I will press him as close to this view as I can in my sixth chapter, but it is not, after all, his view; it

is *my* view. For the purposes of this book, I will try to work within the framework of the problem of immediacy that Royce used, and I will bring him as close to a solution of that problem as can be had on his own terms.

[12] Josiah Royce, *Basic Writings*, ed. John J. McDermott, 2 vols. (New York: Fordham University, Press, 2005), vol. 1, 363–64.

[13] For a further elucidation of the role of feeling and immediacy in the development of this type of pragmatism, see my chapter on "Mysticism and Immediacy" in this book, in which I trace William Ernest Hocking's contributions to these themes.

[14] I have come to appreciate how good a psychologist Royce was as I re-read recently Chapter 2 on the Self in Jacquelyn Kegley's *Royce in Focus*.

[15] See my "Complex Negation, Necessity, and Logical Magic" for a detailed account of how differing levels of generality can be preserved through a series of logical transformations.

[16] It is gratifying to see contemporary logicians return to the serious study of the relations of parts and wholes, now called mereotopology. See for instance, Roberto Casati and Achille C. Varzi, *Parts and Places: The Structures of Spatial Representation* (Boston: MIT Press, 1999). It is unfortunate that contemporary pragmatists do not think they need to study such matters.

[17] This argument, in particular the sense in which hypotheses themselves imply a kind of formal negation, is worked out in great detail in my "Complex Negation" essay cited above.

[18] Peirce's review of Dewey's *Studies in Logical Theory* (Chicago: University of Chicago Decennial Publications, 1903), appeared in *The Nation* in 1904 and is reprinted in *Collected Papers of Charles Sanders Peirce*, ed. Arthur W. Burks (Cambridge: Harvard University Press, 1958), 145–47 (CP8.188–190). There Peirce says that what Dewey is doing simply is not "logic," and that Dewey's collection of inquirers "are not making any studies which anybody in his senses can expect, directly or indirectly, in any considerable degree, to influence twentieth century science." (CP 8.190) Peirce is correct. This is not logic and it had no considerable effect on anything. In a letter to Dewey (although it is not entirely clear whether he actually sent it) Peirce is even more critical of Dewey's project, although he expresses warm personal and philosophical respect. (CP 8.239–244) Larry A. Hickman has nicely analyzed these issues in "Why Peirce Didn't Like Dewey's Logic," in *Southwest Philosophy Review* 3 (1986), 178–189. Royce echoes Peirce's exact criticism of Dewey and James in his 1915–1916 course; see *Metaphysics*, 47. By contrast, there actually is some logic in Dewey's *Logic: The Theory of Inquiry* (1938), which was written after Dewey had awakened to the import of Peirce's criticisms. Most Deweyans, however, treat that work as though it were a natural history of thought rather than a theory of inquiry (a meta-inquiry into logical structures of inquiry). Dewey invites this misunderstanding by beginning the treatise with an epistemology grounding the biological and cultural matrices of inquiry, which are indeed more relevant to the genetic situatedness of logical activity than to formal structures of thinking and the norms and limits governing them. However, in his theory of propositions and judgment, and especially in his account of the relation between mathematics and logic, Dewey demonstrates that he finally did grasp the difference, for pragmatism, between logic and the natural history of thought. As a result, his handling of the issue of possibility greatly improved, and he came to understand the important of the theory of signs for connecting logic to life (even if his subsequent efforts in this domain, the 1949 book with Arthur Bentley entitled *Knowing and the Known*, were quite disappointing and have been justly ignored).

[19] James is so bad at metaphysics that it is no wonder many of his followers have forsaken metaphysics altogether. Most notable among the detractors of metaphysics is Charlene Haddock Seigfried, who, even when she admits James tried his hand at metaphysics, insists ardently that this only proves what a mistake it is even to attempt it. If one's hero is inept at some important undertaking, it seems natural, if sub-philosophical, to attempt to minimize the importance of that activity. I think it is safe to assume that metaphysics will always be a part of philosophy, no matter how vehemently it is rejected by some. See Haddock Siegfried, *William James's Radical Reconstruction of Philosophy* (Albany: State University of New York Press, 1990).

[20] See Richard Rorty, "Dewey's Metaphysics" in *Consequences of Pragmatism* (Minneapolis: University of Minnesota Press, 1982), 72–89.

[21] Royce, *The Philosophy of Loyalty*, in *The Basic Writings of Josiah Royce*, ed. John J. McDermott, two vols. (New York: Fordham University Press, 2005), vol. 2, 858.

[22] Royce, "The Nature and Use of Absolute Truth," Lecture I of The Harrison Lectures in Response to John Dewey, presented February 6th–8th, 1911, typescript, p. 17. These lectures are in the Harvard University Archives, HUG 1755.5, vol. 85, items 3, 4, and 5.

[23] See Thomas M. Alexander, "Dewey's Denotative-Empirical Method: A Thread through the Labyrinth," in *Journal of Speculative Philosophy* 18:3 (2004), 248–256.

[24] It has been pointed out to me by a few Peirce scholars that Peirce usually included "phenomenology" (in his sense of the term) as a branch of philosophy, and only for a brief time did Peirce seem to think that phenomenology was sub-philosophical. These sorts of questions are notoriously tangled and unresolvable in Peirce scholarship and I do not care to enter the controversy. What I will say is that Royce never confused philosophy with empirical activity and believed himself to be following Peirce in this matter. Phenomenology is in fact sub-philosophical (this is not an insult). If Peirce did oscillate on this point, it is not to his credit and Royce is then a better Peircean than Peirce—a point I would defend in more than just this one area.

[25] Royce addresses the issue of the nature and scope of philosophy in many places. The most extended treatment is in the Preface and first chapter of *The Spirit of Modern Philosophy* (1892). This is probably one of the finest essays ever written on the nature and scope of philosophy and the character of the philosopher. I challenge any student of philosophy to read it without reaching for a pencil to mark phrases, jewels of thought and expression so beautifully arranged as to make the reader sigh.

[26] The blending of the Peircean and Roycean accounts is best explained by John E. Smith in *Royce's Social Infinite: The Community of Interpretation* (New York: Liberal Arts Press, 1950), chs. 1–3.

[27] See Gabriel Marcel, *Royce's Metaphysics*, trans. Virginia and Gordon Ringer (Westport: Greenwood, 1975).

[28] See for example, Bruce Wilshire, *William James and Phenomenology* (Bloomington: Indiana University Press, 1968).

[29] See for example, Victor Kestenbaum, *The Phenomenological Sense of John Dewey* (Atlantic Highlands: Humanities, 1977).

[30] See Eddie S. Glaude, Jr.'s "Tragedy and Moral Experience: John Dewey and Toni Morrison's *Beloved*," in *Pragmatism and the Problem of Race*, eds. Bill E. Lawson and Donald F. Koch (Bloomington: Indiana University Press, 2004), 89–121.

[31] Cornel West told David Lionel Smith in an interview conducted on October 12th, 1998, that he was in the process of writing a book on Royce (West, *Cornel West Reader*, [New York: Basic Civitas Books, 1999], p. 561). West has yet to publish this book, but

his address at the 2007 Harvard conference on James and Royce made very clear that he has devoted extensive study to Royce in recent years.

[32] See John E. Smith's discussion of truth in Royce in *Royce's Social Infinite*, 48–59, esp. 56–57 on the "long run."

CHAPTER 5. INDIVIDUALITY

[1] Recalling my statements in the Introduction that Smith has misconstrued the term "appreciation" in Royce's philosophy as denoting private experience, I will show in this chapter how individual experience, even at the level of appreciation, is thoroughly social.

[2] Royce, *The Conception of God*, ed. George Holmes Howison (New York: Macmillan, 1897), 201; hereafter cited as CG.

[3] Many interpreters have suggested that Royce's Absolute is not "God" because it has not been easy to reconcile the ideas about God Royce articulates in "The Problem of Job" with the theories associated with the Absolute. When one reads the material published as "The Problem of Job" in its full context as part of the five Augusts Graham Lectures of 1896, the problem disappears. Unfortunately these lectures are currently unpublished.

[4] Royce, "The Nature and Use of Absolute Truth," Lecture I of The Harrison Lectures in Response to John Dewey, presented February 6th–8th, 1911, typescript, p. 15. These lectures are in the Harvard University Archives, HUG 1755.5, vol. 85, items 3, 4, and 5.

[5] Ibid., 15.

[6] Ibid., 19.

[7] Ibid., 20; the emphasis on "acknowledgement" and "prediction" is mine, the rest is Royce's. Please note that this use of "interpretation" pre-dates Royce's 1912 "Peircean insight."

[8] Ibid.

[9] Ibid., 22–23 (Royce's emphasis).

[10] Ibid., 24. This anticipates Donald Davidson's important principle of charity by fifty years.

[11] See Rudolf Makkreel, *Imagination and Interpretation in Kant* (Chicago: University of Chicago Press, 1990).

[12] Ibid., 28.

[13] Ibid.

[14] Ibid., 29.

[15] Ibid.

[16] Jackie Kegley's most recent work has been setting this right. See her *Josiah Royce in Focus* and her essay "Royce as Psychologist: A Forgotten Aspect of His Thought," presented at "Royce, California, and the World," on August 16th, 2013.

[17] This is John E. Smith's summary of Dewey's argument from the 1916 *Papers in Honor of Josiah Royce*, 26. See the Introduction to this book for a full discussion of this issue about method. The extract is from Smith, *Royce's Social Infinite*, 18.

[18] Royce, "On Purpose in Thought," in *Fugitive Essays*, ed. Jacob Loewenberg (Cambridge: Harvard University Press, 1920), 220–21.

[19] A more thorough discussion of Royce's psychology in relation to the self is in the recent book by Jacquelyn Kegley, *Josiah Royce in Focus* (Bloomington: Indiana University Press, 2008), ch. 2.

²⁰ The literature on mirror neurons has become immense since the first articles appeared in 1997, but a fair collection of the empirical and interpretive results of the discovery, as it bears upon the theory of imitation, is in *Imitation in Animals and Artifacts*, eds. C. Nehaniv and K. Dautenhahn (Cambridge: MIT Press, 2002).

²¹ See Josiah Royce, *Outlines of Psychology* (New York: Macmillan, 1903), 365–66.

²² Royce, *Outlines*, 38.

²³ Ibid., 364.

²⁴ Ibid., 366.

²⁵ Ibid., 367–68; Royce's emphasis.

²⁶ Ibid., 368.

²⁷ Ibid., 369.

²⁸ Ibid.

²⁹ Ibid., 371.

³⁰ Josiah Royce, *The Religious Aspect of Philosophy* (Boston: Houghton Mifflin, 1885), 308–313; hereafter RAP.

³¹ I am using the term "grouping" here for what we would now call a "Gestalt." Royce is quite explicit about the idea that attention operates on Gestalt principles (see for example, RAP, p. 316), he simply did not use that particular term for it.

³² Royce, RAP, 313–14.

³³ Royce was already examining the phenomenon of attention and had landed upon the idea that it strengthens some contents and simplifies, even before he went to Harvard. As he says in 1882: "Any act of attention tends, first, to strengthen the particular set of impressions to which it is at the moment adapted; and secondly, to modify those impressions in such a way as shall make the total impression derived from them all as simple an impression as possible. These two statements could be reduced to one: Attention constantly tends to make our consciousness more definite and less complex; that is, less confused and more united." Much of what later appeared in Chapter 9 of RAP is here in the 1882 essay "How Beliefs Are Made," in *Fugitive Essays*, ed. Jacob Loewenberg (Cambridge: Harvard University Press, 1920), 345–363, including the theory of recognition I will discuss here, but not the theory of construction. This extract is from page 356. I think Royce is responding to Peirce's ideas about the fixation of belief, but his own principle of docility is already at work here, just not by that name. This is part of my justification for thinking that it is unproblematic to use the 1903 *Outlines of Psychology* to serve as empirical ground for the 1885 phenomenology. Royce had all the ideas, but he hadn't yet followed them out in detail.

³⁴ Royce, RAP, 317–18.

³⁵ Ibid., 318.

³⁶ Ibid.

³⁷ Ibid., 320.

³⁸ Ibid., 321; my emphasis.

³⁹ I remind readers here that I am drawing on the results of Dwayne Tunstall's book *Yes, but Not Quite*, in which he defends with a thorough and sustained argument that the unity of Royce's thought is shown in the maintenance and development of a single ethico-religious insight. When I assert the primacy of ethics in Royce's thought, I am presupposing Tunstall's case.

⁴⁰ Royce, CG, 258–59.

⁴¹ Ibid., 260.

⁴² Ibid., 261.

⁴³ Ibid., 262.
⁴⁴ Ibid.
⁴⁵ Ibid., 263.
⁴⁶ Ibid., 265.
⁴⁷ Ibid.
⁴⁸ See Royce, "The Religious Mission of Sorrow," in *Basic Writings*, vol. 2, 1039–1062.
⁴⁹ It should be noted that Royce was not the first in his general philosophical line to treat individuality as an essentially ethical idea, nor was he the first to place emphasis upon the idea of the "unique" contribution of the individual to the divine life. One finds this same emphasis in Schleiermacher, and in a stream of German and other European personalists throughout the nineteenth century, many of whom Royce read. See Jan Olof Bengtsson, *The Worldview of Personalism: Origins and Early Development* (Oxford: Oxford University Press, 2006), 1–30, for the overview of this development, and esp. 16–17 for this point. I think it is fair to say, however, that Royce's adaptation of this development to sociality and practicality was highly original. Bengtsson's book is by far the most comprehensive and thorough survey of the sources that were crucial to American personalism, including Royce, Howison, and Bowne, and mainly through them, also James and Hocking.
⁵⁰ See Auxier and Herstein, *The Quantum of Explanation*, chs. 11–12, for a full account of the relation between philosophy and theology.

CHAPTER 6. TEMPORALISM

¹ See Royce, *The World and the Individual*, Second Series (New York: Macmillan, 1901), 109–151; hereafter "WI2."
² In Jackie Kegley's *Josiah Royce in Focus*, a more thorough discussion of Royce's empirical account of psychological and phenomenological time is included. See Chapter 2, final section.
³ Royce, "On Purpose in Thought," in *Fugitive Essays*, 259, my emphasis. I want to thank Jackie Kegley for drawing my attention to this passage in Chapter 1 of her *Josiah Royce in Focus*.
⁴ In a diary entry of 1879, Royce says: "'The New Phenomenology'; Would this title be Sacrilegious? And this for an opening: Every man lives in a present and contemplates a past and future. In this consists his whole life. The future and past are shadows both; the present is the only real. Yet in contemplation of the shadows is the realm wholly occupied; and without the shadows the real has for us neither life nor value. No more universal fact of consciousness can be mentioned than this fact." This passage is cited by Jacob Loewenberg in his Introduction to Royce, *Fugitive Essays* (Cambridge: Harvard University Press, 1920), 31. Serious readers of Royce do not need to be convinced that Royce was pre-occupied with time from the first to the last, but selective readers may lack this understanding.
⁵ Charles M. Sherover, "Royce's Pragmatic Idealism and Existential Phenomenology," in *From Kant and Royce to Heidegger*, ed. Gregory M. Johnson (Washington, D.C.: Catholic University of America Press, 2003), 107.
⁶ See Royce, *Fugitive Essays*, 31, my emphasis (cited above in note 1).
⁷ See John E. Smith, *The Spirit of American Philosophy*, rev. ed. (Albany: SUNY Press, 1983), 10; cited in Sherover, "Royce's Pragmatic Idealism and Existential

Phenomenology," 96. Smith is here speaking of pragmatism generally, not only Royce, but one can in numerous places find Smith running across this full spectrum of (to my mind important) distinctions without noting them. For example, see *The Spirit of American Philosophy*, 87. And refer to the "Introduction" of this book for a thorough discussion of some other examples from *Royce's Social Infinite: The Community of Interpretation* (New York: Liberal Arts Press, 1950). In addition to what I say in the Introduction, I also think that Smith fails to grasp *The Problem of Christianity* as a work that is restorationist, i.e., Campbellite, in spirit, not Calvinist. Royce's parents were both Campbellites, and anyone familiar with that tradition and its methods and theology will not be able to miss the connection between it and Royce's last major work.

[8] I have argued in detail elsewhere that necessity for Royce is abstracted negation. I identify seven clear levels of generality and suggest still others. See my "Complex Negation, Necessity, and Logical Magic."

[9] Royce, *The Religious Aspect of Philosophy* (Boston: Houghton Mifflin, 1885), 308–09; hereafter RAP. Royce goes on to describe the auditory version of this phenomenological experiment.

[10] Royce, RAP, 298. For Royce scholars, it is instructive to compare this chapter on doubt from RAP with the essay "Doubting and Working," of 1882 (see *Fugitive Essays*, 322–363). There is a clear development during the three intervening years in Royce's understanding of doubt. While he has already, by 1882, framed the fictional ontology, and has already examined the operations of doubt in knowing, he had not yet, apparently, connected the activity of postulating with the operation of doubt, as he did in 1885.

[11] Ibid.

[12] This essay was written for a lecture in March of 1906, but did not appear in print until 1911, in *William James and Other Essays on the Philosophy of Life* (New York: Macmillan, 1911), 257–298. As Royce says, the essay is intended to "repudiate the frequent and groundless assertion that my own form of idealism regards time as 'unreal', or the absolute as 'timeless', or the universe as a 'block'," viii. I fear that Royce had himself invited such an interpretation with his chapter on "The Temporal and the Eternal," and the frequent and groundless assertion is what stuck to him, the repudiation having been largely ignored. I would think that part of the reason is that one does not generally read an essay entitled "Immortality" for a thorough-going expression of temporalism. Happily, this important essay was noticed by John J. McDermott and included in *The Basic Writings of Josiah Royce*, 2 vols. (New York: Fordham University Press, 2005 [1969]), 1:385–417; this is the edition from which I will cite.

[13] Royce, "Immortality," 390.

[14] Ibid.

[15] Ibid.

[16] Ibid., 390–91.

[17] John Elof Boodin, "William James as I Knew Him," in *William James Remembered*, ed. Linda Simon (Lincoln: University of Nebraska Press, 1996), 209.

[18] I have formalized a method drawn from Royce for keeping levels of generalization separate in my "Complex Negation, Necessity, and Logical Magic."

[19] Royce, "Self-consciousness, Social Consciousness and Nature," in *Studies of Good and Evil* (New York: Appleton, 1898), 198–248; this essay, originally a lecture written in 1895, is reprinted in *Basic Writings of Josiah Royce*, ed. John J. McDermott, 2 vols. (New York: Fordham University Press, 2005 [1969]), 1:423–461, which will be cited here. This passage is from 446.

20 Ibid., 447.
21 Ibid.
22 Royce, WI2, 51–52.
23 Royce, RAP, 344–45.
24 Ibid., 345.
25 Ibid., 345–46.
26 This argument by Royce probably derives from his reading of Kant's Critique of Judgment, especially the Antinomy of Teleological Judgment (section 70) and the Methodology (sections 79–84). Royce rarely mentions this work by Kant, but Steven A. Miller did some archival research while a graduate student at my institution, finding two copies of the third Critique owned and annotated by Royce. Miller has not yet published this research and I thank him for sharing it with me.
27 Royce, WI2, 76–77 (original emphasis).
28 See Ibid., esp. 77–79.
29 Ibid., 79. A similar argument was given in RAP.
30 Ibid., 79–80. An analysis of how this triadic argument is related to Royce's later ideas about the semiotics of God and the world was presented by William Elkins under the title "There's Something (Someone) in Between," at the 2013 conference, "Royce, California, and the World." I hope Elkins will publish this excellent analysis soon.
31 What I say here resolves an oft-noted tension in Royce between the theistic finitism articulated in "The Problem of Job" and the supposed absolutism of his metaphysics. When one reads the full 1896 Augustus Graham Lectures (HARP Boxes 52,78), the relation is clearer and accords with the solution I offer here.
32 The best summary I have encountered of this issue about the primacy of value for philosophy is by E.S. Brightman, *Moral Laws* (New York: Abingdon, 1933), Chapter XVI, especially 257–264, where he confronts non-personalist philosophies that depend on aesthetic accounts of value, and 284–87, where he confronts naturalistic accounts of value such as Dewey's. My point here is not whether Brightman is right or wrong, but whether Royce belongs with the personalists or non-personalists, and a survey of the literature will leave little doubt. Charles Hartshorne is an interesting hybrid, being simultaneously a committed personalist and holding that value is aesthetic at bottom. But many variations on this theme are possible within the general field of temporalist philosophy.
33 Royce, "Immortality," 396.
34 Ibid., 397 (my emphasis).
35 Ibid.
36 Ibid.
37 Ibid., 398.
38 Ibid.
39 Ibid., 398–99.
40 Of course, this is Paul's dialectal method in his letter to the Romans.

CHAPTER 7. PERSONALISM

1 See John Clendenning, *The Life and Thought of Josiah Royce*, revised and expanded ed. (Nashville: Vanderbilt University Press, 1999), 239.
2 John Clendenning, ed., *The Letters of Josiah Royce* (Chicago: University of Chicago Press, 1970), 604.

³ An exception to this pervasive problem is Eugene Fontinell, who is sometimes described as having interpreted James as a personalist. I would choose the term "personalistic" for his interpretation, in the sense that Fontinell's work is consistent with a personalist account of James, but goes only part of the way toward a fully articulated personalism. One marker that shows this is Fontinell's association of "self" with "person" in various ways. This is certainly consistent with James's own tendencies in his earlier writings. But there was a development away from this association that Fontinell overlooks. Yet, I must grant a number of points to Fontinell. I will mention only two here. First, he is correct to stress that for James, and for all of us, a conceptual (and especially logical) description of personal experience will always be too abstract and rigid because experience overflows concepts. Thus, what I have to say in this chapter must also be taken in functional rather than logical terms, especially as regards the disjunctive and conjunctive principles in experience. Second, Fontinell rightly stresses that the continuity of the self or person is the central issue, and that *as felt*, the self must be treated as something continuous. This might seem to be at odds with the account I provide here, but I do not think so. When I stress that time is the principle of continuity in experience, I do intend to include the processive "self" as a part of what I mean by "time." Like Fontinell, I intend to be reading James as a process philosopher. But unlike Fontinell, I offer a contrast of the idea of "self" and "person" that I believe suggests an equally important principle of discontinuity, and I do not think we can understand James rightly by privileging continuity over discontinuity. See Eugene Fontinell, *Self, God and Immortality: A Jamesian Investigation* (Philadelphia: Temple University Press, 1986).

⁴ William James, characterizing his philosophy as a whole, in the 1903–04 course "A Pluralistic Description of the World," in *The Works of William James: Manuscript Lectures*, ed. Ignas Skrupskelis (Cambridge: Harvard University Press, 1988), 311. I would like to thank Megan Mustain for calling my attention to this passage.

⁵ For a discussion of the history of the actual term "personalism," see Jan Olof Bengtsson, *The Worldview of Personalism: Origins and Early Development* (Oxford: Oxford University Press, 1006), 1–30; and Rufus Burrow, Jr., *Personalism: A Critical Introduction* (St. Louis: Chalice Press, 1999), 14–18. There was a long-standing claim in the literature that Bowne had actually gotten the term "personalism" from James, who had gotten it from Charles Renouvier, but later scholarship has put this in doubt. On the basis of Bengtsson's research, it seems more plausible that Bowne knew the term from his days studying with Lotze and Ulrici, but only came to apply it to his own thought much later. As Burrow reports, George C. Cell credited James with the first use of the term in American philosophy in *The Varieties of Religious Experience* (New York: Modern Library, n.d. [1902]), 491, and it was long thought by some that Bowne got the term there. James is certainly not the first American philosopher to use the term "personalism." William Torrey Harris, Walt Whitman, and Amos Bronson Alcott had all used the term earlier (see Burrow, 16–17), and Bowne may also have gotten the term from any of them. Some of what I will say in this chapter may actually serve to resurrect the idea that Bowne got the term from James, but it matters very little, except as a historical question whether Bowne did or did not get the term from James. It would be ironic, I suppose, if James were the source of the label, but he is not in any case the source of the philosophical view. Bengtsson traces the view back to Jacobi and makes a thorough case that the worldview of personalism was well defined in the early decades of the nineteenth century.

⁶ Perhaps some would find the omission of Renouvier the most surprising here, since his influence on James was exerted early (1870) and remained important throughout James's life. Indeed, Perry regarded Renouvier as the single most important influence on James's philosophy, imparting significant ideas about freedom and determinism, the will, pluralism, and the part-whole relation, to name only a few. However, as Perry makes clear, by the time Renouvier was explicitly developing his personalism, James had ceased being able to keep up with the voluminous writings and "had become to James an object of veneration rather than a source of light." See Ralph Barton Perry, *The Thought and Character of William James*, 2 vols. (Boston: Little, Brown, 1935), vol. 1, 710. James left most of Renouvier's book *Le Personalisme* unread. My sense is that James might have been emboldened just a bit to use the term "personalism" to describe himself by Renouvier's adoption of it, but perhaps not, since by the time Renouvier began to use it, James's differences with him were very clear. James's use of this new term to refer to himself happened at the same time as Renouvier's book appeared, 1903 (see note 274 above).

⁷ See I.K. Skrupskelis and E.M. Berkeley, *The Correspondence of William James*, vol. 5 (Charlottesville: University of Virginia Press, 1997), 22.

⁸ See Bowne, *The Philosophy of Herbert Spencer: Being an Examination of the First Principles of His System* (New York: Nelson and Phillips, 1874). This book is, of course deeply, even bitingly critical of Spencer's philosophy.

⁹ See James, *Principles of Psychology*, vol. 1, authorized ed. (New York: Dover, 1950 [1890]), 219–220.

¹⁰ Perry notes that James carefully and approvingly annotated his copies of Bowne's 1882 *Metaphysics*, and the 1902 *Theism*. See Perry, *The Thought and Character of William James*, vol. 2, 330.

¹¹ See Skrupskelis and Berkeley, *The Correspondence of William James*, vol. 6, 343–45.

¹² See James' letter of May 21, 1895 in Francis J. McConnell, *Borden Parker Bowne: His Life and Philosophy* (New York: Abingdon, 1929), 274.

¹³ See McConnell, *Bowne*, 272–76. James had gathered books and materials from Bowne in writing *Varieties*, and then Bowne evidently expressed some consternation at having been labeled a "rationalist" in that book, for which James apologized in 1903, even though it was a very laudatory reference in which James enjoined all his readers to read Bowne's three short books on the Christian life. See James, *Varieties of Religious Experience*, 492. The label "rationalist" may seem a negative epithet in James's vocabulary, but I encourage those who think so to consult James's *A Pluralistic Universe* (Philadelphia: McKay, 1909), 12–13 regarding whether rationalism is really such a negative label for James. This is also the sense in which Whitehead uses the term.

¹⁴ See McConnell, *Bowne*, 276. James refers to those who are trying to "weed Bowne out" of the Methodist Church as "the ass and the blatherskite." Bowne was acquitted unanimously of the heresy charge in what is still the only heresy trial in Methodist history, but as Dean of what was then the most important seminary of the Methodists, Bowne's support of the higher criticism of the Bible was controversial, and he was the most obvious target for those among the clergy who were resisting the modern trends in scriptural interpretation. A full account of the trial and some of its excerpted proceedings are in McConnell, 179–206.

¹⁵ Letter from James to Mrs. Bowne, April 14, 1910, *The Correspondence of William James*, vol. 12, 471. I consulted the original held at Boston University, Howard Gottlieb Archival Research Center, Bowne Papers.

[16] William James, "Thomas Davidson: Individualist," in *Essays, Comments and Reviews*, eds. Frederick H. Burkhardt, et al. (Cambridge: Harvard University Press, 1987), 88–89.

[17] See Skrupskelis and Berkeley, *Correspondence of William James*, vol. 5, 182–86. The Henry James, Sr., book was *Society the Redeemed Form of Man*, 1879, and the controversy took place in the *Christian Register* over several numbers. Howison had contended the book led to idealism. Herny James, Sr., was basically "correcting" him.

[18] The history of pluralism in American philosophy is complicated. Jean Wahl's early recognition of the importance of this development is reflected in his book *The Pluralist Philosophies of England and America*, auth. trans. Fred Rothwell (London: Open Court, 1925). Wahl regards pluralism as having reached its maturity in America with James's philosophy, and he catalogues the influences from various places, such as Fechner, Lotze, and Wundt in Germany, Lutoslawski in Poland, and Ménard and Renouvier in France. He overlooks the fact that Howison was a pluralist before James was even a philosopher, but it is possible that Howison came to his emphasis on pluralism through James's affinities with Renouvier. In any case, I think Wahl tends to misreport Howison's views, having too quickly believed what James and others said of Howison without verifying that they were fair in their interpretations. Wahl does recognize that there was a lively controversy between James and Howison over pluralism, but he seems only aware of the episodes between 1898 and 1910, and he comes to the conclusion that Howison had not really achieved the level of radical pluralism of James, accusing Howison in particular of atemporalism. Most of what Wahl says accurately describes the state of the discussion between 1898 and 1910, but fails to document a deeper history of exchange and conversation between James and Howison. More recently in Louis Menand's history of ideas in America, *The Metaphysical Club* (New York: Farrar, Straus, and Giroux, 2001), there is an informative and interesting study of the rise of pluralism, 377–408, which takes the same decade and basic viewpoint as Wahl. However, there is no mention of Howison at all, as Menand concentrates on the students of James and the relationship between pluralistic culture and pluralistic philosophy. Thus, the story of philosophical pluralism in America has not yet been fully told, but when it is, the relationship between James and Howison will surely be the fulcrum. There is more on this topic in my "Editorial Statement" and my essay "The Possibilities of Pluralism" in *The Pluralist*, 1:1 (Spring 2006), v–vii, 1–12.

[19] See George Holmes Howison, *The Limits of Evolution and Other Essays*, second ed. (New York: Macmillan, 1904), xii.

[20] See Perry, *Thought and Character of William James*, vol. 1, 762. The whole of vol. 1, chapter 48 (762–777) is a discussion of Howison, including some correspondence, and some philosophical discussion of their views occurs in vol. 2 of Perry's massive work.

[21] There is a fair amount of discussion of the Howison-James relationship in J.W. Buckham and G.M. Stratton, *Howison: Philosopher and Teacher* (Berkeley: University of California Press, 1934), esp. 108–112.

[22] One can begin the investigation of the James-Royce relationship with Perry's chapters in *The Thought and Character of William James*, vol. 1, 778–824. The latest and most comprehensive study of this relationship, which some will say is definitive, is in Frank M. Oppenheim's most recent book, *Reverence for the Relations of Life: Re-imagining Pragmatism via Josiah Royce's Interactions with Peirce, James, and Dewey* (Notre Dame: University of Notre Dame Press, 2004). Over two hundred pages of this book are

devoted to comparative analysis and biographical interactions (pp. 63–280), and no one who attempts a subsequent study can do anything but respond to Oppenheim. There is much in Oppenheim's treatment that will come as surprising news to James scholars, if they read it.

[23] The most serious offender is probably Gerald Myers's *William James: His Life and Thought* (New Haven: Yale University Press, 1986). In almost every single mention of Royce, Myers pairs him with Bradley on just a list of neo-Hegelians or bad idealists. It is clear to me that apart from their correspondence, Myers may never have read a word of Royce, or if he did, he read it with little understanding and still less sympathy. His story of James's thought is rendered flimsy as a result, in my opinion. It is impossible for me to grasp how a person who has read Perry's biography of James (and Myers certainly did) could pretend that Royce played no greater role in the formation of James's thinking than Myers attributes to him. Among recent contributions to James scholarship that fall into this category, I would note Linda Simon, *Genuine Reality: A Life of William James* (New York: Harcourt Brace, 1998). Simon really does understand the role of Royce in the formation of James's worldview (as is evident in her 1996 edited book *William James Remembered* in which over half of the entries bring up Royce's pivotal role in James's intellectual life), but Simon simply chooses not to give it any importance in her biography. Perhaps still more disappointing is Robert D. Richardson, *William James: In the Maelstrom of American Modernism* (Boston: Houghton Mifflin, 2006). Both Simon and Richardson are content to rehearse the well-known historical facts of the James-Royce friendship, and to dip a small bucket into the sea of their philosophical relationship, and then to pass on. This is typical of James scholarship in the last half-century, and has been a failing in James scholars' understanding of their own subject. A far better job has been done by Timothy L.S. Sprigge in *James and Bradley: American Truth and British Reality* (Chicago: Open Court, 1993), see esp. 26–30, where Sprigge notes the sense in which Royce's defense of the "intentional stance" and its relation to error was "irresistible" to James, as little as James liked it. But Sprigge was not really a James scholar. He was an original idealist in his own right, and a Bradley scholar whose temper was well suited to investigating the niceties of Absolute idealism. My guess is that many James scholars breathed a sigh of relief upon the release of Sprigge's massive tome, thinking "Thank heavens I don't have to do that now . . ." I wonder how many of them read all six hundred pages. More typical is the book by James M. Edie, *William James and Phenomenology* (Bloomington: Indiana University Press, 1987), who actually ignores Royce altogether, as though one could get at the heart of James's intentional stance without so much as reading Royce. This view of things is beginning to look increasingly mistaken as more and more evidence (in Jason Bell's recent work) comes to light that Husserl may have been as much under the influence of Royce's ideas as under James's influence. The sins of the James community are legion. I won't bother to go on listing them.

[24] In addition to what is elsewhere in this book, see for example, my "Introductions" to vols. 1–3 in *Critical Responses to Josiah Royce, 1885–1916* (Bristol: Thoemmes, 2001). Several papers were presented on topics close to this at the Vanderbilt conference "The Relevance of Royce" in April of 2005, and appeared in a volume from Fordham University Press in 2008, edited by Kelly Parker and Jason M. Bell. Other important studies are in *The Pluralist*, 2:2 (Summer 2007), a special issue devoted to Royce, Ethics, and Community.

[25] Recall that for James, psychology is a branch of epistemology that assumes the possibility of knowledge and some sort of "self" to know. See *Principles of Psychology*,

vol. 1, 184. See also Royce, *Outlines of Psychology* (New York: Macmillan, 1903), 274–298, where he argues that the "self" something produced by our social environment. The "person" or "individual" for Royce is an ontological starting place for ethical philosophy, but also for ontology itself, bearing a close resemblance to what Heidegger called "Dasein." What holds the self and the person together for Royce are the temporality of the person, which translates empirically into the "docility" of the self (as we have discussed in Chapter 5), the term Royce chooses for expressing the idea that a self has a history, both of its inner and its outer life. Docility, then, taken ontologically, is the historicity of Dasein's temporality, to make the same point in Heidegger's language. The self is ontic, the person ontological.

[26] See James's review of Royce's *The Religious Aspect of Philosophy* (1885), in *Essays, Comments and Reviews*, 384. In a letter to Frank Thilly in 1895, answering Thilly's remark that James was "the greatest philosopher of our country," James, after remarking "God help the country," suggested that Thilly think of Royce or Bowne as better philosophers, candidates for the (dubious) title. See James, *Essays in Philosophy*, eds. Frederick H. Burkhardt, et al. (Cambridge: Harvard University Press, 1978), 258.

[27] James alludes here to Bergson's discussion of the difference between the two sorts of nervous systems, centralized, as found in vertebrates, and decentralized, as found in arthropods. See Bergson, *Creative Evolution*, auth trans. Arthur G. Mitchell (New York: Holt, 1911 [1907]), 135–175. The broader issue of Bergson's relation to personalism was taken up, unsatisfactorily in my view, by Ralph Tyler Flewelling in *Bergson and Personal Realism* (New York: Abingdon, 1920). I read Bergson as a non-personalist in the sense I described in Chapter 6, and as importantly related to the naturalists such as Dewey, on one side, and the aestheticists such as Whitehead, on the other. I think Bergson is subject to Brightman's critique in *Moral Laws* that I cited in that discussion, and would add that this criticism of Brightman's is helpful in grasping the often observed disconnect between Bergson's moral philosophy and his metaphysics. The key to bridging it, if it can be bridged, lies in Bergson's aesthetics, most notably, his theory of laughter.

[28] See McConnell, *Borden Parker Bowne*, 277–78.

[29] It is possible to treat Bowne as a pragmatist in the sense of idealistic pragmatism as I described it in Chapter 4. This question was taken up by McConnell in *Borden Parker Bowne*, 149–162, and draws the same basic conclusion.

[30] For a full discussion of Bowne's method, see my "Bowne on Time, Evolution, and History," *Journal of Speculative Philosophy* 12:3 (1998), 181–203.

[31] It is interesting to note that the only major work of Bowne's to which I can find no reference in any of James's writings is Bowne's treatise on the relationship between logic and knowledge, what we would, today, call "epistemic logic." Bowne did not write a separate book on logic, as one might have expected, but rather offered this treatise as a discussion of method. See *Theory of Thought and Knowledge* (New York: Harper, 1899). See specifically in the "Preface," v–vi, where Bowne denies that thought (and logic, the science of thought), delivers ontological truths. This is where Bowne sets out his version of what James calls "the philosopher's fallacy," or Whitehead calls "the fallacy of misplaced concreteness." It is worth quoting here at length:

> Apart from these deeper speculative questions [about God, etc.], I have emphasized two points the knowledge of which is of great importance, if not absolutely necessary, for our intellectual salvation. The first point is the volitional and practical nature of belief. Persons living on the plane of instinct and hearsay have no intellectual difficulty here, or anywhere else; but persons

entering upon the life of reflection without insight into this fact are sure to lose themselves in theoretical impotence of practical impudence. The impotence manifests itself in a paralyzing inability to believe, owing to the fancy that theoretical demonstration must precede belief. The impudence shows itself in ruling out with an airy levity the practical principles by which men and nations live, because they admit of no formal proof. These extremes of unwisdom can be escaped only by an insight into the volitional and practical nature of belief. The second point referred to is the almost universal illusion arising from what I have called the structural fallacies of uncritical thought. Spontaneous thought is pretty sure to take its own operations as a double of reality. Thus arises the fallacy of the universal, the parent of a very large part of popular speculation. And when to this are added the omnipresent imposture and deceit of language, there results a great world of abstract and verbal illusion against which we cannot be too much on our guard, seeing that it is the source of so much theoretical error and of so much practical menace and aberration. It is incredible, in the advance of investigation, how much of what is said or written is pompous nothingness. . . it is amazing on looking through philosophical speculation to discover how much of it is nothing but a shadow of our logical processes, in which the abstractions of logic are mistaken for the facts of existence.

One can certainly hear James's will to believe in the first point, and his critique of abstraction in the second. It is difficult to believe that a person who had internalized this point about Bowne's view of reason, logic, and method, could have said what James said in the 1908 letter. Bowne never claimed to resolve *any* problem in the rationalist fashion James described, and James should have known that. Bowne was an empiricist and a voluntarist, like James.

[32] James, *Principles of Psychology*, vol. 1, 225.

[33] Ibid., 225–26.

[34] Ibid., 226.

[35] Ibid. It is worth noting that as his authority for this point on page 226 of *Principles*, James cites none other than Bowne's *Metaphysics*, page 362, where Bowne is making the case that the materialist and the empiricist are not true allies regarding the form of consciousness, since the materialist gives himself to abstractions while the honest empiricist has to acknowledge that consciousness involves the personal form. If the empiricist gives his consent to the materialist claim that impersonal sensations are all that really exists, the empiricist is not a true empiricist but an abstractionist.

[36] James, *Principles of Psychology*, vol. 1, 227.

[37] See for example, James's 1904 essay "Does Consciousness Exist?" reprinted in *Essays in Radical Empiricism* in 1912.

[38] See for examples, James, *Manuscript Essays and Notes*, ed. Frederick H. Burkhardt, et al. (Cambridge: Harvard University Press, 1988), 68, 125. James often associated Bowne's work with Lotze, whom he also admired, and knew of course that Bowne was among Lotze's American students, as was Royce, and indeed, Santayana had written his dissertation on Lotze under Royce's direction. Paul G. Kuntz has made the case for Lotze's influence on James and Royce in the lengthy and admirable "Introduction" to Santayana's *Lotze's System of Philosophy*, ed. Paul G. Kuntz (Bloomington: Indiana University Press, 1971), 48, 63–68; see also Perry, *Thought and Character*, vol. 586–87.

[39] James, *Manuscript Lectures*, 272.

[40] James, *Varieties*, 193.

[41] I do wish to note that the term "energy" becomes simultaneously crucial in Bergson's philosophy, and it was soon to become a very important idea in physics.

[42] James, *Varieties*, 30.

⁴³ Royce, *The Problem of Christianity*, one-volume edition (Chicago: University of Chicago Press, 1968 [1913]), 40–41.

⁴⁴ Muelder points to the deficiencies in Brightman's *Moral Laws* as deriving chiefly from an individualism that is too rigid both epistemologically and ontologically. He corrects this individualism in *Moral Law in Christian Social Ethics* (Richmond: John Knox, 1966).

⁴⁵ James, *Varieties*, 166.

⁴⁶ Ibid., 167.

⁴⁷ James, *Principles of Psychology*, vol. 1, 226.

⁴⁸ A wealth of material criticizing the "individualist" interpretation in James is in the dissertation by Michael W. Allen, "William James, Social Philosopher" (Southern Illinois University Carbondale, 2003).

⁴⁹ I have addressed this issue in a separate essay entitled "Scheler and the Existence of the Impersonal," forthcoming in a collection of essays from the 12th International Conference on Persons, Lund University, August 2013, eds. Phillip Cronce and Anthony L. Cashio.

⁵⁰ The use of "afford" in a manner that alludes to the psychology of J.J. Gibson is conscious and intended. There is a rich area of thinking that someone might pursue in connecting the personalism of Michael Polanyi and Marjorie Grene to that of James by means of a Gibsonian theory of perception.

⁵¹ Chapter 7 of Dwayne Tunstall's book *Yes, but Not Quite* confronts this question directly.

⁵² Apart from the essays cited above, Auxier, "God as Catholic and Personal: A Protestant Perspective on Norris Clarke's Neo-Thomistic Personalism," in *International Philosophical Quarterly* 40:2 (June 2000), 235–252; and the two chapters comparing the thought of Brightman and Hartshorne in *Hartshorne and Brightman on God, Process, and Persons: The Correspondence, 1922–1945*, eds. Randall E. Auxier, Mark Y.A. Davies (Nashville: Vanderbilt University Press, 2001), 100–120, 131–154. A discussion of temporalism in connection with the concept of the person also occurs in "Why 100 Years Is Forever: Hartshorne on Immortality," *The Personalist Forum* 14:2 (1998), 109–132.

⁵³ There is no reason to multiply instances, but an informative discussion of James's temporalism and its connection to the principle of continuity and radical empiricism is given by David L. Miller under the title "James and the Specious Present," in *The Philosophy of William James*, ed. Walter Robert Corti (Hamburg: Felix Meiner Verlag, 1976), 51–79. See also from this same volume Victor Lowe's "The Relation between James and Whitehead," 331–346. Lowe does a nice job of showing some of the senses in which James is a process philosopher, but he mistakenly argues that Whitehead is not "influenced" by James. Regarding Lowe's tendencies in reading Whitehead's influences are inadequate see my "Influence as Confluence: Bergson and Whitehead," *Process Studies*, vol. 28, nos. 3/4 (Fall/Winter 1999), 301–338. A positive account of James as a process philosopher (i.e., temporalist) in the relevant respects is offered by Lee F. Werth under the title "Clarifying Concresence in Whitehead's Process Philosophy," in *Time and Process: The Study of Time VII*, eds. J.T. Fraser and Lewis Rowell (Madison: International Universities Press, 1993), 219–241. Werth argues that Whitehead's own account of concrescing actual entities cannot be understood (as empirical or personal) without reference to James's *Principles*.

⁵⁴ See William J. Gavin, *William James and the Reinstatement of the Vague* (Philadelphia: Temple University Press, 1992). Typical of the anti-metaphysical stance,

interpreters like Charlene Haddock Seigfried tend to be critical of James's notion of pure experience, thinking that he waffles between affirming the metaphysical priority of continuity and discontinuity, in turn. She concludes no metaphysics is needed to get what James wants, philosophically. I think Seigfried may be right that one may have the results of radical empiricism without worrying much over the metaphysics (leaving it implicit), but I do not think James believed that. Among Seigfried's numerous writings on James, see her book *Chaos and Context: A Study in William James* (Athens: Ohio University, Press, 1978), esp. 34–53.

55 Perhaps "characters" or "general guidelines" would be better labels, but if we use the word "principles" as James did in his psychology, or in the sense Dewey spoke of "leading principles," it should not mislead us into seeing time and person as a priori or antecedently formed realities. The only thing antecedent about the givenness of time and person is that both are historical in character, which means that the quality of their availability for any experience is such: all that they have been before is part of the way in which they are present now, i.e., history, or the presence of the past, is what links "person" and "time." A similar point may be made about their futurity.

56 In John J. McDermott, ed. "A Pluralistic Universe," *Writings of William James* (Chicago: University of Chicago Press, 1992), 808 (hereafter cited as WWJ).

57 McDermott, WWJ, 136.

58 James, *Varieties*, 365.

59 Mark Moller, "James, Perception, and the Miller-Bode Objections," in *Transactions of the Charles S. Peirce Society*, 37:4 (Fall 2001), 609–626. I want to thank Russell Pryba of the University at Buffalo for calling this article to my attention.

60 Ibid., 615.

61 James, *Manuscript Essays and Notes*, 70; cited by Moller, 616.

62 Ibid., 70–71; cited by Moller, 616.

63 Moller, "James," 617–18. He is quoting James, *Manuscript Essays and Notebooks*, 83.

64 Moller, "James," 618; James, ibid.

65 Moller, ibid.

66 James, *Essays in Radical Empiricism and A Pluralistic Universe* (New York: Longmans, Green, 1936 [1912]), 53.

67 Ibid., 47.

68 Ibid., 51–52.

69 Ibid., 54.

70 This chapter was greatly improved by close readings and comments by Dwayne Tunstall, Sean Lipham, Kelly J. Booth, and Megan Rust Mustain.

CHAPTER 8. COMMUNITY AND PURPOSE

1 For an explanation of what personalism does with the pseudo-opposition between natural and supernatural, see Borden Parker Bowne, *Theism* (New York: American Book Company, 1902), 230–247; and *The Immanence of God* (Boston: Houghton Mifflin, 1905), 5–32. For the irrelevance of the distinction between natural and revealed theology, see Albert C. Knudson, *The Philosophy of Personalism* (New York: Abingdon, 1927), 255–57.

2 That personalism and pantheism are the enduring foes in the struggle of nineteenth- and twentieth-century philosophy has been noted by a number of interpreters,

including Frederick Copleston, and Albert C. Knudson. But the most thorough documentation of this point, and its importance is Jan Olof Bengtsson's , *The Worldview of Personalism: Origins and Early Development* (Oxford: Oxford University Press, 2006), upon which I drew in the last chapter, and upon which I will heavily rely in this discussion.

³ The best source for this story in the current context is Warren Breckman, *Marx, the Young Hegelians, and the Origins of Radical Social Theory* (Cambridge: Cambridge University Press, 1999). This work is summarized in the context relative to my point in Bengtsson, *The Worldview of Personalism*, ch. 1.

⁴ Douglas R. Anderson, "Royce, Philosophy, and Wandering: A Job Description," in *Philosophy Americana: Making Philosophy at Home in American Culture* (New York: Fordham University Press, 2006), 37.

⁵ I reiterate here something I confessed in my introduction, which is that I need to spend more time studying British idealism. For example, my description to Phil Ferreira of Royce's organic process philosophy in 2006 led him to say that what I had described was precisely Bradley's view. I have read *Appearance and Reality* and a great part of Bradley's *Logic* but was not struck by the similarities with Royce. Yet, Timothy Sprigge's book on James and Bradley has numerous points in common with the present book, and I may be using Bradley as a foil in an inadvisable way that I will have to abandon when time permits me to study Bradley with the care he deserves. I have found the exchanges between Ferreira and Jan Olaf Bengtsson in *The Pluralist* to be a source of my on-going education.

⁶ See my essay, "Bowne on Time, Evolution, and History," *Journal of Speculative Philosophy* 12:3 (1998), 181–203.

⁷ I call attention again to the passage I cited in full in the endnotes of the previous chapter from Bowne's *Theory of Thought and Knowledge*, v; and I would here add a notice of the telling sermon "The Mystery of Life and Its Practical Solution," in *The Essence of Religion* (Boston: Houghton Miffling, 1910), 43–69.

⁸ I do not mean to imply that Bowne regarded philosophy as unimportant. He regarded it as crucial to life, but he simply knew that ordinary people were not going to await its pronouncements, and most people live entirely without it. One must accommodate such a fact of life in one's estimate of the scope of philosophy, and Bowne does so by holding little expectation that a well formed philosophy will actually make much practical difference in the world.

⁹ See Charles M. Sherover, Part III of *Are We in Time and Other Essays on Time and Temporality*, ed. Gregory R. Johnson (Evanston: Northwestern University Press, 2003), 93–159.

¹⁰ Royce, *The Philosophy of Loyalty*, 107–08.

¹¹ Frederick Copleston, *A History of Philosophy*, 8 vols. (New York: Doubleday, 1965), vol. 8, part I, 281; cited in Bengtsson, *The Worldview of Personalism*, 39.

¹² Copleston, *A History of Philosophy*, vol. 8, part II, 52, my emphasis.

¹³ See Alfred North Whitehead, *The Function of Reason* (Boston: Beacon Press, 1958 [1929]), 8.

¹⁴ Copleston, *A History of Philosophy*, vol. 8, part II, 52,, my emphasis.

¹⁵ Copleston not only classes Royce as a personalist, but even is among those rare readers who notices that James is a personalist: "We may also note that the term 'personal idealism' is somewhat ambiguous in the context of American thought. It was used, for example, by William James of his own philosophy. But though the use of the term was doubtless justified, James is best discussed under the heading of pragmatism." Ibid., 23.

[16] I have tried to show the inadequacy of this view in "Immediacy and Purpose in Brightman's Philosophy," in *Hartshorne and Brightman on God, Process, and Persons: The Correspondence, 1922–1945*, eds. Randall E. Auxier and Mark Y.A. Davies (Nashville: Vanderbilt University Press, 2001), 132–154.

[17] Royce makes the distinction between radical empiricism and the type of empiricism he defends, and suggests his own type is "pragmatism." I do not disagree. Radical empiricists are always pragmatists in one of the senses I defended in Chapter 4. But not all pragmatists are radical empiricists. See Royce, "The Eternal and the Practical," in *Presidential Addresses of the American Philosophical Association, 1901–1910*, ed. Richard T. Hull (Dordrecht: Kluwer, 1999), 73.

[18] Sean Lipham, "The Universe as Thou: William James's Religious Personalism," presented in 2007 at the Society for the Advancement of American Philosophy, in Columbia, South Carolina. The paper is available on-line (perhaps temporarily) at <www.philosophy.uncc.edu/mleldrid/SAAP/USC/TP24.html>; accessed May 2nd, 2007.

[19] For a really insightful summary of this aspect of James, see Tadd Ruetenik, "Last Call for William James," in *The Pluralist* 7:1 (Winter, 2012).

[20] The most extensive effort at documenting these activities in the last half-century is Deborah Blum, *Ghost Hunters: William James and the Search for Scientific Proof of Life after Death* (New York: Penguin, 2006).

[21] On Bowne's affirmation of subhuman persons, see Erazim Kohák's "Personalism: Towards a Philosophical Dileneation," in *The Personalist Forum* 13:1 (Spring 1997), 7. Kohák interprets Bowne's progressive statements in *Principles of Ethics* (New York: Harper, 1892), 150, 161, to imply the view that we err when we deal heedlessly with the non-human world as though personal existence were not the source of our community with them. I think Kohák interprets Bowne rightly.

[22] On Hartshorne's personalism and its extent to both sub and superhuman persons, see my "God, Process and Persons: Charles Hartshorne and Personalism," *Process Studies*, 27:3–4 (1998), 175–201; a slightly different and expanded version of this essay is in *Hartshorne and Brightman on God, Process and Persons: The Correspondence, 1922–1945*, eds. Randall E. Auxier and Mark Y.A. Davies (Nashville: Vanderbilt University Press, 2001). Daniel Dombrowski has, without (in my view) due recognition of its personalist roots, taken the implications of Hartshorne's view through to its ethical meaning for animal rights. See *Hartshorne and the Metaphysics of Animal Rights* (Albany: SUNY Press, 1988).

[23] Brightman indicates in several places that so-called "sub-human" personality is real, and animals are persons. See for example, *Moral Laws* (New York: Abingdon, 1933), 58.

[24] This point is made, in essence, by William Ernest Hocking in his essay "On Royce's Empiricism," in *The Journal of Philosophy* 53:3 (February 2nd, 1956), 57–63. Hocking reads Royce's empiricism as being in conflict with his voluntarism, due to the absence of any direct experience of the self, God, and others. I agree that there is a tension here, the problem of immediacy is a real one, as I argued in Chapter 3; but I hope I have shown that the tension is not a contradiction in the account of individuality and will I have provided in Chapter 5 and temporalism in Chapter 6. Thus, even as Hocking is willing to use the term "radical empiricism" to describe Royce's philosophy, on one of its sides, I want to suggest that in other respects he was at the least an empiricist, if not always a radical one, throughout.

[25] Royce, *Studies of Good and Evil* (New York: Appleton, 1898), 230. I strongly recommend that readers who want greater detail about Royce's philosophy of nature and its

ethical meaning consult the following two essays: Thomas W. Price, "The Appreciation of Natural Beings and the Finitude of Consciousness," and Jason M. Bell, "The World and Its Selves: Royce and the Philosophy of Nature," both in *The Personalist Forum* 15:1 (Spring 1999), 153–184. I am drawing on and building on their arguments here. One is also tempted to see in this passage one result of Royce's lifelong study of the Vedas, and to see "Atman" as individuality and "Jiva" as person, although a case could be made for the reversal of the two as well.

[26] Mark Moller, whose article I discussed in Chapter 7, saw no viable alternative, in light of his astute assessment of James's struggles, but to conclude that James had embraced panpsychism at the end. That is not the right term for the position, in my view, but I am not in complete disagreement with Moller either. See Moller, "James, Perception, and the Miller-Bode Objections," in *Transactions of the Charles S. Peirce Society* 37:1 (Fall 2001), esp. 623–25.

[27] This exchange is nicely summed up in the article by Larry Hickman, "Why Peirce Didn't Like Dewey's Logic," in *Southwest Philosophy Review* 3 (1986), 178–189.

[28] I have argued the point in detail that Whitehead is a radical empiricist in my "Whitehead's Radical Empiricism: Mementoes of a Timequake," in *Applied Process Thought II: Following a Trail Ablaze*, ed. Roger Mark Dibben and Rebecca Newton (Frankfurt am Main: Ontos Verlag, 2009), 75–100.

[29] Alfred North Whitehead, *Adventures of Ideas* (New York: Free Press, 1967 [1933]), 226.

[30] In a new book co-authored with Gary Herstein, I call this hypothesis "the quantum of explanation," which is the book's title. We expect to publish it in 2014.

[31] See Royce's critique of Nietzsche's "will to power," in "Nietzsche," *Josiah Royce's Late Writings: A Collection of Unpublished and Scattered Works*, ed. Fram M. Oppenheim, S.J., 2 vols. (Bristol: Thoemmes, 2001), vol. 1, 174–187.

[32] Royce, *The World and the Individual*, Second Series (New York: Macmillan, 1901), 228.

[33] Royce, *The Problem of Christianity*, ed. John E. Smith (Chicago: University of Chicago Press, 1968 [1913]), 235.

[34] Ibid., 236.

[35] Ibid., 237.

[36] Ibid., 238.

[37] Ibid., 243–44.

[38] Ibid., 244–45.

[39] Ibid., 249.

[40] Ibid. Cf., John E. Smith, *Royce's Social Infinite* (New York: Liberal Arts, 1950), 68.

[41] Royce, *The Problem of Christianity*, 254.

[42] Ibid., 255.

[43] Ibid., 80.

[44] Ibid., 82.

[45] Ibid., 82–83.

[46] The misuse of the the US military by its forces is well documented and discussed by Andrew Bacevich in *The Limits of Power: The End of American Exceptionalism* (New York: Holt, 2008).

[47] Nir Eisikovits, "The Corporation Is Not a Person," in *Personalism: Science, Philosophy, Theology* 4 (2003), 57–68. The title is misleading, and was apparently chosen by the editors of the journal. The author's title was "Forensick, Grammatical, and

Corporate Persons: A Family Relationship." This is far more descriptive of the contents, but I suppose the article might also have been called "The Corporation Is Not a Person— Yet."

[48] See Royce, *The Problem of Christianity*, 50–51.

[49] Miroslaw Kowalczyk has done an excellent job of summing up the personalist position on the personhood of nation states, synthesizing the views of numerous other personalists in "The Personal Dimension of the Reality of Nation" in *Personalism: Science, Philosophy, Theology* 7 (2004), 97–102. It is a short essay, but it goes directly to the heart of the issue and gets it right, in my judgment. Of particular importance is Kowalczyk's recognition that not only fascism, extreme forms of socialism, and communism are impersonalist distortions of the personhood of nations, but also "aggressive modern liberalism," which in this country would include both major political parties, including what we call "neo-conservatism," the whole of which Kowalczyk rightly says is "based on leftist views" and "repudiates" forms of national life in exchange for globalism and cosmopolitanism (98). The modernist press is here the issue, for its impersonal treatment of nations and citizens. It is doubtful whether fascism and communism could ever be anything but impersonalist, yet liberalism, classical conservatism, and democratic socialism, along with a variety of economic systems, probably can be institutionalized in ways that do not depersonalize and therefore dehumanize a citizenry. This could be done, but it is not being done.

[50] Of the greatest value, in my judgment, are Oppenheim's two books, *Royce's Mature Philosophy of Religion* (Notre Dame: University of Notre Dame Press, 1987), and *Royce's Mature Ethics* (Notre Dame: University of Notre Dame Press, 1993).

[51] See Reinhold Niebuhr, *Moral Man and Immoral Society* (New York: Scribner's, 1932). For the defense of the prophetic stance, see Niebuhr, *An Interpretation of Christian Ethics* (New York: Harper, 1935).

[52] For Niebuhr's personalism and its relation to educational practice, see my "Is There Room for God in Education?" in *Public Affairs Quarterly* 9:1 (January 1995), 1–13.

[53] Josiah Royce, *California: From the Conquest in 1846 to the Second Vigilance Committee in San Francisco* (New York: Knopf, 1948 [1886]), 123.

[54] The term "common sense" should not be passed over lightly here, not least because Royce so often appeals to it explicitly in his discussions of truth and community, but also because the thorough understanding of "common sense," or *sensus communis* remains at the heart of social philosophy when it is undertaken in its humane and most defensible form. The Scottish common sense school is a factor here also. A personalist philosophy of institutions is being gradually worked out by Thomas O. Buford, and I am especially optimistic about these efforts because he has grounded it in the philosophy of Vico, which I think is a fine guide for such a project. See his essay "Primary Institutions," in *The Personalist Forum* 15:2 (Fall 1999), 205–214; his book *In Search of a Calling: The College's Role in Shaping Identity* (Macon: Mercer University Press, 1995); and his *Trust, Our Second Nature: Crisis, Reconciliation, and the Personal* (Lanham,: Lexington, 2009).

CHAPTER 9. CONSERVATISM AND PROGRESS

[1] Three excellent papers were presented on the topic of the relationship between Royce's conception of the beloved community and King's philosophy at the American

Philosophical Association's Central Division meeting in 2005, only one of which is published, Gary L. Herstein's "The Roycean Roots of the Beloved Community," in *The Pluralist* 4:2 (Summer 2009), 91–107. Herstein traces the history of the concept of the beloved community and showing how it found its way from Royce's philosophy into King's. But there is also a paper by Dwayne A. Tunstall called "Royce and King on *Agape* and the Beloved Community," analyzing the philosophical differences and similarities between King's thinking on this topic and Royce's, and a paper by Rufus Burrow, Jr., that responds to and deepens the other two. Hopefully these other two papers will soon appear in print. In the meantime Burrow's book *God and Human Diginity: The Personalism, Theology, and Ethics of Martin Luther King, Jr.* (Notre Dame: University of Notre Dame Press, 2006) has appeared and contains some discussion of the idea of the beloved community in Royce and how it comes into King's thought (see pp. 161–173). The papers mentioned above are far more detailed.

[2] In an earlier version of this chapter, presented before the Royce Society in 2006, James A. Good, in his commentary, rightly noted that I had neglected to mention the important influence of classical political thought upon the formation of the republic in the United States. His commentary, "Thoughts on Randall E. Auxier's 'Royce's Conservatism'," appears after my own essay in *The Pluralist* 2:2 (Summer 2007), 44–55, 56–62. Since receiving his commentary I have returned to study the matter, especially *The Debate on the Constitution*, ed. Bernard Bailyn, two parts (New York: Library of America, 1993). A close reading of the original documents has led me to conclude, with Good, that the thought of the Roman Republic was perhaps more important in the formation of the American republic than the modern political theories. Nevertheless, this is something not widely known, even in the educated public, and I here report a widely held perception about the origins of American liberalism, not something necessarily supported by a better understanding of the actual history.

[3] Possibly the most important conservative progressive in American history was George Washington, who nicely embodies nearly the whole of what I mean by the term. This combination of traits is nicely brought out in the recent biography of Washington by Ron Chernow (admittedly a bit more conservative an author than I am comfortable with, but a good book is a good book). See his *Washington: A Life* (New York: Penguin, 2010).

[4] Aaron Fortune's work is to be found in a dissertation at Southern Illinois University, Carbondale (2007). The key ideas were presented in a session entitled "Why Liberalism Is Losing: A Missing Voice in American Progressive Politics," for the 14th Annual Philosophical Collaborations Conference, Southern Illinois University Carbondale, March 2nd–3rd, 2006.

[5] Royce makes this point in many places, and we have treated it in some detail in Chapters 5 through 8. Two clear places are, in "Self Consciousness, Social Consciousness and Nature," in *Basic Writings of Josiah Royce*, ed. John J. McDermott, 2 vols. (New York: Fordham University Press, 2005), vol. 1, 427–28; and *The World and the Individual*, Second Series (New York: Macmillan, 1901), 168–174.

[6] See Royce, *The Religious Aspect of Philosophy* (Boston: Houghton Mifflin, 1885), chs. 9–10, and the other sources cited in Chapters 5 through 8.

[7] I readily grant that the mode of expansion Royce has in mind is assimilation of all people to the supposedly superior values and practices of Anglo-european culture, as Tommy J. Curry has argued. One can be a progressive and an assimilationist at the same time.

⁸ Josiah Royce, "The Nature of Voluntary Progress," in *Berkeley Quarterly* (July 1880), 161–189, reprinted in *Fugitive Essays*, ed. Jacob Loewenberg (Cambridge: Harvard University Press, 1920), 96–132, this passage is from p. 97 of the latter.

⁹ For example, Royce draws upon this view in his exclusion of the German government, after the invasion of Belgium by Germany in 1914 (and the slaughter of Belgian civilians), and the sinking of the *Lusitania* in 1915, from any and all hope of inclusion in the progress of humankind. This is not because the German nationalists are being excluded by the progressives, but because, in Royce's judgment, they have chosen to exclude themselves through a willful parochialism, a fixed and unbending conception of who does and does not "count," excluding particularly their innocent victims in Belgium and aboard the *Lusitania*. See Royce, "The Destruction of the *Lusitania*," in *The Hope of the Great Community* (New York: Macmillan, 1916), esp. 22–23; and "An American Thinker on the War" (which is a printed letter to L.P. Jacks) in *Hibbert Journal* 14 (1915), 37–42, reprinted in *The Letters of Josiah Royce*, ed. John Clendenning (Chicago: University of Chicago Press, 1970), 627–631. I do not think Royce's estimation of German action and sentiment in the case of the *Lusitania* are borne out by subsequent history—in part because it appears that the Germans explicitly warned persons considering boarding that ship that it would be considered a transport of war. The following notice was placed in American newspapers by the German Embassy on 1st May 1915, the day the *Lusitania* sailed: "Travelers intending to embark on the Atlantic voyage are reminded that a state of war exists between Germany and her allies and Great Britain and her allies; that the zone of war includes the waters adjacent to the British Isles; that, in accordance with formal notice given by the Imperial German Government, vessels flying the flag of Great Britain, or of any of her allies, are liable to destruction in those waters and that travelers sailing in the war zone on ships of Great Britain or her allies do so at their own risk." This seems like fairly clear notice, taking away the claim that this was a sneak attack. See http://www.gwpda.org/naval/lusika04.htm. Since the Germans had solid reason to believe the *Lusitania* was in fact bearing armaments and that the British authorities were using innocents as human shields, in violation of treaties and international laws of the sea, and because evidence now seems to confirm that the Germans were in fact telling the truth about this, it was the Americans, Canadians, and British who had acted in an unconscionable way by misusing civilians. Royce was probably mistaken in his response to this incident, but it does not follow that he was mistaken in his larger estimate of German nationalism and the appropriate response to it. The German invasion of Belgium and the atrocious treatment of its civilians simply because they happened to occupy the most strategically promising approach to France is not as easily blamed upon others. Even if Royce lost his objectivity in the *Lusitania* case, his overall judgment about whether the Germans had willfully removed themselves from the hope of the beloved community is probably defensible. I would like to thank Zachary Walton for his work on the *Lusitania* case, and Jason M. Bell for his investigations of the Belgium invasion, both currently unpublished, from which my understanding has benefited.

¹⁰ It has been suggested to me by Tommy J. Curry's articles on Royce, that there was a cultural shift at Harvard and among intellectual circles in the 1890s and the first decade of the twentieth century, from an anthropological and biological model of race hierarchy, to a cultural model, involving a hierarchy of "levels of civilization," in which an undeniably racist and colonialist-imperialist model of civilizational development was adopted, using European development as the standard, the high water mark of human

attainment. This idea of "cultural" development became a euphemistic and functional version of racism. I do not doubt that this shift in the propagation of racism happened (the evidence is everywhere), and while those propounding such a model were perhaps largely unconscious of the built-in racism (and at least in the cases of James and Royce, there was even active opposition of imperialism), it is hard to deny that conceiving of civilization along such lines draws upon the presupposed goodness of the white "achievement" and the implied backwardness and inferiority of non-white races. In spite of his opposition to American colonialism and imperialism (from the very beginning, for *The History of California* is a clear indictment of such expansionism, and of the anti-Hispanic racism inherent in it), Royce certainly embraced this implicitly racist model of civilization. It would be difficult to articulate his notion of "progress" without something like the ideal of cultural development exemplified by white Europeans, so it may be impossible to expunge racism from Royce's progressivism—in spite of the fact that he intended to be eradicating racism, as he understood it. This makes Royce's views on progress at least partly "parochial" by our contemporary standard, although they are clearly "progressive" by the standards of his own time. I agree completely with Curry's case and I regard it as decisive to the question of racism and white supremacy in Royce. See Curry, "Royce, Racism and the Colonial Ideal: White Supremacy and the Illusion of Civilization in Josiah Royce's Account of the White Man's Burden," in *The Pluralist* 4:3 (Fall 2009), 10–25. It is also clear that Royce was an anti-black racist of a quite typical stripe in his everyday attitudes; John Clendenning presented an example of this when at the Harvard conference on James and Royce in May of 2007, he read a letter Royce wrote describing poor service he had gotten at a restaurant in Saratoga Springs, due to the inattention of the "nigger" servants. The letter was filled with stereotypes and language that many who admire Royce can wish he had not used. See *Letters of Josiah Royce*, 179–180. Curry works out this strand of thought further in his essay "On the Dark Arts: Problematizing Royce's Assimilative Arts as a Response to LeConte's 'Southern Problems'," yet to be published. Here Curry connects Royce's tendencies to a colonialist tendency and an assimilationist view of race expressed particularly in Royce's essay of 1900, "Some Characteristic Tendencies of American Civilization," now available in the expanded edition of Royce's *Race Questions, Provencialism and Other American Problems*, eds. Scott L. Pratt and Shannon Sullivan (New York: Fordham University Press, 2009), 223–248. Thus, with Curry, I am to some extent disagreeing with the interpretations of Royce on race questions given by Jacquelyn Kegley in "Is a Coherent Racial Identity Essential to Genuine Individuals and Communities? Josiah Royce on Race," in *Journal of Speculative Philosophy* 19:3 (2005), 216–228, and her "Josiah Royce on Race: Issues in Context," in *The Pluralist* 4:3 (Fall 2009), 1–9; and Elizabeth Duquette, in "Embodying Community, Disembodying Race: Josiah Royce on 'Race Questions and Prejudices'," in *American Literary History*, 16:1 (2004), 29–57; and Shannon Sullivan's "Royce's 'Race Questions and Prejudices'," in the expanded edition of Royce's book by that title (cited above), 20–33; and Scott Pratt's "Introduction" to that same volume, all of whom take a more sanguine view of Royce's race theory.

[11] Many scholars have observed that Machiavelli marks the beginning of liberal politics and especially the distinction of ethics and politics, but for one thorough account, consult Ernst Cassirer, *The Myth of the State* (New Haven: Yale University Press, 1946), 116–175.

[12] Obviously this is a very broad generalization about Wilson that would require a thorough analysis to stand. Essentially this claim is made by the Wilson scholar August

Heckscher, among others, when he says: "The emancipation of the individual was not, it should be emphasized, for the purpose of letting the individual do as he desired. The individualism of a man like Wilson was not an invitation to eccentricity; it was a call to duty and honor. For in proportion as a man was disentangled from worldly interests, his relation with the creator becomes the more direct and unshaded. . . .The individual must be righteous." See "Introduction," to *The Politics of Woodrow Wilson* (New York: Harper, 1956), xviii. See also Wilson's writings in chs 3 and 4 of this same book. The Calvinist worldview is largely responsible for the combination of an atomistic metaphysics of person with methodological conservatism in Wilson's case, and such a view is common among Calvinists of many varieties, coming into the present neo-conservative public cant about "moral values." Neo-conservative political leaders in the present are in fact methodological liberals (far closer to Hobbes than to any conservative) who seek to understand and exercise power on its own terms, but many of their supporters among the people are those who would come closer to Wilson's view of things, and who are insensible to the contradiction between the rhetoric and the policies of the neo-conservatives. Part of the reason it is a great mistake to read Royce through a Calvinist lens (as John E. Smith and many who follow him have done) is that Calvinists treat the individual as a fallen metaphysical ultimate, while Royce does not. It is not difficult to account for Royce's progressivism in such an account (there can be Calvinist progressives), but his relational personalism, his ontology, and the underpinnings of his theory of community are made incomprehensible by such a reading. Royce's views are closer to the Restorationist Campbellites than to the Calvinists.

[13] Royce, *The Conception of God*, ed. G.H. Howison (New York: Macmillan, 1897), 258.

[14] Royce developed a social version of the "law of docility" many years before he gave it a psychological form. That is, in the development of Royce's thought, the law of social conservatism—that the past, present and future are so related as to conserve past experience and adapt it to present forms—is the empirical observation he first grasped, and the "law of docility" may now be seen both as an application of the principle of social conservatism, and as a *product* of it. In other words, the reason our individual experience accumulates in such a way as to be docile to its past is because social experience is conserved. In mythic consciousness, social experience is conserved but does not result in the creation of individuals—which is to say, there simply is no relevant distinction between my experience and yours for mythic consciousness, and hence, individuality does not develop. This case is made in great detail by Ernst Cassirer in *The Philosophy of Symbolic Forms, Volume 2: Mythical Thought*, trans. Ralph Manheim (New Haven: Yale University Press, 1955 [1925]). For Cassirer, the "individual," the one who credits the history of his own experience in such a way as to credit the ways in which it is "docile" (in Royce's terms) to its past, is the greatest achievement of human culture. Thus, I am asserting, with Cassirer, that what Royce calls the "law of docility" is the contingent product of a prior social conservatism, and its effect is the creation of human individuals. I do not think it an accident that Royce grasped the social structure first and the psychological outcome of it only later.

[15] This law of social conservation as Royce articulates it ran twenty years ahead of the Progressive Era in the United States, and the basic idea Royce articulates here is one found everywhere during that Era. Clearly the roots of it are to be found in the philosophies of Mill and Spencer, but how important Royce's version of the "law" may have been in giving birth to the Progressive Era would be a study of its own. I will say that the best

application of this idea I have found among the progressives is done by Gifford Pinchot, who was the governor of Pennsylvania, a member of Roosevelt's cabinet, and the founder of the United States Forest Service. In his book, *The Fight for Conservation* (New York: Doubleday, 1910), Pinchot combines pragmatism with progressivism to argue that "conservation," in his sense of it, just *is* democracy. His way of using the term "conservation" comes down to us in our contemporary usage regarding natural resources (water and soil conservation, for instance), but is a mere shadow of what Pinchot meant by the term. I find no mention of Pinchot in Royce's writings, and no mention of Royce in Pinchot's, but they must have known of one another, since Pinchot was among the small handful of people who financially supported Peirce when he lived in Milford, Pennsylvania (Pinchot's home town). But that is not important. The progressive ideas were everywhere by 1900, and the idea that these progressive purposes should be built on "conservation" was common in that time. Royce was well ahead of the curve in this regard.

[16] I have earlier noted that Royce anticipated James in certain crucial aspects of the latter's psychology, and have indicated that I do not think it possible to sort out once and for all who was the "true" originator of the ideas, such as selective attention or the stream of thought. Now I would point out that Royce takes this view of habit in 1880, ten years before James's *Principles of Psychology* was published, and before Royce moved to Boston, but obviously only after there had been very important contact and philosophical discussion between Royce and James.

[17] Royce certainly never thought ontology could be guided solely by science (indeed, it was the reverse), but he does have an interesting discussion of the principle of the conservation of energy in a letter to George Holmes Howison. See *The Letters of Josiah Royce*, ed. John Clendenning (Chicago: University of Chicago Press, 1970), 185–87.

[18] See Reinhold Niebuhr, *Moral Man and Immoral Society* (New York: Scribner's, 1930).

CHAPTER 10. TEACHING

[1] See my article, "A New Class Consciousness," in *Empirical Magazine* (September 2012), 24–31.

[2] Sane people everywhere in the present, and historians of the future, should pay attention to the analysis of the last fifty years of US and world history offered by Andrew Bacevich in his book *The Limits of Power: The End of American Exceptionalism* (New York: Holt, 2009). This adept application of Reinhold Niebuhr's philosophy of history provides, in my judgment, the most insightful assessment of what has happened in recent world history and why. I have my reservations about Bacevitch's grasp of American exceptionalism, however.

[3] See Royce, "Provencialism," in *Basic Writings of Josiah Royce*, ed. John J. McDermott, 2 vols. (New York: Fordham University Press, 2006), 2:1067–088.

[4] Rollo Walter Brown, *Harvard Yard in the Golden Age* (New York: Current Books, 1948), 59.

[5] From a letter to Ellen Axson (soon to be Wilson), February 5th, 1884. In Ray Stannard Baker, *Woodrow Wilson: Life and Letters, Youth 1856–1890* (Garden City: Doubleday, Page, and Co., 1927), 196–97. The impression Royce made on Wilson was enduring. Twenty-four years later Wilson said in another letter to his (now) wife: "The man I met at the Simpsons . . . is a Judge Pennington . . . I had another talk with him the

other day and found him very lively and interesting—though he does not compare with my judicial friend in Bermuda [Henry Cowper Golla, Chief Justice of Bermuda], who affects me in his own field very much as Professor [Josiah] Royce does, —as a walking, sentient mind agog about everything and not to be resisted or put off or mystified or left half answered in its inquiries." Letter of July 27th, 1908, in *The Papers of Woodrow Wilson*, vol. 18 (1908–09), ed, Arthur S. Link (Princeton: Princeton University Press, 1975), 378. The relationship between Royce and Wilson is intriguing and has been little noticed. I am able to place them at the same place and time on a number of occasions: a lunch in Princeton in January of 1894 when Royce spoke there to the "Monday Night Club"; both receiving honorary doctorates from Johns Hopkins in February of 1902; Wilson introducing Royce at the APA, hosted by Princeton in 1903; and both speaking at the International Congress of Arts and Sciences in St. Louis in September 1904. There may have been other meetings. Among Wilson's papers at the Library of Congress is a copy of Royce's "The Duties of Americans in the Present War," and also, interestingly, somehow Wilson possessed a previously unknown letter from Royce to C.A. Cockayne, dated June 17th, 1908. I am not a historian, but there is an article if not a book here in the Royce-Wilson relationship.

[6] Royce, *The Problem of Christianity* (Chicago: University of Chicago Press, 1967 [1913]), 333.

[7] Douglas R. Anderson, *Philosophy Americana: Making Philosophy at Home in American Culture* (New York: Fordham University Press, 2006), 47.

[8] This letter is in the Harvard University Archives, HUG 1755.3.3, Josiah Royce Papers: "Incoming Correspondence to Josiah Royce, ca. 1876–1916," Box 1.

[9] James received a letter from Harry Norman Gardiner on November 12th, 1901, announcing the formation of the APA and inviting him to join. See *The Correspondence of William James*, ed. I. Skrupskelis, et al. (Charlottesville: University of Virginia Press, 2001), vol. 9, 639.

[10] Ibid., 558.

[11] See the essay by Bruce Wilshire, "'The Ph.D. Octopus': William James's Prophetic Grasp of the Failures of Academic Professionalism," in *Fashionable Nihilism: A Critique of Analytic Philosophy* (Albany: SUNY Press, 2002), 31–49; see also Kim Townsend, *Manhood at Harvard: William James and Others* (New York: Norton, 1996), 163–64.

[12] James Campbell, *A Thoughtful Profession: The Early Years of the American Philosophical Association* (Chicago: Open Court, 2006), 69.

[13] The outstanding work of James Campbell in his history of the APA (see above) and also the labors of Richard T. Hull in documenting the presidential speeches have been crucial to our understanding in historical perspective both what was and what might have been. See Hull, *Presidential Addresses of the American Philosophical Association*, currently 7 vols., 1900–1970 (Buffalo: Prometheus, 1999–2006). There are, however, frequent factual errors in Hull's brief biographies of the presidents, regarding dates, book titles, institutions served, and the like. It is advisable to verify independently factual information drawn from this latter source. It is nevertheless a very good thing to have these addresses collected and available.

[14] This essay was originally published in *The Journal of Philosophy*, vol. 12 (January 1912), but is reprinted in *Royce's Logical Essays*, ed. Daniel S. Robinson (Dubuque: Brown, 1951), 232–253.

[15] Campbell, *A Thoughtful Profession*, 73; Hull, *Presidential Addresses*, 1:30–31.

¹⁶ Some notion of what Royce might have said can be gleaned from his "Introductory Statement at the Philosophical Conference of October 19th, 1903," an unpublished manuscript, HARP, Box 73. Here Royce discusses the relation of professional and technical philosophy to the purpose of philosophy in the world. He praises Bergson, the British personal idealists, and pragmatism for making practical concerns primary. He praises Heinrich Rickert for placing moral obligation before the question of Being—something Heidegger didn't learn from his teacher.

¹⁷ I am aware that there is evidence of genuine community in the APA, and I do not wish readers to think that I am asserting it is in every sense bad and always was. For example, I am very much moved by the following letter from E.S. Brightman to Charles Hartshorne in December of 1933:

> Our small band of American philosophers has met with a real loss in the passing of Durant Drake, who was perhaps my best friend in the Association, although I disagreed with most of his characteristic theories. I hardly think his kind of panpsychism would satisfy you any better than it did me. But he was a real man, a loyal friend, and an earnest exponent of moral idealism in his social thinking. I shall miss him.

See *Hartshorne and Brightman on God, Process, and Persons: The Correspondence, 1922–1945*, eds. R.E. Auxier and M.Y.A. Davies (Nashville: Vanderbilt University Press, 2000), 12–13. The on-going will to interpret and the community of memory is clearly here, and seems to be, in Brightman's view, something the APA has facilitated. But it is a "small band" at this point, and the major changes that occurred with the influx of European philosophers displaced by the war is still in the future.

¹⁸ Leonard Harris has notoriously raked the APA over the coals for its institutionalized racism, analogizing it (more rhetorically than historically) to the Ku Klux Klan. See Harris, "'Believe It or Not' or the Ku Klux Klan and American Philosophy Exposed," in *Proceedings of the American Philosophical Association* 68:5 (May 1995), on-line at www.apa.udel.edu/apa/archive/newsletters/v95n1/black.asp. To say that Harris struck a nerve would be an understatement. I would like to go on record as saying that I think Harris has greatly *under*-estimated the damage done by the APA (and its ilk), not only in race relations and reinforcing myths of white supremacy, but in nearly every other domain of genuinely human moral development. I agree with Harris (his point more than his chosen mode of expression), and I do not think he goes far enough in his critique. Organizations like the KKK have a difficult time being "normalized" in their social contexts (although, as the Nazis proved, it *can* happen), and their marginal status usually prevents them from doing the sort of damage that can be done by an institution that *succeeds* in assimilating itself into the wider fabric of society—in this case, occupying a little pigeon hole within the wide range of academic organizations that presume to "speak for" the practitioners of the exalted human endeavors after which they are named—e.g., philosophy, language, history, psychology, biology, and the like. The presumption so to speak is the initial hubris—as though one should have to be a member of the APA to be a "legitimate" philosopher . . . bosh. And then the subsequent effort to foist such hubris on the public as *truth* is the institution's great betrayal of its namesake. It is as if one were to claim that only poets who are published by certain sanctioned publishers are true poets, or only musicians who are signed to a specific set of corporate record labels are true musicians. Nothing could be more ridiculous than to imagine that the APA or any academic or professional organization has a monopoly on what is or is not a fine example of the pursuit or practice of a fundamental human undertaking, like philosophy or medicine or any art. To serve music, for example, is to play and write it well, and to associate with

others who serve it with similar humility. To serve philosophy, philosophize well, sincerely, and to associate with others for whom this ideal is embraced with humility, not hubris. Whatever you do, don't for a moment imagine that pleasing a professional or scholarly organization has any relation to serving an ideal such as the pursuit of wisdom.

[19] Royce, "On Definitions and Debates," in *Royce's Logical Essays*, 232.

[20] Campbell mentions this "defensive" interpretation (see *A Thoughtful Profession*, 75), and mentions that the idea was defended by such scholars as Daniel J. Wilson and C. Wright Mills, but Campbell does not credit the claim, seeing it as a priori rather than well grounded in the historical evidence. I take issue with Campbell on this point because the presidential addresses of both Creighton and Alexander Thomas Ormand, the following year, make this lack of respect for philosophy a central point. These two sober individuals report both the perception and the defensive strategy as received opinion, and both would be in a better position to judge than Campbell, Wilson, Mills, or I. I think it is safe to take Creighton and Ormond at face value on this point, and that doing so is historical rather than a priori. It is understandable that Campbell chooses to devote his efforts to the ideals and aspirations of the APA in his history, but I think it needful to attend to the defensive, nay, "parochial" (in the sense set out in Chapter 9) aspect of the endeavor. This parochialism explains much about the subsequent history and current condition of the APA, even if it is not the most pleasant part of the story.

[21] See John McCumber, *Time in the Ditch: American Philosophy in the McCarthy Era* (Evanston: Northwestern University Press, 2001).

[22] See the essay by Bruce Wilshire, "'The Ph.D. Octopus': William James's Prophetic Grasp of the Failures of Academic Professionalism," in *Fashionable Nihilism: A Critique of Analytic Philosophy* (Albany: SUNY Press, 2002), 31–49. Wilshire shows that the problem goes back much further than McCumber suspects.

[23] Wilshire, *Fashionable Nihilism*, 1–2.

[24] Actually the swindle was exposed in 1998 when the World Congress of Philosophy met in Boston. A reporter from the *New York Times* asked, at a panel of luminaries "What have we learned from philosophy in the twentieth century?" The panel included Willard V. Quine, Donald Davidson, and some others whose names I will not mention since they are still alive. One is not supposed to ask this question. The panelists couldn't answer it. See Sarah Boxer, "At the End of a Century of Philosophizing, the Answer Is, Don't Ask," *New York Times*, August 15th, 1998, B9. Also see Jim Holt, "Quizzing the Philosophers," *Wall Street Journal*, August 21st, 1998, W13. The truth will out. The world took little notice. I was directed to these articles by Raymond Boisvert's "Richard Rorty: Philosopher of the Common Man, *Almost*," in *The Philosophy of Richard M. Rorty*, eds. Randall E. Auxier and Lewis E. Hahn, Library of Living Philosophers, vol. 32 (Chicago: Open Court, 2010).

[25] See Aristotle, *Nicomachean Ethics*, Book X.

[26] William A. Hammond, "James Edwin Creighton," in *Journal of Philosophy* 22:10 (1925), 253–56 (quote on 254).

[27] For an account of how Creighton understood the relationship between periodicals and the APA, see his presidential address, "The Purposes of a Philosophical Association," in Hull, *Presidential Addresses*, 1:31.

[28] An interesting and relatively benign version of this story appears in R.M. Wenley's *The Life and Work of George Sylvester Morris* (New York: Macmillan, 1917), 138–143.

[29] Hull, *Presidential Addresses*, 36.

[30] Ibid.

[31] Campbell recounts how an initially ambitious publishing program in the history of early American philosophy was supposed to be undertaken by the APA, in which Royce was playing an important role, but the effort seems to have died with Royce, producing only one book. See *A Thoughtful Profession*, 81–82.

[32] Cited in ibid., 101.

[33] Creighton, "The Purposes of a Philosophical Association," in Hull, 1:35.

[34] Ibid.

[35] See Katherine Gilbert, "James E. Creighton as Writer and Editor," *Journal of Philosophy* 22:10 (1925), 256–264.

[36] Ibid.

[37] Creighton, "The Purposes of a Philosophical Association," in Hull, 1:33.

[38] Royce, *The Problem of Christianity*, 43.

Bibliography

Works by Royce

An American Thinker on the War. *Hibbert Journal* 14 (1915), 37–42.
Augustus Graham Lectures of 1896. Six Unpublished Lectures. Harvard Archives Royce Papers, Boxes 52, 78.
Basic Writings, ed. John J. McDermott, 2 vols. (New York: Fordham University Press, 2005).
California: From the Conquest in 1846 to the Second Vigilance Committee in San Francisco (New York: Alfred A. Knopf, 1948 [1886]).
The Conception of God, ed. George Holmes Howison (New York: Macmillan, 1897).
The Conception of Immortality, the Ingersoll Lecture (Boston: Houghton Mifflin and Co., 1899).
The Eternal and the Practical. In *Presidential Addresses of the American Philosophical Association, 1901–1910*, ed. Richard T. Hull (Dordrecht: Kluwer Academic Publishers, 1999), 73–93.
Fugitive Essays, ed. Jacob Loewenberg (Cambridge: Harvard University Press, 1920).
The Hope of the Great Community (New York: Macmillan, 1916).
Introductory Statement at the Philosophical Conference of October 19th, 1903, in Harvard Archives Royce Papers, Box 73.
Is There a Science of Education? *Educational Review* 1 (1891), 15–25, 121–132.
Josiah Royce's Late Writings: A Collection of Unpublished and Scattered Works, ed. Frank M. Oppenheim, S.J., 2 vols. (Bristol: Thoemmes Press, 2001).
Kant's Relation to Modern Philosophic Progress. *Journal of Speculative Philosophy* 15 (1881), 360–381.
The Letters of Josiah Royce, ed. John Clendenning (Chicago: University of Chicago Press, 1970).
Metaphysics: His Philosophy 9 Course of 1915–1916, as Stenographically Recorded by Ralph W. Brown and Complemented by Notes from Byron F. Underwood, eds. William Ernest Hocking, Richard Hocking, and Frank M. Oppenheim (Albany: SUNY Press, 1998).
"Mind-Stuff" and Reality. *Mind* 6 (1881), 365–377.
The Nature of Voluntary Progress. *Berkeley Quarterly* (July, 1880), 161–189.
The Nature and Use of Absolute Truth. Lecture I of The Harrison Lectures in Response to John Dewey, presented February 6th–8th, 1911, typescript. Harvard University Archives, HUG 1755.5, vol. 85, items 3, 4, and 5.

Outlines of Psychology (New York: Macmillan, 1903).
The Philosophy of Loyalty (New York: Macmillan, 1908).
The Problem of Christianity, 2 vols. (New York: Macmillan, 1913).
The Problem of Christianity, one volume edition, ed. John E. Smith (Chicago: University of Chicago Press, 1968).
The Problem of Job. *The New World* 6 (1897), 261–281.
Pussy Blackie's Travels: There's No Place Like Home. Eds. Randall E. Auxier and Robin A. Wallace (Penn Valley, CA: Artemis Books, 2013).
Race Questions, Provincialism, and Other American Problems, expanded edition, eds. Scott L. Pratt and Shannon Sullivan (New York: Fordham University Press, 2009).
Royce's Logical Essays, ed. Daniel S. Robinson (Dubuque: Wm. C. Brown Co., 1951).
The Religious Aspect of Philosophy (Boston: Houghton, Mifflin and Co, 1885).
Studies of Good and Evil (New York: D. Appleton and Co., 1898).
William James and Other Essays on the Philosophy of Life (New York: Macmillan, 1911).
The World and the Individual, First and Second Series (New York: Macmillan, 1899, 1901).

Works on and Related to Royce

Anderson, Douglas R. Royce, Philosophy, and Wandering: A Job Description. In *Philosophy Americana: Making Philosophy at Home in American Culture* (New York: Fordham University Press, 2006).

———. Who's a Pragmatist: Royce and Peirce at the Turn of the Century. *Transactions of the Charles S. Peirce Society* 41:3 (Summer 2005), 467–481.

Anderson, Douglas R., and Carl Hausman. Conversations on Peirce: Reals and Ideals (New York: Fordham University Press, 2013).

Auxier, Randall E., ed., *Critical Responses to Royce*, 3 vols. (Bristol: Thoemmes Press, 2000).

———. Josiah Royce. (Relates to this volume, Chapter 1) In *The Dictionary of Modern American Philosophers*, General Editor John Shook (Bristol: Thoemmes Press, 2005), vol. 4, 2089–096.

———. Royce's Fictional Ontology. (Chapter 2) In *The Relevance of Royce*, eds. Kelly Parker and Jason M. Bell (New York: Fordham University Press, 2010).

———. Mysticism and the Immediacy of God: Howison's and Hocking's Critique of Royce. (Chapter 3) *Personalist Forum*, 15:1 (Spring 1999), 59–83.

———. Two Types of Pragmatism. (Chapter 4) In *Dewey's Enduring Impact*, eds. John R. Shook and Paul Kurtz (Amherst: Prometheus Books, 2011); also in *Pragmatic Epistemologies*, eds. Roberto Brigati and Roberto Frega (Lanham: Lexington Books, 2011); also "Due tipi di pragmatismo," (Italian, trans. R. Brigati), in *Discipline Filosofiche* (a special issue on "Epistemologie pragmatiste"), eds. Roberto Brigati and Roberto Frega, XIX:2 (2009), 27–43.

———. Psychological, Phenomenological, and Metaphysical Individuality in Royce's Philosophy. (Chapter 5) In *Josiah Royce: American and European Values, Volume 3*, ed. Krzsytof Piotr Skowronski and Kelly Parker (Newcastle upon Tyne: Cambridge Scholars Publishing), .

———. Royce's Conservatism. (Chapter 9) *The Pluralist* 2:2 (Summer 2007), 44–55; a special issue on Royce's ethical philosophy (the selected proceedings of the Josiah Royce Society Conference in Oklahoma City, Oklahoma, April 2006).

———. Complex Negation, Necessity and Logical Magic. In The Relevance of Royce, eds. Kally A. Parker and Jason M. Bell (New York: Fordham University Press, 2013), 89–131.

———. Josiah Royce: In and of Grass Valley. In Bulletin of the Nevada County Historical Society, 67:3 (July 2013), 1–6.

———. Afterword: A Mystery about History. In Pussy Blackie's Travels by Josiah Royce, eds. Randall Auxier and Robin A. Wallace (Penn Valley, CA: Artemis Books, 2013), 49–59.

Buranelli, Vincent. *Josiah Royce* (New York: Twayne, 1964).

Cesarz, Gary L. Howison's Pluralistic Idealism: A Fifth Conception of Being? *The Personalist Forum* 15:1 (Spring 1999), 28–44.

———. A World of Difference: The Royce-Howison Debate on the Conception of God. *The Personalist Forum* 15:1 (Spring 1999), 84–128.

Bell, Jason M. The German Translation of Royce's Epistemology by Husserl's Student Winthrop Bell: A Neglected Bridge of Pragmatic-Phenomenological Interpretation? *The Pluralist* 6:1 (Winter 2011), 46–62.

———. The World and Its Selves: Royce and the Philosophy of Nature. *The Personalist Forum* 15:1 (Spring 1999), 167–184.

Clendenning, John. *The Life and Thought of Josiah Royce*, revised and expanded ed. (Nashville: Vanderbilt University Press, 1999).

Cormier, Harvey. Royce, James and Logic. *The Journal of Speculative Philosophy* 19:4, 201–214.

Cotton, James Harry. *Royce on the Human Self* (Cambridge: Harvard University Press, 1954).

Curry, Tommy J. On the Dark Arts: Problematizing Royce's Assimilative Arts as a Response to LeConte's 'Southern Problems'. An unpublished manuscript presented to the Josiah Royce Society, at the annual meeting of the Central Division of the American Philosophical Association, February 19th, 2010.

———. Royce, Racism, and the Colonial Ideal: White Supremacy and the Illusion of Civilization in Josiah Royce's Account of the White Man's Burden. *The Pluralist* 4:3 (Fall 2009), 10–25.

Duquette, Elizabeth. Embodying Community, Disembodying Race: Josiah Royce on 'Race Questions and Prejudices'. *American Literary History* 16:1 (2004), 29–57.

Fischer, Marilyn. Locating Royce's Reasoning on Raced. *The Pluralist* 7:1 (Winter 2012), forthcoming.

Futch. Michael. The Dogma of Necessity: Royce on Nature and Scientific Law. *The Pluralist* 7:1 (Winter 2012).

Good, James A. Thought's on Randall E. Auxier's 'Royce's Conservatism'. *The Pluralist* 2:2 (Summer 2007), 56–62.

Harris, Leonard. "Believe It of Not" or the Ku Klux Klan and American Philosophy Exposed. *Proceedings of the American Philosophical Association* 68:5 (May 1995), <www.apa.udel.edu/apa/archive/newsletters/v95n1/black.asp>.

Hartshorne, Charles. Royce's Mistake—And Achievement. *Journal of Philosophy* 53:3 (February 2nd, 1956), 123–130.

Herstein, Gary L. The Roycean Roots of the Beloved Community. *The Pluralist* 4:2 (Summer 2009), 91–107.

Hine, Robert V. *Josiah Royce: From Grass Valley to Harvard* (Norman: University of Oklahoma Press, 1992).

Hocking, William Ernest. Preface to Gabriel Marcel's *Royce's Metaphysics*, trans. Virginia and Gordon Ringer (Chicago: Henry Regnery Co., 1956).

———. On Royce's Empiricism. *The Journal of Philosophy* 53:3 (February 2nd, 1956), 57–63.

Howison, George Holmes. Introduction to *Papers in Honor of Josiah Royce* (originally in the *Philosophical Review*, 1916), reprinted in *Critical Responses to Royce*, ed. Randall E. Auxier, vol. 3 (Bristol: Thoemmes Press, 2000), 9–13.

———. The Real Issue in *The Conception of God* (originally in the *Philosophical Review*, vol. 7, 1898) reprinted in *Critical Responses to Royce*, ed. Randall E. Auxier, vol. 2 (Bristol: Thoemmes Press, 2000), 24–28.

Kegley, Jacquelyn A.K. *Genuine Individuals and Genuine Communities: A Roycean Public Philosophy* (Nashville: Vanderbilt University Press, 1997).

———. Is a Coherent Racial Identity Essential to Genuine Individuals and Communities? Josiah Royce on Race. *Journal of Speculative Philosophy* 19:3 (2005), 216–228.

———. *Josiah Royce in Focus* (Bloomington: Indiana University Press, 2008).

———. Josiah Royce on Race: Issues in Context. *The Pluralist* 4:3 (Fall 2009), 1–9.

———. Royce as Psychologist: A Forgotten Aspect of His Thought. Unpublished manuscript presented at Royce, California and the World: A Conference, August 16–18, 2013.

Lamberth, David, ed. *James and Royce Reconsidered: Reflections on the Centenary of Pragmatism* (Cambridge: Harvard Divinity School, 2008).

Marcel, Gabriel. *Royce's Metaphysics*, trans. Virginia and Gordon Ringer (Chicago: Henry Regnery Co., 1956).

McCumber, John. *Time in the Ditch: American Philosophy in the McCarthy Era* (Evanston: Northwestern University Press, 2001).

McDermott, John J. The Confrontation between Royce and Howison. *Transactions of the Charles S. Peirce Society* 30:4 (Fall 1994), 779–790.

McGinn, Joseph P. The Power to Will: Refiguring Selfhood in Royce's Philosophy. *The Personalist Forum* 15:1 (Spring 1999), 143–152.

McLachlan, James. George Holmes Howison: The Conception of God Debate and the Beginnings of Personal Idealism. *The Personalist Forum* 11:1 (Spring 1995), 1–13.

———. George Holmes Howison's "The City of God and the True God as Its Head": The Royce-Howison Debate over the Idealist Conception of God. *The Personalist Forum* 15:1 (Spring 1999), 5–27.

Oppenheim, Frank M. Josiah Royce's Intellectual Development: An Hypothesis. *Idealistic Studies* 6 (1976), 85–102.

———. *Reverence for the Relations of Life: Re-imagining Pragmatism via Josiah Royce's Interactions with Peirce, James, and Dewey* (Notre Dame: University of Notre Dame Press, 2005).

———. *Royce's Mature Ethics* (Notre Dame: University of Notre Dame Press, 1993).

———. *Royce's Mature Philosophy of Religion* (Notre Dame: University of Notre Dame Press, 1987).

———. *Royce's Voyage Down Under: A Journey of the Mind* (Lexington: University Press of Kentucky, 1980).

Pfeifer, David E. Royce's Influence on Peirce. Unpublished manuscript presented at Royce, California and the World: A Conference, August 16–18, 2013.

Powell, Thomas F. *Josiah Royce* (New York: Washington Square Press, 1967).

Pratt, Scott L. Introduction. In *Race Questions, Provincialism, and Other American Problems*, expanded edition, eds. Scott L. Pratt and Shannon Sullivan (New York: Fordham University Press, 2009).

Price, Thomas W. The Appreciation of Natural Beings and the Finitude of Consciousness. *The Personalist Forum* 15:1 (Spring 1999), 153–166.

Robinson, Daniel S. *Royce and Hocking: American Idealists* (Boston: The Christopher Publishing House, 1968).

Royce, Sarah. *A Frontier Lady: Recollections of the Gold Rush and Early California*, ed. Ralph Henry Gabriel (New Haven: Yale University Press, 1932).

Sherover, Charles M. Royce's Pragmatic Idealism and Existential Phenomenology. In *From Kant and Royce to Heidegger*, ed. Gregory M. Johnson (Washington, D.C.: Catholic University of America Press, 2003), 91–108.

Smith, John E. *Royce's Social Infinite: The Community of Interpretation* (New York: Liberal Arts Press, 1950).

———. *The Spirit of American Philosophy*, revised edition (Albany: SUNY Press, 1983).

Straton, George Douglas. *Theistic Faith for Our Time: An Introduction to the Process Philosophies of Royce and Whitehead* (Washington, D.C.: University Press of America, 1979).

Sullivan, Shannon. Royce's "Race Questions and Prejudices." In *Race Questions, Provincialism, and Other American Problems*, expanded edition, eds. Scott L. Pratt and Shannon Sullivan (New York: Fordham University Press, 2009), 20–33.

Tunstall, Dwayne A. Concerning the God that Is Only a Concept: A Marcellian Critique of Royce's God. *Transactions of the Charles S. Peirce Society* 42:3 (Summer 2006), 394–416.

———. Josiah Royce and the New Realists: Seeing Their Metaphysical Differences Up-Close. In *The Relevance of Royce*, eds. Kelly A. Parker and Jason M. Bell (New York: Fordham University Press, forthcoming).

———. *Yes, but Not Quite: Encountering Josiah Royce's Ethico-religious Insight* (Fordham University Press, 2009).

Tyman, Stephen. Royce and the Destiny of Idealism. *The Personalist Forum* 15:1 (Spring 1999), 45–58.

Other Works Cited and Consulted

Alexander, Thomas M. Dewey's Denotative-Empirical Method: A Thread through the Labyrinth. *Journal of Speculative Philosophy* 18:3 (2004), 248–256.

Allen, Michael W. William James: Social Philosopher. Doctoral dissertation, Southern Illinois University Carbondale (2003).

Auxier, Randall E., ed. Bergson and the Calculus of Intuition. Papers and discussion by Pete A.Y. Gunter, Carl Hausman, and Randall E. Auxier. *Process Studies* 28:3–4 (Fall–Winter 1999), 267–345.

———. Bowne on Time, Evolution. and History. *Journal of Speculative Philosophy* 12:3 (1998), 181–203.

———. The Death of Darwinism and the Limits of Evolution. *Philo* 9:2 (Fall–Winter 2006), 193–220.

———. The Decline of Evolutionary Naturalism in Later Pragmatism. In *Pragmatism:*

From Progressivism to Postmodernism, eds. David DePew and Robert Hollinger (New York: Praeger Books, 1995), 180–207.

———. Editorial Statement. *The Pluralist* 1:1 (Spring 2006), v–vii, 1–12.

———. George Holmes Howison. In *The Dictionary of Modern American Philosophers*, General Editor John Shook (Bristol: Thoemmes Press, 2005), vol. 2, 1179–185.

———. God as Catholic and Personal: A Protestant Perspective on Norris Clarke's Neo-Thomistic Personalism. *International Philosophical Quarterly* 40:2 (June 2000), 235–252.

———. Immediacy and Purpose in Brightman's Philosophy" in *Hartshorne and Brightman on God, Process, and Persons: The Correspondence*, eds. Randall E. Auxier and Mark Y.A. Davies (Nashville: Vanderbilt University Press, 2000), 132–154.

———. Influence as Confluence: Bergson and Whitehead. *Process Studies* 28:3–4 (Fall–Winter 1999), 301–338.

———. Is There Room for God in Education? *Public Affairs Quarterly* 9:1 (January 1995), 1–13.

———. John Elof Boodin. In *The Dictionary of Modern American Philosophers*, General Editor John Shook (Bristol: Thoemmes Press, 2005), vol. 1, 283–88.

———. The Possibilities of Pluralism. *The Pluralist* 1:1 (Spring 2006), 1–12.

———. Whitehead's Radical Empiricism: Mementoes of a Timequake. In *Applied Process Thought II: Following a Trail Ablaze*, ed. Roger Mark Dibben and Rebecca Newton (Frankfurt am Main: Ontos Verlag, 2009), 75–100.

———. Why 100 Years Is Forever: Hartshorne on Immortality. *The Personalist Forum* 14:2 (1998), 109–132.

———. William Ernest Hocking. In *The Dictionary of Modern American Philosophers*, General Editor John Shook (Bristol: Thoemmes Press, 2005), vol. 2, 1128–135.

———. A New Class Consciousness. Empirical Magazine (September 2012), 24–31.

———. Scheler and the Existence of the Impersonal. In Proceedings of the 12th International Conference on Persons, eds. Philip Cronce and Anthony L. Cashio, forthcoming.

Auxier, Randall E. and Gary L. Herstein. *The Quantum of Explanation: Whitehead's Radical Empiricism*. Unpublished book manuscript, forthcoming.

Bacevich, Andrew. *The Limits of Power: The End of American Exceptionalism* (New York: Henry Holt and Co., 2008).

Baker, Ray Stannard. *Woodrow Wilson: Life and Letters, Youth 1856–1890* (Garden City: Doubleday, Page, and Co., 1927).

Bailyn, Bernard, ed. *The Debate on the Constitution*, two parts (New York: Library of America, 1993).

Bengtsson, Jan Olof. *The Worldview of Personalism: Origins and Early Development* (Oxford: Oxford University Press, 2006).

Bergson, Henri. *Creative Evolution*, trans. Arthur G. Mitchell (New York: Henry Holt, 1911 [1907]).

Blum, Deborah. *Ghost Hunters: William James and the Search for Scientific Proof of Life after Death* (New York: Penguin Press, 2006).

Boisvert, Raymond. Richard Rorty: Philosopher of the Common Man, *Almost*. In *The Philosophy of Richard Rorty*, eds. Randall E. Auxier and Lewis E. Hahn, Library of Living Philosophers, Volume 32 (Chicago: Open Court, 2009), 551–570.

Boodin, John Elof, *Truth and Reality* (New York: Macmillan, 1911).

———. *A Realistic Universe* (New York: Macmillan, 1916).
———. *Cosmic Evolution* (New York: Macmillan, 1925).
———. *God* (New York: Macmillan, 1934).
———. *Three Interpretations of the Universe* (New York: Macmillan, 1934).
———. *The Social Mind* (New York: Macmillan, 1939).
———. What Pragmatism Is and Is Not. *Journal of Philosophy, Psychology, and Scientific Methods* 6:23 (November 11th, 1909), 627–635.
———. William James as I knew Him. In *William James Remembered*, ed. Linda Simon (Lincoln: University of Nebraska Press, 1996), 207–232.
Bowne, Borden Parker. *The Essence of Religion* (Boston: Houghton Mifflin, 1910).
———. *The Immanence of God* (Boston: Houghton Mifflin, 1905).
———. *The Philosophy of Herbert Spencer: Being an Examination of the First Principles of His System* (New York: Nelson and Phillips, 1874).
———. *Theism* (New York: American Book Company, 1902).
———. *Theory of Thought and Knowledge* (New York: Harper and Brothers, 1899).
Boxer, Sarah. At the End of a Century of Philosophizing, the Answer Is, Don't Ask. *New York Times*, August 15th, 1998, B9.
Brands, H.W. *American Colossus: The Triumph of Capitalism 1865–1900* (New York: Doubleday, 2010).
Breckman, Warren. *Marx, the Young Hegelians, and the Origins of Radical Social Theory* (Cambridge: Cambridge University Press, 1999).
Brightman, Edgar Sheffield. *Moral Laws* (New York: Abingdon Press, 1933).
Brown, Rollo Walter. *Harvard Yard in the Golden Age* (New York: Current Books, 1948).
Buckham, John Wright, and George Malcolm Stratton, eds. *George Holmes Howison, Philosopher and Teacher* (Berkeley: University of California Press, 1934).
Buford, Thomas O. *In Search of a Calling: The College's Role in Shaping Identity* (Macon: Mercer University Press, 1995).
———. Primary Institutions. *The Personalist Forum* 15:2 (Fall 1999), 205–214.
———. *Trust, Our Second Nature: Crisis, Reconciliation, and the Personal* (Lanham, Lexington Books, 2009).
Burrow, Rufus, Jr. *God and Human Dignity: The Personalism, Theology, and Ethics of Martin Luther King, Jr.* (Notre Dame: University of Notre Dame Press, 2008).
———. *Personalism: A Critical Introduction* (St. Louis: Chalice Press, 1999).
Campbell, James. *A Thoughtful Profession: The Early Years of the American Philosophical Association* (Chicago: Open Court, 2006).
Capaldi, Nicholas, *The Enlightenment Project in the Analytic Conversation* (Dordrecht: Kluwer Academic Publishers, 1998).
Casati, Roberto, and Achille C. Varzi. *Parts and Places: The Structures of Spatial Representation* (Boston: MIT Press, 1999).
Cassirer, Ernst. *The Myth of the State* (New Haven: Yale University Press, 1946).
———. *The Philosophy of Symbolic Forms, Volume 2: Mythical Thought*, trans. Ralph Manheim (New Haven: Yale University Press, 1955 [1925]).
Chernow, Ron. *Washington: A Life* (New York: Penguin Books, 2010).
Copleston, Frederick. *A History of Philosophy*, 8 vols. (New York: Doubleday Image Books, 1965).
Creighton, James Edwin. *An Introductory Logic* (New York, 1898, rev. 1900, 1909, 1920; rev. by Harold Smart, 1932).
———. *Studies in Speculative Philosophy*, ed. H.R. Smart (New York, 1925).

Cunningham, G. Watts. In Memoriam: James Edwin Creighton. *International Journal of Ethics*, 35:2 (1925), pp. 214–16.
Dewey, John. *Later Works of John Dewey*, ed. Jo Ann Boydston, 17 vols. (Carbondale: Southern Illinois University Press, 1981–1997).
Dombrowski, Daniel. *Hartshorne and the Metaphysics of Animal Rights* (Albany: SUNY Press, 1988).
Edie, James M. *William James and Phenomenology* (Bloomington: Indiana University Press, 1987).
Eisikovits, Nir. The Corporation Is Not a Person. In *Personalism: Science, Philosophy, Theology* 4 (2003), 57–68.
Flewelling, Ralph Tyler. *Bergson and Personal Realism* (New York: Abingdon Press, 1920).
Fontinell, Eugene. *Self, God and Immortality: A Jamesian Investigation* (Philadelphia: Temple University Press, 1986).
Fortune, Aaron G. A Philosophical History of American Progressivism. Doctoral dissertation, Southern Illinois University Carbondale (2007).
———. Why Liberalism Is Losing: A Missing Voice in American Progressive Politics. Unpublished address presented at the 14th Annual Philosophical Collaborations Conference, Southern Illinois University Carbondale, March 2nd–3rd, 2006.
Gavin, William J. *William James and the Reinstatement of the Vague* (Philadelphia: Temple University Press, 1992).
Gilbert, Katherine. James E. Creighton as Writer and Editor. *Journal of Philosophy* 22:10 (1925), pp. 256–264.
Glaude, Eddie S., Jr. Tragedy and Moral Experience: John Dewey and Toni Morrison's *Beloved*, in *Pragmatism and the Problem of Race*, eds. Bill E. Lawson and Donald F. Koch (Bloomington: Indiana University Press, 2004), 89–121.
Gould, Stephen J. *The Structure of Evolutionary Theory* (Cambridge: Belknap Press of Harvard University. 2002).
Gunter, Pete A.Y. Bergson, Mathematics, and Creativity. *Process Studies*, 28:3–4 (Fall–Winter 1999), 268–288.
———. Darwinism: Six Scientific Alternatives. *The Pluralist* 1:1 (Spring 2006), 13–30.
Hammond, William A. James Edwin Creighton. *Journal of Philosophy* 22:10 (1925), 253–256.
Hartshorne, Charles, and Edgar Sheffield Brightman. *Hartshorne and Brightman on God, Process and Persons: The Correspondence*, eds. Randall E. Auxier and Mark Y.A. Davies (Nashville: Vanderbilt University Press, 2000).
Hickman, Larry A. Why Peirce Didn't Like Dewey's Logic. *Southwest Philosophy Review* 3 (1986), 178–189.
Hocking, William Ernest. *The Meaning of God in Human Experience* (New Haven: Yale University Press, 1912).
———. Ten Theses Establishing Metaphysical Idealism by Another Route. *Journal of Philosophy* 38 (December 4th, 1941), 688–690.
———. *Types of Philosophy*, revised ed. (New York: Scribner's, 1939).
Holt, Jim. Quizzing the Philosophers. *Wall Street Journal* (August 21st, 1998), W13.
Howison, George Holmes. *The Limits of Evolution and Other Essays*, second ed. (New York: Macmillan, 1904).
Hull, Richard T. James Edwin Creighton. *Presidential Addresses of the American Philosophical Association, 1901–1910* (Dordrecht, 1999), pp. 24–26.
James, William. *The Correspondence of William James*, eds. I. K, Skrupskelis and E.M.

Berkeley, 12 vols. (Charlottesville: University of Virginia Press, 1992–2004).
———. *Essays, Comments, and Reviews*, eds. Frederick H. Burkhardt, et al. (Cambridge: Harvard University Press, 1987).
———. *Essays in Radical Empiricism* (New York: Longmans, Green, and Co., 1912).
———. *A Pluralistic Universe* (Philadelphia: David McKay, 1909).
———. *Principles of Psychology*, 2 vols., authorized ed. (New York: Dover Books, 1950 [1890]).
———. *The Varieties of Religious Experience* (New York: Modern Library, n.d. [1902]).
———. *Writings of William James*, ed. John J. McDermott (Chicago: University of Chicago Press, 1992).
———. *The Works of William James: Manuscript Lectures*, ed. Ignas Skrupskelis (Cambridge: Harvard University Press, 1988).
Kestenbaum, Victor. *The Phenomenological Sense of John Dewey* (Atlantic Highlands: Humanities Press, 1977).
Knudson, Albert C. *The Philosophy of Personalism* (New York: Abingdon Press, 1927).
Kohák, Erazim. Personalism: Towards a Philosophical Dileneation. *The Personalist Forum* 13:1 (Spring 1997), 3–11.
Kowalczyk, Miroslaw. The Personal Dimension of the Reality of Nation. In *Personalism: Science, Philosophy, Theology* 7 (2004), 97–102.
Lipham, Sean. The Universe as Thou: William James's Religious Personalism. Presented in 2007 at the Society for the Advancement of American Philosophy, Columbia, South Carolina. The paper is available on-line (perhaps temporarily) at <www.philosophy.uncc.edu/mleldrid/SAAP/USC/TP24.html>.
Lovejoy, Arthur O. Thirteen Pragmatisms. *Journal of Philosophy, Psychology, and Scientific Methods* 5:1–2 (January 1908), 5–12, 29–39.
Lowe, Victor. The Relation between James and Whitehead. In *The Philosophy of William James*, ed. Walter Robert Corti (Hamburg: Felix Meiner Verlag, 1976), 331–346.
Makkreel, Rudolf. *Imagination and Interpretation in Kant* (Chicago: University of Chicago Press, 1990).
McConnell, Francis. J. *Borden Parker Bowne: His Life and Philosophy* (New York: Abingdon Press, 1929).
McCumber, John. *Time in the Ditch: American Philosophy in the McCarthy Era* (Evanston, 2001).
Menand, Louis. *The Metaphysical Club: A Story of Ideas in America* (New York: Farrar Straus and Giroux, 2001).
Miller, David L. James and the Specious Present. In *The Philosophy of William James*, ed. Walter Robert Corti (Hamburg: Felix Meiner Verlag, 1976), 51–79.
Moller, Mark. James, Perception, and the Miller-Bode Objections. *Transactions of the Charles S. Peirce Society* 37:4 (Fall 2001), 609–626.
Muelder, Walter G. *Moral Law in Christian Social Ethics* (Richmond: John Knox Press, 1966).
Myers, Gerald E. *William James: His Life and Thought* (New Haven: Yale University Press, 1986).
Nehaniv, C., and K. Dautenhahn. *Imitation in Animals and Artifacts* (Cambridge: MIT Press, 2002).
Niebuhr, Reinhold. *An Interpretation of Christian Ethics* (New York: Harper and Brothers, 1935).
———. *Moral Man and Immoral Society* (New York: Charles Scribner's Sons, 1932).
Peirce, Charles S. *Writings of Charles S. Peirce: A Chronological Edition*, eds. Edward C. Moore, et al., vols. 1–6, 8 (Bloomington: Indiana University Press, 1982–2010).

———. Review of Dewey's *Studies in Logical Theory* (Chicago: University of Chicago Decennial Publications, 1903). In *Collected Papers of Charles Sanders Peirce*, ed. Arthur W. Burks (Cambridge: Harvard University Press, 1958), 145–47 (CP8.188–190).

Perry, Ralph Barton. *The Thought and Character of William James*. 2 vols. (Boston: Little, Brown and Co., 1935).

Pierce, Charles P. *Moving the Chains: Tom Brady and the Pursuit of Everything* (New York: Farrar, Straus, and Giroux: 2006).

Pinchot, Gifford. *The Fight for Conservation* (New York: Doubleday, 1910).

Prigogine, Ilya, and Isabelle Stengers. *Order Out of Chaos* (New York: Bantam, 1984).

Richardson, Robert D. *William James: In the Maelstrom of American Modernism* (Boston: Houghton Mifflin, 2006)

Rorty, Richard. Dewey's Metaphysics. In *Consequences of Pragmatism* (Minneapolis: University of Minnesota Press, 1982), 72–89.

Ruetenik, Tadd. Last Call for William James. *The Pluralist* 7:1 (Winter, 2012).

Sabine, George H., ed. *Philosophical Essays in Honor of James Edwin Creighton by Former Students in the Sage School of Philosophy* (New York, 1917).

———. The Philosophy of James Edwin Creighton. *The Philosophical Review* 34:3 (1925), pp. 230–261.

Santayana, George. *Lotze's System of Philosophy*, ed. Paul G. Kuntz (Bloomington: Indiana University Press, 1971).

Seigfried, Charlene Haddock. *Chaos and Context: A Study in William James* (Athens: Ohio University, Press, 1978).

———. *William James' Radical Reconstruction of Philosophy* (Albany: State University of New York Press, 1990).

Sherover, Charles M. *Are We* in *Time and Other Essays on Time and Temporality*, ed. Gregory R. Johnson (Evanston: Northwestern University Press, 2003).

Simon, Linda. *Genuine Reality: A Life of William James* (New York: Harcourt Brace and Co, 1998).

———. *William James Remembered* (Lincoln: University of Nebraska Press, 1996).

Sprigge, Timothy L.S. *James and Bradley: American Truth and British Reality* (Chicago: Open Court, 1993).

Thilly, Frank. The Philosophy of James Edwin Creighton. *The Philosophical Review* 34:3 (1925), pp. 211–229.

Townsend, Kim. *Manhood at Harvard: William James and Others* (New York: W.W. Norton, 1996).

Tunstall, Dwayne A. Being Persons in a Depersonalizing World: Marcel and Gordon on the Human Condition in Late Western Modernity. Doctoral dissertation, Southern Illinois University Carbondale, 2007.

———. *Doing Philosophy Personally* (New York: Fordham University Press, 2013).

Vailati, Giovanni. *Gli Instrumenti della ragione*, ed. Mario Quaranta (Padua: Il Poligrafo casa editrice, 2003).

Wahl, Jean. *The Pluralist Philosophies of England and America*. Trans. Fred Rothwell (London: Open Court, 1925).

Wenley, R.M. *The Life and Work of George Sylvester Morris* (New York: Macmillan, 1917).

Werkmeister, William H. Creighton's Speculative Idealism. In *A History of Philosophical Ideas in America* (New York, 1949), pp. 289–293.

Werth, Lee F. Clarifying Concresence in Whitehead's Process Philosophy. In *Time and Process: The Study of Time VII*, eds. J.T. Fraser and Lewis Rowell (Madison: International Universities Press, 1993), 219–241.

West, Cornel. *The Cornel West Reader* (New York: Basic *Civitas* Books, 1999).

Whitehead, Alfred North. *Adventures of Ideas* (New York: Free Press, 1967 [1933]).

———. *The Aims of Education and Other Essays* (New York: Free Press, 1929).

———. *The Function of Reason* (Boston: Beacon Press, 1958 [1929]).

Wilshire, Bruce. *Fashionable Nihilism: A Critique of Analytic Philosophy* (Albany, 2002).

———. *William James and Phenomenology* (Bloomington: Indiana University Press, 1968).

Wilson, Woodrow. *The Papers of Woodrow Wilson*, vol. 18 (1908–09), ed. Arthur S. Link (Princeton: Princeton University Press, 1975).

———. *The Politics of Woodrow Wilson*, ed. August Heckscher (New York: Harper and Brothers, 1956).

Index

Abbott, Francis Ellingwood, 16, 255, 363
Absolute (the), absoluteness, 11, 18–24, 27, 33, 36, 39, 43–45, 67–70, 72, 77–78, 87, 89, 92, 102, 126–129, 131–135, 137–140, 142, 158–161, 163–164, 166, 177, 182, 188, 190, 194, 196–197, 202, 209–210, 216, 221, 223, 226, 229, 234–236, 240, 244–245, 248, 253, 264, 353 n.21, 360 n.26, 366 n.50, 370 n.3, 378 n.23
  battle of the, 33, 128, 177, 202, 209, 221
  Bradley's, 44, 128, 196, 202, 378 n.23
  ethical character of, 177
  experience (see also experience of the Absolute), 21, 70–71, 89, 127, 142, 160
  as God, 24, 45, 76, 78, 92, 128, 188
  Hegel's, 44, 128, 196
  as infinite system (community), 20
  as interpretant, 19
  as irrevocability of the act, 133–135, 142
  pragmatism, 49, 107
  Spirit, 245
    thought, 20
    as the Whole, 20, 21, 128, 138, 161, 223
acknowledgement (see also anticipation, truth), 39, 47, 60, 62, 130–133, 135, 142, 145, 148, 150, 158–160, 165–166, 169, 176–177, 180, 192, 262, 267, 281, 307, 343, 347, 370 n.7

act (see also action, activity, actuality, dynamis), 21, 39–41, 44, 47, 49, 56, 60–63, 66, 92, 94, 97–99, 101, 117, 128, 130–133, 135, 137, 141–142, 144–152, 154–158, 165, 169–173, 175–176, 178, 182–184, 186–187, 191–193, 195, 214, 219, 224–225, 227, 230, 239, 244, 248, 250, 252, 260, 262, 266–270, 289, 296–297, 302, 304–305, 311, 317, 345, 347–349, 357 n.26, 371 n.33
action (see also act, activity, actuality, dynamis), 23, 40, 48, 59–60, 86, 99, 109, 111–112, 116, 121, 131, 133–135, 141–142, 145–146, 148–151, 153–154, 167–168, 171–174, 178, 181, 193, 195, 199, 219, 227, 229, 236, 240, 244, 248, 250–252, 257, 263, 268, 270, 274, 276, 286, 288–289, 293, 296, 299–302, 357 n.3
  plan of, 147, 167–168, 174, 192, 219, 268, 303, 323
activity (see also act, action, actuality, attention, dynamis), 22, 41, 47, 49, 52, 54, 56–57, 62–65, 67–68, 71, 73, 85–88, 91–92, 101–103, 109, 112–113, 116, 118, 121, 126–131, 135–138, 140–153, 155, 157, 160–161, 166–175, 178, 181, 183, 185, 194, 198, 211, 221, 225, 236, 238, 250, 257, 261, 264–265, 269, 272, 279, 281, 290, 296–297, 301, 311, 314, 327, 331, 336, 338–339,

341, 343–344, 356 n.25, 369 n.24, 373 n.10
actuality (*see also* act, action, activity, *dynamis*, possibility), 13, 19, 22, 25–26, 28, 47, 59–61, 64, 67, 70–71, 85, 87, 95, 102–103, 109, 132–133, 136–138, 140, 142–143, 146, 148–151, 153, 158, 161, 164, 168, 171, 173–174, 178, 181–189, 192–195, 197, 199, 223, 234–235, 237–240, 250, 257, 265, 270, 320, 339, 346, 360 n.17, 367 n.11, 381 n.53
aesthetics (*see also* feeling, value), 31, 47, 63, 194–195, 374 n.32, 379 n.27
agape, agapasm (*see also* love), 35, 44, 48, 50, 346–347, 387 n.1
Alcott, Amos Bronson, 375 n.5
alterity (*see also* non-Ego, Otherness), 227
American Philosophical Association (APA), 201, 315–322, 324, 328–329, 334–341, 343–345, 348, 392 n.5, 392 n.9, 392 n.13, 393 n.17, 393 n.18, 394 n.20, 394 n.27, 395 n.31
  Committee on Definitions 317, 321, 329
American Psychological Association (AΨA), 316, 318
analogy, 38, 49, 83, 87, 101, 122, 164, 222, 254, 262, 267, 270, 272, 274, 278, 300, 349
Anderson, Douglas R., xiii, 315, 353 n.21, 358 n.4, 383 n.4
Anderson, Marc 285
anglo(s), 1–2, 291, 387 n.7
anticipation (*see also* acknowledgement, truth), 39–40, 44, 60, 62–63, 131, 133, 135, 165–166, 169, 179, 181, 192, 194, 260
appreciation, world of (*see also* description, world of), 26–28, 47–48, 57, 81, 88, 90, 125–126, 139, 152–153, 158, 160, 169, 194, 366 n.33, 370 n.1
Aquinas, St. Thomas, 157, 381 n.52

African-American(s), Africana (*see also* Blacks), 277, 291
Aristotle, 3, 18, 31, 36, 54, 80, 292, 325, 329, 341
atheism (*see also* pantheism), 246
Athens, 309, 342
atomism (*see also* individual, individuality, pluralism), 208, 222, 224, 236, 244, 248, 265, 266–267, 287–289, 293–295, 306–307, 390 n.12
atonement (includes reconciliation, redemption; *see also* community), xi, xii, 211–212, 215, 223, 238, 266, 276–278, 281–282, 290–291, 305, 350
attention (*see also* activity, selection, will), 1, 13, 17, 64–65, 112, 127, 138, 145–152, 154, 157, 160, 166–173, 179–181, 189–193, 214, 219, 221, 223–224, 237, 248, 256, 261–262, 270, 272, 310, 371 n.31, 371 n.33

Baldwin, James Mark, 16, 329
Baltimore, 17, 35, 37
Baptist(s), 332
baseball, 83–84, 338
Baylor University 332
Being, 44–46, 53–54, 59, 65, 70–71, 73, 76–78, 80, 84–88, 91, 94, 96–97, 102, 109, 118, 157, 161, 166, 182, 184, 193, 214, 217, 239, 244, 256, 269, 296, 349, 352 n.3, 359 n.13, 363 n.11–12, 393 n.16
  Fourth Conception of 45–46, 50, 96, 126, 159–161, 164, 173, 188, 194, 239
  unity of 94
Beethoven, Ludwig van, 54
Belgium, Belgian(s), 388 n.9
beloved community (*see* community, beloved)
Bell, Jason M., 285, 352 n.7, 364 n.20, 366 n.33, 378 n.23–24, 385 n.25, 388 n.9
Bell, Winthrop, 366 n.33
Bengtsson, Jan Olof, xii, 12, 196–197, 372 n.49, 375 n.5, 383 n.2–3, 383 n.5

Bergson, Henri, 3, 211, 329, 354 n.30, 379 n.27, 380 n.41, 381 n.53, 393 n.16
Berkeley, California, 36, 69, 76, 363 n.11, 364 n.18
  Philosophical Union 44
Berkeley, George, 107, 249
Berlin, 324
black(s) (*see also* African-American), 291, 389 n.10
Boodin, John Elof, 16, 32, 93, 108, 177, 365 n.28, 367 n.8, 367 n.10, 373 n.17
Bosanquet, Bernard, 12
Boston Globe, ix
Boston, ix, 35, 37, 41, 207, 332, 363 n.11, 391 n.16, 394 n.24
Boston Red Sox, 83
Boston University, 202, 330, 332, 340
Boutroux, Émile, 206
Bowne, Borden Parker, 4, 63, 107, 184, 187, 202–207, 209–213, 215–217, 223–227, 235, 237, 241, 246, 248–249, 255, 332, 372 n.49, 375 n.5, 376 n.8, 376 n.10, 376 n.12–15, 379 n.26, 379 n.29–31, 380 n.35, 382 n.1, 383 n.7–8, 384 n.21
Brady, Tom, x
Bradley, F.H., 12, 44–46, 61, 79, 81, 128, 196, 202, 248, 378 n.23, 383, n.5
Brahms, Johannes, 54
Brightman, Edgar Sheffield, 86, 202, 221, 248, 253, 255, 258, 362 n.6, 365 n.30, 374 n.32, 379 n.27, 381 n.44, 381 n.52, 384 n.16, 384 n.22–23, 393 n.17
Britain, British (*see* Great Britain)
Brown, Edmund G. "Jerry," x
Buckley, William F., 295
Buddha, Buddhism, 88, 157
Buford, Thomas O., 386 n.54
Buranelli, Vincent, 10
Burke, Edmund, 299–300
Burrow, Rufus, Jr., 196, 352 n.6, 375 n.5, 387 n.1
Bush, George W. (*see also* Iraq, treason, traitor), 282, 304–305

California (*see also* Berkeley), x, xii, 32, 33, 35–38, 41–42, 44, 76, 208, 332, 363 n.11
  conquest of, 41–42, 68, 281–282, 305, 355 n.12, 361 n.46, 386 n.53, 389 n.10
  Grass Valley 32, 355 n.3
  influence on Royce, 32ff.
  Oakland, 36
Calvin, Calvinism, 35, 98, 373 n.7, 390 n.12
Cambridge, Massachusetts, 32
Campbell, James, 316–317, 320, 335, 337, 392 n.12–13, 394 n.20, 395 n.31
Campbellite(s) (*see* Christianity, Campbellite)
Canada, Canadian(s), 388
Care, xii, 113, 146
Cassirer, Ernst, 85–86, 94, 389 n.11, 390 n.14
Catholic Church, 52, 277, 279, 281, 301, 332, 366 n.34
causation, causal laws, 59–60, 95, 98, 113, 139, 150, 155, 245, 257, 261, 307
  efficient (*see also* mechanism), 261
cause (as something served), xi, 42, 48–49, 155, 165, 173, 211, 252, 266, 272–273, 279, 282, 288, 291, 296–297, 305, 309, 313, 318–320, 337, 346–347
  lost 50, 320, 357 n.26
Cavell, Stanley, 367 n.4
certainty (*see also* necessity), 16, 23–24, 26, 54, 63–64, 130, 134, 158, 172, 258
  Royce's opposition to 130
Cesarz, Gary L., 69, 83, 356 n.19, 361 n.47, 363 n.12, 364 n.24
China, 276
Chomsky, Noam, 338
Christ (*see* Jesus)
Christianity, 9, 35, 48, 50, 98, 127, 274, 276–277, 318, 326, 346, 376 n.13
  Calvinist (*see* Calvin)
  Campbellite (*see also* Pauline), 34, 35, 373 n.7, 390 n.12

412 Index

Pauline (see also Campbellite) 34, 50–51, 91
Churchland, Paul, 271
citizen(s) (see also parochial, progressive), x, 269, 276, 290, 293, 303, 304, 310, 338–339, 386 n.49
Civil Rights Movement, 287–289
Clark University, 331
Clendenning, John, xii, 5, 10, 34, 43, 196, 354 n.1, 355 n.8, 360 n.22, 362 n.10, 363 n.11, 389 n.10, 391 n.17
coherence (see also truth), 82, 101, 122, 158, 164, 198, 211, 215, 267, 342, 389 n.10
colonialism (see also imperialism), 351 n.2, 356 n.14, 388 n.10, 389 n.10
Columbia University, 330–331
communication (see also interpretation, semiotics), 19, 27, 41, 77, 84, 119, 158, 179–181, 184, 199, 216, 236, 254–257, 260–264, 266, 280
communism, 247, 254, 321, 386 n.49
communitarian, 74, 76, 247, 288, 299
community, x–xiii, 14–15, 17–19, 25–27, 33, 35–36, 41–42, 44, 52, 74, 77, 91, 98, 121, 159–160, 166, 173, 199, 220, 243–244, 247–249, 251–252, 254, 260, 263–264, 266–271, 274–279, 281–282, 285–286, 288–291, 296–297, 299–300, 303–306, 312–315, 317–319, 322, 326, 338, 343–344, 346, 348–350, 359 n.12, 362 n.9, 384 n.21, 386 n.54, 390 n.12
  beloved, 7, 22, 25, 41, 49–50, 188, 238, 286, 290–291, 295, 299, 303, 352 n.6, 386 n.1, 387 n.1, 388 n.9
  as communion of saints, 52, 319
  defective, 271–272
  genuine, 27, 252, 270, 286, 288, 295, 312, 337, 389 n.10, 393 n.17
  of hope, xiii, 160, 267, 290
  as infinite system, 20
  of interpretation, 6–7, 13, 20, 39, 62, 279, 290, 326, 352 n.9
  of memory, xiii, 160, 266–268, 277, 282, 314, 339, 393 n.17
  as persons, 220–222, 254, 265, 270, 274, 279, 303, 357 n.26
  revitalization of, xi, 286, 312
  scientific, 272
  triadic theory of, 17, 19, 62, 128, 190–191, 193, 218, 266, 362 n.9
complexity theory, 25, 40, 125, 262, 355 n.7
Comte, Auguste, 271
Conception of God Debate (see God, Conception of)
Concept, 19, 23–24, 30, 36, 38, 47–48, 50, 58, 65, 69, 72–73, 76–78, 83, 88, 90–91, 96–98, 105, 109–112, 114–118, 120–122, 125–126, 128–129, 132, 136, 139, 142, 146, 152–153, 164, 166–169, 175–179, 181–182, 188, 190, 195, 197, 199, 202, 211–213, 231, 233–234, 237, 239–240, 243, 247–248, 254, 261, 266, 268–269, 287, 294, 296, 306, 321, 325, 333, 335, 341–342, 354 n.30, 356 n.25, 359 n.12, 360 n.19, 375 n.3
  of the absolute, 11, 19–24, 27, 45, 127, 132, 134, 164
  of being (see also Fourth Conception of Being), 45–46, 76, 80, 96, 126, 159, 161, 173, 188, 194, 239, 359 n.13, 363 n.11
  of appreciation, 26, 125
  of causation, 60
  of community, 247, 267, 291, 386 n.1
  of description, 26, 47, 125
  of error, 65
  of experience, 100, 117, 172, 231, 233, 240, 256, 267
  of feeling, 195
  of God (see also God, Conception of), 44–45, 71, 193, 243, 246, 359 n.12, 361 n.53–54
  of the individual, 72, 139, 159, 222, 296
  of loyalty, 7, 156
  of person, 196, 198, 201–202, 216, 220, 247, 288, 290, 354 n.32, 381 n.52
  of possibility, 26, 251

of purpose, 28, 202, 269
of rationality, 54–55, 127
of the whole, 20, 24, 44, 69, 72, 111, 113, 126, 128, 136–138, 160, 164, 166
of the will, 28, 129, 141, 146, 166–167, 175–178
conceptualism, conceptualist, 76, 100, 360 n.19
consciousness (*see also* act, action, activity, experience, reflection, unconscious), 21, 39, 42–43, 49, 59, 60–63, 65, 70–71, 75–76, 78, 82, 86–87, 98, 101, 112, 126, 142, 147, 150, 154, 165, 167–168, 170, 173, 176, 180, 183–185, 186, 195, 197–198, 214–217, 219, 248, 256, 261, 266–267, 270, 276, 282, 315, 328, 335, 346, 360 n.26, 365 n.30, 367 n.11, 371 n.33, 372 n.4, 380 n.35
    absolute, 19, 78
    compounding of (*see also* social), 229
    double, 282
    historical, 38, 49, 67
    individual, 219, 229, 251, 262
    mythic, 390 n.14
    personal, 214–215
    self-, 42, 51, 92, 255, 260, 341, 373 n.19
    social, 41, 63, 178, 236, 251, 256
    stream of, 13, 266
conservation (*see also* ontological conservative), 144, 298–299, 301, 390 n.15, 391 n.15, 391 n.17
conservative(s), conservatism (*see also* progress, progressive), 247, 286, 292–294, 297–300, 302–303, 305, 386 n.49, 387 n.3, 390 n.12, 390 n.14–15
    methodological (*see also* relationalism), 287, 291–297, 303–304, 390 n.12
    neo-, 228, 276, 386 n.49
    ontological, 292, 300–302
    progressive, 286–288, 303–306, 387 n.3
    Royce's, Ch. 9, 285ff.
    Social, 297–300, 390 n.14

Constitution, United States (*see* United States Constitution)
construction (*see also* interpretation, recognition), 62, 148–153, 165–166, 171–172, 289, 371n.33
context, 20, 32, 41, 82, 110–112, 114–115, 133, 160, 237, 251, 256, 264, 266, 393n.18
continuity (*see also* discontinuity, generalization, intentional stance), 71, 116, 137, 142, 144, 164, 174, 177–181, 185–187, 189, 192, 197, 199, 212, 214, 216, 223–224, 228, 231, 233, 236–237, 239–241, 244, 249, 258, 262–263, 302, 349, 375n.3, 381n.53, 382n.54
Copleston, Frederick, 252–253, 383 n.2
Coppens, Charles, S.J., 332
Cornell, Ezra, 324, 326
Cornell University, 319, 324, 326–328, 330–336, 340
corporations (multi-national, international), x-xi, 52, 272–275, 278, 280, 306, 311–312, 385n.47
    as defective persons, 273–274, 280
Cotton, James Harry, 353 n.12, 354 n.29–30
courage, xi, xii, 172, 314, 337
creativity (*see also* imitation, novelty), 4, 18, 30–31, 48, 51–52, 54, 69, 74, 85–89, 91, 93, 97, 99, 112–113, 118, 130, 151, 153, 170, 172, 175, 184, 186, 211, 217, 232, 246, 253, 259, 262, 266, 271, 279, 288, 294, 297–300, 303, 309–310, 312, 315, 318–319, 322, 327, 329, 333–334, 342–344, 360 n.28, 365 n.19, 390 n.14
Creighton, James Edwin, 4, 201, 209, 315–318, 320–321, 324–330, 333–343, 395 n.33, 395 n.35
Croce, Jim, 143
Crosby, Joanna, xii
Crouch, Brent, 9
Curry, Tommy J., 6, 355 n.7, 356 n.14, 387 n.7, 388 n.10

Dalhousie College, 324

Darwin, Charles, 36, 357n.1
Davidson, Donald, 370 n.10, 394 n.24
Davidson, Thomas, 77, 203, 207, 223
Dawkins, Richard, 271–272
De Laguna, Grace Andrus, 340
Deleuze, Gilles, 2
Democracy, x, 218, 247, 285-287, 298, 311, 386n.49, 391n.15
Democrat(s) (US political party), 285, 292
Demosthenes, 341
Dennett, Daniel, 271–272
Descartes, René, 3, 117, 329
description (includes world of; *see also* appreciation), descriptive (*see also* metaphysics, phenomenology, philosophy), 26–28, 39–40, 47, 52, 53–54, 57, 59–61, 81–82, 84–86, 88–89, 96, 104–105, 109, 112, 118, 125–126, 129–130, 135–136, 138–140, 143, 147, 149, 152–153, 156, 164–165, 167–169, 174, 193–194, 199, 204, 213, 217, 222–226, 230–231, 235–239, 250, 258, 287, 293–294, 297, 299, 355 n.9, 375 n.3
De Tienne, André, xii, 353 n.15
desire (*see also* will), 87–88, 99, 102, 145–146, 150, 211, 215, 219, 252, 269, 276, 278, 281, 290, 293, 319, 390 n.12
Dewey, John (*see also* situation), ix, 12, 15–16, 23–25, 34, 53–54, 62–63, 84–86, 103–106, 108, 110–120, 122–123, 135, 137, 140, 159–160, 176, 184, 193, 195, 239, 258–259, 271, 354 n.29, 358 n.4, 367 n.3–4, 368 n.18, 369 n.22, 375 n.32, 379 n.27, 382 n.55, 385 n.27
  compared to Royce, 8, 9–10, 16, 24, 31–32, 34, 84, 105, 111–116, 118, 120, 122–123, 137, 259, 326, 352 n.4, 353 n.21
dialectic (*see also* method, dialectical), 1, 23, 46, 81–82, 85, 99–101, 114, 169, 174–178, 180–181, 185, 190, 198–199, 211, 213, 236, 245, 249, 275–277, 287, 292, 325

discontinuity (*see also* attention, continuity, generalization, intentional stance, selection), 164, 174, 178, 180–181, 185, 187, 189, 192–193, 199, 211, 216, 218, 233, 236–239, 241, 262–263, 349, 375 n.3, 382 n.54
disloyalty (*see* Bush, George W.; loyalty; treason)
docility, law of (*see also* instinct, history, imitation, individuality, psychology), 140, 142–145, 147–148, 150, 152, 160, 169, 298, 300, 371 n.33, 379 n.25, 390 n.14
Dombrowski, Daniel, 384 n.22
doubt (*see also* inquiry, problem, situation), 22–23, 38, 42, 49, 57, 87, 89, 92, 111, 113, 117, 121, 171–173, 181, 211, 373 n.10
  genuine, 23, 103, 109, 111, 113, 115–117, 121, 172
  intellectual, 113
  methodological, 22
Drake, Durant, 393 n.17
DuBois, W.E.B., 32, 204, 282
Duquette, Elizabeth, 6, 389 n.10
Duns Scotus, John, 250
duration (includes endure; *see* time-spans), 39, 47, 59, 156, 184, 240, 263, 267, 279–280
dyad, dyadic, 190, 192, 235, 266, 275
dynamis (includes dynamic, dynamism; *see also* act, action, activity, actuality), 47, 256–257, 261–263, 282, 299

education (*see* teaching)
Egypt, 319
Einstein, Albert, 94
Eisikovits, Nir, 273, 385 n.47
Eliot, T.S., 32
Elocution, 330, 332, 334
Emerson, Ralph Waldo, 30, 32, 220–221, 294
Empiricism, 212, 218, 239, 256, 270, 329, 362 n.9, 380 n.31, 380 n.35, 384 n.24

immediate, 104, 117
radical, 3, 110–111, 204, 211, 213, 215, 218, 221, 223–241, 254–255, 259–260, 266, 361 n.53, 381 n.53, 382 n.54, 384 n.17, 384 n.24
transcendental, 211
Enlightenment, the, 38, 245–247, 253, 285–286, 357 n.1
environment, environmentalism (*see also* conservation; philosophy, environmental), 35, 146, 305–306
Epicurean(s), 326, 338
epistemology (*see also* knowledge), 18, 20, 23–24, 27, 31, 41, 44, 69–70, 112, 115, 138, 210, 217, 220, 226–228, 288, 332, 368 n.18, 378 n.25, 379 n.31, 381 n.44
error (*see also* fallibilism, ignorance), 22–23, 42–43, 44, 47, 58, 64–70, 251, 378 n.23
eternity, eternal, eternalism, 26, 47, 64–65, 144, 163–164, 174, 182–183, 187, 193–194, 198, 247, 373 n.12
ethico-religious insight (*see also* Interpreter Spirit, and Tunstall, Dwayne), 11, 28, 74, 201, 292, 362 n.2, 371 n.39
ethics (*see also* value), xii, 19–21, 23, 31, 35, 41, 47–50, 61, 68, 74, 76, 78, 106, 115, 134, 136, 139, 153–154, 156–161, 164–165, 167–168, 173, 193–195, 198–199, 210, 222, 227–228, 230, 243–244, 247, 249, 253, 269, 287, 289, 292–297, 303, 305, 313, 322–323, 352 n.3, 371 n.39, 372 n.49, 379 n.25, 384 n.22, 385 n.25, 389 n.11
as inseparable from politics (*see also* conservative), 292–297
primacy of (as First Philosophy), 68, 134, 139, 153, 159, 167, 193, 198–199, 243, 269, 296
as separable from politics (*see also* liberal), 292–297, 303–304, 389 n.11
virtue, 31, 48, 68, 114–115, 198, 303, 346

Europe, 2, 6, 9, 105, 167, 328, 372 n.49, 388n.10, 393n.17
evolution, 36, 139, 164, 179, 245, 251, 263, 298–299, 357 n.1, 365 n.28, 367 n.4, 377 n.19, 379 n.30, 383 n.6
exclusion (*see also* negation, neglect, selection, will), 26, 42, 65, 114, 137, 143, 145–146, 148–149, 151–157, 159–161, 170–173, 175, 177–178, 181, 186, 190, 192, 199, 213–214, 220, 223, 226, 236, 238, 245, 249–250, 253, 264, 270, 272, 274, 278, 281, 289, 290, 296, 302, 317, 346, 388 n.9
existence, 15, 19, 30, 39–40, 43–46, 48–49, 53–54, 58–61, 63–65, 67–68, 70–72, 76–79, 81–82, 85–87, 95, 97, 101, 104–105, 109, 115–118, 122, 125, 129, 133, 136, 140, 143–145, 148–149, 151, 154, 157, 159, 161, 166–167, 169–170, 173, 178–180, 182–184, 186–187, 189, 191, 195, 197–199, 207, 214–219, 221–223, 225–230, 234, 236, 239, 243–249, 252–262, 265–266, 268, 270, 274, 288–289, 294, 298–299, 301–302, 304, 306, 312, 341, 346, 359 n.12, 367 n.11, 380 n.31, 380 n.35, 384 n.21
existentialism, 5, 74–75, 90, 102, 166
expectation (*see* anticipation), 63, 89, 264, 268, 277, 303, 325, 346, 368 n.18
experience (*see also* existence), 38–40, 46–50, 53, 56–60, 62, 64, 66, 68, 70–71, 73–74, 76, 79, 81–82, 84, 86–89, 91–92, 94–96, 98–101, 103–105, 109–110, 112, 116–117, 125–130, 135, 137–138, 141, 143–150, 154–155, 158, 160–161, 165–169, 171–175, 178–183, 185–188, 191, 194–195, 211, 213, 215–217, 220–221, 224–237, 239–240, 243–244, 249–250, 252–258, 260–264, 267–268, 270–271, 273, 276, 279–280, 283, 288, 300–302, 312, 319, 344, 347,

359 n.12, 367 n.11, 370 n.1, 375
n.1, 382 n.55, 384 n.24, 390 n.14
Absolute, 69–71, 78, 89, 127
of the Absolute (irrevocable), 21, 40,
  91–93, 98, 133–135, 139, 142, 159,
  169, 172, 250, 289, 305, 356 n.25,
  359 n.12
chronosynoptic, 70, 163, 264
concrete, 26, 47, 71, 115, 169, 235,
  259, 270, 271, 300, 356 n.25
conscious, 261
ethical, 156–157, 222
finite, 22, 179–186, 220, 236, 253,
  261
fragmentary, 61, 70, 238
immediate, 21, 27, 48, 54, 72–75, 79,
  90, 92–100, 102–105, 109–110,
  112, 117–118, 125–126, 149, 166,
  168, 170, 199, 204, 229, 233–234,
  237, 239, 249, 264, 266–267, 354
  n.30, 367 n.11
inner, 146, 152, 179, 189, 261
mystical, 74–75, 79, 91–98, 150, 264,
  365 n.31
of necessity, 169–173
non-cognitive (pre-cognitive), 166
other possible (*see also* present,
  truth), 39–40, 49, 59–60, 62, 89,
  160, 165, 174, 181–182, 185–186,
  232, 234, 237, 239–240, 250–251,
  256–257, 261–262, 267–268, 271,
  276, 281, 300, 343, 347–348
particular, 56–59, 82, 99–100, 110,
  112, 127, 137, 184, 221, 225,
  231–232, 234, 237, 262
phenomenological, 147, 171, 183
of possibilities, 71, 73, 143, 173, 183,
  186–187
psychological, 93, 95, 126
pure, 72, 149, 204, 218, 224, 227,
  230–231, 233–241, 382 n.54
religious, 35, 88, 91, 95, 128, 198,
  220–221
sense (includes sensation), 146, 168
social (in community), 178, 236, 251, 268,
  270, 276–277, 298–299, 390, n.14
temporal, 47, 49, 62, 70, 131, 144, 147,
  149–150, 165, 174, 178, 182, 186,
  189, 226, 231, 235–237, 240, 248,
  250–251, 262, 264, 267, 279, 297,
  300–301, 390 n.14
unity of, 244
of universals, 100
whole of, of the whole, 25, 56, 60,
  158, 234

faith, 36, 64, 81, 89, 91–92, 102, 106,
  172, 246, 366 n.34
fallibilism (*see also* error, ignorance),
  30, 44, 68, 72, 140, 169, 195, 213,
  258
fascism, fascists, 254, 272, 295, 386
  n.49
Fechner, Gustav, 377 n.18
Feeling, 61, 74–75, 86–89, 94, 97, 102,
  110–112, 130, 146–147, 173–174,
  194–195, 198, 244, 248, 264–265,
  368 n.13
Ferreira, Philip, 12, 383 n.5
Feuerbach, Ludwig, 245
Fichte, J.G., 12, 247
Fichte, I.H., 12
fiction, fictional ontology (*see also*
  hypothesis), 25, 39, 47, Ch. 2, 77,
  81, 84, 101, 109, 134, 138, 165,
  185, 197, 203–204, 212, 222, 225,
  228, 232, 234, 249, 358 n.4, 364
  n.16, 364 n.23, 373 n.10
finitism (theistic), 71, 127, 186–188,
  374 n.31
Fischer, Marilyn, 6
Flanagan, Owen, 106
Flewelling, Ralph Tyler, 209, 379 n.27
Fontinell, Eugene, 375 n.3
football (*see* sport)
Fortune, Aaron G., 287–294, 297, 302,
  387 n.4
Fourth Conception of Being (*see* Being,
  Fourth Conception of)
fragment, fragmentary (*see also*
  experience), 43–44, 60–61, 70, 76,
  88, 198, 223, 238, 251, 315
Francis, Saint, 156
Friendship, xii, 37, 155–156, 202, 205,
  207, 248, 269, 313, 319–320, 324,

339, 342, 345, 348–349, 378 n.23, 393 n.17
freedom, x, xi, 35, 42, 78–80, 82, 91, 97, 99, 103, 126, 169, 170–172, 182–184, 197, 218, 230, 245, 249, 251, 259, 280, 282, 296–297, 299, 303–304, 309, 311, 319, 329, 338, 340, 346–348, 376 n.6
Frege, Gottlob, 333
Fritzman, John M., xiii
Fuller, Margaret, 294
future (*see also* projection), xi, xii, 17, 23–24, 27, 39–41, 44, 46–47, 49, 58–62, 66, 69, 72, 87, 89, 121–122, 128–129, 132–133, 135–136, 140, 142, 146–149, 151–152, 161, 165, 168–169, 171–172, 174–176, 179, 181–182, 187, 190, 192, 206, 232, 237–238, 240, 250–251, 262, 266–268, 270, 273, 297–300, 320, 327, 333, 372 n.4, 382 n.55, 390 n.14

Gandhi, Mohandas K., 156–157
Garchar, Kimberly, 9
Gardiner, Harry Norman, 316, 336, 392 n.9
Gavin, William J., 231, 381 n.54
generality, generalization, generals (*see also* continuity, universals), ix, 8, 11, 19, 21, 26, 30, 33, 53, 56–61, 64–65, 71, 73, 76, 82, 84, 88–89, 97, 99–101, 105, 110–116, 122, 126–129, 131, 136–145, 150–153, 156–157, 159, 160, 163–166, 168–169, 171, 174–181, 186, 189–193, 199, 209, 212–213, 215, 225–234, 236–237, 240, 243, 249–251, 255–256, 258–263, 267, 270, 279, 287, 290, 293–294, 298–300, 302–303, 320, 349, 368n.14, 373n.8, 382 n.55
Germany, 36, 52, 291, 324, 328, 335, 377 n.18, 388 n.9
  Second Reich, 276, 293
  Third Reich, 272, 276, 293, 357 n.26
Gibson, J.J., 381 n.50

Gifford Lectures, 13, 19, 44–47, 75, 77, 80–81, 163, 202, 316, 352 n.3, 359 n.13, 362 n.9
Gilbert, Katherine Everett, 340–341
Gilman, Daniel C., 36, 331
God (*see also* Absolute), 50, 71–73, 82, 86–87, 89, 91–92, 94, 96–99, 101, 127–128, 156, 160–161, 186–188, 191–193, 197–198, 246–247, 250, 253–255, 264, 273, 279, 283, 296, 330, 352 n.3, 365 n.30, 366 n.50, 370 n.3, 385 n.24
  chronosynoptic (*see also* atemporal), 70, 163, 264
  concept of, 24, 45, 69, 127–128, 193, 197, 243, 246, 254, 356n.25, 359n.12, 361n.53–54
  Conception of, Debate, 44-45, 68, 74–79, 80, 110, 363n.11
  death of (killing of), 245–246
  essence (heart) of, 78, 97, 99, 102
  existence of, 43, 245, 255
  immediate experience of, 91–92, 99–100, 359 n.12
  omnipotence of (*see also* finitism), 71, 127
  omniscience of, 70–71, 127, 253
  personality of, 70–71, 73, 76, 79–80, 127, 184, 198–199, 227, 245, 254
  and possibility, 66, 70, 161, 186–187, 197
  proof of the existence of, 64–65, 69–70,
  as temporal, 127, 186–187, 192, 250, Ch. 6
  will of (*see* will, God's, and will, divine)
Good, the, 294 348, 361 n.54, 373 n.19, 384 n.25
Good, James A., 387 n.2
Goodman, Nelson, 367 n.4
Göttingen, University of, 36
Grace, 98, 276, 278
Grass Valley (*see* California, Grass Valley)
Great Britain, British (includes England, English), 12, 23, 32, 39, 297, 354 n.28, 383 n.5, 388 n.9, 393 n.16

Greene, Thomas Hill, 12
Grene, Marjorie, 381 n.50
grief, grieving, xi, 37, 52, 207, 260
Gunter, Pete A.Y., 354 n.30, 357 n.1

Haack, Susan, 106
Hamilton, Alexander, 286
Hall, G. Stanley, 331
Hare, Peter, xii
Harris, Leonard, 393 n.18
Harris, William Torrey, 328, 375 n.5
Hartshorne, Charles, 32, 74, 87, 94, 98, 102, 230, 248, 255–256, 258, 361 n.53, 362 n.2, 362 n.6, 364 n.23, 365 n.30, 374 n.32, 381 n.52, 384 n.16, 384 n.22, 393 n.17
Harvard University, 16, 32, 40–43, 46, 52, 56, 165, 202, 206, 208–209, 314, 319, 324, 330–332, 340, 352 n.4, 363 n.11, 364 n.19, 366 n.33, 367 n.4, 371 n.33, 388 n.10, 389 n.10
Heidegger, Martin (includes Heideggerian), 51, 53, 157, 161, 166–167, 182, 230, 379 n.25, 393 n.16
Hegel, G.W.F. (includes Hegelian(s)), 12, 36–38, 44–45, 54, 61, 29, 84–85, 87, 105, 128, 169, 178, 190, 196, 205, 208, 245, 247, 378 n.23
Heraclitus, 26, 38
Herstein, Gary L., 352 n.6, 361 n.53, 372 n.50, 385 n.30, 387 n.1
Hibben, J.G., 316
Hindu philosophy (includes vedas), 75, 385 n.25
Hine, Robert V., 10, 354 n.1
Hispanic(s), 389 n.10
history, historian, historical (*see also* consciousness, historical; historicism), x, xi, 3–4, 10, 14, 17, 31, 34, 38, 41–42, 45, 47, 51, 53, 67–68, 78, 80, 85–86, 88, 92–93, 95, 99–103, 105–108, 110, 112, 114, 120, 127, 133–135, 139, 142–145, 153, 157, 175, 180, 194, 197, 199, 204, 209–210, 218, 220–221, 228, 236, 240, 245, 247, 251, 254, 266, 269, 273, 274, 276–279, 281, 286–287, 291, 293, 300–301, 309, 311, 313–315, 318–319, 333, 336, 339, 341, 344, 346, 351 n.3, 366 n.33, 377 n.18, 378 n.23, 379 n.25, 382 n.55, 387 n.2-3, 388 n.9, 390 n.14, 391 n.2, 392 n.13, 393 n.18, 394 n.20
  of ideas (includes intellectual and history of thought), 10, 37, 196, 247, 286, 368 n.18, 375 n.5, 377 n.18
  of philosophy, 3–4, 15, 31, 36, 48, 69, 104, 118, 130, 315, 319, 327, 331–332, 334, 336, 339, 341, 352 n.9, 357 n.26, 362 n.7, 367 n.7, 395 n.31
  philosophy of, 67
historicism, 51, 67, 361 n.45
historiography, 68
Hitler, Adolf, 51, 272, 295, 304
Hobbes, Thomas (includes Hobbesian), 38, 270, 288, 292, 390 n.12
Hocking, William Ernest, 4, 16, 27, 32, 74–75, 78–84, 86–103, 108, 110–112, 201, 204, 209, 248, 251, 264, 354 n.30, 358 n.4, 362 n.9, 364 n.18-19, 364 n.22, 365 n.28, 365 n.30-31, 366 n.34, 366 n.50, 368 n.13, 372 n.49, 384 n.24
Holt, Henry, 36
Holy Spirit, 52
hope (*see also* community), xi, xii, xiii, 30, 42, 52, 60, 70, 87, 114, 156, 160, 175, 180, 261, 264, 266–268, 270, 273, 275, 281–282, 290, 299–300, 305–307, 319, 346, 350, 388 n.9
Howison, George Holmes, 4, 44–45, 63, 69, 71, 76–84, 87–90, 99–100, 102–103, 127, 140, 153, 190, 196, 201–205, 207–210, 215, 237, 241, 248, 362 n.7-8, 363 n.11-12, 364 n.16, 364 n.18, 364 n.24, 365 n.24, 372 n.49, 377 n.17-18, 377 n.20-21, 391 n.17
Hubschmann, Heinrich, 36

humanism, humanist(s), 245–246, 285, 306, 325, 328, 332–333, 336, 342, 348
Hume, David (includes Humean), 3, 107, 273, 299–300, 311
Husserl, Edmund, 90, 118–119, 126, 213, 366 n.33, 378 n.23
hypothesis, hypothetical (*see also* fiction), 22–26, 34, 40, 43, 45–46, 49–50, 54, 56–59, 61–64, 66–68, 70–71, 73–74, 77, 79, 81–82, 112, 114–115, 128, 134–136, 138, 140–143, 151, 153, 158, 163–165, 167, 175, 179–182, 184–189, 191, 193, 195, 221, 223, 225–226, 229, 239, 249, 252, 260–261, 263, 287, 289, 359 n.12, 360 n.17

Ibsen, Henrik, 282
idea(s), x, xi, 1–3, 5–7, 9–21, 24, 30, 32–33, 35–36, 40, 43–47, 50, 52, 55–58, 60, 67–71, 76, 83–84, 86–91, 93–94, 100, 102–103, 105–107, 109–112, 116–117, 119, 121–122, 127–129, 137, 139–140, 142, 149, 151–152, 156–161, 164–165, 166–169, 174, 178, 180, 184–185, 188–189, 194–195, 197–199, 201–202, 204, 208–210, 212–214, 216–219, 221–224, 226, 228–229, 232, 235, 240–241, 243–244, 251, 253–254, 262, 265–267, 270, 273–274, 276, 285, 288, 294, 296–297, 299, 302, 309–311, 313, 316–317, 322, 324–336, 339, 342–343, 346, 348, 351 n.1, 354 n.32, 356 n.22, 356 n.25, 375 n.3, 379 n.25
  ethical, 20, 122, 153, 159, 198, 230, 269, 372 n.49
  living, 1, 7, 11, 53, 55, 72–73, 102, 104, 126, 156, 161, 174, 201, 230, 236, 265, 268, 276, 285, 314, 351 n.1
  of person (*see* person, personalism)
  philosophical, 6, 30, 33, 50, 121, 129, 266, 325

  of self (*see* self, idea of)
ideal, idealize (*see also* actuality, possibility, purpose, reality), xi, 7, 22, 24–25, 44, 48–50, 61, 64, 70, 72, 76–77, 83, 88–90, 104, 108–110, 112–115, 117, 119–123, 127, 133–134, 158, 173, 198, 222, 230, 232–233, 238, 251–254, 266–267, 270, 273, 276, 278, 282–283, 288–292, 294–296, 299, 302–305, 309, 311–312, 314, 319–327, 333, 338, 340, 342–343, 346–347, 349, 351 n.1, 354 n.32, 394 n.18, 394 n.20
  community (*see* community, beloved)
  concrete, 75, 251
  ethical, 48
idealism, 18, 35, 41, 43–47, 50, 63–64, 75, 77, 79–87, 91, 93, 96, 100–103, 107, 111, 113, 115–116, 123, 125, 129, 138–140, 164, 176, 183, 189, 195–196, 202, 207, 209, 212–213, 218, 226, 244–245, 248, 252, 254, 270, 329, 331, 333, 340–342, 352 n.9, 354 n.32, 364 n.16, 373 n.12, 378 n.23, 383 n.15, 393n.17
  Absolute, 140, 196, 226, 244–245, 378 n.23
  British, 12, 23, 196, 383 n.5, 393 n.16
  German, 196, 205
  personal (*see* person, personal idealism, personalism)
impersonal, impersonalism (*see* non-personalism, impersonalism)
inclusion, social-political (*see also* progressive), 290–291
instinct (*see* docility, law of)
institution(s) (*see* person, institutions as)
International Monetary Fund, 52
Interpretation (*see* will to interpret)
Iowa State University, 333
Iraq (*see also* Bush, George W., and treason), 282, 298
Israel, 50, 65
Ithaca, New York, 315, 324, 326

Jacobi, F.H., 247, 375 n.5

420 Index

James, Henry, the elder, 207, 377 n.17
James, Henry, the younger, 206
James, William (*see also* pluralism, pragmstism, radical empiricism), ix, xiii, 3–5, 8, 10, 12–13, 15, 18, 31=34, 37, 40, 45, 52, 61, 63, 72, 74, 77, 82–86, 91, 93, 95–96, 98–100, 102–108, 110–120, 123, 128, 137, 140–141, 145, 149, 156, 176–177, 180, 184, 187, 189, 193, 196, 202–241, 243–261, 266, 271, 315–326, 330, 341, 352 n.4, 354 n.29, 358 n.4, 365 n.28, 366 n.50, 368 n.18, 369 n.19, 372 n.49, 375 n.3–5, 376 n.6, 377 n.13, 377 n.18, 377 n.22
Jefferson, Thomas, 286
Jesus, 50, 65, 157, 274, 281–283, 318
Jevons, William Stanley, 332
John, Saint, 156
Johns Hopkins University, 17, 36–37, 314, 319, 330–332, 334, 340, 353 n.12, 392 n.5
Johnson, Walter, 83
Julius Caesar, 304

Kansas State University, 333
Kant, Immanuel, 3, 12, 37, 46, 54, 57, 59–60, 62, 66, 100, 110, 132, 225, 329, 341, 347, 357 n.3, 374 n.26
Kantian(s), 36–37, 57, 84, 91, 139, 170, 225, 360 n.19, 362 n.2
Kegley, Jacquelyn A. K., xii, 5–6, 11, 196, 285, 351 n.2, 368 n.14, 370 n.16, 370 n.19, 372 n.2–3, 389 n.10
Keller, Helen, 32
Kierkegaard, Søren, 97–98, 311
King, Martin Luther, Jr., 156, 286, 294, 302, 304, 352 n.6, 386 n.1
Knudson, Albert C., 196, 382 n.1, 382 n.2
Kohák, Erazim, 384 n.21
Ku Klux Klan, 393 n.18

LaPlace, Pierre-Simon, 271
Latin America, 105

League of Nations, 52
LeConte, Joseph, 36, 44, 355n.7, 356n.14, 389n.10
Leibniz, G.W., 18, 24, 39, 250
Leipzig, University of, 36, 324
Lenin, V.I., 51
Lévinas, Emmanuel, 167, 227
Lewis, C.I., 55, 367 n.4
Lewis, David, 55
Liberty University, 332
Librescu, Liviu, 348–350
Lipham, Sean, 254, 382 n.70
Locke, Alain, 32
Locke, John, 3, 117, 273, 286–288, 311
Loewenberg, Jacob, 16, 372 n.4
Lotze, Rudolf H., 12, 36, 202, 207–208, 217, 251, 375 n.5, 377 n.18, 380 n.38
Lovejoy, Arthur O., 108, 363 n.11
Loyola University, Chicago, 332
Lusitania, 388 n.9
Lutherans, 98

Machiavelli, Niccolò, 292, 294, 306, 389 n.11
Madison, James, 286, 292
Mahowald, Mary Briody, 285
Many, the (*see* One, the)
Mao Zedong, 51, 276
Marcel, Gabriel, 26–27, 74, 78, 84, 86, 98, 102, 118, 226–227, 248, 354 n.28–30, 356 n.25, 358 n.4, 361 n.39, 362 n.2
Marion, Jean-Luc, 167
Marx, Karl H. (*see also* materialism, dialectical), 245, 383 n.3
Massachusetts Institute of Technology (MIT), 207
Mathematics, 36, 80, 114, 182–183, 259, 264, 368 n.18
McCarthy, Joseph, 321, 328, 337, 342
McCumber, John, 321, 328, 342, 394 n.22
McDermott, John J., xii, 5, 30, 196, 363 n.11, 373 n.12
McGraw, John, 83
McKinley, William, 292

McLachlan, James, 83, 363 n.12
McTaggart, J.M.E., 248
Mead, George Herbert, 32
mediation (*see* immediacy)
Menand, Louis, 377 n.38
Mennonites, 306
Merleau-Ponty, Maurice, 118, 126
Mesopotamia, 319
Metaphysical Club, 207, 377 n.38
Mezes, Sidney, 44
Michigan State University, 333
Mill, John Stuart, 36, 107, 390 n.15
Mills, C. Wright, 394 n.20
mirror neurons (*see also* imitation, psychology), 140, 371 n.20
Mohanty, J.N., 119
Moller, Mark, 233–236, 385 n.26
Monism, 78, 81
Montesquieu, Baron de (Charles-Louis de Secondat), 286
Morrill Land Grant Act, 326
Morris, George Sylvester, 331
Moses, 65
Mozart, Wolfgang A., 54
Muelder, Walter G., 221, 381 n.44
Muhammed, 157
Münsterberg, Hugo, 177
mysticism (*see* experience, immediate)

NASA, 262–263
Nazi(s), 275, 291, 357 n.26, 393 n.18
Neville, Robert C., ix, xii, 184
Niebuhr, Reinhold, 277–278, 300, 303, 386 n.51–52, 391 n.2
Nietzsche, Friedrich (*see also* will), 29–30, 50–51, 97–98, 131, 157, 167, 261, 338, 385 n.31
Nihilism, 51, 322
non-Ego (*see also* alterity, Other), 178
novelty (*see also* creativity, imitation), 147, 184, 203, 301

Oppenheim, Frank M., xii, 5, 7–8, 10, 13, 17, 33, 108, 196, 352 n.8, 353 n.21, 354 n.1, 367 n.7, 377 n.22, 386 n.50

Ormond, Alexander Thomas, 317, 394 n.20
Other, otherness (*see also* alterity, non-Ego)

Palmer, George Herbert, 41, 330
panexperientialism, 64, 256, 258–260, 264, 267
panpsychism, 236, 256, 385 n.26, 393 n.17
pantheism (*see also* atheism, materialism), 245–246, 258, 365 n.24, 382 n.2
Parmenides, 26
Paul, Saint (includes Pauline), 34, 50–51, 91, 156, 277, 318, 374 n.40
Peirce, Charles S. (includes Peircean), ix, 8, 10, 12–13, 15–25, 31–32, 34, 37, 40, 44, 46–47, 55, 60, 62–63, 64, 86–87, 90, 100–103, 105–108, 110–123, 135, 151, 182–185, 187, 190, 195, 205, 213, 237–238, 259, 291, 331, 333–334, 353 n.12, 353 n.15, 353 n.21, 354 n.29, 355 n.10, 357 n.2–3, 358n.4, 362 n.2, 362 n.9, 364 n.16, 368 n.18, 369 n.24, 371 n.33, 391 n.15
Perry, Ralph Barton, 205, 208, 376 n.6, 376 n.10, 377 n.20, 377 n.22, 378 n.23
personal idealism (*see* idealism, personal)
Pierce, Charles P., ix, x, 351 n.1
Pinchot, Gifford, 391 n.15
Plato, Platonism (includes Neo-Platonism), 3, 26, 36, 92, 107, 140, 157, 250, 325, 341
Polanyi, Michael, 381 n.50
Pratt, Scott, 6, 9, 389 n.10
Princeton University, 316–317, 323, 330, 339–342, 392 n.5
Pringle-Pattison, Andrew (Seth), 248
process (*see* temporality)
problem (*see* doubt, situation)
progressive(s) (*see* conservative(s))
projections (*see also* anticipation, construction, recognition), 40, 60, 62, 255

Protagoreans, 245
Protestant(s), 279, 281, 326
psychologism 93, 96, 118
purpose (*see also* action, plan of; ideals, person, telos), 7, 9, 13, 17, 20, 28, 40, 47–50, 56, 58, 60–61, 65, 70–72, 76, 80, 93, 106–107, 112–114, 121, 129, 131–133, 135, 138–139, 142, 153, 156, 158, 160, 165–169, 174–176, 178, 180–181, 184, 186, 188, 191–195, 197–199, 201–202, 204, 219–220, 222, 225, 227, 230, 233, 236, 238, 240, 244–245, 249, 251–252, 254, 257–258, 261–264, 266–274, 276, 278–279, 281–283, 285–290, 294, 296–297, 300–306, 309, 311, 314, 318–320, 322, 326, 335–338, 343, 346–350, 354 n.32, 391 n.15, 393 n.16
Putnam, Hilary, ix, 106, 119, 228, 367 n.4
Putnam, Ruth Anna, ix

Quine, W.V., 367 n.4, 394 n.24
Quintillian, 341

radical empiricism (*see* empiricism, radical)
Rand, Ayn, 288
Rawls, John, 293
reconciliation (*see* atonement)
redemption (*see* atonement)
Renouvier, Charles, 204, 208, 375 n.5, 376 n.6, 377 n.18
Robinson, Daniel, 16, 74, 366 n.35
Roosevelt, Theodore, 292, 391
Rorty, Richard, 104, 106, 115, 119–121, 293, 303, 359 n.10, 394 n.24
Royce, Christopher, 37, 52
Royce, Katherine Head (Kitty), 16, 35, 37
Royce, Sarah Eleanor (Bayliss), 32–33
Russell, Bertrand, 158, 333
Russia (Soviet Union), 276
Rutgers University, 323

Sanskrit, 36
Santayana, George, 31–32, 34, 330, 380 n.38
Scheler, Max, 86, 167, 226–227, 248, 381
Schelling, F.W.J., 12, 84–85, 196, 208, 247
Schiller, Ferdinand C.S., 12
Schleiermacher, Friedrich, 98, 372 n.49
Schopenhauer, Arthur, 29, 30, 37, 47, 50–51, 157, 167, 329
Schurman, Jacob Gould, 324, 327–328, 330, 333
Seigfried, Charlene Haddock, 369 n.19, 382 n.54
semiotics (*see also* Peirce), 16, 18–19, 62, 100, 118, 367 n.11, 374 n.30
Seth, Andrew (*see* Pringle-Pattison, Andrew), 248
Sherover, Charles M., v, xiii, 166–167
Shook, John, 12, 358 n.4
situation (*see also* Dewey, John; inquiry), 24, 82, 93, 115–117, 126, 130–133, 136, 140, 142–143, 145, 160, 166, 197, 246, 256, 259, 368 n.18
Smart, Harold, 333
Smith, John E., 7, 13–28, 47, 56, 135, 168, 352 n.9, 353 n.12, 353 n.14, 353 n.21, 353 n.26, 354 n.28–29, 354 n.32, 358 n.4, 360 n.25, 366 n.49, 369 n.26, 370 n.30, 370 n.1, 370 n.17, 372 n.7, 389 n.12
Sniffin-Marinoff, Megan, xiii
social contract 288, 294
social infinite (*see* infinite, social)
sociality (*see* will, social)
society (*see* experience, social)
Socrates, 92, 107, 157, 309, 342, 347
Spencer, Herbert, 36, 205, 376 n.8, 390 n.15
Spengler, Oswald, 51
Spinoza, Baruch, 37–38, 45, 190, 245, 247, 311, 329
sport (includes football), x, 338, 351 n.1
Sprigge, Timothy, L.S., 12, 378 n.23, 383 n.5
Stalin, Josef; Stalinist, 51, 276

Stikkers, Kenneth W., xiii
Straton, George Douglas, 5, 7, 351 n.3
Sullivan, Shannon, 6, 389 n.10
Syracuse University, 332

teaching, Ch 10
teleology, *telos* (*see also* purpose), 58, 78, 122, 138, 202, 356 n.25
temperament, 4, 81, 83-84, 108, 111, 222, 241, 244–245
temporality, temporalism (*see also* time), 6, 17, 21, 24, 26, 38, 40–41, 44, 46–47, 49–52, 57–58, 60, 62–63, 66–69, 72, 76, 102, 126–127, 129, 131–133, 135, 140, 142, 144, 149–152, 158, 160, 163–166, 168–178, 182–184, 186–190, 192–199, 212, 216, 219, 222–223, 225–228, 230–231, 233–237, 240–241, 249–251, 255–257, 260, 262–263, 266–267, 270, 290, 296–297, 348–349, 353 n.26, 359 n.12, 373 n.12, 374 n.32, 379 n.25, 381 n.53
  continuity (*see also* continuity), 189, 214, 228, 262, 276, 279, 282–283, 287–289
  experience, 236, 240, 251
  form, 47, 181
  order, 47
  and possibility, 26, 49, 95, 112, 173, 250
  structure, 39, 62, 289
theology, 35, 81, 91, 99, 160, 187, 320, 332, 334, 373 n.7, 382 n.1
Thilly, Frank, 335, 379 n.26
Thirty Years' War, 281, 283
Thucydides, 341
time (*see also* temporalism), 15, 24, 38–39, 47, 58–59, 62, 66–67, 98, 117, 137, 159, 161, 163–166, 170, 174–181, 184–185, 189–190, 192–193, 196–198, 202, 204, 211, 214, 222–225, 231–232, 234, 236, 238–240, 244, 248–251, 256–258, 261–263, 267–270, 273, 285, 287, 318, 320, 347, 349, 360 n.19, 367 n.12, 372 n.4, 373 n.12, 375 n.3, 382 n.55
  time-spans, 39, 47, 59, 132, 262–264, 273
  as the form of the will, 165, 177–178, 181, 189, 192
tragedy, tragic, 31, 37, 52, 155–156, 238, 271, 295–296, 357 n.26
traitor, treason (*see also* Bush George W.), xi, 304
triad, triadic, 17, 19, 46, 62, 128, 190–193, 198, 218, 235, 250, 266, 362 n.9, 374 n.30
Trinity, 198
  Unholy, 54–55, 77, 79, 81, 85, 120, 257, 289, 362 n.8
Trotsky, Leon, 299
Trotter, Griffin, 285
Tunstall, Dwayne, xii, 5–6, 11, 20, 28, 63, 67, 70, 73–74, 167, 201, 204, 209, 288, 291, 356 n.25, 358 n.4, 359 n.12, 360 n.28, 361 n.39, 362 n.2, 371 n.39, 382 n.70, 387 n.1
Tyman, Stephen, 75–76, 362 n.5, 366 n.38

unconscious (*see also* consciousness), 33, 70, 216, 219, 246, 256, 276, 282, 323, 328, 389 n.10
unique, uniquifying, uniqueness, uniquity (see Being, Fourth Conception of, exclusion, and Schelling)
United Kingdom (*see* Great Britain)
United States Constitution, 273, 280, 285, 302, 306
unity (*see* experience, unity of)
University of California, Berkeley, 36, 44, 69, 76, 363 n.11, 364 n.18
University of Chicago, 28
University of Illinois, 48
University of Michigan, 331
University of Missouri, 335
University of Pittsburgh, 323
University of Southern California, 332

Vailati, Giovanni, 107

424 Index

Vanderbilt University, 332, 358 n.4, 360 n.22, 278 n.24
Vico, Giambattista, 38, 251, 386 n.54
Virginia Tech University, 348
voluntarism (*see* will)

Wagner, Honus, 83
Wall Street Journal, 394 n.24
WalMart, 273, 275–276, 278, 280
Walton, Sam, 275
Walton, Zachary, 388 n.9
Washington, George, 387 n.3
Wesleyans (John Wesley), 98
West, Cornel, 5, 108, 119–120, 304, 352 n.4, 369 n.31
Western Philosophical Association, 334–335
Whewell, William, 332
White, Andrew Dickson, 326
Whitehead, Alfred North (Whiteheadian), 1, 3, 4, 8, 18, 24, 63, 74, 84–86, 94, 98, 102, 120, 134, 144, 161, 176, 183–184, 193–195, 230–231, 253, 259–260, 333, 341, 351 n.1, 351 n.3, 360 n.17, 361 n.53, 362 n.2, 376 n.13, 379 n.27, 379 n.31, 381 n.53, 385 n.28
Whitman, Walt, 204, 375 n.5
Whole (*see* Absolute, as the Whole)
Will, willing (includes volition; *see also* desire, intentional stance, life), 28, 47, 51, 56, 60, 62, 71–73, 78, 86–87, 89, 97–102, 116, 128–132, 134–136, 139–142, 144, 146–151, 158, 160, 164–169, 171–179, 181, 184, 188–189, 192–193, 197–199, 201–202, 204, 214, 219, 222–223, 230, 238, 240, 245, 248, 250–252, 255–256, 258, 261–264, 266, 269–270, 272, 274, 278, 285, 287, 290, 293–294, 296–298, 301–303, 305, 318, 338, 348–349, 354 n.42, 365 n.31, 367 n.7, 376 n.6, 384 n.24
  broad sense of, 146–147
  collective (*see* social)

conscious (*see also* consciousness), 98
concrete, 99, 157, 211
divine, 193, 360 n.19, 365 n.30
finite, 19, 21, 98–99, 161, 175–177, 197, 252
God's, 127, 129, 186, 188, 279
human, 176
individual, 79–80, 97–99, 136, 141, 153, 157–159, 198, 233, 251, 264, 266, 283, 289, 293, 298, 354 n.32, 384 n.24
infinite, 178
to interpret (*see also* interpretation), 62, 127, 160, 306, 312, 393 n.17
James's, 100, 380 n.31
narrow sense of, 147–148
Nietzsche's concept of, 50, 97, 167, 386 n.31
Rational, 89, 289
Schopenhauer's concept of, 167
Social, 51, 194–195, 220, 238, 251–252, 254, 270, 276, 283, 296, 298, 303
sociality of, 141, 151, 158, 160, 189, 252
volition(al), voluntary, 87, 93
weakness of, 338, 347, 349
world, 158, 177, 197–199, 250
Wilshire, Bruce, 322, 340, 394 n.22
Wilson, Daniel J., 394 n.20
Wilson, E.O., 271–272
Wilson, Woodrow, 292, 294, 314, 389 n.12, 391 n.5
Windelband, Wilhelm, 36
Wittgenstein, Ludwig, 3–4
Women, 291, 301, 306, 326, 340
World Bank, 52
World War I (First World War, the Great War, Guns of August), 51–52, 84
World War II (Second World War), 365 n.28
Worship, 91–92, 96–97, 99, 101, 264, 366 n.34
Wundt, Wilhelm, 36, 377 n.18

X, Malcolm, 294

Yale University, 48, 330–331

www.ingramcontent.com/pod-product-compliance
Lightning Source LLC
Chambersburg PA
CBHW072117290426
44111CB00012B/1688